OVID'S *Met*
Books 1–5

OVID'S *Metamorphoses*
Books 1–5

Edited, with Introduction
and Commentary, by

WILLIAM S. ANDERSON

University of Oklahoma Press : Norman

Other books by William S. Anderson

The Art of the Aeneid (New Jersey, 1967; London, 1989)
(ed. and comm.) *Ovid's* Metamorphoses, *Books 6–10* (Norman, 1972)
Ovidius, Metamorphoses Libri XV (Leipzig, 1977)
Studies on Roman Satire (New Jersey, 1982)
(ed.) *Ovid: The Classical Heritage* (New York, 1995)

The Latin text of Books 1–5 of Ovid's *Metamorphoses* is reprinted from
Ovidius, Metamorphoses, ed. W.S. Anderson, 6th ed. (Stuttgart and Leipzig:
B.G. Teubner, 1993), by permission of the B.G. Teubner Publishing Company
of Stuttgart and Leipzig. All rights in and to the Latin text, including those of
translation, partial reprintings, and reproduction, are retained by B.G. Teubner
of Stuttgart and Leipzig.

Library of Congress Cataloging-in-Publication Data

Ovid, 43 B.C.–17 or 18 A.D.

[Metamorphoses. Liber 1–5]

Ovid's Metamorphoses. Books 1–5 / edited with introduction and
commentary by William S. Anderson.

p. cm.

Includes index.

1. Metamorphosis—Mythology—Poetry. 2. Mythology, Classical—
Poetry. 3. Religious poetry, Latin. 4. Narrative poetry, Latin.
5. Rome—Religion—Poetry. I. Anderson, William Scovil, 1927–
II. Title.
PA6519.M4A49 1996
873'.01—dc20   96–11064

ISBN 978-0-8061-2894 (paper)   CIP

8   9   10

CONTENTS

OVID's *Metamorphoses*
Books 1–5

INTRODUCTION

I. OVID'S CAREER

Publius Ovidius Naso was born on March 20, 43 B.C., almost precisely a year after the murder of Julius Caesar. He spent his boyhood years in his relatively quiet home town of Sulmo, some ninety miles due east of Rome but separated from the metropolis and its political upheavals by the Apennine chain. Shortly after the battle of Actium, early in the twenties, Ovid came to a Rome firmly on the road to restoration after years of war. His father intended him for a career that would be expected to prosper in peacetime, the law, and Ovid duly studied under Arellius Fuscus, one of the prominent teachers of the day. Peace, however, had also enabled poetry once more to flourish in Italy, so Ovid spent much time listening to the many exciting poets of those years: Vergil, Horace, Tibullus, and Propertius, to name the most famous. Rather than toil at oratory and prepare for a life as lawyer and statesman that did not appeal to him, he preferred what was for him the easy, rewarding task of composing poetry. As he modestly put it in that poem which serves us as an autobiography, *Tristia* 4.10, what he tried to write in prose, turned into verse:

> scribere temptabam verba soluta modis.
> sponte sua carmen numeros veniebat ad aptos,
> et quod temptabam scribere, versus erat.
> (24–26)

This introduction has been adapted from my earlier introduction in *Ovid's Metamorphoses, Books 6–10* (Norman: University of Oklahoma Press, 1972), with changes appropriate to Books 1–5.

3

He had scarcely begun to shave when he started reading his own poems in public (57–58). As a close friend and admirer of Propertius and participant in the literary circle sponsored by Messalla, he composed what was the most popular kind of verse in contemporary Rome, love elegy.

Success followed success; elegiac poem followed elegiac poem. First there were the *Amores,* witty love elegies developing a literary genre pioneered by Tibullus and Propertius. Then came the *Heroides,* which utilized another idea of Propertius, the amatory letter written by a girl separated from (or abandoned by) her beloved. Then the subject was examined from the "sober" perspective of the learned expert; Ovid, assuming the persona of *praeceptor amoris,* produced a didactic poem in elegiacs called the *Art of Love* and a sequel called the *Cure for Love.* Successful and only forty, Ovid continued to devise new ways of exploring and displaying his talents. He embarked on two ambitious works, whose relative chronology cannot be determined. The *Fasti,* a poem planned for twelve books covering the commemorative days, month by month, in the Roman calendar, was half-completed by A.D. 8, when Ovid went into exile. Separated from his beloved Rome, whose occasions he longed to commemorate on the spot, and from his reference books, Ovid did not persevere. The six books of the *Fasti* that he did complete continue his technique of elegiac versification; they also follow the model of Propertius (and Callimachus before him) in paying playful honor to national traditions.

Current scholarship infers that Ovid worked at the same time during his final decade in Rome on the *Metamorphoses,* so that it and the *Fasti,* his two major works, influence each other. The *Metamorphoses,* with which we are primarily concerned, apparently proved a more congenial task, even though he had chosen to work in hexameter, for he had completed the fifteen books as we now possess them when Augustus dispatched him to exile, in late A.D. 8, to the shores of the Black Sea. The last decade of Ovid's life was an unhappy one, but not unproductive. He produced many more poems, once again in elegiacs, using the basic tone of lamentation that was traditional with the meter to impress upon the comfortable, urbane audience in Rome a sense of his deprivation as husband, friend, and poet from the environment he needed to survive, and to question also the justice of the Augustan regime that had banished him so arbitrarily. The death of Augustus in 14 did not, as he hoped, terminate his misery; the end came approximately three years later with his own death (unmentioned in surviving documents written before the fourth century).

II. THE *METAMORPHOSES* IN SUBSEQUENT AGES

Ovid reports that when he left Rome his despair impelled him to burn the text of the *Metamorphoses* (*Trist*. 1.7.11 ff.). Whatever he intended by this act, he did not destroy the poem, for other copies were already circulating in Rome by A.D. 8. From exile, then, he talked of the work as a published poem and wished for it the survival that he predicted in its last lines (*Met*. 15.871 ff.), which in fact it has earned.

Explicit comments on the *Metamorphoses* during the first century are not favorable, but they can be largely discounted as the words of rhetoricians and moralists, who judged the poem by the standards of prose oratory and ethical advocacy. Implicit approval, in the form of quotations and imitations, reverses the impression of hostility. Within a few years of his death, Ovid's poem was being quarried by younger orators, particularly for striking *sententiae,* although the Elder Seneca deplored Ovid's talent and its unhealthy influence (cf. *Controv*. 3.7.2, 9.5.17, and 10.4.25). Aemilius Scaurus sneered: *Ovidius nescit quod bene cessit relinquere;* and he cited *Metamorphoses* 13.503 ff. as a choice example (*id*. 9.5.17). Seneca epitomized his dislike of Ovid's defective genius by singling out *licentiam carminum* (*id*. 2.2.12). For Quintilian the critical term to apply to Ovid is *lascivia* (*Inst. orat.* 4.1.77, 10.1.88 and 93). Even more than the young orators, however, the young poets were finding inspiration from the *Metamorphoses*. Regardless of his father's strictures, the Younger Seneca adapted Ovidian techniques enthusiastically in his *Tragedies*. His *sententiae,* his analysis of dilemmas faced by such heroines as Medea and Andromache, his use of fearsome allegorical figures from the Underworld, his eye for the grotesque, and his thematic emphasis on reversed values (such as *pietas*) all remind one of salient characteristics of the *Metamorphoses*.

Lucan, Seneca's nephew, utilized these and similar techniques as well as Ovid's versification for his epic *Pharsalia*. When Pompeii and Herculaneum were destroyed in 79, the graffiti on their walls left a lasting testimonial to Ovid's contemporary popularity.

Throughout the rest of antiquity, then again with the rediscovery of Roman poetry, Ovid had an enormous following. The twelfth century has been described as the *aetas Ovidiana*, not only for the immense number of his manuscripts that were copied all over Europe, but also for the Ovidian poetry that flourished in Latin and in vernacular languages. Italian, French, and Spanish poets lived and breathed Ovid. In England, Chaucer, Shakespeare, and Milton knew and used the *Metamorphoses* thoroughly. Only with the nineteenth century's depreciation of wit and exaltation of direct emotional expression, did Ovid suffer a temporary eclipse. Since classicists, however, have all too often inherited the textbooks and tastes of the nineteenth century, we are still struggling free of its bias against Ovid. This text will present Ovid as a superior poet who deserves admiration for his literary artistry and who gives his readers many kinds of pleasure.

III. THE POEM'S PLAN AND TONE

At the beginning of Book 1, Ovid in four lines rapidly sketches the subject and plan of his poem and perfunctorily invokes the assistance of the gods:

> in nova fert animus mutatas dicere formas
> corpora; di coeptis (nam vos mutastis et illa)
> adspirate meis primaque ab origine mundi
> ad mea perpetuum deducite tempora carmen.

Although he says, to translate him literally, that his subject is "forms changed into new bodies," and the Greek title implies the same emphasis on changed forms, many readers interpret this phrase, as Humphries did in his translation, to mean simply "bodies changed to different forms." However, Ovid does in fact have a greater interest in formal change than in bodily change, for he focuses on the fundamental instability of human experience in its various aspects. For a few hundred lines in Book 1, he deals with the original metamorphosis of formless matter into the various shapes comprising the visible world. Thereafter, he concentrates almost exclusively on human beings whose forms are changed into diverse new bodies, into animals, trees, rocks, birds, springs, flowers, constellations, insects, reptiles, and so on. As lines 3 and 4 indicate, he takes his topic and "draws it out" from the Creation down to his own times, that is, to the Augustan era. Accordingly, in Book 15, Ovid deals with the murder of Julius Caesar and then reaches his own lifetime, but, more to the point, arrives at the amazing career of Augustus. Caesar was metamorphosed into a star; Augustus predictably will be changed into a god when he leaves his loving Romans.

Between that infinitely distant point in the past when human beings were created and that unwished moment in the near future when Augustus will die, Ovid finds material for several hundred metamorphoses, which he recounts with varying detail and manner. Metamorphosis had long been a standard feature in myth. Originally, it had served people's purpose to account for the visible universe in terms which they could grasp: they anthropomorphized nature by claiming that human spirits resided in animals, birds, trees, and the like. Human beings were changed into those animals, birds, and trees. Nowadays, although our rationalism does not need such an explanation of the world, we still instinctively personify nonhuman things. Poets regularly attribute personality to animals and trees. Children and adults alike respond to stories which turn cats, dogs, and other pets into people; and the cartoon world of Mickey Mouse, Bugs Bunny, and Garfield the Cat awakens instinctive response from us all. There is, then, something fundamentally believable about the poetic topic of metamorphosis: our instincts tell us that other beings and objects of nature somehow resemble us in feeling and so can help or hurt us.

Although we all retain some of this primitive instinct that originally inspired many myths of metamorphosis, it is plain to readers of Ovid that he did not retell the old stories simply to appeal to that instinct. He was not trying to account for nature by humanizing it. Both he and his audience were far too sophisticated to spend time on that. For Ovid (who in this respect inherited the ideas of Greek Poets from Euripides' age and more particularly from the Hellenistic era) the myths were opportune stories that could be given contemporary relevance by elaboration of the events leading up to the metamorphosis. The form into which the human being had been changed was the given part of the story, along with a few details about the individual's earlier existence. By, so to speak, fleshing out the story, by exploring the emotions and psychological problems of the characters, by considering the situation in terms of Roman morality and social values, by inspecting the involvement of the gods, by weighing the reasons for metamorphosis and the feelings of that human spirit inside the changing and changed body, Ovid gave new form and meaning to the myth.

Some readers in the past have found Ovid's relevance through allegorizing his poem; "Ovid moralized" was a special passion of the twelfth and thirteenth centuries and a major influence on Renaissance art. But when the "allegory" is stated in too specific terms, especially if colored anachronistically with Christian ideas, it distorts the *Metamorphoses* beyond recognition. Hermann Fränkel has used modern psychological insights to interpret some of the stories. Since, however, the insights purport to define general human behavior, they are not necessarily anachronistic: Fränkel has perceived an important aspect of Ovid's relevance. More recently, readers have discovered in Ovid's theme an expression of our anxieties in the late twentieth century over the instability of every formal entity.

Often in Books 1–3 a girl is raped by a god, then transformed into an animal; or an innocent like Actaeon blunders into trouble with a goddess and suffers unmerited change. In such a context Ovid exploits the opportunity provided him by basic mythical beliefs, that a human sensibility resides in the animal, but his interest differs from that of the primitive myth-makers. He studies the anguish of the essential humanity (of Actaeon, Io, Callisto) as it struggles to cope with its ungainly, alien, bestial form. Thus he alters the original focus of the myth, no longer representing an animal with slight human tendencies, but rather a human being inside an animal form, a human being who accidentally seems to have an animal body. He places us inside the human sensitivity, puts ideas and emotions and unexpressible words in the human mind of the seeming beast, and thus represents what Fränkel rightly considered a basic psychological state of human beings. In dreams and hallucinations we may go precisely through such experiences, imagining ourselves as animals, birds, or reptiles. These dreams dramatize our psychological difficulty in presenting to others what we feel is our real self in all its emotional sincerity and irresistible attraction, when our looks, our clothes, accent, superficial mannerisms, skin color—in short, surface elements that do *not,* we believe, represent us truly—make people misunderstand us and refuse to see the real us. Franz Kafka's short story entitled "Metamorphosis," written in this century, captures the alienation and victimization that Ovid earlier chose to stress. Both writers are attuned to the human struggle to be oneself and to be understood on one's own terms. The poignancy of the human condition emerges acutely, in both, from the fact that one's closest relatives and friends fail to recognize the human being inside the animal body.

So far, I have not referred to the parenthesis in line 2 of the Prologue cited earlier. Addressing the gods in conventional terms as agents of inspiration, Ovid inserts in a *nam* clause a reason why they should assist his poem: they have acted to change his poetry as well as to perform physical metamorphoses. Until recently, the accepted reading for the end of 2 was *et illas,* which obliged the reader to take the demonstrative in connection with *formas*. But a series of cogent arguments (summarized in the notes) have convinced scholars that we should read *illa* and refer it to the nearest neuter plural, namely, *coeptis*. The gods, Ovid suggests, have transformed his poetry from elegiac to hexameter, just as they have transformed human beings. The role of the gods in connection with human metamorphosis constitutes a major concern of Ovid's poem. The myths were quite direct on this point. Jupiter changed Io into a cow; Juno deformed Callisto into a bear; Diana made Actaeon a bear; Mercury turned Battus into stone. The original myths did not speculate: it was simply a matter of offending a god and suffering punishment or occasionally of receiving a new body as a kind of reward.

Ovid, however, sees opportunity to probe the reason for the metamorphosis. Was the deity just? In the early books, the usual reason for change is either that a god is attempting to conceal an extramarital affair or that a goddess, notably Juno, has discovered a wrong to herself and vents her fury on a helpless human victim. As Ovid narrates the circumstances of the divine intervention, we are invited to judge the behavior of the gods. In Book 3 and 4, we consider the role of Bacchus, and in Book 5 the character of Ceres comes under inspection. When Ovid reports the events, we do not always approve of the harshness of the deity, and we often question the omniscience of Jupiter. Moreover, in some of his versions, the poet excludes any reference to gods at the moment of metamorphosis, as if to suggest that we must explain the event in some other way.

The relationship between human beings and gods is very unfair as Ovid presents it in Books 1–5: the gods can do anything they want to mortals, for whatever reason, but the gods never suffer. As soon as they become angry, they vent their wrath, usually on unoffending targets. Human beings can only endure; protest is impossible; prayer is either ignored or malevolently used against the supplicant. The case of Callisto in 2.401 ff. gives us a victim who is abused by three deities, one after the other. First, Jupiter rapes her, disguising himself as the goddess whom she most reveres, Diana, in order to get close enough to perpetrate his crime. Then, when she gets pregnant, Diana angrily banishes her, without a hearing, from her virginal band. Next, when the baby is born, Juno rushes in and turns Callisto into a bear, converting her pleading arms into shaggy paws and her suppliant words into inarticulate growls. Fifteen years later, when Callisto in bear form encounters her son, a hunter, he is on the verge of spearing her in self-protection from her impetuous "bear-hugs." Suddenly, Jupiter, to spare himself ignominy but with no consideration for mother and son, transports both into the sky and makes them constellations. Then, once again Juno angrily enters and secures a guarantee from the gods of the ocean that the Great Bear will never be able to bathe herself there. As Ovid presents the myth, therefore, Callisto enacts the role of the helpless and pathetic victim of unjust cosmic forces. The three deities represent various aspects of divine immorality and amorality. Ovid makes sure that we devote our sympathies to the human victims.

The unjust power of the gods and the weakness of human beings to ward off this injustice and find a way of living justly with divine blessing make Ovid's world very different from that of his Augustan predecessors, Vergil, Horace, and Livy. Livy perceives an intelligible moral pattern in Roman history, where good is rewarded and evil punished. Horace shows how the human individual always makes a difference, and so he regularly concentrates more on what we can do to be happy than on the obstacles that the gods may cause us. Vergil devotes much attention to two gods, namely, Jupiter and Juno. Juno represents hostile fortune, and she dogs the trail of Aeneas and his Trojans until the end of the *Aeneid*. But Jupiter works in a much more far-sighted, dispassionate, and creative manner to promote the ultimate success of Rome. Amid all their troubles, it is clear in Vergil's poem that human beings cause most of their own problems and have the capacity to correct and survive their mistakes. That is one of the key differences between Aeneas and his antagonists: he can go on and fight through obstacles, some of which he created himself, to achieve positive results. His antagonists fail. Ovid proves more pessimistic than Vergil, as he chooses to emphasize human helplessness or failure and divine malevolence or indifference.

When one talks this way about the *Metamorphoses*, it is hard not to be serious. Yet such seriousness risks conveying the impression that we read a dead-solemn poem. Far from it. Many of Ovid's stories are obviously designed to amuse for long stretches, many scenes are written with rapid elegance that dazzles more than it moves us, and often the poet deploys epic conventions for our distinct amusement. Before we get to the rape of Callisto, Ovid lets us divert ourselves with Apollo's inept wooing of Daphne and with his equally unsuccessful attempt to rape her; there follows the rape of Io, but Ovid focuses our attention on the rather silly way that Io, when changed into a cow, tries to cope with her delicate condition. Since Io was restored to human form before her baby was born, her suffering can be played down. Almost every time human beings are allowed by the poet to articulate their miseries—for example, Actaeon inside the deer-form or Narcissus staring at his reflection in the fountain—Ovid consciously oscillates between playfulness and seriousness, making it hard for us to grasp any single uniform tone.

Scholars and readers have entertained widely divergent conclusions about the dominant tone—if there is one—in individual stories and in the whole poem. The Romantic rejection of Ovid in the nineteenth century arose from an erroneous view of how the tone should work in this poem. They faulted Ovid for making light of serious things. There are some who, apparently accepting the ancient bias against Ovid as *lascivus,* believe that the poem is mainly playful. They would emphasize the rhetorical play of the poet as the chief effect of Io's cow-soliloquy, of the love of Pyramus and Thisbe, and of the fantastic killings by Perseus of his enemies at his wedding banquet. Others are so struck by Ovid's human sympathy and understanding that they can only feel the universal pathos in Io, in the lovers, and in the grotesquely unheroic feats of Perseus. The same passages have been judged as both amusing and serious. The conclusion to draw would seem to be that we should not underestimate Ovid by applying a simple label to his narratives. What may seem trivial or playful on the surface may barely conceal frightening perspectives into the helplessness of human beings and the cruelty of the gods (in Books 1–5) or into the vulnerability of mortals to their own destructive passions (in Books 6–12). What may seem respectful evocation of epic themes and specifically of Vergil may instead lead through parody to troubling questions about conventional *virtus.*

The controversy over *Ovidius lascivus,* who supposedly did not "know how to leave well enough alone," involves another fundamental issue: how carefully and purposefully did he organize the *Metamorphoses?* Any reader will observe that he did group some stories together and also jumped surprisingly between groups. In Book 1, for instance, there is a sequence of stories featuring rapists pursuing nymphs, Daphne, Io, and Syrinx, that build upon each other and form an Ovidian narrative pattern. In Books 3 and 4, Ovid creates a framework by focusing on the House of Cadmus at Thebes, from the founding of the city to the forlorn departure of Cadmus after his grandchildren have been wiped out by the gods. Almost immediately, then, the poet shifts to the framework of Perseus' adventures that carries him over into Book 5. There he introduces the scenario of the Muses and their various adventures and variegated song, which acts both as frame for several smaller stories and begins the larger pattern of *certamina* between mortals and gods, that continues into Book 6.

Ovid uses two structural means in the poem: a framing device for seemingly diverse stories and a pattern of thematically related tales. We should not expect that these two narrative strategies function separately in every instance. In fact, the framing devices prove less significant than the diverse stories that they contain, which Ovid makes shimmer with complex interrelationships. The adventures of Cadmus' family in Book 3 are interrupted by the story of an unrelated Boeotian boy named Narcissus, but Narcissus embodies themes (human helplessness in dealing with the dangerous mysteries of existence) that link him more significantly with the princes of Thebes, Actaeon and Pentheus, as well as with Semele their aunt, than these three figures are linked by mere blood. In Book 4, also within the Theban chronicle, Ovid develops a cycle of stories told by the daughters of Minyas not at Thebes, but at Boeotian Orchomenos. The narrative connection is that the Minyeids oppose Bacchus in their city just as rashly as Pentheus had at Thebes, but these stories move us into new themes, of love and of the way women respond to it, that indicate the poet's concern to develop his poem, not to stop it in a narrative frame.

It is frequently noted that the whole poem, besides embodying the plan announced by Ovid (dealing with events chronologically from Creation down to Augustus), also shows a scheme that breaks the *Metamorphoses* into rough thirds: (*a*) gods and men (1.1–6.423); (*b*) human beings as victims of their own passions (6.424–11.478); (*c*) Troy, Rome, and the apotheosis of Roman heroes (11.479–15.870). During the 1960s scholars such as Walter Ludwig and Brooks Otis worked to elaborate a more ingenious and significant "architecture" of the poem. Although such schemes are provocative, most readers of the poem tend to recognize that Ovid produced his architectural framework with impudent brilliance and independence, for the purpose of exploring his and our primary interest, the thematic interrelationships of his stories.

IV. OVID THE POET AT WORK

A. Selection and Organization of the Material

Some of Ovid's material came from finely worked literary or poetic treatments of the same myth; for instance, Lucretius 5 stands behind parts of the Creation story in 1; Vergil's Council of the Gods and councils in earlier epics help to shape Ovid's account in 1.163 ff.; the battle of Perseus at the banquet against Phineus and his motley supporters in 5.1 ff. borrows from the scene of Odysseus and the Suitors in Homer's epic and from heroic battle episodes in the *Aeneid*. The stories of Phaethon in 2 and Pentheus in 3 have models in Euripidean tragedy. And Callimachus stands behind Ovid's pairing of crow and raven in 2.524 ff. Many of the stories, however, apart from Ovid, are known to us only from badly narrated summaries in mythological handbooks or from chance comments. The handbooks of Parthenius, Apollodorus, and Antoninus Liberalis (all in Greek) and of Hyginus (in Latin) have survived from the time of Ovid to the second century; they will be cited where relevant in this commentary. They indicate, of course, that Ovid had much more to work with than we now possess; but they also suggest that he may have used his own creative genius to build upon bare handbook entries.

The consistent quality of the *Metamorphoses,* whether in tales derived from recognizable sources of literary merit or in those so rare (such as Narcissus) as to defy all attempts to identify a source, attests to the fact that Ovid's poetic genius shaped all stories regardless of origin. The story of Io, which we meet early in Book 1, provides a good example of his artistic methods. The general details of the myth were well known to Ovid and his audience and had been adapted for literary purposes as far back as the fifth century by Aeschylus for his *Prometheus* and as recently as the generation before Ovid's by the Neoteric poet Calvus in an epyllion entitled *Io*. Nevertheless, Ovid's account in 1.583 ff. represents a unique elaboration of the material, and it has driven all other Classical versions into obscurity.

As in other stories, the poet makes a transition from a previous tale. He has just dealt with Daphne's desperate escape from the lusty pursuit of Apollo, an "escape" of ambiguous nature since it resulted in her metamorphosis into a laurel tree that the god claimed as his own. Daphne has a father, the river-god Peneus, to whom various rivers come to show their support. But—and this is the ostensible basis of the transition—the river Inachus of Argos fails to appear because he is plunged into misery over his own daughter, who has simply disappeared and left him to imagine a variety of dire events. The narrator wittily words Inachus' anxious thoughts (586–87) and thus starts us off from a distanced vantage, not obliged to be sympathetic. The narrator does not call attention to the many ways in which the fate of this new "heroine," who is Io, will parallel that of Daphne.

Now, the audience learns as background what the father does not know, that Io has been raped and metamorphosed by Jupiter. The rape is presented entirely from the viewpoint of the rapist and the still-objective narrator. No description of the appearance or feelings of Io colors our reactions. Ignoring another version, according to which Io was a priestess of Juno and was raped in the shrine by the god, Ovid shapes his account to resemble the preceding story. Jupiter had spotted her a few moments after her father last saw her (588) and approached her with a short speech of would-be seduction. Ovid wastes little effort on the speech (589–97) because Jupiter put little effort into it himself, and besides, we have just heard a lengthy version of this spiel from Apollo when he approached Daphne (504–24). It has the same result as Apollo's: the girl says nothing, but simply flees in total distrust. However, because Jupiter is omnipotent, he succeeds in the chase where Apollo failed, and he does three things in rapid order: he brings a cloud over the earth, stops Io's flight, and robs her of her chastity (*pudorem* 600). This is our introduction to Jupiter as a lover—before this, we have seen him only as a somewhat unconvincing exponent of divine justice in the punishment of Lycaon and in the decision to destroy humankind by the Flood.

Jupiter has a wife, who regularly plays a role in this story as a tormentor of Io. Ovid introduces her in a comic situation that features a confrontation between the guilty husband and the jealous wife, while the third member of the love-triangle remains silent and featureless. Juno immediately suspects that the cloud over the earth is not natural, but designed to conceal one of her husband's typical amours (605–6), and she determines to investigate. By the time she arrives, however, clever Jupiter has already taken the next step of concealment: he has changed Io into what he expects will be an innocent-appearing cow (610–12). Not in the least deceived, Juno acts the role of a compliant and trusting wife and asks for the cow as a present. This puts the god into an embarrassing position, which Ovid presents as a seriocomic moral dilemma: a conflict between *pudor* and *amor*. The audience easily measures the ethical quality by comparison with similar dilemmas in earlier literature such as those in Terentian comedy or Dido's choices in *Aeneid* 4. Jupiter lacks the commitment and tragic sense of love that human beings exhibit, and he has compromised not only that love but also the very meaning of *pudor*, as we have seen, by the rape. So he makes his decision amorally, in order to save face (having already in fact lost all shame), and he hands over the cow to Juno.

To make sure that the cow or girl causes her no further trouble, Juno assigns hundred-eyed Argus to watch her. Ovid views this situation as an opportunity to play with some motifs of love elegy, as if Argus is both a cowherd and at the same time the guardian of the virtue of the beloved. Only at this point does he give Io any personality, and it is one of those dual personalities that particularly intrigued the poet in Books 1–4, the human being inside the new body, still feeling like the girl Io and articulating her human thoughts, though "pathetically" unable to communicate them to the human beings she encounters, whether Argus her keeper or even Inachus her father. This was apparently a dramatic situation that Calvus had richly exploited, too, in a highly sentimental fashion, it would seem, and Ovid acts to distinguish clearly his narrative tone from his predecessor's. Io appears to be very pathetic, but the narrator remains objective and thus tends to distance us and make us aware of the nature of her self-pity. Though oppressed by her guardian, this girl-cow does not make a very serious elegiac heroine. She seems more concerned over the inedible grass that she must eat, the muddy water that she has to drink, and the lack of a mattress at night (632–34), than she does over her rape. Only by trying to perform certain functions does she realize the extent of her loss. She cannot gesture imploringly to Argus, for lack of hands; she moos when she tries to speak; and finally, as she reaches her river-father Inachus and wants to drink, she sees her bovine reflection in the water and is thoroughly frightened and dismayed at herself. She has become aware of her dualism, but not as aware as we are.

The narrative background has been provided, and Io has now returned, though as a cow, for a "reunion" with her anxious father. But there is a slight problem, which our narrator chooses to examine closely. Although the human sensibility of Io can recognize her father, Inachus cannot see his daughter inside that cow-form. So how can the reunion (642 ff.) be effected? Io acts like a too-tame cow, with some of those sentimental devices that Walt Disney perfected in his representation of creatures like Bambi: she slavers kisses all over her father (who is to be thought of as human rather than river-like in form), her great eyes flow with tears, and she wants to moo her feelings of woe. With a stroke of ingenuity she figures out how to write her simple name with her hoof and she scrawls a line and circle to spell Io. That is the means of recognition and the cue for Inachus to emote with lines of bourgeois sentiments that remind us of Callimachean motifs. The father misses the real issues in this "comedy" and can only focus on the frustration of his marital plans for Io. Now, she will have to mate with a bull, and give him calves for grandchildren (658 ff.)!

Argus breaks up this grotesque scene of pathos—we are expected to keep seeing the father embracing this mooing cow throughout his anguished speech—and drives the cow off. But Jupiter cannot stand the situation and decides to dispose of Argus. He cannot do it directly, because that would be an admission of his guilt to Juno, so he sends Mercury to murder the guard (670). That purpose and the circumstances of Argus' death rather radically affect the playful tone which Ovid has assumed until now, and we can be sure, from comparison with other narratives that resort to sudden shifts of tone, that Ovid has planned this unsettling move. Argus is lulled by a song (689 ff.) that the poet contrives as still another version of the topos of nymph pursued by a lusty deity. He falls asleep before it reaches its expected ending of metamorphosis and, in place of that predictable close, we hear of the bloody murder of gullible Argus. Implicitly, the whole love-comedy, in Ovid's presentation, has turned ugly.

At the death of her servant Argus, Juno angrily re-enters the picture. She assigns a Fury to Io, an Ovidian variant for the customary gadfly, to plague her in body and spirit, and drive her from Argos by land all the way around the Aegean and around the eastern Mediterranean to Egypt, where the exhausted cow-girl, now in an advanced stage of pregnancy from the rape, collapses. With her bovine tears and lowing (732), she attempts to express her human protest to Jupiter over her sufferings. Without defining precisely what Jupiter feels, Ovid describes the god's negotiations with Juno, which, typically, are dishonest and designed only to end his embarrassment. "Never again will there be a reason for pain," he starts off with a show of honest remorse; and we expect him to swear off his libertinism. But then he limits his reform by concluding "from *this* girl." And not long after, the impenitent god will rape Callisto, fully aware of his infidelity, and then Europa. Nevertheless, Juno accepts what she can get, and so, since there is no need to disguise Jupiter's affair by continued metamorphosis, Io recovers her human body. Ovid does not state which deity, if either, is responsible for this reverse-metamorphosis. By devoting some space to it, however, he gives us the sense that Io indeed receives some recompense for all her troubles (738–46). And soon after, she bears a son, Epaphus.

With many stories of Jupiter as rapist to choose from, Ovid has selected this one as his first, and, fully conscious of the varying ways in which Io's adventures have been recounted, he has carefully shaped his narrative for this account. In subsequent stories he intends to be progressively harder on the rapist and other gods and more sympathetic to the human victims, but here he affects to keep his distance, to give the facts of the rape in mild terms, and to ignore the feelings of the victim. The gods have no sense of morality, and Jupiter manipulates ethical terms for his own advantage, uses metamorphosis to conceal his infidelity, and continuously tries to deceive and outwit his wife rather than to settle their dispute honestly. The first sequence of events inserts the rape-account into the anxious search of father for daughter, of daughter for father. When the two do achieve their reunion, Ovid makes it grotesque and comically maudlin, so that we feel little more attracted to the mortals in this story than to the deities. In the second set of events, we study the murder of Argus. Ovid uses a great deal of ingenuity here to ruin the comedy. The boring recapitulation of the chase after Syrinx, which appears to be another elegiac game, is deliberately aborted and replaced with vicious murder. That is enough to suggest how much violence and evil underlie this bourgeois Hellenistic dispute among the gods. Then, in the final sequence, we return to the comic arrangement between husband and wife over this nuisance of a cow, and Io recovers her human body. It is as though nothing has happened. Or is it? In any case, we see Ovid's genius at work here, as he vies with his noted predecessor Calvus and reorganizes familiar material, with innovations, to emphasize some of his favorite topics and embody some of the key themes of this poem.

B. Style and Meter

It used to be assumed that, because Ovid wrote a long poem in hexameters, the *Metamorphoses* was automatically an epic poem. That assumption led to many critical excesses, and in recent years some scholars have reacted by moving toward the opposite extreme, namely by arguing that Ovid really continued to be what he had always been and what he shows himself to be in his other surviving verse, a master of elegy. The hexameter, then, would only be a deceptive mask for his typical non-epic, elegiac mannerisms and techniques. The solution to this controversy lies in taking a middle position and recognizing the fact that Ovid is both an elegiac and epic poet, neither entirely one nor the other. He handles with dexterity the many techniques that he perfected during twenty years as an elegiac poet in Rome, as the great successor to the infinitely ingenious Propertius. He also consciously writes in the perspective of the epic tradition, having closely studied Lucretius and, even more admiringly, the three hexameter poems of Vergil, particularly the *Aeneid*. Remember, writing continuous hexameters, especially those practiced by Ovid, was not so terribly different from producing elegiac couplets. Thus, in the *Metamorphoses,*

we find combinations of elegiac and epic (Vergilian) practices
and the resultant ambiguities of effect: Ovid has planned these.

Let us look again at the story of Io and its narrative
stylistics to get a better sense of Ovid's methods. We focus
first on the father:

> Inachus unus abest imoque reconditus antro
> fletibus auget aquas natamque miserrimus Io
> luget ut amissam; nescit, vitane fruatur
> an sit apud manes, sed quam non invenit usquam,
> esse putat nusquam atque animo peiora veretur.
>
> (583–87)

Notice that the narrative tense is the present, as often in Ovid.
Notice, too, the way Ovid uses the connective *-que* in 583 and
584. Instead of using it as Vergil did to connect semantically
and syntactically similar words, for example, two verbs or two
nouns, Ovid has made *-que* just another *and*—something to be
added to the first word of a new clause or phrase, regardless
of the strangeness. Here is a weeping male, copiously weeping.
To justify such emotions in epic, we would expect a tragic
context, and indeed Ovid starts to spell it out as a death. But
note how the sharp-witted poet has elaborated the sorrow: the
river god adds to his own waters with his tears! (584) Elegiac
wit undercuts epic pathos. It would have been quite enough
for a critic like Scaurus if Ovid had stopped at the middle of
585. But Ovid does elaborate on the father's thoughts about
Io for another two and a half lines. Elaboration is a key tactic
for coloring audience response. Little by little, he shifts our
attention from *where* Io is to *whether* she is. In the witty move
from *non usquam* to *nusquam,* the poet prevents us from taking
the thought of death seriously. And in fact, of course, Io is
not dead. The problem reduces itself to: *what* she is. With this
introduction, then, he drops the father and his tearful anxiety,
to explore exactly what has happened to the girl, her fate worse
than death.

The narrative of events introduces Jupiter brusquely:

> viderat a patrio redeuntem Iuppiter illam
> flumine et 'o virgo Iove digna tuoque beatum

nescio quem factura toro, pete' dixerat 'umbras
altorum nemorum' (et nemorum monstraverat umbras)
'dum calet et medio sol est altissimus orbe.'

(588–92)

Note the pluperfect main tenses, the setting of scene by the
narrator and the added self-serving details by Jupiter, the unepic
introduction of a speech, the obvious unepic deviousness of
this amatory god, and the dramatic use of parenthesis. Ovid
regularly sketches out initial background with the pluperfect.
Thus, even where he does not say so, his use of that tense to
tell us of the time of day, the landscape, or the family of a
character warns us that he is setting the stage for his principal
events.

Ovid is very aware of the dramatic situation in which he
stages his actions. Having just mentioned Inachus and his fears,
he decides to start with the girl's visit to and departure from
her father, who is now viewed simply as a river—which would
offer a second reason for her journey, namely, to fetch water.
Many a girl, in Greco-Roman folktales, was approached and
raped while engaged in the simple virginal task of getting water
at the river or well. Jupiter, seeing her heading home with her
burden of water, affects to be concerned for her comfort, so
he comments on the heat of the day (it is high noon, 592) and
urges her to move into the shade of the woods (and presumably
rest for a while, with him). These scenic details do not just
help our pictorial imagination; they also belong to a cluster of
typical details that collect around attempts on maidenly virtue,
and so they set up expectations that the narrative quickly grati-
fies. The girl drawing water typically is ravished, and the same
is true for the pretty girl resting at high noon in the woods. As
the poem develops, we find that the poet accumulates typical
details around many narrative contexts, so that he creates his
own versions of "type-scenes." They differ strikingly from the
epic models of Homer and Vergil. Ovid's speeches throughout
this poem abandon the epic formalities that Ennius and Vergil
adapted from Homer. Instead of a clear formula at beginning
and end, often precisely a hexameter long, Ovid starts and
ends without sharp separation from the narrative, making the

transition in the middle of a line and of a sentence, as exemplified here: *et . . . dixerat* (589–90).

The speeches themselves are unrealistic, making quick points rather than expanding with an epic spaciousness that evokes a true human situation. Here, Jupiter gets to his purposes with instant seductiveness and no small talk. The first compliment, that Io is lovely enough to merit the attentions of Jupiter himself, is a tactic of dramatic irony, as if the old goat were smirking in our direction as he spoke. We may smile at this dishonest ploy, but we also are meant to distance ourselves from a roué like this. The next compliment is a routine abbreviation of a wooing tactic, used properly to remind the maiden of her future marriage (and therefore also of her need to stay chaste for that time). Homer established an epic model for such a situation and speech in Odysseus' courteous but unamorous words to Nausicaa when he first encountered her on the beach in Phaeacia (*Od.* 6.149 ff.). By contrast with the Greek hero, Jupiter here emerges as an unheroic, subhuman rat, not fit for an epic and rather at the level of the egotistic male speaker in Roman elegy. He manipulates his words to promote his purposes, and the parenthesis helps to remind us of his self-conscious "act." Using the shade as one of his ploys, he makes sure that Io and we give thought to the woods (and their sinister potentialities) by interrupting his spiel with a histrionic gesture. Michael Von Albrecht has devoted an entire, valuable monograph to the unique ways in which Ovid treats parentheses in the *Metamorphoses*. The poet, then, uses several devices to impress upon his audience that they are witnessing the performance of a consummate actor.

I jump a bit to the end of the speech and the way Ovid smoothly fuses it with the next dramatic actions.

> 'ne fuge me!' fugiebat enim. iam pascua Lernae
> consitaque arboribus Lyrcea reliquerat arva,
> cum deus inducta latas caligine terras
> occuluit tenuitque fugam rapuitque pudorem.
> (597–600)

Jupiter has introduced himself to Io as a god—not an ordinary plebeian god, but the god of the lightning himself, the ruler of the other gods. His last words indicate how successful he has been, as he pleads with the girl not to flee and hopelessly gives up his seductive routine. Ovid does not need to tell us, but Io has seen through the words to the intention, so clearly that she does not even believe what is true, namely, that this seducer is Jupiter after all.

So the speech ends abortively, and the narrative resumes with the stage direction from the poet in 597 about Io's flight. With *iam*, Ovid uses another familiar sentence structure: that conjunction with a pluperfect main verb, which in effect gives more background, followed by a subordinate *cum*-clause with verbs in the perfect tense. Since the pluperfect, despite its masquerading as a main verb, proves to present the temporal conditions for the actions of the so-called subordinate clause, it is customary to call that device *cum-inversum,* as a way of noting the true function of the clause to provide the principal facts or actions of the scene. Within the *cum*-clause, Ovid embeds an ablative absolute, another favorite narrative device of his. Although we can easily catch its meaning with a translation, such as: "after bringing darkness over the broad lands," we may find the accusative *terras* a bit unusual. Ovid makes free and frequent use of the somewhat artificial, Greek or archaic Latin syntax that we sometimes call the Greek accusative or internal accusative. We could also call the ablative instrumental and *terras* direct object of *occuluit.* It is a poetic freedom that smacks of epic style, but see how he employs it: to describe the guilty concealment of an elegiac adulterer! He is continuously aware of opportunities to force epic and elegy into significant confrontation.

Having used 599 for the preparatory and subordinated actions of the ablative absolute, Ovid then crowds three main verbs into 600, to give us the rush of decisive actions that result in rape. This is a very careful and deliberate arrangement of his narrative structure. The actions are worded in a dispassionate and objective manner, focusing exclusively on the god and totally ignoring the girl and all feelings. There has been not one word of "love" throughout the speech and the subsequent narrative, and we have no reason to attribute any love to this rape. The third clause, *rapuitque pudorem,* represents the act of rape with a prudish circumlocution, much like our Victorian expression, "stealing a woman's honor," which insidiously introduces the very moral issues that Jupiter has ignored. Ovid likes to get us to think about the ethical factors in his stories from an oblique viewpoint, not that of the trivial characters themselves. Finally, although I intend to deal with meter more extensively below, notice here how the poet uses his metrical skill to reinforce the rush of heedless self-indulgence implied by the three verbs that he crowds into 600: he uses five straight dactyls and no elision to create the maximum impression of unimpeded speed.

When Juno suspiciously descends from Olympus, Jupiter tries to avert possible embarrassment:

> coniugis adventum praesenserat inque nitentem
> Inachidos vultus mutaverat ille iuvencam
> (bos quoque formosa est): speciem Saturnia vaccae
> quamquam invita, probat nec non, et cuius et unde
> quove sit armento, veri quasi nescia, quaerit.
>
> (610–14)

In addition to the loose -*que* (attached here to a preposition in 610), the pluperfect background tenses, and the narrator's parenthetical aside in 611, notice the hyperbaton in *nitentem . . . iuvencam,* the device of epic antonomasia, the terminology of metamorphosis, and the Ovidian comic focus on husband-wife distrust. Separation of attribute and noun is a common poetic device in a language like Latin. But Ovid, as shown here, uses the separation shrewdly. In the first place, he keeps the audience in suspense as to how and into what Jupiter has changed Io; and the participle *nitentem* can function as properly with human beings as with animals. Then, the hyperbaton enables the poet graphically to present the idea that he likes to explore in the *Metamorphoses,* namely, the enclosure of the essential human form and spirit within an intractable alien body, such as that of a cow for Io.

Like *hyperbaton, antonomasia* is an unusual rhetorical term, which simply defines a technique of referring to a character by some substitute word or phrase instead of the name. This was a device that Homer had made familiar to the admirers of the epic tradition: the use of a word defining paternal or maternal connections, the use of an adjectival substantive alluding to family or place of origin, or other variants such as reference to the occupation of the character. Io has the same form in either nominative or accusative, both of which Ovid uses freely, but he avoids the problems of the Greek declension in the oblique forms. Still, that is not the sole reason for using *Inachidos* in 611. He is both reminding us of an epic mannerism and keeping the father in our minds. This in fact is the moment when what Inachus feared as the fate worse than death occurs: not the rape, but the disgraceful cow-form and the loss of a "proper marriage." The second instance of antonomasia introduces Juno on this scene as *Saturnia,* a traditional epic epithet that Ennius had employed and that Vergil had made very familiar. The antonomasia evokes an epic expectation; the actual scene of guilty sexual indulgence and mutual moves to pursue and allay suspicion by wife and husband evokes the far more trivial world of Roman comedy and elegy. Juno sees through Jupiter, but she participates in the comedy that he has tried to manage, only inventing her own lines that work at cross-purposes with his and threaten his "act."

The most common type-scene of this Ovidian poem has to be the description of metamorphosis, the event that gives the work its title. There are more than two hundred tales of such transformation, many of them with multiple changes. This tale has the two alterations of Io, into a cow first, then back into a human woman (738 ff.), plus the tales of how the peacock got Argus' eyes transferred to its plumage (720 ff.) and how the nymph Syrinx turned into a reed that Pan could use for a pan-pipe (705 ff.). Ovid has a variety of different words for the word "form" (here, *vultus, forma* (cf. *formosa* 612), and *speciem;* and he has countless synonyms for the verb of transformation, transitive or intransitive. In 610–11, we meet the most common of such verbal units: a form of *mutare* + accusative object + preposition *in* with accusative noun to cover the action of Jupiter in changing Io's body into that of a cow. Once he has the animal at the end of 611, the poet then carefully uses two further terms for *cow* in 612, each a little less poetic and sympathetic. When Juno approves the appearance of the *vacca,* Ovid expects us to sense the absurdity in her treating a stupid cow as a rival, but not to forget the outrage of what Jupiter has done to the girl Io. The moment of metamorphosis can be packed with much meaning by a poet as skillful as Ovid.

Ovid uses many obvious rhetorical devices, not for their own sakes or to display his cleverness, as critics sometimes assert, but to expose the elements of the narrative to our critical judgment. We have already seen how he analyzed Inachus' feelings of missing Io in 585–87 with skillful elaboration. The devices of anaphora, chiasmus, and zeugma illustrate other aspects of a verbal focus that continually turns away from a merely emotional response to situations.

Anaphora is the repetition of initial words in successive clauses. Jupiter, in his effort to catch Io's favorable attention, introduces himself and his superior qualities:

> nec de plebe deo, *sed qui* caelestia magna
> sceptra manu teneo, *sed qui* vaga fulmina mitto.
> (595–96)

Denying that he is some ordinary deity, he asserts instead his importance as wielder of the heavenly sceptre and hurler of thunderbolts. And in order to make himself seem more impressive, he avoids the simple, unemphatic connective (*et* or *-que*) between clauses and repeats the two heavy syllables. Thus, Ovid stresses the egotism of the god (at a time when a little morality would have been preferable). The repetition gains stress from the identical metrical position at the central caesura, after a pause, in both lines. It also seems to me that Ovid lets Jupiter boastfully refer to his thunderbolts as *vaga* to further sabotage his egotism: what the god thinks are fearsome weapons against sinners have already proved to be rather inaccurate and ineffective in Book 1.

Another example of self-sabotage by anaphora occurs in Inachus' lament over Io's metamorphosis into a cow, which he construes as the frustration of his plans for a dynastic marriage:

> de grege nunc tibi vir et de grege natus habendus. (660)

Like snobbish Jupiter, who boasted of his non-plebeian status, the father of Io had his proud eyes set on an aristocratic marriage. What desolates him now, therefore, is that she must

marry below herself, into the common "herd"; only this is no
metaphor: she must act out the role of her cow-body and find
her marital and domestic future in the cattleherd. It is Inachus'
snobbery that emerges in the anaphora, not his paternal feelings
for poor Io.

Chiasmus is the arrangement of paired ideas in adjacent
clauses so that, if diagrammed, the relationship, when we set
the second clause under the first and connect the key terms,
can be seen as an *X* or as a Greek *chi* (hence chi-asmus). A good
example can be found in the Io-story where Jupiter considers the
ethical issues that affect his decision of whether or not to give
Juno the cow:

> quid faciat? *crudele* suos **addicere** amores,
> **non dare** *suspectum est: pudor* est, qui **suadeat illinc**,
> **hinc dissuadet** *amor*. victus pudor esset amore,
> sed, leve si munus sociae generisque torique
> *vacca* **negaretur**, **poterat** *non vacca* videri.
>
> (617–21)

Three instances of chiasmus in close succession force us to
examine closely the morality about which Jupiter proves so
casual and self-serving. In the first case, he says to himself
that it is cruel to hand over his beloved, but suspicious not to
do so. Ovid has him put it so that in the antithesis of "cruel"
and "suspicious" the emotive terms get the stress by framing
the contrast. Note that Jupiter sees drawbacks in both directions;
he does not declare that it would be "honorable" to refuse
making the gift.

In the second case, the antithesis puts at the emphatic
terminal positions the specifically ethical abstracts *pudor* and
amor. But it is not immediately evident to which of the previous
terms the abstracts and their suasion or dissuasion belong. Only
when we get to "love," do we know how Jupiter uses "shame."
Shame is urging him to hand over the cow; love opposes it.
A very strange sense of shame, which Ovid may be suggesting
by the subjunctive of characteristic, *suadeat*. The negatives
have been switched, and magically Jupiter's predicament is
edging toward a "positive" decision. Forget the fact, of course,
that the god is concerned only about the appearance of honor.

In destroying Io's honor, he of course has lost the reality of his own. In the *Aeneid* and in Roman morality, it is shameful for love to prevail over honor—that, after all, was what ruined Dido. So in the next chiasmus, Ovid shows Jupiter's tawdry sense of shame defeating love (or revealing how trivial his love was in the first place). Briefly inclined to yield to love, the god calculates that he would not get away with it. The issue reduces itself in his mind to the bare amoral decision that the cow could not seem a cow. The repeated chiasmus throws the issues at us and makes us sort them out carefully, not in the sleazy, self-serving manner of the god.

Zeugma, as the Greek term suggests, is the yoking or pairing of two words in connection with a single verb. The two yoked words normally have the same syntax, but their meanings produce a clash, because, for example, one will function with the verb to create an everyday literal description, while the second will extract a figurative meaning from the same verb and raise a serious ethical problem. Ovidian wit aims at that clash, usually to expose the trivialization of morality by characters such as the gods. Ovid's great admirer, Alexander Pope, was a master of this device, and he employs zeugma to get at human duplicity in *The Rape of the Lock:*

> Whether the Nymph shall break Diana's Law,
> Or some frail China Jar receive a flaw,
> Or *stain her Honour or her new Brocade,*
> Forget her Pray'rs, or miss a Masquerade,
> Or *lose her Heart or Necklace* at a Ball.
>
> (II, 105–9)

The linking of concrete and abstract words regularly suggests that people treat ethical values as mere detail: "honour" and "brocade" receive the same kind of stain!

Here are a few examples of zeugma from Books 2 and 3 of the *Metamorphoses:*

> laurea delapsa est audito crimine amanti,
> et pariter *vultusque deo plectrumque colorque*
> excidit.
>
> (2.600–2)

Three nouns, all given the "epic" -*que,* function as subject of the one verb, but the pick that falls clashes with the face and color, which supposedly reveal the deep emotions of the loving god.

> fulmen ab aure
> misit in aurigam pariterque *animaque rotisque*
> *expulit* et saevis conpescuit ignibus ignes.
> (2.311–13)

Two nouns, both ablatives of separation, give us an ambivalent impression of Jupiter's action against Phaethon, that rash driver whom the god dislodged from the chariot and his soul, killing him. Killing and unseating were the same thing for Jupiter. A variant of this device links one noun (usually an accusative object) with another of clashing sense by an ablative of accompaniment, often too adding the adverb *pariter,* which we observe Ovid using in the two examples I have just given, to insist on the clashing connection.

> et *pariter vitam cum sanguine fudit.* (2.610)

Jealous Apollo of the first example shoots an arrow at Coronis; fatally wounded, the girl pours out her blood and life.

> ille diu pavidus *pariter cum mente colorem*
> *perdiderat.*
> (3.99–100)

The "heroic" Cadmus lost his color and his mind in his fear.

We can pause a moment, before going on to metrical features, to summarize some key aspects of Ovid's style. Ovid writes in what I might call a transparent manner. He uses additive structures of clauses linked casually by *et* and -*que* rather than complex subordination. He elaborates one clause by near-repetition that invites us to re-examine it. He constantly asks us to recognize the connections between words and ideas, because he creates verbal clashes. His wit penetrates the careless or amoral use of words by his characters and exposes the duplicitous tendencies of gods and mortals alike. Characters do a lot of talking about feelings, and Ovid places them in situations that would normally, say in Vergilian epic, stir convincing passions and provoke sympathetic response from the audience. Ovid, however, uses his witty, articulate style to question the words and feelings of his supposedly emoting characters. Instead of the powerful symbolic devices of simile and metaphor, which Vergil uses so brilliantly to develop his and our complicated responses to events, Ovid uses figures of speech, such as anaphora and zeugma, to concentrate our attention on the way people use and abuse words and their basic meanings.

Ovid uses the metrical potentialities of the hexameter to support his basic stylistic goals of transparency, speed, and exposure rather than sympathetic masking of our human confusions. An obvious feature of the Ovidian hexameter is its preference for dactyls. He represents the decisive break between the Republican Latin poets, including the first generation of Augustan writers like Vergil, and the poets of the Empire, and his example is significant. Although there are some variations from book to book, the *Aeneid* averages for its eight most common arrangements of dactyls and spondees a ratio of twenty spondees to twelve dactyls. By contrast, with even less variation, the *Metamorphoses* exhibits an average ratio of twenty dactyls to twelve spondees. That is a marked reversal of preferences. We may break down these general statistics to present a table of the most common arrangements in Ovid's Books 1–5. Since the final two feet of any hexameter take a predictable form, it is customary to limit analysis to the first four feet. I use the abbreviations "D" for dactyl, "S" for spondee.

Book	1	2	3	4	5	Average frequency for 5 books
Total vs.	779	875	733	803	678	
DSSS	108	110	97	104	100	13.16%
DDSS	86	137	94	103	79	12.90%
DSSD	98	99	83	110	84	12.25%
DSDS	90	90	90	94	78	11.43%
DDSD	81	96	85	87	77	11.01%
DDDS	69	79	67	56	68	8.76%
DSDD	70	49	55	52	51	7.16%
DDDD	44	35	37	51	27	5.02%
						81.69%

The eight most common patterns of Ovidian hexameter, which account for more than 81 percent of his verses, demonstrate a clear preference for dactyls. All eight have an initial dactyl; only one of the eight uses more than two spondees; four have three dactyls.

Comparison with the preferred patterns of the *Aeneid* brings out the striking differences between Ovid and Vergil. Vergil's preferred eight, used in 72.78 percent of his verses, are in order as follows: DSSS, DDSS, DSDS, SDSS, SSSS, DDDS, SSDS, SDDS. Four of these start with spondees, all eight end with spondees, and only one uses more than two dactyls. The schemes DSSS and DDSS, which Vergil made first and second, retain their respective positions in Books 1–5 of the *Metamorphoses* (though not in every book, as they vie with each other and with DSSD for their ranking). However, SDSS, SSSS, and SSDS, which Vergil made his fourth, fifth, and seventh, were reduced to relative insignificance by Ovid because of their spondaic emphasis: in the *Metamorphoses*, SDSS occurs in about 5 percent of the verses, SSSS in about 1.5 percent, and SSDS in about 2 percent. The change is highly evident in the emphatic patterns SSSS and DDDD: Vergil used SSSS in more than 7 percent, DDDD in 2.1 percent of the verses of the *Aeneid*, whereas Ovid has DDDD in 5.02 percent, SSSS in 1.5 percent, of his verses. Vergil aimed for and achieved a slower, heavier, and graver pace than Ovid, who tells a quick and witty story and supports it with dactyls.

A number of other factors contribute to the impression of lightness and quickness in Ovid's verse. Vergil made elision one of the important features of his hexameter, using it often and skillfully to interlock phrases and reinforce the complexity of his narrative. Ovid aims at a neater verse, and he keeps it smooth and continuously flowing by cutting down on elisions. To take two narrative passages of equal length: in the opening hundred lines of *Aeneid* 4, Vergil elides fifty-one times, applying elision to a variety of significant words; in the first hundred lines of the Io story (*Met.* 1.583-682) Ovid elides thirty-three times, but mainly in an unemphatic way with forms such as *et* and *-que*, connectives between clauses, and *est* with past participle or adjective at the end of clauses and lines.

Ovidian elisions do not materially slow down or condense his flowing narrative.

Ovid's treatment of caesurae contributes to the same clarity of presentation. In the commentary, I shall follow modern techniques of notation. Traditional terminology developed the cumbrous words *trihemimeral, penthemimeral,* and *hepthemimeral* to mark the three most common caesurae ("cuts" in metrical feet produced by word-division). These terms reflect an analysis of the hexameter into twelve half-feet, with caesurae after the third, fifth, and seventh half-feet (hence, tri-, pent-, and hept-hemimeral). While retaining the essential analysis, I shall replace the awkward terminology. I shall talk of the hexameter as a line with twelve *positions;* the conventional caesurae, then, will occur "at positions 3, 5, or 7." For example, in 1.583–87, Ovid gives us an opportunity to adjust to his practice:

> Inachus unus abest imoque reconditus antro
> fletibus auget aquas netamque miserrimus Io
> luget ut amissam; nescit, vitane fruatur   585
> an sit apud manes, sed quam non invenit usquam,
> esse putat nusquam atque animo peiora veretur.

The first four lines have the central caesura at position 5, clearly defined by the organization of clauses. In 583 and 584, a new clause announced by a word + *-que* starts after 5; in 585 and 586, the new clause declares itself with the punctuation at 5. In the fifth line, what might at first sight seem a similar organization, two clauses linked at the caesura by *atque,* has been suppressed by the double elision involving the conjunction, and instead Ovid has resorted to caesurae at positions 3 (after *putat*) and 7 (after *animo*). The frequent use of the caesura by Ovid to reinforce the articulation of his syntatical structures makes for a result that differs significantly from Vergil's effects. Consider *Aeneid* 4.1–5:

> at regina gravi/ iamdudum saucius cura
> vulnus alit venis/ et caeco carpitur igni.
> multa viri virtus animo/ multusque recursat
> gentis honos;/ haerent infixi pectore vultus
> verbaque nec placidam/ membris dat cura quietem.

Only line 2 resembles Ovid's technique of dividing the verse at the central caesura of 5 between two clauses. In lines 1 and 5, the poet also uses the caesura at 5, but he splits adjective and noun thereby, setting adjective at the caesura and noun at the line-end. This produces a quite different structure for the line. The clause begun at the start of 1 does not conclude until the caesura of 2; the clause of 5 has begun with the conjunction *nec* considerably before the caesura. In line 4, the punctuation reinforces the main caesura at position 3. There may be a subordinate caesura at position 5, after the first word in the new clause, but otherwise the sense runs on without interruption. In line 3, a reader would be hard put, while reading, to decide where the main caesura is; Vergil in fact has ended words at positions 3, 5, and 7, and only when we realize that a new clause begins at 7 with *multusque* do we have control of the previous clause. But the breaks all had their effects as we read the line. The greater versatility of Vergil's caesural practices goes with the greater complexity of his syntactical organization to produce the typically dense Vergilian style.

Just as the handling of the middle of the line differs in the two poets, so their treatment of the line-end serves varying ends. The five lines of Vergil consist of two sentences, so that lines 2 and 5 are end-stopped. But line 1 consists of a long metaphorical description of the "wounded" queen Dido that carries over into 2 for its verb and complements. That technique of carry-over or "run-on" is called *enjambement*. We see its different operations in 3 and 4. A short clause begins late in 3 and consists of adjective and verb, which forces us on into 4 to find the rest of the subject, a nominative with a dependent genitive. Then, Vergil begins a new clause, which seems to be complete at the line end until he adds at the start of 5 *verbaque*, a second subject for the verb. The effect of Vergilian enjambement, like his caesura and clausal patterns, is never quite predictable: he is always complicating his narrative and our response to it.

Though at first view Ovid seems to have constructed a longer sentence than Vergil and therefore used more enjambement, it can in fact be shown to be less complex. In the first line of the previously cited passage, he has given us a complete

clause about Inachus' absence. Although he starts a new clause
and has not completed it by line-end, what he has added is
really more about the god's absence, namely, where he is. The
rest of the clause then tells us of his weeping. Ovid then goes
right on to tell us why he weeps, leaving the verb in suspense
to the start of 3, after enjambement. In both 3 and 4, the lines
and clauses end together. We know that 3 will be completed
in 4 by an alternative indirect question. We know that the
relative clause ending 4 will have to be completed by a main
clause, and Ovid does that with witty byplay between *non . . .
usquam* and *nusquam*. In other instances, we encounter a type
of enjambement that Vergil avoided with care: it openly violates
epic practice and allows Ovid's narrative to flow over swiftly
and casually into the next line. Thus, instead of letting the
thought that he plans to continue develop from the middle of
the line or earlier, Ovid starts the clause or phrase of the run-
on in the fifth or sixth foot: for example, *circumspicit, ut quae /
deprensi totiens iam nosset furta marita* (1.605–6); *posset credi
Latonia, si non / corneus huic arcus, si non foret aureus illi*
(1.696–97). There is much art in the Ovidian practice; it simply
differs from that of Vergil and works well in the service of
quite distinct stylistic goals: articulateness by articulation.

Ovid uses a number of devices to emphasize the shape of
certain lines. For example, he imitates the trick known as the
Golden Line, which Catullus and the Neoterics brought into
Latin and Vergil and his generation employed more sparingly.
Strictly speaking, this line should have a specific organization
of two adjectives and their two respective nouns framing a verb
in the center, such as:

pulchra verecundo subfuderat ora rubore (1.484),

a pointed description of the way Daphne blushed with embar-
rassment and annoyance at the mention of marriage; or:

puniceum curva decerpserat arbore pomum (5.536),

the fateful action of Proserpina in picking a pomegranate in
Hades and eating some of the seeds. Note that the adjectives
and nouns may be arranged ABverbAB or ABverbBA. Ovid

sometimes uses the Golden Line organization to describe something that is anything but grand or epic, with obvious parodic intent.

Another popular Neoteric device used by Ovid that Cicero deplored and Vergil severely restricted, employed by Catullus in *C.* 64, is the double spondee at the line end, which violates our expectation of a dactyl in the fifth foot. The first instance in the *Metamorphoses,* in 1.11, with its Greek word, has a distinctly Neoteric feel:

> nec bracchia longo
> margine terrarum porrexerat *Amphitrite.*

One word provides the double spondee. And Ovid avails himself of the opportunity to produce another rarity, a four-word hexameter. A resonant name of Latin origin shows more daring, as in 2.226:

> aeriaeque Alpes et nubifer *Appenninus.*

The double spondee emphatically concludes a list of mountains of Europe and Asia. Still more daringly, Ovid breaks the double spondee between a final word of three syllables and a polysyllabic word that leads up to it, as in 1.732 of the Io-story:

> et gemitu et lacrimis et luctiso*no mugitu*
> cum Iove visa queri.

There can be little doubt that Ovid is impudently slowing down the rhythm and upsetting the smooth accentuation of the fifth foot (by "improper" stress on its last syllable) to suggest the awkward and bathetic mooing of the girl turned cow, just before she becomes human in body once more. He compounds the effect by inventing an "epic epithet" for the mooing; he designs the word *luctisono* for this context, and neither he nor anyone else uses it again. Also clever is the similar pattern of 1.117:

> perque hiemes aestusque et inaequal*is autumnos.*

The irregularity of the meter graphically mirrors the irregularity of the autumn season.

Ovid wrote much faster than Vergil, and he and his elegist friends had developed definite techniques to deal with metrical problems. For example, the reader will encounter instances of apostrophe where perhaps the narrator is being familiar with his characters, but also is availing himself of a means to avoid a long syllable:

> illa quidem nollet, sed te quoque, maxi*me* Python,
> tum genuit, populisque novis, incogni*te* serpens.
>
> (1.438–89)

The short syllable of the vocative enables the poet to achieve the expected dactyl in the fifth foot, whereas the ending of the nominative singular would have made a long syllable with the following consonant. (There is also an appealing impudence in the poet's apparent epic respect for the monster.) The need for a dactyl in the fifth foot helps to explain also the use and localization of third declension nouns, especially invented "epic-sounding" words ending in -*men*. To start from the opening of Book 1, note *origine* 3, *tempora* 4, *semina* 9, *lumina* 10, *aëre* 12, *corpore* 18, *pace* 25, *pondere* 26, *levitate* 28, *litora* 37, *tellure* 48, *frigore* 51, *fulgora* 56, *flamina* 59, *sole* 63, *gravitate* 67. The ablative singular of any such noun and the nominative or accusative plurals of neuter nouns gave Ovid the means of gaining a dactyl in the fifth foot. When you add the feminine nominative singular of first declension nouns and adjectives, the neuter plurals (nominative and accusative) of third declension adjectives and participles (e.g., *omnia*), and the active infinitives, you have accounted for the mass of Ovid's fifth feet. The often mechanical practices by which he ground out the endings of his lines resulted in what seem like stereotyped clausules, such as: *fiducia formae* 2.731, 3.270, 4.687; *crinibus angues* 4.454, 495, 792; *pectora palmis* 2.584, 3.481, 5.473; *causa* plus 3-syllable genitive nouns like *doloris* 1.509, 736, *laboris* 4.739 or genitives of the gerund such as *sequendi* 1.507, *dolendi* 2.614, *videndi* 5.258.

Ovid worked out some initial dactylic formulae also for the beginning of a narrative sequence; e.g., *hactenus* (2.610 and nine other times), *protinus* (1.128 and twenty-eight other lines), *dixerat* (1.367 and ten other times), *dixet et* (1.466 and eight more), *non tulit* (1.753 and ten others); *nec* or occasionally *haud mora* (1.717 and seventeen more). Similarly, we note choriambic units that stretch across the first dactyl to the caesura at 3, e.g., *me miserum (-am), quid faciam (-at)?, obstipui (-it), adspicit hunc (hanc), non* or *haud aliter*. For the simple reason that Ovid so often uses these and other formulae and formulaic localization of words, his narrative vocabulary and style seem easier and swifter than Vergil's and free us to concentrate on the duplicitous words and thoughts of his characters.

Normally, in an introduction to a Latin poet, it would be necessary to spend considerable effort commenting on his special syntactical practices. It does not seem to me that this poet requires extensive grammatical explanation. That, in itself, however, is significant. Ovid wrote with such clarity and relative simplicity that most of his constructions are easy to grasp at sight. One will find some of the typical poetic freedoms that the Neoterics, elegists, and Vergil had established beforehand, such as the so-called Greek accusative, the syncopated forms of the perfect (*mutastis* 1.2), ablative structures without the preposition. But Ovid did not try to be daring with his grammar, only to make it serve his primary stylistic purposes. In general, then, his style is a well-devised, well-executed unity, designed to give his audience a feeling of ease about a narrative that moves along in a genial fashion, told by a narrator who lightly intrudes with somewhat malicious or insidious wit, and with equal celerity removes himself from the story, to let the characters reveal themselves and to keep our minds and emotions alive to the unpredictable possibilities of his tales.

V. THE MANUSCRIPT TRADITION

As I said earlier, the *Metamorphoses* was in effect a published poem at the time of Ovid's exile in A.D. 8. Widely read and extremely influential during the first century and thereafter, it vied with the *Aeneid* throughout antiquity. No manuscript, however, not even a fragment, survives from that period; the tradition of Terence, Vergil, and Plautus is far more complete than Ovid's. Even when the Carolingians gave impetus to a revival of learning and the avid copying of manuscripts, the resurrection of the *Metamorphoses* lagged. We possess good texts of Vergil, Horace, Lucretius, Propertius, and even Juvenal from the ninth century, but the best that chance can offer us for Ovid's poem is a few selections in a ninth century anthology of Latin verse and two short fragments. The tenth century is also represented by mere wretched fragments. Only some mid- and late-eleventh century manuscripts have come down to us in good condition, to give us complete versions of the poem. The next centuries, often called the *aetas Ovidiana,* witnessed the immense popularity of Ovid's poetry, so that even today, we can identify more than four hundred manuscripts of the *Metamorphoses* copied before the time printing began. Of those, the following have been regularly used by editors:

E Palat. 1669	12th cent.
F Marcianus 223	11/12th cent. Books 14 and 15 later.
L Laurent. xxxvi.12	11/12th cent. Ends at 12.298.
M Marcianus 225	late 11th cent. Ends at 14.830.
N Neapolitanus iv F3	12th cent. Ends at 14.851.
P Parisinus 8001	12/13th cent.
U Vat. Urb. 341	11/12th. 15.494 ff. later.
W Vat. lat. 5859	1275 A.D.
a Mus. Brit., King's 26	11th cent.
Fragm. Bern. 363	end of 9th cent. Contains 1.1–199, 304–9, 773–79, 2.1–22, 3.1–56.
Fragm. Lipsiense	end of 9th cent. Contains 3.132–252.
Fragm. Parisin.	end of 9th cent. Contains 1.81–193, 2.67–254 (almost illegible after 160).
Frag. Lond. BM 11967 (β)	end of 10th cent. Contains 2.833–3.510, 4.298–5.389, 588–6.411.
Fragm. Harl. BM 2610 (ε)	end of 10th cent. Contains 1.1–3.622.

Fragm. Vat. Urb. 342 | 10th cent. Contains 5.483–6.45, 7.731–8.104.

Planudes | Maximus Planudes' Greek translation of the *Metamorphoses,* made with great fidelity about 1300 from a lost Latin MS.

As this list indicates, most of the fragments come from the first five books, and thus are useful for this commentary. Many of the fuller manuscripts lack Book 15 or have broken off even earlier.

The Latin text in this edition is published by permission of B.G. Teubner, Stuttgart and Leipzig; it is based on a slightly altered version of my *Ovidius, Metamorphoses* (minus the apparatus criticus), which was first published by B.G. Teubner in 1977.

VI. SELECTED BIBLIOGRAPHY

Below, in alphabetical order, is a list of books and articles concerning Ovid and the *Metamorphoses,* primarily those in English. At the end, I place two major collections of articles written to commemorate the bimillennium of Ovid's birth in 1958. Works cited in the notes are included in this list.

Albrecht, M. von. *Die Parenthese in Ovids Metamorphosen und ihre dichterische Funktion = Spudasmata* VII (Hildesheim, 1964).

Anderson, W. S. "Multiple Change in the *Metamorphoses," TAPA* 94 (1963), 1–27.

———, ed. *Ovidius, Metamorphoses.* Stuttgart and Leipzig, 1993.

Avery, M. M. *The Use of Direct Speech in Ovid's Metamorphoses.* Ph.D. dissertation. Chicago, 1937.

Barkan, L. *The Gods Made Flesh: Metamorphosis and the Pursuit of Paganism.* New Haven, 1986.

Barsby, J. *Ovid.* Greece and Rome: New Surveys in the Classics, 12. Oxford, 1978.

Bernbeck, E. J. *Beobachtungen zur Darstellungsart in Ovids Metamorphosen = Zetemata* 43 (Munich, 1967).

Boillat, M. *Les Métamorphoses d'Ovide: thèmes majeurs et problèmes de composition.* Berne and Frankfort-am-Main, 1976.

Bömer, F. Commentary, *Metamorphosen*. 7 vols. Heidelberg, 1969–86.

Brunner, T. F. "The Function of the Simile in Ovid's Metamorphoses," *CJ* 61 (1966), 354–63.

Curran, L. C. "Transformation and Anti-Augustanism in Ovid's *Metamorphoses*," *Arethusa* 5 (1972), 71–91.

de Lacy, P. "Philosophical Doctrine and Poetic Technique in Ovid," *CJ* 43 (1947), 153–61.

Due, O. *Changing Forms: Studies in the Metamorphoses of Ovid.* Classica et Medievalia, Dissertationes 10. Copenhagen, 1974.

Fränkel, H. *Ovid, a Poet Between Two Worlds.* Sather Classical Lectures 18. Berkeley and Los Angeles, 1945.

Frécaut, J.-M. *L'esprit et l'humour chez Ovide.* Grenoble, 1972.

Galinsky, G. K. *Ovid's Metamorphoses: An Introduction to the Basic Aspects.* Oxford, 1975.

Heinsius, N. Text and collations of 150 manuscripts. Amsterdam, 1652.

Heinze, R. "Ovids elegische Erzählung," *Sitzungsberichte Akademie Leipzig* 71, 7 (1919).

Hinds, S. *The Metamorphosis of Persephone. Ovid and the Self-Conscious Muse.* Cambridge, 1987.

Hofmann, H. "Ovids 'Metamorphosen' in der Forschung der letzten 30 Jahren (1950–1979)," *Aufstieg und Niedergang der römischen Welt* II.31.4:2161–273. Berlin and New York, 1981.

Irving, P. M. C. Forbes. *Metamorphosis in Greek Myths.* Oxford, 1990.

Jahn, J. C. Text and Commentary. Leipzig, 1832.

Keith, A. M. *The Play of Fictions: Studies in Ovid's Metamorphoses Book 2.* Ann Arbor, 1992.

Kenney, E. J. "The Style of the *Metamorphoses*," in *Ovid,* edited by J. W. Binns. London, 1973, 116–53.

———. "Ovidius Prooemians," *Proceedings Cambridge Philological Society,* 202 (1976), 47–53.

Knox, P. *Ovid's Metamorphoses and the Traditions of Augustan Poetry.* Cambridge Philological Society, Supplement 11 (1986).

Kovacs, D. "Ovid, *Metamorphoses* 1.2," *CQ* 37 (1987), 458–65.

Lafaye, G. *Les Métamorphoses d'Ovide et leurs modèles grecs.* Paris, 1904.

Lee, A. G., ed. and comm. *Metamorphoses, Book 1.* Cambridge, 1953.

Ludwig, W. *Struktur und Einheit der Metamorphosen Ovids.* Berlin, 1965.

Mack, S. *Ovid*. New Haven, 1988.

Magnus, H. Text and detailed apparatus. Berlin, 1914.

Martindale, C., ed. *Ovid Renewed. Ovidian Influences on Literature and Art from the Middle Ages to the Twentieth Century*. Cambridge, 1988.

Miller, F. J. "Ovid's *Aeneid* and Vergil's: A Contrast in Motivation," *CJ* 23 (1927), 33–43.

Munari, F. *Catalogue of the Mss. of Ovid's Metamorphoses*. Bulletin of the Institute Classical Studies, Supplement 4 (London, 1957).

Myers, K. S. *Ovid's Causes: Cosmogony and Aetiology in the Metamorphoses*. Ann Arbor, 1994.

Otis, B. *Ovid as an Epic Poet*. 2nd ed. Cambridge, 1970.

Owen, S. G. "Ovid's Use of the Simile," *Classical Review* 45 (1931), 97–106.

Parry, H. "Ovid's *Metamorphoses:* Violence in a Pastoral Landscape," *TAPA* 95 (1964), 268–82.

Richlin, A. "Reading Ovid's Rapes," in *Pornography and Representation in Greece and Rome,* edited by A. Richlin. Oxford, 1992, 158–79.

Segal, C. P. *Landscape in Ovid's Metamorphoses: A Study in the Transformations of a Literary Symbol* = *Hermes Einzelschriften* 23 (Wiesbaden, 1969).

Slater, D. A. Full textual apparatus. Oxford, 1927.

Solodow, J. *The World of Ovid's Metamorphoses*. Chapel Hill, 1988.

Steiner, G. "Ovid's *carmen perpetuum*," *TAPA* 89 (1958), 218–36.

Tarrant, R. "Ovid," in *Texts and Transmission: A Survey of the Latin Classics,* edited by L. D. Reynolds. Oxford 1983, 276–82.

Viarre, S. *L'image et la pensée dans les "Métamorphoses" d'Ovide*. Paris, 1964.

Wilkinson, L. P. *Ovid Recalled*. Cambridge, 1955.

Atti del Convegno internazionale ovidiano. Edited by Istituto di Studi romani. Rome, 1959.

Ovidiana: Recherches sur Ovide. Edited by N. I. Herescu. Paris, 1958.

THE *Metamorphoses*

LIBER PRIMUS

In nova fert animus mutatas dicere formas
corpora: di, coeptis (nam vos mutastis et illa)
adspirate meis primaque ab origine mundi
ad mea perpetuum deducite tempora carmen.
5   Ante mare et terras et, quod tegit omnia, caelum
unus erat toto naturae vultus in orbe,
quem dixere Chaos, rudis indigestaque moles
nec quicquam nisi pondus iners congestaque eodem
non bene iunctarum discordia semina rerum.
10 nullus adhuc mundo praebebat lumina Titan,
nec nova crescendo reparabat cornua Phoebe,
nec circumfuso pendebat in aëre tellus
ponderibus librata suis, nec bracchia longo
margine terrarum porrexerat Amphitrite,
15 utque erat et tellus illic et pontus et aër,
sic erat instabilis tellus, innabilis unda,
lucis egens aër: nulli sua forma manebat,
obstabatque aliis aliud, quia corpore in uno
frigida pugnabant calidis, umentia siccis,
20 mollia cum duris, sine pondere habentia pondus.
    Hanc deus et melior litem natura diremit;
nam caelo terras et terris abscidit undas
et liquidum spisso secrevit ab aëre caelum;
quae postquam evolvit caecoque exemit acervo,
25 dissociata locis concordi pace ligavit.
ignea convexi vis et sine pondere caeli
emicuit summaque locum sibi fecit in arce;

proximus est aër illi levitate locoque,
densior his tellus elementaque grandia traxit
30   et pressa est gravitate sua; circumfluus umor
ultima possedit solidumque coercuit orbem.
    Sic ubi dispositam, quisquis fuit ille deorum,
congeriem secuit sectamque in membra redegit,
principio terram, ne non aequalis ab omni
35   parte foret, magni speciem glomeravit in orbis;
tum freta diffudit rapidisque tumescere ventis
iussit et ambitae circumdare litora terrae.
addidit et fontes et stagna inmensa lacusque
fluminaque obliquis cinxit declivia ripis,
40   quae diversa locis partim sorbentur ab ipsa,
in mare perveniunt partim campoque recepta
liberioris aquae pro ripis litora pulsant.
iussit et extendi campos, subsidere valles,
fronde tegi silvas, lapidosos surgere montes;
45   utque duae dextra caelum totidemque sinistra
parte secant zonae, quinta est ardentior illis,
sic onus inclusum numero distinxit eodem
cura dei, totidemque plagae tellure premuntur.
quarum quae media est, non est habitabilis aestu;
50   nix tegit alta duas: totidem inter utrumque locavit
temperiemque dedit mixta cum frigore flamma.
imminet his aër; qui quanto est pondere terrae,
pondere aquae levior, tanto est onerosior igni.
illic et nebulas, illic consistere nubes
55   iussit et humanas motura tonitrua mentes
et cum fulminibus facientes fulgora ventos.
his quoque non passim mundi fabricator habendum
aëra permisit; vix nunc obsistitur illis,
cum sua quisque regant diverso flamina tractu,
60   quin lanient mundum: tanta est discordia fratrum.
Eurus ad Auroram Nabataeaque regna recessit
Persidaque et radiis iuga subdita matutinis;
vesper et occiduo quae litora sole tepescunt
proxima sunt Zephyro; Scythiam Septemque triones
65   horrifer invasit Boreas; contraria tellus
nubibus adsiduis pluviaque madescit ab Austro.
haec super inposuit liquidum et gravitate carentem

aethera nec quicquam terrenae faecis habentem.
      Vix ita limitibus dissaepserat omnia certis,
70 cum, quae pressa diu fuerant caligine caeca,
sidera coeperunt toto effervescere caelo;
neu regio foret ulla suis animalibus orba,
astra tenent caeleste solum formaeque deorum,
cesserunt nitidis habitandae piscibus undae,
75 terra feras cepit, volucres agitabilis aër.
      Sanctius his animal mentisque capacius altae
deerat adhuc et quod dominari in cetera posset:
natus homo est, sive hunc divino semine fecit
ille opifex rerum, mundi melioris origo,
80 sive recens tellus seductaque nuper ab alto
aethere cognati retinebat semina caeli;
quam satus Iapeto mixtam pluvialibus undis
finxit in effigiem moderantum cuncta deorum,
pronaque cum spectent animalia cetera terram,
85 os homini sublime dedit caelumque videre
iussit et erectos ad sidera tollere vultus.
sic, modo quae fuerat rudis et sine imagine, tellus
induit ignotas hominum conversa figuras.
      Aurea prima sata est aetas, quae vindice nullo,
90 sponte sua, sine lege fidem rectumque colebat.
poena metusque aberant nec verba minantia fixo
aere legebantur nec supplex turba timebat
iudicis ora sui, sed erant sine vindice tuti.
nondum caesa suis, peregrinum ut viseret orbem,
95 montibus in liquidas pinus descenderat undas,
nullaque mortales praeter sua litora norant.
nondum praecipites cingebant oppida fossae,
non tuba directi, non aeris cornua flexi,
non galeae, non ensis erat: sine militis usu
100 mollia securae peragebant otia gentes.
ipsa quoque inmunis rastroque intacta nec ullis
saucia vomeribus per se dabat omnia tellus,
contentique cibis nullo cogente creatis
arbuteos fetus montanaque fraga legebant
105 cornaque et in duris haerentia mora rubetis
et, quae deciderant patula Iovis arbore, glandes.
Ver erat aeternum, placidique tepentibus auris

mulcebant Zephyri natos sine semine flores;
mox etiam fruges tellus inarata ferebat,
110 nec renovatus ager gravidis canebat aristis:
flumina iam lactis, iam flumina nectaris ibant,
flavaque de viridi stillabant ilice mella.
     Postquam Saturno tenebrosa in Tartara misso
sub Iove mundus erat, subiit argentea proles,
115 auro deterior, fulvo pretiosior aere.
Iuppiter antiqui contraxit tempora veris,
perque hiemes aestusque et inaequalis autumnos
et breve ver spatiis exegit quattuor annum.
tum primum siccis aër fervoribus ustus
120 canduit, et ventis glacies adstricta pependit;
tum primum subiere domos: domus antra fuerunt
et densi frutices et vinctae cortice virgae;
semina tum primum longis Cerealia sulcis
obruta sunt, pressique iugo gemuere iuvenci.
125 Tertia post illam successit aenea proles,
saevior ingeniis et ad horrida promptior arma,
non scelerata tamen; de duro est ultima ferro.
protinus inrupit venae peioris in aevum
omne nefas, fugere pudor verumque fidesque;
130 in quorum subiere locum fraudesque dolique
insidiaeque et vis et amor sceleratus habendi.
vela dabat ventis nec adhuc bene noverat illos
navita, quaeque diu steterant in montibus altis,
fluctibus ignotis insultavere carinae,
135 communemque prius ceu lumina solis et auras
cautus humum longo signavit limite mensor.
nec tantum segetes alimentaque debita dives
poscebatur humus, sed itum est in viscera terrae,
quasque recondiderat Stygiisque admoverat umbris,
140 effodiuntur opes, inritamenta malorum;
iamque nocens ferrum ferroque nocentius aurum
prodierat: prodit bellum, quod pugnat utroque,
sanguineaque manu crepitantia concutit arma.
vivitur ex rapto; non hospes ab hospite tutus,
145 non socer a genero, fratrum quoque gratia rara est.
inminet exitio vir coniugis, illa mariti;
lurida terribiles miscent aconita novercae;

filius ante diem patrios inquirit in annos.
victa iacet pietas, et Virgo caede madentes,
150   ultima caelestum, terras Astraea reliquit.
     Neve foret terris securior arduus aether,
adfectasse ferunt regnum caeleste Gigantas
altaque congestos struxisse ad sidera montes.
tum pater omnipotens misso perfregit Olympum
155   fulmine et excussit subiectae Pelion Ossae;
obruta mole sua cum corpora dira iacerent,
perfusam multo natorum sanguine Terram
inmaduisse ferunt calidumque animasse cruorem
et, ne nulla suae stirpis monimenta manerent,
160   in faciem vertisse hominum. sed et illa propago
contemptrix superum saevaeque avidissima caedis
et violenta fuit: scires e sanguine natos.
     Quae pater ut summa vidit Saturnius arce,
ingemit et facto nondum vulgata recenti
165   foeda Lycaoniae referens convivia mensae
ingentes animo et dignas Iove concipit iras
conciliumque vocat; tenuit mora nulla vocatos.
est via sublimis caelo manifesta sereno:
lactea nomen habet candore notabilis ipso;
170   hac iter est superis ad magni tecta Tonantis
regalemque domum: dextra laevaque deorum
atria nobilium valvis celebrantur apertis,
plebs habitat diversa locis: hac parte potentes
caelicolae clarique suos posuere penates;
175   hic locus est, quem, si verbis audacia detur,
haud timeam magni dixisse Palatia caeli.
ergo ubi marmoreo superi sedere recessu,
celsior ipse loco sceptroque innixus eburno
terrificam capitis concussit terque quaterque
180   caesariem, cum qua terram, mare, sidera movit;
talibus inde modis ora indignantia solvit:
     'Non ego pro mundi regno magis anxius illa
tempestate fui, qua centum quisque parabat
inicere anguipedum captivo bracchia caelo.
185   nam quamquam ferus hostis erat, tamen illud ab uno
corpore et ex una pendebat origine bellum;
nunc mihi, qua totum Nereus circumsonat orbem,

perdendum est mortale genus: per flumina iuro
infera sub terras Stygio labentia luco,
190 cuncta prius temptata, sed inmedicabile corpus
ense recidendum est, ne pars sincera trahatur.
sunt mihi semidei, sunt, rustica numina, Nymphae
Faunique Satyrique et monticolae Silvani,
quos, quoniam caeli nondum dignamur honore,
195 quas dedimus certe terras habitare sinamus.
an satis, o superi, tutos fore creditis illos,
cum mihi, qui fulmen, qui vos habeoque regoque,
struxerit insidias notus feritate Lycaon?'
    Confremuere omnes studiisque ardentibus ausum
200 talia deposcunt: sic, cum manus inpia saevit
sanguine Caesareo Romanum extinguere nomen,
attonitum tanto subitae terrore ruinae
humanum genus est totusque perhorruit orbis,
nec tibi grata minus pietas, Auguste, tuorum est,
205 quam fuit illa Iovi. qui postquam voce manuque
murmura conpressit, tenuere silentia cuncti.
substitit ut clamor pressus gravitate regentis,
Iuppiter hoc iterum sermone silentia rupit:
    'Ille quidem poenas (curam hanc dimittite) solvit;
210 quod tamen admissum, quae sit vindicta, docebo.
contigerat nostras infamia temporis aures;
quam cupiens falsam summo delabor Olympo
et deus humana lustro sub imagine terras.
longa mora est, quantum noxae sit ubique repertum,
215 enumerare: minor fuit ipsa infamia vero.
Maenala transieram latebris horrenda ferarum
et cum Cyllene gelidi pineta Lycaei:
Arcadis hinc sedes et inhospita tecta tyranni
ingredior, traherent cum sera crepuscula noctem.
220 signa dedi venisse deum, vulgusque precari
coeperat: inridet primo pia vota Lycaon,
mox ait 'experiar, deus hic, discrimine aperto,
an sit mortalis; nec erit dubitabile verum.'
nocte gravem somno necopina perdere morte
225 me parat: haec illi placet experientia veri.
nec contentus eo est: missi de gente Molossa
obsidis unius iugulum mucrone resolvit

atque ita semineces partim ferventibus artus
mollit aquis, partim subiecto torruit igni.
230 quod simul inposuit mensis, ego vindice flamma
in domino dignos everti tecta penates;
territus ipse fugit nactusque silentia ruris
exululat frustraque loqui conatur; ab ipso
colligit os rabiem solitaeque cupidine caedis
235 utitur in pecudes et nunc quoque sanguine gaudet.
in villos abeunt vestes, in crura lacerti:
fit lupus et veteris servat vestigia formae;
canities eadem est, eadem violentia vultus,
idem oculi lucent, eadem feritatis imago est.
240 occidit una domus, sed non domus una perire
digna fuit; qua terra patet, fera regnat Erinys.
in facinus iurasse putes; dent ocius omnes
quas meruere pati, sic stat sententia, poenas.'
    Dicta Iovis pars voce probant stimulosque frementi
245 adiciunt, alii partes adsensibus inplent;
est tamen humani generis iactura dolori
omnibus, et, quae sit terrae mortalibus orbae
forma futura, rogant, quis sit laturus in aras
tura, ferisne paret populandas tradere terras.
250 talia quaerentes (sibi enim fore cetera curae)
rex superum trepidare vetat subolemque priori
dissimilem populo promittit origine mira.
    Iamque erat in totas sparsurus fulmina terras;
sed timuit, ne forte sacer tot ab ignibus aether
255 conciperet flammas longusque ardesceret axis.
esse quoque in fatis reminiscitur adfore tempus,
quo mare, quo tellus correptaque regia caeli
ardeat et mundi moles operosa laboret.
tela reponuntur manibus fabricata Cyclopum:
260 poena placet diversa, genus mortale sub undis
perdere et ex omni nimbos demittere caelo.
    Protinus Aeoliis Aquilonem claudit in antris
et quaecumque fugant inductas flamina nubes,
emittitque Notum: madidis Notus evolat alis
265 terribilem picea tectus caligine vultum:
barba gravis nimbis, canis fluit unda capillis,
fronte sedent nebulae, rorant pennaeque sinusque;

utque manu late pendentia nubila pressit,
fit fragor: hinc densi funduntur ab aethere nimbi.
270 nuntia Iunonis varios induta colores
concipit Iris aquas alimentaque nubibus adfert:
sternuntur segetes et deplorata colonis
vota iacent longique perit labor inritus anni.
      Nec caelo contenta suo est Iovis ira, sed illum
275 caeruleus frater iuvat auxiliaribus undis.
convocat hic amnes. qui postquam tecta tyranni
intravere sui, 'non est hortamine longo
nunc' ait 'utendum: vires effundite vestras;
sic opus est. aperite domos ac mole remota
280 fluminibus vestris totas inmittite habenas.'
iusserat; hi redeunt ac fontibus ora relaxant
et defrenato volvuntur in aequora cursu.
ipse tridente suo terram percussit, at illa
intremuit motuque vias patefecit aquarum.
285 exspatiata ruunt per apertos flumina campos
cumque satis arbusta simul pecudesque virosque
tectaque cumque suis rapiunt penetralia sacris.
siqua domus mansit potuitque resistere tanto
indeiecta malo, culmen tamen altior huius
290 unda tegit, pressaeque latent sub gurgite turres;
iamque mare et tellus nullum discrimen habebant:
omnia pontus erant, deerant quoque litora ponto.
      Occupat hic collem, cumba sedet alter adunca
et ducit remos illic, ubi nuper ararat;
295 ille supra segetes aut mersae culmina villae
navigat, hic summa piscem deprendit in ulmo;
figitur in viridi, si fors tulit, ancora prato,
aut subiecta terunt curvae vineta carinae,
et, modo qua graciles gramen carpsere capellae,
300 nunc ibi deformes ponunt sua corpora phocae.
mirantur sub aqua lucos urbesque domosque
Nereides, silvasque tenent delphines et altis
incursant ramis agitataque robora pulsant.
nat lupus inter oves, fulvos vehit unda leones,
305 unda vehit tigres, nec vires fulminis apro,
crura nec ablato prosunt velocia cervo,
quaesitisque diu terris, ubi sistere possit,

in mare lassatis volucris vaga decidit alis.
obruerat tumulos inmensa licentia ponti,
310 pulsabantque novi montana cacumina fluctus.
maxima pars unda rapitur: quibus unda pepercit,
illos longa domant inopi ieiunia victu.

Separat Aonios Oetaeis Phocis ab arvis,
terra ferax, dum terra fuit, sed tempore in illo
315 pars maris et latus subitarum campus aquarum;
mons ibi verticibus petit arduus astra duobus,
nomine Parnasus, superantque cacumina nubes:
hic ubi Deucalion (nam cetera texerat aequor)
cum consorte tori parva rate vectus adhaesit,
320 Corycidas nymphas et numina montis adorant
fatidicamque Themin, quae tunc oracla tenebat:
non illo melior quisquam nec amantior aequi
vir fuit aut illa metuentior ulla deorum.

Iuppiter ut liquidis stagnare paludibus orbem
325 et superesse virum de tot modo milibus unum
et superesse videt de tot modo milibus unam,
innocuos ambo, cultores numinis ambo,
nubila disiecit nimbisque aquilone remotis
et caelo terras ostendit et aethera terris.
330 nec maris ira manet, positoque tricuspide telo
mulcet aquas rector pelagi supraque profundum
exstantem atque umeros innato murice tectum
caeruleum Tritona vocat conchaeque sonanti
inspirare iubet fluctusque et flumina signo
335 iam revocare dato: cava bucina sumitur illi,
tortilis, in latum quae turbine crescit ab imo,
bucina, quae medio concepit ubi aëra ponto,
litora voce replet sub utroque iacentia Phoebo.
tunc quoque, ut ora dei madida rorantia barba
340 contigit et cecinit iussos inflata receptus,
omnibus audita est telluris et aequoris undis
et, quibus est undis audita, coercuit omnes.
iam mare litus habet, plenos capit alveus amnes,
flumina subsidunt collesque exire videntur,
345 surgit humus, crescunt loca decrescentibus undis,
postque diem longam nudata cacumina silvae
ostendunt limumque tenent in fronde relictum.

Redditus orbis erat; quem postquam vidit inanem
et desolatas agere alta silentia terras,
350 Deucalion lacrimis ita Pyrrham adfatur obortis:
'O soror, o coniunx, o femina sola superstes,
quam commune mihi genus et patruelis origo,
deinde torus iunxit, nunc ipsa pericula iungunt,
terrarum, quascumque vident occasus et ortus,
355 nos duo turba sumus: possedit cetera pontus.
haec quoque adhuc vitae non est fiducia nostrae
certa satis; terrent etiam nunc nubila mentem.
quis tibi, si sine me fatis erepta fuisses,
nunc animus, miseranda, foret? quo sola timorem
360 ferre modo posses? quo consolante doleres?
namque ego, crede mihi, si te quoque pontus haberet,
te sequerer, coniunx, et me quoque pontus haberet.
o utinam possim populos reparare paternis
artibus atque animas formatae infundere terrae!
365 nunc genus in nobis restat mortale duobus
(sic visum superis) hominumque exempla manemus.'
Dixerat, et flebant; placuit caeleste precari
numen et auxilium per sacras quaerere sortes.
nulla mora est: adeunt pariter Cephisidas undas,
370 ut nondum liquidas, sic iam vada nota secantes.
inde ubi libatos inroravere liquores
vestibus et capiti, flectunt vestigia sanctae
ad delubra deae, quorum fastigia turpi
pallebant musco stabantque sine ignibus arae.
375 ut templi tetigere gradus, procumbit uterque
pronus humi gelidoque pavens dedit oscula saxo,
atque ita 'si precibus' dixerunt 'numina iustis
victa remollescunt, si flectitur ira deorum,
dic, Themi, qua generis damnum reparabile nostri
380 arte sit, et mersis fer opem, mitissima, rebus.'
mota dea est sortemque dedit: 'discedite templo
et velate caput cinctasque resolvite vestes
ossaque post tergum magnae iactate parentis.'
Obstipuere diu, rumpitque silentia voce
385 Pyrrha prior iussisque deae parere recusat,
detque sibi veniam, pavido rogat ore pavetque
laedere iactatis maternas ossibus umbras.

interea repetunt caecis obscura latebris
verba datae sortis secum inter seque volutant.
390 inde Promethides placidis Epimethida dictis
mulcet et 'aut fallax' ait 'est sollertia nobis,
aut (pia sunt nullumque nefas oracula suadent)
magna parens terra est: lapides in corpore terrae
ossa reor dici; iacere hos post terga iubemur.'
395 Coniugis augurio quamquam Titania mota est,
spes tamen in dubio est: adeo caelestibus ambo
diffidunt monitis. sed quid temptare nocebit?
discedunt velantque caput tunicasque recingunt
et iussos lapides sua post vestigia mittunt.
400 saxa (quis hoc credat, nisi sit pro teste vetustas?)
ponere duritiem coepere suumque rigorem
mollirique mora mollitaque ducere formam.
mox ubi creverunt naturaque mitior illis
contigit, ut quaedam, sic non manifesta videri
405 forma potest hominis, sed, uti de marmore coepta,
non exacta satis rudibusque simillima signis.
quae tamen ex illis aliquo pars umida suco
et terrena fuit, versa est in corporis usum;
quod solidum est flectique nequit, mutatur in ossa;
410 quae modo vena fuit, sub eodem nomine mansit;
inque brevi spatio superorum numine saxa
missa viri manibus faciem traxere virorum,
et de femineo reparata est femina iactu.
inde genus durum sumus experiensque laborum
415 et documenta damus, qua simus origine nati.
Cetera diversis tellus animalia formis
sponte sua peperit, postquam vetus umor ab igne
percaluit solis caenumque udaeque paludes
intumuere aestu fecundaque semina rerum
420 vivaci nutrita solo ceu matris in alvo
creverunt faciemque aliquam cepere morando.
sic, ubi deseruit madidos septemfluus agros
Nilus et antiquo sua flumina reddidit alveo
aetherioque recens exarsit sidere limus,
425 plurima cultores versis animalia glaebis
inveniunt et in his quaedam modo coepta per ipsum
nascendi spatium, quaedam inperfecta suisque

trunca vident numeris, et eodem in corpore saepe
altera pars vivit, rudis est pars altera tellus.
430   quippe ubi temperiem sumpsere umorque calorque,
concipiunt, et ab his oriuntur cuncta duobus,
cumque sit ignis aquae pugnax, vapor umidus omnes
res creat, et discors concordia fetibus apta est.
ergo ubi diluvio tellus lutulenta recenti
435   solibus aetheriis altoque recanduit aestu,
edidit innumeras species partimque figuras
rettulit antiquas, partim nova monstra creavit.
illa quidem nollet, sed te quoque, maxime Python,
tum genuit, populisque novis, incognite serpens,
440   terror eras: tantum spatii de monte tenebas.
hunc deus arquitenens et numquam talibus armis
ante nisi in dammis capreisque fugacibus usus
mille gravem telis, exhausta paene pharetra,
perdidit effuso per vulnera nigra veneno.
445   neve operis famam posset delere vetustas,
instituit sacros celebri certamine ludos
Pythia perdomitae serpentis nomine dictos.
hic iuvenum quicumque manu pedibusque rotave
vicerat, aesculeae capiebat frondis honorem;
450   nondum laurus erat, longoque decentia crine
tempora cingebat de qualibet arbore Phoebus.
    Primus amor Phoebi Daphne Peneia: quem non
fors ignara dedit, sed saeva Cupidinis ira.
Delius hunc nuper, victo serpente superbus,
455   viderat adducto flectentem cornua nervo
'quid' que 'tibi, lascive puer, cum fortibus armis?',
dixerat, 'ista decent umeros gestamina nostros,
qui dare certa ferae, dare vulnera possumus hosti,
qui modo pestifero tot iugera ventre prementem
460   stravimus innumeris tumidum Pythona sagittis.
tu face nescio quos esto contentus amores
inritare tua nec laudes adsere nostras.'
filius huic Veneris 'figat tuus omnia, Phoebe,
te meus arcus' ait, 'quantoque animalia cedunt
465   cuncta deo, tanto minor est tua gloria nostra.'
dixit et eliso percussis aëre pennis
inpiger umbrosa Parnasi constitit arce

eque sagittifera prompsit duo tela pharetra
diversorum operum: fugat hoc, facit illud amorem;
470   quod facit, auratum est et cuspide fulget acuta,
quod fugat, obtusum est et habet sub harundine plumbum.
hoc deus in nympha Peneide fixit, at illo
laesit Apollineas traiecta per ossa medullas:
protinus alter amat, fugit altera nomen amantis
475   silvarum latebris captivarumque ferarum
exuviis gaudens innuptaeque aemula Phoebes;
vitta coercebat positos sine lege capillos.
multi illam petiere, illa aversata petentes
inpatiens expersque viri nemora avia lustrat
480   nec, quid Hymen, quid Amor, quid sint conubia, curat.
saepe pater dixit 'generum mihi, filia, debes',
saepe pater dixit 'debes mihi, nata, nepotes':
illa velut crimen taedas exosa iugales
pulchra verecundo subfuderat ora rubore
485   inque patris blandis haerens cervice lacertis
'da mihi perpetua, genitor carissime,' dixit
'virginitate frui: dedit hoc pater ante Dianae.'
ille quidem obsequitur; sed te decor iste, quod optas,
esse vetat, votoque tuo tua forma repugnat.
490   Phoebus amat visaeque cupit conubia Daphnes,
quodque cupit, sperat, suaque illum oracula fallunt;
utque leves stipulae demptis adolentur aristis,
ut facibus saepes ardent, quas forte viator
vel nimis admovit vel iam sub luce reliquit,
495   sic deus in flammas abiit, sic pectore toto
uritur et sterilem sperando nutrit amorem.
spectat inornatos collo pendere capillos
et 'quid, si comantur?' ait; videt igne micantes
sideribus similes oculos, videt oscula, quae non
500   est vidisse satis; laudat digitosque manusque
bracchiaque et nudos media plus parte lacertos:
siqua latent, meliora putat. fugit ocior aura
illa levi neque ad haec revocantis verba resistit:
    'Nympha, precor, Penei, mane! non insequor hostis;
505   nympha, mane! sic agna lupum, sic cerva leonem,
sic aquilam penna fugiunt trepidante columbae,
hostes quaeque suos; amor est mihi causa sequendi.

me miserum! ne prona cadas indignave laedi
crura notent sentes, et sim tibi causa doloris.
510   aspera, qua properas, loca sunt: moderatius, oro,
curre fugamque inhibe: moderatius insequar ipse.
cui placeas, inquire tamen; non incola montis,
non ego sum pastor, non hic armenta gregesque
horridus observo. nescis, temeraria, nescis,
515   quem fugias, ideoque fugis. mihi Delphica tellus
et Claros et Tenedos Patareaque regia servit;
Iuppiter est genitor. per me, quod eritque fuitque
estque, patet; per me concordant carmina nervis.
certa quidem nostra est, nostra tamen una sagitta
520   certior, in vacuo quae vulnera pectore fecit.
inventum medicina meum est, opiferque per orbem
dicor, et herbarum subiecta potentia nobis:
ei mihi, quod nullis amor est sanabilis herbis,
nec prosunt domino, quae prosunt omnibus, artes!'
525   Plura locuturum timido Peneia cursu
fugit cumque ipso verba inperfecta reliquit,
tum quoque visa decens; nudabant corpora venti,
obviaque adversas vibrabant flamina vestes,
et levis inpulsos retro dabat aura capillos,
530   auctaque forma fuga est. sed enim non sustinet ultra
perdere blanditias iuvenis deus, utque monebat
ipse amor, admisso sequitur vestigia passu.
ut canis in vacuo leporem cum Gallicus arvo
vidit, et hic praedam pedibus petit, ille salutem
535   (alter inhaesuro similis iam iamque tenere
sperat et extento stringit vestigia rostro;
alter in ambiguo est, an sit conprensus, et ipsis
morsibus eripitur tangentiaque ora relinquit):
sic deus et virgo; est hic spe celer, illa timore.
540   qui tamen insequitur, pennis adiutus amoris
ocior est requiemque negat tergoque fugacis
inminet et crinem sparsum cervicibus adflat.
viribus absumptis expalluit illa citaeque
victa labore fugae 'Tellus,' ait, 'hisce vel istam,
544a   [victa labore fugae, spectans Peneidas undas]
545   quae facit ut laedar, mutando perde figuram!
fer, pater,' inquit 'opem, si flumina numen habetis!

qua nimium placui, mutando perde figuram!'
547a [qua nimium placui, Tellus, ait, hisce vel istam]
vix prece finita torpor gravis occupat artus:
mollia cinguntur tenui praecordia libro,
550 in frondem crines, in ramos bracchia crescunt;
pes modo tam velox pigris radicibus haeret,
ora cacumen habet: remanet nitor unus in illa.
hanc quoque Phoebus amat positaque in stipite dextra
sentit adhuc trepidare novo sub cortice pectus
555 conplexusque suis ramos, ut membra, lacertis
oscula dat ligno: refugit tamen oscula lignum.
cui deus 'at quoniam coniunx mea non potes esse,
arbor eris certe' dixit 'mea. semper habebunt
te coma, te citharae, te nostrae, laure, pharetrae.
560 tu ducibus Latiis aderis, cum laeta triumphum
vox canet et visent longas Capitolia pompas.
postibus Augustis eadem fidissima custos
ante fores stabis mediamque tuebere quercum,
utque meum intonsis caput est iuvenale capillis,
565 tu quoque perpetuos semper gere frondis honores.'
finierat Paean: factis modo laurea ramis
adnuit utque caput visa est agitasse cacumen.

       Est nemus Haemoniae, praerupta quod undique claudit
silva: vocant Tempe. per quae Peneus ab imo
570 effusus Pindo spumosis volvitur undis
deiectuque gravi tenues agitantia fumos
nubila conducit summisque adspergine silvis
inpluit et sonitu plus quam vicina fatigat:
haec domus, haec sedes, haec sunt penetralia magni
575 amnis; in his residens facto de cautibus antro
undis iura dabat nymphisque colentibus undas.
conveniunt illuc popularia flumina primum,
nescia, gratentur consolenturne parentem,
populifer Sperchios et inrequietus Enipeus
580 Apidanusque senex lenisque Amphrysos et Aeas,
moxque amnes alii, qui, qua tulit impetus illos,
in mare deducunt fessas erroribus undas.

       Inachus unus abest imoque reconditus antro
fletibus auget aquas natamque miserrimus Io
585 luget ut amissam; nescit, vitane fruatur

an sit apud manes, sed quam non invenit usquam,
esse putat nusquam atque animo peiora veretur.
   Viderat a patrio redeuntem Iuppiter illam
flumine et 'o virgo Iove digna tuoque beatum
590   nescio quem factura toro, pete' dixerat 'umbras
altorum nemorum' (et nemorum monstraverat umbras)
'dum calet et medio sol est altissimus orbe.
quodsi sola times latebras intrare ferarum,
praeside tuta deo nemorum secreta subibis,
595   nec de plebe deo, sed qui caelestia magna
sceptra manu teneo, sed qui vaga fulmina mitto.
ne fuge me!' fugiebat enim. iam pascua Lernae
consitaque arboribus Lyrcea reliquerat arva,
cum deus inducta latas caligine terras
600   occuluit tenuitque fugam rapuitque pudorem.
   Interea medios Iuno despexit in agros,
et noctis faciem nebulas fecisse volucres
sub nitido mirata die non fluminis illas
esse nec umenti sensit tellure remitti
605   atque, suus coniunx ubi sit, circumspicit, ut quae
deprensi totiens iam nosset furta mariti.
quem postquam caelo non repperit, 'aut ego fallor
aut ego laedor' ait delapsaque ab aethere summo
constitit in terris nebulasque recedere iussit.
610   coniugis adventum praesenserat inque nitentem
Inachidos vultus mutaverat ille iuvencam
(bos quoque formosa est): speciem Saturnia vaccae,
quamquam invita, probat nec non, et cuius et unde
quove sit armento, veri quasi nescia quaerit;
615   Iuppiter e terra genitam mentitur, ut auctor
desinat inquiri: petit hanc Saturnia munus.
quid faciat? crudele suos addicere amores,
non dare suspectum est: pudor est, qui suadeat illinc,
hinc dissuadet amor. victus pudor esset amore,
620   sed, leve si munus sociae generisque torique
vacca negaretur, poterat non vacca videri.
paelice donata non protinus exuit omnem
diva metum timuitque Iovem et fuit anxia furti,
donec Arestoridae servandam tradidit Argo.
625   Centum luminibus cinctum caput Argus habebat:

inde suis vicibus capiebant bina quietem,
cetera servabant atque in statione manebant.
constiterat quocumque modo, spectabat ad Io:
ante oculos Io, quamvis aversus, habebat.
630 luce sinit pasci; cum sol tellure sub alta est,
claudit et indigno circumdat vincula collo.
frondibus arboreis et amara pascitur herba
proque toro terrae non semper gramen habenti
incubat infelix limosaque flumina potat;
635 illa etiam supplex Argo cum bracchia vellet
tendere, non habuit, quae bracchia tenderet Argo,
et conata queri mugitus edidit ore
pertimuitque sonos propriaque exterrita voce est.
     Venit et ad ripas, ubi ludere saepe solebat,
640 Inachidas ripas, novaque ut conspexit in unda
cornua, pertimuit seque exsternata refugit.
naides ignorant, ignorat et Inachus ipse,
quae sit; at illa patrem sequitur sequiturque sorores
et patitur tangi seque admirantibus offert.
645 decerptas senior porrexerat Inachus herbas:
illa manus lambit patriisque dat oscula palmis
nec retinet lacrimas, et, si modo verba sequantur,
oret opem nomenque suum casusque loquatur;
littera pro verbis, quam pes in pulvere duxit,
650 corporis indicium mutati triste peregit.
'me miserum!' exclamat pater Inachus inque gementis
cornibus et niveae pendens cervice iuvencae
'me miserum!' ingeminat, 'tune es quaesita per omnes
nata mihi terras? tu non inventa reperta
655 luctus eras levior. retices nec mutua nostris
dicta refers, alto tantum suspiria ducis
pectore, quodque unum potes, ad mea verba remugis.
at tibi ego ignarus thalamos taedasque parabam,
spesque fuit generi mihi prima, secunda nepotum:
660 de grege nunc tibi vir et de grege natus habendus.
nec finire licet tantos mihi morte dolores,
sed nocet esse deum, praeclusaque ianua leti
aeternum nostros luctus extendit in aevum.'
talia maerentem stellatus submovet Argus,
665 ereptamque patri diversa in pascua natam

abstrahit; ipse procul montis sublime cacumen
occupat, unde sedens partes speculatur in omnes.
    Nec superum rector mala tanta Phoronidos ultra
ferre potest natumque vocat, quem lucida partu
670 Pleias enixa est, letoque det imperat Argum.
parva mora est alas pedibus virgamque potenti
somniferam sumpsisse manu tegumenque capillis;
haec ubi disposuit, patria Iove natus ab arce
desilit in terras. illic tegumenque removit
675 et posuit pennas, tantummodo virga retenta est:
hac agit ut pastor per devia rura capellas,
dum venit, adductas et structis cantat avenis.
voce nova et captus custos Iunonius arte
'quisquis es, hoc poteras mecum considere saxo',
680 Argus ait, 'neque enim pecori fecundior ullo
herba loco est, aptamque vides pastoribus umbram.'
sedit Atlantiades et euntem multa loquendo
detinuit sermone diem iunctisque canendo
vincere harundinibus servantia lumina temptat.
685 ille tamen pugnat molles evincere somnos
et, quamvis sopor est oculorum parte receptus,
parte tamen vigilat; quaerit quoque (namque reperta
fistula nuper erat), qua sit ratione reperta.
    Tum deus 'Arcadiae gelidis in montibus' inquit
690 'inter hamadryadas celeberrima Nonacrinas
naias una fuit, nymphae Syringa vocabant.
non semel et satyros eluserat illa sequentes
et quoscumque deos umbrosaque silva feraxque
rus habet; Ortygiam studiis ipsaque colebat
695 virginitate deam; ritu quoque cincta Dianae
falleret et posset credi Latonia, si non
corneus huic arcus, si non foret aureus illi;
sic quoque fallebat. redeuntem colle Lycaeo
Pan videt hanc pinuque caput praecinctus acuta
700 talia verba refert'—restabat verba referre
et precibus spretis fugisse per avia nympham,
donec harenosi placidum Ladonis ad amnem
venerit: hic illam cursum inpedientibus undis,
ut se mutarent, liquidas orasse sorores,
705 Panaque, cum prensam sibi iam Syringa putaret,

corpore pro nymphae calamos tenuisse palustres,
dumque ibi suspirat, motos in harundine ventos
effecisse sonum tenuem similemque querenti;
arte nova vocisque deum dulcedine captum
710 'hoc mihi conloquium tecum' dixisse 'manebit',
atque ita disparibus calamis conpagine cerae
inter se iunctis nomen tenuisse puellae.
    Talia dicturus vidit Cyllenius omnes
succubuisse oculos adopertaque lumina somno;
715 supprimit extemplo vocem firmatque soporem
languida permulcens medicata lumina virga.
nec mora, falcato nutantem vulnerat ense,
qua collo est confine caput, saxoque cruentum
deicit et maculat praeruptam sanguine rupem.
720 Arge, iaces, quodque in tot lumina lumen habebas,
exstinctum est, centumque oculos nox occupat una.
excipit hos volucrisque suae Saturnia pennis
conlocat et gemmis caudam stellantibus inplet.
    Protinus exarsit nec tempora distulit irae
725 horriferamque oculis animoque obiecit Erinyn
paelicis Argolicae stimulosque in pectore caecos
condidit et profugam per totum terruit orbem.
ultimus inmenso restabas, Nile, labori;
quem simulac tetigit, positisque in margine ripae
730 procubuit genibus resupinoque ardua collo,
quos potuit solos, tollens ad sidera vultus
et gemitu et lacrimis et luctisono mugitu
cum Iove visa queri finemque orare malorum.
coniugis ille suae conplexus colla lacertis,
735 finiat ut poenas tandem, rogat 'in' que 'futurum
pone metus' inquit, 'numquam tibi causa doloris
haec erit' et Stygias iubet hoc audire paludes.
ut lenita dea est, vultus capit illa priores
fitque, quod ante fuit: fugiunt e corpore saetae,
740 cornua decrescunt, fit luminis artior orbis,
contrahitur rictus, redeunt umerique manusque
ungulaque in quinos dilapsa absumitur ungues:
de bove nil superest formae nisi candor in illa;
officioque pedum nymphe contenta duorum
745 erigitur metuitque loqui, ne more iuvencae

mugiat, et timide verba intermissa retemptat.
Nunc dea linigera colitur celeberrima turba,
nunc Epaphus magni genitus de semine tandem
creditur esse Iovis perque urbes iuncta parenti
750 templa tenet. fuit huic animis aequalis et annis
Sole satus Phaethon; quem quondam magna loquentem
nec sibi cedentem Phoeboque parente superbum
non tulit Inachides 'matri'que ait 'omnia demens
credis et es tumidus genitoris imagine falsi.'
755 erubuit Phaethon iramque pudore repressit
et tulit ad Clymenen Epaphi convicia matrem
'quo'que 'magis doleas, genetrix,' ait 'ille ego liber,
ille ferox tacui. pudet haec opprobria nobis
et dici potuisse et non potuisse refelli;
760 at tu, si modo sum caelesti stirpe creatus,
ede notam tanti generis meque adsere caelo.'
Dixit et inplicuit materno bracchia collo
perque suum Meropisque caput taedasque sororum
traderet oravit veri sibi signa parentis.
765 ambiguum Clymene precibus Phaethontis an ira
mota magis dicti sibi criminis utraque caelo
bracchia porrexit spectansque ad lumina solis
'per iubar hoc' inquit 'radiis insigne coruscis,
nate, tibi iuro, quod nos auditque videtque,
770 hoc te, quem spectas, hoc te, qui temperat orbem,
Sole satum. si ficta loquor, neget ipse videndum
se mihi, sitque oculis lux ista novissima nostris.
nec longus patrios labor est tibi nosse penates:
unde oritur, domus est terrae contermina nostrae;
775 si modo fert animus, gradere et scitabere ab ipso!'
Emicat extemplo laetus post talia matris
dicta suae Phaethon et concipit aethera mente
Aethiopasque suos positosque sub ignibus Indos
sidereis transit patriosque adit inpiger ortus.

LIBER SECUNDUS

Regia Solis erat sublimibus alta columnis,
clara micante auro flammasque imitante pyropo,
cuius ebur nitidum fastigia summa tegebat,
argenti bifores radiabant lumine valvae.
5   materiam superabat opus; nam Mulciber illic
aequora caelarat medias cingentia terras
terrarumque orbem caelumque, quod inminet orbi.
caeruleos habet unda deos, Tritona canorum
Proteaque ambiguum ballenarumque prementem
10   Aegaeona suis inmania terga lacertis
Doridaque et natas, quarum pars nare videtur,
pars in mole sedens virides siccare capillos,
pisce vehi quaedam; facies non omnibus una,
non diversa tamen, qualem decet esse sororum.
15   terra viros urbesque gerit silvasque ferasque
fluminaque et nymphas et cetera numina ruris.
haec super inposita est caeli fulgentis imago
signaque sex foribus dextris totidemque sinistris.
     Quo simul adclivi Clymeneia limite proles
20   venit et intravit dubitati tecta parentis,
protinus ad patrios sua fert vestigia vultus
consistitque procul; neque enim propiora ferebat
lumina: purpurea velatus veste sedebat
in solio Phoebus claris lucente smaragdis.
25   a dextra laevaque Dies et Mensis et Annus
Saeculaque et positae spatiis aequalibus Horae
Verque novum stabat cinctum florente corona,

stabat nuda Aestas et spicea serta gerebat,
stabat et Autumnus calcatis sordidus uvis
30   et glacialis Hiems canos hirsuta capillos.
inde loco medius rerum novitate paventem
Sol oculis iuvenem, quibus adspicit omnia, vidit
'quae' que 'viae tibi causa? quid hac' ait 'arce petisti,
progenies, Phaethon, haud infitianda parenti?'
35   ille refert: 'o lux inmensi publica mundi,
Phoebe pater, si das usum mihi nominis huius,
nec falsa Clymene culpam sub imagine celat,
pignora da, genitor, per quae tua vera propago
credar, et hunc animis errorem detrahe nostris.'
40   dixerat, at genitor circum caput omne micantes
deposuit radios propiusque accedere iussit
amplexuque dato 'nec tu meus esse negari
dignus es, et Clymene veros' ait 'edidit ortus,
quoque minus dubites, quodvis pete munus, ut illud
45   me tribuente feras. promissis testis adesto
dis iuranda palus oculis incognita nostris.'
vix bene desierat, currus rogat ille paternos
inque diem alipedum ius et moderamen equorum.
    Paenituit iurasse patrem, qui terque quaterque
50   concutiens illustre caput 'temeraria' dixit
'vox mea facta tua est. utinam promissa liceret
non dare! confiteor, solum hoc tibi, nate, negarem;
dissuadere licet: non est tua tuta voluntas!
magna petis, Phaethon, et quae nec viribus istis
55   munera conveniant nec tam puerilibus annis.
sors tua mortalis: non est mortale quod optas.
plus etiam, quam quod superis contingere possit,
nescius adfectas; placeat sibi quisque licebit,
non tamen ignifero quisquam consistere in axe
60   me valet excepto. vasti quoque rector Olympi,
qui fera terribili iaculatur fulmina dextra,
non aget hos currus: et quid Iove maius habemus?
    Ardua prima via est et qua vix mane recentes
enituntur equi; medio est altissima caelo,
65   unde mare et terras ipsi mihi saepe videre
sit timor et pavida trepidet formidine pectus;
ultima prona via est et eget moderamine certo:

      tunc etiam, quae me subiectis excipit undis,
      ne ferar in praeceps, Tethys solet ipsa vereri.
70   adde, quod adsidua rapitur vertigine caelum
      sideraque alta trahit celerique volumine torquet.
      nitor in adversum, nec me, qui cetera, vincit
      impetus, et rapido contrarius evehor orbi.
      finge datos currus: quid ages? poterisne rotatis
75   obvius ire polis, ne te citus auferat axis?
      forsitan et lucos illic urbesque deorum
      concipias animo delubraque ditia donis
      esse? per insidias iter est formasque ferarum;
      utque viam teneas nulloque errore traharis,
80   per tamen adversi gradieris cornua Tauri
      Haemoniosque arcus violentique ora Leonis
      saevaque circuitu curvantem bracchia longo
      Scorpion atque aliter curvantem bracchia Cancrum.
      nec tibi quadripedes animosos ignibus illis,
85   quos in pectore habent, quos ore et naribus efflant,
      in promptu regere est: vix me patiuntur, ubi acres
      incaluere animi, cervixque repugnat habenis.
      at tu, funesti ne sim tibi muneris auctor,
      nate, cave, dum resque sinit, tua corrige vota.
90   scilicet, ut nostro genitum te sanguine credas,
      pignora certa petis: do pignora certa timendo
      et patrio pater esse metu probor. adspice vultus
      ecce meos, utinamque oculos in pectora posses
      inserere et patrias intus deprendere curas!
95   denique quidquid habet dives circumspice mundus
      eque tot ac tantis caeli terraeque marisque
      posce bonis aliquid: nullam patiere repulsam.
      deprecor hoc unum, quod vero nomine poena,
      non honor est: poenam, Phaethon, pro munere poscis.
100   quid mea colla tenes blandis, ignare, lacertis?
      ne dubita, dabitur (Stygias iuravimus undas),
      quodcumque optaris, sed tu sapientius opta.'
        Finierat monitus, dictis tamen ille repugnat
      propositumque premit flagratque cupidine currus.
105   ergo, qua licuit, genitor cunctatus ad altos
      deducit iuvenem, Vulcania munera, currus.
      aureus axis erat, temo aureus, aurea summae

curvatura rotae, radiorum argenteus ordo;
per iuga chrysolithi positaeque ex ordine gemmae
110   clara repercusso reddebant lumina Phoebo.
dumque ea magnanimus Phaethon miratur opusque
perspicit, ecce vigil nitido patefecit ab ortu
purpureas Aurora fores et plena rosarum
atria: diffugiunt stellae, quarum agmina cogit
115   Lucifer et caeli statione novissimus exit.
quem petere ut terras mundumque rubescere vidit
cornuaque extremae velut evanescere lunae,
iungere equos Titan velocibus imperat Horis.
iussa deae celeres peragunt ignemque vomentes
120   ambrosiae suco saturos praesepibus altis
quadripedes ducunt adduntque sonantia frena.
tum pater ora sui sacro medicamine nati
contigit et rapidae fecit patientia flammae
inposuitque comae radios praesagaque luctus
125   pectore sollicito repetens suspiria dixit:
   'Si potes his saltem monitis parere parentis,
parce, puer, stimulis et fortius utere loris.
sponte sua properant: labor est inhibere volentes.
nec tibi directos placeat via quinque per arcus;
130   sectus in obliquum est lato curvamine limes
zonarumque trium contentus fine polumque
effugit australem iunctamque aquilonibus Arcton:
hac sit iter, manifesta rotae vestigia cernes;
utque ferant aequos et caelum et terra calores,
135   nec preme nec summum molire per aethera currum.
altius egressus caelestia tecta cremabis,
inferius terras: medio tutissimus ibis.
neu te dexterior tortum declinet ad Anguem,
neve sinisterior pressam rota ducat ad Aram:
140   inter utrumque tene. Fortunae cetera mando,
quae iuvet et melius, quam tu tibi, consulat opto.
dum loquor, Hesperio positas in litore metas
umida nox tetigit; non est mora libera nobis:
poscimur, et fulget tenebris Aurora fugatis.
145   corripe lora manu—vel, si mutabile pectus
est tibi, consiliis, non curribus utere nostris,
dum potes et solidis etiamnunc sedibus adstas

dumque male optatos nondum premis inscius axes.
quae tutus spectes, sine me dare lumina terris!'
150 Occupat ille levem iuvenali corpore currum
statque super manibusque leves contingere habenas
gaudet et invito grates agit inde parenti.
interea volucres Pyrois et Eous et Aethon,
Solis equi, quartusque Phlegon hinnitibus auras
155 flammiferis inplent pedibusque repagula pulsant;
quae postquam Tethys fatorum ignara nepotis
reppulit et facta est inmensi copia caeli,
corripuere viam pedibusque per aëra motis
obstantes scindunt nebulas pennisque levati
160 praetereunt ortos isdem de partibus Euros.
sed leve pondus erat, nec quod cognoscere possent
Solis equi, solitaque iugum gravitate carebat,
utque labant curvae iusto sine pondere naves
perque mare instabiles nimia levitate feruntur,
165 sic onere adsueto vacuus dat in aëre saltus
succutiturque alte similisque est currus inani.
quod simulac sensere, ruunt tritumque relinquunt
quadriiugi spatium nec, quo prius, ordine currunt.
ipse pavet, nec qua commissas flectat habenas,
170 nec scit qua sit iter, nec, si sciat, imperet illis.
tum primum radiis gelidi caluere Triones
et vetito frustra temptarunt aequore tingi,
quaeque polo posita est glaciali proxima Serpens,
frigore pigra prius nec formidabilis ulli,
175 incaluit sumpsitque novas fervoribus iras.
te quoque turbatum memorant fugisse, Boote,
quamvis tardus eras et te tua plaustra tenebant.
ut vero summo despexit ab aethere terras
infelix Phaethon penitus penitusque iacentes,
180 palluit et subito genua intremuere timore,
suntque oculis tenebrae per tantum lumen obortae,
et iam mallet equos numquam tetigisse paternos,
iam cognosse genus piget et valuisse rogando;
iam Meropis dici cupiens ita fertur, ut acta
185 praecipiti pinus borea, cui victa remisit
frena suus rector, quam dis votisque reliquit.
quid faciat? multum caeli post terga relictum,

ante oculos plus est. animo metitur utrumque;
et modo, quos illi fatum contingere non est,
190   prospicit occasus, interdum respicit ortus:
quidque agat, ignarus stupet et nec frena remittit
nec retinere valet nec nomina novit equorum.
sparsa quoque in vario passim miracula caelo
vastarumque videt trepidus simulacra ferarum.
195   est locus, in geminos ubi bracchia concavat arcus
Scorpius et cauda flexisque utrimque lacertis
porrigit in spatium signorum membra duorum:
hunc puer ut nigri madidum sudore veneni
vulnera curvata minitantem cuspide vidit,
200   mentis inops gelida formidine lora remisit.
quae postquam summo tetigere iacentia tergo,
exspatiantur equi nulloque inhibente per auras
ignotae regionis eunt, quaque impetus egit,
hac sine lege ruunt altoque sub aethere fixis
205   incursant stellis rapiuntque per avia currum
et modo summa petunt, modo per declive viasque
praecipites spatio terrae propiore feruntur,
inferiusque suis fraternos currere Luna
admiratur equos, ambustaque nubila fumant.
210   corripitur flammis, ut quaeque altissima, tellus
fissaque agit rimas et sucis aret ademptis.
pabula canescunt, cum frondibus uritur arbor,
materiamque suo praebet seges arida damno.
      Parva queror; magnae pereunt cum moenibus urbes,
215   cumque suis totas populis incendia gentes
in cinerem vertunt; silvae cum montibus ardent,
ardet Athos Taurusque Cilix et Tmolus et Oete
et tum sicca, prius creberrima fontibus, Ide
virgineusque Helicon et nondum Oeagrius Haemus.
220   ardet in inmensum geminatis ignibus Aetna
Parnasusque biceps et Eryx et Cynthus et Othrys
et tandem nivibus Rhodope caritura Mimasque
Dindymaque et Mycale natusque ad sacra Cithaeron.
nec prosunt Scythiae sua frigora: Caucasus ardet
225   Ossaque cum Pindo maiorque ambobus Olympus
aëriaeque Alpes et nubifer Appenninus.
      Tum vero Phaethon cunctis e partibus orbem

adspicit accensum nec tantos sustinet aestus
ferventesque auras velut e fornace profunda
230   ore trahit currusque suos candescere sentit
et neque iam cineres eiectatamque favillam
ferre potest calidoque involvitur undique fumo,
quoque eat aut ubi sit, picea caligine tectus
nescit et arbitrio volucrum raptatur equorum.
235   sanguine tunc credunt in corpora summa vocato
Aethiopum populos nigrum traxisse colorem.
tum facta est Libye raptis umoribus aestu
arida, tum nymphae passis fontesque lacusque
deflevere comis: quaerit Boeotia Dircen,
240   Argos Amymonen, Ephyre Pirenidas undas.
nec sortita loco distantes flumina ripas
tuta manent: mediis Tanais fumavit in undis,
Peneosque senex Teuthranteusque Caicus
et celer Ismenos cum Phegiaco Erymantho
245   arsurusque iterum Xanthus flavusque Lycormas
quique recurvatis ludit Maeandrus in undis
Mygdoniusque Melas et Taenarius Eurotas.
arsit et Euphrates Babylonius, arsit Orontes
Thermodonque citus Gangesque et Phasis et Hister.
250   aestuat Alpheos, ripae Spercheides ardent,
quodque suo Tagus amne vehit, fluit ignibus aurum,
et quae Maeonias celebrabant carmine ripas
flumineae volucres, medio caluere Caystro.
Nilus in extremum fugit perterritus orbem
255   occuluitque caput, quod adhuc latet; ostia septem
pulverulenta vacant, septem sine flumine valles.
fors eadem Ismarios Hebrum cum Strymone siccat
Hesperiosque amnes Rhenum Rhodanumque Padumque,
cuique fuit rerum promissa potentia, Thybrim.
260   Dissilit omne solum, penetratque in Tartara rimis
lumen et infernum terret cum coniuge regem;
et mare contrahitur, siccaeque est campus harenae,
quod modo pontus erat, quosque altum texerat aequor,
exsistunt montes et sparsas Cycladas augent.
265   ima petunt pisces, nec se super aequora curvi
tollere consuetas audent delphines in auras;
corpora phocarum summo resupina profundo

exanimata natant; ipsum quoque Nerea fama est
Doridaque et natas tepidis latuisse sub antris;
270 ter Neptunus aquis cum torvo bracchia vultu
exserere ausus erat, ter non tulit aëris ignes.
alma tamen Tellus, ut erat circumdata ponto,
inter aquas pelagi contractosque undique fontes,
qui se condiderant in opacae viscera matris,
275 sustulit oppressos collo tenus arida vultus
opposuitque manum fronti magnoque tremore
omnia concutiens paulum subsedit et infra,
quam solet esse, fuit siccaque ita voce locuta est:
'Si placet hoc meruique, quid o tua fulmina cessant,
280 summe deum? liceat periturae viribus ignis
igne perire tuo clademque auctore levare.
vix equidem fauces haec ipsa in verba resolvo'
(presserat ora vapor), 'tostos en adspice crines
inque oculis tantum, tantum super ora favillae!
285 hosne mihi fructus, hunc fertilitatis honorem
officiique refers, quod adunci vulnera aratri
rastrorumque fero totoque exerceor anno,
quod pecori frondes alimentaque mitia, fruges,
humano generi, vobis quoque tura ministro?
290 sed tamen exitium fac me meruisse, quid undae,
quid meruit frater? cur illi tradita sorte
aequora decrescunt et ab aethere longius absunt?
quodsi nec fratris nec te mea gratia tangit,
at caeli miserere tui! circumspice utrumque:
295 fumat uterque polus. quos si vitiaverit ignis,
atria vestra ruent. Atlans en ipse laborat
vixque suis umeris candentem sustinet axem.
si freta, si terrae pereunt, si regia caeli,
in chaos antiquum confundimur. eripe flammis,
300 siquid adhuc superest, et rerum consule summae!'
    Dixerat haec Tellus (neque enim tolerare vaporem
ulterius potuit nec dicere plura) suumque
rettulit os in se propioraque manibus antra.
    At pater omnipotens superos testatus et ipsum,
305 qui dederat currus, nisi opem ferat, omnia fato
interitura gravi, summam petit arduus arcem,
unde solet nubes latis inducere terris,

　　　unde movet tonitrus vibrataque fulmina iactat;
　　　sed neque, quas posset terris inducere, nubes
310　tunc habuit nec, quos caelo dimitteret, imbres:
　　　intonat et dextra libratum fulmen ab aure
　　　misit in aurigam pariterque animaque rotisque
　　　expulit et saevis conpescuit ignibus ignes.
　　　consternantur equi et saltu in contraria facto
315　colla iugo eripiunt abruptaque lora relinquunt.
　　　illic frena iacent, illic temone revulsus
　　　axis, in hac radii fractarum parte rotarum,
　　　sparsaque sunt late laceri vestigia currus.
　　　　At Phaethon rutilos flamma populante capillos
320　volvitur in praeceps longoque per aëra tractu
　　　fertur, ut interdum de caelo stella sereno,
　　　etsi non cecidit, potuit cecidisse videri.
　　　quem procul a patria diverso maximus orbe
　　　excipit Eridanus fumantiaque abluit ora.
325　Naides Hesperiae trifida fumantia flamma
　　　corpora dant tumulo, signant quoque carmine saxum:
　　　HIC. SITVS. EST. PHAETHON. CVRRVS. AVRIGA.
　　　　　PATERNI
　　　QVEM. SI. NON. TENVIT. MAGNIS. TAMEN.
　　　　　EXCIDIT. AVSIS.
　　　nam pater obductos luctu miserabilis aegro
330　condiderat vultus: et si modo credimus, unum
　　　isse diem sine sole ferunt; incendia lumen
　　　praebebant, aliquisque malo fuit usus in illo.
　　　　At Clymene postquam dixit, quaecumque fuerunt
　　　in tantis dicenda malis, lugubris et amens
335　et laniata sinus totum percensuit orbem
　　　exanimesque artus primo, mox ossa requirens
　　　repperit, ossa tamen peregrina condita ripa;
　　　incubuitque loco nomenque in marmore lectum
　　　perfudit lacrimis et aperto pectore fovit.
340　　Nec minus Heliades lugent et inania morti
　　　munera dant lacrimas et caesae pectora palmis
　　　non auditurum miseras Phaethonta querellas
　　　nocte dieque vocant adsternunturque sepulcro.
　　　luna quater iunctis inplerat cornibus orbem:
345　illae more suo (nam morem fecerat usus)

plangorem dederant; e quis Phaethusa, sororum
maxima, cum vellet terra procumbere, questa est
deriguisse pedes; ad quam conata venire
candida Lampetie subita radice retenta est;
350   tertia cum crinem manibus laniare pararet,
avellit frondes; haec stipite crura teneri,
illa dolet fieri longos sua bracchia ramos;
dumque ea mirantur, conplectitur inguina cortex
perque gradus uterum pectusque umerosque manusque
355   ambit et exstabant tantum ora vocantia matrem.
quid faciat mater, nisi, quo trahit inpetus illam,
huc eat atque illuc et, dum licet, oscula iungat?
non satis est: truncis avellere corpora temptat
et teneros manibus ramos abrumpit; at inde
360   sanguineae manant tamquam de vulnere guttae.
'parce, precor, mater,' quaecumque est saucia, clamat,
'parce, precor! nostrum laceratur in arbore corpus.
iamque vale'—cortex in verba novissima venit.
inde fluunt lacrimae, stillataque sole rigescunt
365   de ramis electra novis, quae lucidus amnis
excipit et nuribus mittit gestanda Latinis.
      Adfuit huic monstro proles Stheneleia Cygnus,
qui tibi materno quamvis a sanguine iunctus,
mente tamen, Phaethon, propior fuit; ille relicto
370   (nam Ligurum populos et magnas rexerat urbes)
imperio ripas virides amnemque querellis
Eridanum inplerat silvamque sororibus auctam,
cum vox est tenuata viro canaeque capillos
dissimulant plumae collumque a pectore longe
375   porrigitur digitosque ligat iunctura rubentes,
penna latus velat, tenet os sine acumine rostrum.
fit nova Cygnus avis nec se caeloque Iovique
credit ut iniuste missi memor ignis ab illo;
stagna petit patulosque lacus ignemque perosus,
380   quae colat, elegit contraria flumina flammis.
      Squalidus interea genitor Phaethontis et expers
ipse sui decoris, quali, cum deficit, orbe
esse solet, lucemque odit seque ipse diemque
datque animum in luctus et luctibus adicit iram
385   officiumque negat mundo. 'satis' inquit 'ab aevi

sors mea principiis fuit inrequieta, pigetque
actorum sine fine mihi, sine honore, laborum.
quilibet alter agat portantes lumina currus!
si nemo est omnesque dei non posse fatentur,
390 ipse agat, ut saltem, dum nostras temptat habenas,
orbatura patres aliquando fulmina ponat.
tum sciet ignipedum vires expertus equorum
non meruisse necem, qui non bene rexerit illos.'
talia dicentem circumstant omnia Solem
395 numina, neve velit tenebras inducere rebus,
supplice voce rogant; missos quoque Iuppiter ignes
excusat precibusque minas regaliter addit.
conligit amentes et adhuc terrore paventes
Phoebus equos stimuloque dolens et verbere saevit
400 (saevit enim) natumque obiectat et inputat illis.
    At pater omnipotens ingentia moenia caeli
circuit et, ne quid labefactum viribus ignis
corruat, explorat. quae postquam firma suique
roboris esse videt, terras hominumque labores
405 perspicit; Arcadiae tamen est inpensior illi
cura suae, fontesque et nondum audentia labi
flumina restituit, dat terrae gramina, frondes
arboribus laesasque iubet revirescere silvas.
dum redit itque frequens, in virgine Nonacrina
410 haesit, et accepti caluere sub ossibus ignes.
non erat huius opus lanam mollire trahendo
nec positu variare comas; ubi fibula vestem,
vitta coercuerat neglectos alba capillos
et modo leve manu iaculum, modo sumpserat arcum,
415 miles erat Phoebes, nec Maenalon attigit ulla
gratior hac Triviae; sed nulla potentia longa est.
    Ulterius medio spatium sol altus habebat,
cum subit illa nemus, quod nulla ceciderat aetas:
exuit hic umero pharetram lentosque retendit
420 arcus inque solo, quod texerat herba, iacebat
et pictam posita pharetram cervice premebat.
Iuppiter ut vidit fessam et custode vacantem,
'hoc certe furtum coniunx mea nesciet' inquit,
'aut si rescierit,—sunt, o sunt iurgia tanti!'
425 protinus induitur faciem cultumque Dianae

atque ait: 'o comitum, virgo, pars una mearum,
in quibus es venata iugis?' de caespite virgo
se levat et 'salve numen, me iudice' dixit,
'audiat ipse licet, maius Iove.' ridet et audit

430 et sibi praeferri se gaudet et oscula iungit
nec moderata satis nec sic a virgine danda.
qua venata foret silva, narrare parantem
inpedit amplexu nec se sine crimine prodit.
illa quidem contra, quantum modo femina posset,

435 (adspiceres utinam, Saturnia, mitior esses!)
illa quidem pugnat; sed quem superare puella,
quisve Iovem poterat? superum petit aethera victor
Iuppiter: huic odio nemus est et conscia silva;
unde pedem referens paene est oblita pharetram

440 tollere cum telis et, quem suspenderat, arcum.
     Ecce, suo comitata choro Dictynna per altum
Maenalon ingrediens et caede superba ferarum
adspicit hanc visamque vocat: clamata refugit
et timuit primo, ne Iuppiter esset in illa;

445 sed postquam pariter nymphas incedere vidit,
sensit abesse dolos numerumque accessit ad harum.
heu quam difficile est crimen non prodere vultu!
vix oculos attollit humo nec, ut ante solebat,
iuncta deae lateri nec toto est agmine prima,

450 sed silet et laesi dat signa rubore pudoris,
et, nisi quod virgo est, poterat sentire Diana
mille notis culpam; nymphae sensisse feruntur.
orbe resurgebant lunaria cornua nono,
cum dea venatu fraternis languida flammis

455 nacta nemus gelidum, de quo cum murmure labens
ibat et attritas versabat rivus harenas:
ut loca laudavit, summas pede contigit undas;
his quoque laudatis 'procul est' ait 'arbiter omnis;
nuda superfusis tingamus corpora lymphis.'

460 Parrhasis erubuit; cunctae velamina ponunt:
una moras quaerit; dubitanti vestis adempta est,
qua posita nudo patuit cum corpore crimen.
attonitae manibusque uterum celare volenti
'i procul hinc' dixit 'nec sacros pollue fontes!'

465 Cynthia deque suo iussit secedere coetu.

Senserat hoc olim magni matrona Tonantis
distuleratque graves in idonea tempora poenas.
causa morae nulla est, et iam puer Arcas (id ipsum
indoluit Iuno) fuerat de paelice natus;
470   quo simul obvertit saevam cum lumine mentem,
'scilicet hoc etiam restabat, adultera'? dixit
'ut fecunda fores fieretque iniuria partu
nota Iovisque mei testatum dedecus esset!
haud inpune feres: adimam tibi namque figuram,
475   qua tibi quaque places nostro, inportuna, marito.'
Dixit et adversa prensis a fronte capillis
stravit humi pronam; tendebat bracchia supplex:
bracchia coeperunt nigris horrescere villis
curvarique manus et aduncos crescere in ungues
480   officioque pedum fungi laudataque quondam
ora Iovi lato fieri deformia rictu;
neve preces animos et verba precantia flectant,
posse loqui eripitur: vox iracunda minaxque
plenaque terroris rauco de gutture fertur.
485   mens antiqua manet (facta quoque mansit in ursa),
adsiduoque suos gemitu testata dolores
qualescumque manus ad caelum et sidera tollit
ingratumque Iovem, nequeat cum dicere, sentit.
a, quotiens sola non ausa quiescere silva
490   ante domum quondamque suis erravit in agris!
a, quotiens per saxa canum latratibus acta est
venatrixque metu venantum territa fugit!
saepe feris latuit visis oblita, quid esset,
ursaque conspectos in montibus horruit ursos
495   pertimuitque lupos, quamvis pater esset in illis.
Ecce, Lycaoniae proles ignara parentis,
Arcas adest ter quinque fere natalibus actis,
dumque feras sequitur, dum saltus eligit aptos
nexilibusque plagis silvas Erymanthidas ambit,
500   incidit in matrem; quae restitit Arcade viso
et cognoscenti similis fuit. ille refugit
inmotosque oculos in se sine fine tenentem
nescius extimuit propiusque accedere aventi
vulnifico fuerat fixurus pectora telo.
505   arcuit omnipotens pariterque ipsosque nefasque

sustulit et pariter raptos per inania vento
inposuit caelo vicinaque sidera fecit.
   Intumuit Iuno, postquam inter sidera paelex
fulsit, et ad canam descendit in aequora Tethyn
510 Oceanumque senem, quorum reverentia movit
saepe deos, causamque viae scitantibus infit:
'Quaeritis, aetheriis quare regina deorum
sedibus hic adsim? pro me tenet altera caelum.
mentior, obscurum nisi nox cum fecerit orbem,
515 nuper honoratas summo, mea vulnera, caelo
videritis stellas illic, ubi circulus axem
ultimus extremum spatioque brevissimus ambit.
et vero quisquam Iunonem laedere nolit
offensamque tremat, quae prosum sola nocendo?
520 o ego quantum egi! quam vasta potentia nostra est!
esse hominem vetui: facta est dea. sic ego poenas
sontibus inpono, sic est mea magna potestas!
vindicet antiquam faciem vultusque ferinos
detrahat, Argolica quod in ante Phoronide fecit!
525 cur non et pulsa ducit Iunone meoque
conlocat in thalamo socerumque Lycaona sumit?
at vos si laesae tangit contemptus alumnae,
gurgite caeruleo Septem prohibete triones,
sideraque in caelo, stupri mercede, recepta
530 pellite, ne puro tingatur in aequore paelex.'
   Di maris adnuerant: habili Saturnia curru
ingreditur liquidum pavonibus aethera pictis,
tam nuper pictis caeso pavonibus Argo,
quam tu nuper eras, cum candidus ante fuisses,
535 corve loquax, subito nigrantes versus in alas.
nam fuit haec quondam niveis argentea pennis
ales, ut aequaret totas sine labe columbas
nec servaturis vigili Capitolia voce
cederet anseribus nec amanti flumina cygno.
540 lingua fuit damno: lingua faciente loquaci,
qui color albus erat, nunc est contrarius albo.
   Pulchrior in tota quam Larissaea Coronis
non fuit Haemonia: placuit tibi, Delphice, certe,
dum vel casta fuit vel inobservata, sed ales
545 sensit adulterium Phoebeius, utque latentem

detegeret culpam, non exorabilis index,
ad dominum tendebat iter; quem garrula motis
consequitur pennis, scitetur ut omnia, cornix
auditaque viae causa 'non utile carpis'
550   inquit 'iter: ne sperne meae praesagia linguae.
quid fuerim quid simque, vide meritumque require:
invenies nocuisse fidem. nam tempore quodam
Pallas Ericthonium, prolem sine matre creatam,
clauserat Actaeo texta de vimine cista
555   virginibusque tribus gemino de Cecrope natis
et legem dederat, sua ne secreta viderent.
abdita fronde levi densa speculabar ab ulmo,
quid facerent: commissa duae sine fraude tuentur
Pandrosos atque Herse; timidas vocat una sorores
560   Aglauros nodosque manu diducit, et intus
infantemque vident adporrectumque draconem.
acta deae refero; pro quo mihi gratia talis
redditur, ut dicar tutela pulsa Minervae
et ponar post noctis avem. mea poena volucres
565   admonuisse potest, ne voce pericula quaerant.
at, puto, non ultro nec quicquam tale rogantem
me petiit!—ipsa licet hoc a Pallade quaeras:
quamvis irata est, non hoc irata negabit.
nam me Phocaica clarus tellure Coroneus
570   (nota loquor) genuit fueramque ego regia virgo
divitibusque procis (ne me contemne) petebar;
forma mihi nocuit. nam cum per litora lentis
passibus, ut soleo, summa spatiarer harena,
vidit et incaluit pelagi deus, utque precando
575   tempora cum blandis absumpsit inania verbis,
vim parat et sequitur; fugio densumque relinquo
litus et in molli nequiquam lassor harena.
inde deos hominesque voco, nec contigit ullum
vox mea mortalem: mota est pro virgine virgo
580   auxiliumque tulit. tendebam bracchia caelo:
bracchia coeperunt levibus nigrescere pennis;
reicere ex umeris vestem molibar: at illa
pluma erat inque cutem radices egerat imas;
plangere nuda meis conabar pectora palmis,
585   sed neque iam palmas nec pectora nuda gerebam;

currebam, nec ut ante pedes retinebat harena,
sed summa tollebar humo; mox acta per auras
evehor et data sum comes inculpata Minervae.
quid tamen hoc prodest, si diro facta volucris
590   crimine Nyctimene nostro successit honori?
an, quae per totam res est notissima Lesbon,
non audita tibi est, patrium temerasse cubile
Nyctimenen? avis illa quidem, sed conscia culpae
conspectum lucemque fugit tenebrisque pudorem
595   celat et a cunctis expellitur aethere toto.'
      Talia dicenti 'tibi' ait 'revocamina' corvus
'sint precor ista malo: nos vanum spernimus omen.'
nec coeptum dimittit iter dominoque iacentem
cum iuvene Haemonio vidisse Coronida narrat.
600   laurea delapsa est audito crimine amanti,
et pariter vultusque deo plectrumque colorque
excidit, utque animus tumida fervebat ab ira,
arma adsueta capit flexumque a cornibus arcum
tendit et illa suo totiens cum pectore iuncta
605   indevitato traiecit pectora telo.
icta dedit gemitum tractoque a corpore ferro
candida puniceo perfudit membra cruore
et dixit: 'potui poenas tibi, Phoebe, dedisse,
sed peperisse prius. duo nunc moriemur in una.'
610   hactenus, et pariter vitam cum sanguine fudit;
corpus inane animae frigus letale secutum est.
paenitet heu sero poenae crudelis amantem
seque, quod audierit, quod sic exarserit, odit;
odit avem, per quam crimen causamque dolendi
615   scire coactus erat, nec non arcumque manumque
odit cumque manu temeraria tela, sagittas,
conlapsamque fovet seraque ope vincere fata
nititur et medicas exercet inaniter artes.
quae postquam frustra temptata rogumque parari
620   sensit et arsuros supremis ignibus artus,
tum vero gemitus (neque enim caelestia tingi
ora licet lacrimis) alto de corde petitos
edidit, haud aliter, quam cum spectante iuvenca
lactentis vituli dextra libratus ab aure
625   tempora discussit claro cava malleus ictu.

ut tamen ingratos in pectora fudit odores
et dedit amplexus iniustaque iusta peregit,
non tulit in cineres labi sua Phoebus eosdem
semina, sed natum flammis uteroque parentis
630 eripuit geminique tulit Chironis in antrum,
sperantemque sibi non falsae praemia linguae
inter aves albas vetuit consistere corvum.
     Semifer interea divinae stirpis alumno
laetus erat mixtoque oneri gaudebat honore.
635 ecce venit rutilis umeros protecta capillis
filia Centauri, quam quondam nympha Chariclo
fluminis in rapidi ripis enixa vocavit
Ocyroen; non haec artes contenta paternas
edidicisse fuit: fatorum arcana canebat.
640 ergo ubi vaticinos concepit mente furores
incaluitque deo, quem clausum pectore habebat,
adspicit infantem 'toto' que 'salutifer orbi
cresce puer' dixit, 'tibi se mortalia saepe
corpora debebunt; animas tibi reddere ademptas
645 fas erit, idque semel dis indignantibus ausus
posse dare hoc iterum flamma prohibebere avita
eque deo corpus fies exsangue deusque,
qui modo corpus eras, et bis tua fata novabis.
tu quoque, care pater, nunc inmortalis et aevis
650 omnibus ut maneas nascendi lege creatus,
posse mori cupies tum, cum cruciabere dirae
sanguine serpentis per saucia membra recepto,
teque ex aeterno patientem numina mortis
efficient, triplicesque deae tua fila resolvent.'
655 restabat fatis aliquid: suspirat ab imis
pectoribus, lacrimaeque genis labuntur obortae,
atque ita 'praevertunt' inquit 'me fata, vetorque
plura loqui, vocisque meae praecluditur usus.
non fuerant artes tanti, quae numinis iram
660 contraxere mihi: mallem nescisse futura.
iam mihi subduci facies humana videtur,
iam cibus herba placet, iam latis currere campis
impetus est: in equam cognataque corpora vertor.
tota tamen quare? pater est mihi nempe biformis.'
665 talia dicenti pars est extrema querellae

intellecta parum, confusaque verba fuerunt;
mox nec verba quidem nec equae sonus ille videtur,
sed simulantis equam, parvoque in tempore certos
edidit hinnitus et bracchia movit in herbas.
670   tum digiti coeunt et quinos adligat ungues
perpetuo cornu levis ungula, crescit et oris
et colli spatium, longae pars maxima pallae
cauda fit, utque vagi crines per colla iacebant,
in dextras abiere iubas, pariterque novata est
675   et vox et facies; nomen quoque monstra dedere.
    Flebat opemque tuam frustra Philyreius heros,
Delphice, poscebat. nam nec rescindere magni
iussa Iovis poteras, nec, si rescindere posses,
tunc aderas: Elim Messeniaque arva colebas.
680   illud erat tempus, quo te pastoria pellis
texit onusque fuit baculum silvestre sinistrae,
alterius dispar septenis fistula cannis;
dumque amor est curae, dum te tua fistula mulcet,
incustoditae Pylios memorantur in agros
685   processisse boves. videt has Atlantide Maia
natus et arte sua silvis occultat abactas.
senserat hoc furtum nemo nisi notus in illo
rure senex: Battum vicinia tota vocabant.
divitis hic saltus herbosaque pascua Nelei
690   nobiliumque greges custos servabat equarum.
hunc timuit blandaque manu seduxit et illi
'quisquis es, hospes,' ait 'si forte armenta requiret
haec aliquis, vidisse nega, neu gratia facto
nulla rependatur, nitidam cape praemia vaccam',
695   et dedit. accepta voces has reddidit: 'hospes,
tutus eas! lapis iste prius tua furta loquetur',
et lapidem ostendit. simulat Iove natus abire,
mox redit et versa pariter cum voce figura
'rustice, vidisti siquas hoc limite' dixit
700   'ire boves, fer opem, furtoque silentia deme.
iuncta suo pariter dabitur tibi femina tauro.'
at senior, postquam est merces geminata, 'sub illis
montibus' inquit 'erunt', et erant sub montibus illis.
risit Atlantiades et 'me mihi, perfide, prodis?
705   me mihi prodis?' ait periuraque pectora vertit

in durum silicem, qui nunc quoque dicitur index,
inque nihil merito vetus est infamia saxo.
     Hinc se sustulerat paribus Caducifer alis
Munychiosque volans agros gratamque Minervae
710 despectabat humum cultique arbusta Lycei.
illa forte die castae de more puellae
vertice subposito festas in Palladis arces
pura coronatis portabant sacra canistris.
inde revertentes deus adspicit ales iterque
715 non agit in rectum, sed in orbem curvat eundem.
ut volucris visis rapidissima miluus extis,
dum timet et densi circumstant sacra ministri,
flectitur in gyrum nec longius audet abire
spemque suam motis avidus circumvolat alis:
720 sic super Actaeas avidus Cyllenius arces
inclinat cursus et easdem circinat auras:
quanto splendidior quam cetera sidera fulget
Lucifer et quanto quam Lucifer aurea Phoebe,
tanto virginibus praestantior omnibus Herse
725 ibat eratque decus pompae comitumque suarum.
obstipuit forma Iove natus et aethere pendens
non secus exarsit, quam cum Balearica plumbum
funda iacit: volat illud et incandescit eundo,
et quos non habuit, sub nubibus invenit ignes.
730 vertit iter caeloque petit terrena relicto
nec se dissimulat: tanta est fiducia formae.
quae quamquam iusta est, cura tamen adiuvat illam
permulcetque comas chlamydemque, ut pendeat apte,
conlocat, ut limbus totumque appareat aurum,
735 ut teres in dextra, quae somnos ducit et arcet,
virga sit, ut tersis niteant talaria plantis.
pars secreta domus ebore et testudine cultos
tris habuit thalamos, quorum tu, Pandrose, dextrum,
Aglauros laevum, medium possederat Herse.
740 quae tenuit laevum, venientem prima notavit
Mercurium nomenque dei scitarier ausa est
et causam adventus; cui sic respondit: 'Atlantis
Pleionesque nepos ego sum, qui iussa per auras
verba patris porto, pater est mihi Iuppiter ipse.
745 nec fingam causas; tu tantum fida sorori

esse velis prolisque meae matertera dici:
Herse causa viae; faveas oramus amanti.'
adspicit hunc oculis isdem, quibus abdita nuper
viderat Aglauros flavae secreta Minervae,
750   proque minsterio magni sibi ponderis aurum
postulat; interea tectis excedere cogit.
vertit ad hanc torvi dea bellica luminis orbem
et tanto penitus traxit suspiria motu,
ut pariter pectus positamque in pectore forti
755   aegida concuteret. subit hanc arcana profana
detexisse manu tum, cum sine matre creatam
Lemnicolae stirpem contra data foedera vidit,
et gratamque deo fore iam gratamque sorori
et ditem sumpto, quod avara poposcerat, auro.
760   Protinus Invidiae nigro squalentia tabo
tecta petit: domus est imis in vallibus huius
abdita, sole carens, non ulli pervia vento,
tristis et ignavi plenissima frigoris, et quae
igne vacet semper, caligine semper abundet.
765   huc ubi pervenit belli metuenda virago,
constitit ante domum (neque enim succedere tectis
fas habet) et postes extrema cuspide pulsat;
concussae patuere fores: videt intus edentem
vipereas carnes, vitiorum alimenta suorum,
770   Invidiam visaque oculos avertit; at illa
surgit humo pigra semesarumque relinquit
corpora serpentum passuque incedit inerti,
utque deam vidit formaque armisque decoram,
ingemuit vultumque ima ad suspiria duxit.
775   pallor in ore sedet, macies in corpore toto,
nusquam recta acies, livent rubigine dentes,
pectora felle virent, lingua est suffusa veneno.
risus abest, nisi quem visi movere dolores,
nec fruitur somno vigilacibus excita curis,
780   sed videt ingratos intabescitque videndo
successus hominum carpitque et carpitur una
suppliciumque suum est. quamvis tamen oderat illam,
talibus adfata est breviter Tritonia dictis:
'infice tabe tua natarum Cecropis unam.
785   sic opus est; Aglauros ea est.' haud plura locuta

fugit et inpressa tellurem reppulit hasta.
    Illa deam obliquo fugientem lumine cernens
murmura parva dedit successurumque Minervae
indoluit baculumque capit, quod spinea totum
790 vincula cingebant, adopertaque nubibus atris,
quacumque ingreditur, florentia proterit arva
exuritque herbas et summa papavera carpit
adflatuque suo populos urbesque domosque
polluit, et tandem Tritonida conspicit arcem
795 ingeniis opibusque et festa pace virentem
vixque tenet lacrimas, quia nil lacrimabile cernit.
sed postquam thalamos intravit Cecrope natae,
iussa facit pectusque manu ferrugine tincta
tangit et hamatis praecordia sentibus inplet
800 inspiratque nocens virus piceumque per ossa
dissipat et medio spargit pulmone venenum,
neve mali causae spatium per latius errent,
germanam ante oculos fortunatumque sororis
coniugium pulchraque deum sub imagine ponit
805 cunctaque magna facit; quibus inritata, dolore
Cecropis occulto mordetur et anxia nocte,
anxia luce gemit lentaque miserrima tabe
liquitur, ut glacies incerto saucia sole,
felicisque bonis non lenius uritur Herses,
810 quam cum spinosis ignis subponitur herbis,
quae neque dant flammas lenique tepore cremantur.
saepe mori voluit, ne quicquam tale videret,
saepe velut crimen rigido narrare parenti;
denique in adverso venientem limine sedit
815 exclusura deum; cui blandimenta precesque
verbaque iactanti mitissima 'desine' dixit,
'hinc ego me non sum nisi te motura repulso.'
'stemus' ait 'pacto' velox Cyllenius 'isto',
caelestique fores virga patefecit. at illi
820 surgere conanti partes, quascumque sedendo
flectitur, ignava nequeunt gravitate moveri.
illa quidem pugnat recto se attollere trunco,
sed genuum iunctura riget, frigusque per ungues
labitur, et pallent amisso sanguine venae;
825 utque malum late solet inmedicabile cancer

serpere et inlaesas vitiatis addere partes,
sic letalis hiems paulatim in pectora venit
vitalesque vias et respiramina clausit,
nec conata loqui est nec, si conata fuisset,
830   vocis habebat iter; saxum iam colla tenebat,
oraque duruerant, signumque exsangue sedebat;
nec lapis albus erat: sua mens infecerat illam.
　　Has ubi verborum poenas mentisque profanae
cepit Atlantiades, dictas a Pallade terras
835   linquit et ingreditur iactatis aethera pennis.
sevocat hunc genitor nec causam fassus amoris
'fide minister' ait 'iussorum, nate, meorum,
pelle moram solitoque celer delabere cursu,
quaeque tuam matrem tellus a parte sinistra
840   suspicit (indigenae Sidonida nomine dicunt),
hanc pete, quodque procul montano gramine pasci
armentum regale vides, ad litora verte.'
dixit, et expulsi iamdudum monte iuvenci
litora iussa petunt, ubi magni filia regis
845   ludere virginibus Tyriis comitata solebat.
non bene conveniunt nec in una sede morantur
maiestas et amor: sceptri gravitate relicta
ille pater rectorque deum, cui dextra trisulcis
ignibus armata est, qui nutu concutit orbem,
850   induitur faciem tauri mixtusque iuvencis
mugit et in teneris formosus obambulat herbis.
quippe color nivis est, quam nec vestigia duri
calcavere pedis nec solvit aquaticus auster;
colla toris exstant, armis palearia pendent,
855   cornua parva quidem, sed quae contendere possis
facta manu, puraque magis perlucida gemma;
nullae in fronte minae nec formidabile lumen:
pacem vultus habet. miratur Agenore nata,
quod tam formosus, quod proelia nulla minetur,
860   sed quamvis mitem metuit contingere primo:
mox adit et flores ad candida porrigit ora.
gaudet amans et, dum veniat sperata voluptas,
oscula dat manibus; vix iam, vix cetera differt
et nunc adludit viridique exsultat in herba,
865   nunc latus in fulvis niveum deponit harenis

paulatimque metu dempto modo pectora praebet
virginea plaudenda manu, modo cornua sertis
inpedienda novis. ausa est quoque regia virgo
nescia, quem premeret, tergo considere tauri:
870 cum deus a terra siccoque a litore sensim
falsa pedum primo vestiga ponit in undis,
inde abit ulterius mediique per aequora ponti
fert praedam. pavet haec litusque ablata relictum
respicit et dextra cornum tenet, altera dorso
875 inposita est; tremulae sinuantur flamine vestes.

LIBER TERTIVS

Iamque deus posita fallacis imagine tauri
se confessus erat Dictaeaque rura tenebat,
cum pater ignarus Cadmo perquirere raptam
imperat et poenam, si non invenerit, addit
5   exilium, facto pius et sceleratus eodem.
orbe pererrato (quis enim deprendere possit
furta Iovis?) profugus patriamque iramque parentis
vitat Agenorides, Phoebique oracula supplex
consulit et, quae sit tellus habitanda, requirit.
10   'bos tibi' Phoebus ait 'solis occurret in arvis,
nullum passa iugum curvique inmunis aratri:
hac duce carpe vias et, qua requieverit herba,
moenia fac condas Boeotiaque illa vocato.'
vix bene Castalio Cadmus descenderat antro,
15   incustoditam lente videt ire iuvencam
nullum servitii signum cervice gerentem;
subsequitur pressoque legit vestigia passu
auctoremque viae Phoebum taciturnus adorat.
iam vada Cephisi Panopesque evaserat arva:
20   bos stetit et tollens speciosam cornibus altis
ad caelum frontem mugitibus inpulit auras
atque ita respiciens comites sua terga sequentis
procubuit teneraque latus submisit in herba.
Cadmus agit grates peregrinaeque oscula terrae
25   figit et ignotos montes agrosque salutat;
sacra Iovi facturus erat: iubet ire ministros
et petere e vivis libandas fontibus undas.

Silva vetus stabat nulla violata securi
et specus in medio virgis ac vimine densus
30   efficiens humilem lapidum conpagibus arcum,
uberibus fecundus aquis; ubi conditus antro
Martius anguis erat cristis praesignis et auro:
igne micant oculi, corpus tumet omne veneno,
tresque micant linguae, triplici stant ordine dentes.
35   quem postquam Tyria lucum de gente profecti
infausto tetigere gradu demissaque in undas
urna dedit sonitum, longo caput extulit antro
caeruleus serpens horrendaque sibila misit:
effluxere urnae manibus, sanguisque relinquit
40   corpus et attonitos subitus tremor occupat artus.
ille volubilibus squamosos nexibus orbes
torquet et inmensos saltu sinuatur in arcus
ac media plus parte leves erectus in auras
despicit omne nemus tantoque est corpore, quanto,
45   si totum spectes, geminas qui separat Arctos.
nec mora, Phoenicas, sive illi tela parabant
sive fugam, sive ipse timor prohibebat utrumque,
occupat: hos morsu, longis conplexibus illos,
hos necat adflatu funesti tabe veneni.
50   Fecerat exiguas iam sol altissimus umbras:
quae mora sit sociis, miratur Agenore natus
vestigatque viros. tegumen derepta leoni
pellis erat, telum splendenti lancea ferro
et iaculum teloque animus praestantior omni.
55   ut nemus intravit letataque corpora vidit
victoremque supra spatiosi corporis hostem
tristia sanguinea lambentem vulnera lingua,
'aut ultor vestrae, fidissima corpora, mortis,
aut comes' inquit 'ero.' dixit dextraque molarem
60   sustulit et magnum magno conamine misit;
illius inpulsu cum turribus ardua celsis
moenia mota forent: serpens sine vulnere mansit,
loricaeque modo squamis defensus et atrae
duritia pellis validos cute reppulit ictus.
65   at non duritia iaculum quoque vicit eadem:
quod medio lentae spinae curvamine fixum
constitit et totum descendit in ilia ferrum.

ille dolore ferox caput in sua terga retorsit
vulneraque adspexit fixumque hastile momordit,
70   idque, ubi vi multa partem labefecit in omnem,
vix tergo eripuit; ferrum tamen ossibus haesit.
tunc vero, postquam solitas accessit ad iras
causa recens, plenis tumuerunt guttura venis,
spumaque pestiferos circumfluit albida rictus,
75   terraque rasa sonat squamis, quique halitus exit
ore niger Stygio, vitiatas inficit auras.
ipse modo inmensum spiris facientibus orbem
cingitur, interdum longa trabe rectior adstat,
impete nunc vasto ceu concitus imbribus amnis
80   fertur et obstantes proturbat pectore silvas.
cedit Agenorides paulum spolioque leonis
sustinet incursus instantiaque ora retardat
cuspide praetenta; furit ille et inania duro
vulnera dat ferro figitque in acumine dentes;
85   iamque venenifero sanguis manare palato
coeperat et virides adspergine tinxerat herbas:
sed leve vulnus erat, quia se retrahebat ab ictu
laesaque colla dabat retro plagamque sedere
cedendo arcebat nec longius ire sinebat,
90   donec Agenorides coniectum in gutture ferrum
usque sequens pressit, dum retro quercus eunti
obstitit et fixa est pariter cum robore cervix.
pondere serpentis curvata est arbor et imae
parte flagellari gemuit sua robora caudae.
95   dum spatium victor victi considerat hostis,
vox subito audita est (neque erat cognoscere promptum,
unde, sed audita est): 'quid, Agenore nate, peremptum
serpentem spectas? et tu spectabere serpens.'
   Ille diu pavidus pariter cum mente colorem
100 perdiderat, gelidoque comae terrore rigebant;
ecce viri fautrix superas delapsa per auras
Pallas adest motaeque iubet supponere terrae
vipereos dentes, populi incrementa futuri.
paret et, ut presso sulcum patefecit aratro,
105 spargit humi iussos, mortalia semina, dentes.
inde (fide maius) glaebae coepere moveri,
primaque de sulcis acies apparuit hastae,

tegmina mox capitum picto nutantia cono,
mox umeri pectusque onerataque bracchia telis
110 exsistunt, crescitque seges clipeata virorum.
sic ubi tolluntur festis aulaea theatris,
surgere signa solent primumque ostendere vultus,
cetera paulatim, placidoque educta tenore
tota patent imoque pedes in margine ponunt.
115 territus hoste novo Cadmus capere arma parabat.
'ne cape' de populo, quem terra creaverat, unus
exclamat 'nec te civilibus insere bellis.'
atque ita terrigenis rigido de fratribus unum
comminus ense ferit; iaculo cadit eminus ipse.
120 hunc quoque qui leto dederat, non longius illo
vivit et exspirat, modo quas acceperat, auras,
exemploque pari furit omnis turba, suoque
Marte cadunt subiti per mutua vulnera fratres;
iamque brevis vitae spatium sortita iuventus
125 sanguineam tepido plangebant pectore matrem
quinque superstitibus: quorum fuit unus Echion.
is sua iecit humo monitu Tritonidis arma
fraternaeque fidem pacis petiitque deditque.
hos operis comites habuit Sidonius hospes,
130 cum posuit iussus Phoebeis sortibus urbem.
    Iam stabant Thebae: poteras iam, Cadme, videri
exilio felix: soceri tibi Marsque Venusque
contigerant; huc adde genus de coniuge tanta,
tot natas natosque et, pignora cara, nepotes,
135 hos quoque iam iuvenes, sed scilicet ultima semper
exspectanda dies homini est, dicique beatus
ante obitum nemo supremaque funera debet.
    Prima nepos inter tot res tibi, Cadme, secundas
causa fuit luctus alienaque cornua fronti
140 addita vosque, canes satiatae sanguine erili;
at bene si quaeras, fortunae crimen in illo,
non scelus invenies; quod enim scelus error habebat?
    Mons erat infectus variarum caede ferarum,
iamque dies medius rerum contraxerat umbras
145 et sol ex aequo meta distabat utraque,
cum iuvenis placido per devia lustra vagantes
participes operum conpellat Hyantius ore:

'lina madent, comites, ferrumque cruore ferarum,
fortunamque dies habuit satis. altera lucem
150   cum croceis invecta rotis Aurora reducet,
propositum repetemus opus. nunc Phoebus utraque
distat idem terra finditque vaporibus arva:
sistite opus praesens nodosaque tollite lina.'
iussa viri faciunt intermittuntque laborem.
155   Vallis erat piceis et acuta densa cupressu,
nomine Gargaphie, succinctae sacra Dianae,
cuius in extremo est antrum nemorale recessu
arte laboratum nulla: simulaverat artem
ingenio natura suo; nam pumice vivo
160   et levibus tofis nativum duxerat arcum.
fons sonat a dextra tenui perlucidus unda,
margine gramineo patulos succinctus hiatus:
hic dea silvarum venatu fessa solebat
virgineos artus liquido perfundere rore.
165   quo postquam subiit, nympharum tradidit uni
armigerae iaculum pharetramque arcusque retentos;
altera depositae subiecit bracchia pallae;
vincla duae pedibus demunt; nam doctior illis
Ismenis Crocale sparsos per colla capillos
170   conligit in nodum, quamvis erat ipsa solutis.
excipiunt laticem Nepheleque Hyaleque Ranisque
et Psecas et Phiale funduntque capacibus urnis.
dumque ibi perluitur solita Titania lympha,
ecce nepos Cadmi dilata parte laborum
175   per nemus ignotum non certis passibus errans
pervenit in lucum: sic illum fata ferebant.
qui simul intravit rorantia fontibus antra,
sicut erant, viso nudae sua pectora nymphae
percussere viro subitisque ululatibus omne
180   inplevere nemus circumfusaeque Dianam
corporibus texere suis; tamen altior illis
ipsa dea est colloque tenus supereminet omnes.
qui color infectis adversi solis ab ictu
nubibus esse solet aut purpureae Aurorae,
185   is fuit in vultu visae sine veste Dianae,
quae quamquam comitum turba stipata suarum
in latus obliquum tamen adstitit oraque retro

flexit et, ut vellet promptas habuisse sagittas,
quas habuit, sic hausit aquas vultumque virilem
190   perfudit spargensque comas ultricibus undis
addidit haec cladis praenuntia verba futurae:
'nunc tibi me posito visam velamine narres,
si poteris narrare, licet.' nec plura minata
dat sparso capiti vivacis cornua cervi,
195   dat spatium collo summasque cacuminat aures
cum pedibusque manus, cum longis bracchia mutat
cruribus et velat maculoso vellere corpus;
additus et pavor est. fugit Autonoeius heros
et se tam celerem cursu miratur in ipso.
200   ut vero vultus et cornua vidit in unda,
'me miserum!' dicturus erat: vox nulla secuta est;
ingemuit: vox illa fuit, lacrimaeque per ora
non sua fluxerunt; mens tantum pristina mansit.
quid faciat? repetatne domum et regalia tecta
205   an lateat silvis? timor hoc, pudor inpedit illud.
dum dubitat, videre canes: primusque Melampus
Ichnobatesque sagax latratu signa dedere,
Gnosius Ichnobates, Spartana gente Melampus;
inde ruunt alii rapida velocius aura,
210   Pamphagos et Dorceus et Oribasos, Arcades omnes,
Nebrophonosque valens et trux cum Laelape Theron
et pedibus Pterelas et naribus utilis Agre
Hylaeusque ferox nuper percussus ab apro
deque lupo concepta Nape pecudesque secuta
215   Poemenis et natis comitata Harpyia duobus
et substricta gerens Sicyonius ilia Ladon
et Dromas et Canache Sticteque et Tigris et Alce
et niveis Leucon et villis Asbolos atris
praevalidusque Lacon et cursu fortis Aello
220   et Thoos et Cyprio velox cum fratre Lycisce
et nigram medio frontem distinctus ab albo
Harpalos et Melaneus hirsutaque corpore Lachne
et patre Dictaeo, sed matre Laconide nati
Labros et Agriodus et acutae vocis Hylactor,
225   quosque referre mora est: ea turba cupidine praedae
per rupes scopulosque aadituque carentia saxa,
quaque est difficilis, quaque est via nulla, sequuntur.

ille fugit, per quae fuerat loca saepe secutus,
heu famulos fugit ipse suos! clamare libebat:
230   'Actaeon ego sum, dominum cognoscite vestrum!'
verba animo desunt: resonat latratibus aether.
prima Melanchaetes in tergo vulnera fecit,
proxima Therodamas, Oresitrophos haesit in armo:
tardius exierat, sed per conpendia montis
235   anticipata via est; dominum retinentibus illis
cetera turba coit confertque in corpore dentes.
iam loca vulneribus desunt, gemit ille sonumque,
etsi non hominis, quem non tamen edere possit
cervus, habet maestisque replet iuga nota querellis
240   et genibus pronis supplex similisque roganti
circumfert tacitos tamquam sua bracchia vultus.
at comites rabidum solitis hortatibus agmen
ignari instigant oculisque Actaeona quaerunt
et velut absentem certatim Actaeona clamant
245   (ad nomen caput ille refert) et abesse queruntur
nec capere oblatae segnem spectacula praedae.
vellet abesse quidem, sed adest, velletque videre,
non etiam sentire canum fera facta suorum.
undique circumstant mersisque in corpore rostris
250   dilacerant falsi dominum sub imagine cervi,
nec nisi finita per plurima vulnera vita
ira pharetratae fertur satiata Dianae.
      Rumor in ambiguo est: aliis violentior aequo
visa dea est, alii laudant dignamque severa
255   virginitate vocant; pars invenit utraque causas.
sola Iovis coniunx non tam, culpetne probetne,
eloquitur, quam clade domus ab Agenore ductae
gaudet et a Tyria conlectum paelice transfert
in generis socios odium: subit ecce priori
260   causa recens, gravidamque dolet de semine magni
esse Iovis Semelen: tum linguam ad iurgia solvit.
'profeci quid enim totiens per iurgia?' dixit.
'ipsa petenda mihi est; ipsam, si maxima Iuno
rite vocor, perdam, si me gemmantia dextra
265   sceptra tenere decet, si sum regina Iovisque
et soror et coniunx, certe soror. at, puto, furto est
contenta, et thalami brevis est iniuria nostri.

concipit! id deerat! manifestaque crimina pleno
fert utero et mater, quod vix mihi contigit, uno
270 de Iove vult fieri: tanta est fiducia formae.
fallat eam faxo, nec sum Saturnia, si non
ab Iove mersa suo Stygias penetrabit in undas.'
    Surgit ab his solio fulvaque recondita nube
limen adit Semeles nec nubes ante removit,
275 quam simulavit anum posuitque ad tempora canos
sulcavitque cutem rugis et curva trementi
membra tulit passu, vocem quoque fecit anilem
ipsaque erat Beroe, Semeles Epidauria nutrix.
ergo ubi captato sermone diuque loquendo
280 ad nomen venere Iovis, suspirat et 'opto,
Iuppiter ut sit' ait, 'metuo tamen omnia: multi
nomine divorum thalamos iniere pudicos.
nec tamen esse Iovem satis est; det pignus amoris,
si modo verus is est, quantusque et qualis ab alta
285 Iunone excipitur, tantus talisque, rogato,
det tibi conplexus suaque ante insignia sumat.'
talibus ignaram Iuno Cadmeida dictis
formarat: rogat illa Iovem sine nomine munus.
cui deus 'elige' ait, 'nullam patiere repulsam,
290 quoque magis credas, Stygii quoque conscia sunto
numina torrentis; timor et deus ille deorum est.'
laeta malo nimiumque potens perituraque amantis
obsequio Semele 'qualem Saturnia' dixit
'te solet amplecti, Veneris cum foedus initis,
295 da mihi te talem.' voluit deus ora loquentis
opprimere: exierat iam vox properata sub auras.
ingemuit; neque enim non haec optasse, neque ille
non iurasse potest. ergo maestissimus altum
aethera conscendit vultuque sequentia traxit
300 nubila, quis nimbos inmixtaque fulgura ventis
addidit et tonitrus et inevitabile fulmen.
qua tamen usque potest, vires sibi demere temptat
nec, quo centimanum deiecerat igne Typhoea,
nunc armatur eo: nimium feritatis in illo est.
305 est aliud levius fulmen, cui dextra Cyclopum
saevitiae flammaeque minus, minus addidit irae:
tela secunda vocant superi; capit illa domumque

intrat Agenoream: corpus mortale tumultus
non tulit aetherios donisque iugalibus arsit.
310 inperfectus adhuc infans genetricis ab alvo
eripitur patrioque tener, si credere dignum est,
insuitur femori maternaque tempora conplet.
furtim illum primis Ino matertera cunis
educat: inde datum nymphae Nyseides antris
315 occuluere suis lactisque alimenta dedere.
   Dumque ea per terras fatali lege geruntur
tutaque bis geniti sunt incunabula Bacchi,
forte Iovem memorant diffusum nectare curas
seposuisse graves vacuaque agitasse remissos
320 cum Iunone iocos et 'maior vestra profecto est
quam, quae contingit maribus' dixisse 'voluptas.'
illa negat; placuit quae sit sententia docti
quaerere Tiresiae: venus huic erat utraque nota.
nam duo magnorum viridi coeuntia silva
325 corpora serpentum baculi violaverat ictu
deque viro factus, mirabile, femina septem
egerat autumnos; octavo rursus eosdem
vidit et 'est vestrae si tanta potentia plagae',
dixit 'ut auctoris sortem in contraria mutet,
330 nunc quoque vos feriam.' percussis anguibus isdem
forma prior rediit genetivaque venit imago.
arbiter hic igitur sumptus de lite iocosa
dicta Iovis firmat; gravius Saturnia iusto
nec pro materia fertur doluisse suique
335 iudicis aeterna damnavit lumina nocte.
at pater omnipotens (neque enim licet inrita cuiquam
facta dei fecisse deo) pro lumine adempto
scire futura dedit poenamque levavit honore.
   Ille per Aonias fama celeberrimus urbes
340 inreprehensa dabat populo responsa petenti;
prima fide vocisque ratae temptamina sumpsit
caerula Liriope, quam quondam flumine curvo
inplicuit clausaeque suis Cephisos in undis
vim tulit. enixa est utero pulcherrima pleno
345 infantem nymphe, iam tunc qui posset amari,
Narcissumque vocat; de quo consultus, an esset
tempora maturae visurus longa senectae,

fatidicus vates 'si se non noverit' inquit.
vana diu visa est vox auguris, exitus illam
350 resque probat letique genus novitasque furoris.
namque ter ad quinos unum Cephisius annum
addiderat poteratque puer iuvenisque videri:
multi illum iuvenes, multae cupiere puellae;
sed (fuit in tenera tam dura superbia forma)
355 nulli illum iuvenes, nullae tetigere puellae.
adspicit hunc trepidos agitantem in retia cervos
vocalis nymphe, quae nec reticere loquenti
nec prius ipsa loqui didicit, resonabilis Echo.
corpus adhuc Echo, non vox erat; et tamen usum
360 garrula non alium, quam nunc habet, oris habebat,
reddere de multis ut verba novissima posset.
fecerat hoc Iuno, quia, cum deprendere posset
sub Iove saepe suo nymphas in monte iacentes,
illa deam longo prudens sermone tenebat,
365 dum fugerent nymphae. postquam hoc Saturnia sensit,
'huius' ait 'linguae, qua sum delusa, potestas
parva tibi dabitur vocisque brevissimus usus',
reque minas firmat; tamen haec in fine loquendi
ingeminat voces auditaque verba reportat.
370 ergo ubi Narcissum per devia rura vagantem
vidit et incaluit, sequitur vestigia furtim,
quoque magis sequitur, flamma propiore calescit,
non aliter, quam cum summis circumlita taedis
admotas rapiunt vivacia sulphura flammas.
375 o quotiens voluit blandis accedere dictis
et molles adhibere preces! natura repugnat
nec sinit, incipiat; sed, quod sinit, illa parata est
exspectare sonos, ad quos sua verba remittat.
forte puer comitum seductus ab agmine fido
380 dixerat 'ecquis adest?', et 'adest' responderat Echo.
hic stupet, utque aciem partes dimittit in omnes,
voce 'veni' magna clamat: vocat illa vocantem.
respicit et rursus nullo veniente 'quid' inquit
'me fugis?' et totidem, quot dixit, verba recepit.
385 perstat et alternae deceptus imagine vocis
'huc coeamus' ait, nullique libentius umquam
responsura sono 'coeamus' rettulit Echo,

et verbis favet ipsa suis egressaque silva
ibat, ut iniceret sperato bracchia collo.
390   ille fugit fugiensque 'manus conplexibus aufer!
ante' ait 'emoriar, quam sit tibi copia nostri.'
rettulit illa nihil nisi 'sit tibi copia nostri.'
spreta latet silvis pudibundaque frondibus ora
protegit et solis ex illo vivit in antris;
395   sed tamen haeret amor crescitque dolore repulsae:
et tenuant vigiles corpus miserabile curae,
adducitque cutem macies, et in aëra sucus
corporis omnis abit; vox tantum atque ossa supersunt:
vox manet; ossa ferunt lapidis traxisse figuram.
400   inde latet silvis nulloque in monte videtur,
omnibus auditur: sonus est, qui vivit in illa.

Sic hanc, sic alias undis aut montibus ortas
luserat hic nymphas, sic coetus ante viriles;
inde manus aliquis despectus ad aethera tollens
405   'sic amet ipse licet, sic non potiatur amato!'
dixerat: adsensit precibus Rhamnusia iustis.
fons erat inlimis, nitidis argenteus undis,
quem neque pastores neque pastae monte capellae
contigerant aliudve pecus, quem nulla volucris
410   nec fera turbarat nec lapsus ab arbore ramus;
gramen erat circa, quod proximus umor alebat,
silvaque sole locum passura tepescere nullo.
hic puer et studio venandi lassus et aestu
procubuit faciemque loci fontemque secutus,
415   dumque sitim sedare cupit, sitis altera crevit,
dumque bibit, visae conreptus imagine formae
spem sine corpore amat, corpus putat esse, quod unda est.
adstupet ipse sibi vultuque inmotus eodem
haeret ut e Pario formatum marmore signum.
420   spectat humi positus geminum, sua lumina, sidus
et dignos Baccho, dignos et Apolline crines
inpubesque genas et eburnea colla decusque
oris et in niveo mixtum candore ruborem
cunctaque miratur, quibus est mirabilis ipse.
425   se cupit inprudens et, qui probat, ipse probatur,
dumque petit, petitur pariterque accendit et ardet.
inrita fallaci quotiens dedit oscula fonti!

in mediis quotiens visum captantia collum
bracchia mersit aquis nec se deprendit in illis!
430 quid videat, nescit, sed, quod videt, uritur illo
atque oculos idem, qui decipit, incitat error.
credule, quid frustra simulacra fugacia captas?
quod petis, est nusquam; quod amas, avertere, perdes.
ista repercussae, quam cernis, imaginis umbra est:
435 nil habet ista sui: tecum venitque manetque,
tecum discedet, si tu discedere possis.
non illum Cereris, non illum cura quietis
abstrahere inde potest, sed opaca fusus in herba
spectat inexpleto mendacem lumine formam
440 perque oculos perit ipse suos paulumque levatus,
ad circumstantes tendens sua bracchia silvas
'ecquis, io silvae, crudelius' inquit 'amavit?
scitis enim et multis latebra opportuna fuistis.
ecquem, cum vestrae tot agantur saecula vitae,
445 qui sic tabuerit, longo meministis in aevo?
et placet et video, sed, quod videoque placetque,
non tamen invenio: tantus tenet error amantem!
quoque magis doleam, nec nos mare separat ingens
nec via nec montes nec clausis moenia portis:
450 exigua prohibemur aqua! cupit ipse teneri!
nam quotiens liquidis porreximus oscula lymphis,
hic totiens ad me resupino nititur ore;
posse putes tangi: minimum est, quod amantibus obstat.
quisquis es, huc exi! quid me, puer unice, fallis
455 quove petitus abis? certe nec forma nec aetas
est mea, quam fugias, et amarunt me quoque nymphae.
spem mihi nescio quam vultu promittis amico,
cumque ego porrexi tibi bracchia, porrigis ultro;
cum risi, adrides; lacrimas quoque saepe notavi
460 me lacrimante tuas; nutu quoque signa remittis
et, quantum motu formosi suspicor oris,
verba refers aures non pervenientia nostras.
iste ego sum! sensi; nec me mea fallit imago:
uror amore mei, flammas moveoque feroque.
465 quid faciam? roger, anne rogem? quid deinde rogabo?
quod cupio, mecum est: inopem me copia fecit.
o utinam a nostro secedere corpore possem!

votum in amante novum: vellem, quod amamus, abesset!—
iamque dolor vires adimit, nec tempora vitae
470   longa meae superant, primoque extinguor in aevo.
nec mihi mors gravis est, posituro morte dolores:
hic, qui diligitur, vellem, diuturnior esset!
nunc duo concordes anima moriemur in una.'
dixit et ad faciem rediit male sanus eandem
475   et lacrimis turbavit aquas, obscuraque moto
reddita forma lacu est. quam cum vidisset abire,
'quo refugis? remane nec me, crudelis, amantem
desere!' clamavit 'liceat, quod tangere non est,
adspicere et misero praebere alimenta furori!'
480   dumque dolet, summa vestem deduxit ab ora
nudaque marmoreis percussit pectora palmis.
pectora traxerunt roseum percussa ruborem,
non aliter quam poma solent, quae candida parte,
parte rubent, aut ut variis solet uva racemis
485   ducere purpureum nondum matura colorem.
quae simul adspexit liquefacta rursus in unda,
non tulit ulterius, sed, ut intabescere flavae
igne levi cerae matutinaeque pruinae
sole tepente solent, sic attenuatus amore
490   liquitur et tecto paulatim carpitur igni,
et neque iam color est mixto candore rubori
nec vigor et vires et quae modo visa placebant,
nec corpus remanet, quondam quod amaverat Echo.
quae tamen ut vidit, quamvis irata memorque
495   indoluit, quotiensque puer miserabilis 'eheu'
dixerat, haec resonis iterabat vocibus 'eheu.'
cumque suos manibus percusserat ille lacertos,
haec quoque reddebat sonitum plangoris eundem.
ultima vox solitam fuit haec spectantis in undam:
500   'heu frustra dilecte puer!', totidemque remisit
verba locus, dictoque vale 'vale' inquit et Echo.
ille caput viridi fessum submisit in herba,
lumina mors clausit domini mirantia formam.
tum quoque se, postquam est inferna sede receptus,
505   in Stygia spectabat aqua. planxere sorores
naides et sectos fratri posuere capillos,
planxerunt dryades: plangentibus adsonat Echo.

iamque rogum quassasque faces feretrumque parabant:
nusquam corpus erat, croceum pro corpore florem
510 inveniunt foliis medium cingentibus albis.
　　Cognita res meritam vati per Achaidas urbes
attulerat famam, nomenque erat auguris ingens.
spernit Echionides tamen hunc ex omnibus unus,
contemptor superum Pentheus, praesagaque ridet
515 verba senis tenebrasque et cladem lucis ademptae
obicit. ille movens albentia tempora canis
'quam felix esses, si tu quoque luminis huius
orbus' ait 'fieres, ne Bacchica sacra videres!
namque dies aderit, quam non procul auguror esse,
520 qua novus huc veniat, proles Semeleia, Liber;
quem nisi templorum fueris dignatus honore,
mille lacer spargere locis et sanguine silvas
foedabis matremque tuam matrisque sorores.
eveniet! neque enim dignabere numen honore,
525 meque sub his tenebris nimium vidisse quereris.'
talia dicentem proturbat Echione natus.
　　Dicta fides sequitur, responsaque vatis aguntur.
Liber adest, festisque fremunt ululatibus agri:
turba ruit, mixtaeque viris matresque nurusque
530 vulgusque proceresque ignota ad sacra feruntur.
'quis furor, anguigenae, proles Mavortia, vestras
attonuit mentes?' Pentheus ait 'aerane tantum
aere repulsa valent et adunco tibia cornu
et magicae fraudes, ut, quos non bellicus ensis,
535 non tuba terruerit, non strictis agmina telis,
femineae voces et mota insania vino
obscenique greges et inania tympana vincant?
vosne, senes, mirer, qui longa per aequora vecti
hac Tyron, hac profugos posuistis sede Penates,
540 nunc sinitis sine Marte capi? vosne, acrior aetas,
o iuvenes, propiorque meae, quos arma tenere,
non thyrsos, galeaque tegi, non fronde decebat?
este, precor, memores, qua sitis stirpe creati,
illiusque animos, qui multos perdidit unus,
545 sumite serpentis! pro fontibus ille lacuque
interiit: at vos pro fama vincite vestra!
ille dedit leto fortes, vos pellite molles

et patrium retinete decus! si fata vetabant
stare diu Thebas, utinam tormenta virique
550 moenia diruerent, ferrumque ignisque sonarent!
essemus miseri sine crimine, sorsque querenda,
non celanda foret, lacrimaeque pudore carerent:
at nunc a puero Thebae capientur inermi,
quem neque bella iuvant nec tela nec usus equorum,
555 sed madidus murra crinis mollesque coronae
purpuraque et pictis intextum vestibus aurum.
quem quidem ego actutum (modo vos absistite) cogam
adsumptumque patrem commentaque sacra fateri.
an satis Acrisio est animi contemnere vanum
560 numen et Argolicas venienti claudere portas,
Penthea terrebit cum totis advena Thebis?
ite citi'—famulis hoc imperat—'ite ducemque
attrahite huc vinctum! iussis mora segnis abesto!'
  Hunc avus, hunc Athamas, hunc cetera turba suorum
565 corripiunt dictis frustraque inhibere laborant;
acrior admonitu est inritaturque retenta
et crescit rabies, moderaminaque ipsa nocebant:
sic ego torrentem, qua nil obstabat eunti,
lenius et modico strepitu decurrere vidi;
570 at quacumque trabes obstructaque saxa tenebant,
spumeus et fervens et ab obice saevior ibat.
ecce cruentati redeunt et, Bacchus ubi esset,
quaerenti domino Bacchum vidisse negarunt;
'hunc' dixere 'tamen comitem famulumque sacrorum
575 cepimus' et tradunt manibus post terga ligatis
sacra dei quondam Tyrrhena gente secutum.
  Adspicit hunc Pentheus oculis, quos ira tremendos
fecerat et, quamquam poenae vix tempora differt,
'o periture tuaque aliis documenta dature
580 morte' ait, 'ede tuum nomen nomenque parentum
et patriam morisque novi cur sacra frequentes.'
ille metu vacuus 'nomen mihi' dixit 'Acoetes,
patria Maeonia est, humili de plebe parentes.
non mihi quae duri colerent pater arva iuvenci
585 lanigerosve greges, non ulla armenta reliquit;
pauper et ipse fuit linoque solebat et hamis
decipere et calamo salientes ducere pisces.

ars illi sua census erat; cum traderet artem,
'accipe, quas habeo, studii successor et heres,'
590 dixit 'opes', moriensque mihi nihil ille reliquit
praeter aquas; unum hoc possum appellare paternum.
mox ego, ne scopulis haererem semper in isdem,
addidici regimen dextra moderante carinae
flectere et Oleniae sidus pluviale Capellae
595 Taygetenque Hyadasque oculis Arctonque notavi
ventorumque domos et portus puppibus aptos.
forte petens Delon Chiae telluris ad oras
adplicor et dextris adducor litora remis
doque leves saltus udaeque inmittor harenae.
600 nox ubi consumpta est (Aurora rubescere primo
coeperat), exsurgo laticesque inferre recentes
admoneo monstroque viam, quae ducat ad undas.
ipse quid aura mihi tumulo promittat ab alto
prospicio comitesque voco repetoque carinam.
605 'adsumus en!' inquit sociorum primus Opheltes,
utque putat, praedam deserto nactus in agro
virginea puerum ducit per litora forma.
ille mero somnoque gravis titubare videtur
vixque sequi; specto cultum faciemque gradumque:
610 nil ibi, quod credi posset mortale, videbam.
et sensi et dixi sociis: 'quod numen in isto
corpore sit, dubito, sed corpore numen in isto est.
quisquis es, o faveas nostrisque laboribus adsis.
his quoque des veniam.' 'pro nobis mitte precari'
615 Dictys ait, quo non alius conscendere summas
ocior antemnas prensoque rudente relabi;
hoc Libys, hoc flavus, prorae tutela, Melanthus,
hoc probat Alcimedon et, qui requiemque modumque
voce dabat remis, animorum hortator, Epopeus,
620 hoc omnes alii: praedae tam caeca cupido est.
'non tamen hanc sacro violari pondere pinum
perpetiar' dixi; 'pars hic mihi maxima iuris,'
inque aditu obsisto. furit audacissimus omni
de numero Lycabas, qui Tusca pulsus ab urbe
625 exilium dira poenam pro caede luebat.
is mihi, dum resto, iuvenali guttura pugno
rupit et excussum misisset in aequora, si non

haesissem quamvis amens in fune retentus.
inpia turba probat factum; tum denique Bacchus
630 (Bacchus enim fuerat), veluti clamore solutus
sit sopor aque mero redeant in pectora sensus,
'quid facitis? quis clamor?' ait 'qua, dicite, nautae,
huc ope perveni? quo me deferre paratis?'
'pone metum' Proreus 'et quos contingere portus
635 ede velis' dixit: 'terra sistere petita.'
'Naxon' ait Liber 'cursus advertite vestros!
illa mihi domus est, vobis erit hospita tellus.'
per mare fallaces perque omnia numina iurant
sic fore meque iubent pictae dare vela carinae.
640 dextera Naxus erat: dextra mihi lintea danti
'quid facis, o demens? quis te furor' inquit, 'Acoete?'
pro se quisque timet: 'laevam pete!' maxima nutu
pars mihi significat, pars, quid velit, aure susurrat.
obstipui 'capiat' que 'aliquis moderamina!' dixi
645 meque ministerio scelerisque artisque removi.
increpor a cunctis, totumque inmurmurat agmen;
e quibus Aethalion 'te scilicet omnis in uno
nostra salus posita est' ait et subit ipse meumque
explet opus Naxoque petit diversa relicta.
650 tum deus inludens, tamquam modo denique fraudem
senserit, e puppi pontum prospectat adunca
et flenti similis 'non haec mihi litora, nautae,
promisistis' ait, 'non haec mihi terra rogata est.
quo merui poenam facto? quae gloria vestra est,
655 si puerum iuvenes, si multi fallitis unum?'
iamdudum flebam: lacrimas manus inpia nostras
ridet et inpellit properantibus aequora remis.
per tibi nunc ipsum (nec enim praesentior illo
est deus) adiuro, tam me tibi vera referre
660 quam veri maiora fide: stetit aequore puppis
haud aliter, quam si siccum navale teneret.
illi admirantes remorum in verbere perstant
velaque deducunt geminaque ope currere temptant.
inpediunt hederae remos nexuque recurvo
665 serpunt et gravidis distingunt vela corymbis.
ipse racemiferis frontem circumdatus uvis
pampineis agitat velatam frondibus hastam;

quem circa tigres simulacraque inania lyncum
pictarumque iacent fera corpora pantherarum.
670 exsiluere viri, sive hoc insania fecit.
sive timor, primusque Medon nigrescere coepit
corpore et expresso spinae curvamine flecti.
incipit huic Lycabas: 'in quae miracula' dixit
'verteris?' et lati rictus et panda loquenti
675 naris erat squamamque cutis durata trahebat.
at Libys obstantes dum vult obvertere remos,
in spatium resilire manus breve vidit et illas
iam non esse manus, iam pinnas posse vocari.
alter ad intortos cupiens dare bracchia funes
680 bracchia non habuit truncoque repandus in undas
corpore desiluit: falcata novissima cauda est,
qualia dimidiae sinuantur cornua lunae.
undique dant saltus multaque adspergine rorant
emerguntque iterum redeuntque sub aequora rursus
685 inque chori ludunt speciem lascivaque iactant
corpora et acceptum patulis mare naribus efflant.
de modo viginti (tot enim ratis illa ferebat)
restabam solus: pavidum gelidumque trementi
corpore vixque meum firmat deus 'excute' dicens
690 'corde metum Diamque tene.' delatus in illam
accessi sacris Baccheaque sacra frequento.'
    'Praebuimus longis' Pentheus 'ambagibus aures'
inquit, 'ut ira mora vires absumere posset.
praecipitem famuli rapite hunc cruciataque diris
695 corpora tormentis Stygiae demittite nocti!'
protinus abstractus solidis Tyrrhenus Acoetes
clauditur in tectis; et dum crudelia iussae
instrumenta necis ferrumque ignesque parantur,
sponte sua patuisse fores lapsasque lacertis
700 sponte sua fama est nullo solvente catenas.
    Perstat Echionides nec iam iubet ire, sed ipse
vadit, ubi electus facienda ad sacra Cithaeron
cantibus et clara bacchantum voce sonabat.
ut fremit acer equus, cum bellicus aere canoro
705 signa dedit tubicen, pugnaeque adsumit amorem,
Penthea sic ictus longis ululatibus aether
movit, et audito clamore recanduit ira.

      monte fere medio est cingentibus ultima silvis,
      purus ab arboribus, spectabilis undique campus.
710   hic oculis illum cernentem sacra profanis
      prima videt, prima est insano concita cursu,
      prima suum misso violavit Penthea thyrso
      mater et 'o geminae' clamavit 'adeste sorores!
      ille aper, in nostris errat qui maximus agris,
715   ille mihi feriendus aper.' ruit omnis in unum
      turba furens: cunctae coeunt trepidumque sequuntur
      iam trepidum, iam verba minus violenta loquentem,
      iam se damnantem, iam se peccasse fatentem.
      saucius ille tamen 'fer opem, matertera' dixit
720   'Autonoe! moveant animos Actaeonis umbrae!'
      illa, quis Actaeon, nescit dextramque precantis
      abstulit, Inoo lacerata est altera raptu.
      non habet infelix, quae matri bracchia tendat,
      trunca sed ostendens deiectis vulnera membris
725   'adspice, mater!' ait. visis ululavit Agaue
      collaque iactavit movitque per aëra crinem
      avulsumque caput digitis conplexa cruentis
      clamat 'io comites, opus hoc victoria nostra est!'
      non citius frondes autumni frigore tactas
730   iamque male haerentes alta rapit arbore ventus,
      quam sunt membra viri manibus direpta nefandis.
         Talibus exemplis monitae nova sacra frequentant
      turaque dant sanctasque colunt Ismenides aras.

LIBER QVARTVS

At non Alcithoe Minyeias orgia censet
accipienda dei, sed adhuc temeraria Bacchum
progeniem negat esse Iovis sociasque sorores
inpietatis habet. festum celebrare sacerdos
5   inmunesque operum famulas dominasque suorum
pectora pelle tegi, crinales solvere vittas,
serta coma, manibus frondentes sumere thyrsos
iusserat et saevam laesi fore numinis iram
vaticinatus erat. parent matresque nurusque
10 telasque calathosque infectaque pensa reponunt
turaque dant Bacchumque vocant Bromiumque Lyaeumque
ignigenamque satumque iterum solumque bimatrem:
additur his Nyseus indetonsusque Thyoneus
et cum Lenaeo genialis consitor uvae
15 Nycteliusque Eleleusque parens et Iacchus et Euhan,
et quae praeterea per Graias plurima gentes
nomina, Liber, habes; tibi enim inconsumpta iuventa est,
tu puer aeternus, tu formosissimus alto
conspiceris caelo; tibi, cum sine cornibus adstas,
20 virgineum caput est; Oriens tibi victus adusque
decolor extremo qua cingitur India Gange.
Penthea tu, venerande, bipenniferumque Lycurgum
sacrilegos mactas Tyrrhenaque mittis in aequor
corpora; tu biiugum pictis insignia frenis
25 colla premis lyncum; Bacchae Satyrique sequuntur,
quique senex ferula titubantes ebrius artus
sustinet et pando non fortiter haeret asello.

quacumque ingrederis, clamor iuvenalis et una
femineae voces inpulsaque tympana palmis
30 concavaque aera sonant longoque foramine buxus.
    'Placatus mitisque' rogant Ismenides 'adsis,'
iussaque sacra colunt; solae Minyeides intus
intempestiva turbantes festa Minerva
aut ducunt lanas aut stamina pollice versant
35 aut haerent telae famulasque laboribus urgent;
e quibus una levi deducens pollice filum
'dum cessant aliae commentaque sacra frequentant,
nos quoque, quas Pallas, melior dea, detinet' inquit
'utile opus manuum vario sermone levemus
40 perque vices aliquid, quod tempora longa videri
non sinat, in medium vacuas referamus ad aures.'
dicta probant primamque iubent narrare sorores;
illa, quid e multis referat (nam plurima norat),
cogitat et dubia est, de te, Babylonia, narret,
45 Derceti, quam versa squamis velantibus artus
stagna Palaestini credunt motasse figura,
an magis, ut sumptis illius filia pennis
extremos altis in turribus egerit annos,
nais an ut cantu nimiumque potentibus herbis
50 verterit in tacitos iuvenalia corpora pisces,
donec idem passa est, an, quae poma alba ferebat,
ut nunc nigra ferat contactu sanguinis arbor.
hoc placet; haec quoniam vulgaris fabula non est,
talibus orsa modis lana sua fila sequente:
55   'Pyramus et Thisbe, iuvenum pulcherrimus alter,
altera, quas Oriens habuit, praelata puellis,
contiguas tenuere domos, ubi dicitur altam
coctilibus muris cinxisse Semiramis urbem.
notitiam primosque gradus vicinia fecit,
60 tempore crevit amor; taedae quoque iure coissent,
sed vetuere patres; quod non potuere vetare,
ex aequo captis ardebant mentibus ambo.
conscius omnis abest, nutu signisque loquuntur,
quoque magis tegitur, tectus magis aestuat ignis.
65 fissus erat tenui rima, quam duxerat olim,
cum fieret, paries domui communis utrique;
id vitium nulli per saecula longa notatum

(quid non sentit amor?) primi vidistis amantes
et vocis fecistis iter; tutaeque per illud
70   murmure blanditiae minimo transire solebant.
saepe, ubi constiterant hinc Thisbe, Pyramus illinc,
inque vices fuerat captatus anhelitus oris,
'invide' dicebant 'paries, quid amantibus obstas?
quantum erat, ut sineres toto nos corpore iungi,
75   aut, hoc si nimium est, vel ad oscula danda pateres?
nec sumus ingrati: tibi nos debere fatemur,
quod datus est verbis ad amicas transitus aures.'
      Talia diversa nequiquam sede locuti
sub noctem dixere 'vale' partique dedere
80   oscula quisque suae non pervenientia contra.
postera nocturnos Aurora removerat ignes,
solque pruinosas radiis siccaverat herbas:
ad solitum coiere locum. tum murmure parvo
multa prius questi statuunt, ut nocte silenti
85   fallere custodes foribusque excedere temptent,
cumque domo exierint, urbis quoque tecta relinquant,
neve sit errandum lato spatiantibus arvo,
conveniant ad busta Nini lateantque sub umbra
arboris: arbor ibi niveis uberrima pomis,
90   ardua morus, erat, gelido contermina fonti.
pacta placent; et lux tarde discedere visa
praecipitatur aquis, et aquis nox exit ab isdem:
callida per tenebras versato cardine Thisbe
egreditur fallitque suos adopertaque vultum
95   pervenit ad tumulum dictaque sub arbore sedit:
audacem faciebat amor. venit ecce recenti
caede leaena boum spumantes oblita rictus,
depositura sitim vicini fontis in unda;
quam procul ad lunae radios Babylonia Thisbe
100   vidit et obscurum timido pede fugit in antrum,
dumque fugit, tergo velamina lapsa reliquit.
ut lea saeva sitim multa conpescuit unda,
dum redit in silvas, inventos forte sine ipsa
ore cruentato tenues laniavit amictus.
105   serius egressus vestigia vidit in alto
pulvere certa ferae totoque expalluit ore
Pyramus; ut vero vestem quoque sanguine tinctam

repperit, 'una duos' inquit 'nox perdet amantes,
e quibus illa fuit longa dignissima vita;
110   nostra nocens anima est. ego te, miseranda, peremi,
in loca plena metus qui iussi nocte venires
nec prior huc veni. nostrum divellite corpus
et scelerata fero consumite viscera morsu,
o quicumque sub hac habitatis rupe, leones!
115   sed timidi est optare necem.' velamina Thisbes
tollit et ad pactae secum fert arboris umbram,
utque dedit notae lacrimas, dedit oscula vesti,
'accipe nunc' inquit 'nostri quoque sanguinis haustus!'
quoque erat accinctus, demisit in ilia ferrum.
120   nec mora, ferventi moriens e vulnere traxit
et iacuit resupinus humo: cruor emicat alte,
non aliter, quam cum vitiato fistula plumbo
scinditur et tenui stridente foramine longas
eiaculatur aquas atque ictibus aëra rumpit.
125   arborei fetus adspergine caedis in atram
vertuntur faciem, madefactaque sanguine radix
purpureo tingit pendentia mora colore.
       Ecce metu nondum posito, ne fallat amantem,
illa redit iuvenemque oculis animoque requirit,
130   quantaque vitarit narrare pericula gestit;
utque locum et visa cognoscit in arbore formam,
sic facit incertam pomi color: haeret, an haec sit.
dum dubitat, tremebunda videt pulsare cruentum
membra solum retroque pedem tulit oraque buxo
135   pallidiora gerens exhorruit aequoris instar,
quod tremit, exigua cum summum stringitur aura.
sed postquam remorata suos cognovit amores,
percutit indignos claro plangore lacertos
et laniata comas amplexaque corpus amatum
140   vulnera supplevit lacrimis fletumque cruori
miscuit et gelidis in vultibus oscula figens
'Pyrame,' clamavit 'quis te mihi casus ademit?
Pyrame, responde! tua te, carissime, Thisbe
nominat: exaudi vultusque attolle iacentes!'
145   ad nomen Thisbes oculos iam morte gravatos
Pyramus erexit visaque recondidit illa.
quae postquam vestemque suam cognovit et ense

vidit ebur vacuum, 'tua te manus' inquit 'amorque
perdidit, infelix! est et mihi fortis in unum
150   hoc manus, est et amor: dabit hic in vulnera vires.
persequar extinctum letique miserrima dicar
causa comesque tui; quique a me morte revelli
heu sola poteras, poteris nec morte revelli.
hoc tamen amborum verbis estote rogati,
155   o multum miseri meus illiusque parentes,
ut quos certus amor, quos hora novissima iunxit,
conponi tumulo non invideatis eodem.
at tu, quae ramis arbor miserabile corpus
nunc tegis unius, mox es tectura duorum,
160   signa tene caedis pullosque et luctibus aptos
semper habe fetus, gemini monimenta cruoris.'
dixit et aptato pectus mucrone sub imum
incubuit ferro, quod adhuc a caede tepebat.
vota tamen tetigere deos, tetigere parentes:
165   nam color in pomo est, ubi permaturuit, ater,
quodque rogis superest, una requiescit in urna.'
      Desierat, mediumque fuit breve tempus, et orsa est
dicere Leuconoe; vocem tenuere sorores.
      'Hunc quoque, siderea qui temperat omnia luce,
170   cepit amor Solem: Solis referemus amores.
primus adulterium Veneris cum Marte putatur
hic vidisse deus: videt hic deus omnia primus.
indoluit facto Iunonigenaeque marito
furta tori furtique locum monstravit. at illi
175   et mens et quod opus fabrilis dextra tenebat
excidit: extemplo graciles ex aere catenas
retiaque et laqueos, quae lumina fallere possent,
elimat (non illud opus tenuissima vincant
stamina, non summo quae pendet aranea tigno),
180   utque leves tactus momentaque parva sequantur,
efficit et lecto circumdata collocat arte.
ut venere torum coniunx et adulter in unum,
arte viri vinclisque nova ratione paratis
in mediis ambo deprensi amplexibus haerent.
185   Lemnius extemplo valvas patefecit eburnas,
admisitque deos: illi iacuere ligati
turpiter, atque aliquis de dis non tristibus optat

sic fieri turpis: superi risere, diuque
haec fuit in toto notissima fabula caelo.
190   Exigit indicii memorem Cythereia poenam
inque vices illum, tectos qui laesit amores,
laedit amore pari. quid nunc, Hyperione nate,
forma colorque tibi radiataque lumina prosunt?
nempe, tuis omnes qui terras ignibus uris,
195 ureris igne novo, quique omnia cernere debes,
Leucothoen spectas et virgine figis in una,
quos mundo debes, oculos. modo surgis Eoo
temperius caelo, modo serius incidis undis
spectandique mora brumales porrigis horas;
200 deficis interdum, vitiumque in lumina mentis
transit, et obscurus mortalia pectora terres.
nec, tibi quod lunae terris propioris imago
obstiterit, palles: facit hunc amor iste colorem.
diligis hanc unam, nec te Clymeneque Rhodosque
205 nec tenet Aeaeae genetrix pulcherrima Circes,
quaeque tuos Clytie quamvis despecta petebat
concubitus ipsoque illo grave vulnus habebat
tempore: Leucothoe multarum oblivia fecit,
gentis odoriferae quam formosissima partu
210 edidit Eurynome; sed postquam filia crevit,
quam mater cunctas, tam matrem filia vicit.
rexit Achaemenias urbes pater Orchamus isque
septimus a prisco numeratur origine Belo.
axe sub Hesperio sunt pascua Solis equorum:
215 ambrosiam pro gramine habent; ea fessa diurnis
membra ministeriis nutrit reparatque labori.
dumque ibi quadripedes caelestia pabula carpunt,
noxque vicem peragit, thalamos deus intrat amatos
versus in Eurynomes faciem genetricis et inter
220 bis sex Leucothoen famulas ad lumina cernit
levia versato ducentem stamina fuso.
ergo ubi ceu mater carae dedit oscula natae,
'res' ait 'arcana est: famulae, discedite, neve
eripite arbitrium matri secreta loquendi.'
225 paruerant, thalamoque deus sine teste relicto
'ille ego sum' dixit 'qui longum metior annum,
omnia qui video, per quem videt omnia tellus,

mundi oculus: mihi, crede, places.' pavet illa metuque
et colus et fusi digitis cecidere remissis.
230 ipse timor decuit, nec longius ille moratus
in veram rediit speciem solitumque nitorem;
at virgo quamvis inopino territa visu
victa nitore dei posita vim passa querella est.
  Invidit Clytie (neque enim moderatus in illa
235 Solis amor fuerat) stimulataque paelicis ira
vulgat adulterium diffamatumque parenti
indicat; ille ferox inmansuetusque precantem
tendentemque manus ad lumina Solis et 'ille
vim tulit invitae' dicentem defodit alta
240 crudus humo tumulumque super gravis addit harenae.
dissipat hunc radiis Hyperione natus iterque
dat tibi, quo possis defossos promere vultus;
nec tu iam poteras enectum pondere terrae
tollere, nympha, caput, corpusque exsangue iacebas:
245 nil illo fertur volucrum moderator equorum
post Phaethonteos vidisse dolentius ignes.
ille quidem gelidos radiorum viribus artus
si queat in vivum temptat revocare calorem,
sed quoniam tantis fatum conatibus obstat,
250 nectare odorato sparsit corpusque locumque
multaque praequestus 'tanges tamen aethera' dixit.
protinus inbutum caelesti nectare corpus
deliquit terramque suo madefecit odore,
virgaque per glaebas sensim radicibus actis
255 turea surrexit tumulumque cacumine rupit.
  At Clytien, quamvis amor excusare dolorem
indiciumque dolor poterat, non amplius auctor
lucis adit Venerisque modum sibi fecit in illa.
tabuit ex illo demente amoribus usa
260 nympharum inpatiens et sub Iove nocte dieque
sedit humo nuda nudis incompta capillis
perque novem luces expers undaeque cibique
rore mero lacrimisque suis ieiunia pavit
nec se movit humo: tantum spectabat euntis
265 ora dei vultusque suos flectebat ad illum.
membra ferunt haesisse solo, partemque coloris
luridus exsangues pallor convertit in herbas;

est in parte rubor, violaeque simillimus ora
flos tegit. illa suum, quamvis radice tenetur,
270   vertitur ad Solem mutataque servat amorem.'
      Dixerat, et factum mirabile ceperat aures;
pars fieri potuisse negant, pars omnia veros
posse deos memorant: sed non et Bacchus in illis.
poscitur Alcithoe, postquam siluere sorores;
275   quae radio stantis percurrens stamina telae
'Vulgatos taceo' dixit 'pastoris amores
Daphnidis Idaei, quem nymphe paelicis ira
contulit in saxum: tantus dolor urit amantes;
nec loquor, ut quondam naturae iure novato
280   ambiguus fuerit modo vir, modo femina Sithon;
te quoque, nunc adamas, quondam fidissime parvo,
Celmi, Iovi largoque satos Curetas ab imbri
et Crocon in parvos versum cum Smilace flores
praetereo dulcique animos novitate tenebo.
285   Unde sit infamis, quare male fortibus undis
Salmacis enervet tactosque remolliat artus,
discite. causa latet, vis est notissima fontis.
Mercurio puerum diva Cythereide natum
naides Idaeis enutrivere sub antris;
290   cuius erat facies, in qua materque paterque
cognosci possent; nomen quoque traxit ab illis.
is tria cum primum fecit quinquennia, montes
deseruit patrios Idaque altrice relicta
ignotis errare locis, ignota videre
295   flumina gaudebat studio minuente laborem.
ille etiam Lycias urbes Lyciaeque propinquos
Caras adit: videt hic stagnum lucentis ad imum
usque solum lymphae. non illic canna palustris
nec steriles ulvae nec acuta cuspide iunci;
300   perspicuus liquor est: stagni tamen ultima vivo
caespite cinguntur semperque virentibus herbis.
nympha colit, sed nec venatibus apta nec arcus
flectere quae soleat nec quae contendere cursu,
solaque naiadum celeri non nota Dianae.
305   saepe suas illi fama est dixisse sorores:
'Salmaci, vel iaculum vel pictas sume pharetras
et tua cum duris venatibus otia misce!'

nec iaculum sumit nec pictas illa pharetras,
nec sua cum duris venatibus otia miscet,
310 sed modo fonte suo formosos perluit artus,
saepe Cytoriaco deducit pectine crines
et, quid se deceat, spectatas consulit undas;
nunc perlucenti circumdata corpus amictu
mollibus aut foliis aut mollibus incubat herbis;
315 saepe legit flores. et tunc quoque forte legebat,
cum puerum vidit visumque optavit habere;
nec tamen ante adiit, etsi properabat adire,
quam se conposuit, quam circumspexit amictus
et finxit vultum et meruit formosa videri.
320 tum sic orsa loqui: 'puer o dignissime credi
esse deus, seu tu deus es, potes esse Cupido,
sive es mortalis, qui te genuere, beati
et frater felix et fortunata profecto,
siqua tibi soror est, et quae dedit ubera nutrix;
325 sed longe cunctis longeque beatior illa,
siqua tibi sponsa est, siquam dignabere taeda.
haec tibi sive aliqua est, mea sit furtiva voluptas;
seu nulla est, ego sim, thalamumque ineamus eundem.'
nais ab his tacuit, pueri rubor ora notavit
330 (nescit enim, quid amor), sed et erubuisse decebat.
hic color aprica pendentibus arbore pomis
aut ebori tincto est aut sub candore rubenti,
cum frustra resonant aera auxiliaria, lunae.
poscenti nymphae sine fine sororia saltem
335 oscula iamque manus ad eburnea colla ferenti
'desinis? an fugio tecumque' ait 'ista relinquo?'
Salmacis extimuit 'loca' que 'haec tibi libera trado,
hospes' ait simulatque gradu discedere verso,
tum quoque respiciens, fruticumque recondita silva
340 delituit flexuque genu submisit. at ille
scilicet ut vacuis et inobservatus in herbis
huc it et hinc illuc et in adludentibus undis
summa pedum taloque tenus vestigia tingit;
nec mora, temperie blandarum captus aquarum
345 mollia de tenero velamina corpore ponit.
tum vero placuit nudaeque cupidine formae
Salmacis exarsit: flagrant quoque lumina nymphae,

non aliter, quam cum puro nitidissimus orbe
opposita speculi referitur imagine Phoebus,
350   vixque moram patitur, vix iam sua gaudia differt,
iam cupit amplecti, iam se male continet amens.
ille cavis velox applauso corpore palmis
desilit in latices alternaque bracchia ducens
in liquidis translucet aquis, ut eburnea siquis
355   signa tegat claro vel candida lilia vitro.
'vicimus et meus est!' exclamat nais et omni
veste procul iacta mediis inmittitur undis
pugnantemque tenet luctantiaque oscula carpit
subiectatque manus invitaque pectora tangit
360   et nunc hac iuveni, nunc circumfunditur illac.
denique nitentem contra elabique volentem
inplicat ut serpens, quam regia sustinet ales
sublimemque rapit (pendens caput illa pedesque
adligat et cauda spatiantes inplicat alas),
365   utve solent hederae longos intexere truncos,
utque sub aequoribus deprensum polypus hostem
continet ex omni dimissis parte flagellis.
perstat Atlantiades sperataque gaudia nymphae
denegat; illa premit commissaque corpore toto
370   sicut inhaerebat, 'pugnes licet, inprobe,' dixit
'non tamen effugies. ita di iubeatis, et istum
nulla dies a me nec me deducat ab isto.'
vota suos habuere deos: nam mixta duorum
corpora iunguntur faciesque inducitur illis
375   una; velut siquis conducat cortice, ramos
crescendo iungi pariterque adolescere cernit,
sic, ubi conplexu coierunt membra tenaci,
nec duo sunt sed forma duplex, nec femina dici
nec puer ut possit, nec utrumque et utrumque videtur.
380   ergo, ubi se liquidas, quo vir descenderat, undas
semimarem fecisse videt mollitaque in illis
membra, manus tendens, sed iam non voce virili,
Hermaphroditus ait: 'nato date munera vestro
et pater et genetrix, amborum nomen habenti:
385   quisquis in hos fontes vir venerit, exeat inde
semivir et tactis subito mollescat in undis.'
motus uterque parens nati rata verba biformis

fecit et incerto fontem medicamine tinxit.'
    Finis erat dictis, et adhuc Minyeia proles
390 urget opus spernitque deum festumque profanat,
tympana cum subito non apparentia raucis
obstrepuere sonis et adunco tibia cornu
tinnulaque aera sonant et olent murraeque crocique;
resque fide maior: coepere virescere telae
395 inque hederae faciem pendens frondescere vestis;
pars abit in vites et, quae modo fila fuerunt,
palmite mutantur; de stamine pampinus exit;
purpura fulgorem pictis adcommodat uvis.
iamque dies exactus erat tempusque subibat,
400 quod tu nec tenebras nec posses dicere lucem,
sed cum luce tamen dubiae confinia noctis:
tecta repente quati pinguesque ardere videntur
lampades et rutilis conlucere ignibus aedes
falsaque saevarum simulacra ululare ferarum.
405 fumida iamdudum latitant per tecta sorores
diversaeque locis ignes ac lumina vitant,
dumque petunt tenebras, parvos membrana per artus
porrigitur tenuique includunt bracchia penna;
nec, qua perdiderint veterem ratione figuram,
410 scire sinunt tenebrae. non illas pluma levavit,
sustinuere tamen se perlucentibus alis
conataeque loqui minimam et pro corpore vocem
emittunt peraguntque leves stridore querellas
tectaque, non silvas celebrant lucemque perosae
415 nocte volant seroque tenent a vespere nomen.
    Tum vero totis Bacchi memorabile Thebis
numen erat, magnasque novi matertera vires
narrat ubique dei, de totque sororibus expers
una doloris erat, nisi quem fecere sorores.
420 adspicit hanc natis thalamoque Athamantis habentem
sublimes animos et alumno numine Iuno
nec tulit et secum: 'potuit de paelice natus
vertere Maeonios pelagoque inmergere nautas
et laceranda suae nati dare viscera matri
425 et triplices operire novis Minyeidas alis:
nil poterit Iuno nisi inultos flere dolores?
idque mihi satis est? haec una potentia nostra est?

ipse docet, quid agam (fas est et ab hoste doceri),
quidque furor valeat, Penthea caede satisque
430   ac super ostendit. cur non stimuletur eatque
per cognata suis exempla furoribus Ino?'
      Est via declivis, funesta nubila taxo:
ducit ad infernas per muta silentia sedes;
Styx nebulas exhalat iners, umbraeque recentes
435   descendunt illac simulacraque functa sepulcris;
pallor hiemsque tenent late loca senta, novique,
qua sit iter, manes, Stygiam qua ducat ad urbem,
ignorant, ubi sit nigri fera regia Ditis.
mille capax aditus et apertas undique portas
440   urbs habet, utque fretum de tota flumina terra,
sic omnes animas locus accipit ille nec ulli
exiguus populo est turbamve accedere sentit.
errant exsangues sine corpore et ossibus umbrae,
parsque forum celebrant, pars imi tecta tyranni.
445   pars aliquas artes, antiquae imitamina vitae,
exercent, aliam partem sua poena coercet.
      Sustinet ire illuc caelesti sede relicta
(tantum odiis iraeque dabat) Saturnia Iuno.
quo simul intravit sacroque a corpore pressum
450   ingemuit limen, tria Cerberus extulit ora
et tres latratus semel edidit; illa sorores
Nocte vocat genitas, grave et inplacabile numen:
carceris ante fores clausas adamante sedebant
deque suis atros pectebant crinibus angues.
455   quam simul agnorunt inter caliginis umbras,
surrexere deae; Sedes Scelerata vocatur:
viscera praebebat Tityos lanianda novemque
iugeribus distractus erat; tibi, Tantale, nullae
deprenduntur aquae, quaeque inminet, effugit arbor;
460   aut petis aut urges rediturum, Sisyphe, saxum;
volvitur Ixion et se sequiturque fugitque,
molirique suis letum patruelibus ausae
adsiduae repetunt, quas perdant, Belides undas.
      Quos omnes acie postquam Saturnia torva
465   vidit et ante omnes Ixiona, rursus ab illo
Sisyphon adspiciens 'cur hic e fratribus' inquit
'perpetuas patitur poenas, Athamanta superbum

regia dives habet, qui me cum coniuge semper
sprevit?' et exponit causas odiique viaeque
470 quidque velit: quod vellet, erat, ne regia Cadmi
staret, et in facinus traherent Athamanta furores.
imperium, promissa, preces confundit in unum
sollicitatque deas. sic haec Iunone locuta
Tisiphone canos ut erat turbata capillos
475 movit et obstantes reiecit ab ore colubras
atque ita 'non longis opus est ambagibus' inquit,
'facta puta, quaecumque iubes. inamabile regnum
desere teque refer caeli melioris ad auras.'
laeta redit Iuno; quam caelum intrare parantem
480 roratis lustravit aquis Thaumantias Iris.
     Nec mora, Tisiphone madefactam sanguine sumit
inportuna facem fluidoque cruore rubentem
induitur pallam tortoque incingitur angue
egrediturque domo; Luctus comitatur euntem
485 et Pavor et Terror trepidoque Insania vultu.
limine constiterat: postes tremuisse feruntur
Aeolii, pallorque fores infecit acernas,
Solque locum fugit. monstris exterrita coniunx,
territus est Athamas tectoque exire parabant:
490 obstitit infelix aditumque obsedit Erinys
nexaque vipereis distendens bracchia nodis
caesariem excussit; motae sonuere colubrae,
parsque iacent umeris, pars circum pectora lapsae
sibila dant saniemque vomunt linguisque coruscant.
495 inde duos mediis abrumpit crinibus angues
pestiferaque manu raptos inmisit; at illi
Inoosque sinus Athamanteosque pererrant
inspirantque graves animas: nec vulnera membris
ulla ferunt, mens est, quae diros sentiat ictus.
500 attulerat secum liquidi quoque monstra veneni,
oris Cerberei spumas et virus Echidnae
erroresque vagos caecaeque oblivia mentis
et scelus et lacrimas rabiemque et caedis amorem,
omnia trita simul; quae sanguine mixta recenti
505 coxerat aere cavo viridi versata cicuta;
dumque pavent illi, vertit furiale venenum
pectus in amborum praecordiaque intima movit.

tum face iactata per eundem saepius orbem
consequitur motis velociter ignibus ignes.
510   sic victrix iussique potens ad inania magni
regna redit Ditis sumptumque recingitur anguem.
      Protinus Aeolides media furibundus in aula
clamat: 'io, comites, his retia tendite silvis!
hic modo cum gemina visa est mihi prole leaena,'
515   utque ferae sequitur vestigia coniugis amens
deque sinu matris ridentem et parva Learchum
bracchia tendentem rapit et bis terque per auras
more rotat fundae rigidoque infantia saxo
discutit ora ferox; tum denique concita mater,
520   seu dolor hoc fecit, seu sparsi causa veneni,
exululat passisque fugit male sana capillis
teque ferens parvum nudis, Melicerta, lacertis
'euhoe Bacche' sonat: Bacchi sub nomine Iuno
risit et 'hos usus praestet tibi' dixit 'alumnus!'
525   inminet aequoribus scopulus; pars ima cavatur
fluctibus et tectas defendit ab imbribus undas,
summa riget frontemque in apertum porrigit aequor;
occupat hunc (vires insania fecerat) Ino,
seque super pontum nullo tardata timore
530   mittit onusque suum; percussa recanduit unda.
      at Venus inmeritae neptis miserata labores
sic patruo blandita suo est: 'o numen aquarum,
proxima cui caelo cessit, Neptune, potestas,
magna quidem posco, sed tu miserere meorum,
535   iactari quos cernis in Ionio inmenso,
et dis adde tuis. aliqua et mihi gratia ponto est,
si tamen in medio quondam concreta profundo
spuma fui Graiumque manet mihi nomen ab illa.'
adnuit oranti Neptunus et abstulit illis,
540   quod mortale fuit, maiestatemque verendam
inposuit nomenque simul faciemque novavit
Leucotheaque deum cum matre Palaemona dixit.
      Sidoniae comites, quantum valuere, secutae
signa pedum primo videre novissima saxo:
545   nec dubium de morte ratae Cadmeida palmis
deplanxere domum scissae cum veste capillos,
utque parum iustae nimiumque in paelice saevae

invidiam fecere deae; convicia Iuno
non tulit et 'faciam vos ipsas maxima' dixit
550 'saevitiae monimenta meae.' res dicta secuta est.
nam quae praecipue fuerat pia, 'persequar' inquit
'in freta reginam', saltumque datura moveri
haud usquam potuit scopuloque adfixa cohaesit;
altera dum solito temptat plangore ferire
555 pectora, temptatos sensit riguisse lacertos;
illa, manus ut forte tetenderat in maris undas,
saxea facta manus in easdem porrigit undas;
huius, ut arreptum laniabat vertice crinem,
duratos subito digitos in crine videres:
560 quo quaeque in gestu deprensa est, haesit in illo.
pars volucres factae; quae nunc quoque gurgite in illo
aequora destringunt summis Ismenides alis.
     Nescit Agenorides natam parvumque nepotem
aequoris esse deos; luctu serieque malorum
565 victus et ostentis, quae plurima viderat, exit
conditor urbe sua, tamquam fortuna locorum,
non sua se premeret, longisque erroribus actus
contigit Illyricos profuga cum coniuge fines.
iamque malis annisque graves dum prima retractant
570 fata domus releguntque suos sermone labores,
'num sacer ille mea traiectus cuspide serpens'
Cadmus ait 'fuerat, tum, cum Sidone profectus
vipereos sparsi per humum, nova semina, dentes?
quem si cura deum tam certa vindicat ira,
575 ipse, precor, serpens in longam porrigar alvum.'
dixit et, ut serpens, in longam tenditur alvum
durataeque cuti squamas increscere sentit
nigraque caeruleis variari corpora guttis
in pectusque cadit pronus, commissaque in unum
580 paulatim tereti tenuantur acumine crura.
bracchia iam restant; quae restant, bracchia tendit,
et lacrimis per adhuc humana fluentibus ora
'accede, o coniunx, accede, miserrima,' dixit
'dumque aliquid superest de me, me tange manumque
585 accipe, dum manus est, dum non totum occupat anguis.'
ille quidem vult plura loqui, sed lingua repente
in partes est fissa duas: nec verba loquenti

sufficiunt, quotiensque aliquos parat edere questus,
sibilat; hanc illi vocem natura reliquit.
590   nuda manu feriens exclamat pectora coniunx:
'Cadme, mane, teque, infelix, his exue monstris!
Cadme, quid hoc? ubi pes? ubi sunt umerique manusque
et color et facies et, dum loquor, omnia? cur non
me quoque, caelestes, in eandem vertitis anguem?'
595   dixerat: ille suae lambebat coniugis ora
inque sinus caros, veluti cognosceret, ibat
et dabat amplexus adsuetaque colla petebat.
quisquis adest (aderant comites), terretur; at illa
lubrica permulcet cristati colla draconis.
600   et subito duo sunt iunctoque volumine serpunt,
donec in adpositi nemoris subiere latebras.
nunc quoque nec fugiunt hominem nec vulnere laedunt,
quidque prius fuerint, placidi meminere dracones.
      Sed tamen ambobus versae solacia formae
605   magna nepos dederat, quem debellata colebat
India, quem positis celebrabat Achaia templis.
solus Abantiades ab origine cretus eadem
Acrisius superest, qui moenibus arceat urbis
Argolicae contraque deum ferat arma; genusque
610   non putat esse deum: neque enim Iovis esse putabat
Persea, quem pluvio Danae conceperat auro.
mox tamen Acrisium (tanta est praesentia veri)
tam violasse deum quam non agnosse nepotem
paenitet: inpositus iam caelo est alter, at alter
615   viperei referens spolium memorabile monstri
aëra carpebat tenerum stridentibus alis,
cumque super Libycas victor penderet harenas,
Gorgonei capitis guttae cecidere cruentae,
quas humus exceptas varios animavit in angues:
620   unde frequens illa est infestaque terra colubris.
      Inde per inmensum ventis discordibus actus
nunc huc, nunc illuc exemplo nubis aquosae
fertur et ex alto seductas aequore longe
despectat terras totumque supervolat orbem;
625   ter gelidas Arctos, ter Cancri bracchia vidit:
saepe sub occasus, saepe est ablatus in ortus.
iamque cadente die veritus se credere nocti

constitit Hesperio, regnis Atlantis, in orbe
exiguamque petit requiem, dum Lucifer ignes
630 evocet Aurorae, currus Aurora diurnos.
hic hominum cunctis ingenti corpore praestans
Iapetionides Atlas fuit: ultima tellus
rege sub hoc et pontus erat, qui Solis anhelis
aequora subdit equis et fessos excipit axes.
635 mille greges illi totidemque armenta per herbas
errabant, et humum vicinia nulla premebant.
arboreae frondes auro radiante nitentes
ex auro ramos, ex auro poma tegebant.
'hospes,' ait Perseus illi 'seu gloria tangit
640 te generis magni, generis mihi Iuppiter auctor;
sive es mirator rerum, mirabere nostras.
hospitium requiemque peto.' memor ille vetustae
sortis erat. Themis hanc dederat Parnasia sortem:
'tempus, Atla, veniet, tua quo spoliabitur auro
645 arbor, et hunc praedae titulum Iove natus habebit.'
id metuens solidis pomaria clauserat Atlas
montibus et vasto dederat servanda draconi
arcebatque suis externos finibus omnes.
huic quoque 'vade procul, ne longe gloria rerum,
650 quam mentiris,' ait 'longe tibi Iuppiter absit',
vimque minis addit manibusque expellere temptat
cunctantem et placidis miscentem fortia dictis.
viribus inferior (quis enim par esset Atlantis
viribus?) 'at quoniam parvi tibi gratia nostra est,
655 accipe munus' ait laevaque a parte Medusae
ipse retro versus squalentia protulit ora.
quantus erat, mons factus Atlas; nam barba comaeque
in silvas abeunt, iuga sunt umerique manusque,
quod caput ante fuit, summo est in monte cacumen,
660 ossa lapis fiunt: tum partes altus in omnes
crevit in inmensum (sic di statuistis) et omne
cum tot sideribus caelum requievit in illo.
    Clauserat Hippotades aeterno carcere ventos,
admonitorque operum caelo clarissimus alto
665 Lucifer ortus erat: pennis ligat ille resumptis
parte ab utraque pedes teloque accingitur unco
et liquidum motis talaribus aëra findit.

gentibus innumeris circumque infraque relictis
Aethiopum populos Cepheaque conspicit arva:
670   illic inmeritam maternae pendere linguae
Andromedan poenas iniustus iusserat Ammon.
quam simul ad duras religatam bracchia cautes
vidit Abantiades (nisi quod levis aura capillos
moverat et tepido manabant lumina fletu,
675   marmoreum ratus esset opus), trahit inscius ignes
et stupet et visae correptus imagine formae
paene suas quatere est oblitus in aëre pennas.
ut stetit, 'o' dixit 'non istis digna catenis,
sed quibus inter se cupidi iunguntur amantes,
680   pande requirenti nomen terraeque tuumque
et cur vincla geras.' primo silet illa nec audet
appellare virum virgo manibusque modestos
celasset vultus, si non religata fuisset;
lumina, quod potuit, lacrimis inplevit obortis.
685   saepius instanti, sua ne delicta fateri
nolle videretur, nomen terraeque suumque,
quantaque maternae fuerit fiducia formae,
indicat, et nondum memoratis omnibus unda
insonuit, veniensque inmenso belua ponto
690   inminet et latum sub pectore possidet aequor.
   Conclamat virgo; genitor lugubris et una
mater adest, ambo miseri, sed iustius illa,
nec secum auxilium, sed dignos tempore fletus
plangoremque ferunt vinctoque in corpore adhaerent,
695   cum sic hospes ait: 'lacrimarum longa manere
tempora vos poterunt, ad opem brevis hora ferendam est.
hanc ego si peterem Perseus Iove natus et illa,
quam clausam inplevit fecundo Iuppiter auro,
Gorgonis anguicomae Perseus superator et alis
700   aetherias ausus iactatis ire per auras,
praeferrer cunctis certe gener; addere tantis
dotibus et meritum, faveant modo numina, tempto:
ut mea sit servata mea virtute, paciscor.'
accipiunt legem (quis enim dubitaret?) et orant
705   promittuntque super regnum dotale parentes.
ecce velut navis praefixo concita rostro
sulcat aquas iuvenum sudantibus acta lacertis,

sic fera dimotis inpulsu pectoris undis
tantum aberat scopulis, quantum Balearica torto
710 funda potest plumbo medii transmittere caeli,
cum subito iuvenis pedibus tellure repulsa
arduus in nubes abiit. ut in aequore summo
umbra viri visa est, visa fera saevit in umbra;
utque Iovis praepes, vacuo cum vidit in arvo
715 praebentem Phoebo liventia terga draconem,
occupat aversum, neu saeva retorqueat ora,
squamigeris avidos figit cervicibus ungues,
sic celeri missus praeceps per inane volatu
terga ferae pressit dextroque frementis in armo
720 Inachides ferrum curvo tenus abdidit hamo.
vulnere laesa gravi modo se sublimis in auras
attollit, modo subdit aquis, modo more ferocis
versat apri, quem turba canum circumsona terret;
ille avidos morsus velocibus effugit alis,
725 quaque patet, nunc terga cavis super obsita conchis,
nunc laterum costas, nunc, qua tenuissima cauda
desinit in piscem, falcato vulnerat ense.
belua puniceo mixtos cum sanguine fluctus
ore vomit: maduere graves adspergine pennae.
730 nec bibulis ultra Perseus talaribus ausus
credere conspexit scopulum, qui vertice summo
stantibus exstat aquis, operitur ab aequore moto:
nixus eo rupisque tenens iuga prima sinistra
ter quater exegit repetita per ilia ferrum.
735 litora cum plausu clamor superasque deorum
inplevere domos: gaudent generumque salutant
auxiliumque domus servatoremque fatentur
Cassiope Cepheusque pater; resoluta catenis
incedit virgo, pretiumque et causa laboris.
740 ipse manus hausta victrices abluit unda,
anguiferumque caput dura ne laedat harena,
mollit humum foliis natasque sub aequore virgas
sternit et inponit Phorcynidos ora Medusae.
virga recens bibulaque etiamnunc viva medulla
745 vim rapuit monstri tactuque induruit huius
percepitque novum ramis et fronde rigorem.
at pelagi nymphae factum mirabile temptant

pluribus in virgis et idem contingere gaudent
seminaque ex illis iterant iactata per undas.
750   nunc quoque curaliis eadem natura remansit,
duritiam tacto capiant ut ab aëre, quodque
vimen in aequore erat, fiat super aequora saxum.
  Dis tribus ille focos totidem de caespite ponit,
laevum Mercurio, dextrum tibi, bellica virgo,
755   ara Iovis media est: mactatur vacca Minervae,
alipedi vitulus, taurus tibi, summe deorum.
protinus Andromedan et tanti praemia facti
indotata rapit; taedas Hymenaeus Amorque
praecutiunt, largis satiantur odoribus ignes,
760   sertaque dependent tectis, et ubique lyraeque
tibiaque et cantus, animi felicia laeti
argumenta, sonant; reseratis aurea valvis
atria tota patent, pulchroque instructa paratu
Cepheni proceres ineunt convivia regis.
765   Postquam epulis functi generosi munere Bacchi
diffudere animos, cultusque genusque locorum
quaerit Lyncides moresque animumque virorum.
767a   [quaerit Abantiades: quaerenti protinus unus
narrat Lyncides moresque animumque virorum.]
qui simul edocuit 'nunc, o fortissime,' dixit,
770   'fare, precor, Perseu, quanta virtute quibusque
artibus abstuleris crinita draconibus ora.'
  Narrat Agenorides gelido sub Atlante iacentem
esse locum solidae tutum munimine molis;
cuius in introitu geminas habitasse sorores
775   Phorcidas unius partitas luminis usum;
id se sollerti furtim, dum traditur, astu
supposita cepisse manu perque abdita longe
deviaque et silvis horrentia saxa fragosis
Gorgoneas tetigisse domos passimque per agros
780   perque vias vidisse hominum simulacra ferarumque
in silicem ex ipsis visa conversa Medusa:
se tamen horrendae clipei, quod laeva gerebat,
aere repercusso formam adspexisse Medusae,
dumque gravis somnus colubrasque ipsamque tenebat,
785   eripuisse caput collo, pennisque fugacem
Pegason et fratrem matris de sanguine natos.

addidit et longi non falsa pericula cursus,
quae freta, quas terras sub se vidisset ab alto
et quae iactatis tetigisset sidera pennis.
790 ante exspectatum tacuit tamen; excipit unus
ex numero procerum quaerens, cur sola sororum
gesserit alternos inmixtos crinibus angues.
hospes ait: 'quoniam scitaris digna relatu,
accipe quaesiti causam. clarissima forma
795 multorumque fuit spes invidiosa procorum
illa, neque in tota conspectior ulla capillis
pars fuit; inveni, qui se vidisse referret.
hanc pelagi rector templo vitiasse Minervae
dicitur: aversa est et castos aegide vultus
800 nata Iovis texit, neve hoc inpune fuisset,
Gorgoneum crinem turpes mutavit in hydros.
nunc quoque, ut attonitos formidine terreat hostes,
pectore in adverso, quos fecit, sustinet angues.'

LIBER QVINTVS

Dumque ea Cephenum medio Danaeius heros
agmine commemorat, fremida regalia turba
atria conplentur, nec coniugialia festa
qui canat est clamor, sed qui fera nuntiet arma,
5   inque repentinos convivia versa tumultus
adsimilare freto possis, quod saeva quietum
ventorum rabies motis exasperat undis.
primus in his Phineus, belli temerarius auctor,
fraxineam quatiens aeratae cuspidis hastam,
10   'en' ait 'en adsum praereptae coniugis ultor,
nec mihi te pennae nec falsum versus in aurum
Iuppiter eripiet.' conanti mittere Cepheus
'quid facis?' exclamat 'quae te, germane, furentem
mens agit in facinus? meritisne haec gratia tantis
15   redditur? hac vitam servatae dote rependis?.
quam tibi non Perseus, verum si quaeris, ademit,
sed grave Nereidum numen, sed corniger Ammon,
sed quae visceribus veniebat belua ponti
exsaturanda meis. illo tibi tempore rapta est,
20   quo peritura fuit, nisi si crudelis id ipsum
exigis, ut pereat, luctuque levabere nostro.
scilicet haud satis est, quod te spectante revincta est
et nullam quod opem patruus sponsusve tulisti:
insuper, a quoquam quod sit servata, dolebis
25   praemiaque eripies? quae si tibi magna videntur,
ex illis scopulis, ubi erant adfixa, petisses.
nunc sine, qui petiit, per quem haec non orba senectus,

128

ferre, quod et meritis et voce est pactus, eumque
non tibi, sed certae praelatum intellege morti.'
30   ille nihil contra, sed et hunc et Persea vultu
alterno spectans petat hunc ignorat an illum
cunctatusque brevi contortam viribus hastam,
quantas ira dabat, nequiquam in Persea misit.
ut stetit illa toro, stratis tum denique Perseus
35   exsiluit teloque ferox inimica remisso
pectora rupisset, nisi post altaria Phineus
isset: et (indignum) scelerato profuit ara.
fronte tamen Rhoeti non inrita cuspis adhaesit;
qui postquam cecidit ferrumque ex osse revulsum est,
40   calcitrat et positas adspergit sanguine mensas.
tum vero indomitas ardescit vulgus in iras
telaque coniciunt et sunt, qui Cephea dicunt
cum genero debere mori; sed limine tecti
exierat Cepheus testatus iusque fidemque
45   hospitiique deos ea se prohibente moveri.
     Bellica Pallas adest et protegit aegide fratrem
datque animos. erat Indus Athis, quem flumine Gange
edita Limnaee vitreis peperisse sub undis
creditur, egregius forma, quam divite cultu
50   augebat bis adhuc octonis integer annis,
indutus chlamydem Tyriam, quam limbus obibat
aureus; ornabant aurata monilia collum
et madidos murra curvum crinale capillos;
ille quidem iaculo quamvis distantia misso
55   figere doctus erat, sed tendere doctior arcus.
tum quoque lenta manu flectentem cornua Perseus
stipite, qui media positus fumabat in ara,
perculit et fractis confudit in ossibus ora.
hunc ubi laudatos iactantem in sanguine vultus
60   Assyrius vidit Lycabas, iunctissimus illi
et comes et veri non dissimulator amoris,
postquam exhalantem sub acerbo vulnere vitam
deploravit Athin, quos ille tetenderat arcus
adripit et 'mecum tibi sint certamina' dixit,
65   'nec longum pueri fato laetabere, quo plus
invidiae quam laudis habes.' haec omnia nondum
dixerat, emicuit nervo penetrabile telum

vitatumque tamen sinuosa veste pependit.
vertit in hunc harpen spectatam caede Medusae
70   Acrisioniades adigitque in pectus; at ille
iam moriens oculis sub nocte natantibus atra
circumspexit Athin seque adclinavit ad illum
et tulit ad manes iunctae solacia mortis.
      Ecce Suenites, genitus Metione, Phorbas
75   et Libys Amphimedon, avidi committere pugnam,
sanguine, quo late tellus madefacta tepebat,
conciderant lapsi; surgentibus obstitit ensis,
alterius costis, iugulo Phorbantis adactus.
at non Actoriden Erytum, cui lata bipennis
80   telum erat, admoto Perseus petit ense, sed altis
exstantem signis multaeque in pondere massae
ingentem manibus tollit cratera duabus
infligitque viro: rutilum vomit ille cruorem
et resupinus humum moribundo vertice pulsat.
85   inde Semiramio Polydegmona sanguine cretum
Caucasiumque Abarim Sperchionidenque Lycetum
intonsumque comas Helicem Phlegyamque Clytumque
sternit et exstructos morientum calcat acervos.
      Nec Phineus ausus concurrere comminus hosti
90   intorquet iaculum: quod detulit error in Idan
expertem frustra belli et neutra arma secutum.
ille tuens oculis inmitem Phinea torvis
'quandoquidem in partes' ait 'abstrahor, accipe, Phineu,
quem fecisti hostem, pensaque hoc vulnere vulnus!'
95   iamque remissurus tractum de vulnere telum
sanguine defectos cecidit conlapsus in artus.
      Tum quoque Cephenum post regem primus Hodites
ense iacet Clymeni; Prothoenora percutit Hypseus,
Hypsea Lyncides. fuit et grandaevus in illis
100 Emathion, aequi cultor timidusque deorum,
qui, quoniam prohibent anni bellare, loquendo
pugnat et incessit scelerataque devovet arma.
huic Chromis amplexo tremulis altaria palmis
decutit ense caput, quod protinus incidit arae
105 atque ibi semianimi verba exsecrantia lingua
edidit et medios animam exspiravit in ignes.
hinc gemini fratres Broteasque et caestibus Ammon

invicti, vinci si possent caestibus enses,
Phinea cecidere manu Cererisque sacerdos
110 Ampycus albenti velatus tempora vitta;
tu quoque, Lampetide, non hos adhibendus ad usus,
sed qui, pacis opus, citharam cum voce moveres:
iussus eras celebrare dapes festumque canendo.
quem procul adstantem plectrumque inbelle tenentem
115 Paetalus inridens 'Stygiis cane cetera' dixit
'manibus' et laevo mucronem tempore fixit;
concidit et digitis morientibus ille retemptat
fila lyrae, casuque fuit miserabile carmen.
nec sinit hunc inpune ferox cecidisse Lycormas
120 raptaque de dextro robusta repagula posti
ossibus inlisit mediae cervicis, at ille
procubuit terrae mactati more iuvenci.
demere temptabat laevi quoque robora postis
Cinyphius Pelates: temptanti dextera fixa est
125 cuspide Marmaridae Corythi lignoque cohaesit;
haerenti latus hausit Abas, nec corruit ille,
sed retinente manum moriens e poste pependit.
sternitur et Melaneus Perseia castra secutus
et Nasamoniaci Dorylas ditissimus agri,
130 dives agri Dorylas, quo non possederat alter
latius aut totidem tollebat turis acervos.
huius in obliquo missum stetit inguine ferrum:
letifer ille locus; quem postquam vulneris auctor
singultantem animam et versantem lumina vidit
135 Bactrius Halcyoneus, 'hoc, quod premis' inquit 'habeto
de tot agris terrae' corpusque exsangue reliquit.
torquet in hunc hastam calido de vulnere raptam
ultor Abantiades, media quae nare recepta
cervice exacta est in partesque eminet ambas,
140 dumque manum Fortuna iuvat, Clytiumque Claninque
matre satos una diverso vulnere fudit;
nam Clytii per utrumque gravi librata lacerto
fraxinus acta femur, iaculum Clanis ore momordit.
occidit et Celadon Mendesius, occidit Astreus
145 matre Palaestina, dubio genitore creatus,
Aethionque sagax quondam ventura videre,
tunc ave deceptus falsa, regisque Thoactes

armiger et caeso genitore infamis Agyrtes.
plus tamen exhausto superest; namque omnibus unum
150   opprimere est animus, coniurata undique pugnant
agmina pro causa meritum inpugnante fidemque.
hac pro parte socer frustra pius et nova coniunx
cum genetrice favent ululatuque atria conplent,
sed sonus armorum superat gemitusque cadentum,
155   pollutosque simul multo Bellona penates
sanguine perfundit renovataque proelia miscet.
circueunt unum Phineus et mille secuti
Phinea; tela volant hiberna grandine plura
praeter utrumque latus praeterque et lumen et aures.
160   adplicat hic umeros ad magnae saxa columnae
tutaque terga gerens adversaque in agmina versus
sustinet instantes; instabat parte sinistra
Chaonius Molpeus, dextra Nabataeus Echemmon.
tigris ut auditis diversa valle duorum
165   exstimulata fame mugitibus armentorum
nescit, utro potius ruat, et ruere ardet utroque:
sic dubius Perseus, dextra laevane feratur,
Molpea traiecti summovit vulnere cruris
contentusque fuga est; neque enim dat tempus Echemmon;
170   sed furit et cupiens alto dare vulnera collo
non circumspectis exactum viribus ensem
fregit, et extrema percussae parte columnae
lammina dissiluit dominique in gutture fixa est.
non tamen ad letum causas satis illa valentes
175   plaga dedit: trepidum Perseus et inertia frustra
bracchia tendentem Cyllenide confodit harpe.
      Verum ubi virtutem turbae succumbere vidit,
'auxilium' Perseus 'quoniam sic cogitis ipsi,'
dixit 'ab hoste petam. vultus avertite vestros,
180   siquis amicus adest.' et Gorgonis extulit ora.
'quaere alium, tua quem moveant oracula' dixit
Thescelus, utque manu iaculum fatale parabat
mittere, in hoc haesit signum de marmore gestu.
proximus huic Ampyx animi plenissima magni
185   pectora Lyncidae gladio petit, inque petendo
dextera deriguit nec citra mota nec ultra est.
at Nileus, qui se genitum septemplice Nilo

ementitus erat, clipeo quoque flumina septem
argento partim, partim caelaverat auro,
190   'adspice,' ait 'Perseu, nostrae primordia gentis!
magna feres tacitas solacia mortis ad umbras,
a tanto cecidisse viro'—pars ultima vocis
in medio suppressa sono est, adapertaque velle
ora loqui credas, nec sunt ea pervia verbis.
195   increpat hos 'vitio' que 'animi, non viribus' inquit
'Gorgoneis torpetis' Eryx, 'incurrite mecum
et prosternite humi iuvenem magica arma moventem!'
incursurus erat: tenuit vestigia tellus,
inmotusque silex armataque mansit imago.
200   hi tamen ex merito poenas subiere, sed unus
miles erat Persei, pro quo dum pugnat, Aconteus,
Gorgone conspecta saxo concrevit oborto;
quem ratus Astyages etiamnum vivere, longo
ense ferit: sonuit tinnitibus ensis acutis;
205   dum stupet Astyages, naturam traxit eandem
marmoreoque manet vultus mirantis in ore.
nomina longa mora est media de plebe virorum
dicere: bis centum restabant corpora pugnae,
Gorgone bis centum riguerunt corpora visa.
210   Paenitet iniusti tunc denique Phinea belli.
sed quid agat? simulacra videt diversa figuris
agnoscitque suos et nomine quemque vocatum
poscit opem credensque parum sibi proxima tangit
corpora: marmor erant; avertitur atque ita supplex
215   confessasque manus obliquaque bracchia tendens
'vincis,' ait 'Perseu! remove tua monstra tuaeque
saxificos vultus, quaecumque ea, tolle Medusae:
tolle, precor. non nos odium regnique cupido
conpulit ad bellum: pro coniuge movimus arma;
220   causa fuit meritis melior tua, tempore nostra.
non cessisse piget; nihil, o fortissime, praeter
hanc animam concede mihi, tua cetera sunto.'
talia dicenti neque eum, quem voce rogabat,
respicere audenti 'quod' ait, 'timidissme Phineu,
225   et possum tribuisse et magnum est munus inerti,
(pone metum) tribuam: nullo violabere ferro;
quin etiam mansura dabo monimenta per aevum,

inque domo soceri semper spectabere nostri,
ut mea se sponsi soletur imagine coniunx.'
230 dixit et in partem Phorcynida transtulit illam,
ad quam se trepido Phineus obverterat ore.
tum quoque conanti sua vertere lumina cervix
deriguit, saxoque oculorum induruit umor;
sed tamen os timidum vultusque in marmore supplex
235 submissaeque manus faciesque obnoxia mansit.

Victor Abantiades patrios cum coniuge muros
intrat et inmeriti vindex ultorque parentis
adgreditur Proetum: nam fratre per arma fugato
Acrisioneas Proetus possederat arces,
240 sed nec ope armorum nec, quam male ceperat, arce
torva colubriferi superavit lumina monstri.

Te tamen, o parvae rector, Polydecta, Seriphi,
nec iuvenis virtus per tot spectata labores
nec mala mollierant, sed inexorabile durus
245 exerces odium, nec iniqua finis in ira est.
detrectas etiam laudem fictamque Medusae
arguis esse necem. 'dabimus tibi pignora veri.
parcite luminibus!' Perseus ait oraque regis
ore Medusaeo silicem sine sanguine fecit.

250 Hactenus aurigenae comitem Tritonia fratri
se dedit: inde cava circumdata nube Seriphon
deserit, a dextra Cythno Gyaroque relictis,
quaque super pontum via visa brevissima, Thebas
virgineumque Helicona petit; quo monte potita
255 constitit et doctas sic est adfata sorores:
'fama novi fontis nostras pervenit ad aures,
dura Medusaei quem praepetis ungula rupit.
is mihi causa viae: volui mirabile factum
cernere; vidi ipsum materno sanguine nasci.'
260 excipit Uranie: 'quaecumque est causa videndi
has tibi, diva, domos, animo gratissima nostro es.
vera tamen fama est: est Pegasus huius origo
fontis', et ad latices deduxit Pallada sacros.
quae mirata diu factas pedis ictibus undas
265 silvarum lucos circumspicit antiquarum,
antraque et innumeris distinctas floribus herbas
felicesque vocat pariter studioque locoque

Mnemonidas; quam sic adfata est una sororum:
'O, nisi te virtus opera ad maiora tulisset,
270 in partem ventura chori Tritonia nostri,
vera refers, meritoque probas artesque locumque,
et gratam sortem, tutae modo simus, habemus.
sed (vetitum est adeo sceleri nihil) omnia terrent
virgineas mentes, dirusque ante ora Pyreneus
275 vertitur, et nondum tota me mente recepi.
Daulida Threicio Phoceaque milite rura
ceperat ille ferox iniustaque regna tenebat.
templa petebamus Parnasia: vidit euntes
nostraque fallaci veneratus numina vultu
280 'Mnemonides' (cognorat enim) 'consistite' dixit
'nec dubitate, precor, tecto grave sidus et imbrem'
(imber erat) 'vitare meo: subiere minores
saepe casas superi.' dictis et tempore motae
adnuimusque viro primasque intravimus aedes.
285 desierant imbres, victoque aquilonibus austro
fusca repurgato fugiebant nubila caelo;
inpetus ire fuit: claudit sua tecta Pyreneus
vimque parat; quam nos sumptis effugimus alis.
ipse secuturo similis stetit arduus arce
290 'qua' que 'via est vobis, erit et mihi' dixit 'eadem',
seque iacit vecors e summae culmine turris
et cadit in vultus discussisque ossibus oris
tundit humum moriens scelerato sanguine tinctam.'
    Musa loquebatur: pennae sonuere per auras,
295 voxque salutantum ramis veniebat ab altis.
suspicit et linguae quaerit tam certa loquentes
unde sonent hominemque putat Iove nata locutum.
ales erat, numeroque novem sua fata querentes
institerant ramis imitantes omnia picae.
300 miranti sic orsa deae dea: 'nuper et istae
auxerunt volucrum victae certamine turbam.
Pieros has genuit Pellaeis dives in arvis;
Paeonis Euippe mater fuit: illa potentem
Lucinam noviens, noviens paritura, vocavit.
305 intumuit numero stolidarum turba sororum
perque tot Haemonias et per tot Achaidas urbes
huc venit et tali committit proelia voce:

'desinite indoctum vana dulcedine vulgus
fallere. nobiscum, siqua est fiducia vobis,
310   Thespiades, certate, deae. nec voce nec arte
vincemur totidemque sumus. vel cedite victae
fonte Medusaeo et Hyantea Aganippe,
vel nos Emathiis ad Paeonas usque nivosos
cedamus campis. dirimant certamina nymphae.'
315   turpe quidem contendere erat, sed cedere visum
turpius; electae iurant per flumina nymphae
factaque de vivo pressere sedilia saxo.
tunc sine sorte prior, quae se certare professa est,
bella canit superum falsoque in honore Gigantas
320   ponit et extenuat magnorum facta deorum,
emissumque ima de sede Typhoea terrae
caelitibus fecisse metum cunctosque dedisse
terga fugae, donec fessos Aegyptia tellus
ceperit et septem discretus in ostia Nilus.
325   huc quoque terrigenam venisse Typhoea narrat
et se mentitis superos celasse figuris
'dux' que 'gregis' dixit 'fit Iuppiter, unde recurvis
nunc quoque formatus Libys est cum cornibus Ammon;
Delius in corvo est, proles Semeleia capro,
330   fele soror Phoebi, nivea Saturnia vacca,
pisce Venus latuit, Cyllenius ibidis alis.'
    Hactenus ad citharam vocalia moverat ora:
poscimur Aonides—sed forsitan otia non sint,
nec nostris praebere vacet tibi cantibus aures?'
335   'ne dubita vestrumque mihi refer ordine carmen'
Pallas ait nemorisque levi consedit in umbra.
Musa refert: 'dedimus summam certaminis uni.
surgit et inmissos hedera collecta capillos
Calliope querulas praetemptat pollice chordas
340   atque haec percussis subiungit carmina nervis:
    'Prima Ceres unco glaebam dimovit aratro,
prima dedit fruges alimentaque mitia terris,
prima dedit leges: Cereris sunt omnia munus.
illa canenda mihi est; utinam modo dicere possim
345   carmina digna dea! certe dea carmine digna est.
    Vasta Giganteis ingesta est insula membris
Trinacris et magnis subiectum molibus urget

aetherias ausum sperare Typhoea sedes.
nititur ille quidem pugnatque resurgere saepe,
350   dextra sed Ausonio manus est subiecta Peloro,
laeva, Pachyne, tibi, Lilybaeo crura premuntur;
degravat Aetna caput; sub qua resupinus harenas
eiectat flammamque ferox vomit ore Typhoeus.
saepe remoliri luctatur pondera terrae
355   oppidaque et magnos devolvere corpore montes:
inde tremit tellus, et rex pavet ipse silentum,
ne pateat latoque solum retegatur hiatu
inmissusque dies trepidantes terreat umbras.
hanc metuens cladem tenebrosa sede tyrannus
360   exierat curruque atrorum vectus equorum
ambibat Siculae cautus fundamina terrae;
postquam exploratum satis est loca nulla labare
depositoque metu videt hunc Erycina vagantem,
monte suo residens natumque amplexa volucrem
365   'arma manusque meae, mea, nate, potentia' dixit,
'illa, quibus superas omnes, cape tela, Cupido,
inque dei pectus celeres molire sagittas,
cui triplicis cessit fortuna novissima regni.
tu superos ipsumque Iovem, tu numina ponti
370   victa domas ipsumque, regit qui numina ponti.
Tartara quid cessant? cur non matrisque tuumque
imperium profers? agitur pars tertia mundi!
et tamen in caelo, quae iam patientia nostra est,
spernimur, ac mecum vires minuuntur Amoris.
375   Pallada nonne vides iaculatricemque Dianam
abscessisse mihi? Cereris quoque filia virgo,
si patiemur, erit: nam spes adfectat easdem.
at tu pro socio, siqua est ea gratia, regno
iunge deam patruo!' dixit Venus. ille pharetram
380   solvit et arbitrio matris de mille sagittis
unam seposuit, sed qua nec acutior ulla
nec minus incerta est nec quae magis audiat arcum,
oppositoque genu curvavit flexile cornum
inque cor hamata percussit harundine Ditem.
385   Haud procul Hennaeis lacus est a moenibus altae,
nomine Pergus, aquae; non illo plura Caystros
carmina cygnorum labentibus edit in undis.

silva coronat aquas cingens latus omne suisque
frondibus ut velo Phoebeos submovet ictus.
390 frigora dant rami, Tyrios humus umida flores:
perpetuum ver est. quo dum Proserpina luco
ludit et aut violas aut candida lilia carpit,
dumque puellari studio calathosque sinumque
inplet et aequales certat superare legendo,
395 paene simul visa est dilectaque raptaque Diti:
usque adeo est properatus amor. dea territa maesto
et matrem et comites, sed matrem saepius, ore
clamat, et, ut summa vestem laniarat ab ora,
conlecti flores tunicis cecidere remissis,
400 tantaque simplicitas puerilibus adfuit annis:
haec quoque virgineum movit iactura dolorem.
raptor agit currus et nomine quemque vocando
exhortatur equos, quorum per colla iubasque
excutit obscura tinctas ferrugine habenas,
405 perque lacus altos et olentia sulphure fertur
stagna Palicorum rupta ferventia terra
et qua Bacchiadae, bimari gens orta Corintho,
inter inaequales posuerunt moenia portus.
   Est medium Cyanes et Pisaeae Arethusae,
410 quod coit angustis inclusum cornibus aequor:
hic fuit, a cuius stagnum quoque nomine dictum est,
inter Sicelidas Cyane celeberrima nymphas;
gurgite quae medio summa tenus exstitit alvo
agnovitque deam. 'nec longius ibitis!' inquit,
415 'non potes invitae Cereris gener esse: roganda,
non rapienda fuit. quodsi conponere magnis
parva mihi fas est, et me dilexit Anapis,
exorata tamen, nec, ut haec, exterrita nupsi.'
dixit et in partes diversas bracchia tendens
420 obstitit. haud ultra tenuit Saturnius iram
terribilesque hortatus equos in gurgitis ima
contortum valido sceptrum regale lacerto
condidit. icta viam tellus in Tartara fecit
et pronos currus medio cratere recepit.
425 At Cyane raptamque deam contemptaque fontis
iura sui maerens, inconsolabile vulnus
mente gerit tacita lacrimisque absumitur omnis

et, quarum fuerat magnum modo numen, in illas
extenuatur aquas: molliri membra videres,
430 ossa pati flexus, ungues posuisse rigorem,
primaque de tota tenuissima quaeque liquescunt,
caerulei crines digitique et crura pedesque:
nam brevis in gelidas membris exilibus undas
transitus est; post haec umeri tergusque latusque
435 pectoraque in tenues abeunt evanida rivos;
denique pro vivo vitiatas sanguine venas
lympha subit, restatque nihil, quod prendere posses.
     Interea pavidae nequiquam filia matri
omnibus est terris, omni quaesita profundo:
440 illam non udis veniens Aurora capillis
cessantem vidit, non Hesperus; illa duabus
flammiferas pinus manibus succendit ab Aetna
perque pruinosas tulit inrequieta tenebras.
rursus ubi alma dies hebetarat sidera, natam
445 solis ab occasu solis quaerebat ad ortus.
fessa labore sitim conceperat, oraque nulli
conluerant fontes, cum tectam stramine vidit
forte casam parvasque fores pulsavit; at inde
prodit anus divamque videt lymphamque roganti
450 dulce dedit, tosta quod texerat ante polenta.
dum bibit illa datum, duri puer oris et audax
constitit ante deam risitque avidamque vocavit.
offensa est neque adhuc epota parte loquentem
cum liquido mixta perfudit diva polenta;
455 conbibit os maculas et, quae modo bracchia gessit,
crura gerit, cauda est mutatis addita membris,
inque brevem formam, ne sit vis magna nocendi,
contrahitur, parvaque minor mensura lacerta est.
mirantem flentemque et tangere monstra parantem
460 fugit anum latebramque petit aptumque colori
nomen habet variis stellatus corpora guttis.
     Quas dea per terras et quas erraverit undas,
dicere longa mora est: quaerenti defuit orbis.
Sicaniam repetit, dumque omnia lustrat eundo,
465 venit et ad Cyanen; ea ni mutata fuisset,
omnia narrasset, sed et os et lingua volenti
dicere non aderant, nec qua loqueretur habebat;

signa tamen manifesta dedit notamque parenti
illo forte loco delapsam in gurgite sacro
470   Persephones zonam summis ostendit in undis.
quam simul agnovit, tamquam tunc denique raptam
scisset, inornatos laniavit diva capillos
et repetita suis percussit pectora palmis.
nescit adhuc, ubi sit; terras tamen increpat omnes
475   ingratasque vocat nec frugum munere dignas,
Trinacriam ante alias, in qua vestigia damni
repperit. ergo illic saeva vertentia glaebas
fregit aratra manu parilique irata colonos
ruricolasque boves leto dedit arvaque iussit
480   fallere depositum vitiataque semina fecit.
fertilitas terrae latum vulgata per orbem
falsa iacet: primis segetes moriuntur in herbis,
et modo sol nimius, nimius modo corripit imber,
sideraque ventique nocent, avidaeque volucres
485   semina iacta legunt; lolium tribulique fatigant
triticeas messes et inexpugnabile gramen.
tum caput Eleis Alpheias extulit undis
rorantesque comas a fronte removit ad aures
atque ait: 'o toto quaesitae virginis orbe
490   et frugum genetrix, inmensos siste labores,
neve tibi fidae violenta irascere terrae!
terra nihil meruit patuitque invita rapinae;
nec sum pro patria supplex: huc hospita veni.
Pisa mihi patria est et ab Elide ducimus ortus;
495   Sicaniam peregrina colo, sed gratior omni
haec mihi terra solo est: hos nunc Arethusa penates,
hanc habeo sedem; quam tu, mitissima, serva!
mota loco cur sim tantique per aequoris undas
advehar Ortygiam, veniet narratibus hora
500   tempestiva meis, cum tu curaque levata
et vultus melioris eris. mihi pervia tellus
praebet iter subterque imas ablata cavernas
hic caput attollo desuetaque sidera cerno.
ergo dum Stygio sub terris gurgite labor,
505   visa tua est oculis illic Proserpina nostris:
illa quidem tristis neque adhuc interrita vultu,
sed regina tamen, sed opaci maxima mundi,

sed tamen inferni pollens matrona tyranni.'
      Mater ad auditas stupuit ceu saxea voces
510 attonitaeque diu similis fuit, utque dolore
      pulsa gravi gravis est amentia, curribus auras
      exit in aetherias. ibi toto nubila vultu
      ante Iovem passis stetit invidiosa capillis,
      'pro' que 'meo veni supplex tibi, Iuppiter,' inquit
515 'sanguine proque tuo. si nulla est gratia matris,
      nata patrem moveat, neu sit tibi cura precamur
      vilior illius, quod nostro est edita partu.
      en quaesita diu tandem mihi nata reperta est,
      si reperire vocas amittere certius, aut si
520 scire, ubi sit, reperire vocas. quod rapta, feremus,
      dummodo reddat eam! neque enim praedone marito
      filia digna tua est, si iam mea filia non est.'
      Iuppiter excepit: 'commune est pignus onusque
      nata mihi tecum; sed si modo nomina rebus
525 addere vera placet, non hoc iniuria factum,
      verum amor est, neque erit nobis gener ille pudori,
      tu modo, diva, velis. ut desint cetera, quantum est
      esse Iovis fratrem! quid quod non cetera desunt
      nec cedit nisi sorte mihi! sed tanta cupido
530 si tibi discidii est, repetet Proserpina caelum,
      lege tamen certa, si nullos contigit illic
      ore cibos; nam sic Parcarum foedere cautum est.'
      Dixerat, at Cereri certum est educere natam.
      non ita fata sinunt, quoniam ieiunia virgo
535 solverat et, cultis dum simplex errat in hortis,
      puniceum curva decerpserat arbore pomum
      sumptaque pallenti septem de cortice grana
      presserat ore suo; solusque ex omnibus illud
      Ascalaphus vidit, quem quondam dicitur Orphne,
540 inter Avernales haud ignotissima nymphas,
      ex Acheronte suo silvis peperisse sub atris;
      vidit et indicio reditum crudelis ademit.
      ingemuit regina Erebi testemque profanam
      fecit avem sparsumque caput Phlegethontide lympha
545 in rostrum et plumas et grandia lumina vertit.
      ille sibi ablatus fulvis amicitur in alis
      inque caput crescit longosque reflectitur ungues

vixque movet natas per inertia bracchia pennas
foedaque fit volucris, venturi nuntia luctus,
550 ignavus bubo, dirum mortalibus omen.
　　Hic tamen indicio poenam linguaque videri
commeruisse potest: vobis, Acheloides, unde
pluma pedesque avium, cum virginis ora geratis?
an quia, cum legeret vernos Proserpina flores,
555 in comitum numero, doctae Sirenes, eratis?
quam postquam toto frustra quaesistis in orbe,
protinus, ut vestram sentirent aequora curam,
posse super fluctus alarum insistere remis
optastis facilesque deos habuistis et artus
560 vidistis vestros subitis flavescere pennis;
ne tamen ille canor mulcendas natus ad aures
tantaque dos oris linguae deperderet usum,
virginei vultus et vox humana remansit.
　　At medius fratrisque sui maestaeque sororis
565 Iuppiter ex aequo volventem dividit annum:
nunc dea, regnorum numen commune duorum,
cum matre est totidem, totidem cum coniuge menses.
vertitur extemplo facies et mentis et oris;
nam, modo quae poterat Diti quoque maesta videri,
570 laeta deae frons est, ut sol, qui tectus aquosis
nubibus ante fuit, victis e nubibus exit.
　　Exigit alma Ceres, nata secura recepta,
quae tibi causa fugae, cur sis, Arethusa, sacer fons.
conticuere undae, quarum dea sustulit alto
575 fonte caput viridesque manu siccata capillos
fluminis Elei veteres narravit amores.
　　'Pars ego nympharum, quae sunt in Achaide,' dixit,
'una fui: nec me studiosius altera saltus
legit nec posuit studiosius altera casses.
580 sed quamvis formae numquam mihi fama petita est,
quamvis fortis eram, formosae nomen habebam.
nec mea me facies nimium laudata iuvabat,
quaque aliae gaudere solent, ego rustica dote
corporis erubui crimenque placere putavi.
585 lassa revertebar (memini) Stymphalide silva:
aestus erat, magnumque labor geminaverat aestum.
invenio sine vertice aquas, sine murmure euntes,

perspicuas ad humum, per quas numerabilis alte
calculus omnis erat, quas tu vix ire putares;
590 cana salicta dabant nutritaque populus unda
sponte sua natas ripis declivibus umbras:
accessi primumque pedis vestigia tinxi,
poplite deinde tenus neque eo contenta recingor
molliaque inpono salici velamina curvae
595 nudaque mergor aquis; quas dum ferioque trahoque
mille modis labens excussaque bracchia iacto,
nescio quod medio sensi sub gurgite murmur
territaque insisto propiori margine fontis.
'quo properas, Arethusa?' suis Alpheus ab undis,
600 'quo properas?' iterum rauco mihi dixerat ore.
sicut eram, fugio sine vestibus: altera vestes
ripa meas habuit. tanto magis instat et ardet,
et, quia nuda fui, sum visa paratior illi.
sic ego currebam, sic me ferus ille premebat,
605 ut fugere accipitrem penna trepidante columbae,
ut solet accipiter trepidas urgere columbas.
usque sub Orchomenon Psophidaque Cyllenenque
Maenaliosque sinus gelidumque Erymanthon et Elim
currere sustinui, nec me velocior ille;
610 sed tolerare diu cursus ego viribus inpar
non poteram, longi patiens erat ille laboris.
per tamen et campos, per opertos arbore montes
saxa quoque et rupes et, qua via nulla, cucurri.
sol erat a tergo: vidi praecedere longam
615 ante pedes umbram, nisi si timor illa videbat;
sed certe sonitusque pedum terrebat, et ingens
crinales vittas adflabat anhelitus oris.
fessa labore fugae 'fer opem, deprendimur,' inquam,
'armigerae, Diana, tuae, cui saepe dedisti
620 ferre tuos arcus inclusaque tela pharetra.'
mota dea est spississque ferens e nubibus unam
me super iniecit: lustrat caligine tectam
amnis et ignarus circum cava nubila quaerit
bisque locum, quo me dea texerat, inscius ambit
625 et bis 'io Arethusa, io Arethusa!' vocavit.
quid mihi tunc animi miserae fuit? anne quod agnae est,
siqua lupos audit circum stabula alta frementes,

aut lepori, qui vepre latens hostilia cernit
ora canum nullosque audet dare corpore motus?
630 non tamen abscedit; neque enim vestigia cernit
longius ulla pedum: servat nubemque locumque.
occupat obsessos sudor mihi frigidus artus,
caeruleaeque cadunt toto de corpore guttae,
quaque pedem movi, manat locus, eque capillis
635 ros cadit, et citius, quam nunc tibi facta renarro,
in latices mutor. sed enim cognoscit amatas
amnis aquas positoque viri, quod sumpserat, ore
vertitur in proprias, ut se mihi misceat, undas.
Delia rupit humum, caecisque ego mersa cavernis
640 advehor Ortygiam, quae me cognomine divae
grata meae superas eduxit prima sub auras.'
      Hac Arethusa tenus; geminos dea fertilis angues
curribus admovit frenisque coercuit ora
et medium caeli terraeque per aëra vecta est
645 atque levem currum Tritonida misit in urbem
Triptolemo partimque rudi data semina iussit
spargere humo, partim post tempora longa recultae.
iam super Europen sublimis et Asida terram
vectus erat iuvenis: Scythicas advertitur oras.
650 rex ibi Lyncus erat; regis subit ille penates.
qua veniat, causamque viae nomenque rogatus
et patriam 'patria est clarae mihi' dixit 'Athenae,
Triptolemus nomen; veni nec puppe per undas,
nec pede per terras: patuit mihi pervius aether.
655 dona fero Cereris, latos quae sparsa per agros
frugiferas messes alimentaque mitia reddant.'
barbarus invidit, tantique ut muneris auctor
ipse sit, hospitio recipit somnoque gravatum
adgreditur ferro. conantem figere pectus
660 lynca Ceres fecit rursusque per aëra iussit
Mopsopium iuvenem sacros agitare iugales.'
      Finierat doctos e nobis maxima cantus;
at nymphae vicisse deas Helicona colentes
concordi dixere sono; convicia victae
665 cum iacerent, 'quoniam' dixit 'certamine vobis
supplicium meruisse parum est maledictaque culpae
additis et non est patientia libera nobis,

ibimus in poenas et, qua vocat ira, sequemur.'
rident Emathides spernuntque minacia verba
670   conantesque oculis magno clamore protervas
intentare manus pennas exire per ungues
adspexere suos, operiri bracchia plumis,
alteraque alterius rigido concrescere rostro
ora videt volucresque novas accedere silvis,
675   dumque volunt plangi, per bracchia mota levatae
aëre pendebant, nemorum convicia, picae.
nunc quoque in alitibus facundia prisca remansit
raucaque garrulitas studiumque inmane loquendi.'

NOTES

NOTES TO BOOK 1

After announcing that his subject is forms changed into new bodies from the beginning of the world down to his own time, Ovid proceeds in the first part of Book 1 to describe the Creation of the Universe from its original Chaos. With the advent of human beings, the way is open to progress but also to moral degeneration. The Age of Iron (127 ff.) brings such corruption that one man, Lycaon, hosting the supreme deity Jupiter in his palace, conspires to kill him. Jupiter sees to it that this human savage is changed into a bloodthirsty wolf, but he also determines to wipe out all human beings, whom he regards as utterly depraved. He causes a flood to drown out the earth and all its inhabitants (262–312); only Pyrrha and Deucalion, models of goodness, are permitted to ride out the flood in something comparable to Noah's Ark. When the waters recede, they are also allowed to repopulate the earth with stones that change into human beings (313–415).

In his transition to the second section of the Book, Ovid accounts for animal life: it comes about through spontaneous generation from the earth. Some monsters are produced, one of which, a giant snake, Apollo kills at Delphi (416–51). With the new focus on the god Apollo, Ovid turns our attention to the amatory behavior of male deities, in a succession of three stories that portray the impetuous desires of the gods for beautiful nymphs who want only to retain their virginity and enjoy the chaste hunting activities of virginal Diana. Apollo makes an effort to woo the nymph he desires, Daphne, but eventually pursues her in earnest in order to rape her; and her only recourse is to pray for metamorphosis. She escapes by becoming a laurel (452–567). Next, Jupiter acts on his lust for Io (568–746). When Io ignores his perfunctory wooing and runs off, he quickly perpetrates the rape. Then, he turns the girl into a cow in order to conceal his adultery from his wife Juno. Juno, suspecting the truth,

torments the cow (which still has most of the sensibility of the girl
Io), until finally Jupiter confesses his wrong and promises to be good
in the future. Mollified, Juno lets the cow be turned back into Io.
Within this tale is the narration of still another tale of divine desire
for and pursuit of a nymph: this is the story of Syrinx (689–712),
told by Mercury to put his audience to sleep. when almost overtaken
by the god Pan, Syrinx calls upon her sisters to transform her, and
indeed, like Daphne, she escapes, by turning into reeds.

PREFACE (1–4)

Ovid opens his long poem with a brief summary of its contents and
an appeal to unspecified gods for help. He does not use the familiar
language of the epic beginning although it becomes clear in the second
line that he writes in complete hexameters, not elegiac couplets. His
topic covers all time, mythical and historical, without the customary
focus of epic on heroes and great deeds, and it does not substitute for
them the concerns of philosophic or didactic epic (such as that of
Lucretius and Vergil's *Georgics*). In what sense Changed Forms pro-
vide a suitable poetic vehicle remains to be seen.

1   *in nova*: epic poems would regularly open with a noun that specified
    the principal topic or theme, as in Homer and Vergil. Beginning with
    a preposition followed by an adjective and delaying the noun that
    completes the phrase until *corpora* in 2 tends to puzzle expectations.
    At first, *nova* might seem a substantive. *fert animus*: in this unusual
    and untraditional phrase (which works with the infinitive *dicere*), Ovid
    declares that the primary force behind his poem is his own active
    rational intelligence. The phrase occurs earlier in Horace, *Epist.*
    1.14.8, not in a context of poetic activity, and Ovid had tried it in
    Ars Am. 3.467. He uses it once more in the *Met.*, at 1.775, where
    Phaethon's unwise pride takes over his reason. *mutatas . . . formas*:
    the subject of the poem, a Latin translation of the compound Greek
    noun, *Metamorphoses*, which Ovid chose as his title. *dicere*: carefully
    inserted between the two words that define Ovid's subject. In epic
    convention, the poet and his Muse(s) *sing*, although some poets do
    indeed use the verb *dicere*.

2   *corpora*: Ovid's topic is forms changed to new bodies and not bodies
    changed to new forms. It is the instability of form, what normally
    gives things identity in the world, that occupies his attention. *coeptis*:
    dative with *adspirate* in 3. This substantive in the plural became a
    familiar word for poetic "beginnings" after Vergil, *G.* 1.40 (cf. Ovid,
    Ars Am. 1.30). *nam vos mutastis et illa*: before appealing to the gods,
    Ovid inserts a parenthetical explanation of why he addresses them,

namely, because they have manifested their transforming power in the past over poetic beginnings, his own and those of other poets. Recent critics have pointed out that, up to the central caesura of 2 where this parenthesis begins, the audience could easily have assumed that Ovid would be composing in elegiac meter, for which he was so justly famous. With the series of four long syllables that follow, however, there can be no doubt that line 2 is a hexameter like 1. It is as if, against reader expectations, this poem shows a change taking place in its own beginnings. *mutastis*: syncopated form. The sign of the perfect tense, *-vi-*, has been dropped. Syncope is much more common in the third person plural: e.g., *mutarunt* for *mutaverunt*. *illa*: one of the most hotly discussed textual readings in the poem. The MSS agree in transmitting the form *illas*, which would have to refer to *formas*, and that has been accepted by readers for almost two thousand years. However, at least one medieval reader tried to correct his manuscript with *illa*, and now Kenney has made a convincing case for *illa* as Ovid's intended reading, *illas* as a careless error in the early MS tradition that was uncritically accepted. The pronoun in the parenthesis should refer to the noun from which the parenthesis departed, i.e., *coeptis*; the witty change that seems to be transforming the expected elegiac meter into hexameter points to *illa*; and the *et* before the demonstrative would seem to be more logical if it meant "those beginnings also" rather than "those forms also".

3   *adspirate*: originally a nautical metaphor for favorable winds, but Vergil had made it a familiar topos for the Muses' help. Cf. *Aen.* 9.525 *a(d)spirate canenti*. Lee suggested that the nautical theme extends to *deducite* in 4. *primaque ab origine mundi*: this subject starts immediately in 5.

4   *ad mea . . . tempora*: the last verses of his final book, Book 15, reach the death of Julius Caesar and the rise of Augustus in the poet's own lifetime. *perpetuum . . . carmen*: literally, a continuous song. But such a poem was so regularly a long epic on a grandiose theme that the phrase implies the epic genre. Horace's reference in *C*. 1.7.6 to the act of celebrating Athens in continuous poetry (*carmine perpetuo*) could well mean an epic poem. Ovid, however, seems to have aimed to surprise and tantalize his audience. How can changed forms produce a continuous song? Change and continuity appear to be mutually exclusive. And in fact, although the poetic voice remains continuous and the time scheme sweeps steadily toward the present, the subject matter focuses on one metamorphosis after another for a grand total of about 250, devoid of ordinary connection or continuity. Callimachus, in his prologue to the *Aetia* (*Fr*. 1.3), had used a Greek phrase, "one continuous poem," in a programmatic manner to represent what he would *not* write, what his foolish critics idealized. Ovid recalls

this Callimachean context—but not with slavish acceptance. While appearing to reject Callimachus' preference for the small, meticulously crafted poem and to adopt the long continuous one, he delights us by writing what could be considered a series of very Callimachean versions of short individual transformations. *deducite carmen*: the verb's literal sense, "bring down," "lead or guide from," makes sense. However, much scholarly dispute centers on whether Ovid uses a traditional poetic phrase or metaphor and, if so, which one. Both Horace and Propertius had employed *deducere* with object *carmen*: Hor. *C*. 3.30.13, Prop. 1.16.41. Horace's usage is quite literal: he claims to have brought Aeolian song (i.e., from Aeolia) to Italian meters. Propertius may use an image of spinning. Possible metaphors are: nautical (launching), military (leading troops from one place to another), spinning, colonizing. Vergil, *Ecl*. 6.5, uses the participle *deductum carmen* in sharp contrast to "fat sheep," and implicitly secures the meaning "(delicately) spun poetry"; he also declares himself on the side of Callimachean poetics. Ovid might allude to Vergil's creed, but he combines Callimachus with his own program in a different way.

CREATION (5–88)

Beginning, as he promised in 3, from the origin of the universe, Ovid launches into a Creation story. It is neither a scientific or philosophic account, like Lucretius', nor a conventional mythical version, for it does not define a clear divine personality and purpose behind what emerges. Ovid's focus rests on the development of form: that, rather than the agent promoting the change, dominates his and our attention. Thus, the important feature of things at the start is that they were formless or incapable of maintaining a form (17). This curious condition, counter to all our experience and preconceptions, stimulates the poet to explore playfully the state of formlessness. A god and kinder nature brought this chaos to an end by separating out the four basic elements: earth, water, fire, and air. This same indefinite deity then fashioned the Earth into a globe and gave it its familiar features, ending with its various atmospheric conditions: winds, thunder, lightning, rain, and so on (32–68). Since Ovid downplays the god and divine purpose, attention dwells on the clarity, speed, and self-assurance with which the poet records these cataclysmic changes of form. Life then comes to the world without explanation: fish, birds, and beasts just appear—and gods, too! (69–75). The "crown of creation" is human kind. Although Ovid calls this species a more sacred living being (76) whose function is to rule over the rest of things, he offers a muddled, indefinite account of human origins. We may be fashioned from a divine seed or merely formed after the appearance of the gods, and we differ from other animals in that they look down at the earth, while we look up at the sky, standing erect. Again, however, the important theme remains that this change gave the earth an intelligible *imago* and hitherto unknown shapes (87–88).

5   Ovid names the three basic visible realms, skipping fire, to fix our attention on a time when such regions did not yet exist. *quod tegit omnia*: it is a common poetic device to let the relative clause precede the "antecedent" (here, *caelum*) that controls it. Here, this allows Ovid also to expand the third member of his set of three (tricolon).

6   *unus . . . vultus*: the metaphor of a human face does not personify Chaos but implies Ovid's thematic interest in forms and appearance. There was nothing differentiated in this first "aspect" of things. *orbe*: equivalent to *mundo* (cf. 3); the circular implication of the noun should not be pressed.

7   *quem*: although the relative could refer to either of the preceding masculine nouns, it makes better sense with *vultus*. *dixere*: regular poetic form of third person plural, perfect tense (= *dixerunt*). *rudis*: "rough" in that it lacked definitive form or shape, Ovid's thematic concern. So, too, at 87 the earth was *rudis* until it acquired the forms of human beings. *indigestaque*: the first of a series of negatives that help to define the unimaginable quality of Chaos. The fact that Ovid probably invented the word—this is its first attested appearance in Latin—enhances the unusual situation. The first action to make something of this mass is one of ordering (cf. *dispositam* 32).

8   *pondus iners*: dead mass rather than mere weight. *iners*, with its negative prefix, suggests the need of art to turn this Chaos into form (like a statue, cf. *Fast.* 1.108). *congestaque eodem*: the participle is in the same metrical position and rhymes with Ovid's new word *indigestaque* in 7. The elision, unusual at this point in the line, reinforces the sense of being jumbled together.

9   *non bene*: the phrase (= *male*) continues the emphasis on negativity. *discordia*: metaphor of conflict, which will be picked up and developed at 17 ff. Strife can be viewed as a productive process at a later stage in evolution. Thus, at 1.419 ff., after the Flood the *semina rerum* were "fertile", and *discors concordia* (433) helped to regenerate the earth in profusion. *semina rerum*: metaphorical term for constituent matter that emphasizes potential creativity.

10   *nullus . . . Titan*: there was no sun or light, but Ovid puts it in poetic and nonscientific terms. The Sun is a descendant of the early Titans, son of Hyperion (cf. 4.192, 241).

11   With its negation of the moon's existence, this line echoes the previous one in its last three words; gerund *crescendo* has the same ending as

mundo 10. The imaginative description, "repairing the horns," means filling out the new moon's hollow crescent. *Phoebe*: direct transliteration of the Greek nominative form. Ovid uses Phoebe and Phoebus for Moon and Sun and also for Diana and Apollo, originally two quite different pairs.

13   The ancient theory assumed that the weights from all parts of the globe pressed equally on the center and thus created a balance. *bracchia*: having dabbled with a scientific description of the earth's position in the universe, Ovid juxtaposes a poetic picture of the sea. The "arms" here will combine with verb and subject to create an image of a feminine embrace.

14   *margine*: ablative of place where. Ovid refers to a common idea, found in Homeric verse, that water rings the earth (imagined as flat). *Amphitrite*: wife of Neptune and therefore able to stand for the sea here and elsewhere in Greco-Roman poetry. Again, Greek nominative form. In addition to the poetic image built on Greek myth, Ovid makes this line stand out by the double spondee that concludes the hexameter and by composing it in only four words.

15–16   *ut . . . sic*: not so much a comparison as an expression of logical coordination which, as Lee suggests, can best be rendered by "although . . . yet." Lee also urges translation of *-que* in *utque* with "but" after the previous negatives. This hexameter, with its nine short words, makes a sharp contrast with the preceding one.

16   *instabilis*: Ovid plays with the normal Latin sense of this adjective, which should mean "not able to stand, infirm." He turns it into a passive, probably for the first time: "not able to be stood on." When Chaos existed, there was no *terra firma*. *innabilis*: the innovation with the first adjective sets up Ovid's invention of a new word, which occurs in Latin only here. Water is "unswimmable" in that it is not reliably there to swim in.

17   *lucis*: the verb *egere* may take either ablative or, as here, genitive *nulli*: dative of reference.

18   *obstabat*: picks up the metaphor of strife from 9 and starts to develop it through 20. *aliis aliud*: the normal usage would involve either two singular or two plural forms of *alius*. Meter permits neither alternative here, so Ovid mixes his options. He still means that one thing opposed another. *corpore*: Chaos, the sum of all these instable qualities, is here viewed as a containing "body."

19–20   *calidis . . . siccis . . . cum duris*: normal Latin usage calls for a preposition with *pugnare* to apply to the person or thing "with" or "against" whom the fight is being waged. Poets allowed themselves dative without the preposition. Ovid employs poetic usage in 19, prosaic in 20.

20   *sine pondere habentia pondus*: "weighty with weightless things". Ovid

did not have an adjective for "weightless," and Latin lacks a definite article to allow "those without weight." But the clear syntax of the preceding pair, *mollia cum duris*, should make the sense of this second chiastic unit easier to grasp in spite of the deficiencies of Latin.

21 *Hanc . . . litem*: shifts the image of the "war" of elements to a mere legal "dispute". *deus et melior natura*: by not naming the god at work, Ovid keeps our attention fixed on formal change. Neither *god* nor *nature* is to be capitalized; nature is a condition (cf. 6) which now experiences improvement. *diremit*: not the usual legal verb with *litem*. The god "broke up" the dispute, and that action prepares for the definitive separation and permanent formation of the elements.

22 A relatively rare use of the maximum number of spondees to suggest the heavy task being performed. *caelo . . . terris*: ablatives of separation. The close repetition of *terras . . . terris* emphasizes the process of isolation.

23 *liquidum . . . caelum*: the "sky" that was cut off in 22 included everything above earth and water. Now, Ovid separates the light upper air (sky or aether) from the heavier, denser atmosphere (*aër*) of earth. His organization of this line, with its abBA pattern of adjectives and nouns and its final word ringing with the first word of 22, makes the whole procedure of elemental separation very clear.

24 Another line of heavy spondees. Ovid uses this pattern of four initial spondees only nine times in Book 1, but twice in the space of three lines here. *quae*: neuter accusative, referring to the four elements cited in 22-23. *acervo*: chaos.

25 *dissociata*: another word for separation, which Ovid uses only here. It contains a metaphor that makes this line paradoxical: the alienated, politically disunited elements are "bound" by the god into lasting peace. Ovid touches on the philosophic paradox that War "creates" and that clearly "antagonistic" elements are the building blocks of our wonderfully complicated world. *locis*: ablative of respect. *pace*: ablative of means.

26–31 These lines proceed from lightest to heaviest, from highest (*summa* 27) to lowest (*ultima* 31).

26–27 *ignea . . . vis*: aether, which above at 23 was called *liquidum*, receives an important new quality. Its fiery nature accounts for its ability to "flash" to the highest point and also for the light that it will supply. *convexi*: the rounded or, as we say, "vaulted" heaven. *sine pondere*: again, a substitute for the adjective "weightless" (cf. 20). *emicuit* 27: a favorite word of Ovid, used only in the *Met. summa . . . arce*: since the same phrase at 163 refers to the residence of the gods, we probably should take the metaphor here as intentional. The fiery, weightless aether rises to the "citadel" of the universe.

28 *illi*: dative with *proximus*. *levitate locoque*: ablative of respect.

29   *densior . . . tellus*: supply *erat* from 28. *his*: ablative of comparison.
30   This conception of its own gravity pressing down on the earth suppos-
      edly explained its "balanced" position, a characteristic that earlier did
      not exist under Chaos (cf. 12–13). *circumfluus*: Ovid invents the
      adjective for the occasion.
31   *possedit . . . coercuit*: an entirely different metaphor from that of the
      feminine embrace of Amphitrite (14). *orbem*: since the earth has not
      yet assumed a globular form (which will be described at 35), Ovid
      has anticipated himself; or, as Lee suggests, he is still thinking of the
      earth, as at 14, in the Homeric sense of a flat disk.
32–68 Having separated out the four elements and assigned them their appro-
      priate location, the god proceeds to shape them into entities that we
      can recognize: earth as a globe (34–35); rivers and sea (36–42);
      mountains, valleys, and climatic zones (43–51); the air's many differ-
      ent forms of weather (52–66); and the serenity of the aether above
      all this (67–68).
32–33 *ubi dispositam . . . congeriem secuit*: what the syntax makes subordi-
      nate, we should understand as coordinate, e.g., *disposuit et secuit*.
      quisquis . . . deorum 32: whereas at 21 the poet had implied the
      anonymity of the creator-god with his unqualified *deus*, now he flaunts
      his ignorance and/or indifference to the god's identity. *congeriem* 33:
      the original chaos; the noun recalls the participle *congesta* (8). *secuit
      sectamque*: Ovid likes to organize his clauses with this rhetorical
      device known as *anadiplosis*. He uses a main verb that ends at the
      central caesura, then reuses the verb, but now as a past participle,
      accusative object of the next verb. *redegit*: our oldest MS from Berne
      alone offers the reading *coegit*, which is often accepted by editors
      in deference to its age. However, "confined" or "compressed" into
      members hardly gives the desired sense. The lines just previous (26
      ff.) rather suggest considerable freedom, especially for air and aether.
      The Berne MS is far from errorless, and it seems likely that its scribe
      took the prefix *co-* from *coercuit* in 31. The reading *redegit* points to
      the deity's new purpose: it reduces this undifferentiated mass into
      usable parts, specifically "members" of a living entity. What follows
      in 34 ff. describes how these members become functional.
34   *principio*: "first"; to be followed by *tum* (36). This opening adverb
      for a series of facts or arguments was established in the dialogues of
      Cicero and the didactic poem of Lucretius (in this metrical position).
      ne non: double negative device called *litotes*. *aequalis*: the earth needs
      to be uniformly regular over its entire surface so that it can achieve
      a state of "balance" in the universe.
35   *speciem . . . in orbis*: normal word order would be, *in speciem orbis*.
      Delay of the preposition is known as *anastrophe*. We might consider
      this the first metamorphosis, and for its description Ovid uses one of

the synonyms for *forma* in *speciem. glomeravit*: normally, this verb refers to the ordinary formation of a ball, e.g., of yarn, snow, dust. Ovid seems to be the first to extend the usage to our planet, treating the action of the deity with an everyday nuance.

36   *freta diffudit*: the water that ringed the earth before it became globular is now distributed to the appropriate areas we know as seas. *rapidis*: "sweeping."

37   The seas turn the parts of the earth that they touch or "surround" into shores. *terrae*: dative with compound verb.

38–39 After listing three typical bodies of water, Ovid launches into a poetic description of rivers in their course. Bömer usefully notes that the poet reverses the adjectives: we usually hear of sloping banks and winding rivers. Line 39, arranged with noun A, adjective b, verb, adjective a, noun B, shows one of the several artful patterns of Neoteric and Augustan verse.

40   *diversa locis*: "separate in places" = "in various places." *locis*: ablative of respect. *ipsa*: the earth; ablative of agent. Some rivers never make it to the ocean, but appear to be swallowed underground.

41   *campo*: Latin writers had already used this noun metaphorically for the level expanse of the sea. But they regularly gave it a defining attribute: e.g., "fields of salt" or "fields that swim or flow." Ovid implies the metaphor by the genitive phrase of 42. (Cf. *campos* 43.)

45–46 A simile offers the five zones of the heavens as analogue for the five zones that mark out the principal climatic divisions of earth. *duae . . . zonae*: long separation of adjective and noun (known as *hyperbaton*) shapes the entire clause. *dextra . . . sinistra*: ablative of place where. Ovid speaks of directions in the sky like a layman, as if he were merely saying "on either side." *ardentior*: the fifth and central zone will correspond closely to the central (Equatorial) zone on the earth (cf. 49).

47   *onus inclusum*: the Earth, a weighty burden, is closed in by the sky just mentioned.

48   *cura dei*: Ovid attributes "concern" to the indefinite creator-god, but he does not attempt to define a purpose, and the zones do not achieve much more than some kind of symmetry. *plagae . . . premuntur*: the zones are impressed on the earth, just as the heavenly zones cut (46) into the sky.

49–51 The five earthly zones are: the central one running around the equator, what we would call the tropical region, hot and supposedly uninhabitable (49); the two frigid zones at either extreme, what we call the Arctic and Antarctic regions, also hard or impossible to live in (50); and finally the two temperate zones between (50–51), where fortunate humanity resides. *inter utrumque* 50: the reading of most MSS, *utramque*, cannot be right. That term would apply to each of two cold zones only. Since Ovid describes three zones and then fixes on the two regions in between, the simple change to *utrumque*, indicated in the Berne MS and then found also in two MSS of Leiden, restores Ovid's sense. *locavit*: subject is *deus. mixta . . . flamma* 51: ablative absolute.

52–53 The third element, air, is lighter than earth and water and separates them from still lighter aether. *Quanto . . . tanto*: ablative of degree of difference, in a common correlative sentence. *pondere . . . igni*: ablative of comparison.

54–56 *illic . . . illic*: anaphora (repetition of an initial word in successive phrases or clauses). The second adverb follows the caesura, thus articulating the line; and it receives different metrical stress from the first. *consistere*: the activity of the deity allows the poet to get away from the rather prosaic pose of scientific language. Mist and clouds do not, of course, "stand still" in the sky, but they may be said to "make their residence" there. *iussit* 55: same verb for the god's work as in 37 and 43. *motura*: "destined to stir up"; the future participle often implies purpose, which raises the possibility that this deity created and located thunder deliberately to frighten humanity. Winds cause two types of lightning when they drive clouds against each other; cf. the account of Lucretius in 6.160 ff. *fulminibus* 56: forked lightning that strikes in damaging bolts. *fulgora*: flashes, often harmless.

57 *his*: the winds. Dative serves as both indirect object and dative of agent with *habendum. vix . . . obsistitur illis*: impersonal structure; verb of hindering on which subjunctive with *quin* (60) depends.

59 *regant*: subjunctive in *cum*-concessive clause. *tractu*: ablative of place.

60 *tanta . . . fratrum*: Ovid likes to produce a terse *sententia* in the second hemistich (cf. 3.270, 9.630, 10.445). Here, he personifies the winds. Bömer notes that this is the first surviving reference in Latin literature to winds as brothers. Vergil's famous storm-scene in *Aen.* 1.50 ff. would no doubt be in the mind of Ovid and his audience.

61–66 Ovid arranges his description of the four cardinal winds with fine poetic art. The winds get Greek names (except for Auster, which replaces Notus to fit the meter in the significant final position). East and west winds, as Bömer notes, have their opposition emphasized by being placed at the outer extremes of their connected clauses. Boreas, like Eurus, is in the nominative, while Auster, like Zephyrus, takes an oblique case at the end of its clause. *Nabataea*: in what we today call Saudi Arabia. The area was important for Augustan foreign policy. *iuga* 62: Lee thinks of the Himalayas, but Ovid is vague. *matutinis*: double spondee adds to the poetic display and brings the clause to a showy ending after four dactyls. *vesper* 63: the west.

occiduo . . . sole 63: ablative of means. *tepescunt*: the setting sun, of course, gives off only mild heat. *Scythiam* 64: the frozen north. *horrifer* 65: poetic term for something cold that causes shivers. *contraria*: the southern region, Africa. Southerly winds coming across the Mediterranean regularly bring fog and moisture from North Africa. *pluviaque* 66: an elegant emendation for *pluvioque* of the MSS tradition; it changes adjective to noun and makes the structure of the two ablative nouns identical (Means), the syntax of *Austro* separate. That seems neater than assigning two quite different noun-adjective structures to the verb. Both 66 and 67 have the maximum number of dactyls.

67–68 Ovid ends with aether, highest and lightest of the four elements. *liquidum*: cf. 23. *gravitate carentem*: cf. 26. The dactylic lightness of the verse helps to reinforce the sense. *faecis* 68: partitive genitive. *habentem*: the rhyme with the final word of 67 enhances the conclusion of this section.

69 ff Now, Ovid introduces the inhabitants of the four areas, working downward from aether to earth and finally concentrating on human beings.

69   *limitibus*: a technical word for boundaries of property. *dissaepserat*: the subject is the same god, continuing from 67 and earlier. The verb appears in Lucretius; it is another technical word in land measurement, referring to fencing or a barrier that defines an area. This is the first pluperfect tense in the *Met.*

70   *fuerant caligine caeca*: this reading, which is offered in its entirety by the Berne MS alone, is partly supported by *N*; it continues the pluperfect and emphasizes the prior darkness that, in 71, will be dispelled by the gleaming stars. The other MSS agree on *massa latuere sub illa / ipsa*: this would mean that the stars lurked hidden beneath Chaos. Since Chaos has ended back in 21; since perfect with *pressa* does not seem as successful as *pressa fuerant*; and finally since the demonstratives *illa* or *ipsa* make a weak ending, editors tend to reject this reading. Perhaps some damage to the archetype in this hemistich encouraged conjecture.

71   *effervescere*: used only here by Ovid, and not normally a poetic word. It served in Republican prose, especially in Cicero, to describe literal "boiling up" and the figurative "boiling up" of anger. Ovid achieves a unique meaning: "blazed out."

72   *neu*: equivalent to *et ne*, introducing a negative purpose clause. Presumably the implied "purpose" is that of the unknown god.

73   Ovid does not account for the gods or spend any effort defining their higher nature, physical or ethical: he has merely located them in *caelum*.

74   *habitandae piscibus*: same construction as in 57.

75   *agitabilis*: Ovid's felicitous invention. This is the word's only appearance in Classical Latin.

76 ff   Whereas Ovid had casually introduced the gods as mere living beings, without defined qualities, he brings human beings on stage as superior entities, more holy and rational than other beings, and destined to rule them. That leaves the relationship between human and divine beings ambiguous, and ambiguous it remains throughout the poem.

76   *mentis . . . altae*: genitive with *capacius*.

77   *deerat*: read as two syllables, the accented long first *e* causing the second *e* to be combined with it in synizesis. *quod . . . posset*: relative clause of purpose.

78   *natus homo est*: the abruptness of this short trihemimeral unit in strong asyndeton with 77, raises some questions about tone and implication. Is it especially solemn, or does it have a flippant nuance? The long pseudo-philosophic development that follows to the end of 86 offers the reader a choice of explanations: a line and a half starkly proposing that perhaps the same divine creator made men; seven lines offering instead, in vivid detail, the mythical account of Prometheus the creator. It is impossible not to feel that the second and longer account is to be preferred, especially since 87–88 seem to endorse it. *semine*: ablative of source or material, a primarily poetic construction without the preposition.

79   *opifex*: the divine creator is viewed merely as a "workman". Cf. *fabricator* 57. *mundi melioris*: cf 21.

81   *cognati . . . caeli*: through the original mixture of Chaos, the sky is "related" to the earth.

82   *quam*: i.e., *tellus*. *satus Iapeto*: "epic" way of referring to Prometheus by his father that assumes the audience's mythological knowledge. Such circumlocution for a familiar name is known as *antonomasia*. Of course, Ovid has told us nothing of the Titans from which Iapetus and Prometheus arose, nor has he named any gods.

83   *effigiem*: whereas in the first account we are created from a divine seed, here we are only made to look like gods. *moderantum cuncta*: resembling the gods in form, if not in substance, we also imitate their role, ruling the earth and creatures, as implied in 77.

84   *pronaque*: key word in initial position. *cum spectent*: subjunctive in concessive clause; translate "whereas" or "while they look to earth."

85–86 *os . . . sublime*: although Prometheus is not assigned a purpose, the symbolism of our erect position, in contrast to that of animals, is amply suggested by the following clauses. We are meant to look up, away from the beasts, toward the sky and the gods.

87–88 The vocabulary includes some of the common language used to describe metamorphosis: *imagine, induit, conversa, figuras*.

THE SUCCESSION OF AGES (89–150)

Hesiod in his *Works and Days* wrote an influential presentation of the *generations* of humanity: gold, silver, bronze, heroic, and iron. Later poets, especially Aratus in the third century, developed and modified this myth; and Vergil treated it in all three of his works. Essentially, it embraces the idea that people degenerated from the ideal race that was created to enjoy a perfect world. The Romans took the myth over but talked of *ages*. Ovid records the decline of the ages of gold, silver, bronze, and iron. At that point, Jupiter will consider mortals so hopeless that he determines to destroy them and start over. After the Flood, then, a final new age, continuous with our own, ensues.

The Golden Age (89–112)

This fortunate age is characterized by miraculous qualities that can best be expressed, as with Chaos, by negating ordinary experiences, a process that starts with the final word of 89. It was a time of no government, no law and order, no commerce, no fortifications, and no war; life was entirely secure. Human beings did not work for a living, since the natural world was spontaneously bountiful and supplied all necessities. Bömer points out that this twenty-four-line sequence divides precisely in the middle (after 100), and that each part is rounded off by a Golden Line.

89 *aurea . . . aetas*: the key clause of the passage starts with the thematic adjective. *sata est*: this verb is unusual with *aetas*: it implies the natural abundance characteristic of the age but does not specify the sower. *vindice nullo*: ablative of attendant circumstance.

90 *fidem*: refers to social relationships. Human spontaneity never erupted into irresponsibility, so individual freedoms needed no protection from law.

91–93 Ovid elaborates on the happy absence of law. *verba minantia*: the words would threaten punishment. *fixo / aere*: laws, once they had been established, were posted in public places on tablets of bronze (as here) or stone. Numerous such inscriptions survive as precious documents of ancient Greece and Rome. *legebantur*: a likely correction, in *FW*, for the reading of the MSS, *ligabantur*. The words were "read" on the bronze, not "tied" on them nor "bound by" bronze (as in Madness in *Aen*. 1.295). In the next two clauses of 92–93, Ovid refers to two frequent problems that occur when the legal system is corrupted and politicized: the judge becomes an object of fear, and people often need a "defender" and "avenger" against the established manipulators of laws. In such cases, revolution occurs, as it did in first-century Rome, where *vindex* was a standard role claimed in propaganda by dynasts like Caesar and Octavian.

94–95 Ovid varies a familiar theme concerning the damnable origin of sailing: wood was felled and brought down from mountains, unnaturally it is implied, to make ships that then would cross the natural barrier of the sea to visit a foreign land. All this was a mark of people's dissatisfaction with their immediate bounty as they pursued exotic, distant luxuries. *caesa . . . pinus*: ships were so regularly constructed of pine, that the timber constituted a common metonymy for the ship, as in Catullus 64.1. *suis . . . montibus*: the reflexive contrasts with the juxtaposed *peregrinum*.

97–
100 A series of variations on freedom from war and threats of war. As is true today, so in Ovid's time war was an ever-present menace. *praecipites*: cities with steep ditches in front of their walls were a familiar sight in Italy. Ovid fixes our attention on the apparatus of war, not on the bloody effects of human conflict. Amazing as it may seem, there was no such thing as a soldier in the Golden Age. In 100, the description comes to a stately, poetic close with a Golden Line: abVAB. *mollia* 100: often used contemptuously of soft conditions. Here, however, the word emphasizes favorably the unmilitaristic serenity of that first age.

101–
2 *inmunis*: a common technical sense of this word with land was "untaxed"; a common poetic sense was "idle and useless." The paradox here is that the earth, in that make-believe time before taxes and agriculture dominated, gave of itself spontaneously. Cf. Lucretius 5.933 ff. *rastro intacta*: "untouched by plow," but also, in the familiar metaphor, "virginal" in respect to the plow.

103 *nullo cogente*: ablative with *creatis*: "created without anyone's effort." Note the alliteration.

104 The berry of the arbutus (or wild strawberry) and the strawberries in the mountains were regularly instanced as the simple, natural food of early mankind. In Ovid's day, the arbutus was considered almost inedible.

105 Cornel and blackberries were also there for the picking, but would hardly strike Ovid's audience as desirable food. The cornel is almost all inedible pit, and the brambles that surround blackberries reduce their appeal.

106 To end the list of free berries and fruit—human beings were evidently vegetarians at that time—Ovid uses his familiar structure of relative clause + "antecedent." *patula Iovis arbore*: "spreading oak," typically associated with Jupiter's shrine at Dodona. *glandes*: what might seem a climax, because of the connection with Jupiter, is probably an

anticlimax. Acorns, the traditional food of primeval mortals, were fed in Ovid's day to pigs and cattle.

108   Lee notes that this and the next four hexameters are all end-stopped and reinforce "the impression of peace and composure." *mulcebant*: this verb tends to personify the breezes.

109   In a later phase (*mox etiam*), the earth began producing crops, a distinct improvement over the wild berries and nuts with which human beings first had to be content. But the key word here, *inarata*, shows that there was no real "farming." This word was made formulaic by descriptions such as Horace, *Epod.* 16.43 and Vergil, *G.* 1.83.

111   *flumina iam . . . iam flumina*: chiastic form of repetition. Milk and honey (112) often appear in descriptions of marvelous worlds, but nectar, which is rather associated with the food of the gods, has been introduced by Ovid to emphasize his Golden Age.

112   A variant on the Golden Line (abVAB + preposition) serenely ends this account of the Golden Age. Ovid emphasizes in the yellow and green the symbolic colors of the age: gold by definition, green in its eternal Spring.

The Silver and Later Ages (113–150)

In Hesiod's account, the Generation of Silver was itself decadent, and the changes in its living conditions were seen as deserved punishment. Moreover, the arrival of the new age was due to a violent upheaval among the gods. Cronos or Saturn presided over the Golden Age; for that reason, the period is often called the Age of Saturn. Though kind to human beings, Saturn was cruel to his own children, because he knew that one of them was destined to replace him, and so his youngest son, Jupiter, in self-defense overthrew him and dispatched him to Tartarus. Ovid quickly passes over the moral decline implicit in a Silver generation. Jupiter introduced changes, four seasons instead of eternal Spring, the necessity of homes to protect men against the elements, and agriculture; but Ovid assigns no motive for the changes. They just happened.

114   *sub Iove*: under the dominion of Jupiter, instead of Saturn. *subiit*: final syllable is long at the caesura.

115   *auro deterior*: apart from *deterior*, morality is ignored by Ovid.

116   *contraxit*: "drew in, shortened." Spring becomes merely one of four seasons.

117   *inaequalis autumnos*: the unevenness of the fall season, i.e., its erratic weather, shows itself in the unusual meter. Ovid uses a double spondee at the end, but, by apportioning it to the final stressed syllable of the

adjective and the three syllables of the noun, roughens the rhythm. Since we expect accent and stress to coincide in the fifth and sixth feet, the "disagreement" emphasizes *inaequalis*.

118   *spatiis*: these "spaces" or "periods" are the seasons.

119–   With the seasons come extremes of heat and cold, unknown when
20   there was only balmy spring. *canduit* 120: glowed with the heat.

121   *tum primum*: anaphora with 119 suggests cause and effect; some kind of shelter now became necessary because of the difficult temperatures. *domos: domus:* Ovid likes to juxtapose two (usually different) forms of the same noun or verb at a caesura, each in different clauses and receiving different metrical stress. Here, he also avails himself of the double declension of *domus*, which regularly uses second declension endings in the accusative plural, but fourth declension forms in the nominative through accusative singular.

122   *vinctae cortice virgae*: the only instance of "construction" in the three house-types mentioned. It suggests a type of thatching, for walls as well as roof, using branches and bark.

123–   *semina . . . Cerealia*: since Ovid has not yet introduced Ceres or any
24   other deity to teach men agriculture, the adjective, while referring to the grain normally associated with Ceres, paradoxically calls attention to her absence at this juncture. *obruta* 124: "buried" in the process of sowing. *gemuere*: "groaning" of oxen under the yoke's weight symbolizes the increasing painfulness of existence.

125–   The Bronze Race follows the Silver, and Ovid spends little time on
27   it, although Hesiod had described it in much detail. In fact, Hesiod had connected with it the Heroic Age, when great deeds of war and adventure took place. For Ovid, this race was not corrupt, but it had become more savage and more inclined to war.

127–   Ovid finishes up with the Bronze Age at the central caesura, exempting
50   this generation of any blame for *scelus*. Then, in abrupt asyndeton, he introduces what he calls the "final" age of Iron. It is suffused with evil, on which he elaborates at length.

128–   *venae peioris*: refers to both the cheaper value of iron and the degener-
29   ate quality of the age. Lee proposed the witty translation, "of baser mettle." The genitive depends on *aevum*.

130–   *amor sceleratus habendi* 131: the adjective is now thematic (vs. 127).
31   The gerund is an objective genitive.

132–   *vela dabat*: standard phrase, much used by Ovid, for "spreading sail",
34   used independently or, as here, with a dative of the winds. Cf. 15.176–77, the metaphor of the poet's opening up his sail. *noverat*: refers back to *norant* 96 and forward to *ignotis* 134. *navita* 133: Ovid and other poets use the archaic, obsolete form from which *nauta* is derived by syncopation. The heavy syllables and long words result in a rare four-word hexameter in 134.

135–36   Agriculture had already begun in the Silver Age (cf. 123–24). Now, however, human greed causes disputes over ownership and necessitates property lines. *communem*: the idea that earth and water, sun and air are common possessions of all human beings is traditional. *ceu*: a poetic particle that Ovid uses almost exclusively in the *Met*. Here, it simply means "like" and takes the same accusative construction as *humum*. *cautus . . . mensor* 136: the noun, which is technical and rarely found in poetry, emphasizes the sense of violation of freedom that Ovid seeks to express.

137–38   Greed extends into mining. *segetes alimentaque*: accusatives with *poscebatur*. When a verb in the active takes a double accusative, one of the accusatives may be retained if the verb becomes passive and takes the other as nominative subject (e.g., *humus*). *dives*: common poetic epithet for the bountiful earth, but here used to prepare for the greed that forces people to attack and "disembowel" their benefactress.

139–40   *inritamenta* 140: this word, which seems otherwise reserved for prose, occurs only here in Ovid, partly to contrast with the "poetic" effects of 139 (personification of earth and the use of *Stygiis*) and to emphasize the "vulgarization" of humanity's environment. For other passages of the *Met*. Ovid invented the variant *inritamen*.

142   *prodierat: prodit:* nice use of juxtaposed forms of the same verb, but in different senses which are set off by each other. The metals literally do come forth out of the earth, but the same verb tends to personify War both as a force that results from the value on and greed for gold and as a monster that stalks the earth.

143   *manu*: vivid personification enhanced by alliteration of *c*'s.

144   *vivitur ex rapto*: men live off plunder. Such a life constitutes a decline from the peaceful Golden Age and is part of the sinful commitment to violence and greed that fits this corrupt Iron Age. Ovid may be alluding to and correcting the implications of two passages in Vergil, *Aen.* 7.749 and 9.613, where *vivere rapto* seems to be a simple, manly, Italian virtue. *hospes . . . tutus*: whereas everybody was secure (100) in the Golden Age, now not even the host-guest relationship is respected. In myth, hosts could be treacherous toward guests (as we shall soon see in the story of Lycaon, 209 ff.) and vice versa (as for instance when Paris seduced the wife of Menelaus, his host).

145   The troubled connection of *gener* and *socer*, which seems general, had a specific reference in Rome once Julius Caesar used his own daughter to solidify an alliance with Pompey by marriage. Allusions to the two as in-laws start in their own day with Catullus 29.24, then appear prominently in *Aen*. 6.826–31. An even worse stage of *impietas* is the mutual hatred of brothers. That is one of the most typical symbols of the Civil War in Rome (cf. Catullus 64.399 and Lucan).

146   Ovid extends his description to other key family relationships. *inminet*:

originally of inanimate things that projected or leaned toward another thing, the verb eventually included human beings whose "leaning" could be metaphorical and thus signify an eager desire for the thing. *exitio*: dative with compound verb. There were many myths about murderous wives (e.g., Clytemnestra, Eriphyle) but fewer about husbands. However, a good example of each instance is offered by Roman legend: Tarquin murdered his wife and Tullia her husband so that the two, properly in-laws, could be free to marry.

147 This Golden Line (abVAB) contains more examples of an age that is anything but orderly. *lurida*: refers not to the color of the poison aconite, but rather to the yellowish complexion of its victims. *terribiles . . . novercae*: stepmothers were proverbially vicious in Greco-Roman, as in modern, stories.

148 *ante diem*: beforehand, specifically before the day of his natural death. *inquirit in annos*: the greedy son consults astrologers with hostile feelings *against* his father's age.

149– *victa iacet pietas*: the details of 144 ff. have offered examples of
50 *impietas*, the breakdown of family bonds, which might be expected to be the final barrier against general degradation. Now, Ovid epitomizes this state in a picture of crushing "defeat," where *pietas* lies trampled, dying or already dead. *Virgo . . . Astraea*: in Hesiod's account, the last deities to abandon the corrupt human world were Aidos and Nemesis. Aratus later simplified these two into the single goddess of Justice, whom he called the daughter of Astraeus; when she departed, the world was hopelessly unjust and evil. Vergil, in *Ecl.* 4.6, writing of the return of the Golden Age, simply refers to her as *Virgo*; in *G.* 2.473–74, talking of her departure, he calls her *ultima . . . Iustitia*. Ovid, the first Latin writer to use the word *Astraea*, here seems to combine Vergil and Aratus.

War of the Giants: Another Race of Human Beings (151–62)

Ovid has not mentioned the Giants up to this point. Now, he introduces a story of an assault on heaven itself by these monstrous creatures, who are said to be children of Earth; and he attributes the tale to unspecified sources (cf. *ferunt* 152, 158). The sources that we know, namely, Hesiod and Homer, offer parts of Ovid's account, but the combination is either Ovid's own work or that of some now unknown Hellenistic writer. The defeat and destruction of the Giants follow at the hands of Jupiter. This war, the Gigantomachy, in Ovid's own lifetime, was said to parallel the ravages of the Civil War, and Jupiter's triumph to anticipate the victory and peaceful rule of Augustus in a new Golden Age. Augustan poets tend to view the Gigantomachy as a theme to be avoided: it is too gauche for their sophisticated tastes.

Ovid himself pretends in *Am.* 2.11–20 to have embarked upon such a grand epic poem, but to have faltered when his girlfriend shut her door in his face.

151   *neve*: casual connective (= *et ne*), which emphasizes the swift continuity of Ovid's narrative. *Aether* is home of the gods (cf. 73).

152   *adfectasse . . . regnum*: syncopated form of the perfect infinitive (cf. 2). The phrase describes the usurper's and revolutionary's aspiration to illegal power. Julius Caesar was accused by his enemies of seeking to be king.

153   *congestos struxisse . . . montes*: they brought together and piled up mountains. Ovid picks up a story whose earliest version is found in Homer (*Od.* 11.305–20), who called the attackers not Giants, but sons of Aloeus, Otus and Ephialtes.

154   *tum pater omnipotens*: same phrase in same position in *Aen.* 10.100 where Jupiter quiets the uproar of the gods. Elsewhere, Ovid prefers the particle *at* with the noun and epithet (cf. 2.304, 401). *perfregit Olympum*: according to Homer, Otus and Ephialtes piled Ossa on Olympus and Pelion on Ossa; so Jupiter dislodged the structure by striking the bottom-most mountain.

155   *subiectae . . . Ossae*: dative of separation. Ossa was under Pelion, which Jupiter knocked off.

157–   *natorum*: Ovid casually tells us that the Giants were children of the
58   Earth. According to Hesiod, when Uranus was emasculated, Earth caught the blood from the wound and generated numerous offspring, including the Giants. *calidum . . . cruorem* 158: keeping our attention on the blood, Ovid prepares us for the allegorical meaning of the metamorphosis (cf. 161–62).

159   For the double negative or litotes, cf. 34. *monimenta manerent*: human beings, in their diminutive size, are a paltry "monument" for the huge Giants, but they equal them in their bloodthirsty character.

160   Ovid exploited a doublet of the myth of human origins; one or the other was supposed to stand alone, either that we were created by an act of benevolence and then declined from that ideal state (e.g., 76–150) or that an angry earth generated us to be naturally bloody (151 ff.). *et illa*: for Lee, Ovid implies that these men are "like the men of the Iron Age"; but it is preferable to regard these human beings as resembling Earth's previous offspring, the Giants.

161   *contemptrix superum*: Ovid has fashioned a striking phrase, which he will reuse in its masculine form in 3.514 of Pentheus. It varies Vergil's famous characterization of Mezentius in *Aen.* 7.648 as *contemptor divum* (same metrical position). He implicitly prepares here for the tale of Lycaon (209 ff.), who tries to kill a god, lusts for murder, and is violent to his core.

162   *scires e sanguine natos*: another kind of terminal *sententia* (cf. 60). Ovid

invites us, as it were, to cross the distance that separates us from the mythical account, to recognize ourselves in these human beings.

Council of the Gods over Lycaon and Human Viciousness (163–252)

In traditional epics, such as Homer's *Odyssey* and Ennius' *Annales*, the opening human situation is taken under consideration by a Council of the Gods. In the *Iliad* and *Aeneid*, only Zeus/Jupiter and one or two other gods express their concern. Ovid has now come to a point in his partly epic poem at which he can introduce a piece of epic machinery and exploit it for his own purposes. Whereas the traditional Councils help the hero and his people or family, here Jupiter irrationally concludes from the violence of Lycaon that all human beings must be exterminated; so the Council is called to ratify that elimination. Then, Ovid avails himself of a tactic from epic parodies (such as Satire 1 of Lucilius and the later *Apocolocyntosis* of Seneca) that describes the Council as a rowdy meeting of the Roman Senate. It becomes clear that Jupiter plays the role of Augustus and that the gods are the obsequious senators for whom, a century later, Tacitus expressed such contempt. This poetic Council and its mythical subject suddenly have contemporary repercussions, which generates a mixture of tone that is provocatively elusive. We cannot read the Council as just another epic device, therefore serious and even majestic like those in Homer and Vergil; but we cannot read it either as simply humor or parody, because the destruction of mankind is not a patently comic matter.

163   *Quae*: all the degradation just described. *pater . . . Saturnius*: the phrase occurs in different order in *Aen* 4.372 and may go back to Ennius. It also reminds us ironically of Jupiter's unfilial treatment of his father. *summa . . . arce*: same phrase in 27, but now used to evoke a specifically Roman setting, the Palatine Hill.

164–   *facto . . . recenti*: ablative of cause. The event was too recent to have
65   received adequate publicity.

166   *ingentes animo et dignas Iove*: Ovid inspects the wrath: is it huge and worthy, or do these two adjectives clash? *animo*: ablative of place without preposition, a poetic usage. *Iove*: ablative with *dignas*.

167   *conciliumque vocat*: exact repetition of Vergil, *Aen*. 10.2, which invites us to compare throughout the scene the egotistical and domineering Jupiter of Ovid with the impersonal and judicious Jupiter of the *Aeneid*. *mora nulla*: the run of dactyls emphasizes the speed with which the obedient underlings hurry to the Council.

168   *est via*: Ovid embarks on an ecphrasis, a description in epic style. A

paradigmatic example of such a description is that of the landfall in Africa where Aeneas' battered fleet limped to anchor (*Aen.* 1.159 ff.). Such descriptions start regularly with *est* + noun as above (cf. Vergil's *est . . . locus*). After sufficient detail, the poet uses a demonstrative to bring the description to a close and resume his narrative. In *Aen.* 1.167, we find *hic*, followed two lines later by *huc*; Ovid uses in 170 *hac*, but the ecphrasis continues with more detail until 175, *hic locus*.

169   *lactea: nomen habet* functions like *nominatur*, making *lactea* predicate nominative. *notabilis*: rare before Ovid and solely in prose, this word occurs in Ovid only here and in no other Augustan poet.

170   *superis*: dative of reference. *magni . . . Tonantis*: same phrase in 2.466. Since Augustus vowed and then in 22 dedicated a temple to Jupiter Tonans, this epithet became popular. Ovid is the first to bring it into poetry.

171   *regalemque domum*: Augustus lived quite simply and, unlike his imperial successors, did not have a palace.

172   *atria*: Ovid plunges the sublime gods down into Rome, and with *nobilium* he humanizes the deities as Roman aristocrats living on the expensive Palatine Hill. *valvis*: folding doors, appropriate for stately homes (cf. 2.4, the palace of the Sun).

173   *plebs*: if some gods are like Roman aristocrats, others must resemble the *plebs*, living elsewhere in more affordable locations (such as the Subura, Campus Martinus, or areas farther from the city center). *diversa locis*: as in 40, modifies the subject.

174   *clari*: standard adjective for the Roman aristocracy. *posuere penates*: again, Ovid mixes the theoretically separable spheres, by taking an expression that fits normal human behavior—Roman homes all revere their household gods—and applying it to gods—who obviously do not worship other gods. In 5.496, the spring-deity Arethusa also has her own Penates.

175–   *audacia*: Ovid affects to apologize for his bold analogy, but in fact
76   he calls attention to it. *dixisse* 176: perfect infinitive; it looks back from the future less vivid of *timeam*. *Palatia*: since Ovid has been talking about the quarter where Jupiter and the "aristocratic" gods reside, it seems likely that here his "boldness" consists in making the analogy precise: the gods live on a special height like the Palatine Hill in Rome. Other scholars believe that Ovid now returns to his concern with the home of Jupiter (cf. *tecta Tonantis* 170), and they argue that this is the first use of the word to mean "palace." However, the three other times that the poet employs this noun, in *Ars Am.* 3.389 and in the later works from exile, he always refers to the Palatine Hill.

177   *marmoreo . . . recessu*: the Council meets in an inner room which, as is appropriate to Roman decoration in Augustan times, is splendidly veneered in marble.

178   *ipse*: Jupiter sits on a raised chair, like a presiding consul at senate sessions. *sceptro . . . eburno*: the sceptre is a standard symbol of royal power, used on official occasions such as this. For ivory, cf. King Aeetes of *Met*. 7.103.

179–   *terrificam . . . caesariem*: Ovid alludes to the traditional picture of
80   Zeus developed by Homer in *Iliad* 1.528–30. The god nodded his head; his hair swept back magnificently; and the earth trembled. Focusing on something "frightening," which turns out after the suspense caused by enjambement to be only the hair (instead of the majestic nod), Ovid spoils the majesty of the scene.

181   *ora indignantia solvit*: an indignant Jupiter runs counter to the self-controlled, calm, or even smiling god of Vergil and Horace. For Ovid Jupiter regularly lacks self-control; and *a fortiori* the other gods let their emotions dominate them.

183–   *tempestate*: archaic-poetic use of the noun in the sense of "time."
84   *centum* with *bracchia* 184. Ovid conflates the war of the Giants (cf. 152 ff.) with that of the Titans and their monstrous allies. Horace in *C*. 2.17.14 calls one of them, Gyges, *centimanus. anguipedum* 184: Ovid's invention for effect; only appears here.

187–   *perdendum* 188: sudden surprise in initial position of line. The neces-
88   sity in the participle is self-evident only to Jupiter.

189   *Stygio . . . luco*: traditionally, the Styx, a river or cold swamp, lacked anything so attractive as a grove. But Vergil in *Aen*. 6.154 had vaguely mentioned "groves of Styx." The solemn oath by the Styx, which bars even the gods from lying, can enforce an assertion about the past (*Il*. 15.37) or about the future. In this passage, it depends on the punctuation adopted by the editor, comma or period after *luco*, and on the text of 190, which time and which verb is defined by the oath.

190   *temptata*: adopting this reading, found in the not especially reliable Berne MS, we assume a comma at the end of 189, so that, supplying *esse* here, we assign to Ovid an indirect statement depending on *iuro* 188. The reading favored by most other MSS is *temptanda*. That would presuppose a period at the end of 189 and require supplying *sunt* to produce a passive periphrastic; and it would make the oath of 188–89 refer back to the assertion by Jupiter at the start of 188 that humanity must be destroyed. The clarification with *temptanda* would fall back on a medical commonplace, namely, that doctors should try every remedy short of surgery, but as a last resort surgery, removal of an incurable growth, say, is the only way to save the patient. There are similar difficulties with either form of *temptare*: on the one hand,

Ovid has given us no indication that Jupiter has been at all worried about human degeneracy or made any efforts to "cure" it; on the other, Ovid will not show any efforts by Jupiter in succeeding episodes that contribute to healing: he has made up his mind on destruction.

190–
91
inmedicabile: an epic compound, apparently coined by Vergil for *Aen.* 12.858 to describe a poisoned arrow, then borrowed by Ovid three times and applied to a clearly medical context (cf. 2.825 of spreading cancer). Reading *temptata*, we enter the medical image only with this striking word. *corpus*: not the entire human body, but a growth or possibly a limb. *ense* 191: this should mean surgical knife. Its customary meaning of "sword" may have stimulated the false reading *vulnus* for *corpus*. *pars sincera*: the adjective can be applied to medical situations as here (cf. also 12.100 for meaning "unwounded"). *trahatur*: "infected"; rare usage to keep up the image.

192–
93
semidei: apparently Ovid's invention, modeled on the Greek "hemitheos." The neologism is meant to attract attention, and the expansion of Jupiter's argument around these demigods becomes a critical problem. What is Ovid's tone; how should his reader respond? *Faunique* 193: the *-que* counts as a long syllable. In imitation of a Homeric pattern, when Roman epic poets used a pair of nouns with double *-que*, and the first *-que* fell at the thesis (first syllable) of the second foot, they could treat it as long regardless. *monticolae Silvani*: a particularly striking "poetic" phrase to conclude Jupiter's list of preferences. The adjective, a unique epic compound invented by Ovid, together with *Silvani*, forms an unusual type of the already unorthodox double spondee, polysyllable + tri-syllable, which forces a prominent stress on the final syllable of this showy first word.

194–
95
Ovid assigns to Jupiter a neat rhetorical organization that echoes Roman politics. *dignamur honore*: this picture of discrimination among the gods tends to reduce them to the human level. *certe*: to be taken with *habitare*. Nobility obliges the gods, since they have imposed separate residences on the demigods, at least to give them security (cf. *tutos* 196). *sinamus* 195: hortatory subjunctive.

196–
98
Jupiter comes to the point. He is generalizing from his own experience on earth. If a man has tried to kill him, the supreme deity, then how will mere demigods be safe from human beings? The gods let themselves be overwhelmed by Jupiter's rhetoric, but that does not mean that Ovid's audience is to agree tamely. *illos / cum mihi*: the close positioning of the pronouns helps emphasize the rhetorical antithesis. Then, the speaker delays the villain's name until the end of 198. *habeoque regoque*: both verbs should be construed in zeugma (cf. my introduction) with both objects, though each is more appropriate for one of them. The zeugma suggests the god's pompous self-assurance.

notus feritate 198: the principal characteristic of the man has now been thematically stated: "wild" like an animal, he will aptly be changed into an animal in punishment.

199   *confremuere omnes*: Ovid has invented the verb for this passage and never uses it again; it defines the total uproar of rage that greets Jupiter's revelation of the plot against him. Some readers might detect an oblique allusion to *Aen.* 2.1 *conticuere omnes*, which has an identical metrical shape. The sympathetic silence that Aeneas can command by his heroic presence puts the violent uproar, caused by the angry rhetoric of Jupiter, in a negative light. *ausum*: accusative object of *deposcunt* 200, itself having *talia* 200 as object.

200   *deposcunt*: technical word of law and politics for demanding that someone be punished. Ovid uses this word only here in the *Met.* (and once more in a late poem), and it continues the process of "depoeticizing" the god and his listeners. Then, to make the effect obvious, the poet moves into an anachronistic simile that compares Jupiter/Lycaon and Augustus/impious plotter.

201   *sanguine Caesareo*: the adjective refers to Augustus as the heir of Julius Caesar, *divi Caesaris filius* as he styled himself. Some interpreters wrongly see an allusion to the actual assassination of Caesar; but the point of the simile is that there was an *attempted* assassination, as there was in the failed attempt against Jupiter, and both plotters were savagely punished after their detection. *exstinguere*: unusual syntax, infinitive of purpose with *saevit*. Both Cicero and Livy use this verb with the same object as Ovid.

203   Ovid patently exaggerates the world's response to the plot against Augustus, but the exaggeration is consistent with Augustan propaganda.

204   *tibi . . . /Auguste*: this apostrophe, which affects to be admiring and worshipful, establishes the equation for the entire Council of the Gods, which meets on the Palatine where Augustus, too, resides.

205   *illa*: the gods have reacted to the reported impiety of Lycaon in 199–200 just as the Roman world did to the "impious hand" raised against Augustus. *voce manuque*: words and gestures appropriate to bring the noisy assembly to order.

206   In the *Aeneid*, for example in the Council of the Gods in 10.100 ff., when Jupiter speaks, there is silence during and after his words, which are full of authority and impartiality. But Ovid's Jupiter has first roused his own passions and those of his audience, and now his gesture for silence lacks grandeur. He seems to combine the discordant qualities of Vergil's savage Juno and the imperious qualities of his Jupiter.

207   The line repeats what Ovid has just said in new words. The fullness of description here has been criticized as otiose by some readers, who have proposed to "improve" it by cutting out 204–6. But repetition

by variation is a favorite device of the poet, and it serves to clarify the details and our response. *pressus gravitate*: the participle picks up *conpressit* 206, but now functions in a potentially irreverent metaphor (which Ovid often exploits). Political authority is "grave," but also "heavy" in a literal sense.

208   *silentia rupit*: Vergil uses the phrase of Juno in the Council of *Aen.* 10.63–64. "Breaking" the silence is exactly what Juno did there and what the Ovidian Jupiter does here: an uproar ensues.

209   *curam hanc dimittite*: Ovid likes the device of parenthesis, which also, by interrupting a syntactical unit, such as object and verb here, introduces suspense. Cf. the first example at 2.

210   From this point through 239, the story of Lycaon serves as the first narration of human metamorphosis, and we might expect it to be paradigmatic. It is in some ways, but not in all. An important special feature here is the narrator, a very biased Jupiter. Thus, when he makes the tale very moral, of a crime punished and punishment that fits the crime, we might expect that all cases of metamorphosis could be so easily moralized and rationalized. That is not the case, however. Ovid as narrator will turn in the remainder of Book 1 to crimes committed by gods against human beings, notably rape. These crimes remain unpunished, and the metamorphosis rarely provides a clear, comforting moral meaning.

210   *sit*: goes with *quod . . . admissum* also, in indirect question. The interrogative is an adjective like *quae*, so *admissum* must be a substantive.

211   *infamia temporis*: as the first story about Jupiter—we have had only the details of his majestic defeat of the Giants at 154–55—this account seems to represent the supreme deity as an aloof god who has had no direct contact with men and women until this ill report finally reaches his ears.

213   *deus humana . . . sub imagine*: careful juxtaposition of the first two words. *imago* is one of the standard synonyms for "form" or "shape" or "appearance" in the accounts of metamorphosis.

216–   Ovid names three widely separated mountains, to indicate that Jupiter
17   wandered all over Arcadia. *et cum Cyllene* 217: ablative of accompaniment to vary the syntax.

218–   *Arcadis*: genitive with *tyranni*. *inhospita*: an important negative theme
19   planted by the moralistic god. With its final syllable, it begins an alliterative series that builds up to *tyranni*. This noun Ovid uses mainly and frequently in the *Met.* Here, it acquires negative associations from the preparatory adjective, but it can be argued that Ovid expected the word to connote a cruel ruler. He limits its use to genuine "tyrants," Thracian monsters like Tereus, fearsome gods like Dis of the Underworld, and rulers who, in their context, are behaving violently. Thus,

he does not carelessly, at 276, refer to the domain of Neptune who is about to inundate mankind, with the same phrase, *tecta tyranni*.

220–
21   *signa dedi*: it is not clear what signs of divinity Jupiter produced. He could have performed some quick changes of his appearance, as Lee· suggests, or staged a miracle. The story contrasts the pious response of the ordinary people with the sneering disbelief of Lycaon.

222–
23   *an sit*: the alternative clause helps the reader to supply the omitted parts of the first alternative: *utrum deus sit hic*. Lee attributes the ellipsis to Ovid's attempt to capture Lycaon's "excitement." *dubitabile* 223: Ovid seems to have invented the adjective here, to enhance the ironic boast of the menacing villain. It occurs once more in *Met.* 13.21, then in late Latin admirers.

224–
25   *nocte . . . me parat*: the narration creates suspense by leaving unclear throughout 224 the person about to be victimized, then shocks us with the abrupt initial pronoun of 225. We can easily imagine the indignation and gloating satisfaction with which the god speaks. *haec . . . experientia veri*: it is a tour de force to get such a long word as this noun into the hexameter, but Vergil had already shown Ovid the way, in a quite different context, in *G*. 1.4.

226–
27   In this unique variant, Lycaon decides to test the divinity of Jupiter by offering him a meal of human flesh. (Scholars think that the idea may go back to a prehistoric practice of human sacrifice in Arcadia.) In other versions, the victim was one of Lycaon's sons; Ovid absolves the ruler of such a crime, but ascribes to him one more thematically relevant, namely, the murder of a hostage, which violates sacred customs of hospitality. *unius* 227: an example of the unemphatic use of the number, which would help it eventually become the Romance indefinite article.

228–
29   *semineces*: Ovid derives this epic compound from Vergil, who seems to have invented, then used it on five occasions. This is the only occurrence in the *Met*, and it extends Vergil's usage, which was limited to people.

230–
31   *quod*: a few MSS have tried to "correct" this reading to *quos* (i.e., *artus*), not realizing that neuter singular effectively emphasizes the change of the hostage into mere cooked meat. *simul*: a common shortening of the conjunction *simul ac*. The word order of 231 may be reconstituted as follows: *tecta everti in penates domino dignos*. Ovid has arranged this not so much to confuse us as to surprise us with *penates*. The god overturned the palace of Lycaon, bringing down the roof on the household gods and claiming that they deserved it because of their loyalty to such a "master" as the king.

232   *ipse fugit*: although the audience might have expected the avenging flame to have struck Lycaon first, it turns out instead that he has escaped. He flees to the countryside, the natural habitat of the wolf

he becomes. The human beast turns into the literal beast that his behavior most suggests: a perfect moral allegory.

233 *exululat*: it is now clear why Ovid mentioned the *silent* countryside: the howls seem to sound all the more. *frustraque loqui*: a standard detail of human metamorphosis in Ovid is the inability to speak, the loss of that capacity which helps to differentiate us from all other beings. *ab ipso*: from the essential wildness (cf. *feritate* 198) of Lycaon, which now provides allegorical meaning to the changes.

235 *nunc quoque*: these words, so common as to be formulaic in Ovid's descriptions of metamorphosis, indicate that essential elements of the human being are continuous in the new form.

236 *in . . . abeunt*: another frequent formula for metamorphosis in Ovid.

237 *servat vestigia*: once the transformation into wolf has been effected, interest turns to what traces of the human being and his savage nature remain. Both words regularly appear in Ovid's accounts of change.

240– Jupiter makes a transition from the single case of Lycaon to his
41 proclaimed denunciation of the whole human race, from the destruction of one clearly delineated villain to the annihilation of all (whose guilt is not demonstrated). *fera* 241: all humanity resembles Lycaon. *Erinys*: not the Fury who punishes evil, but a representation of the criminal madness that requires the Fury to act.

242– *in facinus . . . putes*: supply as subject accusative *omnes*, implied by
43 the last word of 242. The second person singular and hypothetical subjunctive indicate that Jupiter is now working rhetorically on his audience to get assent to his proposal. *dent*: jussive subjunctive.

244– Ovid analyzes the response of Jupiter's audience. This Council, like
45 the Roman Senate in so much of Tacitus' *Annales*, consists of yes-men who merely explore the possibilities of obsequiousness. *frementi*: not a dignified word to describe the tone and manner of Jupiter's speech. It indicates the shrill nature of his claims in 240 ff. And it agrees with the tone of wild indignation with which his speech opened (cf. 181) and the implications of the neologism *confremuere* (199): i.e., they shared his roaring. In the *Aeneid*, as Ovid well knew, this verb characterized the representatives of *furor* and *impietas*. *partes . . . inplent* 245: Lee detects an acting metaphor and translates: "they play their parts."

246– *est . . . dolori / omnibus*: when we read so far, we expect that these
47 gods feel sympathy for human beings. However, the next lines show that they care for humans no more than Jupiter does; their grief is selfish, at the thought that they are going to lose out on offerings.

247– *terrae mortalibus orbae*: the first word is a dative of possession; its
49 adjective then governs the ablative *mortalibus*. *forma* 248: Ovid earlier implied that when first created (cf. 87–88), human beings gave a definite appearance to earth; that now is threatened. Human beings

were also made to rule over the other animals (cf. 76–77); that function, too, is about to be nullified, and the gods see no merit in turning over the world to wild animals to ravage. *ferisne* 249: both indirect object with *tradere* and dative of agent with *populandas*.

250–
52
sibi . . . curae: "for he would take care of everything else." Another parenthesis typically occupying the final hemistich, this is rather bold in form. Its indirect discourse depends on a verb of saying implicit in *vetat* 251, and the reflexive refers forward to Jupiter. *priori . . . populo* 251–52: dative with the adjective which the phrase frames. *origine mira*: ablative of description.

The Deluge (253–312)

Jupiter is accustomed to relying on his trusty thunderbolt for carrying out punishments, and his original intention is to use it on humankind. However, on second thought, he realizes that the resultant damage to the rest of the universe would be too risky, so he decides to drown human beings. That requires immense amounts of rain and the enthusiastic cooperation of his brother Neptune. After getting the wet south wind into action (262 ff.), he receives help from Neptune (274 ff.), who plays the destructive role of Aeolus of *Aen.* 1, not the reconstructive part of Vergil's Neptune. Rivers and seas run riot. Once this paradoxical transformation of the world has been described, Ovid focuses on human beings and living creatures, who become the victims of the Flood (293 ff.). To the indignant amazement of readers like Seneca, the poet injects little emotion into his description, avoiding opportunities for pathos. Instead, he assumes a clear distance from the scene and records with precise detail its paradoxical effects. Then, he focuses on the animal life (299–308). At first, here too his attention is dominated by the paradoxes: e.g., that seals "graze" where cattle once browsed, that wolf and sheep swim together (instead of preying and being preyed upon). He ignores the fact that these creatures are all innocent and caught up in the human destruction because of the indiscriminate violence of Jupiter. Nevertheless, we fail badly if we conclude that the poet lacks sympathy and is merely displaying his wit inopportunely. Our discomfort with this objective account (which reflects the gods' viewpoint, not ours) is a response designed by Ovid.

253   *erat . . . sparsurus*: the future participle with *erat* could mean either of two things: Jupiter was about to act, and then did, or he was about to act and then (as in this instance) changed his mind.

255   *axis*: the imaginary pole passing through the earth and extended into the heaven, around which supposedly the rest of the universe revolved. By common metonymy, it signifies the skies.

257– *correptaque . . . ardeat*: Lee rightly notes that participle and verb
58   function with all three nouns. *mundi moles*: an alliterative phrase for
the massive universe that goes back to Lucretius 5.96. The MSS offer
two main traditions here: either *moles operosa* or *proles obsessa*; and
a number have conflated the two to produce *moles obsessa*. Since
everyone agrees that *proles* is wrong, it should follow that *obsessa*
is equally suspect. Bömer argues that a concept like "the ingeniously
worked universe" is Christian. However, Ovid's own language for
Creation refutes that claim: his Creator is *opifex rerum* (79).

259– *tela . . . Cyclopum*: myth and poets imagined that the Cyclopes under
61   Mount Etna fashioned Jupiter's thunderbolts at Vulcan's forge (cf.
Aen. 8.424 ff.). *placet* 260: a word that frequently expresses the
formal decision of a political group; it also may connote the "pleasure"
of the decision: drowning all human beings!

262   *Aeoliis . . . in antris*: Ovid uses this scene as a symbol of Disorder
caused by the highest gods; and he takes the storm of *Aeneid 1* as a
counter-symbol. There, Aeolus cooperated wrongly with angry Juno
in causing a storm that was both a violation of Neptune's rule and
also of Jupiter's intentions; accordingly, Neptune moved in, cleared
away the storm, and saved Aeneas' fleet. So Ovid puts Jupiter, then
Neptune, in the roles of the furious and disorderly gods of Vergil.
Aeolus' function was to keep the winds under control in his caves,
and he failed in his duty when he let them loose. *Aquilonem*: defined
here as useful for clearing clouds (and so used after the Flood has
done its destructive job, 328). In *Aen.* 1.85–86 and passim, Aeolus
releases the winds that typically cause storms on the Mediterranean
(where Aeneas sails), Eurus, Notus, and Africus, which come from
southeast, south, and southwest; later, Vergil names Aquilo (102) and
Zephyrus (131). By penning up Aquilo and releasing Notus, then,
Jupiter acts like Vergil's renegade Aeolus.

264– *Notum*: the stormy wet wind from the south. *madidis . . . alis*: now
65   begins a personification of the South Wind that continues through
271. Vergil's winds, once released, sallied forth like a destructive
army and immediately began their stormy task against Aeneas' helpless
ships (*Aen.* 1.84 ff.). Vergil used metaphors to emphasize the warlike
effect. Ovid makes us linger over his humanizing details. *tectus . . .
vultum* 265: Latin poets availed themselves of a special structure,
Greek or archaic Latin ("Greek accusative"), using passive participles
of clothing, covering, etc., as though they were reflexive (or middle
voice) and could take a direct object. Here, the wind has concealed
his face in a pitchy darkness.

268– For scientists and poets like Lucretius, winds cause thunder and light-
69   ning as they compress clouds and rub them against each other (cf.
56). To personify this process, Ovid has Notus squeeze the clouds

with his "hand." *fit fragor* 269: the leisurely picture of 268 comes to a sudden conclusion with the crash of thunder in this alliterative initial dactyl.

270– Iris, Juno's messenger, e.g., in *Aen*. 9.2, is normally the personifica-
71   tion of the rainbow, beautiful, but, for the ancients, a potential omen of more rain. *induta colores*: for syntax of accusative with passive participle, cf. 265.

272– Focusing on the destruction of crops, the poet hardly touches upon
73   the flood's danger to people and animals. *deplorata colonis*: the human despair puts the emphasis on the crops, the essence of farmers' hopes. A few reliable MSS offer the reading *coloni*, genitive singular, which certainly could be possible. But they do not negate the validity of this dative plural. Since *deplorata colonis* gives shape to the end of 272 without minimizing the effectiveness of the first two words of 273, I accept *colonis*.

274   *nec . . . contenta*: same connective phrase at 226. *suo*: Jupiter has done all he could in his personal area of power, the sky.

275   *caeruleus frater*: Neptune is blue, it appears, like the sea he controls. *auxiliaribus*: the metaphor goes with the personification and the picture of the gods' combined war against humankind.

276   *convocat*: like Jupiter at 165, Neptune calls a council to give his bellicose orders. There is no debate here either, and Ovid implies that Neptune acts like a cruel tyrant.

277– *non est . . . utendum*: this verbal unit frames the entire clause, the
78   passive periphrastic finally explaining ablative *hortamine*, a rare word of archaic tone. Neptune, autocratically ignoring the "soldiers'" feelings, dispenses with a standard "battlefield speech."

279– *sic opus est*: same trihemimeral unit in the context of a command as
80   at 2.785. Lee attempts to unify the imagery of the scene here, taking his cue from the final word *habenas*: he assumes a consistent racetrack picture. But in fact Ovid seems to be recalling sporadic details from Vergil's narrative about Aeolus in *Aen*. 1: *domos* (140), *mole* (61), *habenas* (63). Thus, Neptune becomes a symbol of Vergilian disorder, the absolute reverse of his role when he stopped Vergil's storm. See Solodow's discussion, pp. 111 ff.

281– *iusserat*: for this abrupt dactylic unit to end a speech, cf. *dixerat*
82   (367). *ora relaxant . . . defrenato*: both expressions continue the metaphor of horse control from 280. The first is a variation on Vergil's *laxas . . . habenas*, and the second is a unique invention of Ovid for this passage. *in aequora*: rivers normally make for the sea, but these flooding streams presumably also sweep over the plains and merge into the "plain" of the sea.

283– Neptune/Poseidon was traditionally the *Earthshaker*. He also carried
84   a special three-pronged sceptre known as a *trident*. Vergil refers to

it in *Aen.* 1.138 and 145 as a symbol of the god's authority and an
instrument by which he dispels the storm. Ovid's Neptune, like
Aeolus, uses his sceptre to cause trouble.

285   *exspatiata*: Ovid has invented this word for his special effects here.
Seneca in *Q Nat.* 3.27.14 admired this line (and 290) as an outstanding
example of Ovid's characteristic ingenuity. It seems to pick up the
image of *vias* (284) and represent the rivers as wandering off the
beaten track.

286–   The rains of Jupiter have already flattened and ruined the crops (272–
87   73); now, Neptune's flooding streams sweep everything away. *cumque
satis*: momentarily deceptive, but *cum* is a preposition and *satis* (from
sero) a substantive, ablative of accompaniment. *penetralia* 287: this
substantive, regularly poetic, often, as here, refers to the sanctuary
of the Penates. Similar anachronism in representing pre-Roman times
has already occurred at 174 and 231. The rivers' indiscriminate ram-
page destroys sacred and profane alike.

288–   *indeiecta* 289: Ovid's unique creation, more poetic flavor to distance
90   us from the reality of the flood. *malo*: dative with *resistere*. *culmen
. . . tegit*: prose order would be, *tamen altior unda huius [domus]
culmen tegit*.

291–   Line 291 sets up the wit of 292, which again elicited the approving
92   notice of Seneca in *Q Nat.* 3.27.13. He believed that Ovid achieved
a tone suitable to the seriousness of the situation (*pro magnitudine
rei*), but that he spoiled it later at 304. The narrator seems fascinated
by the metamorphosis of all things to an undifferentiated sheet of
water. Without land, the sea must be shoreless. *omnia pontus erant*:
the MSS tradition divides between a plural and a singular verb. Ovid
and Latin can do either; Latin allows a singular predicate noun to
attract its verb into the singular. I believe the plural here enhances
the parallelism between the line's two clauses, whose verbs Ovid
carefully juxtaposed.

293–   The description at last turns to the reactions of human beings, otherwise
94   only noticed in passing at 272. Ovid's human beings here are a variety
of undistinguished demonstrative pronouns, without qualifying adjec-
tives or adverbs, with verbs that merely imply the strange (but unmen-
acing) topsy-turvy situation. *collem*: people took to the hills; that
would have to have happened before the Flood reached the stage
described in 291–92. *ararat* 294: syncopated form of pluperfect.
Horace plays with the flood in *C.* 1.2.7 ff.

295–   *navigat* 296: in contrast with the rower, another sails, and still another
96   is a nonchalant fisherman. *ulmo*: surprise ending of clause and line,
to point up the amazing effects of this "drowned" world. In normal
circumstances, *unda* would have been expectable.

299–   *graciles . . . deformes* express a value judgment: beauty has been

300   "deformed." Modern taste might tend to regard the seal as a more attractive and graceful animal than the goat, but we have seen seals more frequently than did Ovid, at zoos. *ponunt sua corpora*: should mean that the seals lie down to rest (as in the famous scene with Proteus of *Od.* 4.400 ff., used by Vergil in *G.* 4.432). If so, Ovid has momentarily ignored the fact that the earth is totally inundated.

301–   *mirantur*: a regular reaction to metamorphosis in Ovid's poem is
3   simple astonishment. Here, in his first use of the verb in the poem, Ovid assigns it to unaffected demigods (not, as elsewhere, to the people directly touched by the change). What this marveling conceals, of course, is the drowning of human beings and land animals. The Nereids could care less! *agitataque* 303: past participle instead of a coordinate finite verb. Horace mocked the stereotype of dolphins in trees (*Ars P.* 30) after using it himself in *C.* 1.2.9.

304–   *nat lupus inter oves*: Ovid focuses his attention on animals, which
6   are forced to swim and plunged into a paradoxical predicament (before they finally drown). Seneca *Q Nat.* 3.27.13 singled out this passage as inept because of its playfulness within a context of universal destruction. The wolf is regularly the predatory enemy of sheep. A commonplace in visions of the ideal world (Vergil's Fourth Eclogue, Horace's Sixteenth Epode, and the Old Testament prophets such as Isaiah 11:6) is that hostility among animals will cease: the wolf will dwell with the lamb. Ovid takes that idyllic theme and shows the two species sharing the same activity without hostility, but not as a symbol of peace and security. They are both swimming for their lives. *vires fulminis* 305: the lightning bolt is a favorite Ovidian metaphor for the power of the boar (cf. *Met.* 8.289 and 355).

307–   Ovid's final vignette of the animal world comes closest to obvious
8   pathos, as he focuses on the exhausted birds. *lassatis . . . alis* 308: the sound patterns are interrupted by the fatal verb.

309–   *novi* 310: a motif of metamorphosis is the novelty of change. Cf. 1,
10   437, 554. Here, the "new" waves violate nature; they beat on the mountain tops, since no shores remain (cf. 292).

311–   *maxima pars*: only with *illos* in 312 can we be sure that this vague
12   "largest part" refers to human beings, the original targets of Jupiter's devastation. *unda . . . unda*: different cases and metrical stress. *pepercit*: sets up ironic expectations, which the next line quickly disappoints. *inopi . . . victu* 312: relies on the Roman audience's familiarity with a phrase such as *inopia victus*, "lack of food."

DEUCALION AND PYRRHA (313–415)

Ovid has left the impression that every surface of the earth, even the highest mountains (310), has been submerged and that every human being has been destroyed. Now, it suddenly turns out that the summit of Mount Parnassus rises above the flood and that two individuals have ridden out the deluge and safely landed on Parnassus. These two have survived because of their extraordinary justice and piety, to become, by a curious nonsexual process, the source of the new race of human beings. Their names are Pyrrha and Deucalion.

The story of Pyrrha and Deucalion, a familiar one, was told in many variants. Two readily available versions are those of Apollodorus 1.7.2 and Hyginus 152. The former offers some interesting details; the latter is brief. For Apollodorus, it is important from the beginning that Deucalion is the son of Prometheus; Ovid mentions the fact late (390) and without emphasis. Prometheus advised Deucalion, because of the impending flood, to build an ark for himself and Pyrrha (like the Biblical Noah); with that, the couple were able to ride out the water for nine days (while everybody else was being drowned), then make land on Mount Parnassus after the rain had stopped. In the more Roman account of Hyginus, the landfall is Mount Etna in Sicily. Both accounts then have the refugees pray to Zeus/Jupiter for fellow human beings to relieve their loneliness. Ovid, who has been emphasizing Jupiter's role as destructive deity, allows the "Father" god no part in the re-creation of humanity: he introduces Themis, whose kindly oracle instructs the pious couple how to repopulate the devastated earth. The accounts of Apollodorus and Hyginus both report briefly that, following the god's orders, Deucalion and Pyrrha cast stones behind them, and that Deucalion's stones become men and Pyrrha's women. Both writers also comment on the etymology that goes into the aetiology: the Greek word for stone (*laas*) seems temptingly related to the word for people (*laos*). Ovid, on the other hand, devotes his artistic talent to making the couple come alive in a special light, both sympathetic and somewhat ironic. They are devoted to each other, a perfect example of mutuality in marriage; totally devout toward the gods (an obvious disproof of Jupiter's sweeping condemnation); but incredibly simple-minded. This is shown in Pyrrha's shocked and indignant response to the ambiguities of Themis' oracle, but also in the comically naive problem they seem to have about how children are made (379–80).

313   Ovid starts the new sequence by setting the geographical scene; this line contains three Greek place names, to tantalize the reader. The medieval scribes were as baffled as most modern audiences, and one name became hopelessly corrupted by late antiquity. All extant MSS read *Actaeis* as the second name: that would mean Attic and is geographically impossible. Phocis, which lies northwest of Boeotia, cannot separate the Aonians from lands *south* of themselves (as Attica is).

The emendation proposed by Gierig—*Oetaeis*—refers to the region of Mount Oete in southern Thessaly, where Hercules died.

314–
15   Phocis was a very fertile region, but now it and all lands are undistinguishable tracts of the flooding sea. *subitarum* 315: suddenness is often associated by Ovid with metamorphosis.

316–
17   In Phocis, north of Delphi, towers Mount Parnassus, a group of peaks of which the two most prominent face Delphi. *cacumina* 317: the same two peaks referred to by *verticibus*. A common but inferior MSS variant offers *superatque cacumine*, which keeps the same subject as in the previous clause, but sacrifices the number of peaks.

318–
19   Here at last Ovid names Deucalion, without explaining his origin or the reason for his unique escape. *consorte tori* 319: instead of the name of Pyrrha (postponed to 250); perhaps an ironic reflection on her sexual naiveté? *rate*: usually, a raft, but here the ark which, in Apollodorus, Prometheus advised his son to build.

320–
21   *Corycidas*: nymphs who lived in a cave of Parnassus known as the Corycian. Ovid seems to have invented this poetic adjective, which is unique here. *fatidicamque Themin* 321: the compound adjective was used in prose and poetry during the generation before Ovid. Themis, the goddess of justice, is said to be the oracular deity at Delphi in this early time, before Apollo (whose story follows [441 ff.]) takes control of the site. No prayers go to Jupiter. *oracla*: to ease metrical problems, poets could drop the *u* of *oracula* (a process called syncope by linguists). Ovid does it only here (cf. 392 and 491).

322–
23   *illo . . . illa*: ablative of comparison. *amantior . . . metuentior*: rare uses of the comparative forms of present participles in poetry. Each takes an objective genitive.

324–
26   Jupiter, last mentioned at 274, now reappears to find that he has not destroyed every human being and that these two, who have escaped death, do not deserve to die. *stagnare paludibus orbem*: "the world is inundated with waters." A very similar phrase occurs in 15.269. The infinitive, like the next two, depends on *videt* 326 in indirect discourse. In the line that almost word for word repeats 325, *virum* is dropped and *videt* (which starts off like it) replaces it. The very repetitiveness of the two lines resulted in 326 being omitted by a group of good MSS. As Lee suggests, the similarity between man and woman emphasizes their like-mindedness, an ideal marital quality.

328–
29   Leaving it to us to infer Jupiter's motives, Ovid merely describes the god's actions to end the Flood. He reverses what he did in 262 ff., where he locked up the north wind, then let the rain clouds take over the skies.

330   *tricuspide*: Ovid playfully disarms Neptune's feared trident (cf. 283) with this unique adjective.

331   *mulcet*: soothing the waters ends their *ira* (330).

331–   Triton is depicted in Classical art as a man above the waist, who then
32   tapers off into a sea monster below. Artists found it convenient, then,
        to submerge that lower part and show only the human upper part
        rising above the surface of the water, as Ovid does here. His description
        of Triton through 340 gives a pictorial but ethically neutral picture of
        the Flood's cessation. This should be contrasted with the morally
        loaded symbolism of Vergil's description of Neptune as he ends the
        storm that buffeted Aeneas' fleet off Sicily in *Aen*. 1.124 ff. *umeros
        . . . tectum* 332: for this syntax, cf. 265 and 270.

333–   *vocat*: echo and reversal of *convocat* 276, where Neptune called to-
35   gether his "military host" and sent them off to war. *conchae*: Triton
        is regularly equipped with a large conch shell that serves him as a
        horn. This is probably the first time in myth that it functions as a
        military trumpet (cf. *bucina* 335).

335–   *illi*: dative of agent with present passive, a poetic freedom. *tortilis*
38   336: unlike the familiar military trumpet made from a curved animal's
        horn, this is a shell, conical in outer shape. *in latum . . . ab imo*:
        "which expands in width (or diameter) from the base of a spiral."
        litora 338: shores have reappeared (cf. 329, 343). *sub utroque . . .
        Phoebo*: east and west, where Phoebus the sun rises and sets.

339–   Subject of all the verbs here is *bucina*. *iussos . . . receptus* 340: cf.
42   334–35. Triton has now carried out his orders. *omnibus . . . quibus*
        341–42: dative of agent. *coercuit*: the verb implies restraint on wild
        spirits, such as horses or soldiers.

344   *exire*: the correlative effect of subsiding water is the apparent emer-
        gence of the hills.

345–   *diem longam* 346: unusual way of referring to a long time. *nudata*: be-
47   cause the trees still have their leaves in 347, covered with mud from the
        flood, Lee suggests that we are not to think of bare-branched trees, but
        of tops freed of water.

348–   *redditus orbis*: the restoration of the world rounds off the description
49   which began at 324 with the picture of the world under water.
        Deucalion and Pyrrha, whom Ovid left just landed on Parnassus at 323,
        notice the emptiness, the lack of other life and hence their own loneli-
        ness. An utterly quiet earth would be eery indeed. *desolatas*: an emphatic
        word created by Augustan writers (probably Vergil, who used it twice
        in *Aen*. 11), made especially impressive by its long syllables.

350   *lacrimis . . . obortis*: the preparation in 348–49 might have led to
        some heroic speech from Deucalion, but Ovid moves us precisely
        away from conventional epic self-control and fortitude with the first
        of many tearful talks by a male character. Contrast Aeneas' powerful
        self-restraint in his first speech to his men after landing in North
        Africa: *Aen*. 1.198 ff.

351–   *o soror, o coniunx*: Ovid seems to overdo the pathos of Deucalion

53   here, letting him double his exclamatory *o* and address Pyrrha in a
somewhat ambiguous manner. She is of course not his sister, but his
cousin, daughter of Prometheus' brother Epimetheus (*patruelis* 352;
cf. 390). Although Latin permits children of brothers to be called
soror (or *frater*), the primary meaning of the word remains sister; and
the Roman audience was familiar with the incestuous relationships of
the Ptolemies and those of Jupiter and Juno, the latter of whom proudly
claims in *Aen.* 1.47 to be *Iovisque / et soror et coniunx* (also later in
Met. 3.266). The identical metrical shape of Ovid's passage with
Vergil's suggests a deliberate echo. In this first speech of a human
being, Ovid creates a sharp contrast with the assertive egotism of
Jupiter's recent harangue to the cringing gods.

354–   *terrarum . . . turba*: as the only survivors, the pair are, in a striking
55   way, the "crowd" of the earth. *cetera*: we might have expected *ceteros*
(other human beings), but the neuter, besides solving a metrical prob-
lem, applies to all animate beings once on earth. Cf. similar use of
cetera in parenthesis of 318.

356–   The word order, which undermines *fiducia* by negating it in advance,
57   can be restored to prose form as follows: *haec quoque vitae nostrae
fiducia adhuc non est satis certa.*

358–   Bömer finds the pathos of these rhetorical questions barely tolerable
60   for "modern taste." However, it brings out the significant contrast
between Jupiter's rhetoric and Deucalion's; the human being is filled
with love, concern, and trust for another. And these were the people
Jupiter tried to exterminate as hopelessly degenerate! *quo consolante*
360: ablative absolute.

363–   With another pathetic *o*, Deucalion confesses his feeling of help-
64   lessness about repopulating the earth: he is not his father Prometheus.
However, the alliteration of *p* in four successive words ending in
paternis in 363 could suggest a more humorous nuance. Deucalion
does not know how to be *a* father.

366   The parenthesis (*sic visum superis*) works with Ovidian ambiguity: it
conveys Deucalion's simple piety, but it invites the audience to wonder
about divine judgment in sending the Flood.

367–   *dixerat*: abrupt, unepic transition from a speech, all in a single dactyl
68   (cf. 281). *et flebant*: Ovid frames, so to speak, the speech of Deucalion
in tears (cf. 350). The pious pair now decide to appeal to divine help
in their childless plight. Here, we understand the function in Ovid's
narrative of Themis, who is unknown to Apollodorus and Hyginus:
an appeal to Jupiter or the other Olympians, who had agreed to destroy
humankind, might be vain. Jupiter's promise to take care of things
(250–52) is never personally fulfilled. *per sacras . . . sortes* 368: by
oracle, as also at 381 and 389.

369–   *nulla mora est*: replaces an introductory phrase like "without delay"

70   or "immediately". For this purpose, Ovid regularly prefers the dactylic
     unit *nec mora*: cf. 1.717 and 3.46. *Cephisidas undas*: presumably,
     the Castalian springs of Delphi. Themis acts as a predecessor of
     Apollo. Although Delphi lies along the south slopes of Parnassus,
     and the Cephisos River runs through the Phocian plain north of Parnas-
     sus, Ovid knew of a tradition in which the waters of the river partly
     flowed into the springs of Delphi. *ut nondum . . . sic iam* 370: "al-
     though not yet . . . still already". *liquidas*: "clear."

371– *libatos . . . liquores*: implies some sort of sacred libation. But Pyrrha
74   and Deucalion are ritually cleaning themselves before approaching
     the deity, with water taken from the spring. *delubra* 373: cf. *templi*
     375. Ovid suggests a sacred building somewhat like the majestic
     Temple of Apollo known to all ancient visitors at Delphi. *fastigia*:
     the flood had topped the roof of the temple and all the decorations of
     the pediment.

375– Perhaps because the altars, which would have been in front of the
76   temple, have been deprived of fire and function, the couple go right
     to the steps and make their prayer. They do not enter the shrine: that
     is not customary in Greco-Roman worship. *pronus humi*: they do not
     just fall to their knees, but prostrate themselves face downward on
     the ground (*humi*, locative).

377– *atque ita* + delayed verb of saying: cf. 4.476. If-clauses (protases),
78   beginning this prayer, are standard rhetorical elements of such pleas;
     they remind the deity of her functions. *remollescunt* 378: the softening
     of Themis anticipates that of the stones which will turn into the new
     inhabitants of earth: cf. below, 402.

379– *qua . . . arte*: Ovid has used hyperbaton (cf. my introduction) to
80   separate noun-adjective units. When restored to normal order, the
     indirect question would be: *qua arte damnum generis nostri reparabile
     sit. mersis fer opem . . . rebus* 380: the plea for help, *fer opem*, is
     common in the *Met.*; next occurrence will be in Daphne's story, 546.

381– *mota dea est*: same words at 5.621 and 7.711. Deities in this poem often
83   ignore prayers and deserving piety. The oracle that Themis gives the
     couple baffles them; they puzzle over it until 398, when they start to
     carry it out (and Ovid repeats its key terms, in formal epic manner).
     Delay of *parentis* to the final word emphasizes the puzzling enormity
     of Themis' response. A different word would have made all rapidly
     understandable, with no agony (or comedy). The "great mother" is the
     earth (now less hostile); her "bones" are stones (cf. 393–94).

384– *obstipuere*: this emphatic verb regularly has initial position in the line.
85   *recusat* 385: with the infinitive, when not negative, is rare in prose but
     allowable in poetry.

386– *detque . . . veniam*: indirect command with *rogat*. Pious Pyrrha imme-
87   diately controls her outrage and prays for pardon. *pavido . . . pa-*

vetque: repetition implies her fearful dilemma. Ovid is the first to use *pavet* with an infinitive.

388   *caecis obscura latebris*: Ovid's word order implies that the ablative phrase goes with *obscura* and means "puzzling, unclear in or because of dark hidden meaning."

390   An epic device, refers to both Deucalion and Pyrrha by patronymics. *placidis . . . dictis*: in contrast to Pyrrha's emotional response above, Deucalion acts as a wise and calming influence.

391–   In our idiom, Deucalion says: "Either I am wrong or this is the meaning
94   of the oracle." *sollertia*: skill (in interpreting). *nobis*: for *mihi*, dative of possession. After *aut* 392, the parenthesis reveals the simple piety of Deucalion that can disarm the seemingly threatening divine command of 383.

395–   *Titania*: Pyrrha's grandfather was the Titan Iapetus. *nocebit* 397: the
97   couple said: "What harm *will* there be in trying?"

400–   Parenthesis to produce suspense. We know that the stones are su-
402   premely important. The Romans had great respect for *vetustas*, what we might call venerable tradition, but Ovid's query undermines such credulity. *ponere duritiem* 401: beginning of metamorphosis. The noun can be in either the first or fifth declension. Since Ovid otherwise uses the first (e.g., 3.64 and 65, 4.751), some MSS have wrongly tried to regularize the reading here. *molliri* 402: the verb echoes that of the prayer in 378. For the anadiplosis with *mollita*, cf. 33. *mora*: a loose instrumental ablative used as our adverb *gradually*.

403–   *creverunt*: the stones need to expand somehow from their originally
6   small, portable size to that of human beings. *mitior*: this word, too, reflects the kindly answer of Themis to the prayer for help (cf. 380, *mitissima*). *ut . . . sic . . . hominis* 404–5: "while some form could be made out, nevertheless a clear human form could not be perceived." The sculptor Rodin liked to leave his marble statues unfinished, in order to achieve the effect of an emerging form that the viewer's imagination could complete.

407–   Ovid now analyzes the contents of the formative rocks, first imagining
8   moisture or earth, still adhering to the stones from the flood, which could be transformed into corporeal forms. *in corporis usum*: "into usable or functional body."

409–   *solidum*: residual hardness accounts for bones.
10

411–   Ovid starts to end his story by careful recapitulation of key words
13   and themes. *superorum*: the couple had appealed to the gods at 377–78, and so we may infer that Themis answers for the gods in general. *saxa / missa*: cf. 399–400. *viri*: the man Deucalion. *de fēmineo . . . iactu* 413: "from the woman's (Pyrrha's) throw." The noun echoes

the verb of the oracle: cf. 383 and 394. *reparata*: final answer of the problem stated in 363 and 379.

414–   The narrator affects to reduce the significance of the whole story to simple
15   aetiology: why human beings are hardy and used to toil. The audience should not feel so restricted. *laborum*: objective genitive. *documenta*: a prosaic word captures the didactic manner of the aetiologist.

CREATION OF NONHUMAN ANIMAL LIFE AND THE MONSTER PYTHON (416–51)

Once human beings have reappeared by the merciful intervention of the gods, Ovid is content to attribute the return of other animal life to spontaneous, natural, nondivine forces. Moisture and heat combine to foster the "seeds of things" (wherever they come from). On the analogy of the Nile, which seems to cause life by its annual floods, the narrator argues that, with the end of the Deluge, the sun's heat brought countless creatures into existence in the still-moist fields. Having offered this semi-scientific explanation for life, Ovid shifts to mythology and concentrates on one extraordinary creature produced at this time, the huge snake Python. After it terrorized Delphi, Apollo finally killed it with many arrows and, to commemorate his feat, founded the Pythian Games. In those early days, before the laurel had come into existence, the prize was a crown of oak leaves. (The laurel would be the metamorphosed Daphne.)

416–   *diversis . . . formis*: ablative of description. *animalia*: the rest of the
21   animate world except human beings. *tellus . . . peperit*: Ovid starts with the image of "mother" earth, which is a commonplace for Greek and Roman writers; it will inspire the simile of 420–21. But the narrative insists on impersonal spontaneous creation. Had Ovid wanted to use a mythological explanation that would agree with his emphasis on water and heat, he could have followed Lucretius (e.g., 1.250 ff.), who unites *pater aether* and *mater terra* in a productive "marriage". *ab igne*: instead of the instrumental ablative, Ovid uses preposition + ablative of source; the construction provides a convenient metrical alternative. *intumuere* 419: the expanding mud resembles a pregnant womb; the related adjective *tumidus* often modifies *venter* and connotes pregnancy. *semina rerum*: a technical term in Lucretius and scientific/ philosophic writers for "atoms"; Ovid means normal seeds, as the similes that follow indicate. *morando* 421: the gerund functions in the same way as the ablative noun *mora* (cf. above 402) to mean "gradually."

422–   The long simile resembles the exuberance of Lucretius' extensive

29   comparisons and tumultuous enjambement. (The simile actually con-
      tinues to the end of 433, for Ovid expands it with a Lucretianic *quippe
      ubi* at 430 ff.) Lucretius had discussed possible causes of the Nile
      flood in summer (6.712 ff.), and Vergil in *G.* 4.287 ff. had talked
      of spontaneous generation of bees in Egypt by the Nile, but Ovid
      develops details that come from Greek or lost Latin sources. *ubi . . .
      Nilus* 423: the withdrawal of the Nile after annually flooding the fields.
      septemfluus: Ovid invented this epithet to refer to the seven mouths
      of the river at its delta. He uses it once more at 15.753; it occurs
      nowhere else. *alveo*: the meter requires synizesis or coalescence of
      the two final vowels into one syllable (cf. 77). Ovid arranged 424 as
      a Golden Line (AAVNN). *animalia* 425: same position in line as 416.
      quaedam modo coepta . . . quaedam inperfecta 426–27: although
      these two phrases mean substantially the same thing, they imply two
      different viewpoints, as the added language indicates. The first stresses
      the birth process; the second, the incomplete creation. Ovid uses a
      somewhat rough enjambement here in three successive lines (426–
      28), with final adjective or adverb *per ipsum, suisque, saepe*; it reminds
      his audience of Lucretius and also reinforces the sense of unfinished
      creation. *numeris* 428: "parts, limbs", ablative of specification.

430–   *quippe ubi*: commentators like Bömer and Lee focus on *quippe* alone
34   (which Ovid employs only in the *Met.* and *Tristia*). However, it is
      the two words that define the style here, for they are characteristic of
      Lucretius and the "natural science" that Ovid affects in this long
      simile. (Cf. Lucr. 1. 167, 182, 242, etc.) *temperiem sumpsere*: the
      noun is an Augustan formation, to create a metrically usable equivalent
      for such words as *temperatio*. Ovid used it before at 51. For the
      importance of moisture and heat, cf. 417–18. *concipiunt* 431: preg-
      nancy occurs merely from the mixture of hot and cold, which then
      generates every animate thing. *aquae*: dative with *pugnax*, a bold
      poetic syntax that Ovid may well have invented here, later to be used
      by Silver Latin writers. *vapor umidus*: the combination of heat and
      moisture. *discors concordia* 433: this phrase had already been used
      by Horace of the operation of the physical universe in *Epist.* 1.12.19,
      reversing the words to make a hexameter ending; and Manilius has
      Horace's phrase in 1.142. Ovid has ingeniously transferred the sense
      specifically to the creative opposition of moist and hot. *fetibus apta*:
      "fosters the creation of living things."

434–   With *ergo*, Ovid returns to the situation after the Deluge, which he
35   left at 422. Thus, he repeats earlier words: *tellus* 434 and 416, *solibus*
      435 and 418, *aestu* 435 and 419. *recanduit*: Ovid seems to have
      invented this verb and used it always in this form. It occurs four
      times, in the *Met.* only; cf. 3.707 and 4.530. Here, the prefix should
      be translated, as Lee notes: "grew hot *again*."

436– Ovid divides the countless living kinds into two groups: those that
37   exhibit a form like earlier beings who drowned and those that are
      monstrous and new. The mention of monsters provides the transition
      to the mythical Python, and here we leave "natural science."

438– *nollet*: imperfect subjunctive in hypothetical clause of contrary to fact,
40   imperfect probably standing for the pluperfect. "She (the earth) of
      course would have refused (if she could have), but . . . " *te quoque*:
      the poet familiarly apostrophizes the monster and, in the process,
      reduces his fearsome aspects. *novis*: for this adjective in connection
      with metamorphosis, cf. 437. *incognite*: in two senses. It is unknown
      to human beings who have never lived before; also absolutely unknown
      to the world, a "new monster." *tantum spatii de monte* 440: "so great
      an extent of the mountain," referring to Parnassus. Since *spatii* is
      partitive genitive Ovid did not want to repeat the syntax (with *montis*)
      and used instead the alternative ablative with preposition *de* that later
      became the standard genitive form in the Romance languages.

441– *arquitenens*: the epithet and antonomasia come from archaic Latin
42   epic (Naevius) and identify Apollo, killer of Python, in a seemingly
      solemn epic manner. In fact, Apollo emerges as egotistic and rather
      comic. *armis*: ablative with *usus* 442.

443– *mille gravem telis*: the adjective, linked to *hunc* 441, makes us imagine
44   the serpent (or dragon), looking like a pin cushion and weighed down
      by a thousand arrows. The precision in the next clause of 443, an
      ablative absolute, also seems comic: the quiver (which would have
      been incredibly capacious for one thousand arrows) *almost* ran out of
      bolts. *nigra*: poison traditionally turns everything black.

445– *neve*: for this Ovidian alternative to *et ne*, cf. 72 and 151. *vetustas*:
47   time, thought of as enemy of fame. For a different view of this Latin
      abstract ("tradition"), cf. 400. *sacros . . . ludos* 446: Bömer notes
      that Ovid is the first to associate the adjective with this noun, which
      regularly receives a word denoting the opulence and impressiveness
      of the "show", from the spectator's viewpoint. *Pythia . . . dictos* 447:
      the Greek name of this festival, like the name of many Roman holidays
      (Floralia, Megalensia), took the form of a neuter substantive. *perdomi-
      tae*: the prefix emphasizes the total mastery of Apollo. Some MSS
      indicate that readers missed a preposition with *nomine* and so insisted
      on "correcting" to *de domitae . . . nomine*. A different Greek etymol-
      ogy assumes that the Python had no name, that the word Pythia arose
      from the rotting (*pyth-* in Greek) of the monster's corpse.

448– Ovid describes a period of the Pythia before the laurel served as
49   the characteristic prize of Apollo. Hence, the tenses: pluperfect and
      imperfect. *manu . . . rotave*: the metonymy refers to standard contests,
      e.g., throwing of discus or javelin, running, chariot races.

450– *nondum laurus erat*: Ovid, who likes to allude to a subsequent meta-

51   morphosis, prepares for the immediately following story: Daphne
     changes into the laurel tree. *longo . . . crine*: the long hair of the
     ever-youthful Apollo, like that of Bacchus, was a standard element
     in his pictorial representation. *de qualibet arbore*: having blithely
     dropped a preposition in 447, Ovid here inserts one, to make instru-
     mental ablative into one of source (cf. 440).

APOLLO AND DAPHNE (452–567)

The brief account of Apollo's victory over Python ends Ovid's
interest in the area around Parnassus and in mighty feats, and he now
elaborately develops a second and unheroic myth about Apollo, which
features him as a frustrated elegiac lover, farther north in Thessaly.
Boasting of his prowess with the bow, Apollo incurs the anger of
Cupid, who quickly demonstrates that he is the superior archer by
striking Apollo with an arrow of love and thus subjecting him help-
lessly to amatory passions. To insure that the god will have no success,
Cupid wounds Daphne, the nymph Apollo desires, with an arrow that
repels love. The main development in Ovid's narrative, then, focuses
on erotic symptoms that rob the god of his powers and reduce him
to human elegiac level (490 ff.), especially in the wooing speech
which he calls out to fleeing Daphne as he pursues her (504 ff.).
When polite wooing fails, Apollo presses on, determined to force his
will on the nymph, and, what the nymph has feared all along, namely,
rape, is almost perpetrated. But just as the long chase (530–44) seems
destined to end in Daphne's misery, she appeals for rescue, asking
that the beautiful form, which has so attracted the god, be changed.
In answer to that prayer, her feminine body becomes a laurel. Apollo
does the best he can with this defeat of his lust and takes possession
of the tree, making it his emblem.

This highly polished story is essentially Ovid's free invention,
constructed to fit into the themes of his poem and indeed to provide
the first representation of love, a major topic of the *Met.* Earlier
versions of Apollo's love for Daphne existed, but they seem to have
been late Hellenistic creations, and they were set in the area of Laconia
in the Peloponessus, not in Thessaly. Parthenius 15 summarizes their
narratives, which differed substantially, in detail, theme, and tone,
from the account here produced. Ovid uses Apollo to develop a the-
matic representation of male erotic desire, an obviously flawed kind
of love. Exploiting the familiar motifs of elegy, he lightly mocks the
god's almost human helplessness and also lightly hints at the selfish
violence that lurks underneath those trite elegiac formulae of wooing.
Daphne, too, proves a loser: she cannot survive as a virgin and prefers
to sacrifice her human form rather than yield to an undesired god.

Yet she is not being punished for insisting on virginity. The next stories, featuring lusty gods who gratify their rapist desires on reluctant nymphs, will elaborate the wretched disorientation that results from such selfish violence. So Ovid does not invite the audience to fault Daphne here; the main stress of his account dwells on the distorting effects of *amor* on a god (and implicitly on human males).

452–
53
primus amor: as in English "first love," the abstract noun stands for the person loved. Ovid slyly emphasizes "first," because Apollo was no more "monogamous" than the other gods. Cf. the way Tacitus in *Annals* introduces Nero's reign of terror with the phrase *primum facinus*, "the first crime." *Peneia*: as the daughter of the river Peneus, Daphne lives in Thessaly near the idyllic vale of Tempe. Various forms of the patronymic occur at 472, 504, 525, and finally Ovid presents the father himself at 569. *quem*: i.e., *amor*. Naturally, many MSS have "corrected" this reading to *quam*, i.e., Daphne. *fors* 453: though blind chance often accounts for love, in this case a special explanation exists.

454–
55
Delius: the first of numerous references to Apollo in connection with Delos, the island of his birth (an event later discussed in greater detail at 6.186 ff.). *hunc*: Cupid. *victo serpente*: Latin and Ovid feel free to treat this noun as masculine or feminine; cf. above 439 and 447. Ablative of respect. *adducto . . . nervo* 455: Cupid was bending his bow by pulling back the string. Since some ancient bows were not only tipped with horn but actually made of two horns connected by a central piece of wood that could bend and give spring, *cornua* by metonymy could denote the bow. Ovid compares two archers, the arrogant Apollo and the playful but powerful Cupid.

456–
58
quidque . . . dixerat: using *-que* as a casual connective, Ovid continues in the pluperfect with a speech by Apollo that sets him up for humiliation. *quid . . . tibi . . . cum*: like English "What do you want with?" or "What are you doing with?" The pronoun is dative of reference and functions with an assumed verb such as *vis* or *vis facere*. Apollo, sneers at Cupid: dangerous weapons should not be trusted to a boy. *gestamina* 457: a word borrowed from epic poetry, used twice by Vergil in the *Aen.* and three times by Ovid only in the *Met.* It characterizes proud Apollo. In 458, the unconvincing rhetoric of his boast is further diminished by the lilting series of dactyls.

459–
60
Note the pompous "editorial we." Compare the god's version in 459 of the serpent's sprawling size with the Ovidian narrator's casual familiarity (urbane apostrophe) in 440. The epic epithet *pestifero* is no accident. For the actual killing, 460 corresponds to earlier 443–44. What Apollo calls "countless" arrows were comically counted by the narrator.

461–   *face . . . tua*: Apollo tries to limit Cupid to the use of his characteristic
62   torch. As Bömer points out, in the *Aeneid* Vergil described Cupid's
       work to create in Dido love for Aeneas entirely in the metaphorical
       terms of fire (1.657 ff.). *nescio quos*: the tone of contemptuous indiffer-
       ence is obvious. *inritare . . . nec . . . adsere* 462: more offensive
       language to Cupid. Instead, for example, of using an appropriate
       metaphorical verb such as *inflammare*, Apollo reduces the importance
       of Cupid's activities.

463–   *figat . . . arcus*: an example of the so-called *apo koinou* structure; cf.
65   *certa . . . vulnera* 458. The verb from the first clause must be used
       in the second (though in the future indicative); the noun from the
       second functions in the first. That leaves "your" and "my," *omnia*
       and *te*, to create the desired antithesis. Assigning a concessive sense
       to *figat* and supplying future *figet* in the second clause, translate:
       "Although your bow may strike everything else, my bow will strike
       you." *quanto . . . tanto* 464–65: coordinate clauses using ablative of
       degree of difference. Since Ovid has unbalanced the structure of the
       two clauses by using *cedunt* in the first to be equivalent to *minor est*
       in the second, translation should bring out the emphasis on inferiority.
       nostra: ablative of comparison. Cupid's speech ends on the key word
       asserting *his* superiority.

466–   *eliso . . . pennis*: as Bömer notes, Ovid contrives a description of
67   flying which, because of the unusual verbs employed, gives to Cupid
       an impression of heroic energy. As his wings beat along, they force
       the air out of the way. This sounds like the action of a mighty eagle
       more than that of the boy with usually small wings. *inpiger . . .
       arce* 467: the adjective "heroizes" Cupid. He takes his stance in a
       dominating spot atop Parnassus, again like a melodramatic hero. *arce*:
       ablative of place where, without the preposition.

468–   *sagittifera*: epic compound to counter Apollo's in 459. Both Catullus
69   and Vergil had used it of warriors or hunters who bear arrows. Ovid
       extends the usage. Note that Cupid needs only one arrow for Apollo,
       then a second one for Daphne. *hoc . . . illud* 469: since we lack
       details yet about the two arrows, the pronouns can be loosely translated
       as "this" and "that" or "one" and "the other." However, from this
       point on, we have to pay attention so that we correctly assign the
       pronouns at 472. The arrow that banishes love comes as somewhat
       of a surprise, and Ovid keeps us briefly in suspense as to how the
       two arrows of contrasting effects will be employed.

471   *sub harundine*: at the end of the shaft, where we would expect the
       point.

472–   *hoc . . . illo*: when two items have been described, the pronoun *hoc*
73   refers by "this" to the nearer of the two, the last mentioned. Hence,
       Latin regularly specifies "the latter" before "the former," unlike En-

glish. *deus*: Ovid calls Cupid a god as he demonstrates his power, not *puer* (which fits metrically), as Apollo contemptuously has done. *in nympha . . . fixit*: an easy variation for the construction used in 463–64. *Apollineas* 473: Ovid has invented this word here.

474   *fugit*: if the arrow has put love to flight in her, then logically she flees the word *lover* and the role it implies. But the verb also fixes attention on literal flight and chase, which will be enacted now (cf. 502). *nomen amantis*: the "lover" is not herself, but a male, like Apollo.

475–   These lines characterize Daphne as a virginal huntress; hunting is her
77   passion, an alternative to love. *innuptae*: properly applied to unmarried human maidens, who were destined to become wives in the future, this word became a fixed epithet for certain goddesses who never married, but were permanently virginal. Diana is one such; another is Minerva, to whom Vergil had applied the word in *Aen.* 2.31. Ovid uses the adjective to introduce the theme of marriage, a natural future for Daphne, one that her father very much desires (cf. 478 ff. and 481 ff.). *aemula Phoebes*: the first word, whether adjective or substantive, usually has a pejorative sense in Ovid, but not here. Daphne does not compete with but admiringly copies Diana. The word takes objective genitive. Ovid used Phoebe in 11 to denote the moon; here, she is sister of Apollo (called Phoebus above at 463). In 477, Ovid captures several typical features of the virginal huntress in connection with her hairstyle: she wears a simple ribbon, no fancy jewelry, and the hair hangs freely, not braided or curled by any maid. Thus, Daphne fits the role of a simple outdoors person. *sine lege*: not according to law, hence freely.

478   Folktales and myths regularly stage the competition of suitors for the hand of the beautiful maid (often princess). Such a situation can be developed several ways. When Ovid does it with *multi (-ae) illam (-um)*, the many serve as a foil to the decision of the person wooed; either nobody or a surprising individual is preferred. Cf. the description of Narcissus in 3.353 ff. and that of the centaur Cyllaris (a comic variant) in 12.404. For other scenes where men compete for the attention and hand of a girl, cf. 2.571 (Coronis), 10.315 (Myrrha), and 10.582 (Atalanta). We find this motif earlier in Catullus 62.42 and in Vergil's account of the suitors who vied for Lavinia (*Aen.* 7.54). The three elisions that Ovid allows himself in 478 are, as Lee notes, unusual.

479–   *viri*: "husband"; genitive with both preceding adjectives. *nemora avia*:
80   Ovid imitates a phrase of Lucretius 2.145. Daphne avoids frequented places and thus escapes male attention.

481–   The exact repetition of the initial half-lines led to understandable
82   problems in part of the MSS tradition: line 481 had to be written in the margin, when its omission was noticed.

483–   *velut crimen*: Daphne's hostility to marriage sounds extreme here,
84   almost as if she were a Vestal Virgin. *taedas*: by metonymy, the
       torches stand for marriage. *exosa*: this word first appears in Latin in
       Vergillian epic.

485–   An embrace around the neck frequently accompanies words of request
87   to a beloved parent or mate; cf. 1.734 and 762. *blandis* . . *lacertis*:
       same phrase in 2.100, when Phaethon embraces and pleads with his
       father, the Sun, to borrow the fatal chariot. The word order entangles
       the separate phrases: *inque patris* . . . *cervice* and *blandis* . . . *lacertis*.
       virginitate frui 487: the noun occurs more often in Ovid than in all
       his predecessors put together; that probably reflects his interest in
       erotic situations. *dedit* . . . *Dianae*: Daphne appeals to the experience
       of her model (cf. 476) and Jupiter's tolerance toward her virginity.
       As commentators note, Ovid is citing Callimachus' *Hymn to Artemis*,
       where the young goddess sat on her father's lap and successfully
       begged him for this favor.

488–   *quidem*: emphasizes the first clause, to enhance the antithesis with
89   the second. It is an irony of the *Met.* that beauty (or form) frustrates
       conscious plans and efforts. Daphne's own beauty literally fights
       against her desire. *quod optas / esse*: i.e., *virgo esse*. *tuo tua*: juxtaposi-
       tion stresses the conflict.

490–   *amat*: links with 474. The particular cruelty of Cupid's vengeance
91   now emerges: the god has been made to fall in love with a girl who
       hates love. *conubia*: Apollo does not use this word as Daphne had
       earlier in 480: she meant "marriage," whereas the selfish god merely
       desires sexual intercourse. *quodque* 491: the connective goes with the
       main verb, *sperat*. A typical elegiac lover, Apollo lets his passion
       create a false hope, and then Ovid comments on the irony, that the
       god of prophecy is failed by his own oracles.

492–   The rural fires in these similes do not lend Apollo's love much dignity.
94   *adolentur*: this verb, which originally meant "to make an offering at
       the altar," came to describe burning anywhere and under any circum-
       stances, as here. *viator* 493: like a careless traveller, Cupid has caused
       Apollo to burn up with love.

495–   *in flammas abiit*: the verb with the preposition forms a synonym for
96   "change," as earlier at 236 with Lycaon. Subject to love, the mighty
       god suffers psychological transformation, as if becoming fire. *sterilem*
       . . . *amorem* 496: the love would be "unproductive," vain because
       of Cupid's arrow to Daphne. *sperando*: links with *sperat* 491, the
       point from which the simile had taken off.

497–   *inornatos*: cf. 477, *positos sine lege*. Her hair, not being braided or
501   curled or piled up on her head, hangs freely and, to Apollo's eye,
       attractively. However, he tries to imagine how it would look if care-
       fully arranged. *quid si comantur* 498: hypothetical question in unreal

condition. *igne . . . oculos*: we would probably simply say "eyes flashing like stars," but Ovid has specified that they flash with fire. *oscula* 499: kisses, since they are given and stolen from the lips, can by metonymy suggest lips themselves. Alternatively, since this word for kiss derives from a lost Archaic Latin diminutive of the word for mouth, *os*, it may mean "darling little mouth." Apollo's eyes are beginning to work their way down from the hair; they reach hidden parts at 502. *laudat . . . lacertos* 500–501: although we might have expected the god to start with the shoulders and travel down the arms of Daphne with his glance, Ovid reverses the order of the anatomy lesson. That is probably because the upper arms, being half-bared, arouse erotic excitement. This passage provides a good illustration of the difference between *bracchia* and *lacerti*, forearms and upper arms.

502–3   What is witty and amusing here, when adapted in remarkably similar terms to a vicious rapist like Tereus (6.451 ff.), will be revealed as ruthlessly selfish lust. Like Tereus at 6.492, Apollo's imagination fires his passion. *fugit ocior aura*: this clause is closely modeled on *Aen.* 12.733, *fugit ocior Euro*, Turnus' last desperate flight when his sword shatters (cf. also *Aen.* 8.223, of Cacus). Ovid has eroticized the heroic life-and-death flight. *haec revocantis verba* 503: this announces the speech that follows (504–24) and the rather comic dramatic situation: Apollo, running after Daphne and trying to get her to stop and listen, breathlessly calls to her back as he calls her back.

504–7   *Penei*: vocative of *Peneis*; cf. 472. The final two syllables are separately sounded, not a diphthong. Consequently, the caesura in this line is the so-called "weak" or trochaic. Lee calls attention to the fact that Ovid uses this caesura with unusual frequency in Apollo's speech (six lines up to 521). He suggests that "it is used to express the hurry of the race." Alternatively, since this caesura itself is less important than the fact that, where it occurs, the line breaks into three distinctive units, with caesurae also at 3 and 7, Ovid is indicating by these brief units the breathlessness of the running god. *non insequor hostis*: the verb reveals that Apollo is chasing the fleeing nymph, not just standing still and calling after her (cf. 507). The animal similes of the next two lines form a tricolon, and, in standard rhetorical organization, the third member is longer, occupying the entire line of 506. *hostes . . . amor* 507: Apollo creates his own special definition of "enemy", namely, predators intent on killing and eating their prey. By contrast, he implies, love, the antithesis of enmity, absolves him from all blame.

508–9   *me miserum*: accusative in an exclamation. Apollo pretends to be in great distress. The following three clauses, all subjunctives, introduced by *ne*, might be prohibitions, i.e., negative commands; but negative wishes seem more likely. The god hopes that Daphne will not trip or be scratched on her pretty bare shins by brambles.

510   *moderatius*: the word is prosaic, the idea is absurd, and the calculating lover is revealed.

512–   Apollo tries a second ploy: to identify himself as an important god.
16   *cui placeas*: indirect question. The verb, though it may seem rather tepid in English, regularly occurs in an erotic sense in elegiac poetry and in the *Met.*; cf. 2.543, again of a girl who has attracted the attention of Apollo. With a tricolon of negative clauses, the god scornfully denies that he is a usual inhabitant of this rustic realm. The longer third member, with its adjective *horridus* 514, conveys the prejudice of a citified snob. *temeraria*: she is rash to flee him and so lose a chance for a good match, he suggests. *quem fugias* 515: indirect question. *ideo*: argumentative conjunctions do not appear often in epic or amatory poetry; this is the only occurrence in the *Met.* Its very usage may undermine the god's pose of sincerity. *mihi . . . servit*: Apollo now indirectly reveals himself without giving his name. Various lands, from Delphi to Patara, act as his slaves. The three places named in 516 are all situated in Asia Minor: Tenedos, an island near Troy, mentioned in *Iliad* 1.452 as a cult-site of Apollo and later in *Met.* 13.174; Claros, a famous oracle-site on the Ionian coast, cited in *Met.* 11.413; and Patara in Lycia, whose cult explains why Apollo is occasionally called by Roman poets "the Lycian god." By naming sites increasingly remote from nearby Delphi, he suggests the vast extent of his domain. The god ends his list with a florid phrase that gives inaccurate emphasis to Patara—it had no "palace" or royal residence—and thus falsely stresses his supposed mastery.

517–   Continuing with clues to his identity, Apollo names his father Jupiter,
18   then some of his attributes. Notice the pompous anaphora, *per me*, and the excessive use of *-que*. *concordant*: normally used with *cum* + ablative; Ovid has dared a dative without preposition. Apollo regularly appears in art and poetry with the lyre.

519–   *certa . . . certior*: clever chiastic arrangement, as Apollo reveals his
20   weakness and defeat by Cupid; cf. 463 ff. The second *nostra* is ablative of comparison. *vacuo . . . pectore*: an "empty" breast connotes a heart free of love.

521–   Paradoxically, the god of medicine cannot cure his own "wounds"
22   and "sickness" of love. *opifer*: Apollo claims this epithet, but this is its first appearance in extant Latin. Possibly Ovid has revived the epic compound from Ennius; he uses it a second time in 15.653 to refer to the god's son Aesculapius, also a doctor.

523–   *ei mihi*: a convenient dactylic verse-opening, of the same meaning as
24   *me miserum* (508), which extends to position 3. *sanabilis*: introduced to Latin probably by Cicero; Ovid is the first poet to employ it. The "incurability" of love was an elegiac topos. *prosunt . . . prosunt* 524: typically in such repetitions, Ovid alters the metrical position and

hence stress that the word receives. *domino . . . artes*: Ovid plays with a rhetorical commonplace that can be used with tragic overtones, as in Thucydides' (and imitators' such as Ovid in 7.561–62) account of plagues, where self-sacrificing doctors are caught up in the contagion and perish.

525–
26   Ovid likes to cut speeches short and vary the usually stately epic formula for closure. *plura locuturum . . . fugit*: Apollo may have become so intent on his verbiage that he failed to keep up with Daphne. *cumque ipso verba* 526: for this variation on a pair of accusative objects, cf. 217. It is easy to imagine Apollo with still-open mouth.

527–
29   *decens*: Ovid, who has already stated the paradox that Daphne's *decor* militates against her virginal wishes (488–89), here concentrates on the blowing of long robes away from the limbs to reveal more of the desired body. That theme is fully repeated in the Golden Line, 528; and 529 adds pictorial detail about Daphne's windblown tresses.

530–
32   *auctaque forma fuga est*: summarizes the paradox, that flight only makes Daphne seem more beautiful. *sed enim*: a common emphatic "but" in Vergil, as later in *Met.* 5.636, this expression seems somewhat unusual here because Ovid has separated it radically from the context which it will alter, namely 525–26. Yet what he has reported in the intervening lines about that increased beauty has much to do with the sudden change in Apollo's line of action. The god has been left unheard by the fugitive, *but* that does not matter anymore because he has no further interest in words. *blanditias* 531: signifies in elegy and love poetry the soft and often deceptive words of lovers. *amor* 532: the "love" that Apollo declared pure, friendly, and selfless in 507 reveals its essential nature. *admisso sequitur . . . passu*: back in pursuit (cf. 504, 507, 511), Apollo has a pace that has suddenly been freed from restraint. The usual noun with the participle is *equo*, and the phrase means "at full speed" (for the horse has been given the rein). However, as the following simile suggests, Ovid may have been thinking of a hunting dog on a leash, when set loose to track the quarry. Hence, the use of *vestigia* here and in 536.

533–
34   *ut canis . . . Gallicus*: Apollo has now become the animal "enemy" of Daphne that he expressly disclaimed earlier in 504 ff. The "Gallic hound" was one of many hunting dog types used by Romans. *hic . . . ille* 534: not the idiomatic arrangement of "latter" and "former" that appeared earlier at 472; Ovid maintains attention on Apollo and refers to him as *hic*.

535–
38   *alter . . . alter*: Ovid neatly divides the four lines, allotting two to each beast, dog first, then hare. *inhaesuro similis*: "as though he were about to hang or fasten on to" the hare. The verb *inhaereo* can also be used to describe the embrace of a lover (cf. *Trist.* 1.3.79). *iam iamque tenere*: with these words, Ovid reveals the model for this part

of the simile, namely, Vergil's comparison of the pursuit of Turnus
by Aeneas in *Aen.* 12.754 to the chase of a deer by a baying, snapping
hound (*haeret hians, iam iamque tenet similisque tenenti*). Ovid has
transferred the grim epic situation to this erotic context, where, as we
shall see, the outcome is ambiguous (though Daphne, like Turnus,
ceases to be human). *sperat* 536: Apollo still hopes in vain (cf. 491,
496). *extento . . . rostro*: a literal picture of a hound just grazing the
feet of its prey as it strains its muzzle (and snapping teeth) forward.
an sit conprensus 537: indirect question, *an* replacing *utrum*, as Roman
writers often did. The perfect passive is not entirely logical; surely
the hare would have known whether it had been caught (for there
would be pain to inform it). The form presumably replaces present
passive subjunctive, unmetrical *comprehendatur*; the shorter and met-
rical *comprendatur* does not appear in Augustan literature. *eripitur*
538: passive for reflexive (or middle); "it tears itself away." *relinquit*:
the simile ends with the same verb as in 526.

539   *virgo*: first use of this word for Daphne or for any human female. It
will recur frequently hereafter in contexts of rape or near-rape. The
synaloephe (elision) with *est* at the caesura is not in itself unusual,
but normal practice links the *est* syntactically with the elided word
and makes the caesura functional as a sense-pause. Here, the caesura
and synaloephe obscure the sense-units.

540–   *insequitur*: obviously, Apollo (cf. 504, 511, 532). *pennis adiutus*
42   *amoris*: as Bömer nicely observes, it is important not to capitalize
amoris, because Cupid has decisively doomed Apollo's passion and
the winged "help" he gets from his own love will result in a most
ironic "catch." With these wings, he becomes like a bird of prey (cf.
506). Four clauses crowded into 541–42, each slightly longer than
the previous one, emphasize the gradual superiority of Apollo as he
overtakes Daphne. *crinem sparsum cervicibus* 542: the loose hair,
which Ovid has described as catching Apollo's attention (497–98)
and blown back by the breeze while she flees (529), here seems to
him, as he looms over her, to spread over her neck. For a similar
description of a pursuer breathing on the hair and neck of a fleeing
nymph, cf. Arethusa's story in 5.616–17.

543–   *expalluit*: this verb is restricted to the perfect tense and, in Ovid, to
45   this particular form. Pallor serves as a sign of exhaustion. *victa labore
fugae* 544: cf. Arethusa *fessa labore fugae* (5.618). *Tellus*: Ovid has
not mentioned her before, and there is no evidence that Daphne appeals
to her as her mother, but as a common refuge available to any human
being. It is thus conventional for people in desperation to ask the
earth to open up and swallow them. Cf. Dido's prayer in *Aen.* 4.24;
her phrase is *tellus . . . dehiscat*. Since death and total physical
disappearance run counter to the themes of Ovid's poem, Daphne

proposes an alternative, metamorphosis, in *istam . . . figuram*. Her beauty has caused her crisis—the imminence of rape—so her only recourse is to destroy it. For a similar situation, where loss by change of body answers the appeal for help, cf. 13.669 ff.

546   Daphne also appeals to her father with the formulaic *fer . . . opem*: cf. 1.380, 647, 2.700, 3.719, and 5.618. Unlike the Olympian deities, rivers in Ovid's poem do not possess the power to transform others. It is with the roles of Earth and Peneos that some of Ovid's readers and thence the MSS had trouble. Our earliest extant evidence (not all that early) gives lines 544–46 as this text does. That means that Daphne makes a stronger appeal to Tellus than to her father, that Tellus is invoked as the agent of transformation. The two MSS that most commonly seem to preserve the authentic text, *MN*, apparently had those same three lines, but subsequently parts of 545 and 546 were erased. Those erasures suggest that a later scribe wanted to change *MN* to fit a different text found in other traditions. In those other traditions, the role of Peneos is expanded. A new line 547 appears, which assigns to the river the task of destroying Daphne's beauty by metamorphosis. To prepare for it and make the father the first to whom Daphne prays, 544 is altered to *victa labore fugae, spectans Peneidas undas* [=544a]. In fact, Ovid does not say which deity, if either, answered the prayer. But the transformation into a tree (and the later confusion as to Peneos' reaction to the change, 578) imply that Tellus alone has acted with her earthly powers.

548–   The juxtaposition of metamorphosis to the prayer requesting it sug-
50   gests, but does not prove, that the gods have responded. *torpor*: since the limbs are in active motion of flight, this sudden heaviness is especially striking. It might well inspire a statue such as Bernini's famous group, where Daphne has just begun to turn into a laurel. *occupat*: a benevolent "occupation" in place of hostile or erotic (cf. 11.239) possession. *cinguntur* 549: Daphne's form now becomes clothed or girt, as it were, with a thin covering of bark. Bernini shows this effect nicely. The bark, of course, finally destroys the female beauty, as Daphne wanted.

551–   For feet to become roots is traditional; Ovid adds pathos by contrasting
52   "slow" with the recent "speedy". *remanet nitor unus* 552: the only bit of physical continuity between the girl Daphne and the laurel is the sensuously healthy glow of its leaves (= skin).

553–   *hanc*: Daphne in this altered form; but the feminine could also apply
54   to *arbor* and *laurus*, the new genus. *stipite*: the lovely body of the girl has turned into a tree trunk. *adhuc . . . novo* 554: different aspects of metamorphosis: continuity on the one hand and novelty on the other.

555–   *ramos, ut membra*: above at 550, Ovid identified the source of branches

56   as *bracchia*. Here, he needs a shorter word. Apollo is throwing his
arms around what once were Daphne's arms, in order to kiss her; but
the botanical detail makes the scene silly rather than sentimental.
oscula 556: earlier, at 499, Apollo had been excited by her mouth
and the thought of kisses that could be planted there. But Daphne
continues to avoid the touch of the god.

557–   *cui*: Apollo addresses the wood and personifies it, a comic touch that
59   Ovid emphasizes by moving back and forth between botanical and
human terms. *coniunx*: it has been clear that Apollo has not intended
more than a passing sexual gratification for himself in his pursuit and
"love" of Daphne. Moreover, Apollo in myth never did have a long-
term consort or "wife." *arbor . . . mea* 558: the exchange of tree for
wife, emphasized by the repeated but delayed possessive, should be
an anticlimax. *laure* 559: the new form is at last named in a vocative.

560–   The speech of Apollo to the laurel, because of its subject and its
61   formal use of second person singular pronouns, follows the pattern
of hymns and prayers. Ironically, after causing Daphne's destruction
by his "disrespect," the god appears to treat the "wood" with reverence
and to appropriate it as a fit attribute of his own worship. *ducibus
Latiis*: the laurel was a regular symbol of a Roman triumph in the
crown worn by the celebrating generals. The MSS all give the reading
laetis, which would be acceptable in itself, but seems otiose when
the same adjective recurs in the line. Heinsius' brilliant conjecture,
Latiis, fits with Ovid's tendency to modernize myths, to stress their
non-Greek applications. *canet . . . visent* 561: the verbs point to
regular action of the future (Ovid's and his audience's present). Trium-
phal parades started in the Campus Martius and, after passing through
the Circus Maximus, made their way through the Forum and up the
Via Triumphalis to the Temple of Jupiter on the Capitoline Hill.

562–   *postibus Augustis*: Augustus lived in a rather modest home on the
63   Palatine Hill. In the Senatorial actions that focused on making his
official name Augustus (instead of Octavian) in 27 B.C., it was also
decreed that a crown of oak leaves (which symbolized his salvation
of citizens by ending civil war) be awarded him and permanently hung
on his door, along with laurel to commemorate his victories. *stabis
. . . quercum* 563: the detail indicates that laurel bushes were probably
planted on either side of Augustus' doorway and thus could "look at"
the oak crown in between.

564–   Apollo ends up with a comparison between himself and the laurel that
65   seems strained syntactically and logically. The immediate connection
between god and bush consists in the likeness of long hair on Apollo's
head and foliage crowning the laurel bush. Therefore, he may be
thought to be saying that, as his hair is the eternal crowning glory of
his handsome young head, so the laurel will have an eternal crown

of evergreen foliage. The recent translation of A. D. Melville has made that point: "My brow is ever young, my locks unshorn; / So keep your leaves' proud glory ever green." The repetition of "ever" regularizes the comparison that Ovid made patently irregular. Even after explicating the comparison and its syntax, problems remain. First, the exact sense of *frondis honores*. Is the genitive, as translation and discussion so far have implied, objective? Does the foliage receive honor from its greenery, and is that what Apollo, in his still warm affection for Daphne, desires? The parallel phrase at 449, *frondis honorem*, at the beginning of this narrative, seems to negate that interpretation. There, the foliage is possessive; it confers honor. And that, after all, is what Apollo wants. The second problem arises as to the start of the comparison. Is it neutral, or is the god naively proud of his youth? Does he aim to exploit this laurel, which he has now appropriated, as his eternal ornament?

566– *Paean*: this name properly attaches to Apollo in his capacity as healer.
67   However, Apollo has healed nothing; he has promoted his own triumph over frustration. *factis modo*: another formulaic way of referring to metamorphosis. *ramis / adnuit*: the verb, which means to nod assent (by a forward movement among the Romans), would assume that the instrumental ablative refers to the head. Earlier, Ovid said that the girl's arms became branches (550) and that Apollo embraced them (i.e., her arms and waist) with his arms (555). Now, apparently we must ignore that equation and imagine the branches that lead into the crowning foliage, which are then part of the whole nodding movement. *utque caput . . . cacumen*: at 552, Ovid made the treetop take over the human face. At the end, then, the humanity inside the laurel, which resisted Apollo's efforts to continue his amatory purposes, acquiesces in the "nobler" designs of the god. Ovid leaves it unclear whether Apollo's triumph is her defeat or her victory, too. Such ambiguity is not an atypical conclusion.

Io (568–746)

The final story of Book 1 reuses elements of the Daphne-story, but in this case Ovid features Jupiter as lover of the nymph, and the love (or lust) quickly results in rape. Ovid then continues with new story-motifs: namely, the guilt of Jupiter as not only rapist but also adulterer, his trivial sense of morality and commitment as lover, the jealousy of Juno, a new reason for metamorphosis, the continued human aware-ness of Io after metamorphosis and her half-comic, half-tragic sense of suffering, and finally her restoration as a human being (or nymph). Ovid is a master of this technique of theme and variation.

The story of Io can be traced back to the Greek epic cycles, but the chief transmitter of the story in early literature is Aeschylus in his *Prometheus*. As part of a tragedy, the story serves a serious purpose: in obvious ways, the misery of Io parallels that of Prometheus at the hands of a cruel Zeus, and her happy escape alerts the audience to the possibility of Prometheus' eventual reconciliation with the god. Much came between Aeschylus and Ovid, which we cannot trace. In Neoteric literature, Calvus composed an epyllion about Io, and Ovid knew it well enough to allude to one of its pathetic lines at 632, where the earlier poet had sympathetically apostrophized Io turned cow. Ovid himself, in an earlier and briefer account of Io's sufferings (*Her.* 14.85–108), had let the narrator, Hypermestra, treat her as a pathetic prototype.

It is notable that Ovid does not apostrophize Io, whether as nymph or cow. Thus, he refrains from projecting sentimental sympathy for the victimized girl. Moving rapidly past the rape, which he renders in circumlocution (600), he exposes in a light and playful manner the cheap morality of Jupiter and the selfish reasons for which the god inflicted metamorphosis, another outrage, on Io. But our sense of outrage is attenuated by the way the narrator focuses on minor details: we hear nothing of Io's indignation or her puzzled sense of wrong; instead, Ovid talks of her discomforts in having to lie on grass rather than a luxurious couch (633), of her frustration in lacking hands to appeal for pity, and of lacking a human voice to communicate with Argus or later with her father (647). Similarly, when Inachus realizes that the cow is Io metamorphosed, Ovid makes his reactions bathetic: he is appalled because she moos in response to his words, because she will ruin his dynastic plans by marrying a bull. That technique does not appear to have been Calvus', but playful grotesquerie was one of the tactics of Callimachus, notably in his story of Erysichthon; he played with the family's bourgeois responses instead of emphasizing the monstrosity of Erysichthon.

Ovid also takes us away from the half-comic plight of Io by turning his and our attention to her guard Argus (668–723), a sequence of fifty-five lines that replays, in a story that Mercury sings to the guard about the lovely nymph Syrinx, the motifs of pursued nymph and escape by metamorphosis, but in such a dry and monotonous manner that it takes life and feeling from the story. In fact, Mercury uses the tale to put Argus to sleep, all hundred of his eyes: it was that boring. Then, when we are perhaps smiling at Ovid's clever self-referentiality, the poet surprises us: as Argus nods in sleep, Mercury seizes a sword and slashes at his neck, probably decapitates him, and pushes the corpse over a cliff. The monotonous story has been used to perpetrate a murder; the murderer has been a god displaying consummate musical ability; and he in turn has been carrying out the unscrupulous will of Jupiter.

This unfunny conclusion to the inserted story of Syrinx and to the life of simple Argus changes the tone of the remainder of Io's tale: Juno gets furious (724) and harrasses the cow over the entire world with a new and more savage "attendant," a Fury (instead of the traditional gadfly). Finally arriving at the Nile, at the end of her endurance, Io appeals to guilty Jupiter, who weasels out a specious promise to his wife. When Juno becomes mollified—though Jupiter will soon arouse her fury with another nymph—it is possible for Io to recover her human form.

The Transition from Daphne to Io (568–87)

The story of Io is going to resemble that of Daphne, in that she, too, will be pursued by a god, but it will quickly acquire new features, once that god, Jupiter, succeeds in his rapist designs. Characteristically, however, Ovid masks the relationship in his transition. He focuses first on Daphne's father, who has played a minor role in her experiences: Peneus is attended by subordinate rivers who, in their obsequious desperation, cannot figure out whether what has happened to Daphne is cause for congratulation or sympathy. Ovid gives a short catalogue of the rivers who are present (579–82), then focuses on the sole absentee, Inachus, father of Io. His daughter is missing and he fears her dead. Thus, through the two fathers and Inachus' preoccupation with his own child instead of Peneus', Ovid moves us into curiosity over Io's fate.

568   *est nemus*: the scene is set with a place-description or ecphrasis (cf. 1.168) of traditional form. In the tale of Daphne, only the identification of the nymph as daughter of Peneus suggested the locale in Thessaly. Now we move to a specific valley along the course of the Peneus River. *praerupta*: the steepness of the terrain, which affects the layout of the trees in Ovid's description, was to the Greeks and the Romans who saw the spot the major feature. They described the place, Tempe, as a vale or valley, not as a grove. *claudit / silva*: Ovid likes to set the stage, so to speak, in a natural amphitheatre. Cf. the scene of Pentheus' death in 3.708 ff.

569   *Tempe*: since this word is indeclinable neuter plural, it is followed by relative *quae*. The Vale of Tempe struck the ancient mind as an idyllic spot, but it was a strategic as well as beautiful location. The great Plain of Thessaly is surrounded by mountains. In the northeast, the only feasible exit has been made by the Peneus River which, emerging, as Ovid says in 570, from the Pindus Mountains, makes its way across the Plain to the northeast corner, where it has carved a course through a gorge to the sea. That gorge or vale, well-watered and therefore

well-wooded, the Greeks called *Tempe*. *Peneus*: the first actual naming of the river, though of course Ovid has prepared for it by the various patronymic adjectives used for Daphne (cf. 452, 472, 504). *ab imo /
. . . Pindo* (570): "from the depths of the Pindus," not simply from the base of the mountains.

570   *spumosis . . . undis*: the foam suggests the swift and turbulent movement of rapids, appropriate in a narrow gorge. For another description, which seems more emphatic of the idyllic details, Lee cites Pliny *NH* 4.31.

571   *deiectu*: a rare word, prosaic before and after Ovid until Statius, and only here in Ovid. Besides rapids, he also imagines falls, another typical element of river gorges. A standard side effect of falls, as is well known at Niagara, for example, would be a cloud of water spray or mist rising from the bottom. The falls of the Anio River at Tibur near Rome (modern Tivoli, still impressive) were familiar to many in Ovid's audience.

572   *summis . . . silvis*: to emphasize the extent of the spray, Ovid specifies the very tops of the trees in the steep woods (cf. 568). Alliteration of *s* in this half-line emphasizes the sound of spray. *adspergine*: a poetic alternative to the word that Cicero regularly uses, *aspersio*, which becomes unmetrical in the oblique cases.

573   *inpluit*: only a few MSS preserve this reading; *N* changed the order of two letters and transmits *impluit*, and most MSS have *influit*. Clearly, however, the river does not "flow" but "rain" with spray on the tree-tops. *sonitu*: concludes the description with another standard detail for falls: thunderous sound. *plus quam vicina*: "more than the neighborhood". The indirect phrase creates rhetorical emphasis. Other examples of this usage are more notable: e.g., *plus quam civiliter* (12.583), which Lucan admired and imitated in the first line of his epic, and *plus quam femina* (13.451) for the heroically brave Polyxena.

575   *in his*: the last noun in the list of 574 is plural; simply translate "here." *antro*: ablative of place where; the preposition may be supplied from the earlier *in*. A cave in the side of a cliff is a common sight in gorges.

576   *iura dabat*: having depicted Peneus as a river, Ovid now visualizes him as a powerful ruler of waters (i.e., tributaries) and water-nymphs. That image allows him both to play with the problem caused by political power, the necessity for courtiers to please, and to transfer his attention to Peneus as father of Daphne.

577   *popularia*: the local rivers are viewed as the "people" under his rule. In Rome, the word had strong overtones during the factional struggles of the first century B.C. *primum*: prepares for *mox* (581).

578   *nescia gratentur*: the adjective introduces an indirect question. Although the grammar books teach us to use such particles as *an* or *utrum* before the subjunctive, Roman writers, in prose and poetry,

did not feel obliged to do so in what are called "disjunctive" questions (where there were two options). In such cases, simple *-ne* could be added to the second term (cf. 5.167). *parentem*: not "their father," but the father of Daphne.

579–
80
Ovid produces a two-line catalogue of Peneus' neighbors, giving each a dignifying epithet (except the last one). The epithets seem to be typical of rivers rather than specific to the chosen river. Those in 579 are Ovid's invention: *populifer* he had already first used of the Po River in *Amores* 2.17.32; *inrequietus* has its first occurrence here. The first four rivers are all major, but widely distributed Thessalian streams. The Enipeus and Apidanus are tributaries of Peneos; the Sperchios runs far to the south in Thessaly; and the Amphrysos to the north. And the Aeas does not even flow in Thessaly, but in Epirus on the far side of the Pindus range. *Apidanus*: a correction for the MSS reading, *Eridanus*, which would refer to the Italian Po. No Italian river belongs in this catalogue.

581–
82
Ovid seems to be thinking of all the other rivers of Greece, since he singles out as the sole absentee the Inachus, which flows through the Argolid. *impetus*: the combined effect of current and natural course. *deducunt* 582: since a river's course has to be slightly graded in order for the water to flow, it regularly can be said in Latin to bring its waters *down* to the sea. *fessas erroribus*: personifies the waters, as if they have "wandered" like a tired traveller.

583
Inachus unus abest: the preamble concludes by abandoning the rivers in Peneus' cave and focusing on the sole absentee (cf. 6.421). *reconditus antro*: like Peneus, Inachus is in a cave, alone and weeping inconsolably.

584
fletibus auget aquas: exploits the double view of Inachus as both person and river. His tears increase his own supply of water! *natam . . . Io*: since the name of Io is indeclinable, this form is accusative.

585–
86
amissam: whereas we meet Peneus at the end of Daphne's adventures, when we and he know all, here Ovid starts the father Inachus midway, so to speak, in Io's experiences. She is mysteriously lost. During the next fifty lines, the story will fill in the background, then continue with the scene when the father "finds" Io (now a cow, 639 ff.). *vitane fruatur / an sit*: the more conventional form of alternative indirect question: cf. above 578.

586–
87
Witty phrasing suggests the attitude with which the narrator interprets this story. *non usquam = nusquam*, that is, no longer alive. *animo peiora veretur* 587: Lee suggests that this means that Inachus fears the worse of the two alternatives, hence that Ovid repeats himself and emphasizes how strongly the father believes Io dead. However, the Latin could also mean: "he fears worse things in his heart." Io may have met what we call a fate "worse than death," the obvious one of

dishonor. And when Inachus does recognize his lost daughter in the cow (651 ff.), we shall see that as a cow she is worse than dead for her "conventional father."

Flashback: How Io Was Lost (Raped and Transformed) (588–638)

In the typical manner of an explanatory flashback, the narrative starts in the pluperfect tense. Gradually, it moves to the perfect, then to the vivid present (605 ff.), where for the most part it stays. In working out his account, Ovid ingeniously starts the "loss" at the moment Io was coming back from a visit to her beloved father. Approached by a suspicious male who claims to be Jupiter, she flees and is rather swiftly overtaken by the superhuman god not far away in Lerna. Rape and metamorphosis follow in that spot, and, as a cow, Io is handed over to Juno, then entrusted to Argus, the specially vigilant "cowherd." The cow ambles through the countryside and eventually comes back to meadows along the Inachus (her father). Thus, the narrative reunites the father with Io, but not as he desired.

588–
89   *a patrio redeuntem . . . flumine*: it might seem, as Bömer suggests, that Io ought to be going to her father's home, like a modest ancient virgin. However, the hyperbaton that separates adjective and noun indicates the sense of the narrative. Io resembles the typical virgin who has gone out to draw water. Cf. Tarpeia in Propertius 4.4, Rhea Silvia at *Fast.* 3.11 ff., or the innocent young daughter of Cnemon in Menander's *Dyskolos*. *o virgo Iove digna*: the speech starts abruptly without any verb of saying (which is postponed until late in 590). Jupiter appears to be using an ordinary wooing formula, by which he implies the superior attractions of the girl. However, at a second crasser level, he in only telling us of his lust for this virgin. The praise from the god's lips in these two lines, though abbreviated, fulfills the motif which, in the story of Daphne, is elaborated into a full description of the lovely feminine features. Hypermestra in *Her.* 14.99 calls Io *Iove digna*, too.

589–
90   *tuoque beatum . . . factura toro*: this wooing formula goes back to *Od.* 6 (and earlier), where Odysseus arouses the interest of Nausicaa by envying the man who marries her. *torus*, which refers to any couch or bed, can also apply to the marriage bed and hence by metonymy to marriage: cf. 319 and 353 for its use with the married pair Pyrrha and Deucalion. In raping Io, however, Jupiter uses no bed; for him, *torus* dwindles into simply meaning sex.

590–
92   *pete umbras*: Jupiter tries to lure Io into the woods, where she will be at his mercy, by pretending to be concerned for her comfort. It is very hot, and therefore it would make sense to find a shady spot to

rest. This is a standard reference for Ovid, the first of many, to a time and place for rapes. At noon, when the maiden seeks a place under the trees to rest, perhaps also some water in which to drink or bathe, she exposes herself to the lust of the gods. *altorum nemorum et nemorum* 591: Heinsius rescued this reading, universally accepted, from some of his precious, now lost MSS. The line has been partially erased in *M* and totally erased in *N. M, U,* and *ε* all start with the first two words, but then become corrupt; other MSS are more desperate. None apparently perceived that Ovid was launching into a stage direction in parenthesis. Once Heinsius found the right text, the art of Ovid's parenthetical wit was rescued. Jupiter makes a large gesture toward the woods, in order to convince Io of his real concern. In 592, the sun high up in mid-course poetically indicates midday or what we call high noon. Cf. the description in 2.417, where Jupiter accosts Callisto: *ulterius medio spatium sol altus habebat.*

593   *times . . . intrare: timeo* with the infinitive is not uncommon in prose and especially poetry. Caesar used it, and it obviously helps the poets crowd more words into a line (cf. earlier 1.176). Io, no huntress like Daphne, might be frightened of wild animals in the woods.

594   *praeside tuta deo*: Jupiter uses the solemn language of Roman religion (*praeside*) as he starts to present what he expects to be his irresistible attractions. Of course, the "protection" he is offering is spurious. *nemorum secreta*: the genitive depends on the adjective in neuter plural, which functions as a substantive. These "secret haunts" will be convenient for the god's lust.

595–   *de plebe deo*: Ovid has already distinguished the "aristocrats" and the
96   "common people" among the gods in his first description of Olympus (168–74). When Jupiter tries to win favor by boasting of his social superiority, he sounds like a spoiled Roman noble. *caelestia magna*: neuter accusative and feminine ablative, so that each of the following nouns may have its adjective. The credentials that Jupiter here specifies have been shown in somewhat incompetent operation during the Lycaon episode earlier. He was a bigoted wielder of the sceptre, and his thunderbolt proved ineffective twice (230, 253). Hence *vaga* 596 seems ironic.

597   *ne fuge me! fugiebat enim.* Before the god can develop a long speech, as Apollo had with Daphne, Io, like Daphne, starts to run away (cf. 525–26). Ovid then inserts a stage direction.

597–   Lerna and Lyrcaea, in the Argolid, were not far from the Inachus.
98   The flight does not last long.

599–   *inducta . . . caligine terras / occuluit*: ablative absolute or ablative
600   of means. The god hid the earth in a pall of darkness that he brought over it. Three verbs in the perfect end the sequence of background pluperfects and also register the selfish and inhuman swiftness of the

god's lust. Each has its own object, but the last one, *pudorem*, transfers
us from the literal into the moral sphere. Jupiter has perpetrated what
Apollo failed to do, and it ceases to be amusing. Nothing in this affair
suggests the ordinary process of love. Thus, when Jupiter pretends
to balance the rival claims of *amor* and *pudor* (617 ff.), he will only
emphasize his loveless selfishness and his total lack of shame or honor.

601 Here Juno enters the poem. She plays the comic role of the deceived
and angrily suspicious wife; her anger lacks the grandeur that Vergil
assigned to it in the *Aeneid*. *despexit*: the preposition in the compound
implies that Juno is in Olympus looking down.

602– Jupiter has concealed the earth with a dark mist, for a reason that was
4 not immediately obvious. Now, we understand: he is an adulterer
trying to escape the notice of his wife. *sub nitido . . . die* 603: "in
bright daylight."

605– *ut quae . . . nosset*: relative clause of characteristic with causal over-
6 tones. The introductory words might more commonly be *quippe quae,
utpote quae*, as Lee notes. *nosset* for *novisset*. Jupiter's regular role
as adulterer in Ovid's poem vastly outweighs his function as supreme
ruler. *furta*: this word, which properly refers to ordinary theft, comes
to mean "stolen love" as early as Catullus (68.140, of Jupiter); Ovid
uses it frequently (cf. 1.623, 2.423).

607 *quem*: her husband Jupiter. *aut ego fallor . . . laedor* 608: Lee suggests
the witty translation, "either I am wrong or I am being wronged."
The exactly equal rhythmical quality of the two clauses invites appreci-
ation of Ovid's wit.

608– *delapsa*: Juno glides down in easy flight, perhaps planning to approach
9 the scene quietly. *nebulas . . . iussit* 609: she exerts authority over
clouds, much as the sky god Jupiter himself.

610– The pluperfect tenses indicate that Jupiter (*ille* 611) had already acted
11 to outwit his wife. *mutare in* + accusative of the object changed and
accusative of the entity into which it changes constitute one of the
most familiar phrases of metamorphosis; Ovid uses the passive form
in line 1. *nitentem . . . iuvencam*: effective hyperbaton, which delays
the noun, the whole phrase enclosing the victim of the change. The
gleaming whiteness of Io's body easily fitted the sleek whiteness of
a cow. *Inachidos vultus*: Greek genitive and patronymic for Io. Since
the entire body, not just the face, was turned into a cow—more than
the face aroused the god's lust, after all—treat *vultus* as synonymous
with *formam*.

612 *bos*: the monosyllabic word, coming after *iuvenca*, causes some sur-
prise, as though the pretty young calf has suddenly become nothing
but a cow! *speciem*: regular synonym for *formam*.

613 *quamquam invita:* this construction of conjunction and adjective is
rare before the next generation of writers. In Ovid, it occurs only

here, as Bömer notes. *nec non*: double negative merely means: "and."
Ovid next uses it again at 2.615.

614 *sit*: subjunctive in indirect question, with each of the interrogative
words that have preceded. *armento*: ablative of description. *veri quasi
nescia*: objective genitive with the adjective Ovid sketches out a do-
mestic comedy of mutual pretense and dishonesty.

615– The comedy grows. Embarrassed by Juno's questions, none of which
616 he can answer truthfully, and unwilling to pretend ignorance, Jupiter
tries a simple lie: the cow was earth-born. In the idiom of contemporary
Augustan Rome, that meant it was of unknown origin. It is part of
Ovid's wit, that we should hear the everyday idiom. *auctor*: Juno's
questions have artfully circled around her real interest, which is quite
bluntly where the cow came from, or more bluntly, who brought it
into existence. Ovid leaves amusing gaps in his narrative, inviting his
audience to fill in the real motives and feelings of this divine couple.
Thus, we can assume that Juno recognized Jupiter's lie. Pretending
to believe him, she asks him to present her the cow (since, it seems,
it means nothing to him).

617– *quid faciat?* Ovid sets up with the deliberative subjunctive the dilemma
619 that Juno has created for her liar husband, first in terms of the adjectives
crudele and *suspectum*, then with the abstract nouns *pudor* and *amor*.
Jupiter feels no emotional obligations to his wife; his dilemma focuses
on how to enjoy his love and get away with it. It follows that he also
does not feel any serious emotional obligations to Io, his victim. His
entire dilemma is subjective: it feels cruel to lose his sexual partner—
the cruel sufferings she may experience are of little and secondary
concern. But he does not want to be suspect. Next, Ovid mockingly
translates Jupiter's motives into normally serious Roman ethical terms
and by the demonstrative adverbs makes clear the application: *illinc
. . . hinc*. A supposedly right sense of shame (*pudor*) urges him to
bite the bullet, suffer a bit, but give the gift; a supposedly full awareness
of what love entails (*amor*) impels him to refuse. The conflict between
these two values was traditional in Roman comedy, Roman elegy,
and in Hellenistic epic. Vergil had thus defined Dido's inner conflict
in *Aen.* 4.27–28 and 54–55. Ovid's audience, then, knew precisely
what significance these terms should bear in a serious moral context.
But this almighty god of Ovid is a casuist, bound by no moral ties.
When Jupiter comes close to letting love defeat shame (619), he may
seem to resemble the typical tormented lover, but it does not take
long to realize that he is exclusively self-interested. It is no accident
that Ovid earlier described the act of rape as the violation of Io's
pudor. Jupiter, in destroying her honor, has lost honor already; and
he certainly has exhibited a low level of *amor*.

620– *sociae generisque torique*: since it was conventional to hail Juno as

21   sister and wife of Jupiter (cf. 3.265–66, *Aen.* 1.46–47), Ovid uses somewhat high-flown language to over-emphasize the relationship, which was in human terms incestuous. Double *-que* is also a mark of epic diction. *negaretur, poterat* 621: where one might expect *posse* in the imperfect subjunctive (as here, in present contrary to fact), Latin frequently allows imperfect indicative.

622–   *paelice*: Ovid deliberately confuses the double nature of Io, who is a
24   cow in form, but in significance a rival of Juno. By handing over his wife's rival, the god seems to play the role of the penitent guilty husband. However, he has never admitted his affair and is in fact hoping that he has fooled Juno into believing the cow a cow and himself a loyal mate. *exuit . . . metum*: "threw off her fear"; the image is of removing clothing, the opposite of *induere*. *anxia furti*: this is the first known instance in Latin where the adjective *anxius* takes an objective genitive. *furti* has both the figurative sense of 606 and the literal sense of theft. Jupiter might try to steal the cow from his wife. *Arestoridae . . . Argo* 624: this patronymic for Argus, which originates in Greek myth and appears in Apollonius of Rhodes 1.111 and 325, has its first and only occurrence here in Latin poetry. Ovid flaunts his erudition. *servandam*: traditionally, Argus just used his many eyes to keep the cow in sight. Ovid, however, turns him into a typical herdsman (cf. below 630 ff).

625   *luminibus*: the lights of the eye reappear in the witty epitaph for Argus at 720. As Bömer notes, the number and location of Argus' eyes was never fixed: by Aeschylus' time, they were countless (which is what a hundred would suggest to a Roman), usually all on the head, as here; but some vase painters distributed them all over the body (since there was hardly room on the head for so many eyes).

626–   *inde*: "of these (eyes)." In strict rotation, two eyes rest while the others
27   stand watch, and then by twos each sleeps. This prepares us for the abnormal problem faced by Mercury: how to put all hundred eyes to sleep at one time.

628–   Ovid plays with the incredible situation and varies the metrical stress
29   on Io. Argus had Io before his eyes though he had turned his back to her.

630–   *luce*: in the light of day, by day. *pasci*: to graze; this is the first word
31   since 621 to fix on the cow. The scene extracts humorous pathos from the tension between human and animal. Hence, *indigno* 631: Io did not deserve to be tethered like a beast; the beast that Argus sees does of course have to be tied up.

632   Ovid retraces ground previously worked by the once-famous Neoteric poet Calvus in his epyllion *Io*, already reworked in *Her.* 14.85 ff. Calvus had created an unforgettable hexameter to which Ovid alludes here and in 634: *a virgo infelix, herbis pasceris amaris*. Ovid refrains

from the overly sentimental apostrophe. He wants to be more amused than tearful over the paradoxes of Io's predicament: this girl whose human sensibility is trapped temporarily inside a cow!

633–
34
Ovid conveys (*infelix* 634) Io's misery with her sleeping conditions: like a fussy princess (cf. the Princess and the Pea) she objects to the ground for a bed. *terrae*: dative with *incubat*. *limosa*: the drinking places of cattle strike us as muddy, which does not bother cows, of course, but appalls the girl inside the cow-shape.

635–
36
Now, Ovid moves on to paradoxes available to him in the metamorphosed body. This is the first of many times when he will describe the frustration of the human desire to supplicate help that emerges in a metamorphosed creature who lacks human hands (cf. Actaeon at 2.240–41). *Argo*: loose dative; with *tendere*, the more common construction would be *ad* + accusative. *quae bracchia*: reverses normal prose word order and pulls the "antecedent" of the relative into the characteristic clause, so as to make the verbal echo of *bracchia . . . tendere* above more effective.

637–
38
et conata: Ovid takes 637 almost verbatim from *Her.* 14.91. The emphasis falls on the frustration of the human being who, when she tried to complain (the typical stance in elegy), merely moos! The next line also represents a variation on *Her.* 14.92.

Reunion of Father and Daughter, Inachus and Io (639–63)

639–
40
After this flashback, Ovid brings Io back to her father's river and ends his uncertainty. In the innocence of her girlhood, Io used to play in the meadows, gathering flowers, dancing with her friends. Now, all that has come to a pathetic end, and the spot evokes predictably sad memories. *venit et*: Io has been drinking muddy water from nameless Argolid rivers, and now at last she reaches the Inachus.

640–
41
nova . . . cornua: as noted at 437, the adjective *novus* regularly refers to the results of metamorphosis, either in the whole form or, as here, to a significant part. Ovid postpones that self-recognition for this poignant moment. He is reusing here a couplet from *Her.* 14.89–90. The horns convey it all to Io; there is no need to go into other grotesque features of the cow's head and body. *seque* 641: although Ovid used *pertimuitque* above at 638 with a direct object, the verb can be used absolutely, or, if necessary, we can assume *ea* (the horns). Terrified by the sight of the horns, Io fled from herself (as though running away from a dangerous beast). *exsternata*: rare poetic word, which Ovid uses only here and at 11.77.

642–
44
Repeating the verb (anadiplosis: cf. 33 and 402) at the caesura of 642 also achieves chiasmus in the two clauses. *quae sit* 643: indirect question. The whole line, with the maximum number of dactyls,

repetition of *sequitur* and the *s*-sounds, fits the anxious (but rather comic) movements of this girl-cow. *sorores*: the naiads of 642. *seque* 644: the pronoun functions also with *patitur*. The tame actions of this animal surprise Io's relatives.

645   *senior*: as Lee notes, the comparative form means no more than *senex*. In a century or two, this word would function simply as a respectful title and prepare the way for Romance words such as *signor, senor,* and *seigneur*. Ironically, Io dislikes the grass that her father gives her, because it is bitter (cf. 632).

647–   Io's tears mean less to Inachus than to us and her. The chief obstacle
48   to communication after metamorphosis stems from lack of human speech to vent the compelling force of human feelings inside the "new" animal. *sequantur . . . oret . . . loquatur*: since the narrative has used the historical present, Ovid continues with a conditional sentence in the unreal future.

649–   Ingenious Io finds a way to identify herself: by pawing on the earth
50   the two letters of her name. *indicium* 650: legal metaphor. The letters complete the evidence for Io's metamorphosis.

651–   *me miserum*: this exclamation has already occurred at 508, and will
52   be used eight more times in the poem (cf. 3.201). Bourgeois Inachus registers consternation: his daughter has become a cow and confounded his dynastic plans! *inque*: the preposition with *pendens* captures the difference between English "hang from" and "hang on." *gementis*: the word's flexibility for human or animal sounds captures Io's double being and the ambiguous quality of her "lowing." All the language of 652 insists on her bovine features.

653–   A more prosaic word order for 653–54 would be: *tune es nata mihi*
55   *quaesita per omnes terras?* Construe *nata* as predicate noun and *mihi* as dative of agent. *non inventa reperta*: Ovid plays with the curious results of Io's being lost and found. The second participle is ablative of comparison with *levior*. *luctus* 655: Inachus overstates his "tragedy" with this alliterative term.

655–   *mutua nostris / dicta: dictis* is implied for *nostris*: "words that respond
57   to mine." *remugis* 657: Io's response is a moo! This is the only occurrence of this verb in all Ovid's poetry.

658–   On the father's expectations for a son-in-law and grandchildren, cf.
59   Daphne's father Peneos at 1.481–82. *thalamos taedasque*: both words connote marriage by metonymy.

660   *de grege*: emphatic repetition; each time, the preposition receives stress. For this use of *de*, cf. 595. Ovid has fun with Inachus' social prejudices. *tibi*: dative of agent with *habendus*. *vir*: the short syllable is lengthened at the caesura when it receives the stress.

661–   *finire . . . morte dolores*: irreverent allusion to a truly poignant scene
63   of *Aen*. 12.879 ff., where Turnus' immortal sister Juturna laments

the cruel fact that she cannot share his death. She too uses the phrase *finire dolores*. *esse deum* 662: serves as subject of the impersonal verb *nocet*: "it hurts me to be a god." *praeclusaque ianua leti*: the entire phrase comes from a passage in Lucretius 5.373 where he argued that the physical universe was *not* immune from destruction; the door to death was *not* shut.

Argus' Death: The Fatal Power of Another Story of Rape (664–723)

Argus, the many-eyed cowherd whom Juno has set over Io, irritates Jupiter by his careful watchfulness, and the god orders Mercury to get rid of him. Posing as a goatherd, Mercury joins Argus and entertains him with the tune he produces on his pipes, a new invention. When he goes on to tell of the origin of these pipes, his story (which traces the familiar lines of the rape-tales of Daphne and Io and is to end with the metamorphosis of Syrinx, a nymph, into the Greek reed known as syrinx) puts Argus to sleep long before its climax. Mercury then kills the helpless cowherd, but Juno transfers the numberless eyes to the plumage of her bird the peacock.

664   *talia maerentem*: a striking phrase for the formulaic close of an epic speech. *talia* is a cognate accusative, to be translated: "with such words," "in such a way." *stellatus*: like the star-spangled heaven, Argus is covered by light-filled eyes with which he watches Io. *submovet*: this verb regularly described the actions of guards and lictors in Rome who cleared space for officials such as consuls. Argus thus shoves the father aside without sympathy.

665   *ereptam . . . natam*: the hyperbaton (cf. 45) helps to emphasize the separation of father and daughter. Prose order would have brought participle and noun close together. *patri*: dative of separation.

666–   *ipse procul*: Ovid now focuses on Argus, who will be the next victim.
67   The cowherd relaxes, sitting on a hill from which he can easily survey his charge. *partes . . . omnes* 667: humorous double meaning. Anyone from a hilltop has a panoramic view, but Argus, without even turning his head, can see in all directions with his hundred eyes.

668–   *superum rector*: cf. *rex superum* (251). *Phoronidos*: antonomasia.
70   Somewhere in his handbooks, Ovid had discovered that Io had a brother Phoroneus; no previous writer who has come down to us referred to that brother or loosely used the patronymic to refer to Io. *natum . . . quem . . . enixa est* 669–70: again, Ovid avoids the name, and introduces the third member of the cast by a relative clause. Mercury is Jupiter's son by Maia, daughter of Pleione and one of the seven Pleiades, and an earlier amour. *lucida*: appropriate for both a

214   OVID's *Metamorphoses*

white-skinned female and a star. *leto det*: subjunctive of indirect command without the conjunction *ut*.

671–
72
parva mora est + infinitive: for the opposite (*longa mora*), cf. 214. Mercury quickly gathers and puts on the three standard items of his wardrobe: his sandal-wings (elsewhere called *talaria*), his *caduceus* or staff, and his traveller's *petasus* or brimmed cap. Ovid continues to use circumlocutions. *somniferam* 672: this seemingly otiose "epic adjective" in fact refers to the crucial function of this staff; cf. below 716. *tegumen*: although Plautus had used *petasus*, it had not become a familiar Latin word; Ovid preferred the periphrasis.

673–
75
haec: as Bömer points out, Mercury took more than these three items. He typically carried a curved sword, and that item shows up in the killing of Argus (cf. 717). *patria . . . arce*: the height of Olympus, where father Jupiter usually resides. *desilit* 674: he does not simply jump down, but uses his winged sandals to fly. Once on earth, he gets rid of unneeded items. The narrator leaves us briefly in suspense as to why the staff is not also left behind, then shows Mercury putting it to strange use.

676–
77
hac: the traveller's staff has now become a pastoral item. *capellas . . . adductas*: the goats are massed together in a flock while he proceeds. Heinsius proposed emending to *abductas* and understood a reference to Mercury's notorious thieving. We do not need to know where the god got the animals. *structis cantat avenis* 677: as goatherd, Mercury plays a tune—he does not "sing"—on a pipe.

678
nova et . . . arte: the adjective is to be construed with the noun that follows it (at some distance), and the connective, as often, is out of prose order. The MSS were confused by this sequence: some offer *nova* without *et*, which gives the ablative phrase no intelligible structure; others resort to *novae . . . artis*, which may have been designed to cope with the problem, or may have come from writing one consonant where two of similar form were needed (e.g., *novaetcaptus*, because of the similarity of *t* and *c*, dropped the *t*). That produces the wrong sense, as the resumptive line proves at 709: *arte nova vocisque . . . dulcedine captum*. It is the instrumental art that is novel.

679–
81
Argus does not recognize Mercury and so greets him as an interesting young goatherd. *poteras*: the imperfect does not refer to the past, but gives a polite potential quality to what is essentially an invitation. Thus, "You might sit down with me" or simply "Why not sit down?" *hoc . . . saxo*: already referred to as *montis . . . cacumen* (666). The demonstrative indicates a dramatic gesture. *pecori* 680: dative with the adjective *fecundior*. Argus refers, of course, to the herd that Mercury has driven to this spot.

682–
84
Atlantiades: another antonomasia appeals to the audience's mythological lore: Mercury is grandson of Atlas (father of Maia); cf. 670. Ovid

avoids giving Mercury's name throughout this story; it first appears at 2.741. *euntem*: with *diem* (683). *multa loquendo*: ablative of gerund with its own object in neuter accusative plural. A little more specific than, but roughly synonymous with *sermone* (683). *detinuit*: goes with the metaphor of motion in *euntem*: he "held back" (i.e., "occupied") the passing day. *iunctis . . . harundinibus*: the reeds referred to as "oaten" at 677. *canendo*: rhymes with the gerund of 682. *vincere* 684: the bellicose verb reminds us of Mercury's true purpose of murder. *servantia lumina*: "watching eyes." Restful pastoral music has become a murderous lullaby.

685   Lee calls attention to the metrical organization in the first four feet that produces conflict between ictus and accent and therefore reinforces the sense of Argus' struggle against sleep.

686–   Although *quamvis* commonly takes the subjunctive (as in 2.495), Ovid
87   freely uses it, as here, with the indicative; cf. 2.177.

687–   The parenthesis announces the subject to be assumed in the next
88   clause. *fistula* 688: this Latin word for the reed pipe, to which the narrator has twice indirectly referred (677 and 683–84), exactly corresponds to the Greek syrinx, for which Ovid now begins an aetiological tale of metamorphosis.

689–   *tum deus*: we know that a god is speaking, but Argus is fatally ignorant
91   of that fact. Arcadia, the rough and mountainous region in the interior of the Peloponnesos, abounded in wild animals and inspired much hunting. *gelidis*: not frigid, but simply cool and idyllic. A good storyteller, Mercury (Ovid) postpones introduction of the heroine until 691. Line 690 is a tour de force: a rare four-word unit, made all the more exotic by the Greek word for mountain-nymphs and the unusual double-spondee *Nonacrinas* (which follows four dactyls). Nonacris is a mountain in Arcadia. In 691 both *naias* (Greek nominative) and *nymphae* are synonymous with hamadryads. *Syringa*: Greek accusative. The Roman audience, knowing Greek well, would immediately catch the significance of the word in an account of the origin of the *fistula*. Pre-Ovidian accounts about the nymph Syrinx, which probably once existed, have not survived. Still, Ovid was probably the first to weave her into the larger narrative of Io and Argus.

692–   *non semel*: the negative phrase, a form of litotes (cf. 34), means
94   "often." Mercury's bald, unsentimental manner of narration permits no details about the personality, feelings, or even looks of Syrinx. Nymphs traditionally attracted satyrs' pursuit; this was a common subject of literature and of Greek vase painting. *umbrosaque*: the -*que*, not needed as a connective, seems to be a free use of "epic" double -*que*.

694–   *Ortygiam . . . deam*: Diana, who was born on Delos, known also as
97   Ortygia (as in fact Ovid calls it at 15.337). As a devotee of Diana,

Syrinx, like Daphne earlier, dedicated her interest to hunting and her chastity to eternal virginity. *ritu . . . cincta Dianae*: she had her long robe hitched up above the knees, so that she could move quickly in the hunt. Cf. Venus as huntress: *vestem ritu succincta Dianae* (10.536). *falleret et posset* 696: imperfect subjunctive for pluperfect in past contrary to fact. Normally, *fallere* takes a direct object; as Bömer notes, here and at 698 are the only occasions where Ovid uses the verb absolutely. *Latonia*: Diana, daughter of Latona. Syrinx thus becomes the epitome of Diana, archetype of chaste, beautiful huntress. Only a trivial difference distinguishes in 697 goddess and Syrinx, namely, the composition of respective bows. *corneus* 697: there are two distinct adjectives of this spelling; Ovid here means "of horn." The natural curve of horns was ideal for the bow's shape. *huic*: although it would be idiomatic for this pronoun to refer to the second of two people ("the latter"), here it refers to Syrinx who, as the subject of the story interest, is "this person we are watching." *aureus*: a golden bow is either a fantastic instrument for a god—gold has no spring and would crumple under the pressure of a tight string—or it would actually be a bow of wood or horn that was then sheathed in gold. In Homer, Diana's brother Apollo had a silver bow; this gold bow seems to be a post-Homeric attribute of the goddess.

698–
700
redeuntem: same verb to open the account of Io's rape (cf. 588). Syrinx has been hunting. *Lycaeo*: Lycaeus (named at 217) was also a favorite haunt of Pan. Like Jupiter at 588 ff., no sooner does Pan spot Syrinx than he starts talking, to try to win her compliance. Since we have already heard this routine twice (Daphne and Io), we do not need any elaboration. *pinuque* 699: the *-que* provides the link between the two main verbs. *pinu caput praecinctus acuta: caput* is accusative with the past participle as in 265 and 270. Pan's head was crowned with "sharp pine", i.e., pine needles. *talia* 700: Mercury uses an obvious formula for introducing a speech, which Ovid surprisingly interrupts.

700–
701
restabat verba referre: the repetition of two words from the first hemistich of 700 invites us to assume, at first, that Pan is still the focus and that we should translate: "it remained for him [Pan] to speak his words [as promised in *talia*]." In fact, as we see in 701–12, the poet summarizes what is left to tell, then ends in 713 with *talia dicturus*. Thus, we must correct our initial assumption and translate: "It remained for him [Mercury] to narrate." In subsequent lines, all the infinitives will be indirect discourse, dependent on this new sense of *referre*. *precibus spretis* 701: both Daphne (at 525) and Io (at 597) ignored the wooing words (or prayers) of their would-be lovers and fled, leaving the gods still talking.

702– *donec . . . venerit*: the dependent clause in indicative discourse takes
4   subjunctive. Ovid seems to choose perfect subjunctive (rather than
      pluperfect in secondary discourse) because he relates the act of coming
      to the earlier act of fleeing, which was perfect infinitive. *Ladonis*:
      this river flows out of a mountain lake toward and into the Alpheus
      in southwestern Arcadia. In this sequence, Syrinx resembles Daphne,
      who also fled until she became exhausted and desperate. *illam . . .
      orasse* 703–4: a second clause of indirect discourse depending on
      referre. *se mutarent*: the reflexive refers not to the subject of this verb
      (her sister nymphs) but to the subject of *orasse* (Syrinx).

705– *Panaque . . . tenuisse palustres*: indirect discourse continues. We
6   have not been told that Pan chased the fleeing Syrinx, but that is so
      basic an element in these stories—flight triggers chase by both Apollo
      and Jupiter—that we can assume it. *cum . . . putaret*: subjunctive
      with subordinate clause in indirect discourse. *prensam sibi*: past parti-
      ciple and dative of agent. *corpore pro nymphae* 706: anastrophe of
      preposition and its noun allows Ovid to move up to the emphatic
      initial verse position the body that defines Pan's frustration. He gets
      no sexual gratification, and only dubious compensation for his pains.
      The sudden transformation of the female body into reeds, though
      preceded by prayer, has no specific divine agent.

707   *dumque . . . suspirat*: unlike the other dependent clauses, which took
      subjunctive, this *dum*-clause quite idiomatically takes indicative. The
      -que actually connects the infinitives *tenuisse* and *effecisse*. *motos in
      harundine ventos*: the breath of Pan's sigh causes an air current that
      flows through the reed(s) with sympathetic sound.

709– *arte . . . captum*: Pan reacts with the same pleasure to the unusual
10   music from the reeds that Argus had exhibited above at 677. All these
      repeated motifs, presented without any interesting elaboration and
      individuation, add inevitably to the monotony for Argus and help to
      induce sleep in all hundred eyes. In 710, Pan's little apostrophe to
      the plant he holds instead of the girl is reminiscent of Apollo's speech
      of appropriation to the laurel that was Daphne (557 ff.). *conloquium*
      710: a reading that only *M* preserves; like Apollo, Pan deceives himself
      about the personality of the plant. Syrinx had never spoken a word
      to Pan, any more than Daphne had to Apollo, and Pan has no right
      to expect conversation now.

711– *disparibus calamis . . . iunctis*: Pan now creates the first Pan-pipe,
12   by picking reeds of different lengths and fastening them together.
      Same participle in 683 means another repeated motif. *nomen tenuisse
      puellae*: in the context, we may reasonably expect that Pan continues
      to be the subject from 709–10; that results in the strange translation:
      "he held the name of the girl." Editors have pinpointed the difficulty

in *tenuisse*, without finally solving it. In aetiological stories such as this, the narrative regularly ends with a reference to the name acquired by the item under discussion (usually from a person or a detail in the story). The formula then is, that the metamorphosed had or, as here, "retained" the name of the girl from which it was changed. Same construction in 4.415 to account for the name of the bat. Proposed emendations keep Pan as subject and *nomen* as object (e.g., *tribuisse*), or they turn the participial clause into dative and make *nomen* subject (e.g., *mansisse* or *venisse*). The emendations, however, alter so considerably the letters of *tenuisse* that they fail to explain the origin of the "error."

713–   *talia dicturus*: the material summarized in 700–12 produced a deliber-
14   ate sense of suspense: Pan was about to do all this, but *his* narrator Mercury realized that it was unnecessary to report it. *Cyllenius*: Mercury, born on Mount Cyllene of Arcadia. *omnes*: all hundred eyes close in sleep. *adopertaque* 714: supply *esse*; this is a second infinitive in indirect discourse.

715–   *supprimit . . . vocem*: the narrative resumes, as Mercury interrupts
16   his story precisely where Ovid had intervened. The god, despite his invention of the lyre, has no real interest in poetry and song, but exploits his new art coldly to perpetrate murder.

717–   *falcato . . . ense*: Mercury and Perseus (cf. 4.427) both traditionally
18   use a hooked sword called *harpe*. Ovid has not mentioned this as part of the god's original equipment. *nutantem*: Argus nodding with sleep appears even more of a victim and Mercury that much more vicious a murderer. *vulnerat* 718: the "wound" is fatal; the god probably beheads the herdsman. *collo*: dat. with the adjective *confine*. The bloody disposal of the corpse adds to the grim tones of this passage.

720–   The Ovidian narrator now intrudes, with an apostrophe to the dead
21   that turns into an epitaph. He does not express any particular grief, but displays funereal wit with an epigram. *quodque . . . lumen*: plays with the two related senses of *lumen*: namely, the literal sense of light and the metonymous sense of eye. All those eyes had one single kind of light, and that has been snuffed out; now they have a single night of darkness and death.

722–   The story offers one more metamorphosis: the "darkened" eyes of
23   dead Argus become, by action of Juno, the "eyes" on the plumage of the peacock, her particular bird. *excipit*: like a surgeon, she "takes out" the eyes (*hos*). *Saturnia*: Juno is Saturn's daughter; Vergil uses this epithet frequently. Just why the peacock became Juno's bird is unclear. It acquired symbolic prominence on her island of Samos after 200 B.C.; but originally it would have been imported form its native habitat in India. *gemmis . . . stellantibus* 723: Ovid compares the "eyes" in the feathers to glittering jewels.

The Release of Io from Torment (724–46)

The killing of Argus, which vents Jupiter's anger, does not save Io from suffering. On the contrary, since that murder confirms for Juno her husband's guilty relation with the girl who is inside the cow, she sets out to makes her life miserable. In Aeschylus, a gadfly stings Io and drives her over the landscape, at the orders of Juno. Ovid substitutes a Fury for the gadfly. When the cow arrives at the Nile, her plight finally stirs Jupiter to proper steps, as "proper" as he is capable of. He goes to Juno, admits his wrong, and promises not to repeat it. Mollified, Juno either herself changes the cow back into the human Io, or she allows Jupiter to do so; Ovid says that the change occurs, but does not specify its agency.

724–
27
exarsit: Ovid likes this form in this metrical position of this vivid verb of fire. Angry or furious Juno had played a central role in the *Aeneid*, but Ovid trivializes that epic wrath by making it arise from petty jealousy here. *oculis animoque* 725: dative with compound verb. Io both sees and imagines the savage Fury. *Erinyn*: Greek accusative. *paelicis* 726: used earlier of Io at 622, when Jupiter surrendered his "beloved", Juno's rival, to his wife. *stimulos . . . caecos*: cf. the action of the angry Erinys in *Aen*, 7.445 ff., who plants a smoky torch in the chest of Turnus. The basic meaning of *stimulus* is a cattle prod, which is apt here. *per totum terruit orbem* 727: compounding *terrere* with the preposition *per*, to mean "drive in terror all over the world," is unusual for Ovid or any writer.

728
ultimus: Io's bovine form has been chased a huge distance, when she arrives at last in Egypt. *restabas, Nile*: the apostrophe seems mainly to serve metrical convenience. Had Ovid used the third person, as the narrative leads us to expect, *restabat Nilus* would have lost him the short syllable of the vocative. But Ovid also likes to bring himself as narrator into the story.

729–
31
quem: the Nile. *positisque . . . procubuit genibus resupinoque . . . collo . . . cum Iove visa queri* (733). According to this punctuation and text, Ovid links two coordinate main clauses by transferred double *-que*. His interest focuses on what Io did after reaching the Nile. Alternatively, as Lee notes, all the clauses in 729–33 might depend on *simulac*; the sentence would then continue up to its main clause at 734 ff. That, however, postulates a sentence of un-Ovidian length and subordinates the suffering of Io—on which Ovid lavishes much attention—to the trivial negotiations of Jupiter. Ovid represents in 729 ff. the clumsy, bathetic efforts of this lumbering cow-form to maneuver itself into the praying position that Io inside the cow requires. The cow can kneel, all right, but then she has trouble looking prayerful.

quos potuit solos . . . vultus 731: a human being would lift up his or her hands in a praying gesture; Ovid has already once described the frustration of the girl-cow's efforts as suppliant (cf. 635 ff.).

732– *luctisono mugitu*: the "epic" compound, unique to Latin, Ovid's inven-
33   tion here, emphasizes the sound that this prayerful cow produces and, artfully disposed with its noun, produces a double spondee of most unorthodox rhythm, thus even more strongly stressing the comical mooing. *cum love . . . queri* 733: for English "complain to." *visa*: supply *est. finem . . . malorum*: Io asks, and eventually receives what her father despaired of gaining at 661.

734– Jupiter now re-enters the story, in response to Io's plea. *finiat ut*
37   *poenas* 735: the god takes over the girl's prayer. Subjunctive of indirect command, with *rogat. inque*: Ovid now continues with direct speech, starting the quotation with a preposition, on which he tacks his connective *-que*. Jupiter seems to address himself carefully and guiltily to Juno's rightful jealousy. What he should be saying and honestly mean is that he will never play around with *any* nymph or other female; but what he says, as Ovid emphasizes by the enjambement and the initial position of *haec*, is: "There will never be any occasion of pain again from *this* girl." That allows this faithless and lecherous deity ample room to rape Callisto and then Europa in Book 2. Swearing by the river Styx is supposed to guarantee a statement of promise: cf. 188 ff.

738– The process of reverse metamorphosis begins with those pathetic
40   bovine features (*vultus*) that above at 731 so desperately tried to pray. *fitque . . . fuit* 739: a nice example of the distinction in Latin, emphasized by alliteration, between becoming and being. *saetae*: bristles do not belong with any other Ovidian cows and seem odd in this context; they characterize boars and other fierce animals.

741– *rictus*: the mouth of a cow, as anyone knows who has observed it in
43   the act of mooing or eating, is large and ugly, with slobbery lips and gross teeth. Much needs to be "contracted" to recover the lovely mouth of a nymph. *redeunt* 741: as the metamorphosis is reversed, so the usual verb of change, *abire in* (cf. 236), is inverted. *dilapsa absumitur* 742: both verbs, synonyms for "vanishing," help to stress miraculous change. *nil superest* 743: this verb is often used in descriptions of metamorphosis, to indicate what survives or, in this case, does not survive (cf. 3.398 and 4.584). It helps to pinpoint the one detail of continuity, *formae candor*, which earlier was continuous between girl and cow (cf. *nitentem* 610 and *formosa* 612). *in illa*: Io, now a nymph.

744– *nymphe*: Greek nominative form, used for metrical purposes. A nymph
46   obviously needs only two feet. *erigitur* 745: a standard distinction between human beings and beasts (and thus between the cow and Io) consists in the erect stature of the former versus the prone position

of the latter (cf. 85–86). Ovid concludes the scene with a delicately humorous picture of Io as she uncertainly tests out that other definably human quality, speech.

Epaphus and Phaethon (747–79)

Ovid is moving toward a representation of the Great Fire, which in Book 2 will match the Great Flood of Book 1. To effect his transition, he uses Isis' son Epaphus, who gets into a boyish argument with a playmate named Phaethon over whose father is more important. Both children have gods for sires, and both gods raped the child's mother. The argument allows Ovid to transfer our attention from Epaphus, who questions the divinity of Phaethon's father, to the embarrassed and unsure Phaethon, who goes back to his mother and demands proof that the Sun is his father. This leads to the fateful visit that will be described at the beginning of Book 2. The contents of this transition are everyday, and the tone is light and ironic, as the juveniles boast emptily over their bastard state. In the contrast between this almost bourgeois ending of Book 1 and the magniloquent beginning of Book 2, in the Palace of the Sun, Ovid achieves one of his typically delightful changes of pace. (For further background to the story of Phaethon, see the introduction to Book 2.)

747 *nunc*: refers to the familiar deity Isis, who made such an impression among Roman women in Ovid's own lifetime. *dea*: best rendered as a predicate noun. *linigera . . . turba*: the throng of priests attendant on Isis stood out in Rome because of their un-Roman attire, linen robes. Ovid had devised this compound epithet earlier in *Am.* 2.2.25 to refer to Isis and her shrine. *celeberrima*: Ovid likes to use this superlative form at this point in the line (cf. 3.339 and 5.412).

748– Epaphus derives his name by Greek etymology from the verb "to
50   touch," as if Zeus (Jupiter) had "touched" Io fruitfully to sire the son. *magni . . . Iovis*: a considerable hyperbaton, whose effect is ironically undercut by the verb *creditur*. What is "believed" is not necessarily a fact. *iuncta parenti*: we cannot determine for sure, because of the common declension, masculine and feminine, of *parens*, whether Ovid means Io (Isis) or Jupiter. Apis (Epaphus) did not apparently share religious space with either parent.

50   *huic*: dative with *aequalis*. Epaphus now yields center stage to the new subject, Phaethon. *animis . . . et annis*: a carefully chosen alliterative pair. The more important word proves to be the first, since the high spirits of Phaethon will cause him not only his original embarrassment with Epaphus, but will also eventually lead to his death in the Sun's chariot.

751   *Sole satus*: the Ovidian narrator treats Phaethon's divine birth as a fact (vs. *creditur* 749). The same phrase will be part of the oath of Phaethon's mother to him in 771. *Sole*: ablative of origin. *quem*: Phaethon now becomes the object of a verb that Ovid postpones until 753 (*tulit*), in the meantime collecting around this new character three clauses that typify his proud spirit. *magna loquentem*: "big talk" irritates here, as in most instances.

752   *nec sibi cedentem*: the reflexive refers to Epaphus, the subject of the delayed verb. Since Epaphus' father is Jupiter, and Phaethon's is only the subordinate Sun, Epaphus might well be impatient with his brash companion.

753   *non tulit*: this phrase regularly connotes in Latin the intolerant feeling of anger and indignation. *Inachides*: Io's father, Epaphus' grandfather, was the River Inachus. Ironically, Inachus represents the inferior side of Epaphus' family tree, not the boasted connection with Jupiter.

753–   *matrique*: Epaphus' speech begins with the abruptness that Ovid likes
54   in unepic moments. All Phaethon's boasts, it appears, depend on what his mother has told him, not on anything he knows for sure about his father. *omnia*: cognate accusative: "in all things". *demens*: Epaphus calls Phaethon a fool to believe his mother, but his crowning insult comes in the final word of 754. *credis* 754: balances *creditur* above in 749, both initial words. There is general belief in Epaphus' divine father, but Phaethon alone credits his mother's dubious story about the Sun. *tumidus*: an unflattering synonym for *superbus* (cf. 752). *genitoris*: this noun for "father" belongs to the high style of epic. Coupled with the nasty *falsi*, it mocks Phaethon's illusions about his father. *imagine*: in the language of Ovid's poem, Phaethon deludes himself with an insubstantial form or fiction.

755–   Two competing forces seethe inside the boy, anger and a sense of shame,
56   and it is to his credit that he controls his wrath out of concern for his good name. Then, having controlled himself outwardly and not given Epaphus the pleasure of knowing that his insults hurt, the boy goes off to his mother (now at last named, *Clymene*).

757   Again, the speech starts swiftly with a simple *-que* acting as link and introduction. Phaethon is very excited. *quo . . . doleas*: relative clause of purpose. The pain that he expects his mother to feel involves anger; cf. below, 765. *genetrix*: female analogue for solemn *genitor*, used here for the first time in the poem. Phaethon's dependency on his mother at this stage seems obvious. *ille ego liber*: "I that outspokenly free person you know." An automatic association of free birth is the right and practice of free speech. Yet Phaethon has felt unable to speak out freely.

758   *ferox*: "hot-tempered" as befits his pride. *pudet*: understand *me* as object, the infinitive clauses as subject.

760   *si modo*: "if in fact." *caelesti*: at first, it seems as though Phaethon
       merely wishes to be assured that his father is divine, like Epaphus'.
       See *caelo* in the next line. However, his father's functions in the sky
       will prove fatally relevant. *stirpe creatus*: a grandiose epic phrase
       borrowed from Vergil (*Aen.* 10.543).

761   *ede notam*: Clymene is to provide proof of his birth. *meque adsere*
       caelo: as Bömer aptly notes, Ovid has here made something new out
       of a familiar prosaic expression. The technical legal expression in
       Latin for "making someone a free man" is *aliquem libertati adserere*.
       Changing the noun to *caelo* indicates the boy's overweening ambition.
       In effect, he is asking Clymene to declare him a god!

762   Children hug their parents as they ask for a favor, and Ovid uses this
       gesture often in intimate and potentially pathetic moments. Cf. Daphne
       at 485 pleading with her father to let her remain a virgin. Phaethon
       will use the same ploy on his father at 2.100, as he makes the request
       that will lead to his death. *collo*: dative with compound verb.

763–   The boy appeals to what he believes she holds most precious,
64   namely, himself, her current husband Merops, and his sisters.
       Although this may seem to be a needless list, designed to test our
       esoteric knowledge of myth, in fact Ovid makes use later of both
       the stepfather and the sisters (cf. 2.184 and 340 ff.). *traderet* 764:
       subjunctive of indirect command, omitting the conjunction *ut* as
       at 670.

765–   *ambiguum Clymene*: commentators usually claim that Ovid means
66   here to employ a typical parenthesis; that readers should understand
       the following word order: *Clymene (ambiguum utrum precibus Phae-*
       thontis an ira dicti sibi criminis magis mota sit) utraque, etc. However,
       Ovid has two ideas to present in close order: namely, the unclear
       motivations of Clymene, then her dramatic and visible actions. Al-
       though he could have contrived a parenthesis, as on many other
       occasions, I believe that he had no intention here of doing so. He has
       compressed into one what English would render in two separate
       clauses: "It is unclear . . . but she stretched out both hands . . . "
       ira: like her son, Clymene was prone to anger. *criminis* 766: objective
       genitive with *ira*. Epaphus implied she lied about her divine mate,
       cloaking an ordinary act of sexual promiscuity.

66–   Clymene's gesture of lifting her arms to the sky—*caelo* is a poetic
67   dative for *ad caelum*—is particularly relevant. Phaethon's mysterious
       father is, as the narrator told us at 751, the Sun. Thus, *solis* uncapital-
       ized changes at 771 to *Sole*.

68–   *per iubar hoc*: Clymene starts off in conventional manner by invoking
69   the all-seeing Sun as witness of her truth. But then she proceeds in
       an unusual fashion, for she swears that the witnessing Sun is the
       father Phaethon seeks. *auditque videtque*: that the Sun hears and sees

everything was a commonplace of Greco-Roman thought from the time of Homer (cf. 4.172).

770–72   *hoc te . . . Sole satum*: the demonstrative is masculine ablative, agreeing with its noun in 771; Clymeme points. The personal pronoun is accusative and subject of the infinitive *satum (esse)*. In typical fashion, Ovid varies the metrical stress in the two instances of *hoc te. neget . . . sitque*: jussive subjunctive. *videndum / se mihi*: the verb is a gerundive, modifying *se*, and governing a dative of agent. *novissima*: Roman use of "newest" to mean the "last."

773   *patrios . . . penates*: the phrase seems to echo the solemnity of the Vergilian words in *Aen.* 2.717. As is clear from *domus* in 774, Clymene means little more than "the home of your father." However, her use of *penates* conjures the ironic image of gods like the Sun having household gods of their own!

774   *unde oritur*: relative clause placed, as often in Ovid, before its "antecedent" *(domus)*. *terrae contermina nostrae*: it might seem odd that Clymene can declare the Far East, where the sun rises, to be bordering on her land. However, Ovid can justify the statement as follows: (1) From Egypt, where Io and Epaphus reside, we have moved to the country of Phaethon's stepfather Merops, which is Ethiopia. (2) There was a historical Aethiopia which, from Herodotus' time, was placed south of Egypt. That is where Clymene and Phaethon have been talking. (3) There was also a mythical Aethiopia (mentioned by Homer, *Od.* 1.23), which extended to the rising of the sun. That is now what Clymene refers to. Ovid has combined fact and myth.

775   *fert animus*: this phrase appeared in the first line of the poem. Phaethon is invited to have the same ambition as the epic poet beginning on his demanding task. *gradere*: imperative, but a solemn word; not ordinary "go" (*i*). *scitabere*: the future can often work with a previous imperative. Thus, here: "Set out, and you may inquire," which amounts to the same as: "Set out and inquire."

776–77   *laetus*: his unhappy mood of suppressed anger and frustration has vanished, thanks to Clymene's answer. *concipit aethera mente* 777: in Ovidian diction, human beings "conceive in the mind" (*mente, animo*) an emotion or some idea. Phaethon is imagining the aether as his ultimate goal, to be attained through his father.

778–79   *Aethiopasque suos*: Greek declension, accusative plural. They are "his" Aethiopians because, as noted at 774, Merops, Phaethon's stepfather, ruled in Aethiopia. *Indos*: Phaethon races eastward, past the Indians and their sun-exposed land. His haste receives emphasis from the five dactyls of 778. *patrios . . . ortus*: once again, the adjective is emphatic. *inpiger*: conventional for the intrepid epic hero (cf. 467). Phaethon's "heroic" ambitions are rash and fatal.

NOTES TO BOOK 2

The story of Phaethon, which Ovid started at the end of Book 1, takes up almost half of Book 2. Phaethon locates his father, asks to use the Sun's chariot for a day, and the poet embarks on a spirited description of how the world almost burned up when Phaethon lost control of his vehicle and its horses. This disaster balances to some extent the account of the Flood in Book 1, except that the destruction seems less severe in this case, and Ovid is not recording the punishment of human beings but the fatal wilfulness of Phaethon. He does die (320 ff.), and his fond but foolish sisters erect for him a tomb and epitaph that overstates his heroism. Then, they and others devote themselves so wildly to lamentation that one metamorphosis after another occurs among the mourners (340–400).

The second half of Book 2 concentrates again on the gods and their unsatisfactory behavior. Jupiter turns from concern for the fire-damaged earth to another amatory adventure (401–531), which quickly leads to the satisfaction of his lust through a despicable rape of the virginal nymph Callisto. But the story goes on with the merciless anger of two other deities: Diana expels guiltless Callisto from her chaste band; Juno then metamorphoses the girl as punishment for attracting Jupiter. Callisto is helplessly exposed to one misery after another, and even after changing into a bear, she is humanly aware of her unjust suffering.

Then follows a carefully worked series of tales that deal with inform-ers, who faithfully, maliciously, or treacherously pass on incriminating information. The informers are human, and they deliver their reports to deities. To their surprise, the god or goddess then punishes the informer. First, we hear of two black birds, the raven and the crow, who truthfully report the misdeeds of others, and for their pains are ousted from their positions of honor with Minerva and Apollo (532–632). Next, Ocyroe, who by her special powers as prophetess threatens to reveal information that the gods want hidden, is silenced by meta-morphosis into a horse (633–75). Then, Mercury, who has stolen cattle from Apollo and bribed an observer to keep the truth hidden, unscrupulously disguises himself and offers a larger bribe to his victim, who then does inform, but fatally to the very culprit, and Mercury gleefully turns him into a kind of monument of informing, a rock that points (676–707).

The next long story (708–832) combines the theme of the punishment of informers with the familiar scheme of divine lust and a well-developed allegorical description. This time the lusty god is Mercury. His target starts out to be the lovely Athenian Herse, but then an obstacle arises in the form of her sister Aglauros, already marked as guilty by an earlier informer, but now threatening to profit by acting herself as informer unless suitably bribed. Mercury recedes from attention for awhile, and another deity asserts herself to punish Aglauros. Minerva, angry at Aglauros and then jealous of her possible success as recipient of a large bribe, activates Jealousy herself from her remote and cheerless abode to subject Aglauros to jealous envy of Herse. When Mercury comes with his bribe, Aglauros is too sick with envy to accept the gift, and she provokes the god to metamorphose her. That seems to satisfy the god, who ignores his desire for Herse and quickly flies off from Athens on a mission from Jupiter, who once again is driven by his typical lust and comically plans to approach his victim, in the "disguise" of a bull (833–75). Thus, Ovid frames this half with stories of lustful Jupiter, but within the frame he studies other gods and goddesses, who are driven by motives that seem to us subhuman.

PHAETHON (1–366)

The results of Phaethon's search for and location of his father, the Sun, are drastic, and Ovid creates a story of considerable versatility and skillful modulations. First comes an epic ecphrasis or description of the Palace of the Sun (1–18) and then of his attendants (days, years, seasons), which promises grandeur and dignity in the ruler of this realm. The initial conversation between Phaethon and his father (31–48) exhibits some of the formality that might be expected. Phaethon asks for reassurance that the Sun indeed fathered him, and the Sun all too readily promises it. Indeed, he commits himself to whatever Phaethon asks of him, and binds himself beyond recall by swearing on the Styx (an oath that earlier Jupiter misused). The father's rashness allows the rash son to ask for what will inevitably cause his own death: the opportunity to drive the Sun's chariot for a day.

Too late, when Phaethon has asked what he cannot, on oath, refuse, the Sun tries to persuade his son to moderate his wild ambition (49–102). This vain speech (like the *suasio* of the rhetorical schools) moves into the pathetic vein and so borrows more from the style of elegy than from epic. The father warns in general of the dangers Phaethon faces, of the fatal presumption that asks to do what no mortal can accomplish; and then he sketches out in detail the various terrors of the heavens (treating the allegorical symbols of astronomy as so many real monsters). The boy resists every argument, ardently pursuing his goal of driving the chariot. Ovid introduces an interlude of further description, again in a loftier vein, as the Sun leads Phaethon down to the place where the chariot waits, and the time approaches for setting forth (105–21).

His previous speech had been summarized as warnings (*monitus* 103). Now the Sun proceeds to produce a second speech, pathetic and elegiac in manner, which consists of vain advice (*monitis* 126) about the safe route to take through the skies (126–49). Incapable of paying attention either to his father's worry or to his directions, Phaethon springs up on the chariot and seizes the reins with childish pleasure (150–52).

Very quickly, the horses run out of control and the chariot careers from its normal path (161 ff.). Twice, Ovid compares the vehicle to a ship, whose lightness makes it a plaything of the waves (163–64) and whose battering by the north wind obliges the helpless steersman to give up his efforts (184–86). Similarly, Phaethon grows afraid (169), then terrified (180), loses control of the powerful steeds, and finally abandons the reins altogether (200). What follows is an Ovidian tour of the heavens and a tour de force of metamorphoses as the earth reacts geologically and anthropologically to the unusual proximity of the scorching sun (214–71). In this crisis, when even Neptune could not risk emerging from the protection of his waters to appeal to Jupiter, Mother Earth exhibited the necessary fortitude. She raised her head and spoke out as long as she could (272–300), with passion, indignation, and urgency, and finally caught the ear of Jupiter. He is *omnipotens* (304), so, even though somewhat inconvenienced by the lack of his usual attributes (clouds and rain, because of the excessive heat), he nevertheless strikes Phaethon with his thunderbolt. The charioteer falls lifeless from the chariot; the horses bolt in terror; and the vehicle is smashed to bits. When Phaethon, like a falling star (321), strikes the earth, far from his home in Ethiopia, he receives burial by the Po River and an epitaph that inappropriately hails his grand audacity (327–28).

In the course of this long story, Phaethon experiences considerable psychological change, from doubt to pride to terror, from youthful ambition to vain desire of escaping his proud wish; but his death is no metamorphosis. His wild route through the sky and too close to the earth has produced a rash of changes in the world, and now his death brings in its train a number of metamorphoses among those who mourn him: first his sisters, the Heliades (340–66), who turn into trees that ooze amber, then Cygnus, who turns into a swan (367–80). And finally the Sun, whose grief has temporarily metamorphosed his brightness into unrelieved gloom, yields to the persuasion and veiled threats of Jupiter, and glumly returns to the skies with his horses, whom he angrily blames and lashes for the death of Phaethon (381–400).

There were many accounts of Phaethon's death available to Ovid. Writers had used the myth and embellished it since the time of Hesiod at latest. Aeschylus dealt with the story in his tragedy about Phaethon's sisters, *Heliades*. Euripides then humanized the account in his *Phaethon,* of which two sizable and several brief fragments survive, to indicate the plot. Totally different from the initial occasion devised by Ovid, Euripides starts from the wedding day of Phaethon, which has been arranged by his stepfather Merops. Only at this late moment does Clymene reveal to Phaethon that his true father is the Sun. Phaethon goes off to the Palace of Helios to test the story of his mother and makes the fatal choice to drive the chariot. But Helios rides with him, advising him as a sort of "back seat driver," with the usual disastrous result. Then, Phaethon's corpse is brought back to the scene of wedding festivity, where Euripides exploits to the full the tragic irony. The only sustained version now extant in surviving mythographers can be found in Hyginus 154. (He has another thoroughly garbled account in 152 A.) Hyginus credits his tale to Hesiod, but also cites Pherecydes for a detail about the Eridanus (Po). In this Hesiodic version, Phaethon is indeed the natural son of Merops and Clymene, but grandson of Helios. Nevertheless, he presumes upon this relationship, uses the chariot, and dies; and Hyginus devotes half his account to the metamorphosis of the Indians into dark-skinned people and the transformation of the Heliades (seven of whom he names) and of Cygnus.

This review of the sporadic source material proves fairly clearly that Ovid owes very little to any of these—indeed, Hyginus may owe *his* various metamorphoses to Ovid. The speeches of the Sun might be inspired by some tragic prototype, but, if so, Ovid has pretty well removed the tragic themes and emotions and given to the scenes at the Palace an elegiac tone. And that section (31–149) occupies Ovid's attention far less than, and does not carry over thematically into, the longer sections about the metamorphic effects of Phaethon's wild ride and of his death (150–380). This is very much Ovid's story, then; and it is only appropriate that Ovid's version had the surviving power that all others lacked and so became the canonic account of Phaethon right into the Renaissance.

The Palace of the Sun (1–30)

Book 1 has brought Phaethon vaguely to the place where his father, the Sun, rises; but the final phrase of the book, *patrios ortus,* might refer to the boy's paternal origins or "roots." Ovid starts Book 2 with the formulaic words that announce an ecphrasis. He first describes the exterior of the Palace of the Sun (a description that vies with the earlier one concerning the domain of Jupiter as a glorified Palatine Hill [1.168 ff.]. Emphasis falls principally on the two doors, on which Vulcan has ingeniously engraved a representation of the cosmos (5–18). Then, Phaethon enters and sees his father surrounded by a host of allegorical figures that symbolize his close association with the orderly passage of time (19–30). Although some critics have considered this section otiose and an example of Ovidian self-indulgence, others have suggested that Ovid sounds the minor theme of order here, to set off the major theme of disorder that will prevail with Phaethon's rashness.

1   *Regia Solis erat:* the noun plus the form of the verb "to be" announces an ecphrasis (cf. 1.168 and 568). It extends to the end of 18, and the initial word of 19, *quo,* functions as the demonstrative that closes off the description. Seneca, *Ep.* 19.115.12 cites the first line and a half here, and later 107-8, as though the passage was already well known, and he criticizes Ovid for putting so much emphasis on gold and ignoring other more important divine qualities. However, Ovid does not want to emphasize much about the gods but the trivial, sensual, and materialistic; and furthermore it was conventional in descriptions of palaces and temples to focus on their rich decoration. *sublimibus alta columnis:* Hellenistic poets made it a topos to talk of the gigantic temple or royal dwelling that towered on its many columns; and that was the style of royal architecture in Ovid's day. Vergil had already imagined the palace of Latinus (despite its antiquity) as an imposing structure with one hundred columns! (Cf. *Aen.* 7.170–71.) As Bömer notes, Augustus' Temples of Apollo and Mars Ultor provided contemporary examples, and the poets responded with ecphrasis.

2   *clara micante auro:* Ovid here describes another conventional feature of rich buildings in poetry: namely, gilt roofs, *aurea tecta* (cf. *Aen.* 6.13), what he himself calls *aurata tecta* (8.702) in his description of the monumentalized hut of Philemon and Baucis. *auro:* ablative of respect. *pyropo:* same syntax; here, though, equipped with a participle that is not simply attributive, but has its own object. The noun,

from the Greek, is rare; Lucretius and Propertius each used it once, and Ovid has it only here. Its Greek etymology connected with fire functions here with *flammas* to emphasize the dazzling effect of the metal sheathing on the palace. Apparently, Ovid refers to something like gilded bronze.

3   *cuius:* referring to the *regia*. Ivory was also used as a precious architectural veneer, but in places not exposed to weather, on paneled ceilings for instance. Thus, *fastigia* should denote either ceilings or the undersides of the cornice.

4   Arranged like a Golden Line: the verb stands in the middle, and *argenti* goes with *lumine, bifores* with *valvae*. Ovid now draws our eye down to the front of the palace and its monumental doors in silver relief. Such gigantic doors were described on the Temple of Apollo by Propertius 2.31.12–14 and by Vergil in the imaginary temple built by Daedalus at Cumae (*Aen.* 6.20 ff.). Visitors to Rome today can gain an idea of their effect from the doors to St. Peter's. *bifores:* Vergil had apparently invented this word as a picturesque way of referring to the two pipes used in exotic Asiatic song (*Aen.* 9.618). Ovid restores the compound to its basic sense to refer to the two doors on which Vulcan displays his artistry.

5   *materiam . . . opus:* having emphasized the dazzling silver material of the sheathing on the doors—which would have had to be tough iron inside the decorative soft silver—Ovid moves to an even more valuable feature: the artistic scenes worked into the silver. The superiority of artwork to unworked precious metal was a topos. *Mulciber:* archaic term for Vulcan, derived from the verb *mulceo* and referring to the smith's practice of softening metals before working them. It appears in Latin literature as early as Plautus, but Ovid probably picked it up from *Aen.* 8.724, where Vergil described Vulcan's work on Aeneas' shield.

6   *caelarat:* usual shortened poetic form of the pluperfect. The verb denotes the process of engraving metal to produce a bas relief. What follows through 18 is a detailed description of the universe, as Vulcan represented it on the doors. The artistic work parallels Ovid's own artistic representation of the Creation in Book 1. Vulcan depicts three of the four basic elements (leaving out *aether,* home of the Olympian deities). Ovid names first the sea, and deals with it in detail in 8–14.

7   The table of contents is expanded to include the earth and sky, each occupying a half-line, linked by the repetition *orbem . . . orbi*.

8   *caeruleos . . . deos:* Ovid playfully reverses a half-line of Propertius, which declared that there are no gods in the sea: *non habet unda deos* (3.7.18). That same poem of Propertius later called Neptune *caerulo . . . deo* (62). The adjective properly means the color of blue-green

associated with sea water. It was almost exclusively employed by poets, who began to use it, without reference to color, as meaning simply "of the sea." In this passage, Ovid may want the proper sense of color, in order to suit his selection of strange sea deities. Instead of Neptune in all his majesty, he portrays a set of grotesque creatures who might well be thought of as blue-green in complexion. *Tritona canorum:* Ovid has already described this creature's use of the conch as a horn in 1.331 ff. and mentioned that his shoulders were covered with seashells. Generally, the Triton (as in Bernini's famous Baroque statue or in the Trevi Fountain) appears as the counterpart of the mermaid, with a human torso and then a fish tail instead of legs. Why all this emphasis on the sea (instead of the sky) and odd creatures instead of noble gods in Vulcan's doors for Helios? Probably not because they actually were so dominant, but because the poet Ovid is slightly distorting our viewpoint and foreshadowing the confusion and disorder that will eventually prevail in this story.

9–10 *Proteaque ambiguum:* although the ability of Proteus to change shape was well known since the *Odyssey* and had been reused in Vergil's *G.* 4, no poet had ever called him by this epithet. It emphasizes the instability of his form rather than the wisdom that, for Homer and Vergil, was the primary feature of Proteus. Aegaeon traditionally had a hundred arms: here Ovid imagines him as grasping sea monsters (e.g., whales) with those countless limbs. How all this could fit on two doors, Ovid does not say. The subject matter seems more appropriate for the countless mosaic floors (especially in large baths) that favored such marine motifs.

11–13 Doris is the mother of the Nereids or sea-nymphs; we saw them in 1.302 admiring the strange disorder of the Flood; one of them, Galatea, plays an important role later on in 13.740 ff. They are not normally represented as mermaids with fishtails, and Ovid chooses to focus on their pretty variety, distinguishing three groups (in three infinitive clauses). *videtur* 11: Ovid catches the artistic illusion. Only the green hair, which is conventional, indicates their unusual appearance. Nymphs swimming or being carried along by dolphins form regular motifs for marine mosaics. For the nymph sitting on a rock and drying her hair, cf. Galatea's stance in *Met.* 13.

13–14 *facies non omnibus una:* supply *est,* and read *omnibus* as dative of possession. Vulcan's artistic talent enables him to individualize each of the sea-nymphs while maintaining a general family resemblance among them. Minerva shows similar skill in distinguishing the Olympian gods on her tapestry in 6.73–74. *sororum* 14: genitive with understood *faciem;* to continue the dative syntax would have been metrically impossible.

15–16 After the seven lines for the sea, Ovid allows only two each for earth
and sky. He lists what the earth contains (*gerit*), without assigning
the seven items emphasis by way of adjective or clause.

17–18 *haec super imposita est:* Ovid has a very similar clause in 1.67. *haec:*
neuter accusative plural, collectively referring to all the various items
on earth just mentioned. *caeli fulgentis:* as promised at 7; but the
participle refers to the brightness of the sun as well as the other stars,
presumably also to the metal with which Vulcan depicted them. Only
in the last line, does Ovid indicate how material was distributed over
the two doors: six of the twelve signs of the zodiac on each. *foribus*
18: ablative of place without preposition.

19–20 *adclivi . . . limite:* ablative of means. Phaethon had to climb a path
to enter the palace. That could signify that the palace, like the lordly
homes of Roman nobles, was prominently situated on a commanding
elevation; or possibly the boy rose into the heavens, where the Sun
has its natural position. Ovid does not specify, and he may well play
with both possibilities. The sun is both an anthropomorphic "father"
and a stellar body. *Clymeneia . . . proles:* typical "epic" antonomasia
for Phaethon. The adjective, formed by analogy with other more
familiar words (such as *Neptunia*), is Ovid's creation; it occurs only
here. *dubitati . . . parentis* 20: a reminder of the theme that dominated
the end of Book 1, resulting from the argument between Epaphus and
Phaethon. His mother is certain; his father is dubious. Ovid allows
himself a grammatical innovation here: as Bömer notes, no writer
prior to Ovid employed the passive forms of *dubitare* with human
beings.

21   *patrios . . . vultus:* the narrator comments decisively, as before, on
Phaethon's doubts. The Sun *is* his father. Notice the alliterative pat-
terns at each end of this line.

22–23 *consistitque procul:* with typical realism, Ovid intrudes on this senti-
mental reunion of father and son the "practical" problem that the sun
is too hot for the boy to approach. The poet notes the fact, and then
explains it, playing on the meanings of *lumina*. The "face" of the Sun
has burning "eyes." The physical distance between father and son
implies the difference between god and human being, which dooms
Phaethon's ambition.

23–24 Having referred to the "light" of the Sun, implicitly unendurable
because both hot and dazzling, Ovid gives a quick sketch of him in
his palace. The royal purple robe and throne briefly define the king,
though they do not normally function as the attributes of the Sun. A
radiate crown, for example, would be much more consistent with
artistic representations (cf. below, 40–41). *smaragdis* 24: a Greek
loan word, covering several greenish gems such as emeralds and
jasper. Ovid uses it only here. The glitter of the gems is appropriate

to the Sun, but the greenish light and the exotic nature of the jewels fit the monarch more than the star. Ovid calls the Sun Phoebus, having earlier in 1.451 ff. more correctly called Apollo by that name. (He had already claimed this freedom in 1.336.) The distinction between Helios and Phoebus Apollo, which prevailed in Homer and earlier Greek literature, has vanished by this time.

25–30 Like a king attended by his courtiers, the Sun is flanked by the "nobility of time." In 25–26, Ovid lists allegorical figures associated with the procession of hours, days, years, etc. No verb occurs, but it is easy to supply one, from the repeated *stabat* in 27–28. The Sun, of course, determines our earthly day, year, and century. The Greeks had already given a poetic and artistic personality to the Hours, but not to the other figures that Ovid's imagination evokes. In this passage, as in the description of the wind Notus in 1.265 ff. and in many later passages of this poem, Ovid is a major poetic inspiration of later allegory. The Sun also determines the seasons of the year, and Ovid in 27–30 allots a neat line to each. (He will create a much longer series of personifications of these seasons in the final book of this poem, 15.199–213.) Although he has declared that these figures stand on the right and left of the throne, the poet leaves it imprecise how this arrangement is to be imagined. *novum* 27: Spring is new and implicitly young, as in artistic representations of ancient and Renaissance painters and sculptors, while the last of the series, Winter, is patently imagined as an elderly, white-haired (as befits snow) man. Ovid does not indicate any age for Summer and Autumn, but it became conventional to assign them distinct ages: Summer as fully mature and in the pride of life, Autumn as middle-aged. The poet also gives each season an agricultural attribute appropriate to its place in the farmer's year, all except Winter (who typically prevails when farming is impossible). For Spring and the floral crown, cf. Horace *C.* 1.4.9–10. *cinctum . . . corona*: this hemistich recurs in *Pont.* 3.1.11. *spicea serta* 28: the phrase may come from Tibullus and his description of Ceres; Ovid uses it four times. *Autumnus . . . uvis* 29: the identical phrase occurs in *Fast.* 4.897. Bömer calls this a "self-citation" from the *Fasti*. However, we do not know the relative chronology of the two poems, which were composed almost simultaneously, as Ovid says. It could be argued that, if he were composing both poems at about steady rate, Ovid would not have been at the end of Book 4 of the *Fasti* (which after all only extended to the end of Book 6 at the time of exile) *before* he started Book 2 of the *Met.* (which averaged two books a year and had reached Book 15 at the time of exile). So this rich passage may have been used for *Fast.* 4, as it would serve *Pont.* 3. Support may also be found in the tenses of the verbs that anchor these clauses in their respective contexts: *stabat et* seems

exactly appropriate, whereas pluperfect *venerat* of *Fast.* 4.897 is
inconsistent with the other tenses of its passage. Bömer claims that
the epithet *sordidus* is inappropriate to this royal setting, but Ovid is
intent on the allegory here, not on the royal elegance. *et glacialis
Hiems* 30: a quote from *Aen.* 3.285. *capillos:* poetic accusative of
specification. Cf. *alba capillos* in the parallel passage of 15.213.

First Conversation of Father and Son, Both Foolish (31–102)

Leaving behind the allegorical stage-setting, Ovid moves us to a
sentimental, half-tragic dialogue between Phaethon and his father.
Instead of developing the theme of "doubted father," the poet plunges
ahead to the folktale motif of the "fatal gift." The father is trapped
into giving what he knows will kill his son, who insists on having
that lethal present, in spite of every effort of the Sun, too late, to
dissuade him. By viewing all this pathos cooly from a distance, the
poet makes sure that we do not identify with either character.

31   *inde:* this temporal conjunction serves to mark a transition away from
       the allegory. Magnus sought to improve the transition by emending
       to *ipse;* clever but unconvincing. *loco medius:* a reminder of 25, where
       the allegory started. The ablative noun is otiose, but not uncommon.
       Ovid delays his identification of the individuals until 32. But it should
       be clear who is in the middle and who is pale with amazement at
       these novelties. *novitate:* this word, which the other Augustan poets
       employ only five times all together, occurs nine times thematically
       in the *Met.* and eight times in other Ovidian works. This line has four
       dactyls, and the next two each have five, to help mark the change of
       pace in this "dramatic" section.

32   *oculis:* now the Sun is clearly humanized and personified, by contrast
       with the double meaning of *lumina* 23. Normally, the fact that the
       Sun sees all means that he knows all; Ovid plays with this idea, for
       example, in 3.171–72 and 226–28. But here the eyes are only human,
       and this glance from the all-seeing Sun merely prefaces a question
       that, as Bömer remarks, the father need never have asked: he should
       have been fully prepared for Phaethon's arrival. Thus, we may well
       infer that Ovid is slyly poking fun at the god's ignorance and preparing
       for foolish, fatal "generosity."

33–34 *quaeque:* the *-que* is the usual casual Ovidian connective between
       narrative and direct speech. A visitor is regularly asked why he or
       she has come. Homeric epic made this initial question formulaic, and
       Ovid regularly alludes to it; e.g., in 2.511, when Juno visits Tethys.
       However, the Sun really answers his own query in 34, when he affirms

that Phaethon is undeniably his offspring. That, after all, is what the boy came to ascertain. Heavy alliteration of *p, ph,* and f, along with the pompous verbiage, lends a somewhat unreal emphasis to his assertion. *parenti:* dative of agent.

35–36 *o lux . . . mundi:* Phaethon starts by addressing the Sun formally almost as though in prayer. But Ovid's language is carefully chosen. The light of the world becomes central to the story that unfolds. *Phoebe pater* 36: it is not usual in Roman ritual to address either Apollo or the Sun as *pater;* this epithet springs from the story, not religious belief.

37–39 *falsa . . . sub imagine:* the boy refers to the charge of Epaphus in 1.754, that Clymene cloaked her sexual indulgence by claiming that the Sun raped her. *pignora da* 38: the request for proof (often fatal) is a regular story-motif. Perseus proves his powers in these terms (5.247). Notice that Phaethon calls the Sun *genitor* as he asks for proof. He is, as he says, very confused and desperate that others believe his noble status. *animis* 39: ablative of separation.

40–41 *dixerat:* for the use of a single verb in the pluperfect to close a speech in Ovid, cf. 1.367. *circum caput . . . radios:* here, Ovid refers to the radiate crown regularly shown in paintings and statues of the Sun. He puts it down, apparently, because its brightness has kept Phaethon at a distance (cf. 22).

42–43 *nec . . . et:* the two clauses here answer the two conditional clauses of Phaethon's speech (36–37): he is indeed the god's son.

44–46 *quoque:* the *-que* is a connective; *quo* introduces a relative clause of purpose. The father now answers the request for proof, promising to grant any wish of Phaethon. *adesto* 45: future imperative, common in solemn vows. *dis iuranda palus* 46: the Styx, strongest confirmation of a divine oath (cf. 1.188–89). Ovid, however, undercuts the solemnity of the vow by his witty gloss: the Sun could never behold the river, which runs through the Underworld. *dis:* dative of agent.

47–48 *vix bene desierat:* after this pluperfect opening, Ovid most commonly uses the *cum-inversum* structure, but he sometimes, as here, places the two clauses in parataxis, without a conjunction; the purpose is perhaps to emphasize the headlong, headstrong speed of the boy's response. *currus . . . equorum:* Phaethon cannot just borrow the family car, as today; he has to specify both the chariot and the horses. *inque diem:* the *-que* actually connects the accusatives *currus* and *ius.* The prepositional phrase means: "for a day." *alipedum . . . equorum:* treat this as one sense-unit: "the right to drive the swift horses." Vergil had used the epic epithet for horses. Ovid adds to the display of epic diction his own invented "archaism," *moderamen* (used seven times, only in the *Met.*). The noun takes the objective genitive.

49–50 *patrem:* Ovid keeps emphasizing the father, here in his recognition
of his fond folly. *terque quaterque / concutiens:* an obvious echo of
1.179–80, where a somewhat foolish Jupiter was mightily moved.

50–52 Ovid assigns the Sun now the longest speech he has so far contrived
in the poem, just over fifty lines. *temeraria:* a word found in comedy
and prose before Ovid, who uses it often, especially in this metrical
position. He likes the irony of rashness punished. *vox mea facta
tua est* 51: because of the aphaeresis (elision) in *tuast,* we do not
automatically know whether *tua* is ablative; but since *mea* has to be
nominative, we can infer the case of *tua. utinam . . . liceret . . .
negarem:* the unreal quality of *liceret* smoothly prepares us for the
imperfective subjunctive and contrary-to-fact aspect of *negarem.*

53 *dissuadere:* this verb announces the rhetorical type of the speech, a
suasio against the boy's suicidal wish.

54–55 *magna petis . . . munera:* to do what his father, a god, does only
with great effort is impossible for Phaethon, a *puer,* and, as the next
line emphasizes, mortal. Ovid comes back to this point when he
ironically calls Phaethon *magnanimus* (111) and then gives him a
hero's epitaph that calls attention to his "great daring" (328). The
logical word order would be: *magna petis munera quae nec viribus
nec annis conveniant.* The last verb is subjunctive in a clause of
characteristic; it takes the dative.

56 Ovid has contrived a near-perfect chiasmus, missing only the *est* that
we easily understand in the first hemistich. *non est mortale:* ironically,
Phaethon is usurping an immortal's role, which will be the death of
him.

57–60 Further emphasis: only one god could handle the chariot, and that is
Helios himself. *plus:* refers back to *magna* (54). *placeat . . . licebit*
58: "No matter how self-satisfied people may be." *ignifero . . . in
axe* 59: epic language, compound adjective and metonymous noun,
to refer to the special chariot of the Sun. *me . . . excepto* 60: ablative
absolute, with effective emphasis of the pronoun by metrical position.

60–62 The climactic point: not even Jupiter can drive the chariot. Line 61
is essentially Golden; its emphasis on the fierce lightning bolt might
remind us of Jupiter's incompetent use of the weapon on Lycaon
and his reluctant abandonment of it in the destruction of mankind.
However, in this story, he does employ it effectively, if somewhat
unorthodoxly (cf. 304 ff.). *quid Iove maius habemus?* 62: a rhetorical
question such as this, especially at the end of a speech, can be highly
effective. Ovid has been harping on the theme of greatness, and we
know that Jupiter is supposed to possess supreme *maiestas* and to be
omnipotens. But to ask the question, and especially using the neuter
gender, invites doubts. Jupiter has not been very "great" in Ovid's
representation; at the end of this book (847), his *maiestas* will be

seriously compromised, when he chooses to pursue an amatory adventure and trade his "greatness" for bull-form.

63–64   The Sun proceeds to describe the frightening features of the route through the sky, in hope of dampening the boy's rashness. He begins by representing the course as a great arc (like the path of an airplane today): a steep climb, leveling out for the main distance, then a steep descent. Seneca knew Ovid's story and this passage so well, that he cited 63 through 69 from memory to illustrate a moral point in his essay *De Providentia* 5.10. As Seneca interprets the scene, the dangers that the Sun sets forth only act as a challenge to the heroic nature of Phaethon, and he actually attributes to the boy a speech of dashing resolution that Ovid never wrote and which, in fact, runs counter to Ovid's characterization. Ovid's Phaethon is not heroic, but foolish, headstrong, and ambitious, in a way that does not earn sympathy. So Seneca's passage gives us both an early textual version and an early misreading of the Latin. *prima:* Ovid will define the three stages with this adjective, along with *medio* (64) and *ultima* (67). *qua:* ablative of means. *recentes:* when the horses are fresh. *medio:* the reader is expecting Ovid to continue his syntax and use feminine nominative singular to refer to the mid-course; and several scribes, e.g., *LM* have written *media* (which the aphaeresis will allow). However, the form guaranteed by the meter, *altissima,* preempts nominative singular and proves that Ovid has used the familiar variation of a transferred epithet, making *medio* go with *caelo.*

65–66   *ipsi mihi:* dative of reference. If even the Sun admits his terror, then Phaethon should know how frightened he can expect to be. And indeed he will be: cf. 180 below. *sit. trepidet* 66: subjunctive in a relative clause of characteristic; *unde = a quo.* It is so high that, when he looks down, he gets dizzy with fear. Seneca's text helps to confirm this reading. Some early MSS, following the lead of *PU,* read indicative *fit . . . trepidat.* That may have been encouraged by the easy misreading of the initial *s* of *sit* as *f.*

67   *prona:* the reverse of *ardua;* it slopes steeply down. *moderamine certo:* ablative with special verb. This is the second use of this invented noun (cf. above 48). Phaethon's fear, once he reaches the height of the heavens, robs him of the power to use a "sure" hand on the reins; in fact he will abandon them (cf. 200), the prelude to total disaster. Five dactyls help to emphasize the speed of the descent.

68–69   *quae:* the "antecedent" (*Tethys* 69), as often in Ovid, comes later. *subiectis:* the waters of the sea that lies beneath the sky are regularly imagined, even today, as "receiving" the setting sun. *in praeceps* 69: a common phrase of adverbial quality: "precipitately." Ovid will use the same phrase again when Phaethon plunges to the earth (320). *Tethys:* goddess of the sea, who fears for her waters. Ovid plays with the dualism of mythology, treating Tethys partly as a person, partly as a figure of speech.

70–71   *adsidua . . . caelum:* it was common belief in Ovid's day that the sun moved in one direction and the sky and stars "behind it" in the reverse direction. It took the telescope and the Copernican Revolution to elaborate more correctly the movements of the solar system and the various galaxies. In these two lines, Ovid poetically renders, as part of the father's warning, the movement of the sky in three successive, basically repetitive, clauses. The only difference between *vertigine* and *volumine,* for instance, is that Ovid first specifies how the sky turns, then how it turns the stars with it.

72–73   *nitor in adversum:* as if the rotation of the sky exerts a pull on the Sun (as well as on the lofty stars), Ovid says that the Sun must struggle against that motion, in order to pursue his course (in the reverse direction). *impetus* 73: the rotational pull of the sky. *rapido . . . orbi:* again, the swift rotation of the sky; dative with the adjective *contrarius,* which refers to the opposite motion of the sun.

74–75   *finge:* "suppose." Seneca, in his dramatic misreading, imagined that Phaethon replied to the fatherly list of dangers: *iunge datos currus.* That does not mean that he read *iunge* in his text, but rather that he took off from line 74 freely on his own. *rotatis . . . polis:* still another variation on the rotation of the sky that is counter (hence *obvius*) to the motion of the sun. Dative with the adjective. *citus . . . axis:* another variant on the same heavenly motion, here conceived as rotating on an axis.

76–78   Next, the father tries to frighten Phaethon with a description of the fearsome creatures that exist in the skies as constellations. He reverses the usual process of the human imagination, which has strained to "people" the heavens with creatures suggested by the patterns of stars; he takes the imaginative names of these constellations and represents them menacing his son. In a standard rhetorical tactic, he postulates that Phaethon pictures the heavens as a pleasant place where the gods dwell in comfort, in groves and cities. (Ironically, of course, Ovid has described precisely that kind of "Palatine" existence for Jupiter and his companions in 1.168 ff.) Then, he asserts the reverse. *esse* 78: the verb, not strictly necessary and no doubt already understood in the previous lines, comes emphatically at the beginning of the line, only to be denied. It is replaced by a totally different statement of fact (*est*). *insidias . . . formasque:* taking both nouns with *ferarum,* we should picture beasts lying in wait, ready to spring on the careless traveller.

79   *ut . . . teneas:* subjunctive in a concessive clause. The second clause says the same thing, in negative form. *errore:* literally, wandering

off course. In fact, Phaethon, once in the chariot and en route, quickly strays from the correct course; cf. 167 ff.

80–81   The creatures mentioned by the Sun are some of the signs of the Zodiac. Strictly speaking, however, the course of the Sun in a single day would not pass through the entire Zodiac, but through one prevailing sign (e.g., through Leo the Lion in late August). *adversi:* the Bull is represented as charging against Phaethon. *gradieris:* not strictly correct, since the boy will not be on foot, but driving. *Haemoniosque arcus* 81: a learned allusion to the Archer or Sagittarius, who was commonly imagined to be a centaur and hence a native of Thessaly in origin. His bow would supposedly be aimed in hostility at the charioteer. *violentique:* the Lion is introduced with a menancing epithet.

82–83   *saevaque:* the cleverness of Ovid's verbal repetitions here undermines the supposed savagery of Scorpio and the Crab; the adjective presumably goes with both cases of *bracchia*. *aliter* 83: the range of the Crab's "arms" would be quite "other" than that of the gigantic Scorpion with its wide sweep.

84–87   *nec tibi quadripedes . . . in promptu regere est:* these words, which frame the rest of the passage, provide the essential syntax. *quadripedes:* accusative direct object of *regere. in promptu . . . est* + infinitive: "it is easy to . . ." The Sun adds a final danger to his list of vain deterrents: the difficulty of controlling the spirited horses. No ordinary horses, they breathe fire out from their lungs through their nostrils. *incaluere animi* 87: cf. *animosos ignibus* 84. Their inner fire fires their spirits. *habenis:* dative with compound verb.

88–89   As he reverts to his direct appeal, the Sun speaks in slow, serious spondees at the start of 88. *funesti . . . muneris:* we are back to the theme of the fatal gift. *dum resque sinit* 89: the -*que* actually connects the two imperatives, *cave* and *corrige.*

90–92   *scilicet:* often ironic, but not here. It means "clearly," and it modifies *petis* 91. The Sun is reminding Phaethon and us of the boy's request earlier at 38–39, to which he foolishly acceded, thus precipitating this crisis. Now, however, he wants to extract a rhetorical argument from this anxious moment; and so he pointedly repeats *pignora certa*. To believe him, he has already given Phaethon the desired proof now, not by the promise of the chariot, but by his evident fear! To make sure that we savor the point, Ovid then repeats it in *patrio . . . probor* 92, a clause that kills pathos with its tripping four dactyls and its obsessive alliteration. The Sun here is too much the self-conscious speaker of Roman rhetorical schools, not the truly anxious father.

92–94   *adspice vultus:* we may understand that the Sun's usually bright and cheery countenance here is supposed to be "clouded" with fear. But many a clever speaker or actor would start squeezing out tears at this point, using them as evidence of deep feeling. Later, when the fear is actually realized and Phaethon dies, the father does indeed go into decline, almost as though "eclipsed"; cf. 381 ff. *ecce* 93: this adverb is often used, as here and at 112, with a verb of seeing, to emphasize the dramatic effect. *utinamque oculos . . . posses inserere:* in his most ingenious ploy, the Sun wishes for the impossible and tries to use that very impossibility as sure proof. Ovid's audience would love this, but certainly not be engulfed with tears. *in pectora:* the MSS divide between this reading and ablative singular *pectore*. Although it might seem that the ablative form is the "more difficult reading," it also might simply be an error resulting from the common use of the phrase *in pectore* (e.g., 85 above), from the postponement of the controlling verb until the next line, and from the unfamiliarity of this expression. The accusative reading has been preserved in our oldest witnesses, two fragmentary MSS of the ninth and tenth centuries respectively. Presumably, then, the division goes back to the ancestors of all extant MSS. The popping alliteration starts again with this word.

95–97 This sentence can be reorganized as follows: *circumspice quidquid . . . habet mundus [et] e . . . tantis bonis . . . posce aliquid.* The connective is supplied by Ovid's typically casual *-que* added to the preposition *e* (96). Notice the artful correspondence between *quidquid* and *aliquid*. The Sun has already said that the chariot is the only gift he would like to refuse (cf. 52); now he offers anything else. *nullam patiere repulsam* 97: Ovid ironically repeats this clause verbatim in 3.289, where Jupiter repeats the Sun's folly, offering his beloved Semele any gift she wants and binding himself by the Styx, with the same fatal result.

98–99 *hoc unum:* cf. *solum hoc* (52). *poena, / non honor:* Ovid likes to analyze issues in terms of the correct terminology to be used for them. It was undoubtedly a rhetorical trick of his day, but he can often employ it quite powerfully. Not here, I think. Childish Phaethon gives it no answer whatever. *poenam . . . poscis:* in the reiteration of his point, the Sun again betrays himself by his insistent alliteration.

100 The question indicates that Phaethon has moved forward to use his childish wiles on his father, like Daphne in 1.485, who also got her father to promise something against his better judgment. *ignare:* ignorance is an essential element of Phaethon's melodrama.

101– Here, the Sun returns to the point from which he departed. All his
2 words have been futile, and he once again weakly capitulates to the foolish boy, bound as he is by his unwise oath. *optaris* 102: future perfect, with syncopation of *-ve-*. *sapientius:* the god urges his son to be wiser in his choice, but this supposedly all-seeing and omniscient father has been inexcusably unwise himself.

The Father's Sad Farewell (103–49)

The dramatic interruption from Phaethon during the Sun's speech, his embrace and silent appeal (100), has been a powerful response that the weak father cannot resist. His "warnings" collapse before he has finished. So Phaethon hurries toward the chariot and welcomes the moment when, with dawn, he must set out. Not so, his father. He embarks on a second series of warnings (*monitis* 126) that vainly advise the headstrong boy how to drive safely. Safety is impossible for Phaethon once he drives away.

103–
4

dictis . . . repugnat: Ovid skips over Phaethon's response, which a less gifted poet would have elaborated; its gist can be inferred from this half-line. The boy fights against good advice.

105–
6

qua licuit: read this with *cunctatus.* The Sun delayed in every possible way, but finally had to make good on his promise. *altos . . . currus:* the hyperbaton encloses the entire clause, namely, the verb, its object, and the apposition that should logically follow *currus. Vulcania munera:* Ovid seems to have been the first to credit Vulcan with major artistic work for the Sun, on his palace doors (above, 5 ff.) and on this chariot. He may be imagining a friendly link between the two ever since the Sun helped Vulcan detect the adultery of his wife Venus with Mars (cf. 4.171 ff.).

107–
8

Seneca cited these two lines in *Ep.* 19.115.12, taking exception to all this emphasis on gold. But he had a moral theme that had little to do with Ovid's narrative themes. The skillfully repeated forms of *aureus* go with the dazzling brightness of everything to do with the sun, but also indicate why Phaethon is both dazzled and eager to possess the chariot. All the necessarily metal parts of the wagon are of gold or silver; or, if we insisted on realistic details, they would consist of hard iron and be gilded with the softer ornamental gold and silver.

109–
10

The yokes for the horses are studded with flashing jewels. Exactly what chrysolites are, is not clear, but the Latin word comes from a Greek compound meaning "goldstone." They must have looked golden. *positaeque ex ordine:* cf. 12.211, *positis ex ordine.* Ovid likes to place this phrase *ex ordine* or synonymous *in ordine* so that the noun occupies the fifth dactyl. The "orderly disposition" of these gems would presumably be determined by artistic effect. What interests Ovid is not the richness of these gems, but the fact that they reflect the light of the sun, a point that is elegantly made in the Golden Line 110. *repercusso* 110: this participle determines the fact that Phoebus himself is being reflected to himself.

111–   *dumque ea:* same initial dactyl at 2.353. *magnanimus:* Ovid probably
14   recalls the passage in Lucretius 5.399 ff., where his predecessor briefly
       referred to this myth and used this "heroic" epithet of Phaethon. Ovid
       has not heroized the rash boy, so the epithet has an ironic ring in this
       context. The boy is simply excited by all the glitter of his father's
       chariot (in today's terms, the new sports car). *perspicit* 112: he looks
       it over. This is the first of five dactyls in this smooth line. *ecce:* cf.
       above 93. *vigil . . . fores:* Ovid describes dawn without the sun,
       because the Sun's chariot has yet to depart on its ill-fated journey.
       The three adjectives collectively give a sense of literal dawn and Dawn
       as an anthropomorphic figure. There is a bright purplish light early
       in the morning, as the goddess, fully awake, opens the doors on the
       east. *ortu:* by metonymy, the place of sunrise—which has not hap-
       pened yet, of course—is the east. *atria* 114: poetic plural; Ovid imag-
       ines the "house" of Dawn to have a rosy atrium (as "rosy-fingered"
       Dawn should), not the smoke-blackened walls that the name, etymo-
       logically interpreted, suggests.

114–   *diffugiunt:* the calm, colorful appearance of Dawn at her open door
15   has a violent effect on the end of night, which Ovid catches with his
       sudden series of military metaphors. *Lucifer:* the morning star; Ovid
       has personified it as a commanding general.

116–   *quem petere ut . . . vidit:* this clause early became corrupted in the
18   archetype MSS, so that the prevailing reading has come down as *quem
       pater ut.* Apparently, the elision caused scribes to hear a more familiar
       phrase, of which 8.145 is a clear example. They expected a subject
       early in the sentence, and what more appropriate subject than "father"?
       However, *quem* and *terras* both need a verb. An early ingenious
       corrector hit upon the true reading in *MN.* Ovid simply delays the
       subject until 118, while telling us of more effects of morning that are
       visible. *cornuaque extremae . . . lunae* 117: the moon in its latest
       cycle can be imagined as a slim crescent or, very commonly by Ovid,
       as a pair of horns: cf. 1.11. Here, the "lateness" goes with the picture of
       the moon fading before daylight. *velut:* prose writers often "apologize"
       with this word for a metaphor, but we would not expect Ovid to do
       so. *Titan* 118: used of the sun earlier in 1.10, but only here of
       Phaethon's father. *Horis:* the only allegorical figures of 25 ff. who
       play any role in the story. They yoke the fire-breathing horses. Dative
       with *imperat* and infinitive is a poetic construction, which Ovid likes:
       cf. 3.4.

119–   *iussa deae celeres:* Ovid picks up and varies the last three words of
21   118. *ignemque vomentes . . . quadripedes:* Ovid has already described
       these horses at 84, using the same epic substantive, so he can presume
       on the audience's ability to cope with his hyperbaton here. *ambrosiae
       suco saturos* 120: Ovid has used here a phrase from Vergil, *Aen.*

12.418 (about the ambrosial juice that Venus put on Aeneas' wound)
for the divine food eaten by the horses. He seems to have been the
first to have adapted this detail: cf. below 4.214–15, where he makes
much of this hay-substitute. The alliteration also implies the poet's
playfulness. *praesepibus:* since the Sun has horses, he has to have a
stable where they are kept at night. Ablative of place from which.
sonantia frena 121: the traces and reins by which the charioteer has
to control the horses. They probably "sound" because, like many such
riggings, they are adorned with bells. Phaethon grabs them at 151,
but abandons them at 200.

122–   *pater . . . sui . . . nati:* a final emphasis on the relationship between
23   Sun and Phaethon as the father vainly addresses the son with his last
        appeal. *medicamine:* this word, which Cicero used once in a speech,
        became poetic after Ovid, who employed it eighteen times, even in
        the title of one of his works. Here, he refers to some salve that would
        make the boy immune to the heat of the sun. In earlier literature, we
        hear of mortals being anointed with ambrosia, but that is to render
        them immortal. *rapidae . . . flammae* 123: the adjective suggests the
        way fire swiftly ignites and consumes other things. Ovid uses it later
        in 8.225 to describe the way the sun's heat destroyed Icarus' wings.
        Objective genitive with *patientia,* which in turn modifies *ora* (122).

124–   *imposuit . . . radios:* he placed on Phaethon the radiate crown that
25   he himself had removed at 41. Thus, he decks the boy with his
        powerful symbols. *praesagaque luctus:* the compound adjective is
        epic in form, and Vergil introduced it twice in Book 10 of the *Aeneid.*
        He may well have inspired Ovid by the scene in *Aen.* 10.843, where
        Mezentius senses what has happened to his son Lausus; Vergil also
        used the objective genitive. *pectore* 125: ablative of place from which.

126–   *his saltem monitis:* alluding to the failure of the previous speech of
27   warning (cf. 103). Dative with *parere. parere parentis:* Ovid presum-
        ably plays with the two verbs of similar form but quite different root
        meanings. (Their participles are identical.) *stimulis* 127: dative with
        verb *parce.* The noun, which generally refers to cattle goads or some-
        thing like spurs for riders, must here apply to a whip one uses with
        a team of steeds. Instead of urging the horses on, this charioteer should
        use his reins.

128   A nicely structured Ovidian line, framed by the repeated stress on the
        natural inclination of the horses, both an advantage and a danger.
        Five dactyls stress the natural speed that needs slowing.

129   *directos . . . via quinque per arcus:* the first adjective should be
        considered transferred and hence translated as though with *via.* The
        five "arcs" that Ovid mentions here are the five heavenly zones, what
        he earlier also calls *plagae* (above, 1.45 ff.).

130–   *sectus . . . limes:* since many Roman roads were literally cut across

32   the countryside, Ovid imagines a similar route marked out in the heavens. This path of the sun, which we call the ecliptic, runs at an oblique angle in a broad arc across the three central zones, avoiding the extremes at north and south.

133   *sit:* jussive subjunctive. *vestigia cernes:* Ovid imagines not only that the path is cut but also that the wagon and horses have left ruts and hoofprints, so that Phaethon will be able to trace his route.

134–   *aequos . . . calores:* Ovid has the Sun sketch out what can be allego-
35   rized as a *via media,* the "moderate way". Similarly, when Daedalus tries to guide his son Icarus on the safe way through the skies, he also recommends the "middle way" (8.203). Here, though, the Sun's concern is for the world. *nec preme* 135: Phaethon is not to drive down too low or, as the next clause indicates, up too high. Both verbs with *currum* express in striking manner the power that the charioteer ought to possess.

136–   Here, Ovid elaborates what he meant by the phrase "equal heat" above
37   at 134. *altius . . . inferius:* "too high . . . too low." The damage that Phaethon later will cause will result from his getting too low and close to the earth (cf. 206 ff.). *medio:* this is the substantive, not the adjective used without the preposition *in. tutissimus:* the Sun's concern for the safety of the heavens and earth involves that of Phaethon, for which the father fears so rightly.

138–   A carefully balanced pair of lines, again illustrating two extremes,
39   between which the charioteer should steer. If the right wheel veers off too far, then it will be because the right horses are being allowed to pull more strongly. The comparative use of *dexter* is rare, especially in poetry. Ovid employs it twice more in the *Met. tortum . . . Auguem:* this coiled Snake is situated near the Bears in the highest part of the sky. *pressam . . . Aram* 139: the Altar lies correspondingly low on the horizon, "pressed" by that boundary and implicitly close to earth.

140–   *inter utrumque tene:* supply an object like *cursum.* Cf. the similar
41   advice given to Icarus by his father: *inter utrumque vola* (8.206). *Fortunae cetera mando:* the father desperately commits his son to the care of Fortune, who just might save him if she feels benevolently disposed. Bömer suggests that Ovid refers to that Fortune which, in many Roman sayings, is said to help the brave. However, if so, Ovid does it ironically. Phaethon is not brave: he is rash and foolish; and his father clearly believes so as he speaks here. *iuvet . . . consulat* 141: optative subjunctive with *opto. melius . . . opto:* with all the understood words included, this would read: *melius tibi consulat opto quam tu tibi consulis.*

142–   Ovid has already described the end of night and coming of dawn
44   above at 112 ff. Now, the Sun goes over the same detail, though

more briefly, as a way of focusing attention on the critical moment when Phaethon either drives off to destruction or listens to the anxious words of his father. In contrast to the other passage, this one is ostentatiously epic and Vergilian. The first clause about night touching the limits set on the western shore owes much to *Aen.* 5.835–36; the clause about the lack of freedom to delay is reminiscent of a very serious passage about Turnus in *Aen.* 12.74; and the image and last two words of 144 come from *Aen.* 3.521. However, the echoes of Vergil here help us to appreciate the unepic situation and characters. *poscimur* 144: "we are called upon," i.e., to carry out our function. Elsewhere, in 4.274 and 5.333, Ovid uses this verb in the same metrical position, but specifically of poetic speakers.

145–46   *corripe lora manu:* this would be the Sun's normal response to the time; and it will be Phaethon's response (cf. 151 below). But the father checks himself and launches one final vain appeal. *si mutabile pectus / est tibi:* Ovid also uses this rare construction in *Fast.* 4.601. The unchangeable emotion or driving characteristic that persists when the external form is metamorphosed becomes an increasingly prominent theme of Ovid's poem as of this book: cf. below the account of Callisto at 2.485. In this instance, Phaethon's driving ambition seems so childish that it wins him little sympathy. *consiliis non curribus utere:* as we saw at 98–99 above, Ovid likes to manipulate pairs of opposing terms. Here, he gains emphasis from the alliteration.

147–48   The three *dum*-clauses, organized in a tricolon of ever-longer units, emphasize the critical choice. *solidis . . . sedibus:* Ovid uses allilteration to emphasize the idea of what we would call "solid earth." *male optatos* 148: the father has already stressed this, e.g., at 56. *inscius:* cf. *nescius* 58. *premis . . . axes:* if Phaethon mounts the chariot, as he will at 150, he will press down on the axles.

149   *quae tutus spectes:* the relative purpose clause before the noun that it limits (*lumina*) brings out the father's main concern, the safety of Phaethon (cf. 137). Earlier, at 22–23, Phaethon was unable to bear the proximity of the Sun's light or eyes.

Phaethon's Disastrous Drive (150–259)

Phaethon shows total disregard for his father's anxiety by leaping into the chariot and seizing the reins, exactly what the Sun tried to dissuade him from doing. A brief period of pleasure allows the boy to feel in charge of the mighty apparatus. Then, as soon as he starts out on the road, he loses control. The horses realize that they have a powerless charioteer and run away with the carriage. As the vehicle swoops too close to the earth, Ovid records the damage its heat causes in a series of cleverly worded metamorphoses.

150–   *occupat:* instead of closing off the father's words with an epic formula,
52   as Vergil would have done, Ovid brusquely introduces a vigorous
        action by Phaethon to end and answer the speech. *levem iuvenali:*
        both adjectives are important. The lightness of the chariot makes it
        hard to control, and the youthful and therefore light (cf. 161 ff.) body
        of the new charioteer makes the vehicle far less steady than usual.
        statque super 151: although this phrasing is normal enough, it could
        be regarded, with Bömer, as an example of tmesis; in that case, for
        metrical reasons Ovid would have broken up the compound *superstat.*
        However, there are few examples of this compound verb in Augustan
        verse; Ovid himself uses it only once in all his poetry (*Her.* 10.123).
        The stance suggests the arrogance and pride of the young brat. *mani-
        busque . . . habenas:* for closely similar wording, cf. 7.221. The
        adjective *leves* is not the only epithet Ovid could have used for the
        reins; elsewhere, he has *lentes* and even *graves.* Their lightness perhaps
        implies the need for a "heavy hand", which Phaethon cannot apply.
        An early stylist tried to "improve" this wording and get rid of the
        repeated adjective; the alternative reading *datas* has been inserted in
        many MSS. In 152, Ovid brings out the irony of the scene in the
        juxtaposition *invito grates.*

153–   Ovid lists four horses by name. It is traditional to assign the Sun a
55   mighty four-horse chariot, but the names of the steeds were optional.
        These four are otherwise known only from Hyginus, who credits Ovid.
        All the names are Greek in origin. Eous, connected with the east and
        dawn, may have been in Eumelus earlier; the other three all suggest
        the sun's fiery quality. Individually pronounced vowels of the first
        two names help to make line 153 exceedingly mellifluous and dactylic.
        Solis equi 154: Ovid punctuates his list before going on to the fourth
        horse. Since the same two words open line 162 below, it was to be
        expected that at least one scribe would let his eyes drop and then skip
        the passage in between as he hurriedly copied his quota of lines. Such
        an error appears in *U.* The rhythm continues to be primarily dactylic
        in 154 and 155, and the language becomes more poetic. *hinnitibus
        . . . flammiferis:* a vivid elaboration of a picture Ovid presented above
        in 84–85. The compound adjective seems to have been revived from
        Ennius, once in the *Heroides* and four times in the *Met. repagula*
        155: Ovid uses this word three times and only in the *Met.* In the other
        cases, he clearly aligns himself with the standard prose meaning of
        the word, denoting the bolts of a door. Here, the first time he employs
        it, we might also expect him to be content with the alliterative effect
        and also refer to normal bolts, on a gate or paddock.

156–   Tethys, first mentioned above at 2.69, serves here with double aptness.
57   As goddess of the sea, she properly sends the Sun forth at sunrise;
        as mother of Clymene, known to Ovid from wide reading, she can

be used to sound the ironic note of pathos for her grandson. The rhythm slows down with four straight spondees. *facta . . . copia* 157: the vast expanse is opened up.

158– *corripuere viam:* Ovid borrows an epic phrase from Vergil, *Aen.*
60   1.418, where, however, the poet described the hurried pace of Aeneas (not horses). Ovid stresses speed by using five dactyls. *pedibusque per aera motis:* normally, this clause would suggest vain movement, beating the air; but Ovid cleverly makes the air provide traction, as the earth does for ordinary horses. *nebulas* 159: the morning mists. *praetereunt . . . Euros* 160: rising into the heavens, the horses and their chariot outdistance and soar above the east winds that have sprung up at daybreak.

161– *leve pondus:* see above at 150 ff. on the use of the adjective. *nec*
62   *quod . . . possent:* a special kind of relative clause of characteristic that amplifies a previous phrase and so starts with a conjunction. For an earlier example with *et quod,* cf. 1.77. *gravitate* 162: opposite of *leve pondus* (161) and *levitate* (164). If we take the yoke literally, not as metonymy for the whole chariot, then the lighter weight of Phaethon affects the feel of the yoke.

163– It is easy to imagine any object moving through the air as "sailing,"
64   as we say of kites, blimps, airplanes, and even orbiting space vehicles. So Ovid, comparing the chariot to a ship that is not properly ballasted or weighted with cargo, continues the theme of 161–62 with *pondere* and *levitate*. His rhythm of dactyls in 164 also mirrors the sense.

165– Moving from the comparison, the poet delays his subject until the
66   penultimate word of 166. *onere adsueto:* another synonymous thematic phrase: cf. 162. Ablative with *vacuus. dat . . . saltus:* a convenient alternative for the verb *salit,* which enables Ovid to get the meter. This phrase and the rare verb *succutitur* (166), both of which catch the bobbing movement of the uncontrolled chariot, may have been suggested to Ovid by the context of Lucretius 6.549–51. *inani:* the theme reaches a final development, as the light weight becomes comparable to no weight.

167– Changed subject delayed to first word of 168. *ruunt:* our verb "bolt"
68   captures the sense. *tritum . . . spatium:* the ruts made by the chariot wheels in previous trips; cf. 133. *quadriiugi* 168: the team of four horses named at 153–54. Ovid seems to have been the first to use this poetic adjective as a substantive. He was later imitated by Silver Latin poets. The horses run off course in complete disorder. *quo . . . currunt:* typically, Ovid places the relative before its "antecedent" and omits the parallel form of *currunt.* In full form, the passage would read: *nec ordine currunt quo prius currebant.*

169– *ipse:* Phaethon. Bömer nicely observes that Ovid has captured the
70   uncertainty of the boy in his many short clauses and words crowded

into these two lines, in radical contrast to the previous expansive lines. *qua . . . flectat:* indirect question depending, with *qua sit,* on *scit. commissas:* the Sun has most doubtfully entrusted reins and chariot to the boy, who heedlessly grabbed them, happy until now: cf. 145 and 151. *si sciat, imperet* 170: subjunctive in a future less vivid condition. Probably, we should link the indirect question also with *imperet* and translate: "he would not know how to command or control the horses."

171–
72 Ovid now starts to focus on paradoxical effects resulting from a disordered universe: here, a sun off course. Compare his playful fascination with the effects of the Deluge in Book 1. *tum primum:* for the first time, a constellation so far north that it was never warmed by the sun's rays suddenly gets hot. *Triones:* the plow-oxen who were imagined as at work in the seven stars that the Romans regularly called *Septemtriones* (cf. 1.64). The ancients also thought of them as a wagon (cf. British "Charles' wain"), and their mythology turned them into the Great Bear or Callisto. *vetito . . . aequore* 172: a clever allusion to a part of the myth that Ovid, with deliberate anachronism, plans to tell us later in this book at 527 ff. Since this constellation never sets into the ocean, under stress from the heat here it "tries" vainly to cool off in the water. By calling the stars oxen, Ovid can catch the animation without anticipating his story of Callisto turned into a bear.

173–
75 *quaeque . . . Serpens:* = *et Serpens quae*. Like the Oxen, the Serpent has always been in the frigid northern sky. Exploiting his opportunity to animate the imaginary celestial shape, Ovid pictures it as a reptile in hibernation, normally cold and sluggish, but suddenly acquiring "new anger" from the unwonted proximity of the Sun. *sumpsit novas* 175: the language of metamorphosis; Ovid has first given the constellation a "real" physical nature, then amused himself and us by transforming it. *fervoribus:* ablative of cause. The connection between anger and heat is a common one.

176–
77 Ovid grows increasingly charmed with his opportunities and disarms the "tragedy" of Phaethon more and more. Here, he chattily addresses another constellation, the plowman who supposedly drives the Oxen. The paradox he realizes is that this man, who normally is so slow in movement (= setting), now flees in terror from the heat that has invaded his normally chill northern heaven. *memorant:* the poet affects to fall back on narrative tradition, and thereby he moves us farther from Phaethon. *plaustra* 177: the Wagon, a.k.a the Oxen (*Triones*), a.k.a the Great Bear. The alliteration with *t* slows down the pronunciation of the line, hence reinforces the sense.

178–
79 The boy climbs to the point whence, as his father warned, it was scary to look down; cf. above, 64 ff. *summo despexit ab aethere:*

closely parallel to Vergil's description of Jupiter in *Aen.* 1.223. Phaethon is no almighty god; he is pathetically *infelix,* like some of Vergil's mortal characters, e.g., *infelix Dido (Aen.* 1.749). *penitus penitusque* 179: rhetorical doubling; translate "far, far below." *iacentes:* the MSS tradition divided here by the Middle Ages between the above reading and *patentes,* both transmitted by the earliest fragments. Either makes sense and could have been corrupted into the other, but *iacentes,* I believe, goes better with the frightening height.

180–
81
Ovid renders the sudden swift attack of terror with five dactyls. *genua intremuere:* same phrase at 10.458 of Myrrha. Vergil made the verb an effective element of his poetic vocabulary. *suntque . . . obortae* 181: unusually wide separation of the two parts of the verb, so as to frame the line. Then Ovid creates a paradoxical subject, *tenebrae,* which metaphorically renders the attack of dizziness or sense of dimness produced by a dazzling light. Literally, it seems as though light creates darkness! Rhetorical play, not "tragic" Phaethon, dominates his attention and, he trusts, ours.

182–
83
iam mallet: potential subjunctive. *paternos:* now, it becomes a source of regret to have exploited his father's permissiveness. *iam . . . piget* 183: By omitting the personal subject of the infinitives, Ovid makes the phrase seem to resemble that of 182, but it differs considerably, both in mood and its impersonal form. These are not the feelings of heroic magnanimity (cf. 111), but of a frightened boy. *rogando:* i.e., when he asked to ride the chariot.

184–
86
Meropis: understand *filius* with this genitive. As noted earlier, Merops was Clymene's husband and reputed to be Phaethon's father. As the boy is vainly indulging in his desire, he is carried off helplessly *(ita fertur),* and Ovid represents that state with a second ship-comparison. No longer concerned with the balance and weight of the craft (cf. 163–64), he describes a ship that is borne along by a northern gale while the pilot abandons the tiller and entrusts the boat to the gods. Obviously, Phaethon resembles that useless pilot. *acta . . . pinus:* pine serves in metonymy for the boat made of this wood. *victa . . . suus:* for metrical and poetic reasons, Ovid has reversed the adjectives from their expected nouns. *remisit / frena:* the noun "reins" is a metaphor that reminds us of the charioteering base of this simile. Ovid uses the same phrase properly of Phaethon at 191 and a synonymous one (with the same verb) at 200, when finally the boy does abandon the reins. *rector:* properly, a ruler; then, regularly extended to cover humbler activity, where guiding or steering occurs. Ovid, thus, commonly uses the word for a pilot (e.g., 6.232); but he also occasionally uses it, as here, for a charioteer (cf. *Ars Am.* 2.433). *quam:* the boat.

187–
88
quid faciat: deliberative subjunctive, which prepares us for analysis of a dilemma (cf. 1.617), as the poet expresses the anxiety of his

character. *caeli:* partitive genitive with both *multum* and *plus;* the chariot has not quite completed half its course.

189–
90
quos: by placing the relative clause before its "antecedent" Ovid captures added pathos and irony. *prospicit . . . respicit* 190: the line has been constructed to highlight antitheses.

191–
92
quidque agat: the *-que* is a connective, and the clause is simple indirect question depending on *ignarus. stupet:* the verb suggests the shocked helplessness and paralysis of the boy. Ovid will use the verb rather comically of Perseus at 4.676, when the sudden sight of lovely Andromeda almost stuns the flying hero into a tailspin. *nomina* 192: we have been told the horses' names at 153–54; but Phaethon has not mastered them.

193–
94
miracula: Ovid uses this word five times, and only in the *Met.*; in the other four instances (cf. 3.673), he refers specifically to the marvel of metamorphosis, but here he is more general. *vario . . . caelo:* the heaven is variegated with diverse constellations. The adjective initiates a system of alliteration for 194. *simulacra* 194: Ovid has already played with the opportunity to animate the imaginary shapes of the constellations; cf. 171 ff. Now, Phaethon is terrified by their "reality."

195–
97
est locus: the formula for starting an ecphrasis; cf. above 1.168. The demonstrative *hunc* (198) ends the development. The remainder of 195 produces a rather puzzling picture of something doing something unique with its "arms," before Ovid finally resolves the mystery by naming Scorpio at the start of 196. The puzzle is a game for the audience, which removes us from the terror of the boy. *concavat:* invented by the poet for this passage, the verb does not appear again in Ovid and has few imitators. It describes the threatening way a scorpion curves its claws. The poet goes on to describe the huge size of this monstrous constellation, extending over the space of two zodiacal signs with its tail and claws on either side.

198–
200
hunc: despite the formulaic expectation of the ecphrasis, this demonstrative refers not to *locus,* but to Scorpio. *madidum sudore:* "soaked in moisture." *curvata . . . cuspide* 199: the curved tail and stinger. Ovid's alliterative phrase makes a metaphor of war—the stinger is a spearpoint—which goes with the other words of this line. *mentis inops* 200: Ovid invented this phrase, using it twice in the *Met.* and once in the *Fasti,* always in initial position, and once elsewhere in *Her.* 15.139. Phaethon is frightened out of his mind. *gelida formidine:* ablative of manner without preposition. *lora remisit:* now Phaethon fully resembles the frightened pilot of the simile at 185–86.

201–
3
quae: the reins. Once Phaethon drops them, they fall idly on the necks of the horses, which immediately sense their freedom. *exspatiantur* 202: Ovid has used this word once before, at 1.285, to describe the beginning of the Flood as the rivers overflowed their courses and

spread over the countryside. Here, the heat of the sun is about to go outside its course and create widespread damage. *nullo inhibente:* ablative absolute. Nobody, certainly not Phaethon, restrains the horses. *auras / ignotae regionis:* a somewhat unusual phrase; we might have expected *aurarum ignotas regiones.*

203–   *quaque . . . hac:* = *et qua* with the coordinate *hac.* The horses can
5   go wherever their instincts take them; no human "law" governs them. *fixis / incursant stellis:* we know that stars move, too; but the Romans assumed that they were fixed against the backdrop of aether. The verb, "rushing into or upon, encroaching on," also occurred in the description of the Flood (1.303) to report the way dolphins abandoned their natural element and invaded the forests and branches of trees. *per avia:* Ovid uses this phrase elsewhere only at 1.701, there literally, here metaphorically. The skies are "pathless" except in a myth like this, where the poet has stressed the well-marked route of the Sun.

206–   Ovid has already recorded results that arose when Phaethon drove
7   too near the northerly constellations. He makes his transition to the alternative of dropping too low and too close to the earth, where he concentrates our attention for the next fifty lines. *per declive:* the route sloping back down toward the earth. The Sun already mentioned its terrifying steepness; cf. 67–69. *spatio terrae propiore* 207: "in the region that lies too close to the earth." The first noun is ablative of place; the second is dative with the adjective.

208–   Now, Ovid suddenly makes the Moon a witness of the unnatural
9   course of the Sun. *inferius:* Phaethon has been warned and the audience prepared by this word in the Sun's speech at 137. *suis:* ablative of comparison. *fraternos:* it is not so much that Sol and Luna were brother and sister, but Apollo and Diana (who could be thought of by the Romans as respectively sun and moon) were siblings. *admiratur* 209: Ovid likes to call attention to the marvelous or the sense of marvel in his characters, and often to define the way we should respond to metamorphosis. The verb takes indirect discourse in this passage. *fumant:* we sometimes imagine clouds as swirling smoke; here, they literally smoke because they are scorched.

210–   *ut quaeque altissima:* "all the tallest parts" of the earth catch fire,
11   i.e., the mountains and hills. Then, the heat cracks it open, and its "juices," i.e., its waters, dry up. The effects of the scorching sun extend ever deeper.

212–   *canescunt:* the proper color for ripe grain is yellow. If it becomes
13   white, then it has dried up. Usually, that would be for lack of rain or irrigation; here, it is because of the closeness of the sun. *cum frondibus . . . arbor:* this is a forest fire caused in a special manner. *suo . . . damno* 213: Ovid likes to point up paradoxes in situations by using reflexive pronouns and adjectives. The dry crops provide

material, in the form of fuel, for their own destruction. Farmers do burn their fields, but only after they have reaped; so that what normally burns is not the crop, but the dry stubble.

214–
16
parva queror: the narrator intrudes. Not that he has in any way been "complaining." He has introduced the note of marvel at 209; and what he has said about the crops, inasmuch as he has ignored the effect on farmers and other human beings—cf. the way Ovid generally avoided speaking of the human victims of the Flood—has been devoid of pathos. Now, however, he allots a perfunctory two lines, still devoid of feeling, to the destruction of cities and their populations. *in cinerem vertunt* 216: the language of this synonym for "burn up" suggests that Ovid's interest focuses primarily on the fascination of metamorphosis. *vertere in* + accusative constitutes the most common phrase for transformation in the poem. Ovid's model seems to be Horace, *Epist.* 1.15.39. *silvae . . . ardent:* we have already heard of forest fires at 212, but Ovid initiates here a sequence of dramatic mountain-burnings by repeating this verb.

217–
26
What follows through 226 is a catalogue of mountains, mostly in the Greek and Asiatic world, but concluding with a resonant line that brings the audience back to Italy. Ovid is a master of catalogues, and he invites his audience to enjoy his art. There is no geographical order to the arrangement—as Bömer notes, two neighboring mountains like Oete and Orthrys appear in different lines (217 and 221)—but Ovid plays with variety, sound, and the occasional adjective or identifying phrase. At 239, he will play with a catalogue of rivers. Nothing could make clearer the untragic tone of this narrative. In 217, the poet names four mountains from widely separated regions: Athos in Macedonia, Taurus in Cilicia (as he notes), Tmolus in Lydia, and Oete in Thessaly near Thermopylae. In 218, he restricts himself to a single Ida (without telling us which of the two Idas, that of Troy or that of Crete, he means) and amuses himself with the transformation of the well-watered height to dryness. And in 219, he introduces two poetic heights with their epithets: Helicon in Boeotia already can be called "virginal" because the Muses supposedly inhabit it; Haemus in Thrace does not yet merit the name of Oeagrius, because our poet has not yet told us of how Orpheus, supposed son of Oeagros, retired there and met his death. That will be material for the beginnings of Book 10 and 11.

220–
23
The catalogue continues, with the repetition of *ardet*. Line 220, devoted to Sicilian Etna, captures the paradox that its natural volcanic fires are "doubled" by the flames ignited by the too close sun. Eryx in 221 rises in western Sicily, but Ovid sweeps us back to Greece to view Parnassus rather than grouping the two Sicilian mountains together. *biceps* 221: Ovid referred to the twin peaks of Parnassus in 1.316. Cynthus takes us out into the Aegaean Sea, to Delos, where

this height was connected with the birth of Apollo and Diana; it provides them one of their identifying adjectives. Othrys rises in Thessaly, not far from Oeta (cf. 217). After line 221, with its widely separated four mountains, Ovid confines himself to two in 222: Thracian Rhodope, characteristically snowcapped, but now experiencing an unusual transformation, destined to be snow-free as a result of the unique proximity of the sun; and Mimas, one of two so named, either in Ionia or Thrace (and, given the separated order elsewhere, Ovid perhaps meant the Ionian Mimas here, to keep the audience hopping geographically). To complete the numerical variety of these four lines, 223 contains three mountains. Dindyma in Asia Minor near Troy was sacred to Cybele; Cithaeron held its rites for Apollo, master of nearby Delphi. Between these two, Ovid introduces Mycale, a summit on the Carian peninsula, off which the Athenians fought and won a naval battle against the Persians in 479.

224–26   The last sequence in the catalogue gets an introduction, then settles down with the same verb *ardet*. Even where there are no snows, mountain heights have very cold atmospheres. But the fires of the sun negate this characteristic. Scythia, imagined as so far north as to be prey to what we would call arctic climate, now briefly loses its chill. Line 225 transports us back to Thrace and three more of its peaks, ending with the towering Olympus. And 226 moves us west and north into the Roman world, to the lofty Alps in the north of the Italian peninsula and the Apennine Chain that abuts on the Alps, then turns south and constitutes so to speak the backbone of Italy far down the peninsula. The highest point of the Chain is the Gran Sasso in the north, but the next highest section towers near Ovid's native town of Sulmo. Vergil mentions the snow that is typical of the heights (*Aen.* 12.703); Ovid achieves a striking effect by inventing the poetic epithet *nubifer* and then placing the mountain-name artfully so that its double spondee ends both the line and the catalogue with resonance.

227–28   We left Phaethon at 200, to focus on other subjects. Now, Ovid brings him back, to register the boy's reactions before embarking on another catalogue (239 ff.). Line 227 is heavily spondaic, apart from Phaethon's name. *aestus* 228: Phaethon cannot endure the heat he has produced in the burning world.

229–30   Ovid gets us to imagine the effect of the hot air by comparing the way the sudden blast of heat from a furnace or oven, when the door opens, sears the lungs. Lucretius and Vergil in the *Georgics* uses the furnace-comparison, as one of those practical similes that fits the genre of didactic poetry. *candescere* 230: the chariot, which Ovid has described as sparkling with precious metals and jewels (107 ff.), glows white with the heat, and Phaethon feels it.

231–   Surrounded by fire, as in a burning city or forest or near an erupting

32   volcano, the boy feels a steady rain of ash and embers and is engulfed in smoke. Lucretius, describing the fires of Mount Etna in 6.690–91, ends his lines with the same two words as Ovid here.

233–
34   *quoque* = *et quo*, introducing indirect questions with *nescit* 234. *picea caligine:* a vivid expansion on *fumo* (232). *arbitrio* 234: Since Phaethon has given up the reins and abandoned his rightful authority as charioteer, the "control" has passed over to the horses (cf. 201 ff). *volucrum:* the horses are "winged" as at 153. The prosody of this word, because of the mute + liquid in the second syllable, was optional to the poets. Ovid counts the syllable short except when the word appears in the sixth foot of the hexameter, which requires a long syllable (cf. 1.602 and 5.364).

235–
36   *sanguine . . . vocato:* ablative absolute. Ovid asks us to imagine that the scorching heat brought the blood (as when we blush) to the surface of the body, where it permanently colored the skin. *credunt:* the poet refuses to claim authority for his quite incredible tale: others believe it. A popular etymology for Aethiopia connected the first part of the name (Aethi-) with the Greek verb for burning. *nigrum . . . colorem* 236: blood turns dark when exposed to the air.

237–
40   *Libye:* because the normal word *Libya* consists of three short syllables, it cannot fit into the hexameter, and Ovid resorts to the Greek nominative with long -*e*. *raptis umoribus:* Ovid describes the process of evaporation, but his verb conveys the violence of rapine or rape, which then prepares us for the mourning of 239. From Libya near Aethiopia, which has turned into a desert from loss of water, Ovid makes his transition, as water-nymphs lament their lost waters, to a catalogue of waters. Whole regions in Greece miss their famous springs. He names Dirce near Thebes, Amymone near Argos, and Pirene near Corinth (Ephyre in its archaic name).

241–
42   Ovid then shifts to rivers, which normally because of the large amount of water that runs between their wide banks would be expected to be immune from fire. *loco:* ablative of specification; the riverbanks are vastly separated. The catalogue starts with the remote Don River in Southern Russia, which flows into the Sea of Azov. It produced the paradox of smoking in the middle of its billows—or, as we might say, in spite of all its waves.

243–
45   In 243, Ovid's entry consists of two rivers, each equipped with an epithet, so that the line restricts itself to four words only. We have already encountered Daphne's father Peneus, notably by Tempe in Thessaly (cf. 1.568 ff.). The second river, the Caicus, with its exotic adjective, flows in Asia Minor in Mysia, from the mountains near Pergamum and out into the Aegean by Lesbos. Two more rivers, also widely disparate, fill 244: the Ismenos of Thebes and the Erymanthus

of western Arcadia near Elis. Ovid uses a rare epithet, *Phegiaco*, to refer to Arcadia, and adds to the exotic tone by availing himself of hiatus between final and initial vowels. *arsurusque iterum Xanthus* 245: play with the chronology of myth; the Xanthus of the Troad is one of the rivers that will engage in battle with Achilles. When the mortal hero's life is endangered, the firegod Hephaestos will attack and humiliate Xanthus, who at that time will burn again. The verb, which prevailed in the mountain-catalogue above, will be reused in this catalogue; cf. 248 and 250. To locate the Lycormas, we jump all the way across the Aegean and over to western Greece, to Aetolia; Ovid gives it one of the standard epithets for a river, yellow, i.e., with soil after the spring thaws.

246–47 *recurvatis ludit . . . in undis:* the Maeander, which springs from the mountains of Caria and flows into the sea near Miletus, was so famous for its winding course that it gave its name to that desultory back-and-forward movement that we call "meandering." Ovid imagines that the river is playing games by its deceptive flow. *recurvatis:* probably Ovid's invention; he used it earlier in *Am.* 1.8.6. *Mygdonius* 247: the epithet identifies the Mela as Thracian. From there, Ovid leaps to the Eurotas of Sparta in the southern Peloponnesus. *Taenarius:* properly, this should refer to the southern tip of Laconia, at least forty miles from Sparta. But it could serve vaguely to refer to Laconia and, as here, be associated with Sparta's river, the Eurotas. Ovid lengthens the final syllable and makes it part of a double spondee.

248–49 *arsit:* the previous rivers, all ten of them, were subjects of the verb *fumavit* (242). Ovid here increases the rhetorical level, to make the next set of rivers burn, using anaphora in 248 and variations in 250. The Euphrates runs a long distance before it reaches and passes Babylon. The Orontes is the major river of Syria. We stay in Asia with three of the four rivers of 249: the Thermodon, a favorite haunt of the Amazons near the Black Sea; the Ganges far away in India; the Phasis back near the Thermodon in Medea's native region of Colchis. The Hister is Europe's mighty Danube.

250–51 For 250, Ovid arranges his two rivers and their clauses in chiastic pattern. The Alpheus flows in the northwestern Peloponnesus through Olympia. The Thessalian Sperchios we have encountered in 1.579. *quodque . . . aurum* (251): = *et quod . . . aurum*. Ovid frames the line with the relative and its antecedent, playing games with our ability to anticipate the allusion. Like the Pactolus of Asia Minor, the Spanish Tagus contained rich amounts of gold in its sandy bed. Paradoxically now, because of the heat, that gold melts and "flows" with the water! Five dactyls add to the lightheartedness.

252– These two lines introduce a welcome variation: the subject changes

53   to the famous swans that frequent the Cayster in Lydia (= Maeonia).
        They get hot as they sail and sing in the water. Note the alliteration
        with *c* and the five dactyls in 253.

254–   Three lines deal with the great Nile. Ovid personifies it and asks us
56   to imagine it as terrified by the heat and fleeing for refuge into the
        most remote part of Africa and there burying its head. In effect, that
        means that the Nile flowed backward and, in burying its head, con-
        cealed its source; which, as Ovid declares, was still unknown in his
        day. In fact, it remained so until late in the nineteenth century. Thus,
        the poet achieves a diverting aetiology out of this pseudo-tragedy.
        With all the water vanished from its bed, the famous Nile delta, with
        its seven mouths, turns to dust, seven dry valleys.

257–   Ovid ends his catalogue by linking the desiccation of two Thracian
59   and four rivers of the west, the final one being, as happened in the
        mountain-catalogue, a resonant item for the patriotic ear. *Ismarios:*
        local adjective derived from the mountain and city of Ismaros in
        Thrace. Its noun is *amnes* (258). *cum Strymone:* ablative of accompani-
        ment, to take advantage of the meter, instead of the more correct, but
        less metrically adaptable form of a conjunction (*et* or *-que*) with
        accusative. The three western rivers of 258 bring us progressively
        southward, from the frontier of Germany down to Northern Italy;
        which then prepares us for the Tiber in 259. *cuique . . . promissa
        potentia* 259: Ovid reuses these words in a more dramatic context, a
        speech of Mars, in *Fast.* 6.358. Here, the ostentatious anachronism
        once again calls attention to the narrator, audience, and their times,
        away from this fantastic myth.

Tellus Protests to Jupiter (260–303)

        As the soil cracks and the sea dries up, the Underworld and marine
        deities exhibit ungodly panic, all except Tellus, who braves the heat
        and speaks out to Jupiter (who so far has been entirely uninvolved in
        this disaster, as stupid in his carelessness as he was in his vengefulness
        with the Flood). She succeeds in making him aware of the crisis and
        of his responsibility.

260–   The effective position of the verbs in 260 emphasizes the sense of
61   violence and disruption in the natural order. *rimis:* ablative of means;
        Ovid picks up on the cracking mentioned in the first clause and
        ingeniously imagines that daylight reaches the normally dark Under-
        world, to terrify its mighty king. *cum coniuge* 261: same use of
        ablative of accompaniment to solve a metrical problem as above
        at 257.

262–   The sea contracts and then disappears for the most part. Ovid imagines

64   a stretch of dry sand where once the water billowed. *quod modo:* the relative refers back to *mare* (262); the adverb often appears in the details of metamorphosis. *quosque . . . aequor:* the poet reverses the order of relative and main clauses in this sequence. This enables him to double the relative clauses about the normal natural order of the sea in 263 and also to create playful suspense about the actual "antecedent" of *quos.* The passage ends with a witty conceit: that once entirely submerged mountains, becoming visible, increase the known number of islands in the Cyclades. With seeming solemnity, the poet slows down 264 by four spondees.

265–   Ovid seems to recall some of the details of his Flood and to reverse
66   them. Whereas in 1.296, because of the prevalence of water, people caught fish in the tops of trees, here fish make for the bottom. Whereas dolphins also occupied the forests and encroached on tree branches in 1.302–3, here they do not dare to make their customary leaps into the unusually hot air.

267–   In 1.299–300, seals had a wonderful time with their bodies, laying
69   them out to rest in the grass once grazed by cattle. But in this passage the deceptive wording leads up to a picture of death. *summo . . . profundo:* this seems like a paradox, especially when we take the bait and treat both words as adjectives. In fact, though, the verbal trap makes a game out of a scene that could produce considerable pathos with different handling. The phrase means: "on the surface of the deep or water." *resupina:* when a body is on its back, we often imagine idle resting and ease. But when a fish is on its back, it is dead or dying. This adjective then prepares us for the unambiguous participle at the start of 268. *natant* 268: this verb regularly connotes the active movements of fish, human beings, and animals through water. However, it also can apply to the movement of inanimate and dead creatures in water: not swimming, but floating, washing about lifelessly. In 1.301–2, the poet registered the amazement of the Nereides at the Flood, thus stressing marvel rather than pathos in the dramatic situation. Here, he introduces Doris and her daughters (using the same words as in 2.11, where he made the Nereides one of the striking scenes on the Sun's palace doors) along with their father, all of whom are taking refuge in caves that offer less coolness than usual. *tepidis* 269: Ovid's wonderful precision hits upon this adjective, to catch the unique moment and to charm his audience. The expected adjective for caves would have been *gelidis.*

270–   A nice example of anticlimax at the expense of Neptune. The first
71   longer clause, with its choice of words like *torvo,* the main verb of daring, and the action of stretching out arms, seem to promise a truly impressive result. Many in Ovid's audience might well have been reminded of the magnificent presentation of Neptune in *Aen.* 1.124

ff. He raised his head above the water and quickly brought order into the chaotic situation created by Juno, Aeolus, and the storm. In 271 here, Ovid, deliberately using the anaphora of *ter* to link his two clauses, lets Neptune dwindle into bathetic impotence: he can't stand the heat!

272–74   *alma tamen Tellus:* in contrast to all the marine deities, even mighty Neptune, who exhibit weakness, the Earth shows some strength of character. The Earth regularly struck the Greek and Roman imagination as a "mother." Lucretius again and again became poetically stirred by the maternal image: e.g., 1.251 ff., 2.589 ff., 5.821 ff. In 2.992–93, he referred to *alma mater terra.* Thus, although Ovid's epithet for *Tellus* seems unique, it is a short step from Lucretius; and in 274 Ovid carefully uses the mother-image. *circumdata ponto:* cf. the account of the creation of the sea in 1.37. The earth surrounded by the sea constitutes a basic image of stability, which here Ovid qualifies. *contractos . . . fontes* 273: same verb in 262 for the sea; a short list of affected springs occurred above at 239–40. *condiderant in . . . viscera matris* 274: the image is unusual enough to upset any grand notions of this deity. We can understand how the rivers sank into the depths or "bowels" of the earth. But when the poet insists on the personification, it is hard not to picture some version of Freud's "back to the womb."

275–78   *sustulit . . . vultus:* this parallels the action of Neptune in 270–71, but without the empty posturing. Earth maintains her head in the heat until 303. *oppressos:* the reading of *M* alone, it may well be a clever conjecture of a medieval scholar, to deal with a meaningless text. Except for *Harl* 2610, which presents what seems, in *omps,* an abbreviation that has been interpreted as pointing either to *omnipotens* or *omniparens,* the manuscripts agree in *omniferos.* That would be a unique word, not unexpected in Ovid, but it makes no sense with the noun *vultus.* Because the reading of *M* does make sense and there is too much guess work in the abbreviation *omps* (which in addition is uniquely transmitted), most editors accept *oppressos,* even though it in no way explains the origin of the corruption *omniferos. collo tenus:* exactly how we are to imagine this, is not clear. Whereas Neptune tried to raise his head above his dwindling water, what is Tellus doing? Is she lifting her head above the earth, that is, above herself? To judge from 303, Ovid may be keeping us guessing until he supplies the answer. Our interest in the neckline of the goddess is probably provoked intentionally; Ovid does the same in the scene of Diana bathing in 3.182, using the same phrase. *fronti* 276: dative with compound verb. The gesture shields her face somewhat from the heat. It is not "epic" or grandiose, but very human. *magnoque tremore:* what seems to start off as a description of human physiology, in response to the terrible effort against the heat, turns into a geological symptom. Ovid takes advantage of every opportunity to play with the dualism of Tellus, viewed both anthropomorphically and geologically. So now he moves into language of earthquakes. *subsedit* 277: doubly employed, to continue the earthquake description and also to depict a female crouching down in fear and dismay. *infra . . . fuit:* similar doubling: the physical earth has collapsed in the quake, and the divine Tellus has been much diminished. Bömer asks whether Ovid deliberately reduced the stature here of Tellus or whether he just could not match the height of Vergil's style. We should give Ovid more credit. *siccaque ita voce:* a specific detail that would never appear in an epic introduction to a speech; again, Ovid indicates the approach that the audience should be prepared to take. Heinsius rescued the reading from the single MS *U;* all other MSS give the uninteresting *sacraque,* which is the "easier reading."

279–
81

The rhetoric of Tellus (and Ovid) is obvious. Earlier readers grew impatient with such display and treated it as an artistic mistake on Ovid's part. But Ovid chose to throw an amused light on this entire situation, and the stylized verbiage of Tellus serves that purpose. She starts by hypothesizing that this conflagration (like the Flood) constitutes condign punishment for some sin she has committed. If so—and she really does not think of herself as sinner—why cannot she perish with dignity, i.e., by Jupiter's thunderbolt? *quid o . . . summe deum:* the interrogative goes with the clause and means "why"; the separation of interjection and vocative unit is striking, but it does incidentally help Ovid to crowd five dactyls into 279. Tellus sounds like a society snob who resents being insulted by an inferior, but will take a snub from someone above her. Note the artful juxtaposition across enjambement of *ignis / igne. clademque auctore levare* 281: it will lighten her disaster to die at the hands of supreme Jupiter, even though it is also by a kind of fire.

282–
84

vix . . . fauces . . . resolvo: Tellus ostentatiously calls attention to the difficulty of speaking conditions, and then, to our wry amusement, plunges verbosely on for seventeen more lines. *presserat . . . vapor:* a typical parenthetical interruption by the narrator, of which Ovid has his first example in 1.2. It occupies a half-line and provides dramatic background with the pluperfect verb. The verb may provide some support for the reading *oppressos* in 275. *tostos . . . crines:* next, the speaker melodramatically points to her singed hair and to the film of ash that covers her face. Such grotesque detail distances us from the speaker and make us smile at her rhetorical egotism. Repeated *tantum* at the caesura of 284 gives special resonance to her cinder-covered visage; *favillae,* partitive genitive, goes with both.

285–

hosne . . . hunc: rhetorical organization; repeated forms of the demon-

87   strative, in parallel phrases. Having affected to consider her "sins,"
     Tellus now indignantly demands an answer about her honorable de-
     serts. *fertilitatis . . . officiique:* objective genitive. She presents herself
     as Mother Earth here, the source of all productivity in the agricultural
     world, a role that overlaps to some degree with that of Ceres. *vulnera*
     aratri . . . fero: in her self-dramatization, Tellus represents herself
     as enduring wounds from the plow, heroically and selflessly! *exerceor:*
     the active verb appears often in Vergil's *Georgics* to describe the
     vigorous, often aggressive behavior of the farmer toward the soil in
     cultivation. Turning the verb into a personal passive is a clever tour
     de force on Ovid's part. As Tellus appeals for sympathy, Ovid makes
     us smile.

288– This clause consists of three parallel units, each containing a direct
89   and indirect object, all dependent on the final word *ministro*. The
      alliteration of objects in 288 and the even more artful disposition
      create two successive chiastic pairs: i.e., dative and accusative, accusa-
      tive and dative, dative and accusative. *alimentaque mitia:* really an
      apposition describing *fruges,* with which the connective *-que* would
      properly go. The verb chosen by Tellus conveys her self-pitying sense
      of herself as a long-suffering "servant".

290– *fac me meruisse:* a standard courtroom argument: "grant that I did
92   deserve." Tellus returns to her initial starting-point in 279, but only
      to move to a new rhetorical question. How did Jupiter's brother and
      his waters deserve such torment? *tradita sorte* 291: the first of many
      references to the story that the three brothers, Jupiter, Neptune, and
      Dis drew lots to determine which areas of the universe each would
      control (cf. 5.368). It is Neptune's right to hold a third of the universe
      with his waters, and that right has been violated by the effects of the
      heat; he has been deprived of some of his realm as his waters recede,
      dried up.

293– The next step in Tellus' rhetoric moves up from herself and Neptune
95   to Jupiter and his kingdom, the heavens. The argument resembles that
      of 290: forget me (us), but how about you? *gratia:* this word often
      applies to political favoritism, especially in Ovid. Tellus employs
      every manipulative device that she can. *at* 294: "at least." *miserere:*
      more rhetoric; she urges him to pity an inanimate space, thereby
      inviting him to imagine it animated with the divine inhabitants of the
      sky. *utrumque:* borrows the noun of *uterque* in 295. If the two poles
      smoke, that signifies that the entire heaven stands in danger of destruc-
      tion from fire.

295– *vitiaverit:* Tellus represents the heavens as a complicated structure,
97   which the fire could seriously damage. This would endanger the pal-
      aces of the gods. *vestra* 296: of Jupiter and the other Olympians. To
      confirm the danger, Tellus points out Atlas, who is having a precarious

and painful time trying to hold up the skies; being white hot, they burn his bare shoulder. *axem* 297: also linked with the heavenly pole above at 75.

298–
300

Tellus continues her rhetoric of conditional sentences. She affects to divide the universe into three parts, namely, water, earth, and heaven. It follows that, if all three perish, nothing will remain but chaos. To make that division valid, however, she would have to substitute Dis for herself or at least make clear that she subsumes Dis in with her account of earth. *confundimur* 299: note the deliberate use of first person plural. *flammis:* ablative of separation. *summae* 300: dative with the verb. The speech ends on the same word with which Tellus hailed Jupiter at the start (280). Unmoved by Tellus' plight, but disturbed by his own danger, the god finally does something useful.

301–
3

dixerat: typical Ovidian ending of a speech (cf. 1.367), but here the poet goes on with unepic elaboration. The parenthesis extends farther than most (more than a hexameter), as it offers two explanations for stopping: she could not stand the heat (*vaporem;* cf. 283 and the last parenthesis), and she apparently ran out of words. *rettulit os in se* 303: this seems to be the first instance in the poem of a practice that becomes notable, the playful double view of something as simultaneously an anthropomorphic being and an inanimate physical entity, and the verbalization of this view by reflexives to produce a paradox. Here, Tellus is said to withdraw her face inside herself. That is nonsense at the literal level. But as soon as we let the two aspects of Tellus operate simultaneously, it is possible to imagine the goddess sinking her face into the earth for protection. Ovid has carefully ended this sequence, then, with this witty conceit. He still expects us to be amused with what, in Tellus' shrill rhetoric, is a frightful crisis for the universe.

The Almighty Father Acts to Destroy Phaethon (304–28)

304–
6

at pater omnipotens: the epithet makes its appearance in epic as early as Ennius. The whole phrase, filling a half-line, has occurred in *Aen.* 6., where Vergil described the god hurling a thunderbolt, as Jupiter will here, at a notorious sinner. However, before Vergil, Lucretius had already used the phrase in what must be the principal source of Ovid (*DRN* 5.399–401): he was describing this very situation, when Jupiter slew Phaethon. Without saying a word about whether and how the god reacted to the speech of Tellus, Ovid depicts, in fact, a rather careful politician in action, not the autocrat we saw in Book 1. Anxious to justify himself and pacify his critics, the god delivers an oration of some extent, which Ovid rapidly summarizes. The argument, in indirect discourse (*nisi . . . gravi* 305–6), depends on *testatus*. All the gods, and especially the Sun himself, are to bear witness to the truth of his claim. *ferat:* subjunctive for subordinate clause with indirect discourse. Present subjunctive because Ovid has embarked on the narrative present: cf. *petit* (306). *interitura* 306: infinitive: supply *esse. summam . . . arcem:* the same phrase (in ablative) located Jupiter in his first major scene in 1.163.

307–   As if to dignify the god, Ovid tells us in parallel relative clauses,
8   linked by anaphora (*unde*), of Jupiter's customary activities as fear-
        some weather god in heaven. However, it turns out in 309 ff. that,
        because of the heat, Jupiter himself has suffered loss of his usual
        powers. *nubes . . . terris:* the last time we saw Jupiter bringing clouds
        over the earth, it was in very undignified circumstances, as he tried
        to veil his act of raping Io from jealous Juno: cf. 1.599, *inducta latas
        caligine terras / occuluit.* As for hurling thunderbolts, we last saw
        Jupiter histrionically prepare to devastate the earth that way (1.253),
        then give it up as an inefficient means of punishment. Thus, these
        seemingly decorative clauses have a somewhat ironic overtone for
        Ovid's audience. *vibrata . . . iactat* 308: Ovid uses the participle with
        the direct object, where other Romans and most English translators
        would employ two coordinate verbs.

309–   With witty precision, the narrator corrects expectations. In both lines,
10   he enhances his wit by placing his relative purpose clause before the
        "antecedent."

311–   *intonat:* the dactyl quickly reports all that the great god can do under
13   the circumstances, for lack of clouds and rain. However, Ovid manages
        to produce a special effect, because thunder, sounding out suddenly
        in a cloudless sky, is regarded by Greeks and Romans as a special
        sign of divinity (cf. Horace *C.* 1.34.5 ff). *libratum . . . misit:* same
        construction as above in 308. Jupiter, like a warrior with a spear,
        balances his weapon, then hurls it at his victim. For similar language
        of an actual battle context, cf. *Aen.* 9.417. It was, of course, a
        notorious fact in antiquity that the thunderbolt, supposedly the instru-
        ment of divine justice, missed guilty targets and usually hit nothing
        but trees, but sometimes was so badly aimed that it damaged the
        temples of the very gods on earth! So here Jupiter aims very carefully
        and does strike his target: cf. by contrast his clumsy aim in the story
        of Lycaon (1.230 ff.). *aurigam* 312: Ovid uses this word only of
        Phaethon in the poem, here and at 327 in the epitaph. Since its
        etymology refers to one who wields the reins (*aureas*), it is pathetically
        ironic of this boy who has quickly dropped the traces. *pariterque
        animaque rotisque / expulit:* first example of a type of zeugma on
        which Ovid puts his witty stamp, establishing a model for later writers,
        such as Alexander Pope in Augustan English verse. The essence of
        this zeugma (my introduction) is letting two words of highly disparate

usage be governed simultaneously by a single verb; when one tries
to apply the verb, which works on the first noun, to the second, the
clash is felt and the wit savored. As a result, this scene of death loses
its pathos as the audience recognizes the light-hearted and self-serving
rhetorical moves of the narrator. Knocking Phaethon off his life and
also his wheels makes for a shocking anticlimax. Ovid does not want
us to wallow in tears for Phaethon. Distance from the boy at this fatal
moment means that we will not identify with his grieving relatives
and friends below. *conpescuit ignibus ignes:* if the audience missed
the wit in the zeugma, then it can hardly ignore it in this oxymoron.
This is not only fighting fire with fire, but quenching fire with fire!
Again, the logic of the phrase depends on Ovid's clear insistence on
the two disparate kinds of fire, which he forces together.

314–   *consternantur:* this is the standard word that Roman historians use
15   when describing the confusion of animals (horses, even elephants) in
the crisis of battle. *saltu in contraria facto:* they rear up and conse-
quently are able to slip from the yoke. *abrupta . . . relinquunt* 314:
same structure as in 308 and 311.

316–   The structure of 316 and 317 links three clauses by using the single
18   verb *iacent* and anaphora *illic . . . illic* + the variant *in hac . . .
parte*. Then 318 adds a fourth complete clause. Taking off from
abrupta (315), Ovid now describes the shattered chariot. As Bömer
notes, it is as though we look up and watch the parts float down
toward us. Readers might be reminded of the appalling sight on the
television screen when the American space shuttle Challenger ex-
ploded after take-off. *temone revulsus / axis:* with the traces broken
and the horses bolted, the pole to which they were attached also breaks
away from the front axle, as the wheels are smashed and disintegrate.
radii 317: spokes of the broken wheels. *laceri* 318: more usually of
a living thing. With alliterative *late,* Ovid almost creates pathos for
the inanimate chariot instead of for Phaethon.

319–   *at Phaethon:* in the zeugma at 312, Ovid told us that the boy had been
22   killed and his body thrown from the chariot. Now, we follow the trail
of the corpse down to the earth. *rutilos:* the poet here introduces his first
reference to Phaethon's hair and its flaming color, to make the scene
more vivid. *volvitur* 320: he is whirled headlong. *longo . . . tractu:* the
corpse, with its burning hair, seems like a comet with a long train (or
tail) of fire. This terminology for comets goes back at least to Lucretius
2.206–7. *ut . . . stella* 321: Ovid's simile invokes his audience's own
experience. Had he stopped at the end of 321, he would have produced
a rather pretty, potentially pathetic picture. (A "falling" or "shooting
star" is more exactly a meteor). In 322, however, he takes away the
emotional power of the picture by getting fussy and scientific about the
term "falling." Once again, he has robbed the young fool of his pathos.

323–
24
procul a patria: to perish and be buried far away from one's home and family is of course a sad fate. *diverso . . . orbe:* ablative of place where. Born and raised in Ethiopia, Phaethon's corpse plummets down by the Po River in North Italy. *maximus . . . Eridanus:* the Po is the longest river of Italy, flowing from the Alps some four hundred miles into the Adriatic. At 258, in his catalogue of rivers that were desiccated by the heat, Ovid mentions the Padus. Eridanus is the more exotic name for the same river, derived from the Greek mythical tradition, which was not too sure of its exact location. Sometimes, Phaethon seems to be more closely connected to the present Rhone than to the Po. *excipit . . . abluit:* the verbs suggest a living being who tenderly receives the body and washes it off.

325–
26
Hesperiae: this Greek loan-word properly means the "West," but Vergil had used it in the *Aeneid* to refer specifically to Italy, which is what Ovid means here. *trifida:* Ovid invented the word and uses it only here, but his many admirers borrowed it liberally in the first century A.D. Jagged or forked lightning may be imagined as triply divided, but we may suspect, too, that Ovid chose this neologism for its alliterative utility. *carmine* 326: Ovid imagines that the tomb, like a contemporary Roman one, would have an inscription, and he invents an effective epigram.

327–
28
hic situs est: a familiar formula for the Romans, common in ordinary tomb inscriptions, also used by the poets as early as Ennius for Scipio Africanus, but only here in Ovid. *currus . . . paterni:* objective genitive. This phrase echoes the request of Phaethon for this fatal present in 47 above. This first line, with its clear organization and simple statements, sets up the second line and its ostentatious rhetoric. *quem* 328: i.e., the chariot. *si non . . . tamen:* for a similar development of a clever point, cf. 322 above. We have reason to question the claim of the inscription (attributed by the poet to the sentimental Naides). That Phaethon perished in a dubiously "great," but surely rash, enterprise has less importance than the fact that he caused an incredible amount of inexcusable damage. Ovid, then, in abandoning the story of Phaethon, makes sure that he leaves it on a falsely pathetic note.

THE AFTERMATH: MOURNING BECOMES ELECTRON (329–400)

In Euripides' tragedy, the corpse of Phaethon was brought back to his home in Ethiopia, and so his wedding became a funeral, dominated by the grief of his mother Clymene. Ovid's account buried the boy far away by the Po River. His tomb collects little by little a series of mourners and offers Ovid the opportunity to present human metamorphoses that were absent from the main narrative, crowded out by the possibilities of spectacular changes that the Burning of the Universe provided. The Sun goes into "eclipse"; Clymene arrives and welters in tears; his sisters, the Heliades, lament themselves into poplars, and their teardrops become precious amber; and lastly an old friend Cygnus turns into a dolorous swan. After all that, it is time to restore order, and Jupiter gets the Sun to come out of his sulks and return to his normal task of lighting up the sky.

The Grief of Father and Mother (329–39)

329–
32
nam pater: the conjunction offers an explanation to an unexpressed question, such as, "Where was his all-seeing father? Why didn't he take care of the funeral?" The bumbling Sun, who in other versions closely attended Phaethon at death, here in Ovid can only wallow in self-pity. *obductos luctu:* it was a standard gesture and sign of grief to cover the head with the robe; there are many examples in Greco-Roman art. Note the pair of sentimental adjectives that end 329. What the narrator has denied Phaethon throughout his story, he lavishes on the unworthy father. *condiderat vultus* 330: Ovid exploits the double view of the Sun, as a heavenly body and as an anthropomorphic deity. Thus, hiding the face in grief equals going into eclipse. *si modo credimus:* the narrator intrudes with a remark that prepares for an incredible detail. Such a distancing technique has a stronger effect than merely reporting that others believe (or believed) a story: e.g., *credunt* (2.90), *creditur* (1.749). Other variants: questions like *quis hoc credat* (1.400) and *credere quis posset?* (7.690); personal statements like *vix ausim credere* (6.560–61) and *nec credite factum* (10.302). *unum:* effective emphasis before enjambement. Eclipses never last long, and Ovid is not describing anything so mundane as an overcast sky for a whole day; he refers to the sudden, unexpected disappearance of the sun, which always caused alarm among humankind (that is, before eclipses were explained). The incredible duration of the Sun's histrionic eclipse should have made the narrator's tone clear. If it did not, the concluding comments (331–32) are unmistakable. The poet cleverly realizes that an alternative source of light has become providentially available and so affects to find a consoling utility in the otherwise devastating fire that had ravaged heaven and earth and necessitated the death of incompetent Phaethon.

333–
35
quaecumque fuerunt . . . dicenda: the poet calls attention to the conventional speech of lamentation from a mother, but refuses to develop its dramatic aspects. A fragmentary example of Clymene's lament has been preserved in the tattered remains of Euripides' tragedy. In sparing his audience, the narrator also makes sure that we do not hear any convincingly sympathetic regret for Phaethon. From the scanty details here, it appears that we should understand that a message came

to Clymene in Ethiopia and reported the death of her son, at which she burst out in the customary words of maternal grief. She also put on mourning clothes and beat her breast in the conventional female gesture of sorrow (334–35). Only then did she set out from Africa and travel the long distance to the banks of the Po. *percensuit orbem* 335: the verb is not poetic, and Ovid uses it elsewhere only once in *Fast;* it often refers to official administrative travel.

336–37   *artus primo:* Clymene started out before learning of the burial by the nymphs, so she expected to perform the last rites herself. Over the course of time, she gave up on finding the body and reconciled herself to merely locating the fleshless bones. Effective chiasmus in 336 backs *mox ossa* up to the above unit at the hepthemimeral caesura. When she does find the bones, the poet introduces another qualification: they have already been entombed.

338–39   *incubuitque:* from *incubo,* not *incumbo;* she lay down on the tomb in total grief. *nomen in marmore:* the inscription of 327 gave the name of the dead on the stone, which now we learn is marble (an anachronism, to fit the splendid tastes of Ovid's time). *perfudit lacrimis* 339: she "bathed" the name with her tears. Not content with that, the poet has Clymene clutch the name to her bared breast. The gestures are conventional; but they focus on one word in an inscription rather than the body (already burned), so seem melodramatic. *aperto pectore:* elsewhere, Ovid will use the adjective *nudus* in such contexts of female grief and despair (Cf. 2.584–85, 3.481, 4.590). Bömer suggests that the poet has here produced his first definitely erotic description, but the choice of adjective, when *nudo* would have fitted comfortably into the same metrical position, contributes to an alliterative pattern. It is emotional bathos, yes, but not an appeal to our libido.

Phaethon's Sisters Become Poplars and Weep Amber/Electron (340–66)

340–43   *nec minus . . . lugent:* the connective is merely a negative way of saying "and also" (cf. 13.358). The verb links the daughters with the mood of their parents: cf. *luctu* (329) and *lugubris* (334). *inania morti / munera* 340–41: the reader can decide whether this is sympathetic or ironic. Ovid places this unit, which technically functions as an apposition, before (rather than after) the noun (tears) that it illustrates. The rhetorical effect resembles that of the relative clause preceding its "antecedent." *caesae pectora palmis:* although we may probably presume that, like their mother Clymene, the girls beat their bare breasts, in standard fashion, Ovid does not specify it. Nor does he exaggerate the alliteration by also using a verb beginning with *p:* e.g., *pulsae* or *plangens* (cf. 5.473). In these first descriptions of human grief, he restrains his wit, even if he is not inclined to be sympathetic. *miseras . . . querellas* 342: again, the narrator spares us a speech while indicating its formulaic content, material very congenial to elegy. *adsternunturque* 343: this verb, with its series of long syllables, juxtaposed to a verb at the central caesura, has been invented by Ovid for this context. It calls attention to itself, no doubt deliberately. Unlike the description of Clymene in 338, this scene is crowded with too many bodies prostrating themselves on the tomb: there are three sisters.

344–
46
luna . . . orbem: Ovid treats this method of recording time as a personal formula; Bömer notes the close imitation in 7.530–31 and *Fast.* 2.175. The pluperfect tense sets the temporal background. Four months of continuous grief at the tomb is fantastic. *more suo* 345: the narrator's fussy precision about their habit and how it developed, as is often the case with Ovidian parentheses, distracts and distances us from the passionate wildness of the actors.

346–
49
Metamorphosis begins appropriately with the eldest sister; her name resembles that of Phaethon, also containing the same verbal reference to her father, the burning Sun. *terra procumbere* 347: for the verb, cf. 338. Phaethusa has apparently beaten her breast while standing and then tried to fall on the ground by the tomb, only to find herself rooted to the earth! *questa est:* again Ovid spares his audience a speech. When Dryope turns into a tree in 9.370 ff., she does get a long oration. *deriguisse* 348: Ovid chooses here to emphasize the rigidification of the grief. With Daphne in 1.548 ff., he stressed the hard tree-surface that enabled the nymph to escape the lust of Apollo. Elsewhere, turning into a tree produces more emphasis on the creation of greenery, even of long-lasting vitality. Cf. the benevolent change of Philemon and Baucis in 8.711 ff. *conata venire:* Ovid likes to present situations where a helpful individual, in the very act of bringing assistance, is struck down by an unfeeling force. Here, Lampetie, whose name is connected with the Greek verb of shining bright, finds her attempt to approach Phaethusa frustrated as she becomes rooted in place. *subita* 349: Ovid emphasizes the surprising suddenness of the change.

350–
52
tertia: Ovid teases his audience, testing its knowledge of mythology and the name of a rather obscure character. Our sources tell us she was called Aigle; the name would have fitted perfectly in the meter here. *crinem . . . laniare:* the gesture of tearing one's hair is a standard sign of despair and grief. Since Phaethon has been dead a long time and the sisters' sorrow has confined itself to less violent acts, Ovid probably views Aigle's wild gesture as her reaction to the immediate crisis, Lampetie's rooting. Improving on this effect in 9.354–55, Ovid describes how Dryope, seeing herself start to become a tree, tries to

tear her hair and fills her hand with leaves! *avellit frondes* 351: verb
and noun both indicate metamorphosis. Since the hair has turned into
leaves, the verb must change to the appropriate category, to describe
"plucking." All this becomes more effective as a result of the roughly
chiastic pattern of words. Thus far, Ovid has delineated a metamorpho-
sis of the first two sisters that began at the feet = roots; and with the
third he introduces a new detail about the hair = foliage, which may
indicate either that Aigle has started to change at the other extremity
or that she is in the second stage of metamorphosis, already rooted.
From her, at any rate, the poet turns back to the other two. The
verb *dolet* (352) goes with them both, as they grieve now over their
transformation. *stipite crura teneri*: her feet are rooted, and now her
legs are contained by the bark of the tree. *bracchia ramos* 352: one
of the most familiar equivalents in tree-metamorphoses (cf. Daphne,
1.550).

353–   *mirantur:* Ovid often describes, as here, the reaction not only of
55   onlookers but also of victims themselves to metamorphosis. Marvel
is the archetypal response. Ironically, as the girls are amazed at what
has happened, the remaining stages of transformation overtake them.
The bark, which has enclosed the legs of one (351), now moves up
the body, and Ovid catalogues the parts. The last part left before the
change is complete is the mouth that can still express human feelings.
With their final words, the girls cry out to Clymene. Cf. Proserpina's
shriek for her mother in 5.396 ff.

356–   *quid faciat mater:* the poet intrudes with his rhetorical question and
57   thereby concentrates on what Clymene might do and does, rather than
on her feelings. *inpetus:* her (maternal) instinct. *huc . . . illuc* 357:
although this pair usually functions to describe two opposite directions,
we must assume that Clymene dashed from one to the other of the
three girls. *oscula iungat:* the verb indicates that the kisses were
exchanged, given and received, until the faces turned to wood. Ovid
likes to describe the desperate race of loved ones to anticipate the
metamorphosis and kiss the disappearing human faces. Apollo the
lover kisses mere wood (cf. 1.556).

358–   *non satis est:* a favorite transitional unit, negative and positive, de-
60   signed by Ovid to occupy the first foot and a half. Clymene finds no
satisfaction in these last kisses, and she tries to tear the wooden exterior
from her girls. *truncis:* ablative of separation. *teneros . . . ramos* 359:
presumably, because those branches were just now the "tender arms"
of the girls, they may still retain some of that feminine softness.
And the adjective helps to explain why they are so easily breakable.
sanguineae . . . guttae 360: Ovid's model here is the passage in *Aen.*
3.26 ff. where Aeneas pulls up the myrtle under which the murdered
Polydorus has been buried and into which his blood has drained. This

passage has none of Vergil's solemnity. The fond mother Clymene does more harm than good by her wild efforts. Ovid creates another incident like this later when Dryope accidentally picks a lotus flower (9.344 ff.). *tamquam de vulnere:* this prepares for the metaphorical language in 361–62.

361–
63
parce, precor, mater: "Stop, mother, please!" *nostrum . . . corpus* 362: significant word position. "That's *my* body that you are tearing." *verba novissima* 363: the pathos of the last words is treated rather grotesquely, as the girl does not die, but has bark grow over her and silence her voluble mouth. For a more affectionate description of the last farewell and final transformation into a tree, cf. Philemon and Baucis in 8.716 ff.

364–
66
According to Hyginus 154, the Heliades were transformed into poplar trees. That is not inappropriate for the banks of a river. *lacrimae:* grieving for themselves as well as their brother still, the girls inside the poplars weep, and the tears emerge as sap. *stillataque:* this neuter plural participle looks forward to a new noun, to the transformation of human tears into electrum or amber. For the same collocation of words, cf. the description of the tears of Myrrha in 10.501 ff. Altering the poetic word order to more prosaic arrangement would give: *stillataque de ramis novis electra sole rigescunt.* The reference to "new" branches reminds us that they were arms a short time ago. This metamorphosis must be understood as something miraculous. Amber did not and does not come from poplar trees and is not suddenly hardened by the sun. It was a resin, but a fossilized one, found in prehistoric Tertiary levels, especially those of northern Europe. Greeks and Romans considered it a precious gem and imported it as a luxury item. Some amber was washed out by the Po, as Pliny reports, but its main source was modern Denmark. *nuribus . . . Latinis* 366: dat. of agent. Ovid ends his long myth by bringing us up to contemporary times. Electrum was a Greek loan word; the Romans called amber *sucinum.* As Ovid suggests, it adorned women, its association with tears forgotten.

The Transformation of Cygnus into a Swan (367–80)

Ovid deals with the metamorphosis of two other men by the name of Cygnus, also into swans: cf. 7.371 ff. and 12.64 ff. Drawing upon a brief narrative in *Aen.* 10.189 ff., he here tells how a relative of Phaethon—living in Italian Liguria, but somehow connected through Clymene—was so desperately in love with him that grief turned him into a sorrowing water bird, the swan that presumably haunted the quiet reaches of the Po in Ovid's day. Ovid, who rarely shows much sympathy with homosexual love, plays down Vergil's emphasis.

367–   *monstro:* simply, "marvel," in keeping with regular Latin usage. Ac-
69   cording to context, this word can mean anything from "monster" and
      "bad omen" to "wonderful event." Dative with compound verb. *proles
      Stheneleia:* Ovid gives Cygnus parentage phrased in epic terms; but
      scholars today do not know who Sthenelos was, and we may doubt
      whether Ovid did either. *quamvis . . . sanguine . . . mente tamen*
      368–69: careful chiastic organization of antithesis, to bring the stress
      in 369 on the basic feelings of Cygnus, which, as usual in this poem,
      overwhelm the individual. *mente:* ablative of respect. In the apostrophe
      to the dead Phaethon, the narrator affects to be sympathetic at last.

369–   *relicto . . . imperio* (369–71): a good instance of Ovid's use of paren-
72   thesis—the entire line of 370—to create suspense and also cause some
      doubt about the narrator's engagement with his character. If he can
      interrupt his story to give this fussy and useless information, his
      attention is not well focused. For hyperbaton in an ablative absolute,
      this sequence is remarkable. *querellis:* we have seen at 342 that the
      Heliades plunged into laments. For Cygnus, the mournful sound of
      his sorrow becomes the rationale for his metamorphosis. Used with
      implerat, the grief becomes rather extravagant. *silvamque sororibus
      auctam* 372: this self-conscious reference to the account just given of
      the Heliades, who after all added only three trees to the woods, creates
      another diversion from the story to the storyteller.

373–   The metamorphosis is recounted in a *cum-inversum* structure. It starts
76   with the key feature, the voice: its masculine deepness must be light-
      ened, to fit a bird. *viro:* dative of reference. In what follows, Ovid
      spells out for this first description of a man turning into a bird, the
      substitution of human for swan parts. He works down from hair to
      toes, then returns up past the wings to the face, which is now fully
      that of a bird. *dissimulant* 374: a striking choice of verb, which
      prepares us to be fascinated by the transformation rather than sympa-
      thetic with Cygnus' sorrow. *collum . . . porrigitur:* a swan's neck is
      lengthened, but Ovid makes no effort to suggest anything but the
      grotesqueness of the change; many find the swan's neck extra-
      ordinarily beautiful in its graceful curve. *digitos . . . rubentes* 375:
      the toes, not the fingers (which become part of the wings in other
      bird-transformations); the narrator is accounting for the webbed feet.
      The human toes are apparently imagined as reddish (like flesh) before
      the change. *penna latus velat* 376: the great wings of the swan, folded
      while they swim, and raised while they walk on land, can properly
      be said to "veil" the side. *tenet os . . . rostrum:* the swan has a bill,
      not a pointed beak. Ovid ends his description, as with the Heliades,
      at the face, the most identifiable feature of the individual and, espe-
      cially in the case of Cygnus, the area from which his lugubrious
      lament emerged.

377–   *fit nova Cygnus avis:* the verb and adjective are both standard parts
78   of the vocabulary of metamorphosis. As with the change of Lycaon
       in 1.237 ff., Ovid is moving on to the continuity of feeling between
       the human being and the new creature. It may be that he deliberately
       uses the feminine gender of *avis* to poke fun at the effeminate Cygnus.
       Latin had borrowed the Greek word *kyknos* for swan and used it long
       before Ovid; but it had its own native word *olor,* which Ovid will
       use in the Cygnus-metamorphosis at 7.372. *caeloque Iovique:* the
       double *-que* construction links the two nouns closely, to exploit the
       dual sense of Jupiter as the embodiment of the sky—he is the Sky-
       god—and the anthropomorphic deity who killed Phaethon. *credit* 378:
       the texts of the often better MSS *MN* and *Harl.* transmit *tradit.*
       Although that surely is the more "difficult" reading, it is easy enough
       to account for the change of letters either way. However, Ovid does not
       elsewhere use *tradit* with the reflexive (which would mean "surrender
       oneself" and be more appropriate to events in Caesar and the histori-
       ans), but does use *credit* and reflexive (e.g., 4.627 and 13.900) to
       capture the more general sense of "entrust oneself". *ut iniuste missi
       memor ignis:* Ovid likes to attribute memory of some traumatic event
       that continues from human into animal form. Thus, in 8.259, Perdix,
       who has become a partridge when his uncle Daedalus tried to throw
       him from the Acropolis, remembers that fall and refuses as a bird to
       fly very high above the ground. The narrator takes no position as to
       whether or not Jupiter was unjust to use the thunderbolt on Phaethon;
       he reports the feelings of the biased lover, still resentful after metamor-
       phosis.

379–   Ovid works up to the antithesis, emphasized by the alliteration ending
80   380, between fire and water. *quae colat* 380: subjunctive in relative
       purpose clause, which, as often, the poet places before its "ante-
       cedent."

The Sun Gives up His Sulking (381–400)

381–   *squalidus:* self-neglect under the possession of grief was and is a
85   standard reaction. Romans, for instance, did not shave when first in
       mourning. Ovid uses the same word in 10.74 to characterize Orpheus'
       appearance as he mourned dead Eurydice. In the remainder of 381
       and 382, the narrator collects more attributes of the grieving father,
       then finally comes to the main verb at *odit* in 383. *expers . . . decoris:*
       another sign of mourning, the refusal to wear bright, happy clothes.
       In reference to the Sun, of course, Ovid exploits the usual dualism
       and links the grief with the natural phenomenon of a sun that fails to
       shine as usual. *quali, cum deficit, orbe / esse solet:* this text rests
       upon a brilliant emendation advanced by Passerat. All MSS agree on

the nominative form *qualis;* they divide unequally over *orbem* (a few valued MSS) and *orbe* (many good and mediocre MSS). Conservative editors, determined to preserve the authority of *M,* have tried to defend *cum deficit orbem* as possible Latin, at any rate uniquely possible for Ovid. However, we are not interested, nor is Ovid, in elaborating a normal phrase (*ut deficit*) about eclipse into something abnormal (= "when he is deficient in relation to the globe of the earth"); the "orb" Ovid calls to our attention is that of the Sun itself. Following Passerat, then, we should interpret *quali . . . orbe* as ablative of description: the Sun showed a globe like that which he customarily has when he is in eclipse. *lucemque* 383: the *-que* is part of the polysyndetic structure with the two other objects of *odit.* Ovid enhances his dualistic wit by adding the emphasis of the reflexive: the Sun, like a standard mourner, loves darkness and hates all light; but that means that he hates himself, since he is the source of daylight. There is little indication, however, that the father feels remorse or guilt over the death. For the most part, the Sun prefers to take the easy, self-serving route of blaming others, first Jupiter, then the poor horses. *datque animum in luctus:* the prepositional phrase is a quick Ovidian alternative for the normal grammatical structure of dative of indirect object. *officium* 385: Ovid shapes the behavior of the Sun as petty and irresponsible. Often in tragedy characters struggle with the differing claims of public and private duty, political and ethical responsibilities, and we honor their rejection of ordinary duty as heroic. Think of Socrates or Antigone. Plainly, Ovid's Sun does not belong to this heroic class; his emotions are petty.

385–
87

The unheroic, plaintive speech takes off unepically after the hepthemimeral caesura. Its word order exhibits awkwardness that presumably characterizes the irrational thought of the Sun, not Ovid's lack of artistry. A more prosaic order would be: *mea sors fuit satis inrequieta ab aevi principiis. inrequieta* 386: on Ovid's invention of this word, see 1.579, where it is used somewhat differently. The Sun here overstates his ceaseless, unresting toil. He is not like the continuously flowing river of 1.579. At the end of each day, he enjoys a long period of rest and honor. In fact, when we and Phaethon first encounter him at the beginning of this very book, he is seated in glory among his subjects, idling away the hours until dawn and the moment when his chariot sets out. *sine fine . . . sine honore* 387: rhetorical presentation that fails to mask the self-serving distortion. He argues from his "daily grind" that he works endlessly, and he claims, in spite of his regal powers, that he lacks honor mainly because of what happened to his son. *mihi:* dative of agent with passive verb (participle here).

388–
91

quilibet alter: "someone else, anyone but me." The negative condition of 389 implies the absence of competent drivers among the gods, and that lets the Sun focus invidiously on the deity who has roused his wrath. *ipse* 390: Jupiter, as the nasty continuation demonstrates. This challenge to Jupiter to drive the chariot balances the earlier assertion to Phaethon, by way of warning, that even Jupiter could not handle the vehicle. *agat . . . ponat:* jussive subjunctive. *orbatura patres:* a perversely egoistic way to describe the situation in which Jupiter has recently acted. Although earlier the thunderbolt seemed a poor instrument of warped justice, in the case of Phaethon its use has done more good than harm. Left alone, he and his chariot would have burned up the universe. *aliquando:* in our idiom, "for once." This adverb appears rarely in poetry before Ovid: Vergil used it twice only, in Book 8 of the *Aeneid;* Ovid uses it only here in this poem, but five times more in other works.

392–
93
sciet: the shift to the future lets the Sun assert that Jupiter will not be able to handle the chariot and so can discover the "innocence" of Phaethon. *ignipedum:* preferable to the reading of *MN* and *Harl.,* *igniferum,* which would involve using this first and second declension adjective in an unusual genitive form. The epithet is Ovid's creation here; earlier, at 48, the horses were epically styled *alipedum. non meruisse* 393: supply a pronoun subject such as *eum* or *illum,* to serve as antecedent for the relative clause. Again, the paternal bias, further indicated by the meiosis *non bene* (instead of *male*), makes for distortion of the truth. A drunken driver or teenager who steals a bus and crashes may earn pity, but each does earn death by losing control of the vehicle. Ovid has let the Sun argue a mythical *controversia* in this section.

394–
97
circumstant: the Sun gets some of the reaction he seeks: all the gods collect around him and jointly beg him to perform his regular and necessary function. *neve* 395: = *et* (with *rogant* of 396) and *ne* with *velit.* For this use of *neve,* cf. 1.445. *tenebras inducere rebus:* same construction as in 307. Strictly speaking, the Sun does not bring darkness over the world; but his absence allows the shadows to prevail. *supplice voce* 396: Ovid conveys the idea of the many requests without indulging in a speech. *excusat* 397: similarly, the poet could have given Jupiter a lengthy bit of rhetoric, to match that of the father; but he summarizes its two main phrases. It would have begun with a line like: "I'm sorry I had to do it, but it was necessary." Then, it would have moved to some sterner stuff: "You've had enough time to grieve and we've let you go this far; now it's time to get back to normal business, and stop this protracted self-indulgence. I expect you to be back at work at dawn tomorrow, or else." *regaliter:* used by Livy, this word appears here for the only time in Ovidian or Augustan poetry. Ovid uses it precisely and ironically to characterize the manner of Jupiter; as if all kings used their power to make threats and to

disguise their own dubious actions. This differs sharply from the positive conception of rulers like Vergil's Jupiter, advanced until the end of the *Aeneid*.

398–
400

The narrative jumps right to the compliance of the Sun, as if he rapidly saw reason to yield to the combination of prayers and threats from Jupiter. We last saw the horses at 315 as they broke their traces and galloped in panic from the shattered chariot and their dead driver. *adhuc terrore paventes:* the narrative link with 314–15. *stimulo . . . et verbere* 399; in a world, such as Ovid's, where horse-driven vehicles were a common item, the savagery of brutal drivers against terrified animals would often be seen. I suspect that Ovid enlists us here on the side of the beasts against this violent deity, who is shifting his anger from himself and his guilt to the innocent animals. *dolens . . . saevit:* these two verbs go together in the regular characterization of raging anger; pain in the form of grief and suppressed remorse leads to savagery. *(saevit enim)* 400: the parenthesis not only repeats the verb of 399, taking advantage of the enjambement for emphasis, but it also implies the shock and disapproval of the narrator. This god, like most Ovidian deities, is evidently inferior to human beings. *obiectat et inputat:* these all too ordinary verbs, describing the unjust blaming of the animals, end the long myth with little honor for the Sun.

CALLISTO (401–530)

The second major story of Book 2 makes an artless, yet comical transition from the scene of fire damage occasioned by Phaethon, to a focus on Jupiter, who had finally restored the operation of the sun and was checking on structural dangers and the general conditions of humanity in the world. But the god suddenly reverts to the familiar adulterer of the Io-story, and Ovid traces out a story of divine lust that forms a variant on the type established in Book 1. This narrative is less playful; indeed, it portrays Jupiter and the other gods as almost viciously immoral, sadistic, and hypocritical, and thus makes the nymph Callisto into a near-tragic victim.

Ovid organizes his dramatic narrative into a sequence of Acts. First, when Jupiter spots the nymph (whom Ovid never names) and burns with passion for her, the poet pauses to describe her virginal ways. She is the typical devotee of Diana, a modest huntress, not a young maiden interested in domestic tasks and self-adornment who is preparing herself for marriage. But she is not a fanatic opponent of men and the marital state, as Daphne was. Callisto has won special favor with Diana; yet, the narrator adds as foreshadowing, no advantage lasts long. The second Act concentrates on the rape of the nymph. Overtly referring to the difficulties he had with Juno over Io, Jupiter consciously defies morality and decides that stolen pleasure (*furtum* 423) is worth any amount of angry denunciations from his wife. So he disguises himself ingeniously as Diana, which allows him to get close to Callisto as she relaxes from the hunt; at this point, without a word of wooing, he rapes her. Callisto puts up a fight, of course in vain. Then Jupiter, ironically called "the victor" by the narrator, departs back to Olympus, leaving the nymph to face her trauma and the long-range consequences by herself.

In the next scene, shortly after, Callisto stumbles from her violated place of rest and encounters the real Diana. At first suspicious, when she reassures herself that her rapist has indeed gone, the nymph is overwhelmed with shame, but unable to tell the story of the outrage. There is a considerable gap in time before the following Act, during which the inevitable pregnancy declares itself. So when, after the usual hunt, Diana and her band arrive at a shaded spot and an inviting pool, and the goddess proposes that they all bathe to relieve the heat and fatigue, Callisto is too embarrassed to expose himself. Her companion nymphs maliciously strip her, and the truth is out. Scandalized, without inquiring into the facts that prove her innocence, Diana dismisses the ex-virgin from her band.

Meanwhile, Ovid now reports, Juno has been aware of the situation (as she had penetrated the plot involving Io), but she has decided not to react spontaneously, but to postpone her vengeance for a "suitable time". She makes no effort to confront the guilty Jupiter, her husband, but instead concentrates all her ill feelings on Callisto, whom she regards as the criminal for attracting the impressionable rapist. The "suitable moment," then, turns out to be the time when, after Callisto has lost the protection of Djana, she slinks off alone and gives birth to a son, Arcas. As if she did not know that the pregnancy would result in a baby, Juno now plunges into paroxysms of rage and whips herself into malignant fury at Callisto. Now she declares herself determined to deform that beauty which had attracted Jupiter and so resulted in this disgrace! The process of metamorphosis constitutes an essential topic of this poem, and so Ovid describes it at length; and he clearly presents it as deformation, the unjust punishment of an innocent female, whose very pleas for mercy are savagely spurned. This is the first case in the poem of metamorphosis that springs from divine rage against an innocent individual. Callisto has suffered a worse fate than Io. She is no pretty white cow: she has become a shaggy bear.

Without given us any indication of what happens to the newborn baby, the narrator follows the fate of the new bear. Like Io before her, Callisto is a woman imprisoned in an animal's form, and she retains her human sensibility. Ovid specifically stresses this point: *mens antiqua manet* (485); and he explores the paradoxes that are available when one imagines a gentle girl taking a brute bear's outer shape without altering personality. For Callisto, it is all terror, a further emblem of the suffering visited on her by the rape: she fears hunters; she fears other animals, even the bears and wolves (into which her father had been turned). Human dismay when coping with animal metamorphosis is a unique theme of Ovid's poem.

In the penultimate Act, we are to assume that fifteen years have elapsed since Arcas was born and Callisto became a bear. Having become a stalwart young man, Arcas naturally spends time hunting, and inevitably he chances on his mother. Here is another opportunity for Ovid to develop, and he does so skillfully. Arcas does not know anything about his past and of course cannot distinguish his mother in her ursine shape. Callisto, however, somehow has the ability not only to identify a fellow human being in this hunter but also to recognize her own son, even after all this time, having lost him as an infant! As she halts in her tracks and starts to move towards him, as if recognizing him, Arcas shrinks back and interprets the staring beast as an obvious danger. At this near-tragic conclusion, Jupiter finally intervenes, to prevent a disaster that would redound on himself, and suddenly transports the pair into the heavens and transforms them into constellations, namely, the Great Bear (Ursa Major) and the Bear-Watcher (Arctophylax, more commonly the Oxdriver, Bootes). There remains one final, rather anti-climactic Act, in which Juno continues to urge her hatred against Callisto in this second transformation: she visits the goddess of the sea, Tethys, and passionately pleads with her never to allow the constellation of the Bear to descend into her waters and bathe. And accordingly the Bear never does set.

Ovid has drawn his material here from many layers of myth and presumably from a variety of sources—his achievement is too evidently Ovidian to be derivable from a single writer. Apollodorus 3.8.2.2 ff. provides a list of Greek recounters of this myth or portions of it: he cites Eumelos, Hesiod, Asios, and Pherekydes, plus a number of anonymous sources. Thus, the name of Callisto's father was disputed; only Eumelos and his followers agreed that Lycaon was the parent. Then, it was customary to stage a scene that Ovid here ignores: where Callisto swore to Diana to remain a virgin forever. The device of assuming disguise that Jupiter used to engineer his rape is known to Apollodorus, who, however, mentions two versions: the god pretended to be either Diana or her brother Apollo. The rest of Apollodorus' story proceeds differently from Ovid's: as in the case of Io, Jupiter changed his victim into a bear, to avoid the wrath of Juno. Juno was not deceived, and she maneuvered Diana into shooting dead the bear (the unchaste nymph who had sworn perpetual virginity). Alternatively, Diana did it without prompting. Before her death, Callisto had

had a baby, and so now Jupiter assumes responsibility for his son, takes him to Arcadia, and entrusts him to Maia for rearing. As for dead Callisto, the god transports her into the skies and turns her into the Great Bear. The detail of Apollodorus permits us to see how wide a choice of incident and of causation Ovid had; and it also suggests that the special emphasis he gives to the act of metamorphosis and the conception of the human consciousness inside the animal shape are peculiarly Ovidian realizations of the myth's possibilities. Ovid wrote another account of Callisto's fate in *Fast*. 2.155–92. Since he was writing both works contemporaneously, it is impossible to prove that Book 2 of the one poem preceded Book 2 of the other. The two poems have no common lines, not even half-lines. The version of the *Fasti*, clearly much shorter, gives no details of the rape and ignores the irrelevant stress on metamorphosis and its psychological meanings (which is central to the *Met*.), but it does have Callisto swearing eternal virginity, and it does recount the scene that fits its own themes: the catasterism of mother and son, as the *Met*. does.

Omnipotent Jupiter Becomes a Lover Again (401–16)

We have seen Jupiter, in a clumsy and authoritarian manner, restore order in the sunburnt universe. He disposed of Phaethon, and, when the Sun sulked in grief, the supreme god combined excuses and threats to force the father back to his chariot and proper role as deliverer of light. Thus, when Ovid continues to describe Jupiter's concern with his world, he lulls us into inattention, only to spring on us the scene of Jupiter spotting Callisto and declining from his sublime paternal role to a kind of paternity that is no joke.

401   *at pater omnipotens:* same resonant epic phrase as in 304. Ovid has different, sardonic uses for it this time. Near the conclusion of this myth, Ovid will remind us caustically of this opening, when he has *omnipotens* intervene (505) to fix an impasse of his own criminal creation. *ingentia moenia caeli:* this sounds like an echo of Lucretius, who liked to end lines with the phrase *flammantia moenia mundi* (e.g., 1.73), but Ovid does not need any more references here to "burning."

402   *circuit:* this prosaic action connotes the serious concern of a structural engineer. The verb, an initial dactyl, takes the form that satisfies poetic euphony. Its equivalent, *circumit*, would be metrically permissible, but Vergil and Ovid reject it, while Caesar uses it in his *Commentaries*. Of the seven different cases of this verb in the *Met*., Ovid permits the *m* only at 15.290. *labefactum:* although this verb can be conjugated, the Romans tended to limit themselves to this participle. Cicero uses it alone; Ovid has it six times and *labefecit* in 3.70 as his sole variation.

403–   *ne . . . corruat, explorat:* "he checks, to see that nothing might
4   collapse." Ovid is the first to use this verb *explorat* to introduce a
       negative purpose clause. *quae:* the walls. *suique / roboris:* genitive
       of description with an unusual separation produced by enjambement.
       The walls have their normal strength. *hominumque labores:* keeping
       up the expectation that he is describing the epic and grand Jupiter,
       Ovid borrows from epic predecessors. Homer had a Greek equivalent.
       Vergil created a genitive doublet with the final noun: e.g., *hominumque
       urbisque labores* (*Aen.* 2.284).

405–   *perspicit:* same initial dactyl at 2.112 and 7.226, but here Ovid uses
6   it to end a sequence. The juxtaposed proper noun focuses our and
       Jupiter's attention on Arcadia. *Arcadiae . . . suae:* these widely sepa-
       rated words enclose their clause. The older and better known tradition
       had Jupiter / Zeus born in Crete and there brought up by the Curetes.
       Ovid, however, follows a second venerable tradition, according to
       which the birth took place in Arcadia; hence, the god regards the
       region affectionately as "his." *inpensior:* the comparative adverb is
       well attested in prose and poetry before Ovid, but this is the first
       known appearance of the comparative adjective.

406–   In keeping with the traditional bucolic landscape of Arcadia, Ovid
8   has Jupiter restore flowers, rivers, grass, and trees. Ironically, these
       will prove a trap for Callisto, inviting her to an idyllic spot where
       Jupiter will rape her (cf. 418 ff.). Note the way the poet chooses
       nouns that alliterate with *f* in 406–7 and disposes the nouns that serve
       as double objects so as to frame their respective clauses. *nondum
       audentia:* the rivers are personified. *laesas* 408: we can imagine them
       as charred and blackened, like modern woods after a forest fire. That
       sets up the color contrast for *revirescere,* which Ovid here and at
       7.305 seems to have been the first poet to employ.

409–   *dum redit itque:* not quite the same as our idiom "comes and goes."
10   The idea of coming *back* is too strong. The natural Latin arrangement
       of this doublet, for which we have ample evidence before Ovid, would
       be *itque reditque,* as in *Aen.* 6.122. Ovid might have used this more
       logical phrasing here with his conjunction *dum,* but it would have
       produced a graceless elision of the monosyllable. *virgine:* Callisto
       can be vaguely called a nymph, as companion of Diana in the wood;
       but her virginity, as was the case for Daphne, is her main qualification
       for Diana's band and, alas, Jupiter's lecherous interest. Although her
       name is perfectly metrical, with three long syllables, and Ovid does
       employ it to begin his narrative in *Fast.* 2.156, he never names her
       in this account and prefers this mellifluous antonomasia, with the
       double-spondee *Nonacrina.* He plays to his audience's erudition. For
       a similarly flamboyant use of this adjective for Arcadia, in the introduc-
       tion of a new character, cf. 1.690. *haesit* 410: Ovid chooses to empha-

size somewhat ironically the sudden stopping of Jupiter's purposeful movements *in* lust concentrated on the nymph. Literally, the image of "getting stuck on" seriously diminishes the god's grandeur. The same verb, without the prepositional phrase, captures sudden passion in the case of Narcissus (3.419) and Glaucus (13.906).

411–
12   The narrator switches attention to the girl who has captured Jupiter's eye. Two negative clauses establish the fact that she is not herself romantically inclined, not preparing herself for marriage or the pleasures of courtship. *lanam mollire:* this phrase (or the more familiar *lanam facere*) connotes the dutiful woman, the "perfect wife," who weaves wool at home, rather than gadding about. Lucretia established her superiority over other noble wives by staying home and weaving. When Clinia needs reassurance about his beloved Antiphila in Terence's *Haut.* 275 ff., all he has to hear is that she and her maids were "at the wool," and he becomes ecstatic with joy. First, then, Callisto is not domestically inclined. Secondly, she takes no interest in arranging her hair stylishly: a detail which signifies that she is not looking for a husband. *positu variare comas* 412: Ovid has a similar clause in *Medic. fac.* 19, *positu variare capillos;* and there he affects to believe that it is a most desirable goal for young girls to arrange their hair artfully. The fourth declension *positu* + verb is equivalent to *[com]ponere* + adverb or noun. Although Ovid and his audience obviously saw in Rome everywhere women with attractive hairstyles, and hairdressing was a necessary part of the life of any woman with social ambitions, nevertheless the *Met.* seems to speak only of women who have either ignored the rite of hairdressing or have had their hair disarranged when they suffered violence or did violence to themselves in grief or passion. Thus, Daphne had *positos sine lege capillos* (1.477); and her carelessness parallels the neglect of Callisto (see the next line). In cases of passion, the participle changes to *passi, sparsi, laniati,* and the like. This poem does not feature courtly modern women. In the *Fasti,* however, the poet can divide women up without prejudice into two groups: those who do not comb their hair and those who appear in public *positis arte manuque comis* (1.406).

412–
14   Against this negative portrait, Ovid now places a positive. *fibula:* Roman ladies in general used one or two pins or brooches to fasten their robe at the shoulders. Presumably what distinguishes the modest, unstylish Callisto is the fact that her brooch is simple, not bejewelled or designed with figures by some expensive artist. Thus, Atalanta has a brooch that is undecorated (*rasilis* 8.318). *vitta . . . capillos* 413: the use of a simple hairband instead of formal hairdressing was established as a defining characteristic of Diana's followers in the first example, Daphne, in a line that Ovid here clearly echoes: *vitta coercebat positos sine lege capillos* (1.477). Finally, in 414, Ovid com-

pletes the portrait by giving Callisto the attributes of a huntress: a spear and bow. To enhance the picture, the poet employs a smooth rhythm of five dactyls in both 412 and 414.

415–
16   *miles erat Phoebes:* we expect Callisto to be called a follower or rival (cf. 1.476) of Phoebe (Diana), but Ovid permits himself a provocative variation here. It is extremely rare to call any woman a "soldier." Some critics have assumed that such a usage here indicates anti-Augustan criticism of the militarism of the day. Others have read the metaphor in terms of the erotic topic favored by the elegists and loudly proclaimed in *Amores* 1.9, that every lover is a "soldier." I would put more emphasis on the themes of this story, where the account of Callisto's rape emphasizes the crude but "victorious" violence that overwhelms her desperate, but vain, efforts to fight off Jupiter. Thus, Ovid has portrayed the woman as well-armed and then called her a "soldier" in order to set up an ironic reversal, as 416 will show. *Maenalon:* a mountain of Arcadia, first mentioned in 1.216, in connection with Callisto's father Lycaon. Ovid omits the traditional scene of the nymph swearing to uphold her virginity. *Triviae* 416: another title for Diana. *nulla potentia longa est:* Ovid likes to introduce foreshadowing in his narrative by isolating an abstract noun and making some general assertion about it. I have noted his use of a terminal *sententia* introduced by *tanta est* at 1.60 (cf. 2.731 and 3.270). Here, the *sententia* is negative; cf. 7.453, *usque adeo nulla est sincera voluptas.* Ovid refers to the "power" that derives from the favor of the goddess Diana. That "power" and the "military status" of Callisto prove null against the omnipotence of Jupiter.

The Rape (417–40)

The rape of Io had taken place at high noon as she fled from the shaded resting spot that Jupiter had designed for his conquest (cf. 1.590–92). Ovid repeats the same timing and setting for this rape and thus establishes an ironic pattern for subsequent stories: an idyllic site disturbed by divine violence against a human being. He begins with background tenses, as he brings Callisto, tired huntress, alone to the shaded grass and has her lie down to rest. Enter Jupiter (last mentioned at 410 as "stuck on" the virgin) who finds the scene all too inviting. The god's soliloquy reminds us of his amoral egoism in pursuit of Io, but his behavior is even worse. Not even attempting to woo the nymph, he disguises himself so as to be able to perpetrate his rape without chasing his prey all over Arcadia. The rape then displays his victorious omnipotence in a sinister way and, with pathos, her helpless lack of power. (In the story of Callisto from *Fast.* 2, Ovid skips over setting and details of the rape, but uses the noon-timing and idyllic

description for the forest pool, where Diana exposes and expels the
nymph from her band; cf. *Fast.* 2.163–66.)

17– *ulterius medio spatium:* "'s place or position past the midpoint of its
18   course"; it was slightly past noon. *medio* is ablative of comparison
with the comparative adjective *ulterius*. *nemus* 418: the woods connote
shade, as Jupiter specifically mentioned in 1.590–91 when speaking
to Io. *nulla ceciderat aetas:* at no time had any human disturbed the
spot with an axe, so the trees were thick and as nature planned them.
This motif, that the place has never been invaded and so is "virginal,"
like the huntress who finds it so appealing, becomes an added element
of Ovid's idyllic descriptions. Cf. the elaborate ecphrasis for
Narcissus' forest pool in 3.407 ff.; Cadmus in 328 encounters woods
that have not been "violated by any axe."

19– Callisto's actions indicate what elsewhere Ovid typically notes, that
21   the hunter/huntress has grown tired (cf. *fessam* 422). Then follows
relaxation. However, removal of the quiver and unstringing of the
bow signify more than readiness for rest: they also reduce the defenses
of the hunter, who now cannot act as "soldier" of Diana, whether to
chase animals or to defend virginity. *herba* 420: grass for comfortable
reclining is a necessary element, too, of the idyllic spot. *pictam . . .
pharetram* 421: as Bömer acutely observes, Greeks and Romans did
not use bows and arrows for hunting: archery is a mythological topos.
The decorated quiver serves Ovid as a pictorial motif. The alliteration
of *p* is striking here in this last moment of serenity for Callisto: it
may suggest the imminent explosion of violence.

22– *custode vacantem:* Ovid alludes to a theme of Roman elegy, where
24   the lover seeks to attain access to the beloved in spite of, or by bribery
of, the "guard" set on her chastity by husband, father, or family.
Callisto would not have had a literal guard, but her hunting companions
and Diana would have served the purpose. In a later rape-account,
the Sun enters a girl's room disguised as her mother, dismisses the
servants so as to have a "private conversation," and then, without
these "guards," becomes a rapist. (cf. 4. 218 ff.). *hoc certe furtum*
423: Jupiter had deceptively promised Juno after the debacle with Io
(1.736–37) that he would not renew his adultery. However, this noun
furtum has so far occurred only during the Io-story (plural in 1.606,
singular in 623). Thus, there can be no doubt that Jupiter is thinking
of that episode and Ovid reminding us. Jupiter's certainty of outwitting
his wife comically evaporates in 424, but that does not deter him.
What is a little scolding? *sunt, o sunt* 424: the interjection *o* reveals
the god's comically lyrical eagerness for this sexual adventure. *tanti:*
genitive of value.

25   *induitur faciem:* a standard way of referring to disguise as "putting

on a face." For *indutus* with Greek accusative or accusative of respect, cf. 1.270. Here, the verb functions like the Greek middle voice, in a reflexive sense, while taking a direct object. (See the similar instance in 2.850.) The origin of this element in Callisto's story (mentioned by Apollodorus) can be traced as far back as the fourth century comic poet Amphis, but it could also antedate him. It is no mere comic trick, Ovid shows.

426–
27 To make his impersonation plausible, Jupiter-Diana affects to identify Callisto and then asks her where she has been hunting. The use of *virgo* is correct for the last time. *pars una:* a member.

427–
29 Sitting up from her recumbent position (cf. 420), Callisto hails this Diana-shape in enthusiastic words. *me iudice* 428: ablative absolute. *audiat . . . licet* 429: the subjunctive acquires a concessive sense from *licet. maius Iove:* the adjective refers to *numen*. This is the second time in Book 2 that we have been invited to consider something grander than Jupiter (Cf. 62).

429–
31 Jupiter plays the comic intriguer, immensely enjoying himself and relishing the irony of this self-comparison. As noted at 213 and 303, Ovid likes to play with reflexive conceits, but not always in the same manner. Here, he assigns the play to the rapist Jupiter, and it serves to condemn the deceiver. As if pleased by the compliment, then, he starts kissing Callisto effusively, in a way that Ovid distinguishes from merely friendly kissing between women. Callisto is probably too innocent to realize what is happening. *virgine* 431: Diana, whom Jupiter impersonates.

432–
33 *qua . . . silva:* the indirect question refers to the direct query with which Jupiter approached Callisto in 427. *parantem:* i.e., Callisto. She now becomes the object of the verbs of 428, victim of the rapist. The two lines bring out the disparity of thoughts and actions of the two people. *nec . . . sine crimine* 433: the litotes or double negative helps to stress the real criminality of this situation. By contrast, in the *Fasti* Ovid ignores the scene of rape and briefly states: *de Iove crimen habet* (2.162).

434–
37 *illa quidem . . . pugnat* 436: Ovid skillfully delays the verb and increases the suspense by the parenthetical apostrophe of Juno in 435. *posset:* the potential subjunctive and the choice of verb comment ironically on the *potentia* that Callisto once proudly possessed. *adspiceres utinam . . . esses* 435: the vain wish in *utinam* gives the narrator's intrusion somewhat greater force than the conjunction *si*. Imperfect subjunctive goes with the narrative present tenses. *pugnat . . . superare* 436: note the military imagery at this ironic moment where Callisto's status as *miles* disintegrates. *sed quem:* all MSS except the early fragmentary *Harl.* have *quae,* which would be an interrogative adjective. Following Bentley's conjecture, seemingly confirmed by

the subsequent discovery of *Harl.*, we get two quite distinct clauses. Can a woman fight off a male? Ovid first asks. Then he makes his question even stronger: Can anyone overcome Jupiter? *poterat* 437: indicative has the force of subjunctive. No human being can master the god because he is *omnipotens* (401, 505).

437–
38
superum: this adjective normally is taken with the following *aethera*, as the punctuation indicates. Ovid uses it regularly to refer to the breezes and homes "above," in the heavens, not to the Olympian gods. Thus, the ingenious suggestion of Jahn, to repunctuate and place the question mark after *superum*, so as to link the adjective with *Iovem*, has been rejected. There is no literary evidence that Jupiter ever had the epithet *superus*. Ovid piles up the dactyls in 437: this is not a lordly ascent, but a hasty withdrawal after quick pleasure. *Iuppiter: huic* 438: Ovid juxtaposes the two unequal members of this "union," giving the god his full dignity, name, and epithet, but assigning Callisto, who has lost her essential being, only a simple pronoun. She remains in the real world to grapple confusedly with the effects of her rape. The dative functions as part of a double dative with *odio*. What she once loved, the friendly woods, has now become for the rape victim hateful. *conscia:* Callisto is ashamed at what the woods have witnessed. In a similar vein, when Philomela suffers rape from Tereus, she threatens to fill woods and *conscia saxa* (6.547) with her outcries.

439–
40
unde pedem referens: "withdrawing from there [the woods]." This verbal compound, *pedem* + a form of *referre*, has metrical and pictorial advantages over a bare verb. *oblita:* in almost forgetting her hunting equipment, Callisto reveals how radically her psyche has been confounded by violence.

Callisto Suffers the Angry Rejection of Diana (441–65)

Callisto goes from one ruthless, unsympathetic deity to another. Trapped in her helpless shame, she tries to remain with Diana as long as possible. Ultimately, she has to endure the malice of her companion nymphs and reveal her shame to the prudish, outraged deity. With no womanly concern for this victim of male aggression, Diana banishes her from the sacred band. (At least, Ovid does not follow the version in which she actually killed her.)

441–
44
ecce: as in 112, the narrator calls attention to a new actor entering. *Dictynna:* a Cretan goddess, with whom Artemis (Diana) became amalgamated. Ovid names her otherwise only in *Fast.* 6.755, but the educated audience would already have met the name in Tibullus (and in the *Ciris*, depending on its date). He is not simply finding a metrical

alternative for Diana, to avoid its short first syllable. Although Ovid primarily treats *Diana* as having a short first syllable and so regularly places it at the end of the hexameter, he knows that the archaic form of the word has a long *i* and avails himself of that spelling on occasion: so, in 5.619. *Maenalon* 442: the scene implied by the proper noun in 415 is confirmed. As in that instance, Ovid uses the Greek declension for the accusative, to avoid elision and retain the mellifluous effect of the word. *ingrediens:* with its epic associations, this verb adds drama to Diana's entrance. *caede superba ferarum:* the narrator regularly includes in the details accompanying a hunter or huntress some reference to his or her success. Nevertheless, the formulaic detail can be worded in various ways. This arrogant slaughterer foreshadows the pitiless and proud Diana who dismisses her nymph. *visamque vocat: clamata* 443: The two participles act as vivid substitutes for uninteresting pronouns and enhance the connection between the three clauses of which 443 is composed. Often, Ovid juxtaposes forms of the same verb, as in 4.316. Here, although he could have used *vocata,* he refrained. *esset in illa* 444: since earlier Jupiter "put on" (425) Diana's form, Callisto now fears that he still lurks inside her shape.

445–46   The sight of other nymphs entering, unraped, with Diana proves reassuring.

447–49   The poet intrudes in 447 to gain empathy for Callisto. *crimen:* the "crime" that Jupiter perpetrated (cf. 433) has now, as often today with innocent victims, become hers. She then in 448 ff. enacts the trauma that she has suffered. In effect, the rape has already transformed her, and the bear-form that will be inflicted on her by her next divine tormenter will only serve to symbolize her total brutalization. *nec . . . prima* 449: she instinctively avoids the favorite's position, aware of her lost "power."

450–52   A woman's blushing silence is a favorite poetic vignette; perhaps the most famous such scene is that of Lavinia in *Aen.* 12.64 ff. *laesi . . . pudoris:* this phrase applies generally to any injury to the sense of shame. Here, we know that it refers to the outrage of rape; in the story of Cephalus and Procris (7.751), the same phrase covers Cephalus' false accusation against his wife's chastity. *est, poterat* 451: this seeming mixture of tenses is only apparent. As we have seen earlier, the imperfect indicative of *posse* can stand for a subjunctive (here, *possit*) in an unreal condition. *mille notis* 452: the narrator implies that he has provided us with only a few of these thousand indicators. *nymphae sensisse feruntur:* unlike the essentially chaste and virginal goddess, the nymphs possess some practical feminine knowledge, like young ladies in the Roman court; and they have been able to figure out what Diana has not suspected. (But the narrator affects not to invent this motif.)

453   Time now leaps forward nine months from the day of the rape, and Ovid uses the moon to measure it, in one of his many variants. The horns of the new moon are rising with its ninth sphere, that is, for the ninth time. For similar wording, cf. 8.11. This entire sequence, 453–65, adopts past tenses.

454–   *dea venatu . . . flammis:* the two ablative nouns strike readers as
56   unusual. The second is of course normal, with its alliterative adjective-noun arrangement framing the word *languida* on which it depends. But *venatu* at the central caesura exhibits loose syntax at best: it is usually explained as a second instrumental ablative with *languida*, but also as a local ablative with the participle (= "from or after the hunt"). Some MSS have inserted a "correction" by adding *et* and thus forcing the connection with *languida*. Modern scholars have also tried conjecture: Heinsius proposed *dea venatrix;* Slater, *de venatu.* Both sacrifice more than they gain. With the reference to "her brother's flames" (i.e., Apollo's = the sun's), Ovid brings in high noon and starts on the stereotypical scene of the idyllic spot where paradoxically some brutal victimization will occur. (Cf. above 417 ff. and the scenario of Callisto's rape.) *nemus gelidum* 455: woods are cool because well shaded against the rays of the sun. *cum murmure labens . . . rivus:* the same descriptive phrase occurs in 11.603 for the somniferous river of Lethe. Here, Ovid is talking more of a forest brook, which babbles along in its sandy bed. This is a new element in his idyllic scene, but familiar from Horace's *Odes.* The water may slake thirst and/or bathe tired limbs.

57–   By echoing *laudavit* with *laudatis* (458), in the same metrical position,
59   Ovid links the climactic steps by which Diana decided to bathe. She liked the pretty spot, and then she liked the temperature of the water. *procul est* 458: Diana declares that every alien presence (male) is absent. Soon, however, she discovers that Callisto, because her virginity has been ruined, is alien; and she dispatches her from the sacred spot that she "pollutes": *i procul* (464). *arbiter* 458: a witness. The noun seems to be derived from *ad* + *bito* and to mean "go to," an archaic form of *adeo* (like *abito/abeo* and *perbito/pereo*). Originally, the person who arrived as a presence was merely a chance spectator or auditor; then, the noun came to denote someone who was sent or chosen to decide a dispute or a legal problem. In 459, Diana proposes her bath in a highly stylized Golden Line, beginning, however, with the attention-getting word *nuda. tingamus:* in the parallel account of *Fast.* 2.167, Diana says: *lavemur.* But that seems to suggest a full bath. Ovid alters his verb to imply just a cooling dip. As Bömer

observes, the final verb in both accounts conforms to the earlier: in
Fast. 2.192, Juno asks Tethys that Callisto/The Bear not be allowed
to wash (*ne lavet*) in the sea; in *Met*. 2.530, she says: *ne tingatur*.

460–
62

Parrhasis: antonomasia that Ovid first introduced to Latin. By way
of a town in Arcadia, it refers to Callisto. Ovid used it first in *Her*.
18.152 and twice elsewhere, as an adjective; and in all three instances
he describes the constellation that Callisto became, the "Parrhasian
Bear." *erubuit:* Ovid does not need to explain this second blush (cf.
450). *velamina ponunt:* the other nymphs take off their clothes and
so obediently become *nudae*. Again, the narration in 461 divides our
focus at the caesura. *una* 461: since we have just heard about "all the
rest," it is obvious who this individual exception is. *dubitanti:* dative
of separation and disadvantage. Callisto's efforts to delay may be
called "hesitating." It can only be the all too worldly and envious
fellow nymphs who strip Callisto. *qua posita* 462: same verb for this
ablative absolute as in 460, with same sense. *patuit cum corpore
crimen:* a nice variant of Ovidian zeugma (both nouns taken in different
senses with the single verb) enhanced by alliteration. Diana reacts to
crimen without ascertaining the real criminal.

463–
65

attonitae . . . volenti: the two participles frame the line and briefly
capture Callisto's desperation. Of more than twenty uses of the first
verb in the *Met*., only one is not the past participle. There are many
factors, we might imagine, in Callisto's thunderstruck state: dismay
at the cruelty of the other nymphs, despair over her past suffering,
and helpless innocence, shame, and terror before Diana. The gesture
with which she attempts to conceal her pregnant belly seems reminis-
cent, especially because of this bath-setting, of the well-known statues
of nude and bathing Aphrodite/Venus, who uses her hands to shield
her sexual attractions from prying eyes. Only after he has painted the
nymph's misery, does Ovid clarify the syntax of the dative participles:
they go with the verb *dixit,* indirect object of Diana's indignant out-
burst. The one-line speech of 464 does not correspond very closely
to reality and is certainly not an "epic speech," but it quickly gets to
the point and allows Ovid to move rapidly to the next narrative se-
quence. *sacros . . . fontes* 464: Bömer suggests that, behind the use
of this adjective, lies an ancient ritual to test chastity. *Cynthia* 465:
Propertius was the first to bring this name into Latin, and he of course
did not refer to the goddess, but to his talented and inspiring beloved.
Then, Horace *C*. 3.28.12 uses it properly of Diana. Ovid has eight
instances of the name, the earliest in *Her*. 17.74. *deque:* the expected
preposition would have been *a;* but to avoid the metrical problem
with elision, Ovid chose *de. secedere:* the MSS *NU* change to *dece-
dere,* perhaps to go with the unusual preposition. However, Ovid
never uses *decedere,* and he is unique among Augustan poets in his

ample exploitation of *secedere*. This verb also contributes to the sound patterns of 465.

Callisto Suffers Brutalization from Juno (466–95)

Apollodorus reports a version according to which, when Juno found out before Diana of Callisto's rape, she maneuvered Diana into angrily shooting the girl dead. Ovid cannot use that detail, because he intends to record the catasterism of the Great Bear from a living, if threatened, being. So he builds up a Juno who is even more venomously vengeful than the Juno who harassed Io. Instead of acting instantaneously, Juno nurses her wrath and waits for a cruelly apt opportunity (namely, when the baby has been born). She attacks the rape victim; and she whips up her fury with a ranting speech that alienates us by its unfairness. She brutalizes the girl's form into an ugly, fearsome bear. Ovid goes on to record the bewildered suffering of the girl, who now has to face existence in a form that completely belies her essential nature, but reflects the callous cruelty of three deities toward her innocence.

466–
67
senserat: Juno's suspicious nature and previous experience make her far more knowledgable than Diana (cf. 451). The pluperfect tenses provide background through 469; then, Ovid moves into the narrative perfect until after the metamorphosis (481). The psychological confusion of the girl inside the bear emerges in the narrative present (482–88) and then in a series of actions once again in the perfect (489–95). *magni matrona Tonantis:* this half-line for identifying Juno takes the form of an epic circumlocution, which seems totally inappropriate for this situation and therefore ironic. Jupiter has been anything but "great" and "thundering" in this rape. Now, Juno herself behaves well below the level of a proper Roman matron. *distuleratque* 467: Juno had to wait for her moment of vengeance so that Arcas could be born and thus available for catasterism himself. But Ovid's narrative portrays a vicious deity, one who acts not with quick and spontaneous justice, but chooses the cruelest moment to afflict the innocent. *poenas:* Juno has no question about the necessity and rightness of punishing the girl.

68–
69
At the birth of Arcas, Juno has no reason (nor does the traditional story) to postpone the punishment, which will be metamorphosis. With the chronology that Ovid uses, Callisto was already in her ninth month when Diana dismissed her; the birth would have taken place shortly after. *Arcas:* Arcas should be the originator of the Arcadians and give his name to their region, but Ovid has already set the scene in Arcadia at the beginning of this story (405: cf. 1.689). *indoluit*

469: Ovid is the first poet to make extensive use of this expressive verb. He builds, of course, on the Vergilian characterization of Juno as a person of fierce *dolor* and *furor*. *paelice:* as in the case of Io (cf. 1.622 and 726), the narrator's pejorative noun presents the victim as viewed by angry Juno. The word is probably taken over from Roman elegy, where mistresses do mount serious threats to legitimate wives. But to call Io or Callisto a concubine is to commit a grave injustice against either.

470– *quo simul:* as in 2.19, the second word is a conjunction (in prose,
73   customarily *simul ac*). *saevam cum lumine mentem:* the same virtual zeugma as in 462: she turned her eye and her savage purpose. Evidently Juno swooped down on Callisto right after her childbirth and began to rail directly at her. *scilicet* 471: an angrily sardonic opening. *hoc:* this pronoun prepares for the result clause that Ovid holds in suspense until the beginning of 472. *adultera:* a word banned from traditional epic as undignified. Ovid has taken it into the *Met.* from elegy. Again, Juno's choice of the term reflects her low level of understanding; neither the narrator nor we accept it as literally apt. *fecunda* 472: more prejudice. Juno holds against the victim that she became pregnant! Of course, omnipotent Jupiter seems to have been so potent that all his rapes resulted in progeny. The alliteration here catches the sputtering fury of the goddess. *iniuria:* Juno still seems to mean some injury committed by the girl. However, especially in combination with the next clause and its reference to Jupiter's *dedecus,* the audience would tend to correct Juno's bias. In 473, we hear the small-minded bigotry of the jealous wife, whose principal complaint is over the fact that her husband's disgrace has hit the front pages! After all, she has known about it a long time (cf. 466). *mei:* not a sign of affection, but of personal possession and public arrogance.

474– *haud inpune feres:* the formulaic language of indignant menace, pref-
75   acing the actual punishment. Such calls for punishment are thematic in Senecan tragedy and in the angry Satires of Juvenal. *adimam . . . figuram:* Juno announces her power confidently. She will take away, destroy the form that Callisto naturally possesses. The same collocation of verb and noun recurs at 8.615, where sceptic Pirithous challenges the report that gods can give or take away forms. *namque:* for the metrical utility of this form, cf. 1.361 and 687. *places* 475: with two different words in different senses of pleasing. Callisto is accused of taking pleasure in her looks: but it is doubtful that such a plain-dressing virgin ever did look at her reflection. It is true, however, that she pleased, though involuntarily, her rapist Jupiter. She did not, as Juno implies, set out to catch his attention and interest. Thus, Juno's unjust fury makes of Callisto's person and physical beauty a target for abuse

just as her lascivious husband had selfishly abused them in his lust. *inportuna:* another unfair epithet: something like "trouble-maker."

76–
77
dixit et: this initial dactylic unit, like *dixerat,* moves us on quickly to the action. For Ovid's unepic transitions from speech, cf. 1.281 and 466. *adversa . . . capillis:* she seized the hair on Callisto's forehead as the girl faced her. The MSS had difficulty with the first word, unable to decide whether it should be *ad-* or *a-versa* and whether ablative or accusative. The context decides the first question: Callisto can hardly offer her forehead to Juno's savagery if she has turned away. As for the choice between ablative and accusative, it seems smoother Latin to attach the adjective to *fronte* than to have a double accusative without connective. For a similar description of an angry goddess throwing a victim to the ground before metamorphosing her, cf. Lucina's treatment of Galanthis in 9.317 ff. *humi* 477: locative. *pronam:* face-forward, Callisto can quickly raise herself into praying position. *tendebat bracchia:* for the gesture and its special opportunities for pathos used by Ovid, cf. the scene of Io in 1.635–36. Here, the poet outdoes the earlier scene, for he has Juno rob the girl of supplicating arms by changing those limbs into an animal's.

78–
79
The smooth girlish arms suddenly bristle with shaggy black hair: a grotesque divine answer to her prayer! *horrescere:* the conative force of the verb, with its suffix in *-scere,* seems redundant, when the main verb is *coeperunt.* However, Ovid may be deliberately emphasizing this beginning of brutalization. In 479, he then follows the arms down to the hands, which are bent, and the fingernails that grow out into hooked claws.

80–
81
officioque pedum: since the bear is a quadruped, human hands now serve as animal forefeet. Callisto, already thrown to the ground, can immediately use her new feet. *laudataque . . . Iovi:* dative of agent with passive verb. Ovid refers back to Juno's threat in 474–75 to destroy the beauty that delights her husband. *deformia:* Juno does more than destroy the lovely face: she distorts it into something truly ugly and frightening.

82–
84
In the act of prayer, the girl has become a beast. But that still in theory leaves her the chance to verbalize her prayer even if she has been robbed of the gesture. *preces . . . precantia:* emphasis on the conscious effort of the goddess to stifle the girl's prayers, making them unheard. Juno does not want to let any pleas be articulated. *posse* 483: serves as subject of the verb. Perhaps another ironic echo of *potentia* 416. *eripitur:* a strong verb to emphasize the cruel violence of Juno. With the destruction of human speech, Ovid then turns at the caesura to the voice that remains, now that of a beast. For Callisto, the worst thing about her transformation is that her new form belies

the unchanged *mens* or personality that it conceals. Her new guttural roar, with its implicit menace, totally frustrates her.

485–
86   *mens antiqua manet:* here is the ingenious theme that Ovid discovered in metamorphosis and made the inspiration for later writers such as Kafka. He had implied it in the case of Io; here, he states it to accord with the greater seriousness of his presentation. He will restate it once more to capture the greater tragedy of Actaeon: *mens tantum pristina mansit* (3.203.). Continuity between new and old form was a traditional topic, and Ovid emphasizes the point not only with this verb (in contexts referring to physical changes) but also by such words as *servare, nunc quoque, adhuc, etiam, idem.* Continuity of human consciousness is Ovid's innovation. *facta . . . mansit in ursa:* the narrator intrudes with a parenthetical remark that informs us that the self-conscious beast is a bear. *gemitu testata* 486: the subject is now *ursa.* One of the sounds which human beings and animals share is that of groaning. Callisto voices her agony. As the adjectives in 483–84 suggest, in bears that same sound usually connotes anger, menace, and fearsomeness.

487–
88   *qualescumque manus:* Juno has been satisfied with her vengeance and departed. Left to herself, Callisto still tries to use her "hands" in a gesture of appeal and protest to the god who caused all her suffering. Bears can stand on their hind legs and somewhat duplicate human gestures with their paws. Callisto will do this again at 500 ff. *ingratumque Iovem . . . sentit* 488: the adjective, it turns out, is predicative; it is what she cannot say, but feels. Nevertheless, the narrator implies that Jupiter's ingratitude is a cruel fact. He has taken his pleasure and departed, without the slightest consideration for his "pleasurer." *nequeat:* concessive subjunctive.

489–
90   *a, quotiens:* the interjection and exclamatory adverb, repeated in anaphora at 491, represent a sympathetic intrusion of the narrator, who imagines how frightened the girl must be inside the bear-shape. *sola . . . silva:* the alliterative phrase represents the forest from the perspective of a human being. There are plenty of other animals there, indeed many other bears, as Ovid notes (494). *quiescere:* ironically, her previous rest in the woods had led to her rape. *ante domum* 490: afraid to sleep like a bear, Callisto haunts her former human environs, but of course cannot safely enter the building or be seen in the fields. Ovid explores the same frustrating paradox in the story of Actaeon (cf. 3.204–5). The parallel passage in *Fast.* 2.181–82, devotes a single couplet to Callisto after metamorphosis, merely recording that she wandered over the wild mountains. *quondamque suis:* special pathetic emphasis on the possessive (which also applies to *domum*).

491–   *venatrixque metu venantum* 492: another paradox. As Ovid words it,

92　　Callisto still regards herself as a huntress, but now she is terrified of
　　　hunters and baffled by her helplessness.

493–　Ovid concludes this sequence by pointing up paradoxes in this new
95　　"animal"'s relationships with other animals. *feris . . . visis:* ablative
　　　absolute. The bear hides, though she would be one of the largest and
　　　most feared beasts, immune from attack. *oblita quid esset:* with her
　　　human consciousness, Callisto does not just "forget": she never can
　　　realize and come to terms with her animality. The subjunctive in an
　　　indirect question has her as its subject. *ursa . . . ursos* 494: Ovid
　　　captures and emphasizes this paradox, a more poignant one than that
　　　of 493, by the artful placing of the repeated words. The she-bear is
　　　afraid of male bears. *pertimuitque* 495: for his final paradox, the
　　　narrator chooses the encounter between bear and wolf, i.e., Callisto
　　　and Lycaon. Although he affects to reach a climax in his verbs of
　　　fearing, the series of conceits by which he engineers the situation
　　　makes it seem more witty than pathetic. This is the first time we have
　　　been told about the relationship between Lycaon and Callisto; and the
　　　marked separation of the two stories suggests that it is gratuitous
　　　information, cleverly saved for this moment's paradox. *in illis:* the
　　　ambiguity of these words is, I think, intended. Logically, her father
　　　should be inside *one* wolf (as she is inside a single bear-shape). How
　　　is it comforting that her father is in a wolf-pack, when she cannot
　　　distinguish him and he cannot identify her?

The Bear and Her Son Arcas: More Suffering and a Second Metamorphosis by Catasterism (496–507)

　　　For fifteen years, Callisto in her bear-shape wanders miserably and
fearfully in the woods. Meanwhile, her son Arcas, whose birth (cf.
468) had occasioned the vengeful metamorphosis by Juno, has grown
into a young man and hunter. Inevitably, then, hunter and bear,
Arcas and mother, encounter each other, but Arcas of course cannot
recognize his mother inside the animal, whereas she easily identifies
her son. Inclined to avoid the large beast, Arcas interprets her eager
"maternal" approach as an attack and prepares to defend himself. To
prevent the crime of matricide, which would be blamed on him, Jupiter
intervenes, transports the two to the heavens, and turns them into
constellations. Thus, he solves his problem, but continues to ignore
Callisto's misery. This catasterism is no honor or consolation for the
abused nymph.

496–　*ecce:* a new phase of the long story, as in 441. *Lycaoniae:* now that
97　　he has just mentioned the connection with Lycaon, Ovid uses the

patronymic for the first time. *ignara parentis:* objective genitive with the adjective. As often, Ovid introduces a character with a mythological circumlocution (plus sexual ambiguity), but quickly names Arcas in 497. *ter quinque . . . natalibus* 497: since *quindecim* rarely would fit into the hexameter, Ovid uses multiplication: 3 × 5 = 15. Arcas is an adolescent, like Narcissus in 3.351.

498– In three *dum*-clauses, of which the third, as in most tricola, is the
99   longest, Ovid summarizes the hunter's activities. Since Arcas lays nets, we may infer that he does not hunt larger animals such as bears. *nexilibusque plagis* 499: woven nets, ablative of means with *ambit* (to be taken as transitive verb in the sense of "surround, ring"). *Erymanthidas:* never at a loss for a new word to vary a familiar geographical area, Ovid invents this synonym for "Arcadian." Erymanthus is the name of a mountain chain in Arcadia, and Ovid has also called it an Arcadian river in 2.244.

500– *incidit in matrem:* although the verb can refer to hostile attack, it
501   very commonly describes a chance meeting of any kind, as here. By using *matrem,* however, Ovid emphasizes the irony of Arcas's ignorance. He sees only a bear and a threat. *restitit:* at sight of the boy, the bear does not take flight (as many bears would do), but stops. To Arcas, that means trouble, and the corresponding verb assigned to him is the unheroic, if prudent *refugit. cognoscenti similis* 501: dative with *similis.* As in *Fast.* 2.185, Ovid says that the mother/bear appeared to recognize her son. That has to be an intrusion from the narrator; Arcas certainly did not suspect this, or he would not have turned tail.

502– *immotosque oculos . . . tenentem:* since the subject is Arcas, this
4   participial clause in accusative must refer to the other individual in the scene, Callisto or the bear. What Arcas sees is a beast with fixed, staring, and, in his interpretation, wild eyes. Staring eyes connote a number of different feelings. Knowing that there is a mother inside the bear, we can understand that stare sympathetically as fond love desperately trying to communicate itself without speech. The scene symbolizes the basic lack of communication between any two people, who often cannot even see or hear each other as human beings. *nescius* 503: Ovid underlines the dramatic irony. *aventi:* the participial clause again, since the subject remains stable, refers to the mother/bear, now indirect object. Having first stopped and stared fixedly at Arcas, she now lumbers toward him, with an eagerness that we understand quite differently from the fearful boy. In *Fast.* 2.186, Ovid has the bear give a groan/roar that served as "a mother's words." *vulnifico* 504: Ovid has picked up a neologism of Vergil, *Aen.* 8.446. The ostentatious language of this line seems to emphasize the melodrama. *fuerat*

fixuras: this periphrastic structure with the future participle, our grammars tell us, equals the pluperfect subjunctive *fixisset.* It functions as the conclusion of a past contrary-to-fact clause, leaving unstated the if-clause. It also creates emphatic alliteration (connected with the initial striking adjective) and uses a verbal form that puts more emphasis on the future action than on the fact that it will not happen. *pectora:* exploits the similar anatomy of bear and human female. Spearing his mother in the breast would have been a terrible *nefas* (cf. 505) for Arcas.

505–
7

arcuit omnipotens: having avoided the conditional structure in 504 and teased his audience with his grand suspense, Ovid quickly dissipates the problem by an indicative verb. The almighty father (literally true here) stops his son. Fine, we might say. And will he not restore Callisto to her human form, as he did for Io, reuniting mother and child, so that they will live happily ever after? Unfortunately, that is not how this story ends. The Almighty here is terribly inhuman and incompetent. He acts swiftly, as the three straight dactyls suggest, but he makes an unholy mess. *pariterque ipsosque nefasque:* a prize example of the sly Ovidian zeugma of which Alexander Pope and his era were such admirers and imitators. The adverb and the double *-que* construction all emphasize the simultaneity of the verb's operation, but the two objects cannot take the same sense of that one verb. *sustulit* 506: from *tollere,* not *suffere.* The basic sense of the verb is "to lift up"; from which comes "to exalt", but also "to lift away from, remove". Here, the ambiguous meanings in the zeugma are best captured in the translation: "he removed." Jupiter snatched the pair into the air and placed them as adjacent constellations in the sky. But, in a sense closer to what was needed for the object *nefas,* he removed them from existence, destroying them as he wiped out the possible sin. Cicero produced a deadly pun with this verb when he declared that Octavian was to be praised, honored, and lifted out of existence: *laudandum adulescentem, ornandum, tollendum (Fam.* 11.20.1). Bömer cites a lampoon about Nero after his matricide: Nero, it begins, is undeniably descended from Aeneas: *sustulit hic matrem, sustulit ille patrem* (Suet. *Ner.* 39.2). Aeneas lifted his father Anchises on his shoulders and carried him from burning Troy; Nero removed his mother. Politicians often prefer to eradicate a troublous individual rather than deal with the humane and personal issues that she or he raises. In effect, Jupiter eliminates his son and the woman he loved. *pariter raptos:* the next two lines concentrate on the disposal of the difficult pair. *inposuit* 507: literally, "he set them in," and, figuratively, "he imposed them on." Another hint at the autocratic behavior of the god. *sidera fecit:* the second metamorphosis for Callisto. In the sky, the Great Bear is followed by the Bear-Watcher.

INSATIATE JUNO TRIES TO HARASS CALLISTO FURTHER (508–30)

Callisto has been removed from existence and no longer possesses her human *mens* and the capacity to suffer or protest: she has become an inanimate star, the mere outline of a figure that Ovid here calls a bear, but elsewhere a wagon (cf. 2.176–77). However, Juno believes herself foiled by Jupiter because her rival has been honored (515) by catasterism. Raging with fury, she goes to the sea goddess Tethys and delivers a long ranting speech (which exaggerates the Junonian rhetoric familiar in the *Aeneid*). Her ultimate purpose is to request that the sea never receive the hated Callisto into its waters to bathe, any more than the forest pool of Diana received the unchaste nymph. *Fast.* 2 has no such dramatic speech, only a couplet, for this scene.

508–11   *intumuit:* not a dignified word or picture. Horace used it once in *Epod.* 16.52 in a literal sense, but Ovid brought it into poetry, particularly in the *Met.* and *Fast.* to capture the ridiculous swollen wrath and arrogance of deities. Same initial hemistich in *Fast.* 6.487. Ovid confines himself to the metrically convenient perfect active, predominantly, as here, in the initial position. *inter sidera paelex / fulsit* 509: Ovid offers a new perspective on what he sparely described in 507, the invidious viewpoint of Juno, who cannot help but think of Callisto as a kept concubine (cf. 469). Juno thinks that the glittering constellation is indeed an exaltation, not an elimination. *canam . . . Tethyn:* Tethys, wife of Oceanus, can be imagined as white-haired, because she belongs to the older generation of gods. *quorum* 510: objective genitive. Ironically, though the gods supposedly often show their respect for the pair, Juno exhibits none. She came to get something from them. *causamque viae scitantibus* 511: as hosts of the visitor, the elderly pair graciously inquire the reason for her visit, in traditional Homeric manner. For this technique of introducing a speech cf. 2.33. 549, 747. *infit:* a Vergilian epic word and in the metrical position preferred by Vergil, but Ovid has removed the larger epic formula with which his predecessor began an epic speech (cf. *Aen.* 5.708 and 10.860).

512–13   *regina deorum:* Juno starts off arrogantly assigning herself a pompous title, something that no doubt was *not* a part of the inquiry. She intends to make much use of her regal status, as in *Aen.* 1.46. Juno was not queen merely in Roman myth; she was also worshipped as *Regina* and had a major temple built in her honor on the Aventine Hill early in the fourth century B.C.E. *aetheriis . . . sedibus hic adsim:* ablative of place from which. The MSS disagree on the prepositional prefix, offering *ad-, ab-,* and *as-.* Although the ablative with *adesse* is rarer than with *abesse,* it is well attested; and the verb *adesse* otherwise seems required by the context and the adverb. *pro me tenet altera caelum:* Juno puts the situation in extremely distorted terms. Callisto has a place as a constellation, a bear deformed by Juno, set in a remote part of the skies, not in Olympus; and she surely has not replaced Juno.

514–
17
mentior . . . nisi: not an epic formula, but taken from colloquial language. Cf. our idiomatic: "Call me a liar if . . . not." In a sense, Juno is lying, because of her hysterical interpretation of the fact of catasterism. *obscurum . . . orbem:* when night makes the world dark. *nuper honorates* 515: there is the lie. *summo, mea vulnera, caelo:* the device of interrupting an adjective-noun unit with an apposition goes back to Neoteric poetry. Ovid uses it flamboyantly here and elsewhere. Juno claims that she has been wounded by the creation of Ursa Major. In fact, we could invert the image and suggest that the Bear testifies to the wounds that Juno has inflicted on Callisto. *ubi . . . ambit* 516–17: "where the outermost circle, smallest in circumference, goes around the farthest point of the axis." Juno's description seems to stress the fact of how far this constellation is removed from Olympus: it does not supplant her.

518–
19
et vero quisquam: amid all the variety in the MSS, this text comes closest to being "the more difficult" and at the same time to alluding to the Vergilian passage to which Ovid here refers. All MSS start with *est.* Then *Harl* and *MN* read *vero quisquam, L, vero quisque,* and *W, vero quis qui.* From this series, it appears that an error at *est* created nonsense, which *L* and *W* try to fix by emending *quisquam,* to set up a proper indirect question. That effort later triggered a major "improvement" in *EFU,* namely *est vero cur quis.* Once we recognize that the source of all the differences is the attempt to deal with the problem caused by *est,* which is a simple early scribal error for *et,* then the reading of the generally reliable *MN Harl* can be adopted. In *Aen.* 1.48, Juno asks rhetorically: *et quisquam numen lunonis adorat | praeterea?* It is typical of Ovid, just as he misused the claim of Juno to be queen at 512 (cf. *Aen.* 1.46), that here he trivializes the angry rhetoric of Vergil's Juno. Ovid's Juno, in a situation with no epic significance, shrilly asks, overusing her spondees: "Would anyone refuse to outrage Juno?"—and then adds the acid comment: "since I alone seem to help by injuring!" *offensamque* 519: although a noun of this type exists, this is the past participle (referring to Juno), and the following relative clause depends on it. *prosum . . . nocendo:* Juno means by this paradox that she has helped Callisto become a star and gain eternal honor by turning her into a bear. Callisto would disagree.

520–
22
o ego: the self-pity is obvious in these opening words. It then shades into heavy irony, as the goddess affects to discredit her efforts and her power. *quam vasta . . . est:* "I certainly have an immense amount

of power!" This insincere rhetoric about *potentia* connects with the tragic theme that earlier focused on the nymph. *facta est dea* 521: another lie. To be made a constellation (cf. 507) hardly equals becoming a goddess; nothing in the narrator's more objective description supports Juno's wild assertion. *sic . . . sic*: effective anaphora. "That's how I punish the guilty; that's how great my power is!" Heavy sarcasm makes the goddess even less appealing.

523–
24

vindicet: subject has to be Jupiter, here and for the next lines. That seemingly sudden shift in turn throws light back on the sarcasm of 520 ff. Juno rages because she believes—or claims to—that Jupiter has acted to rescue his beloved and put her in heaven in her own (Juno's) place. She appropriates the jussive subjunctive to sneer: "Let him go ahead and . . ." The verb and its noun *vindex* had legal and political connotations, quite powerful in the propaganda of the recent Roman Revolution. Jupiter, the angry wife suggests, should act as Callisto's *vindex* or protector and lay claim to her original human form (in all its beauty, of course). Then, he could metamorphose her back from her animal appearance, just as he had done with Io. *Argolica . . . Phoronide* 524: Ovid had invented this special reference to Io at 1.668. This is the last parallel between Callisto and Io that Ovid uses. In every instance, in fact, the story of Callisto is more serious, filled with crueller divine behavior than the story of her predecessor. The rhythm of 524–27 is striking: the four lines alternate between five dactyls and four spondees! Ovid is, I think, exposing the calculated rhetoric of the goddess.

525–
26

cur non et . . . ducit: Juno slightly changes her grammatical forms, but the nasty tone remains the same as with the subjunctive above. The verb is a standard one for marrying. *pulsa . . . Iunone:* ablative absolute, effectively framing the verb that points to Jupiter's marriage to her rival. *socerumque Lycaona sumit* 526: a particularly catty remark, since, as we have seen, Jupiter hated Lycaon and used all his efforts to destroy him.

527–
28

at vos: Juno has at last finished her rhetorical build-up, and she is ready now to appeal directly to her audience, Tethys and Oceanus. *laesae:* her injuries, it is evident, are grossly exaggerated. *contemptus alumnae:* objective genitive. She has suffered scorn, she claims. *gurgite caeruleo* 528: ablative of separation. *Septem . . . triones:* Ovid divides the word, a process called tmesis, to make it metrically tractable. In using this word for the seven stars that form Ursa Major, he takes some liberty. The literal meaning of the word is "the seven plow oxen"; it goes with the conception of the constellation, not as a bear, but as a farming implement, plow, or wagon.

529–
30

sidera: i.e., Callisto (cf. 507). *stupri mercede:* objective genitive and ablative of cause. *stuprum,* a particularly precise word, is what is generally called "unpoetic"; it does not fit the decorum of grand poetry. This is the only place in the *Met.* that it does occur, and that says more about Juno's vitriolic temper than about Ovid's violation of decorum. *ne . . . tingatur* 530: as mentioned earlier, this verb seems chosen to echo that of 459 and remind us of Callisto's banishment from Diana's bath. *paelex:* Juno's last word is that which sprang to her mind earlier (cf. 469, 508). She hates the women that Jupiter dallies with.

THE RAVEN AND THE CROW (531–632)

Ovid drops the continuous theme of the lustful god and his human victim (until Europa at 836 ff.), and he makes his transition from Juno and her winged chariot to a pair of interrelated tales about similar birds: the large, black, and raucous-voiced crow and raven. Adapting an account made famous by Callimachus, he starts with a white raven, favorite of Apollo, who spies on the girl the god loves, observes her in adultery, and flies hurriedly off to inform the god. This initiates a story-motif about informers who are variously punished for their information, whether by the recipient of the news or by the person who is being informed on. Before the raven reaches Apollo, a crow intervenes, learns what is happening, and then tries to deter the raven from its purpose by telling a warning story about itself. It had also seized a chance to spy on, and inform Minerva about, the disobedience of Cecrops' daughters. For this seemingly loyal action, Minerva dismissed her from favor and put in her place the owl Nyctimene, who was notorious for incest with her father. Undeterred by the ominous parallel, the raven spurns all advice, tattles on beloved Coronis, and, when Apollo acts too rashly and causes her death, suffers the principal blame for the disaster. Apollo turns it into a bird of bad omen, with black plumage, as we know it.

Transition from Juno to Raven (531–41)

531–
32
di maris: Tethys and Oceanus. *adnuerant:* they had assented to Juno's request, so that finishes that and allows the narrator quickly to move on. *habili . . . curru:* Saturnian Juno rises from the scene, back up to Olympus, in her handy chariot (which the poet mentions only now because he can make use of it). *pavonibus . . . pictis* 532: since the peacocks draw the chariot, this must be an instrumental ablative, though it seems somewhat awkward in the same clause with ablative *curru.* The key detail is the final one of 532, because the recent change in the plumage of the peacocks offers a parallel to the destined change of the raven.

533–
tam nuper pictis: carefully picks up the final word of 532 and starts

35   a comparison that will unfold over the next lines. For the story of
how Argus was killed and his hundred eyes transferred to the peacock,
cf. 1.715 ff. *quam tu nuper eras . . . versus 534–35:* The correlation,
because not quite exact in either structure or terminology, exposes
the factitious nature of the comparison and Ovid's too clever transition,
no doubt as he wanted. The temporal adverb is repeated, but *pictus*
does not exactly balance *versus*. Both birds experienced a change in
their plumage, one as honor and the other as dishonor. The narrator
apostrophizes his new character, the raven, with undue familiarity
that enables him also to fit *corve loquax* 535 into the opening trihemim-
eral space. *versus in alas:* the Latin says that the raven was turned
into black wings, but Ovid means that the white wings which it already
had turned black.

536–   In the *nam-* clauses, the narrator explains how the raven once was,
39   contrary to all present experience, white. *haec . . . ales:* although the
substantive *ales* commonly is feminine—*avis* is definitely feminine—
it does not have to be. Thus, in the very next occurrence of the word,
544–45, the same *ales* becomes masculine. *corvus,* as masculine noun,
would tend to make *ales* masculine too. However, in 536–37, Ovid
not only teases his audience by the long hyperbaton, as if introducing
a new character, but he also uses the new gender to facilitate the
metrical employment of *argentea. niveis . . . pennis:* ablative of re-
spect with *argentea. ut aequaret . . . nec . . . cederet* (537–39): first
in a positive form, then a negative, Ovid compares the white raven
to unblemished doves, geese, and swans. By postponing the verb
cederet and the key noun *anseribus,* he makes 538 a problem for the
erudite audience. In spite of the obvious anachronism, the Roman
audience is supposed to appreciate an allusion to the famous geese
whose loud quacking awoke the sleeping soldiers on the Capitoline
Hill and alerted them to the attack of the Gauls in the early fourth
century B.C.E.

540–   *damno:* dative of purpose. *lingua . . . loquaci:* ablative absolute;
41   "because the tongue acted so talkatively." Notice the two different
forms of the same word (*lingua*) in one line, as often in Ovid. In 541,
dividing the line at the central caesura, the poet captures the contrast
between past and present, white and its opposite.

The Crow Warns the Raven against Informing (542–65)

542–   Bömer calls attention to the artful word order in 542–43: the arrange-
44   ment of *pulchrior . . . Coronis* to frame 542, of *tota . . . Haemonia*
to mark the central caesurae in both lines. *Larissaea:* ever since
Hesiod, Coronis was traditionally assigned to Thessalia, of which
Larissa is a principal city. *placuit* 543: as we saw in 475, "pleasing"

a deity has the obvious meaning of sexual pleasure for a lustful god. That was how Juno accused Callisto. Apollodorus 3.10. 3.6 gives much the same account of Coronis, except to suggest that she was not unchaste, but obeying her father's wishes. Hyginus 202 agrees that she was guilty. The name of the other man was Ischys. *tibi Delphice:* the vocative is unduly familiar, as Ovid starts to undermine the deity, and also metrically helpful. *inobservata* 544: this negative compound was invented by Ovid and used three times, probably here first in this witty manner. Affecting to give two exclusive alternatives, the poet compares chastity to being undetected, as though both were on the same ethical level.

544–   *ales . . . Phoebeius:* for the gender, cf. 537. The raven was considered
47   the emblematic bird of Apollo, as the owl was for Minerva, and it possessed augural significance. Later, at 5.329, Ovid reports that the god chose to take the form of raven to escape from Typhoeus. Hyginus declares that Apollo had set the raven as guard (*custos*) over the pregnant Coronis, but Ovid more interestingly suggests that the bird was a self-appointed spy. *sensit* 545: same verb and context as in 466. *adulterium:* again, as in Juno's abuse of 471, a biased term. Apollo has not married Coronis, only selfishly appropriated her. *non exorabilis* 546: Horace had earlier produced this collocation for the same metrical position in *Epist.* 2.2.179. In 5.244, Ovid manages the single word *inexorabile*. *index:* the role, motivation, and frequent punishment of the informer become basic themes of the poem from this point. Later, in the story of Aglauros (especially, 797 ff.), Ovid shows how envy frequently distorts the purpose of apparent helpfulness. In Book 3, both the Sun and Clytie are punished for self-righteous interference in "adultery." There is no implication that Coronis tried to dissuade the raven (as later thievish Mercury tries with Battus, 692 ff.); the adjective suggests the rigidity that will make the bird spurn the warning of the crow. *dominum:* Apollo.

547–   *quem:* the raven. *garrula . . . cornix:* wide hyperbaton, to collect
50   details about the crow before identifying it. It is notoriously noisy, hence talkative; that trait helps to link these birds. *consequitur:* "catches up with." Alliteration with the delayed *cornix* to frame the line. *viae causa* 549: cf. above, 511. *carpis . . . iter:* Ovid likes to use this verb with this object or similar words, such as *viam* (cf. 3.12) or *aera* (cf. 4.616). *ne sperne* 550: the raven does indeed spurn this warning: cf. 597. *praesagia:* first attested use of this word in Latin. Ovid has it five times in the *Met.* and four times in later poems.

551–   The indirect questions invite the raven and audience to consider the
52   essential change in the crow, as though it had been metamorphosed. But color of plumage has no relevance to the crow's fate. It has been demoted from its position of honor, as it predicts will happen to the

raven. *meritum:* literally, what is deserved. As it will say later (562),
the crow received a "reward" that it in no way expected, namely,
punishment. Or, put in the ironic manner of 552, loyalty has hurt it.

552–
56
With the *nam-* clause and the pluperfect tenses, the crow lays the
background for its disaster. *tempore quodam:* a filler for a temporal
adverb like *olim. Ericthonium:* as the apposition indicates, he was
generated without a mother, but all the piquant details are ignored.
The audience was familiar with the fuller story, which may be found
in Apollodorus 3.14.6 and Hyginus 166. For several possible reasons
(abandoned by Venus, instigated by Poseidon), Vulcan passionately
desired to mate with Minerva. When she came to his forge to ask
him to make her some weapons, he started to pursue her. But she,
being a determined virgin, was able to elude him, especially since he
was lame. In the heat of his passionate pursuit, he ejaculated. When
some semen landed on her leg, she disgustedly rubbed it off with
some wool, which she then threw to the ground. The earth provided
some of the maternal functions, and so Ericthonius came into being.
Once that happened, Minerva took special interest in him. She placed
the baby in a chest and entrusted that to the care of the three daughters
of Cecrops of Athens, with express orders that they should never open
it. One of them conspired secretly to open the forbidden container, and,
when she did, discovered the baby and a snake stretched beside him. The
trouble was, that the spying crow observed not only her disobedience but
also the forbidden sight that she witnessed. So, although the crow claims
to have been punished for his loyalty (552), in fact he suffers for uninten-
tional *dis*-loyalty, having seen a secret of Minerva that is forbidden to
all, friends and enemies alike. *Actaeo* 554: Attic, a detail that situates
the episode in Athens. *gemino . . . Cecrope* 555: Cecrops had a human
torso and snake's coil for his lower body. His three daughters are named
in 559–60. The structure of the clause in this line indicates that Minerva
entrusted the baby (accusative *Ericthonium* functions as first object of
dederat 556) to the girls. *et legem* 556: second object of *dederat,* with
the indirect command: *ne . . . viderent.*

557–
61
abdita: modifies the first-person subject, the crow-narrator, who now
returns to herself after the background. She is hidden and spying,
with no authorization either (like the raven in 545), so she will not
be a welcome *index* to Minerva. *commissa* 558: we could merely call
this a poetic plural used for metrical convenience; but Ovid may also
be reminding us that more than one item has in fact been entrusted
to the girls: the chest and, unbeknownst to them, a baby. Here the
narration moves into the present tense. *una* 559: when in stories there
are three siblings or three members of a family or three deeds to
perform, it is regularly the third that has the special interest. Punish-
ment for Aglauros is postponed until 748 ff. In other versions, all

three disobey, and all are quickly destroyed, by Minerva or the snake. *nodosque . . . diducit* 560: the chest was a woven basket and apparently closed by knotted ropes. Aglauros opens it by undoing the knots. *et intus:* Ovid creates unorthodox enjambement beginning in the middle of the fifth foot. The result is suspense followed by the surprise of 561, an unusual four-word hexameter consisting of the expected baby and the unexpected snake. *adporrectumque* 561: this word, invented for this passage and never used again by Ovid or any Latin writer, emphasizes the surprise of the second, monstrous sight in the basket.

562–65   *acta deae refero:* the crow wastes no time explaining her action as informer. *gratia talis . . . ut dicar:* subjunctive in result clause. The crow does not understand Minerva's hostility to herself, expecting gratitude. *tutela:* ablative of separation with *pulsa. noctis avem* 564: the owl, well-known symbol of Athenian coinage and of the wisdom of Minerva/Athena. Whether or not the crow ever was a favorite of the goddess before the owl, this story accounts for the observable hostility between crows and owls, about which Aristotle was the first to leave comments. Crows are day birds and robbers, stealing the eggs of owls by day when the latter, being night birds, are sleeping (*Hist. An.* 9, p. 609a 8). *admonuisse* 565: perfect for present. The crow has assumed the role of warner; her warning can be ignored only with great risk. "Don't court danger by speech" means: don't tell tales on others, don't be an informer; but it sounds more like: loose talk costs lives, especially that of the talkative (*loquax;* cf. 535, 540).

How the Crow Became a Favorite of Minerva (566–95)

Although the warning has concluded and the crow could now let the raven respond to her advice, she is still too talkative; and she insists on continuing with an apparently otiose account of how Minerva chose her as her favorite bird. It is another story of rape attempted, this time by Neptune, and frustrated by the intervention of virginal Minerva on behalf of the would-be virgin. By changing the girl into a bird, the goddess effected her escape. Her interference, about which the crow entertains some legitimate doubts, may also reflect her traditional rivalry with Neptune, which came to a head in their dispute over major status in Athens. Having narrated that episode (566–88), the crow then appends some nasty gossip about the origins of the owl who, she claims, was once an incestuous daughter and escaped from daylight and public condemnation through her metamorphosis. We end up with a negative impression, I think, of all three characters involved: the goddess and her two bird-favorites.

566–
68
at, puto . . . me petiit: "But, I suppose you'll say, she did not seek me [for her companion] of her own accord, when I had no such idea in mind." The transition here, which I translate according to my interpretation, seems designed to justify the crow's feeling of disappointment in the goddess. She did not ask to be companion of Minerva, she now proposes to show, and it follows that she has done nothing to deserve losing the status of companion. However, the crow has missed the point. Nobody can safely see divine secrets. *nec quicquam:* a variant in *NU, nequiquam,* is tempting, but, in spite of its Vergilian and Ovidian pathos, is not pertinent to this context. *petiit* 567: the third syllable counts as naturally long. *ipsa:* the scansion tells us that this is ablative with *Pallade*. The unusual form of *petiit* and the expectation that the demonstrative would refer to the subject of *quaeras* led to a number of corruptions in the MSS. But the crow is addressing its audience (the raven) and inviting it to check with Minerva herself, who will back up her claim that she became without asking a companion of the goddess. *quamvis irata est* 568: for the indicative with *quamvis,* cf. 1.686 n.

569–
71
In the *nam*-clauses, the loquacious crow starts to prattle about her origins. She was, of course, of distinguished, even royal birth and so, when she became nubile, she was wooed by the cream of Greek society. *Phocaica:* Ovid invented this adjective for Phocis here. *Coroneus:* Ovid seems also to have invented this character; and indeed he may have invented this whole long-winded crow's story of her human origins. Hence, the ironic humor of *nota loquor* 570, the parenthetical comment with which the crow clamors for our respect. As the Roman audience knew, Greek for *cornix* is *korônê.* So Ovid imagines a girl Corone, daughter of King Coroneus. This is particularly confusing, because, as we recall, the raven prattles about Coronis. The crow's volubility gains emphasis from the five dactyls in 570. *procis . . . petebar* 571: although this is the first Ovidian use of the noun for suitors (cf. 4.795), Ovid already used the basic story pattern of the princess with many seeking her hand (cf. 1.479 ff.), familiar in German as well as Greek myth. The second parenthesis in two lines continues the characterization of anxious garrulity.

572–
77
forma mihi nocuit: the way that form injures has become a fundamental theme of the poem. Ovid has shown how beauty frustrates the virgin's wishes, from the story of Daphne to that of Callisto. Corone's beauty, like Callisto's, rouses a god's lust. *per litora:* it is easy enough to imagine a girl walking idly along the sand at the seashore, especially today, but Ovid makes it somewhat difficult to picture Corone doing this in Phocis, the place she claims as home. Traditionally, except when it warred to control the region around Delphi, Phocis was landlocked. It cannot be the shore of a lake or a river bank, because the

sea-god appears at 574 as would-be rapist. Alliterations in 574 and 575 are notable. *vidit et incaluit* 574: a quick, witty sketch of love at first sight. Ovid reuses it for Echo's passion on seeing Narcissus; cf. 3.371. More dactyls in this line make Corone seem very wordy. *precando . . . verbis:* another stereotype: Neptune tries courting, then decides that it is a waste of words. The paradigm here is Apollo with Daphne. However, there the girl made it clear that words were useless by running away and leaving the speaking deity flat. Here, Corone mentions flight only after the god decides to try rape. Did she listen to a long spiel, or did she weary the god by her loquacious replies? *sequitur; fugio* 576: effective use of the caesura to divide the correlative actions of pursuit and flight, a typical amatory pattern. *in molli . . . harena* 577: Ovid devises a unique setting for the rapist's pursuit. Running through the sand, because it is so soft and lacks traction, is exhausting, and Corone soon is helpless. The rhythm of 577 uses successive spondees to give that sense of struggle with the sand.

578–81   *deos hominesque voco:* the rapist's victim typically invokes the help of her family (as Daphne did) and of the gods. The latter source has not proven helpful so far, since a major deity has been intent on rape. This case proves an exception when no human being responds, but a goddess does. *pro virgine virgo* 579: Minerva (the *virgo*) preserves the essential virgin's personality at the expense of her dangerous beauty. *tendebam bracchia . . . bracchia coeperunt* 580–81: Ovid's audience has heard exactly these words, in identical metrical position, at 477–78, as Callisto suffered her metamorphosis from angry Juno. Minerva acting from concern takes the prayer gesture and makes it the beginning of escape by flight. The crow does not say that she actually saw or heard Minerva, and her reaction to the metamorphosis seems to have been one of shock and dismay at first. She felt the transformation of her beautiful arms to be a deformation. But crow's wings seem less horrible than shaggy bear's forefeet.

582–83   *reicere . . . vestem:* Ovid uses this collocation once again, at 9.32, and it might be thought to illuminate this passage, but it does not. There, in preparation for a wrestling match with Hercules, Achelous strips. Corone is doing nothing of the sort. She is throwing off her upper robe so as to beat her bare breast in grief and dismay. The verb in this situation is usually "pull apart" (*diducere*) or "rip" (*scindere*). Cf. the action of despairing Narcissus in 3.480–81. This response of the girl to metamorphosis shows indeed that she did not exactly welcome it. *molibar:* Ovid treats this verb as deponent, along with most Latin writers, except in present infinitive (which he makes *molire*). *inque cutem radices* 583: the description suggests that Corone met only frustration and agonizing pain when she struggled to throw off the now-rooted dress.

584–
85   Ovid regularly contrives triple alliteration with *p* when describing the
        beating of bare breasts: the repeated plosives suggest the actual sound
        of beating, but the effect on the audience seems often to be humorous.
        In this couplet, he sets up the intention in the first line and frustration
        in the second, the result of metamorphosis. Just as we start imagining
        the bared body, we discover, with Corone, that she does not have the
        human body to carry out her purpose.

586–   *currebam:* Ovid reverts to the earlier description of her arduous flight
88   (cf. 576–77). The sand now offers no resistance at all, because she
        no longer runs through it, but above it, in the air. She has taken off.
        summa . . . humo 587: ablative of place from which. *tollebar:* same
        verb as that which recorded the catasterism of Callisto in 506. Here,
        the "helpful" intervention of Minerva can be regarded, from the human
        perspective of Corone and Ovid's audience, as rather inept. *evehor*
        588: a second passive verb conveys the girl's lack of free choice. All
        this happens to her. *data sum comes:* a final passive to describe her
        involuntary role as companion. *inculpata:* Ovid invented this word
        here for special emphasis; he reuses it in 9.673. The crow insists that
        she was blameless when taken into Minerva's band; her virginity was
        intact. The adjective bears also on her sense of injured innocence in
        two respects: she protests the "reward" that her loyalty has received,
        and she particularly protests the fact that she has been replaced by a
        girl-turned-owl whose human past was definitely not blameless.

589–   *diro facta volucris / crimine:* the metamorphosis of her rival was the
90   result of a dreadful crime. That raises grave objections in the human
        sensibility about the fairness and ethical judgment of Minerva. How
        could the goddess replace Corone/crow with such a bird? *Nyctimene:*
        according to Corone's story in 591–95, she lived on Lesbos and was
        guilty of aggressive incest with her father, for which she subsequently
        felt shame, remorse, and public disgrace. Hyginus 204 tells the tale
        differently, making her the victim of her father's lust and the object
        of Minerva's pity, too. Since incest commonly originates from an
        older male relative, we might be inclined to trust Hyginus' version
        and be cautious about Corone's. Remember, it is she, not Ovid, that
        voices this pejorative interpretation of Nyctimene; and she has obvious
        reasons for bias. Thus, we are left in ambiguity about this situation:
        although Nyctimene has been harshly blamed, she may not have been
        blameworthy.

591–   *res . . . notissima:* the talkative crow has previously (570) insisted
95   that what she reported was common knowledge—and there she was
        telling a tale that Ovid may well have invented. Here, too, her insis-
        tence on the total familiarity of her facts may ironically mask her
        bias. She pounds home her assurance with four straight spondees in
        591. *patrium temerasse cubile* 592: Corone assigns the blame for the

incest to her rival. *conscia culpae* 593: we may contrast this full awareness of fault in the owl with the crow's confidence in faultlessness (cf. 588). *conspectum* 594: the sight of others. *lucemque fugit:* everybody knows that owls are night birds. The name of Nyctimene, in Greek, suggests one who inhabits the night. *a cunctis expellitur* 595: from another point of view, the owl has become a night bird because "everybody" is agreed on barring it from the bright pure air of daytime. *aethere toto:* ablative of separation. The bitter crow suggests that Nyctimene has changed into an owl as the result of universal repulsion. Her sense of shame has supposedly effected the metamorphosis. The crow cannot know what she asserts here. Hyginus' version credits Minerva with the change: she acted in pity for the girl's unmerited self-disgust.

The Ruinous Results of the Raven's Informing (596–632)

Unimpressed by the crow's warning, the raven proceeds on its flight and delivers its baneful information. First, Apollo felt the typical lover's dismay; then, overwhelmed by anger against Coronis, he thoughtlessly shot an arrow at her that fatally wounded her. So he plunged into remorse and blamed himself and all his archery equipment and the informing bird. Ovid wastes no sympathy on this foolish god, who should have known better. But we do not pity the bird either when its plumage turns black. It is now a fitting companion for the crow, a disgraced informer, with plumage that symbolizes behavior that the ancients associated with blackness.

596–
97

talia dicenti: Ovid uses this nonepic participial clause to achieve a swift close of the crow's long speech. *tibi . . . malo:* double dative. The two words frame the sentence. *revocamina* 596: Ovid invented this noun and used it in three different works, once only. No later writer picked it up. It helps to increase the feel of contemptuous rejection in the raven. "All your efforts to call me back I pray will bring you trouble." *vanum spernimus omen* 597: the verb picks up the crow's opening remark at 550. The "vanity" of the omen serves to characterize the stubborn egotism of the raven.

598–
99

iter dominoque: these words echo 547. What the raven reports is summarized by *adulterium* (545).

600–
602

laurea: the laurel was the standard attribute of Apollo, but in this poem it has somewhat dubious associations, being connected with another female victim of the god, Daphne. *audito crimine:* ablative absolute. *amanti:* dative of separation. All MSS give the genitive form, which Heinsius brilliantly emended. For Ovid, the "lover" who needs studying is the inadequate and selfish Apollo (cf. 612). In what follows, the low quality of Apollo's love emerges. *et pariter . . . excidit* 601–2: three subjects, emphasized as a group by the adverb, are listed with this singular verb, to produce a striking instance of zeugma. Face, plectrum, and natural color all fall together! The wit is at the expense of Apollo's dignity and his inept pose as an elegiac lover. *deo* 601: dative of reference. *tumida . . . ira* 602: the god swells with anger, as Juno had at 508, and launches into deadly and reprehensible vengeance.

603– *arma adsueta:* bow and arrow, as the sequel shows. *flexumque . . .*
5   *arcum / tendit:* English style would make the participle a coordinate verb; "he pulls on and bends the bow from its tips." Plainly, he has an arrow in the bow and pulls on that, but Ovid leaves that implicit until the carefully delayed final word of 605. *illa . . . iuncta . . . pectora:* planned hyperbaton. *indevitato:* Ovid has planted this word here with multiple stylistic and tonal effect. First, he has created it for this context; it will never again occur in writing by him or anyone. Second, it starts a succession of four spondees. And third, it initiates a four-word hexameter. The slow rhythm, the striking word, the emphasis on inevitability, and the fact that the god ruthlessly and selfishly kills the woman who has given him so much love add up negatively for Apollo.

606– *icta:* i.e., Coronis. The participle picks up *traiecit* (605). *tractoque*
9   *. . . ferro:* a standard reaction of a wounded person; cf. 4.120, 6.251–53. In the statue-group of the Niobids, who were victims of the archery of Apollo and Diana, many of the dying are reaching to pull out the agonizing arrows. *candida puniceo* 607: with this careful juxtaposition of white and red, Ovid builds a line that is also Golden and effectively alliterative. All the chosen details of this scene incline us toward the human victim. Her crime, if it was such, has little bearing now in the perspective of this intolerable divine crime. Coronis' last words in 608–9 avoid all self-pity, but gently and powerfully rebuke the god for killing his baby as well as her. *duo nunc moriemur in una* 609: "two of us—mother and baby—die in one [i.e., me]." Bömer points to the similar statement by dying Narcissus at 3.473, about himself and his reflection perishing together. Ovid alludes to the theme of union, in love and friendship, of two separate individuals. As Narcissus and later Pyramus and Thisbe in 4.151 ff. show; as Horace's similar response to Maecenas' gloomy thoughts of dying in *C.* 217 and the imminent dangers of Vergil at sea (1.3.8) emphasizes, the lover/friend is one's other half, without whom one is incomplete, with whom one wants, needs to share even death. Here in 609, Ovid twists the theme significantly. The self-styled "lover" Apollo, instead of dying with his beloved, kills the two whom he should love simultaneously.

610– *pariter vitam cum sanguine fudit:* at 463 and 470, Ovid used the

11   construction of accusative direct object and ablative of accompaniment
as a metrically convenient variant for a double object to achieve
"virtual zeugma." Here, the poet reinforces the effect with the adverb
pariter (cf. 505 and 601). In most instances, Ovid contents himself
with a conclusion such as that of 610. Here, however, to emphasize
the pathos of the victim, he adds an epic-sounding line about the cold
that invades the corpse. Cf. the final two lines of the *Aeneid* and their
concentration on the cold corpse and angry spirit of dead Turnus.
animae: genitive with adjective *inane;* "void of spirit."

612–   *heu sero:* Apollo wallows in self-pity, but the true victim is Coronis.
13   *poenae crudelis:* in normal fashion, *paenitet* takes accusative of the
person involved and genitive of the thing that is regretted. The adjective
belongs to the thoughts of both narrator and of Apollo (though the
god uses it less honestly). *quod audierit . . . sic exarserit* 613: perfect
subjunctive in causal clauses. The question is: do the subjunctives
carry any special nuance or not? Some think not. I note that Apollo's
self-hatred and -blame end with this single line. Accordingly, Ovid
may slyly indicate that the god loudly emotes with words of self-
reproach, but then quickly moves on to words and acts that betray
his real feelings, his need to pin the blame on others. So he is just
saying things in 613 to be heard.

614–   *odit avem:* the verb, repeated in enjambement, marks the transition
16   from self- to other-hatred. Apollo hates the informer, as the crow
predicted. *arcumque manumque* 615: as though the inanimate bow
were guilty and his hand belonged to someone else, Apollo invents
culprits for his own act of murderous jealousy. *temeraria tela* 616:
an apposition placed before its noun. The god personifies the arrows,
so that he may more easily blame them.

617–   *conlapsamque fovet:* having recognized and regretted his long-range
18   archery, Apollo now has apparently come down to the corpse and too
late shown some love. *seraque ope:* echoes *sero* (612). *vincere fata:*
Apollo tries to overcome death. In only a few myths does a mortal
come back from death, and Coronis is not one of those few. But her
son, Aesculapius is so privileged; cf. below 648. *medicas . . . artes*
618: Apollo Medicus, protector and supporter of doctors, was familiar
to the Roman audience. But the doctor-lover fails to find the medical
skill to revive Coronis.

619–   *quae:* neuter plural, referring to the three actions of 617–18. *temptata*
23   *[esse] . . . parari . . . arsuros [esse]:* indicative statements, all with
sensit. The funeral preparations prove that the girl is really dead, and
the god has to realize that her once-loved body will be consumed in
fire. *gemitus* 621: Ovid is going to draw a parallel between the groans
of the god and those of a sorrowing cow. For the common capacity
to groan among mortals and beasts, cf. Callisto as a bear at 486. In

the parenthetical remark of 621–22, the narrator comments that Apollo can exhibit his feelings only by groans; he is barred from weeping. The tearless nature of the gods often receives Ovid's comment, most often when we would expect a god to show sympathy with human troubles. In the *Hippolytus* of Euripides, Artemis cannot weep for her dying favorite, the hunter Hippolytus. Ovid has twisted the motif, to reflect on the egoist Apollo, who cannot weep to show his own sense of loss.

623– As if he intended to express his respect for the god's groans, Ovid
25 launches into a simile, which has the superficial markings of an epic device. However, the comparison emerges in a nonparallel fashion: Apollo's groans (over the dead girl) are like the occasion when a young bull is sacrificed at the altar in the sight of a young cow (who then presumably bellows her grief). Each half of the comparison lacks an element that would complete the balance. It seems evident that Ovid has deliberately altered a traditional simile for a mother's grief, in which the human mother is likened to a mother cow whose young has been slain at the altar. He develops such an image in *Fast.* 4.459 ff., to portray the feelings of Ceres when her daughter Proserpina is kidnapped; and that picture in turn is based on a scene in Lucretius 2.352 ff. about a mother cow. By changing the grieving, groaning animal from a mother to a cow of the same age as the victim, Ovid suggests the possibility of an erotic element in the grief. The two animals are just approaching the mating stage perhaps and are already playmates. So although the sexes have been reversed, to fit the simple fact that males were the standard sacrificial victims, the young cow has something in common with Apollo. But she threatens the seeming epic seriousness of the context with her lovesick sounds. Moreover, whereas the cow stands by as an innocent, suffering spectator, while the cruel sacrifice (the smashing of the young bull's head by the hammer 624–25) takes place, Apollo cannot claim to have been an idle spectator. He has been the perpetrator of Coronis' death, which, though he is a deity, was far from divine sacrifice. In the end, I think, the suffering of the cow tends to downgrade the trivial grief of the god. *dextra libratus ab aure* 624: the hammer was lifted in the right hand and poised at the right ear before the attendant brought it down hard on the skull of the animal, felling it. As Bömer correctly notes, this description is typical of anyone, mortal or god, who prepares to make a heavy stroke or throw a weapon. Cf. the similar language for Jupiter poised to hurl the thunderbolt in 2.311. Many statues show gods and warriors in this pose. Note the long delay of the noun *malleus* and the alliteration with *c* and *t* (brought together in final *ictu*) in 625. Might the sound suggest the cracking of the skull?

626– *ingratos . . . odores:* Bömer argues that Ovid means to transfer the

27   epithet to *pectora,* and he cites this adjective in connection with
      amatory situations such as 2.488. However, Ovid views Coronis as
      a victim; Apollo is the ungrateful lover and killer, and his offering
      of incense is indeed ungrateful. *in pectora fudit:* Apollo pours scent
      on the breast that his arrow has pierced. *iniustaque iusta peregit* 627:
      a strikingly self-contradictory phrase or oxymoron contrived by Ovid,
      to emphasize that Apollo performs the rites, but that the very funeral
      arises from his injustice. Therefore, his ritual acts are flawed; he is
      an impious, subhuman deity like the others.

628– *in cineres . . . semina:* the infinitive clause functions as the object of
30   *non tulit.* Ovid briefly moves to the miraculous birth of Apollo's son
      Aesculapius. With the mother dead and on the pyre, the father acts
      fast to save the child. The details closely parallel those in the earliest
      known version of Pindar, *Pyth.* 3.40 ff. *flammis uteroque parentis /
      eripuit* 630: zeugma of ablative pair. *geminique:* as a centaur, Chiron
      is both human and animal. He is the teacher, in his cave, of many
      demigods, such as Achilles.

631– The long-awaited punishment of the raven, already foreshadowed at
32   614, now takes place to bring the story full circle back to its starting
      point. *sperantemque . . . praemia:* the raven is as surprised by the
      god's displeasure as the crow was. *inter aves albas* 632: Ovid has
      earlier listed the series of white birds with which the proto-raven could
      vie (537–39). Now, it cannot find a place (*consistere*) with them
      because it has indeed become a true raven—emphatic final word—
      and black. The changed alliteration after *vetuit* further stresses the
      metamorphosis.

CHIRON'S DAUGHTER OCYROE (633–75)

      Having disposed of the raven, Ovid returns to the baby of Coronis
      and Apollo, whom he still does not name. Chiron duly starts to raise
      the child. A visit from his daughter Ocyroe, who has uncanny prophetic
      powers, leads to a rash of predictions: about the greatness of
      Aesculapius as a doctor and his death from the thunderbolt of angry
      Jupiter; about her father's painful effort to be allowed to die to escape
      the agony of a snake bite; about her own destiny—which overtakes
      her before she can foretell it—to be turned into a mare.

633– *Semifer:* the centaur Chiron. This word has been used, by Vergil, to
34   refer to a variety of half-human monsters, such as Cacus or a Triton.
      Ovid restricts it to centaurs (also, at 12.406). *interea:* after the details
      of 631–32, the narrator reminds us of where he left off, at 630. *divinae
      stirpis alumno:* more "epic" language, circumlocution for the divine
      baby entrusted to Chiron to bring up. The imperfect tenses indicate

background. *mixtoque oneri . . . honore* 634: dative with participle *mixto*. If the meter had permitted, a simple pair of ablative nouns connected by *et* or *-que* would have done the job. Chiron has taken on an honor and a responsibility. Ovid also puns on the sounds of *honos* and *onus*.

635–
39   *ecce:* dramatic entrance of a new character and change of tenses. *rutilis . . . capillis:* Ovid picks out a vivid detail for a young girl, long reddish hair covering her shoulders. Like other heroines, she lets her hair flow freely. But it serves more than a picturesque purpose. When Ocyroe turns into a mare, a key aspect of the transformation will be the loose hair that becomes her mane (cf. 673–74). *nympha Chariclo* 636: centaurs mate, or try to, with human beings. Hence, their progeny is human in form, not half-horse. The nymph, to judge from her habitat near water and the name she chose for her baby, may have been a naiad. *fluminis . . . rapidi . . . Ocyroen* 637–38: the name, which means "swiftly flowing", was apparently suggested by the place of her birth. *artes . . . paternas:* Chiron was the great educator, promoter of culture and civilized skills. His daughter cultivated a skill that was available and honorable for women, prophecy. *fatorum arcana* 639: the phrase comes from *Aen.* 1.262 (same metrical position); Ovid makes a show of epic diction for this unepic situation.

640–
41   *vaticinos . . . furores:* the adjective looks like an epic compound, but it has never been seen before, and Ovid uses it only here. Madness and prophecy go together in literary descriptions. Vergil's presentation of the Sibyl in *Aen.* 6.98 ff. is a familiar example. Perhaps even better is a passage of Cicero, where the source of this adjective also emerges: *vaticinantibus per furorem* (*Div.* 1.18.34). *incaluitque deo* 641: Ovid likes this verb (cf. 87, 175, 574) for heated emotions. *deo:* unusual instrumental ablative; no particular god is meant. As the relative clause insists, she has her own personal deity inside.

642–
46   *infantem:* now begins the prophecy to and about Aesculapius (642–48). For sources, see Apollodoros 3.10.3.7 and Hyginus 49. *salutifer orbi:* Ocyroe hails the baby as the "savior of the world," as if in parody of the enthusiasm with which Vergil hailed the "divine" baby in *Ecl.* 4. A few years later, and it would be tempting to compare this with the treatment of baby Jesus. Ovid has invented this epithet earlier in *Her.* 20.174, but, except for that passage, he uses it exclusively for Aesculapius in the *Met.*, namely, here and in 15.632 and 744, where he describes the transferral of the god from Epidauros to the Tiber Island in Rome. *cresce* 643: "grow up." *tibi . . . debebunt* 644: Aesculapius, the supreme doctor, cured many human ills. *animas . . . reddere ademptas:* Aesculapius brought the dead back to life (thus violating the harsh rules of nature). Ovid, however, has contrived a clever play on words with this clause. Simple *anim-am, -as reddere*

conventionally means "to die" by giving back the soul to the gods or nature. Cf. 8.505 or *Fast.* 6.745. The latter passage is particularly significant: after Hippolytus has "given back his soul," Aesculapius intervenes and restores him to Diana. The sudden addition of *ademptas* completely reverses the sense here. *idque semel . . . ausus* 645: the single instance of resuscitation is the case of dead Hippolytus, which Ovid briefly covers in the passage cited above from *Fast.* 6.745 ff., and more extensively in a story narrated by once-dead Hippolytus, now Virbius ("twice a man") in *Met.* 15.497 ff. The gods resented the fact that Aesculapius had done a favor to one individual, bribed by Diana, when so many sons of gods had been allowed to die in the past. *posse dare hoc iterum* 646: "to be able to give this again"; instead of a subjunctive clause introduced by *ne* or *"quominus,* as our Latin grammars recommend, Ovid uses an infinitive clause with *prohibebere.* That verb form is very unusual in verse, and Ovid fits it only by allowing himself elision in the fifth foot (not customary). *flamma . . . avita:* more games for the erudite audience to play. Assuming that they figure out the one occasion when a human being was revived, they will decipher the reference to Aesculapius' grandfather (Jupiter, father of Apollo), who uses the flame of his thunderbolt to kill the savior of the world.

647–
48
eque deo: Aesculapius was not a full god like his father, but he had special privileges and powers. If a full god, he could not have been killed. *corpus . . . exsangue:* a bloodless corpse, after being struck by the thunderbolt. Same phrase for a dying person in 4.244. *deusque . . . corpus:* careful positioning of both words, to emphasize the dramatic reversal. *bis tua fata novabis:* this is the first time, of many, that Ovid uses this verb in the poem to refer to metamorphosis. It means "make new" (but not "renew") something that previously existed, here "fate." Translating it as "change" gives the easiest sense. Thus, Aesculapius changed first from god to corpse, then from corpse back to god. For *novus* and newness as part of the total thematics of change in the poem, cf. note at 1.437.

649–
50
care pater: Ocyroe now turns to Chiron and launches on her second prophecy (649–54). She links Chiron with Aesculapius, in that both are "gods" and immortal, yet both will die. However, as she points out in 651, Chiron will want to die and be frustrated by his condition of immortality. *inmortalis:* surprisingly, this is the sole instance of this word in all Ovid's poetry. *et aevis / omnibus ut maneas:* purpose clause precedes the participle *creatus* on which it depends. The ablative is a loose grammatical variant for *aevum per omne.* Chiron was unique among the Centaurs in possessing immortality, being the son of Jupiter and Philyra (cf. below 676).

651–
posse mori: the double infinitive construction creates a contrast with

52   Aesculapius' situation in 646. The form of *cruciabere* also echoes
        the verb of 646. *sanguine serpentis* 652: on Chiron's painful wound,
        see Apollodoros 2.5.4.4. He was with some rowdy Centaurs when
        Hercules attacked them. A poisoned arrow pierced the arm of one of
        them, Elatos, and went through, ending up in Chiron's leg. Chiron
        suffered terrible agony, but could not overcome his immortality. Even-
        tually, he was able to strike a bargain with Jupiter, to exchange his
        immortality for the mortality of Hercules; and thus he could finally
        die. Note the hissing alliteration in 652.

653–   *ex aeterno:* parallel with *eque deo* 647. Chiron will change from an
54   immortal to a mortal (*patientem . . . mortis*). *mortis:* objective geni-
        tive. *triplicesque deae* 654: the three Fates, goddesses over the length
        of life.

655–   *restabat fatis:* Ocyroe begins a third prophecy, about herself, but it
56   is swallowed up by her metamorphosis, as she loses the power of
        speech. Deep sighs and dripping tears melodramatically insist on
        pathos. *lacrimae . . . obortae* 656: standard Ovidian phrase for weep-
        ing (cf. 1.350). *genis:* ablative of place from which. The tears are
        streaming down and falling from the cheeks.

657–   *atque ita:* unepic opening of speech. *praevertunt:* Ovid uses this
58   prosaic verb only here in all his poetry. Bömer infers that he is thereby
        straining to achieve the heights of hymnic style. On the contrary,
        he aims to point up the grotesque and to use a verb that hints at
        metamorphosis: she is being "prevented" because she is being
        "changed ahead of time." *plura loqui* 658: part of the cruelty of some
        changes consists in the deliberate silencing of human speech at a
        desperate moment of needed communication. Juno frustrated Callisto's
        efforts to speak her prayers (cf. 482–83). Here, the silencing of the
        prophetess by metamorphosis keeps a thematic link with earlier "in-
        formers," the birds who were disgraced, and the next "informers,"
        Battus and Aglauros. *praecluditur:* again, as with *praevertunt*, Ovid
        has chosen a nonpoetic, commonplace word, in order to make special
        use of its prefix (cf. *vertor* 663). Ocyroe does not indicate what agency
        effects the change. In 677–78, however, we hear that the commands
        of Jupiter have operated.

659–   *tanti:* genitive of price. *contraxere* 660: perfect indicative in ordinary
60   clause of fact. Her skills have concentrated the god's wrath on her.

661–   The repeated *iam* emphasizes the sensation of progressive change.
64   *subduci:* "to be withdrawn, stolen, undermined." Ovid uses this com-
        mon verb, for the process of change, only here. In the paired clauses
        of 662, the girl imagines stages of her change into a mare (*equam*)
        while still possessing speech to describe it. *cognataque corpora* 663:
        alliteration enhances the clever allusion to the fact (elaborated in 664)
        that, as daughter of a centaur, she is "related" to the horse-family.

She protests: why must I be changed into an entire horse? *biformis* 664: this compound, used by Vergil of the Minotaur and Horace (not so seriously) of himself as a swan-poet in *C.* 2.20.2, serves the theme of this poem well; Ovid employs it three times for centaurs, once for Hermaphroditus, and once for the Minotaur.

665–66   *querellae:* although complaint is rather an elegiac than an epic emotion, Ovid frequently features this emotion in the *Met. intellecta parum* 666: whereas the narrator has apparently quoted her in full, he now declares that the end of her speech could not be understood. Her words degenerated into the whinnies of a mare.

667–69   Once the words became unintelligible, the next stage is an intermediate one (667): not words, but not convincing horse-sounds either. The progress is toward a horse, so that the final condition of genuine whinnies marks that goal. *bracchia movit in herbas* 669: Ovid here continues with other visible aspects of the metamorphosis. The girl's arms, always considered an attractive and prominent physical feature in ancient times, have now become forelegs, as she turns into a quadruped mare, advancing into the grass.

670–75   The rest of the metamorphosis is represented in one long sentence, without the usual pauses at the end of the hexameter. Having mentioned arms in 669, Ovid follows them out to the hands and fingers, in order to record the creation of hooves. This unwanted transformation of the red-haired girl has to seem a brutalization. The enlargement of the feminine neck and face (671–72) adds to the cruel dehumanization. Next, we glance at the other end (672–73), where the characteristically long robe (*pallae*) has turned into the horse's tail. Finally, the flowing red hair, with which alone he described the girl originally (cf. 635), turns into the tossing mane (673–74). It can all be summarized in the final clauses: her voice, the only offensive part of her as seeress, and her external form have simultaneously been changed. *novata est* 674: cf. *novabis* 648. Passive form emphasizes the fact of Ocyroe's victimization. The double subject, connected by *et . . . et* and reinforced by *pariter,* shows the "overkill" that seems typical of divine vengeance in Ovid. *nomen* 675: as often in cases of metamorphosis, Ovid alludes to the new name that the changed being acquired. When possible, he actually inserts the new name (cf. 2.377, 485, and perhaps 632); but often, because of metrical problems or to play with his audience's erudition, he merely says that a new name arose after the transformation, related to some part of the total event (cf. 4.415 and 541). In this instance, Ocyroe apparently changed her name to Hippe (Greek for mare). *monstra:* earlier, glossed as "marvel." The series of animal metamorphoses in this book have not been marvelous since the change of Callisto. They have been angry and small-minded, if not totally unjust, reactions of gods to innocent human activities. The transformation of Ocyroe, then, in eradicating her amazing human talent and beauty, can be considered the creation of an unnatural thing, a monster. For a more playful use, see 4.591.

BATTUS THE INEPT INFORMER (676–707)

To make his transition to the next story, Ovid has to leave behind Chiron, Aesculapius, and Apollo. He does so by having the first vainly pray for help to Apollo, who is no longer available. The god has become a herdsman in love with a handsome young man on earth, in the region of Pylos. Ignoring the cattle to pursue his passion, Apollo lets them be rustled by the clever thief, his younger brother, Mercury. The story of this first theft of Mercury is familiar from the Homeric *Hymn to Hermes* and many other later accounts, such as Horace *C.* 1.10. Ovid merely uses it to get to Mercury and leave Apollo behind. Another herdsman named Battus spotts the rustler, and Mercury tries to bribe him with a cow not to inform against him. Battus takes the cow and promises silence. However, when he tries to outsmart Mercury, he is himself outsmarted. Mercury disguises himself and asks Battus about the missing cattle, offering two animals, cow and bull, as reward for information. When Battus succumbs to the temptation, the god turns him into a stone, the paradigm of inanimate silence. Apart from Ovid, the only ancient source surviving for this story is Antoninus Liberalis 23; but he cites as older sources Hesiod, Nicander, Apollonios, Didymarchos, and Antigonos.

676–79   *flebat . . . heros:* here, in Ovid's first use of the Latin word for hero, he depicts a "heroic" centaur, odd in itself, who is crying! For a supposedly epic poet, he shows a rather curious and even comic sense of heroes. Cf. 3.198, where a hero turns tail. *Philyreius:* this resonant adjective, with a final noun, has all the hallmarks of an epic formula. Philyra, as noted above (cf. 650), was Chiron's mother (his least important parent in respect to his heroic status). Note the alliteration on the *f*-sound, which helps to emphasize *frustra.* The vain efforts of Chiron end our interest in him, and Ovid's apostrophe of Apollo (*tuam* 676, *Delphice* 677) shifts attention briefly to that god, sponsor of prophets and presumably concerned with the fate of Ocyroe. *nec . . . poteras nec . . . aderas* 677–79: a parallelism that trivializes Apollo, who, like other gods, concerns himself with amorous adventures more than with divine responsibilities. Ovid makes *poteras* formally parallel to the properly imperfect verb, by availing himself of the potential sense of imperfect indicative. *Elim . . . colebas:* the god frequents these places in the Peloponnesos, not farming them. He has become a herdsman.

680– Still chatting with Apollo, the poet describes the odd attire and attri-
82   butes of the god. The dignified deity, so regularly depicted idly strum-
      ming his lyre, with long artistic hair, has become a pastoral character,
      wearing a shaggy skin and carrying staff and rustic pipes. Rural people
      often wore goatskins and no doubt the warmer sheepskins. Cf. the
      crude attire of John the Baptist. Ovid, in exile on the Black Sea, often
      comments on the skins that were worn by the barbarians there. *onusque
      . . . sinistrae / alterius* 681–82: playfully, the poet talks about the
      "burden of the left hand and of the other," i.e., the right. *dispar . . .
      fistula:* the adjective has been transferred, because *cannis* already has
      its adjective. The pan-pipe or flute consists of seven reeds of graduated
      length, each of which will produce a different note. Blowing such a
      pipe stands in sharp contrast to the playing of the lyre.

683– *amor est curae:* dative of purpose. Apollo is not even a very responsible
86   herdsman; rather, he is a typical pastoral lover, paying no attention
      to his herd and mooning away on his pipe. Ovid has here greatly
      simplified a complicated story and, as a result, complicated the job
      of his commentators. In one central tradition, Apollo was sentenced
      to a year's service on earth, as punishment for his violent reaction to
      the killing of his son Aesculapius; and he worked as the herdsman of
      King Admetus of Thessaly. That old Hesiodic version is repeated by
      Apollodoros 3.10.4.1 and Hyginus 49. The god was honorably treated
      by the king, toward whom he responded in a friendly, even erotic
      manner, and made his cattle unusually productive. It has several
      inconsistencies with Ovid's version here: Apollo has gone to be a
      herdsman long before Aesculapius has grown up and met his death;
      and the locale of the theft here is not Thessaly, but the southern
      Peloponnesos. The version of Antoninus Liberalis 23 (which claims
      Hesiod as one of its sources) smooths out those problems and suggests
      how Ovid has proceeded. Liberalis makes it a love story, not bothering
      to explain how Apollo happened to be working for Admetus. But the
      god falls in love with Admetus' grandson Hymenaios. While he is
      distracted, then, Mercury steals his cattle, there in Thessaly, and then
      drives them the incredible distance from northern Greece into the
      Peloponnesos, where the encounter with Battus can take place. Ovid
      has made it a love story, too, without background, and he has then
      unified the locale in southern Greece. *incustoditae* 684: this kind of
      compound, a negative *in-* with the participle, is a favorite source of
      Ovidian neologisms (cf. 588, 605). Ovid seems to have created the
      word here, but used it often hereafter; and it had a productive life in
      Silver Latin, especially in the poetically sensitive Tacitus. It consists
      entirely of long syllables and thus here occupies the entire first hemi-
      stich. *Pylios:* the fields of Pylos, home of Homeric Nestor and family,
      lay west of Messenia. The untended cattle have strayed and become

an easy target for rustling. *Atlantide Maia / natus:* Mercury, son of Maia who was daughter of Atlas. He played an earlier role in 1.668 ff. in killing Argus, but Ovid used different epithets of him there. Bömer noted another anachronism with the tradition that Mercury was a mere child at the time of the theft and indeed inaugurated his thievish career with this notorious feat. In the next story Mercury, erotically aroused by sight of Herse, clearly has grown up into a typically amorous and ruthless deity. *occultat abactas:* English prefers coordination; hence, "he drives them off and hides them."

687–
88
senserat: this informer parallels the raven (cf. 545). *Battum* 688: the name implies lack of control over speech and often refers to one who stammers.

689–
90
Battus tends the mares of Neleus, father of Nestor. Homer had attributed rich herds of cattle and horses to this family.

691–
94
timuit: i.e., Mercury. *blandaque manu:* as a consummate deceiver and manipulator of people, the god exudes friendliness, to get Battus to abet his crime. *vidisse nega* 693: the thief bribes the old man to lie, then later entraps him to commit perjury, for which he then drastically punishes him. How could Battus have succeeded? *neu* 693: for this convenient variant for *et ne* + purpose clause, see 1.72 and 445 n. *gratia:* Battus gets gratitude for not being an informer, whereas the crow received hostility, not the expected reward (cf. 562), for faithfully informing. *praemia* 694: a contrast with the tattling raven (cf. 631).

695–
97
accepta: ablative absolute with understood *vacca*. Battus takes the bribe and assures Mercury of his silence. He uses what is called an *adynaton* to back his promise: sooner will some fixed quality of nature be changed than he will ever tell about the stolen cattle. The stone will inform before he will. That determines the eventual punishment he will suffer. The five dactyls of 696 reinforce the glibness of this promise. *simulat* 697: the trickster Mercury trusts nobody, knowing himself, so he immediately launches into a pretense that will lead to a test of Battus' fidelity. Antoninus Liberalis, in his prosaic account, explains everything; Ovid artfully leaves Mercury's purpose implicit, but emphasizes his doubts from the start.

698–
701
As Liberalis dutifully notes, the god had to hide his stolen animals somewhere well out of sight and hearing. *pariter cum voce* 698: Ovid's standard use of ablative of accompaniment instead of coordinate *et voce*, emphasized with standard adverb. *rustice* 699: although Ovid could have used the form *hospes* as before (692, 695), he wants to show that the god has changed identity and assumed a new manner; and Ovid prefers an initial dactyl for his hexameter. *vidisti:* a crucial verb for an informer (cf. 599, 693). *fer opem* 700: urgent request for help (cf. Daphne in 1.546). *furtoque:* ablative of separation. Mercury

names his own crime, but with no sense of guilt. In 701, glibly promising with five dactyls, Mercury more than doubles the bribe: a cow plus a bull. *iuncta suo pariter* 701: again, a poetic variant for a double-noun unit.

702–3   *sub illis / montibus . . . erunt:* "they'll be (= you'll find them) at the foot of those mountains." The whole clause is carefully devised and the words placed so that the narrator can comment with a kind of echo. Future and imperfect almost juxtaposed.

704–7   *risit Atlantiades:* the triumphant laugh of the rogue, who has outwitted his rival, has much appeal to any audience. But Ovid has not given this divine rogue attractive qualities, and so this story features victimization. Mercury laughs more like a villain than a likable rogue. The epic epithet, used and invented earlier at 1.682, emphasizes the unfair competition. *me mihi, perfide, prodis:* the god relishes the play of reflexives, of which he has total control, and he rolls off the alliteration. Poor Battus hears this gloating stranger and his taunting speech, but he has spoken his last. *periuraque pectora* 705: the narrator seems to take Mercury's side and tamely condemn, in full agreement with the god, the old man. As if the conscious being (*pectus* or *mens*) were corrupt, the whole body turns into voiceless, inanimate stone, hardened in feeling, hard to the touch, totally "dead." Mercury, who has killed simple-minded Argus, now uses his capital punishment on this miserable old man. Is it excessive? *silicem* 706: the general word *lapidem* (cf. 696, 697) would have fitted the meter here, but this particular kind of hard stone, flint, effectively symbolizes what has happened to Battus. He is supposed to be a "hardened criminal" and worthy of execution, but what about the executioner, an admitted criminal, who escapes from his guilt by this "legal murder?" *nunc quoque:* for this phrase to emphasize continuity after metamorphosis, cf. 1.235. Battus was an informer; the flint crag or cliff into which he is turned is named after him. Perhaps the mountain top has the appearance of an old man's head, and, when the wind surges around it, it seems to be speaking. Liberalis simply declares that wayfarers call the crags after Battus. Ovid's point is that Battus has become a particular stone formation in a specific location, providing an aetiology for the spot; in the same way, he transfers petrified Niobe in 6.310 ff. from Greece back to Phrygia and makes her the top of Mount Sipylus (whose summit reminds some of the head of a weeping woman), to agree with a local aetiology.

MERCURY INVOLVES HIMSELF WITH HERSE, BUT EVEN MORE WITH HER SISTER AGLAUROS (708–832)

Mercury now gets a major role in connection with the daughters of Cecrops whom the crow mentioned as the objects of his spying (cf. 555 ff.). As he lightheartedly flies off from the scene of theft and vengeance, he passes near Athens and spots Herse, with whom he falls in love on sight. He immediately determines to visit her, for the usual erotic purposes, and approaches the palace. Unfortunately for him, he is spotted by Herse's sister Aglauros, and she is not impressed by his open lust or flattered by the chance to become the aunt of Mercury's baby (746). For her service, which would be like that of Battus, namely, not informing her parents about this divine lecher, she demands a sizable sum of gold and sends the god packing until he can produce it. Already, she is inferior to Battus, because she proposed the fee for her cooperation, and this crime of Mercury would be worse than cattle-rustling. But she degenerates still more as a result of the intervention of hostile Minerva. This goddess has been stewing over Aglauros' earlier disobedience, and now she finds the right occasion for her vengeance. She makes a long trek to the House of Envy (which gives Ovid an opportunity to display his talent for allegorical description) and gets that malign deity to poison the girl. Aglauros becomes a human incarnation of Envy. Envy infects her attitude toward Herse's prospective love affair and the lover Mercury. No longer interested in gold, she merely wants to spoil things. Thus, when Mercury reappears, she simply opposes his entry in a challenging way that he eagerly takes up. He turns her to stone, too, a stone of mottled color that entirely fits her jaundiced *mens*.

Mercury Becomes a Lover (708–36)

708–
10
hinc: Mercury has been in the fields of Pylos (684), robbing cattle and abusing Battus. The tenses of the verbs move from background pluperfect and imperfect to foreground present at 714. *paribus . . . alis:* the wings on his two feet (cf. 1.671). *Caducifer:* Ovid has invented this epic compound here and uses it once more in the *Met.* and twice in the *Fasti.* As we have seen, Mercury has not displayed any epic grandeur with the cattle of Apollo or poor Battus, and the epithet promises no improvement in the erotic scenes that follow. Mercury carried a staff called *caduceus.* That word, however, because of the arrangement of its long and short syllables, is virtually unmetrical. Ovid employs substitutes, such as *virga* (cf. the earlier description of Mercury at 1.671 and 675) and *baculum. volans* 709: the god is flying northeast to Athens. Ovid picks out two parts of the city that would be familiar to many in his Roman audience who visited the city: the Munychian fields near the harbor and the groves of the learned Lyceum, where the Peripatetic school of Aristotle had its center. No doubt, the audience would enjoy the obvious unmythical anachronism.

711–
Ovid imagines an occasion much like those in New Comedy, when

13   a young man first sees a girl of good family in public. Religious
celebrations gave rare opportunities for girls to escape the confines
of their houses. In New Comedy, such occasions almost inevitably
lead to the rape of the girl; and Mercury looks for a similar conclusion.
castae . . . puellae: Athens in historical times annually celebrated the
Panathenaia, at which one of the ritual events was the procession of
girls of the upper classes, each carrying on her head a basket containing
items needed for sacrifice to Minerva. Called canephori, they are
represented by the caryatids in the Porch of the Maidens of the
Erectheum and in many statue-copies, e.g., those at Hadrian's Villa.
For Ovid's purposes, emphasis falls on the virginal aspect of these
maidens; the one Mercury spots, Herse, becomes a natural victim.
vertice subposito 712: ablative absolute. *festas . . . arces:* they were
heading up to the Parthenon on the holiday. The elaborate description
reaches its stately end in a Golden Line at 713.

714–   *revertentes:* the maidens on their way home. *deus . . . ales:* the second
15   word is an adjective here, referring to the wings of 708; but, since
Ovid regularly treats *ales* as a substantive, it easily prepares for the
bird-simile that follows. In 715, the poet explains the flight pattern
of the god: he does not fly straight on—"as the crow flies," we say—
but starts circling in the same tight arc, around Herse, like the bird
of prey of 716 ff. Ovid gets us curious about the sudden change of
Mercury's flight before explaining it.

716–   *volucris:* substantive, feminine since the noun *avis* is feminine. *miluus:*
19   this bird, the kite, is basically a nuisance, trying to snatch the meat
of the sacrifice while the priest and servants are not alert. I know of no
instance when Romans or Greeks represented the kite as an attractive or
humanly appealing bird. *extis:* a point of parallelism with the original
scene. However, the "meat" that interests Mercury the kite is Herse,
not the proper food of the sacrifice (which contented Minerva). The
dum-clause of 717 again suggests a parallel between Mercury, waiting
until the end of the celebration, and the kite, waiting until the altars
were left accessible. *flectitur in gyrum* 718: this circling flight parallels
that of 715. *spemque suam* 719: the object of his hope. Ovid regularly
describes hope in connection with amatory desire. Cf. Apollo's hopes
for pleasure from Daphne (1.491, 496, 536, and 538, also linked with
the simile of a predatory beast in 533 ff.). Narcissus will love a
bodiless hope in a later paradox, 3.417. The bird's wild circling for
carrion trivializes the god's movements. *avidus:* adjective for a greedy
bird, beast, or human being, definitely not ennobling. Ovid repeats
it outside the simile, specifically applied to the god in 720. But he
artfully postpones specifying the object of Mercury's greedy desires
until 722 ff.

720–   *super Actaeas . . . arces:* above the Acropolis, echoing 712 and the

21   scene of 709 ff. Ovid pretends to have composed an epic simile and
        to be returning formally, like Vergil or Homer, to the point from
        which he started. *Cyllenius:* already used of Mercury in 1.713. *easdem
        circinat auras* 721: parallel to 715, but rendered by a unique extension
        of the verb in the sense of "circling through."

722–   Now Ovid introduces the object of the god's desire as a girl of outstand-
25   ing, dazzling beauty, like the morning star or the moon in the sky.
        All this elaborate preparation creates expectation that Ovid flagrantly
        will disappoint; for eventually Mercury will fly off, content with
        vengeance rather than Herse's beauty. *quanto . . . quanto . . . tanto*
        722–24: ablative of degree of difference. *virginibus praestantior:*
        ablative of comparison, a variation of the comparative + *quam* in
        722–23. For this fairy-tale motif of unique beauty, cf. Daphne's
        irresistible and self-defeating beauty (1.488–89) and the attraction of
        Atalanta (10.563). *eratque decus pompae* 725: she was literally the
        "beauty" of the procession, which Ovid earlier described.

726–   *obstipuit forma:* the verb has epic connotations from Vergil, but Ovid
29   here misuses it for an erotic context, thus in effect taking an elegiac
        situation and giving it a mock-epic color. *aethere pendens:* Ovid does
        not seem to mean that Mercury hung there in the air, in one place,
        but rather that he was in flight, suspended in air. The simile that
        follows, especially in 728, continues to stress his swift motion. *exarsit*
        727: heat of passion is a commonplace for Ovid's audience, but he
        colors it with exaggeration and mockery, as in the earlier simile for
        Apollo "going up in flames" (1.492 ff.). This verb has so far been
        employed to represent the thoughtless emotionality of gods (cf. 1.724,
        2.613). Having established that biased connotation, the poet now starts
        to focus it on divine "love." *Balaerica plumbum / funda iacit* 728:
        the inhabitants of the Balearic Islands off Spain were famous for their
        use of the sling or catapult. Ovid has taken a comparison that Lucretius
        made famous in connection with atmospheric phenomena (cf. 6.178
        ff.), talking about the lead shot in general; Ovid has tied it down with
        the adjective and even more by its application to a flying, erotically
        excited god. The result cannot be epic: Mercury made to resemble a
        heated ball of lead is a joke. *incandescit eundo:* we know how projec-
        tiles and space vehicles heat up in the atmosphere because of their
        speed. This was a scientific curiosity; but Mercury's heat is not, nor
        is it caused by his movement but by what he has seen. His movements
        are incidental. In 729, the poet wittily captures the situation of the
        lead shot: he does not take it any more seriously than he does Mercury.
        quos . . . habuit . . . ignes: typical Ovidian placing of relative clause
        before its "antecedent." That helps to enhance the byplay between
        the verbs.

730–   *vertit iter:* the god's peculiar route (714–15) now changes. *caeloque*

31   . . . *relicto:* ablative absolute, which frames the main action of going
        down to earth. *terrena:* only instance of this substantival usage in
        Ovid; rare in general. *nec se dissimulat* 731: Mercury shows his
        difference from the most recently described lover, Jupiter, who dis-
        guised himself to approach Callisto (cf. 2.425). *tanta est fiducia
        formae:* a fine terminal sententia (cf. 1.60) enhanced by alliteration
        of the key words. Among human beings, *forma* causes nothing but
        frustration and trouble. On the next two occasions, confidence in
        human beauty brings on disaster for Semele (3.270) and for the mother
        of Andromeda (4.687). But a god enjoys special advantages, even
        beyond those Ovid urged males to recognize in *Ars Am.* 1.505 ff.

732–   *quae:* i.e., his beauty. *cura:* Mercury acts with ideal, almost feminine
36   courtliness to make himself attractive. In *Ars Am.* 3.105 and *Medic.*
        1, the poet addresses women and urges them to enhance their looks
        with cosmetic attention. Usually in Ovid men need not worry about
        their appearance. *permulcetque comas:* the verb is common in prose.
        As the first of a series of actions in which Ovid shows Mercury
        primping, it is amusingly specific. The god pats his hair, adjusts his
        cloak to hang nicely and show off its golden border. In 735–36, the
        ut-clauses continue, but they cannot logically depend on the arrange-
        ment of the chlamys (733–34); we may supply a verb like *curat,* "he
        sees to it" (cf. *cura* 722). Mercury is now concerned that his staff or
        caduceus (cf. 708) seem polished and that the wings (here called
        talaria, as in *Aen.* 4.239) gleam white on his well-wiped feet. He is
        quite a dandy.

Aglauros' Interference Provokes Minerva's Envy (737–59)

737–   *pars secreta:* the women's quarters of a home were considered highly
39   private. *ebore et testudine cultos:* use of ivory and tortoise shell to
        provide rich and colorful veneer or inlaid decoration characterized
        wealthy homes in Augustan times. *tu, Pandrose* 738: since any form
        of Pandrosos except vocative, with its short final vowel, is difficult
        or impossible to fit into the hexameter, Ovid adopts the vocative and
        a narrator's casual familiarity with his characters. Pandrosos is the
        least important of the three sisters and disappears from the narrative
        after this. Aglauros is assigned the left room, which implies the sinister
        role that she is to play. Herse, the apparent star and focus of the tale,
        gets central billing. Note the arrangement of 739 in virtual chiasmus.

740–   Despite the promise of the beginning, Herse never enters, speaks, or
42   gets to play the indicated love scene. Aglauros, on the left, immediately
        preempts the lead and spoils the drama. *venientem:* his name appears
        in 741, ironically, as the girl inquires about his identity. In the hexame-

ter, this name fits conveniently only at the initial or second dactylic position. Aglauros asks the typical epic questions: his name and the reason for his visit (cf. above, 511).

742–
44

respondit: with this punctuation, it is assumed that the audience has no difficulty recognizing that the god serves as subject. However, beginning a speech in the last word of a line disagrees with convention, and other editors change the punctuation to begin the speech at *ego* in 743, thus supplying a subject for the verb in the genealogy of Mercury. But though that seems to solve one problem, it creates more awkwardness than is appropriate to Ovid. In this form, then, Mercury boasts of his maternal grandparents, Atlas and Pleione (leaving unmentioned those on his father's side), then mentions his almighty father. *verba patris* 744: Mercury is most typically imagined as messenger of Jupiter, as Vergil uses him in *Aen.* 4.222 ff. However, up to this point in the *Met.*, the god has been only killer, thief, and sadistic transformer; and now he intends to follow his father's noble example as lecher. Thus, his boast serves to remind us of what a special role Ovid has assigned him.

745–
47

nec fingam causas: again, Mercury makes a virtue out of his direct-ness—sheer bluntness, from our viewpoint—and reminds us of Jupi-ter's deviousness with Callisto. *fida sorori:* loyalty, for this lustful male, means abetting his purposes. He assumes without question a very dubious assumption, that Herse will answer his passion and want to use Aglauros as trusty co-conspirator. Mercury's urgent solemnity gains emphasis from the four straight spondees of 745. *velis* 746: volitive subjunctive. *prolisque meae matertera:* here, the god's blunt-ness becomes shameless impudence. Why should Aglauros want to be the aunt of his bastard? Only after he has revealed his basic sexual desire does Mercury lamely indicate that he is interested in a particular person, inspired by "love." Thus, he has exposed his love as typical divine lust.

748–
51

oculis isdem: Ovid carefully connects this moment with a scene that the crow briefly described above at 558 ff. He is not so concerned with the "same eyes" as with the same significant expression perceptible in the eyes. The crow did not say anything about her look, and we must therefore infer the connection. Bömer suggests that a wild or hot look would serve the purpose, but would not provide a significant link. Perhaps, the larger context of 750–51 provides a clue to what Ovid would now have us read into 558 ff. Aglauros asks for a bribe for her silence (similar to Battus), and thus we can imagine her looking at Mercury in a calculating, greedy manner. And that could have been her motivation for opening and looking at the contents of the secret chest of Minerva; she expected to find treasure. This is a common motif in fairy tales. *ministerio* 750: Vergil had used this word seriously in *Aen.* 6.223 and 7.619 to describe solemn "services"; the prose writers Cicero and Caesar had not employed it at all. Thus, it seems to have been a solemn word for Augustan poetry; and Ovid continues to use it so: four times in the *Met.* and otherwise once only in *Am.* 1.11.3, always in this metrical position. *tectis excedere cogit* 751: Aglauros shows equal bluntness with the god. She is telling him in no uncertain terms to get out—and he does—until he produces the money. These two unappealing characters deserve each other.

752–   Having already reminded us of Aglauros' disloyal connection with
55   Minerva, Ovid brings the goddess on, angry and nursing a long grudge. *vertit . . . luminis orbem:* an elaborate way of putting the conventional *vertit lumina* or *vultum.* The elaboration puts emphasis on the look, to which the poet has added the adjective *torvi.* The goddess's looks can "kill." She is angry and savage, but why? In devoting the next two and a half lines to Minerva's violent sighs, the poet indicates that a great deal of feminine envy has twisted the goddess. She is ready to use Envy as her ally, because already sharing that feeling. As she looks at Aglauros' apparent good fortune achieved through evil (or what annoys her), the goddess responds exactly as Envy will at sight of the mighty goddess: with deep sighs (cf. below 774). Together these two malevolent beings conspire to make Aglauros subject to the same destructive emotion. Ovid's emphasis on Minerva's sighs produces a result clause in 754–55 that undermines her dignity; note the popping alliteration and the zeugma with its typical over-emphasis by *pariter.* The "simultaneous" shaking of her breast and her aegis, rather different processes, invites our comic reaction.

755–   *subit:* "the thought occurs to her." The remainder of the sentence
59   consists of a system of indirect statements. *hanc:* Aglauros, who is the subject of the indirect discourse. *arcana profana:* another reminder (cf. 748–49) of the episode of Ericthonius in 558 ff. *sine matre creatam / Lemnicolae stirpem* 756–57: for Vulcan's siring of Ericthonius without a mother, see above 553 n. *gratamque . . . fore* 758: Minerva can predict that, without her intervention, Aglauros will reap the gratitude of Mercury; but she exhibits the same naive confidence as Mercury in predicting the automatic response of Herse to the god's impetuous lust. Will Herse's attitude be identical with that of Mercury? Herse never has a chance to display her feelings, while Mercury's passion evaporates after his display of "ingratitude." *ditem* 759: the infinitive *fore* continues to function. *sumpto . . . auro:* ablative absolute. Translated: "if she received the gold." *avara:* this adjective creates an interesting parallelism between Aglauros and Mercury (cf. 719–20) as well as between Aglauros and Battus.

The House of Envy (760–86)

Ovid embarks on the first of his great allegorical descriptions, capturing a prevalent interest of the Hellenistic period but applying it in an individual and creative manner. Vergil had composed an allegory on *Fama* in *Aen.* 4.173 ff., focusing not on where Rumor lived, but on how it operated in the human world. (In 12.23 ff., Ovid attempts to vie with Vergil and produce a home for Rumor, similar to the House of Envy here.) Ovid's allegory concentrates on the native region of Envy, which he describes by itself first (760–64), before zooming in on its sole inhabitant. Envy herself. We see her as Minerva perceives her (768–70), then as the narrator portrays her responding to the sight of the powerful goddess (770–82). The etymology of *Invidia* and its verb *invideo* stresses the act of seeing. Envy's view of the conditions of others is hostile. Starting from the envious observation of Aglauros by Minerva, Ovid proceeds to the envious observation of Minerva by Envy herself (773–74), then to her dismay and tears at the happiness of Athens (794–96), and finally to the effects that Envy's infestation has on Aglauros, with special stress on the girl's eyes and what she sees (803 ff., 812). Dante knew this section well when he composed the cantos of *Purgatorio,* which deal with the Circle of Envy.

760–
64
nigro squalentia tabo: Envy is so busy looking and thinking hatefully, that she neglects her own home, which is filthy and rotten with black corruption. The symbolism of Envy features black or morbid colors, discoloration, and warped, off-color perception. *imis in vallibus* 761: we should imagine a valley with narrow walls that prevent the sun and breeze from reaching its floor. *sole carens* 762: Envy lives in almost funereal darkness. Lack of wind suggests changelessness of climate, absence of nature's sound and movement. *ignavi . . . frigoris* 763: the numbing cold causes listlessness. One feels no energy, only depression. *et quae . . . vacet . . . abundet:* subjunctive in relative clause of description, still referring to *domus.* Note the careful balance of the six words in 764.

765–
67
huc ubi pervenit: Ovid gives no indications as to the location of Envy's home in relation to the human or divine world. Thus, he does not say that Minerva went *down* to it, only that she came to it. *belli metuenda virago:* the unusual construction of *belli* with *virago,* to make "warlike maiden of war," caused many MSS to change the genitive to ablative *bello,* to make a standard ablative of respect with the gerundive. As the more difficult reading, the genitive receives priority. Ovid uses *virago* only twice, of Minerva and solely in the *Met.* In 766–67, Minerva acts out her supposedly antithetical nature in respect to this

foul goddess and her polluted home. However, Ovid has already suggested that the two are kindred spirits, that Minerva feels envy before visiting Envy. Why did she not send one of her underlings if Envy was in fact so antipathetical to her? *extrema cuspide* 767: standing at some distance, the goddess reaches out prudishly (arrogantly?) and strikes the door with her spearpoint.

768–
70
patuere: from *patesco;* "they became open." No servant opened the doors, nor did Envy: they yielded to the imperious presence of the goddess. *videt:* i.e., Minerva. She has no reason to envy the disgusting life of Envy, so turns her gaze away. *edentem / vipereas carnes:* as 772 puts it more clearly, Envy is chewing on snakes, poisonous ones (cf. 777), which will nourish her own poisonous nature. The adjective *vipereus,* like other adjectives formed with the suffix -*eus,* is a creation of Augustan poets designed to facilitate their search for picturesque vocabulary that would also yield easy dactyls. Vergil made good use of the word in *Aen.* 6 and 7 to color the activities of the Furies and of Allecto in particular. Ovid has it nine times in the *Met. Invidiam visaque* 770: as if the definition of Envy was "She Who Must Not Be Seen," the goddess looks away from her. The participle is ablative of separation.

770–
74
Once the goddess averts her face, the narrator enters in full force to elaborate on the looks and actions of Envy. She now becomes the continuous subject until 782. *humo pigra* 771: ablative of place from which. The soil is frozen and "lifeless." Presumably, she was sitting or sprawled on the ground, gnawing away at the snakes like a demented person. *semesarumque . . . serpentum:* a striking phrase, using the adjective specially, making the noun feminine (perhaps for euphony), and securing alliteration. *passuque incedit inerti:* Ovid regularly uses the verb to describe the dramatic entrance of women in the *Met.* Here, he immediately qualifies the movement of Envy with another reference to her listless ways. When Eurydice rejoins Orpheus in 10.49, she is slowed down by her snakebite: *incessit passu de volnere tardo. formaque armisque decoram* 773: double -*que* construction enhances the ablative of respect, which serves to define the enviable attractions of Minerva. *ingemuit* 774: first reaction of envy. *vultumque ima ad suspiria duxit:* a troubled passage. Most of the MSS read *deae* instead of *ima* (influenced by *deam* 773); that would seem to give: "She extended her look to the sighs of the goddess," e.g., the sighs mentioned in 753. However, this makes no sense in the context. Envy is envious of Minerva: she is not comforting herself over the sighs of the goddess. She reacts as the goddess did earlier, with sighs that connote envious feelings. After all, Minerva does not sigh here; Envy is sighing with envy of the goddess' good looks. But the text with *ima* is also strange; it seems to mean: "She brought her look to the

deepest sighs." That, I think, means that what she saw resulted in
deep sighs on the part of Envy. A third possibility is to accept *deae*
and assume that Ovid made a single phrase out of the words *vultumque
deae ad* (availing himself of a rare form of anastrophe, postponement
of the preposition); this would yield: "She drew sighs at the look of
the goddess." The metrical organization of the line, with caesurae at
3 and 7 (after *ad*), might lend support to this interpretation.

775–
77
Ovid now gives a more particular description. Envy is pale and gaunt
(775), a result of the dark place she inhabits, the limited food she
eats, and her total sleeplessness (to be mentioned in 779). He gives
six characteristics, two per line; and in each line he varies the positions
of the two subjects. In 776, she never looks directly at anyone, always
eying people "askance," invidiously. Her teeth are black with mold.
The "tooth of Envy" is often a potent symbol. *pectora felle virent*
777: her breasts are apparently visible (at least to the poet's imagina-
tion). Far from having maternal milk in them, they are green with
the bile of Envy. Lastly, her tongue is covered with poison, as a result
of the snakes she gnaws.

778–
82
Ovid now passes on to her habits. She never laughs except when she
sees another's pains. That is a typical version of envy, which the
Germans call *Schadenfreude*. She is racked by sleepless misery, not
over her own problems, but over the prosperity of others. *vigilacibus*
779: the MSS disagree on the ending of the word, giving *-acibus,
-atibus,* and *-antibus.* I choose the first reading, because the spelling
with *c* goes better with the sound-patterns. This sole instance of *vigilax*
in the entire Ovidian corpus would have been derived from Ovid's
admired Propertius (4.7.13). *videt ingratos . . . successus* 780–81.
Once again, the sight of others' happiness ruins the feelings of *In-
vidia.* Similarly, Minerva was highly disturbed that Aglauros might
be in a happy position with Mercury and Herse (cf. 758, *gratam*).
intabescitque 780: she wastes away, just as her home is falling down
with decay (*tabo* 760). The coordination between her seeing and
rotting away at the sight is spelled out in a more obviously clever
pairing: *carpitque et carpitur una* 781. The adverb emphasizes the
link between the active work of envy in tearing down another and the
passive condition of being "torn apart" by another's prosperity. Fi-
nally, with the reflexive notion, *suppliciumque suum est* 782, Ovid
captures the fact that envy tends to cause its own torment. Envy is
in the eye of the beholder, not in the person and happiness of the one
observed.

782–
86
The story turns back briefly to Minerva, who rushes out her request
to Envy, then departs, leaving the stage to this thwarted creature.
oderat: pluperfect form, but, because of the absence of all but perfect

forms in this verb, imperfect in translation. *illam:* with change of
subject (*Tritonia* 783), Envy becomes object. Minerva's epithet comes
from Lake Triton in North Africa, where some myths place her birth.
Vergil had already used this word in *Aen.* 2.171. The brief speech
of a line and a half lacks all epic impressiveness and does not seem
dramatically convincing. We might expect that Minerva needed to
work more to convince Envy of the pleasure of ruining the happiness
of Aglauros, of making her as miserable as herself. *infice* 784: Envy
is to "infect" Aglauros, make her sick with envy. Thus, at the end,
the girl's infected mind "infects" (832) the livid stone into which she
is turned by Mercury. *tabe:* related to *tabo* of 760, but more general.
Ovid can use both as metrical alternatives, but he chooses the second
declension noun to refer specifically to the putrid liquid of corruption,
whereas the fifth declension noun covers the abstract condition of
corruption as well as its concrete putridity. In 785, Ovid assigns
Minerva a particularly graceless pair of clauses, each of three words,
each using the dreary verb *est,* each occupying a metrical unit. *fugit*
786: Ovid slyly chooses this verb to comment on the undignified or
"cowardly" departure of the goddess whose warlike attributes have
received much emphasis up to this point (cf. 754–55, 765, 767, 773).
inpressa . . . hasta: she has used her mighty spear only to knock on
the door and now to hasten her "flight." Minerva's dependence on
the spear evokes a parallel in the way Nestor uses his lance to catapult
himself into a tree in 8.365–68 to escape the deadly charge of the
Calydonian Boar. Ovid seems to describe both Minerva and Nestor
as pole-vaulting escapists.

Envy Possesses Aglauros (787–815)

787–   *illa deam:* subject and object are now reversed, as Envy remains alone
90   on stage. *obliquo . . . lumine:* Ovid has already said that Envy never
       looks directly at anyone (776). Her look betrays her feeling: Minerva
       is already grand and will be made happy, alas, by what Envy will do
       to Aglauros. *murmura . . . dedit* 788: the muttering of unhappiness.
       successurumque Minervae: indirect discourse; the infinitive is used
       impersonally and governs the dative; "She is pained that there will
       be success for Minerva." Envy pines away to see others' successes
       (780–81). (The reading of the infinitive is due to the brilliance of
       Heinsius; the MSS tradition is hopelessly corrupted.) Nevertheless,
       she immediately starts to carry out the divine request. *baculumque*
       789: traveller's staff, an indication that she prepares to set out on a
       journey to Athens. *spinea . . . vincula:* Bömer seems right to insist
       that the staff is of a wood that bristles with thorns, appropriate to the

prickly personality of Envy. The adjective again shows the form familiar to Augustan poetry, providing a natural dactyl with its *-ea* ending; Ovid invented it for this effective description. *nubibus atris:* black clouds clearly fit this personage who lives ordinarily in light-denying frigidity and never sleeps.

791–
94

ingreditur: now her step is confident and authoritative. She is in the destructive phase of envy. *florentia:* anything that flowers provokes her hostility. *exuritque* 792: Ovid may be thinking of the way farmers burn their fields of grass and other growth. *summa papavera carpit:* the verb has already been emphatically attached to Envy in 781. Ovid also seems to be alluding to the infamous action of the tyrant Tarquin, who conveyed thereby a message to his son to get rid of all the more eminent men of Gabii; which the son then did. Closely similar language in the account of Livy 1.54.6. She is attacking the tallest poppies. *adflatuque . . . polluit* 793–94: Ovid has not mentioned Envy's breath, but its foulness is easy to infer from 775 and 776.

794–
96

Tritonida: a more obvious Greek form of *Tritoniam,* to fit the meter here (cf. 783). *virentem* 795: the color green here has markedly different associations from 777; it connotes flourishing aspects of city life that stir Envy. Epigrammatic 796, with its perverse portrait of Envy almost weeping over the totally cheerful aspect of Athens, closes this long sentence.

797–
801

thalamos: poetic plural. *Cecrope natae:* Aglauros. Ovid has used the same phrase in this position in the plural at 555. Instead of ablative of origin, he has the genitive *Cecropis* in 784. *ferrugine tincta* 798: Envy touches Aglauros' breast, the center of her feelings, with a dark rust-stained hand, to communicate the malignity of her poisonous self. *hamatis . . . sentibus inplet* 799: thorny associations of Envy have already been connected with her staff at 789. *nocens virus piceumque . . . venenum* 800–81: these two nouns refer to similar poisons, and Ovid uses the double description to gain emphasis. He describes the witch Circe in much the same way at 14.403. Poison has been on Envy's tongue (777) and in the snakes she has been eating. *piceus* is another poetic adjective favored by Vergil and Ovid (five times in the *Met.* only); it continues here to stress the sinister color black.

802–
4

mali causae . . . errent: Envy works to concentrate the specific cause of Aglauros' "sickness"; she prevents it from being dissipated on irrelevant enviable things. *germanam ante oculos* 803: the sight of Herse focuses Aglauros' envy. *pulchraque . . . sub imagine* 804: then Envy works on the "eye" of the imagination. Since, as Ovid tells the story, Herse has not yet talked with Mercury, the marriage with the handsome young god cannot be an actual event. Ovid is interested, here and elsewhere, in the way that the imagination functions to affect the personality. In other accounts, Mercury does indeed meet Herse, and from their "marriage" is born Cephalus (who grows up to be an Athenian hero and play a leading role in *Met.* 7).

805–8   *cunctaque magna facit:* Envy exaggerates the happiness and prosperity enjoyed by Herse in this imaginary union, to incite a predictable response from the envious sister. *dolore . . . occulto* 806: the secret aspect of this pain suggests a desperate "sickness". For pain and illness at another's pleasure, cf. 774, 780 and 789. Aglauros responds precisely as sick Envy has done, because she is *Invidia altera.* *mordetur:* cf. *carpitur* 781. *anxia nocte:* cf. 779. *gemit* 807: cf. *ingemuit* 774. *miserrima tabe:* the girl has been infected, as Minerva asked (784). *liquitur* 808: since the corruption of *tabes* regularly functions to dissolve into putrid moisture whatever it affects, the girl is said to dissolve into foul liquid. *glacies . . . saucia:* when ice starts to melt in the tepid sunshine of late winter or early spring, it softens and produces much water, but remains mostly ice. The metaphor "wounded" keeps the focus on the hostile infection that Envy has planted. (For an entirely different association of melting ice in spring, cf. Byblis' turning into a fountain 9.661–62: Ovid makes that attractive.)

809–11   *felicisque bonis . . . Herses:* the felicity of Herse is a figment of jealous imagination. *uritur:* another passive verb (cf. 806) to stress the helpless suffering. It is a steady burn (*lenius*), like that of bramble-filled grass or thornbushes. Ovid builds a two-line simile and explains in 811 that the grass burns without visible flames, just as Aglauros' "fire" is unseen.

812–15   *ne quicquam tale videret:* Aglauros, a typical victim of envy, is ready to die to avoid seeing what triggers or might trigger—remember, she is also a prey to her imagination—her suffering. *rigido narrare parenti* 813: a reminder of the theme of the informer (of which Ovid makes no use here). The father is stern and unbending in his morality. *in adverso . . . limine* 814: "on the threshold opposite or facing." Aglauros sits there to stop the approach of Mercury. *venientem:* moved up from its logical position near *deum.* The separation enables Ovid to build his clause up slowly, postponing to the end the person who negates all the girl's efforts, a ruthless, unstoppable god. *exclusura* 815: Aglauros has assumed a role common in one of the situations of Roman elegy, when a lover stands at the closed door of his or her beloved and expresses frustration over being excluded. When the excluder is someone other than the *amata,* such as a guard or servant, that person receives the lover's appeal. The complaint of the *exclusus amator* is a commonplace for Tibullus, Propertius, and Ovid in elegy. On this occasion, Ovid aborts the love theme, deprives Mercury of amatory appeal, and maintains his focus on the invidious negator of love, Aglauros.

Envious Aglauros is Petrified by Mercury (815–32)

815–
19

In five brief lines, Ovid stages the entry of Mercury and his rapid reaction to the vain antagonism of human envy; then he turns back to study the final metamorphosis of Aglauros. *blandimenta precesque / verbaque iactanti* 816: the nouns show that Mercury is covering the familiar topics of the excluded lover in elegy. But Ovid refuses to give him the speech. *mitissima:* soft words to soften the heart of the beloved or doorkeeper, who, like Aglauros here, cannot be softened, being *immitis*. The word order of 817 could be adjusted to prosaic form as follows: *hinc ego me non motura sum nisi te repulso;* the last two words form a convenient ablative absolute, in place of a more conventional conditional clause, e.g., *nisi te reppulerim*. If Aglauros were acting as a faithful guardian of her sister's virtue, these words would be blameless. As is clear from the narrative, her sick motivation of envy exposes her to punishment that, though coming from a heartless god, devoid of the sense of justice, still comes justly to her. *stemus . . . pacto . . . isto* 818: the three words of the god's sardonic reply, distributed over the whole line, effectively destroy the confidence of Aglauros' future tenses. As though she had made a promise or contract to sit there, Mercury plays the casuistic lawyer—cf. his laughing treatment of Battus whom he had lured into his trap at 704—and insists on pressing the words she has spoken. "It's a deal," we might say; "let's stick to those conditions of yours." *velox Cyllenius:* the adjective + antonomasia (used earlier at 1.713) sounds like epic, but the situation has been designed by Ovid to strike us as grimly mock-epic. The speedy deity has seized upon her words. *fores virga patefecit* 819: Mercury uses his trusty caduceus (cf. 735–36), which normally serves nobler purposes, to open the doors that Aglauros is trying to block and keep closed against him. Thus, he demonstrates that he has the opportunity to carry out his lustful purposes, in spite of her. But instead of proceeding with his easy amatory conquest (and the siring of Cephalus), Ovid ignores his "victory" and concentrates on the "defeat" of the human victim. We do not enjoy Aglauros' misery as much as the sadistic god does.

819–
21

at illi: Aglauros, now gradually coming back into focus, first as dative of reference. *surgere conanti* 820: she strains to rise, that is, to "move" to fulfill her threat at 817; but Mercury is holding her to the *nisi*-clause. *partes quascumque sedendo / flectitur:* although the MSS show amazing fidelity to the reading of the final verb, it is apparent that ancient readers had trouble with its grammar and tried emendation. But all are so obviously efforts to escape the transmitted difficulty that editors stick determinedly with *flectitur*. For the prosaic mind, what we need is either some active form of the verb, such as *flectimus,* or a change of accusative *quascumque* to nominative *quaecumque* with *flectuntur*. Ovid's verb in the third person singular present passive means he has chosen the impersonal construction. But that goes oddly with the accusative. We have seen him use the passive as a reflexive and then couple with it an accusative of the body part involved, when, for example, he describes putting on armor or clothes (e.g., *induitur faciem* 2.425). It has been argued that he is merely doing the same thing here, passive for reflexive, and that we should understand: "the parts that she bends in sitting". However, logic would have required Ovid to say "the parts that she bent already when she sat down." I prefer, then, to take the passive as impersonal, to which the familiar limiting accusative has been added, and translate: "the parts that people bend when sitting". This is sequel to the moment when Aglauros stubbornly sat down (814) to block the god's approach. *ignava . . . gravitate:* this listless heaviness when trying to rise parallels Envy's sluggishness at the arrival of Minerva (771–72). *moveri:* the key verb of 817 echoed.

822–
24

illa quidem pugnat: an ironic repetition of 436 echoing Callisto's hopeless battle against her conqueror. Here, Aglauros is not innocent, but she gets sympathy in her "fight" to stand straight. *genuum iunctura* 823: the knee joint will not bend. Her affliction resembles that of retired athletes today, whose knees, repeatedly injured, have permanently stiffened. But she is turning into unmoving, inanimate stone. *frigusque:* this cold is related to the "sluggish cold" of Envy's home in 763, but its effects are much worse, for they petrify. She is becoming "stone-cold," another lifeless stone-victim of Mercury. Ovid ingeniously chose the parts affected by the cold that in our experience suffer numbness, namely, the tips of the fingers. *pallent* 824: more than the pallor of Envy (775), this is the bloodless pallor as death approaches. For a similar conjunction of paleness and the freezing of the blood, during metamorphosis into a stone, cf. Anaxarete at 14.754–59.

825–
28

malum . . . inmedicabile cancer: apposition before proper noun; on the striking adjective see 1.190 n. Although Ovid frequently refers to the astronomical Cancer, this is the only passage in his poetry to name the frightening disease. Bömer usefully notes that in fact Ovid is the only Latin poet to mention it. *serpere* 826: the disease works like a snake; it seems an extension of the poison and venom from the snakes of Envy (cf. 771–72 and 801–2). *inlaesas vitiatis addere:* the word arrangement graphically reinforces the picture. *letalis hiems* 827: the cold of Envy (cf. 763 and 823) becomes deadly winter. *in pectora venit:* clearly, this replaces the effects of Envy, which started there (798). *vitalesque vias* 828: alliteration to refer generally to the passages of air, liquid, and blood. *respiramina:* this word invented by Ovid raises the image of asphyxiation or strangulation, to generate a stronger sense of the suffering of Aglauros at the hands of cruel gods.

829–
32

nec conata loqui est: since the effort to speak, which metamorphosis frustrates, has become a familiar motif, Ovid plays with it. This motif appeared in the first human transformation, that of Lycaon, at 1.233; then, again at 1.637 with Io. Speech, an essential attribute of human beings, stops with death, petrifaction, or bestialization. *vocis . . . iter* 830: Ovid immediately explains this by his focus on the neck and mouth, now turned into rock. *duruerant* 831: pluperfect tense paves the way for imperfect. Battus had similarly hardened (706), but he did not become a statue. *signumque exsangue sedebat:* each of the words has importance, and all reinforce each other with the sibilant alliteration. For a human being to become a statue reverses the creative process of art, which tries to capture life in an inanimate medium, not snuff it out. Perseus uses the Gorgon head to create a statue gallery for his beloved (cf. 5.185–86 and 223 ff.). Bloodlessness means death (cf. 824), but also suggests the "dead" color of stone, especially the white marbles used for statuary. And the verb fixes Aglauros permanently in the pose she defiantly assumed at 814. We should imagine her, I think, not stubbornly and confidently seated, looking powerful, but struggling to rise and move, pathetic in her impotent agony. *nec lapis albus* 832: in fact, she is not white Pentelic or Parian marble such as most statues of women and goddesses. *sua mens infecerat illam:* note the gender of the pronoun, referring to her, not the stone. The infection that Envy had started in her, which became extended by the "cancer" of petrifaction that Mercury produced, ends by discoloring her essential being and ensuring that the stone she turns into will be of dark, livid hues. Minerva, abetted by Mercury, has achieved an inhuman result with a punishment actuated more by her own envy than a true sense of justice. She has tampered with Aglauros' *mens,* after which the girl had little control over the strange person she became, an easy victim for sardonic Mercury to finish off.

Jupiter and Europa (833–75)

In the final story of Book 2, Ovid puts Mercury briefly to work as an ignorant abetter of another amatory escapade of Jupiter, then dismisses him. Jupiter has spotted beautiful, desirable Europa and decided to try another approach in disguise, this time as a white bull. Fascinated by the "tame" beast, innocent Europa becomes too trusting and climbs up on the animal. The bull slowly lumbers to its feet, enters the Mediterranean, and carries its prize off to Crete, where, as the god, it will satisfy his ardor. Since Ovid stops before the predictable rape and the despair of Europa that ensues, the tone of his narration remains light, and the book closes picturesquely on the scene of the

girl astride the bull as it disappears across the water. It was a scene
that artists liked for wall-paintings; and Ovid himself elaborated on
it more fully in *Fast*. 5.605 ff. Apollodoros 3.1.1 and Hyginus 178
give standard brief summaries of the myth. Moschos and Horace *C*.
3.27 have different literary presentations. Ovid's account, however,
remains especially engaging.

833–   Transition from Athens and the fate of Aglauros, in ostentatiously
35   epic manner. *has . . . poenas . . . cepit* 834: the narrator is either
being very "objective" here or presenting the viewpoint of egotistic
Mercury. *mentisque profanae* 833: if we are to understand by this a
reference to Aglauros' first sin, when she "profaned" the chest en-
trusted to her by Minerva, then Mercury has no right to take credit
for the punishment. But if he is putting her envy down as "profane"
and insisting that he has the right to punish it, we would still be
dissatisfied; because the girl has been made a victim of Envy by two
terrible goddesses. Here is where Ovid sends Mercury off without
concern for Herse. *ingreditur . . . aethera* 835: a somewhat strange
expression, "stepping into the air," but Ovid used it earlier of Juno
in her peacock-drawn chariot at 532. Mercury heads for Olympus.
pennis: the wings are beating at his ankles.

836–   *sevocat:* this verb brings the tone sharply down from that of epic to
38   everyday politics. Cicero employed it often to describe the machina-
tions of himself and fellow Romans; and Ovid, who uses it only here
in all his poetry, borrows those connotations to color the calculating
behavior of Jupiter. *genitor:* his father Jupiter. *nec causam fassus
amoris:* without revealing to Mercury the amatory purpose in his
orders, Jupiter dispatches him on a mission that must seem odd indeed
to the dutiful son. This clause gives Ovid's audience the advantage
of dramatic irony over Mercury. *iussorum* 837: objective genitive with
minister. celer delabere 838: for the speed of Mercury, cf. 818. Here,
the adjective stands for an adverb. The verb is an imperative, parallel
to *pelle*. Having just flown up from the earth at Athens, Mercury is
now told to go back down again.

839–   The reason for his journey must puzzle the god. In two separate
42   commands, using the suspenseful construction where the relative
clause precedes its "antecedent," Jupiter orders him to go to Sidon
and drive a herd of cattle from the mountains to the shore. *quaeque
. . . tellus . . . suspicit . . . hanc pete:* the structure of this unit
sprawls, and its meaning is elusive. Looking down from the heavens,
as though from north to south, Jupiter has on his left a large part of
Asia Minor, of which he names, for confused Mercury, the place that
its natives call *Sidon*. It looks up to Mercury's mother Maia among
the Pleiades (cf. 1.669–70), obviously from the left, too. *quodque . . .*

armentum . . . vides . . . verte 841–42: this detail about Mercury's job as a cowherd may well be Ovid's invention; it goes well with the god's recent work as a cattle-rustler. Mercury might suspect that now he is to rustle for his father.

843– *dixit, et expulsi . . . / . . . petunt:* Ovid quickly signs off the short
45   unepic speech with the single word *dixit,* and then he records the fulfilment of Jupiter's orders without again referring to Mercury, who now disappears until 8.627 (when he enters in disguise with his father to visit the earth). *monte:* ablative of separation. *litora iussa* 844: from the vague orders, Mercury was apparently able to divine that a specific section of the shore near Sidon was the goal of his cattle drive. *magni filia regis:* Europa is not named at all, but the audience may have already identified her and, if not, will certainly do so from the circumlocution that names her father Agenor at 858. The scene briefly sketched out with five smooth dactyls in 845, of a girl playing with her companions by the seashore, was so conventional for Europa and, with minor variations, for other rape victims like Persephone, that the audience had little difficulty imagining that Europa was wandering through meadows picking flowers (cf. 861 and Horace, *C.* 3.27.29); she was not sunbathing or swimming. With the mention of the girl, we now know that the love of Jupiter, his motive announced at 836, will at last be explained.

846– Ovid wittily sets up an ethical dilemma for Jupiter, which the god
47   will solve in his own predictable manner, as he did those involving Io in 1.617 ff. and Callisto 2.423 ff., with priority given to his selfish erotic purposes and no attention paid to moral values that most members of the Roman audience recognized as supreme. As the poet words the dilemma, it is evident that moral majesty should not be paired with love, its inferior. Because of the expectation designed by the poet's wording, the surprise of Jupiter's choice has that much greater an effect.

847– *sceptri gravitate relicta:* Ovid moves from the abstract terms of moral
51   choice to concrete details by which Jupiter's sleazy decision can be conveyed. The sceptre connotes regal authority, and *gravitate* serves as a physical synonym for the ethical term *maiestas.* The verb of this ablative absolute ends the expectation produced by the apparent declaration of 846–47. *ille pater rectorque deum* 848: Ovid has separately referred to Jupiter as father (frequently and often irreverently when the god pursued and raped a nymph) and ruler (1.668 and 2.60), but this is the first time he has united these emphatic titles. Evidently, Jupiter disgraces himself. The same title will next occur in 9.245, in a self-congratulatory speech of the god, where again he falls woefully short of the majesty implied by the words. The demonstrative + the relative clauses of 848–49, further emphasizes the anticlimax. *cui:*

dative of reference. *trisulcis / ignibus:* the lightning bolt, which was triply jagged, as Ovid stressed in 2.325 with his neologism *trifida*. In earlier stories, Ovid has often described the incompetent way that Jupiter has used this weapon. *nutu concutit orbem:* Ovid introduced this earthshaking nod in a mocking way at 1.179 ff. His Jupiter notoriously lacks the grandeur of Vergil's great god, already by his past performance; but here he exceeds expectations. *induitur faciem* 850: same unit in 2.425, to describe the god's previous disguise with Callisto, but the genitive *tauri* here makes his simulation as Diana petty by comparison. All that majesty has been forsaken for the fine physique of a bull. *mugit* 851: the animal bellowing further conveys the god's degradation. *formosus obambulat:* in a different context these words could describe a handsome young man approaching a girl; the adjective particularly belongs to the vocabulary of love elegy, where men and women are alike beautiful. Ovid abuses the terms to describe a somehow well-formed bull ambling up to the band of maidens, to initiate this conquest by Jupiter.

852– Ovid proceeds comically to anatomize the comely form of the bull.
53   First, he is gleaming white, like the driven snow, we might say. Io was thought beautiful as a white cow (cf. 1.610–12). For snow as the epitome of whiteness, cf. 8.373–74 *nive candidioribus . . . equis*. Ideally white snow has never been walked on nor been discolored by melting. Cf. the reference to ice "wounded" by the sun in 808. All that whiteness could never make Jupiter a handsome bull.

854– The narrator admiringly adds details in 854 about the bulging neck
56   muscles and the hanging dewlaps, then goes on to the tiny horns, inviting the audience in by apostrophe (*possis* 855) to attest to these attractions. Usually, bulls have large, majestic, and frightening horns. But Ovid intends to make this bull an attractive dandy (like Mercury in 731 ff.), so gives him small, handcrafted, gem-like horns. *perlucida* 856: the translucence of gems has always been admired, and so was that of horns by the ancients.

857– *nullae . . . minae:* because of the small horns, the bull's head seems
59   unthreatening. *formidabile lumen:* usually, bulls are imagined as wild-eyed, not contented and mild-looking like this bull or Ferdinand of the modern children's story. *pacem* 858: Ovid plays with metaphors of peace and war (859), but he omits the relevant image of treachery, *insidiae*. *Agenore:* Agenor is father of both Europa and of Cadmus, whose family preoccupies Ovid in Books 3 and 4. *minetur* 859: subjunctive in *quod*-causal clause that expresses Europa's personal (and erroneous) feelings. As the narrator has made clear to us, this "bull" threatens rape, not attack.

860– *mitem:* tame and gentle, it seemed. Europa acts cautiously at first,
61   then proceeds to adorn the animal with her flowers.

862–   *gaudet amans:* as usual, Ovid depicts this metamorphosis in a fashion
65   similar to that of Callisto, except that this disguise has been voluntarily
        assumed and can of course be removed at will. But there is a nonbestial
        person inside the beast-form. It is a gratified lover, happily pursuing
        his goal to success. In later stories, the person inside the form will
        tend to be a human being who is a frustrated lover. *dum veniat:*
        subjunctive in clause of anticipation. *voluptas:* regularly sexual plea-
        sure in Ovid (cf. 3.321, 4.327). *oscula dat* 863: the slobbering kisses
        of the bull contrast comically with the passionate kisses of the anthro-
        pomorphic lover. Jupiter is one who kisses in disguise, as with Callisto
        in 430. *vix cetera differt:* the impatience of the aroused male is a
        topos that Ovid frequently describes. He will later word it: *vix . . .
        sua gaudia differt* (of Tereus in 6.514; but same phrase also for
        female Salmacis in 4.350). *cetera* for erotic things is a witty elegiac
        periphrasis, notoriously used in *Am.* 1.5.25 with the impudent ques-
        tion, *cetera quis nescit?* The playful, gamboling bull makes Jupiter a
        comic lover. *viridique* 864: Ovid reveals his eye for color, emphasizing
        green, white, and yellow (the latter two in significant juxtaposition
        in 865). *niveum* 865: cf. 852.

866–   *metu dempto:* ablative absolute; the fear is Europa's (cf. 860). Jupiter
69   gets her to approach and pat his chest and garland him with flowers.
        Ovid emphasizes the sound of patting with alliteration. *cornua sertis /
        inpedienda* 867–68: the horns are not seriously "hampered" by the
        garlands; the verb captures the symbolic way the points are adorned
        and pacified. Poets before Ovid had already begun to use *inpedire* for
        bedecking (e.g., Horace *C.* 1.4.9). *ausa est:* Europa becomes fatally
        daring. *Nescia, quem premeret* 869: subjunctive in indirect question
        (not relative clause of characteristic with *tauri*). The masculine pro-
        noun refers to Jupiter and should be translated as "whom." The verb
        often occurs with *tergum* or its plural to describe horsemen sitting on
        the back of an animal (cf. 6.223 and 8.34).

870–   *cum deus:* Ovid uses the *cum*-inversum construction to change the
73   focus from innocent Europa to lecherous Jupiter, who now starts to
        emerge from his disguise, a ridiculous god. Note the repeated preposi-
        tion *a;* the bull moves Europa *away from* the security of dry land.
        falsa . . . vestigia 871: the adjective, emphatically placed in initial
        position, stresses the deliberate deception of the bull-form; cf. 511,
        6.125, 7.360. *primo:* Ovid regularly uses this adverb in an initial
        clause, followed by a second clause with another temporal adverb,
        such as *inde* here or *mox* (860–61). As the bull swims farther away
        from land, Ovid enhances his smooth success in 872 with five dactyls.
        Then, he creates a contrasting rhythm at the start of 873 with three
        long syllables and full stop. The supposedly "peaceful" bull has waged
        his "war" and come away with his "booty." In *Ars Am.* Ovid uses

metaphors of war and hunting (especially *praeda*) to define the corrupt
relationship between men and women.

873–
75
pavet haec: in contrast with the god's triumph, Ovid ends the scene
and book studying the girl's pretty fear. It is less specific than that
of Leucothoe, who faces rape from the Sun in 4.227, but that is only
because Europa knows less than we do about the bull. *ablata:* follows
up *fert*. Passive implies her role as victim. *relictum / respicit* 874:
she looks back at all she has left, not just the shore. Horace's Europa
bewails the *relictum / filiae nomen* in *C.* 3.27.34–35. Catullus' Attis,
coming to his senses after his self-mutilation, apostrophizes his distant
homeland and all that he has completely left and lost (*C.* 62.49 ff.).
For Europa's hands, as Bömer nicely notes, poets and artists felt free
to use variety. Here, Ovid seems to emphasize the insecurity of the
girl by having her cling to the animal, grasping his horn with her
right hand and balancing herself with her left on his back. In *Fast.*
5.607, the poet describes her holding the hair on the bull's neck with
her right and clutching her mantle with her left, as if cold in the sea
breeze. *sinuantur . . . vestes* 875: her skirts blow out like a sail.
For this pretty effect of movement and its appeal to the eager male
imagination, cf. Daphne running in 1.501 and 527 ff.

NOTES TO BOOK 3

At the end of Book 2, we might expect Ovid to go on at length with the adventures of Europa, a familiar rape victim. However, he disposes of her summarily in the first two lines of Book 3 and transfers his attention to her brother Cadmus, founder of Thebes. The family of Cadmus, especially his grandchildren (plus a useful Boeotian youth, Narcissus), dominates Book 3 and much of Book 4 until Cadmus and his wife finally decide to abandon their city Thebes, which has proved so disastrous for their descendants, and depart (4.576 ff.).

CADMUS FOUNDS THEBES (1–130)

Dispatched by his father Agenor to find Europa or else remain an exile, Cadmus wanders vainly until he reaches the oracle of Apollo at Delphi. Consulted, it offers a helpful answer. On leaving the oracle, he will see a cow, which he should follow from Delphi to where it stops and lies down in the grass. There, he should settle down, found his city, and name the region (etymologically) *Boeotia*, from the Greek for cow. Nothing in the response points to the procession of troubles that will come to Cadmus and his children from their settlement. When he follows the oracle dutifully and prepares to sacrifice to Jupiter before founding his city, he innocently comes into a clash with the serpent of Mars that fiercely guards the region. It kills some of his companions who have disturbed it, and Cadmus heroically avenges their deaths in a violent battle. But as his spear nails the serpent to a tree and completes his victory, he hears an ominous voice that dooms him mysteriously to ultimate metamorphosis as a serpent and casts a gloomy pall over the entire origin of Thebes, his foundation. The mysterious prophecy (97–98) introduces a theme that Ovid will pursue in other stories of the Book: the sight of something or someone who is sacred/divine is automatically tragic for a human being, regardless

338

of his or her innocent intentions. Cadmus, however, rejects his first reactions of terror because another deity, Minerva, shows up and commands him to proceed with the establishment of Thebes. He takes the serpent's teeth, sows them in the ground, and then copes with the warriors who spring from the soil. Five survive from the internecine combat that arises, and these five, who replace his dead companions, help him to start Thebes and give a special character to its citizens.

1   *iamque*: the temporal adverb plus *-que* tends to obliterate the book-division and keep the story running. It is therefore somewhat of a surprise when Ovid immediately drops Jupiter and Europa after line 2. He begins Books 7 and 14 the same way. *posita . . . imagine*: ablative absolute. The metaphor for doffing a disguise corresponds to that of donning one at 2.850, *induitur*.

2   *se confessus erat*: Ovid devises a witty circumlocution to cover the easily imaginable scene when Jupiter resumed his male form and raped Europa; the verb points to the god's guilt (from our perspective), something that the amoral god would never recognize. Pluperfect tense, as usual, creates a background for the main narrative that starts in 3. *Dictaea*: Cretan, from Mount Dicte on Crete. Europa became the mother by Jupiter of Minos.

3–5   *pater ignarus*: Ovid has already defined this type in the fathers of Daphne and Io, so he spares us elaboration here. In other accounts, Agenor sends the whole family in search of Europa. Ovid concentrates exclusively on Cadmus, so as to get quickly to the founding of Thebes. *perquirere*: a technical verb used of researchers, spies, and scouts and restricted to prose. Ovid has it only here; it emphasizes the kind of "investigation" that the king commands. *si non invenerit* 4: future perfect, to go with the implied future in the "added penalty": he will suffer exile. *pius et sceleratus* 5: a careful pairing to emphasize favorite Ovidian theme: family loyalty can also be criminal. Agenor's exaggerated concern for Europa makes him harsh to Cadmus.

6–8   *orbe pererrato*: Ovid somewhat exaggerates the wanderings of Cadmus in order to start a Vergilian echo. Vergil had brought this verb into epic in connection with the wanderings of Aeneas, and in *Aen.* 2.295 had used the same perfect participle in a prophecy of the founding of Rome. This somewhat inappropriate comparison between Cadmus and Aeneas, Thebes and Rome will be developed with considerable irony here. *quis enim*: the parenthetical question, which interrupts the narrative, affects to create sympathy for Cadmus in his impossible search, but in fact it keeps reminding us of the criminal guilt of the rapist Jupiter and his complete escape from punishment which would have overtaken a human culprit. We have even heard how often Juno his wife has caught him in the act (*deprensi . . . furta mariti* 1.606).

Thus, although the apparent answer to the rhetorical question is: nobody, the poet has made sure that we answer it: everybody. *profugus* 7: another Vergilian word, taken from *Aen.* 1.2, the same metrical position, where it characterizes Aeneas. Ovid is intent on forcing a similarity between Cadmus and Aeneas despite the radical difference in the reasons for their exiles. *patriamque iramque*: the double object forces zeugma on the verb *vitat*. The two words clarify the distinction from Aeneas also. *Agenorides* 8: making good epic use of the patronymic, Ovid emphasizes ironically—in sharp opposition to Vergil's *Anchisiades* for Aeneas—the absence of paternal affection.

8–9 *Phoebique oracula*: the oracle at Delphi, as the later topographical detail at 14 confirms. The proximity of Delphi to Thebes has importance in the story of Oedipus, too. *quae . . . habitanda* 9: in historical times as well as in myth, Apollo advised on colonial settlements.

10–13 *bos . . . occurret*: prophecies often make use of the first thing or being the inquirer will see. Here, the verb suggests that the cow will voluntarily approach Cadmus. *solis . . . in arvis*: the adjective, which would have been *sola* with *bos*, has been transferred to the fields, at least partly for metrical reasons. *nullum passa iugum* 11: the fact that the animal is untamed and wandering free marks it out as a special sign. *hac duce* 12: ablative absolute. *carpe vias*: same verb with *iter* as object in 2.549. *requieverit*: future perfect indicative. Ovid has compressed an ordinary relative clause, which might be restored as: *in herba qua req. fac condas* 13: the imperative *fac* with the subjunctive belongs to the language of solemn injunctions like those of an oracle or religious commandment. Hence, too, the future imperative *vocato*. Once again, Ovid's language is reminiscent of Vergil's at *Aen.* 1.276–77, where Jupiter predicts the founding and naming of Rome.

14–16 *Castalio . . . antro*: the adjective Castalian referred to the famous spring of that name at Delphi, and thereby it came to connote Delphi in general. Thus, here it is associated with the cave from which the oracle spoke. Ablative of place from which. *incustoditam* 15: used earlier in 2.684, but here, supported by the slow syllables of *lente*, emphasizes the sedate amble of the prophesied animal (cf. 11). Since cows were so valuable, it would be unusual in Greece to find one untended; Ovid is not referring to range cattle such as we know in the American West and Southwest. Line 16 merely expands the detail of the first half of 11: the beast shows no trances of having ever been yoked.

17–18 *presso . . . passu*: "he follows in its tracks matching its pace." *taciturnus adorat* 18: Greeks and Romans characteristically prayed aloud, but here, without a place of worship and in the heat of pursuit, Cadmus confines his piety to silent prayer.

19–21 The Cephisus River and the town of Panopeus (simplified to Panope by Ovid) marked the border of Boeotia on the west near Delphi. The pluperfect thus indicates background; once it passed these points, the cow stopped to signify arrival in the region it would name. But they still are many miles from the site of future Thebes. Ovid's description of the cow here seems comic and anticlimactic: a long participial clause to describe its handsome horned head leads into a series of moos in the main clause. The founding of Thebes hardly matches that of Rome.

22–23 There are five dactyls in 22 and three more to open 23, all of which speed the verse up and probably contrast the haste of Cadmus and his companions with the sedate slowness of the cow. Line 23 describes the fulfillment of the prophecy in the second hemistich of 12; note repeated *herba*.

24–25 Kissing the earth on arrival at one's destination is a ritual practice known in all times. Brutus did it on return to Italy from Delphi; the Pope does it today on his trips. *ignotos* 25: a nice effect, contrasting the ignorance of the stranger with the familiarity of his descendants and many of Ovid's audience with the terrain of Boeotia.

26–27 *sacra Iovi*: since Jupiter has not been mentioned as the inspirer of this settlement and in fact may be considered rather as the criminal cause behind it, Ovid may again be contrasting the rules of Jupiter in Thebes and Rome. *ministros*: Cadmus' companions (22) or *socii* (51) perform here the duties of sacrificial attendants. The sacrifice is interrupted by the deaths of the companions and the vengeful assault on the dragon, and it is never resumed in Ovid's account. It might have included dedication of the cow; cf. the sacrifice of the portentous sow which appeared to Aeneas on the way to the site of Rome (*Aen.* 8.84–85). *vivis . . . fontibus* 27: fresh running water was required for religious rituals.

28–30 Ovid describes a seemingly idyllic spot in the woods, but he will turn it into a scene of violence. He has already done this with the grassy areas in the forest where tired huntresses like Callisto have rested and been raped. The new overtone here is indicated by the word *violata*. The place has religious taboos on it, and the companions of Cadmus, then Cadmus himself, are unwitting violators of its sanctity, for which they must suffer punishment. Regardless of their pious purpose, they disturb a sacred area and its apparent guardian. The cave in the middle of the woods quickly becomes the focus of attention. Thickly overgrown with vines, it seems to create a natural arch. Ovid here combines traditional items, woods and cave that go back as far as Homer, with more recent features such as this arch, which reflects the interests of contemporary artists and designers of rich gardens. There will be a similar description at 3.155 ff., with a similarly ironic function, for the forest pool (backed by cave and arch) of Diana. This arch (30) Ovid clearly explains: the vines have lodged in the cracks of the stone.

31–32   *uberibus fecundus aquis*: Ovid transfers to the waters of the spring its effects on agriculture and growth in general. Water is often the final element in a description of a *locus amoenus*, but it can have different connotations. For the tired hunter/huntress, water provides a cool drink and a place to bathe; for Cadmus' men, it provides the object of their quest, water for pious sacrifice. And it turns out that the spring constitutes only the penultimate element, for now Ovid adds the serpent or dragon, which implicitly functions as the menacing guardian of the spot. *Martius anguis* 32: it is not clear why Mars should be associated with a dragon, but the association was employed to explain his connection with Thebes and to add a warlike element to its founding myth. As Bömer notes, Ovid exploits this serpent from myth to reuse Vergilian details from the twin snakes that destroyed Laocoon and his sons in *Aen*. 2.203 ff. However, Bömer misses the artistry of Ovid and deals severely with what he considers inadequate and bombastic efforts to outdo Vergil. Ovid has a more playful and thematic purpose: to color the founding of Thebes with mock-epic touches and contrast it with Rome's Vergil-ennobled origins. *cristis praesignis et auro*: Ovid starts with his own details and vocabulary. The adjective is his own invention, perhaps first used here (or in *Ars Am*. 3.773, depending on the date of its Book 3). Vergil does not assign his serpents crests, but Ovid regularly does. When Cadmus is later metamorphosed, he will have a crest (4.599); and so will the similar dragon that Jason confronts in Colchis (7.150). Where the gold appears, on the crest or flecked over the entire snakeskin, is not evident, but it supports the deceptive attractiveness (a non-Vergilian motif), which Ovid will quickly dissipate in the next lines. Vergil's snakes are entirely menacing in color and physical stance from the start.

33–34   *igne micant oculi*: for fiery eyes in snakes, cf. *Aen*. 2.210; but the phrase itself comes from the wild-eyed description of Turnus in 12.102. Ovid has reversed the grammatical functions of the two nouns. Poison and snakes go together: cf. the earlier description of Python at 1.444 and *Aen*. 2.221. *tresque micant linguae* 34: Vergil limited himself to mentioning the hissing tongues of his snakes at *Aen*. 2.211, but at 2.475 he described in a simile a snake: *linguis micat ore trisulcis*, where the verb as well as the three-forked tongue is significant. Ovid uses the same verb at 6.557 with a snake's tongue, too. Thus, although our taste tends to reject the seemingly otiose repetition of verbs in successive lines, it is probably better to accept the unwavering tradition of the MSS and Latin usage. Heinsius did find *vibrant* in two MSS that have never been identified and urged its adoption. That would gain some support from Ovid's use of that verb with a snake's hissing tongue in 15.684 (also Vergil's in *Aen.* 2.211). However, there and elsewhere he always treats the *i* as long. To accept *vibrant*, then, it would be necessary to drop *-que* from *tres*; and that seems like too many changes on very slight authority. Ovid aims to exaggerate the three-forked tongue into three separate tongues and then give the mouth three sets of teeth. This is a cartoon monster.

35–38 *quem . . . lucum*: the separation of adjective and noun deceives the audience at first into believing that Ovid continues to refer to the snake with the accusative masculine. *Tyria . . . de gente profecti*: epic circumlocution to refer to the Tyrian companions of Cadmus (cf. 2.845). *infausto . . . gradu* 36: the adjective sounds a note of forewarning. *demissaque in undas*: the men are carrying out the orders of 27. The sound of the urn dipping out the water would not have been noisy, but it would have disturbed the serpent in his formerly inviolate environment. *longo . . . antro* 37: the MSS evidence again is uniform for the ablative form. Although that adjective is unusual for describing a deep or extensive cave, it is appropriate for the lair of the huge dragon. We need not adopt the emendation in some late MSS of Naugerius and read *longum*. *caput extulit*: same phrase and metrical position in *Aen.* 1.127. *caeruleus* 38: the color of an angry serpent in *Aen.* 2.381.

39–40 Ovid sketches the sudden terror of the Tyrians in a tricolon of ever larger units. *urnae*: a reading preserved by the Bern fragment; the subsequent MSS tradition agrees in *undae*, which is manifestly inferior.

41–42 Ovid describes the snake as it coils for the strike, in highly poetic and melodramatic language. The pattern of 41, with its two literary adjectives followed by their two nouns, and the postponement of the verb until 42, shows the poet ostentatiously at work on the trite myth. In 42, Ovid reminds his audience of Vergil's clause, *sinuatque immensa volumine terga (Aen.* 2.109), but outdoes his predecessor with his alliteration of slithering *s* and his arch-metaphor.

43–45 *media . . . parte*: ablative of comparison with *plus*; the snake towers over the men with more than half its body. *leves erectus in auras*: Ovid reuses this clause, varying only the adjective, in 15.512, where he describes the monstrous bull from the sea that caused the death of Hippolytus. *tantoque est corpore quanto* 44: ablative of description. The ending of the line with *quanto* creates an unusual run-on, which gains emphasis from the parenthetical condition at the beginning of 45. *si totum spectes* 45: Ovid invites the audience to participate in the experience, but also adds to his exaggeration. Roughly half this dragon is as large as the entire constellation, obviously colossal, that snakes its way between the two Bears. The wilder the scene, the more intimate the poet seems to get with his audience, as if inviting our smiling incredulity.

46–48   *Phoenicas*: Tyre (cf. 35), with Sidon, was a principal city of the coastal region of Phoenicia, whose inhabitants, then, are Phoenicians. In the remainder of 46 and 47, by a clever tricolon, Ovid analyzes the possible responses of the men, only to deny the utility of any action by the sudden *occupat*, a single dactyl that opens 48 and then comes to an abrupt stop with punctuation at the caesura.

48–49   This tricolon might, but probably does not, deal with the same three groups analyzed in 46–47, but it certainly displays artful rhetorical organization, with its ascending pattern and the careful placement of the demonstratives. *funesti tabe veneni* 49: the Bern fragment preserves the correct *funesti*, which most of the later MSS have changed to ablative. Ovid's somewhat cumbrous syntax results from his desire to crowd emphasis into the line-end on the foul, poisonous, and noxious breath of the dragon. The Latin then actually talks of the "breath of poison deadly with pestilence."

50   A variant on high noon, that deceptively quiet time which Ovid ironically chooses for many occasions of violence. Cf. the rape of Callisto at 2.417.

51–54   *Agenore natus*: cf. 3.8 and 2.858. *vestigatque viros* 52: deliberately trivializes a clause in identical metrical position from *Aen.* 12.482, where Aeneas is hunting Turnus down. Cadmus, for all his hunting uniform here, is no Aeneas. *tegumen . . . pellis*: the lion skin evokes mighty Hercules, as in *Aen.* 7.666. *leoni*: dative of separation. Ready for anything, the hunter carries both hunting spear and javelin. To cap the heroic build-up, the poet makes sure that we grasp the superior quality of Cadmus' courage, mightier than any weapon. *teloque . . . omni* 54: ablative of comparison; in such cases, *omni* = "any."

55–57   *letataque*: rare poetic verb. presumably chosen to prepare us for Cadmus' "heroism." *victoremque . . . hostem* 56: it sounds as though Cadmus is looking at a gigantic human warrior towering over the corpses. Then 57, patterned as a Golden Line, with its grotesque description of the reptilian behavior, undercuts this confrontation— not epic but merely fabulous.

58–60   Cadmus apostrophizes his dead companions and bravely takes on the task of avenging their deaths. His speech starts off in solemn spondees. *mortis*: objective genitive. *molarem* 59: literally, a millstone. The only earlier use we know of this substantive is *Aen.* 8.250, where Vergil describes Hercules' battle with Cacus and uses the plural form to refer to large stones. The word choice seems designed to fit Cadmus' Herculean costume in accordance with Ovid's allusive program. It is no doubt odd that this hunter, with his two spears, should have first resort to a stone for a weapon. The ostentatious alliteration of 60 makes too much of the effort to throw the thing. *conamine*: Ovid, who has picked up this archaic poeticism from Lucretius (or Ennius before him), has it five times, always in this useful metrical position.

1–64 Ovid playfully goes on, setting up an expectation of complete annihilation (*mota*) in his conditional clause of 61–62, then dismissing it with the simple indicative *mansit* 62. He relies on his audience's knowledge of the use of ballistic weapons in military sieges. In 63–64, the serpent assumes the status of a warrior equipped with impenetrable armor in the form of thick scales and tough skin.

5–67 The same subject and the same instrumental ablative operate in 65, but with a negative. Why the spear is more effective than the huge stone is not explained. Presumably, the point on the spear succeeds where the mere mass of the stone failed. *quod* 66: the spear. It has pierced the dragon's back at the center of the spine and sticks out from there, but its iron point has driven on into the entrails.

8–69 *ille*: the dragon. In duels between men, a wounded hero regularly tries to wrench out a spear that has pierced him and fight on. Hunted animals also attack the weapon that has hurt them. So this dragon feels pain, looks back to see what has caused it, and then tries to bite the spear. *fixumque* 69: cf. 66, where Ovid uses the same participle, but varies the noun.

0–71 *partem labefecit in omnem*: by tugging the haft in every direction, the dragon has weakened its purchase. *tergo* 71: singular vs. plural in 68; here, ablative of separation. Though he manages to dislodge the shaft, the real source of his agony, the point, remains fixed in spine and vitals.

2–73 *solitas . . . iras*: like most snakes in Greco-Roman literature, this dragon is imagined to be prone to anger, which in this instance is aggravated by the wound. In the manner of poisonous snakes like the adder, it puffs up menacingly at the neck (rather than inside the throat, as the normal usage of *guttura* might suggest).

4–76 A Golden Line in 74 artfully renders the supposed horror of the foaming mouth. Then, Ovid makes the scales, which normally produce no special sound, give off a rasping noise. Finally, the dragon's breath is black, that is, deadly, and it pours out of its hellish mouth. *vitiatas inficit* 76: Ovid uses the subordinated participle where we would probably use a double verb, e.g., "pollutes and dyes."

7–80 *ipse*: the snake. Ovid develops another tricolon, which he clearly articulates by the three temporal adverbs. The snake coils—Ovid says it is ringed by coils creating huge circles—then straightens out like a beam (78), then launches itself in an attack on Cadmus. *ceu concitus . . . amnis* 79: like a flood, especially the familiar torrent that rushes down the mountains and out into the Italian plains during the spring. *obstantes proturbat* 80: Caesar and other prose writers use the main verb regularly in contexts of battle, and Ovid has reinforced the metaphor here with the participle. In its wild attack on Cadmus, the dragon knocks down the trees in its path as if they were enemies.

81–84 *spolioque leonis / sustinet* 82: a normal lion skin would never stop the deadly charge and breath of a dragon, but, as Bömer suggests, this lion skin resembles that of Hercules, which came from the unwoundable Nemean lion. *cuspide praetenta* 83: Cadmus jabs at the face of the dragon and thus keeps it from biting him. *furit ille*: in its frustration, the beast snaps at the point.

85–86 *venenifero*: Ovid here invents this word, along the lines of epic compounds. Note the use of colors: red blood dyeing the green grass. Pluperfects mark background events.

87–89 Though all that blood seemed significant, Ovid now plays with our expectations, and expatiates for three lines on how the snake pulled itself back from serious wounds. Note *retrahebat, dabat retro, cedendo*.

90–92 *coniectum in gutture ferrum*: Ovid now compresses his description. Two phases of the action become one: first Cadmus threw his spear into the throat (*in guttura telum*) of the dragon, then followed it and pressed the iron point lodged in the throat (*in gutture ferrum*). Notice the two different syntaxes and two different parts of the spear involved. *retro . . . eunti* 91: the snake continues to retreat, but now its way is blocked by an oak. Never mind that earlier it knocked over any tree in its way (cf. 80): now it is stopped and nailed to the trunk by the spear. *pariter cum robore cervix* 92: an instance of virtual zeugma dear to Ovid (cf. 2.610).

93–94 Final details: the oak bends under the weight of the dragon, and it is lashed by the death throes of the tail. *imae / parte . . . caudae*: the MSS reading *imae* has bothered some, and Hartung proposed emending to ablative *ima*. However, Ovid and other Latin poets like to frame their clauses with an adjective-noun unit as here, and they felt no difficulty with a transferred epithet. *flagellari*: this seems to be the first occurrence of this verb, invented for this picturesque detail. *gemuit*: this verb governs indirect discourse with neologism *flagellari*. The tree groans that its wood is being whipped. Ovid has apparently freely devised this novel death for the legendary serpent.

95–98 *spatium*: cf. *spatiosi* 56. *victor victi . . . hostis*: Ovid stresses the heroic pose of Cadmus in familiar Roman propagandistic terms. But as he proudly looks at the dragon, Cadmus falls under the curse for beholding the sacred and taboo. *audita est . . . laudita est* 96–97: Ovid engineers the repetition, which insists on the audibility of the voice, to occur in the same metrical position in successive lines. The parenthesis has a standard Ovidian organization, occupying the second hemistich of one line and the first of the next, divided between *neque-*

and *sed*-clauses. Line 98 presents one of Ovid's riddling prophecies, enhanced by chiastic repetition around the central caesura, and rendered gravely resonant by four successive spondees and alliteration. Although no effort is made to explain here why Cadmus should not look at the dead dragon or why he should be punished—if it is that—by metamorphosis as snake, subsequent stories in Book 3 suggest that there are sights that mortals may not behold without penalty.

99–
100   *pariter cum mente colorem*: another case of virtual zeugma (cf. 92), this one rather comical in reference to the "hero" Cadmus, whose *animus*, we heard, was so outstanding (cf. 54). Alliteration of *p* also undercuts. Apparently, his hair stands up stiffly with fright, but only for this line. Ovid then dismisses the momentary effect and moves on to a new mood and situation in 101.

101–
3   *fautrix*: this word has the prosaic connotations of political patronage, and Ovid seems to have used it rather daringly and uniquely in hexameter poetry here of a goddess. In tradition, Minerva (Athena) has a long association with Cadmus and the sowing of the dragon's teeth. Her sudden arrival ends the hero's terror and launches him enthusiastically into his next adventure. *adest* 102: with its subject, the verb connotes help. *motaeque . . . supponere terrae*: Ovid devises unusual language for ordinary plowing and sowing. Since we see Cadmus in 104–5 obeying Pallas' command, it is not clear why she should have been so pompous here. "Moved earth" could, as the modern Italian word terremoto, allude to an earthquake. And *supponere* does not have any agricultural connotation; rather, it refers to hiding or even dishonestly substituting something. Perhaps, Ovid implies that the order of the goddess was obscure, like the voice from the tree, and its meaning only became clear later. In that case, we may imagine Cadmus puzzled by what he was doing with the teeth, but dutifully obeying. *populi incrementa futuri* 103: "growth of a future people," i.e., which will grow into a future people. The line, divided at the caesura between two seemingly irreconcilable sets of words, points up the confusion inherent in Pallas' words.

104–
5   *spargit* 105: common verb for sowing. *iussos . . . dentes*: picks up key words of 102–3. Ovid splits this phrase with its logical apposition. *mortalia semina*: the adjective is variously relevant: to the death of the serpent, the human beings who will be produced from the seeds, and finally to the deaths of those creatures in mutual warfare. Those possibilities should not be limited by translation; use our ambiguous word "mortal."

106–
8   *inde (fide maius)*: identical preparation for a marvel in the contemporaneous *Fasti* 2.113. The parenthesis, extremely abrupt, involves ablative of comparison and an understood verb like *est*: "it is beyond belief." *glaebae . . . moveri*: this has nothing to do with Pallas'

command in 102, although the words are similar; here, the earth moves not from plowing, but from the sprouting seed. Then, growing up before Cadmus' eyes, from head to foot, appears a set of warriors. He sees first the spearpoint (which normally set on a long shaft stands above the armored soldier), and then he marks the crest and helmet of the warriors themselves. *tegmina . . . nutantia* 108: what is waving is obviously the helmet crest, which is attached to the top (*conus*) of the decorated headgear.

109–
10
In a pair of clauses of chiastic arrangement, where the verbs of growth are juxtaposed in 110, Ovid gets more of the men to sprout, up to the bottoms of their shields (which normally extend down to their upper legs or even knees). *seges clipeata* 110: the noun repeats the agricultural metaphor that has been operative since 102; the adjective refers to the round bronze shield of the Roman soldier, the *clipeus*. The anachronism occurs also in Vergil, who equipped his warriors with this shield.

111–
14
To clarify the scene and also to make it more pictorial than frightening, Ovid develops a simile from the familiar Roman stage, where curtains were raised from the floor to close off the setting and action, not to reveal it. When the painted curtain appeared, rising to end an act or a full drama, the picture on its surface unfolded in the same general way as the warriors, sprung from the dragon's seed, steadily rose to their full form before Cadmus. *theatris*: ablative of place where. *surgere signa solent* 112: the noun indicates that statues have been depicted on the curtain, not living beings. The audience first sees heads and, as more of the curtain rises into view, it gets to look at more complete bodies until finally the feet appear. The alliteration in 112 has no precise effect except perhaps to suggest the steady unrolling of the curtain. Cf. *placidoque educta tenore* 113. *imoque . . . in margine* 114: at the bottom of the drape, where the artfully drawn statues seem to set or plant their feet, both completing the figure for the audience and assuming a lifelike pose as a standing person.

115
territus hoste novo: poor Cadmus, completely unprepared by Pallas for what is happening, plunges into terror again (cf. 100). In other versions, as in the parallel account of Jason's trial with the men he harvested from his dragon's teeth, Cadmus was fully ready to cope with the crisis and calmly did so. Ovid seems to want to stress his character's fears and constant recourse to weapons. He thinks he must defend himself, whereas usually Cadmus throws a stone among the warriors and so starts them fighting, perfectly safe himself.

116–
17
Ovid contrives a unique variant, which appears to bear directly on key political themes of the Augustan era. For no apparent reason, one of the warriors addresses Cadmus, telling him to put down his sword and not interfere in the fight, which he pointedly labels *civilibus bellis*.

Thus, though "civil war" occurs at the founding of Thebes, the founder is untainted by the conflict, and he embodies ideals of peace and civic accord, ideals that Augustan propaganda continuously sounded. Ovid makes his Cadmus a cardboard angel, who lacks the complex and compromised personality of Vergil's Aeneas. I assume that he was playing with the Augustan themes, expecting the courtiers to smile at the audacity with which he treated such ideals.

118–
21
terrigenis . . . fratribus: the epic compound goes back at least to Lucretius. Ovid uses it of these men and of the similar product of Jason's dragon seed in 7.36 and 141, but also of the more properly "earthborn" giant Typhoeus in 5.325. The reference to brothers applies to the theme of Civil War, when typically brother fights brother. In this "war" we hear of no motivation (such as the rock traditionally thrown among them by Cadmus); the speaker of 116–17 simply hacks at a nearby "brother" with his sword, for no reason. The three related terms of the two clauses in 119 do not quite fall into a full chiasmus, but they do balance each other. The one who has sliced his brother close at hand with his sword falls, struck by a flying spear from a distance. To take away serious engagement with this scene, Ovid keeps us at a distance, too, records no pain or blood, and prances lightly over the events of 119 with five dactyls. In a third death, elaborated over 120–21, the poet reveals the spiral effect of killer being killed and uses the rhetorical paradox that, dying, the warrior breathes the last of the air he has just started to inhale.

122–
23
exemploque pari: ablative of attendant circumstances, roughly "in the same manner." *furit*: appropriate verb for savage warfare. *suoque / Marte*: in war among themselves, i.e., civil war. The unusual enjambement between these two words helps to make the delayed noun, an instance of metonymy, that much more effective. We probably should remember, too, that Mars, as the patron of the dragon, would be involved in the fate of the men who sprang from its teeth. *subiti*: they have, as we have seen, sprung up very suddenly from the ground.

124–
26
Ovid registers with fake pathos the short life of these men in 124, then develops a Golden Line in 125 to catch the picture of their death throes, after which he quickly dismisses them to focus on the survivors. *superstitibus* 126: ablative absolute. The most important survivor, for the poet's purposes, is Echion, who will marry Cadmus' daughter Agave and sire Pentheus, the central character of 3.511 ff. (introduced as *Echionides* at 513 and also called *Echione natus* at 526). The name in Greek implies a connection with snakes.

127–
28
iecit humo: a locative form *humo* existed in Ovid's day parallel with the more familiar *humi*. As the more difficult reading, preserved by some of the earliest MSS, it has earned acceptance. *monitu Tritonidis*: Ovid once again makes Minerva intrude, to take matters out of the

helpless Cadmus' hands and settle this civil war once and for all. Echion takes the lead in 128 and arranges a firm peace. Note the alliteration.

129–
30   In a highly formal pair of lines, Ovid brings this first narrative of Book 3 to a stately close, referring to Cadmus in circumlocution as a "stranger" and reminding us of the oracle of Delphi that initiated events. The MSS tradition divides in 130 between *iussus* and *iussam*, but the former gains preference because it has good early support and is more difficult.

TRANSITION TO CADMUS' MISFORTUNES (131–37)

Ovid jumps over many years, during which Thebes began to prosper, and Cadmus' loneliness turned into a large family of three generations. As we meet him now, he enjoys happy domesticity with Harmonia, who, as daughter of Venus and Mars, helps to insure those divinities' favor. By Harmonia, he has had four daughters, all of whom we will encounter in Book 3. Each has at least one son, three of whom will also play roles in Book 3. On the surface, then, Cadmus has a thriving family and the promise of a long-lived dynasty. Alas, his hopes were even more frustrated than the notorious dynastic plans of Augustus (of which no doubt Ovid's audience thinks), and Ovid waxes sententious, in the fashion of Herodotus and his times, to remind us that we should count no man happy before death. It is ironic that Cadmus will not die, but change into a snake, so the Herodotean sentiment does not apply. The stories that follow about Cadmus' family do not illustrate the Greek commonplace, but rather work out the semiliterary, folklore theme about the danger of seeing the forbidden holy.

131–
33   *iam stabant Thebae*: in this solemn spondaic series, Ovid at last names the city that Cadmus founded. The adverb indicates the passage of time, which works out to almost fifty years, two generations grown to maturity. *poteras*: although this tense might simply continue the imperfect indicative, it is probable that it serves as the equivalent of the imperfect subjunctive in an unreal condition. The apostrophe of Cadmus by the narrator is a frequent device of familiarity by Ovid. *exilio felix* 132: a paradox for any ancient (whose whole existence depended upon belonging to a city and state), but especially for Ovid, whose experience of exile proved totally miserable. However, these words were probably written before he had to leave Rome and sail for the Black Sea, never to return. *soceri*: still addressing Cadmus, Ovid tells him and us of the in-laws that he acquired by marriage to Harmonia. Note the pluperfect tense: the wedding was the beginning of his seeming happiness. That was followed in due course by children and grandchildren.

133–   *huc adde*: the imperative might continue to refer to Cadmus, or it
35   might now address the Ovidian audience. *genus de coniuge tanta*:
        one might have expected *tantum* with *genus*, but the MSS universally
        agree on the ablative, which emphasizes the eminence of this semi-
        divine wife. *natas natosque* 134: a few MSS have chauvinistically
        assumed that sons would always take priority over daughters and
        reversed the nouns. However, Cadmus seems to have had only one
        son, named Polydorus; he disappears rather quickly, yielding center
        stage to his four sisters, whose tragic stories inspire Ovid in most of
        Books 3 and 4. *pignora cara*: children and grandchildren are consid-
        ered "guarantees" of the family and its prosperous survival. The meta-
        phor is ironic in the case of Cadmus' grandsons. *iam iuvenes* 135:
        the third generation has already reached young manhood; about fifty
        years had passed.

135–   *homini* 136: dative of agent with passive periphrastic. The sentiment
37   is particularly attributed to Solon by Herodotus 1.32, who then demon-
        strates the truth of Greek wisdom by tracing the ruin of Croesus.

ACTAEON (138–252)

Having mentioned Cadmus' grandsons, Ovid proceeds to follow
their wretched fates, ignoring strict chronology in favor of narrative
importance. The two who appear in Book 2 are Actaeon and Pentheus,
and Ovid places them not together, but at the start and end of the
book. Why he chooses to start with Actaeon, Autonoe's son, instead
of Pentheus, he does not say. I suspect that Actaeon serves immediate
poetic purposes better because he is a hunter who suffers the wrath
of Diana, and his story can be seen as parallel to those of other
unfortunate hunters, notably Callisto.

The myth of Actaeon knew several variants. Always a hunter, young
Actaeon was early presented as one who outraged Diana, whether by
challenging her to a competition in hunting, by violating her sanctuary,
or by trying to rape her (cf. Hyginus 180), and for his guilt he was
changed into a deer and hunted to his death by his own hounds. At
latest by the time of Callimachus, Actaeon's "crime" had become less
outrageous: he had chanced upon Diana bathing. Ovid takes that
situation and builds it into a powerful story of human innocence
abused, as was Callisto's innocence, by a ruthless deity. Actaeon, in
Ovid's narrative, had no intention of spying on Diana, accidently
stumbled onto her bathing, and, before he even had a chance to
react, was branded as guilty and punished with metamorphosis by the
indignant, plainly unjust goddess. As a deer, Actaeon does not stand
a chance. Trapped inside the animal form, he cannot communicate
his human feelings, and he dies a helpless beast of prey, torn to

bits by his own dogs who are urged on by his own recent hunting companions. The pathos of this human deer and the cruelty of angry, unreasonable Diana align us with the innocent victim. In terms of the basic theme of beholding the forbidden and holy, Actaeon is even less guilty and more abused than his grandfather Cadmus, who was innocent in his trespassing on the dragon's lair, but brought trouble on himself by attacking and killing this creature of Mars.

138–40   The poet begins his story, avoiding the name of Actaeon and describing him for the clever audience through key details, namely, the horns on his head (an allusion to his becoming a deer) and his death as victim of his own dogs. The name *Actaeon* will finally first appear when the deer vainly tries to identify itself as the prince before falling prey to the hounds (cf. 230 below). The word order of 138–39 may be simplified as follows: *prima causa luctus inter . . . secundas fuit nepos.* Notice that the poet once again addresses Cadmus. The circumlocutions to avoid naming Actaeon allow the poet to introduce (in 139–40) key elements of the tragic tale he plans to tell. But they do not seem tragic at this stage, especially with the apostrophe to the dogs.

141–42   *si quaeras . . . invenies* 142: a mixed condition of subjunctive and indicative. The second person may continue the conversation with Cadmus and offer him comfort, but the audience would naturally feel addressed by it, too. The narrator is raising the common question about a sudden, cruel death: what did the dead man do to deserve his death? He insists, against earlier tradition about Actaeon, that, if there was a misdeed, it should be attributed to fortune. Then, he goes on to contrast *scelus* and *error: scelus* would be an act of deliberate evil (such as openly insulting Diana from foolish pride); *error* would be accidental wandering, whether literally from the path or figuratively from the truth. It turns out that Actaeon's mistake is one of literal wandering (cf. 174 ff.). He did not mean to intrude on Diana's bath, and he certainly does not have time to think of *scelus* before she angrily punishes him.

143–45   *infectus*: the verb of dyeing has so many bad connotations, e.g., "soaked, infected, poisoned," that it is hard to read this description of animal slaughter as neutral. Ironically, the blood of other animals that he has copiously shed as the story opens will be matched (and avenged) by the hunter's own blood at the end, blood shed from a seeming animal. *dies medius* 144: Ovid devotes two lines to the representation of high noon (cf. 50). In the *Met.*, this is a frequent setting for disaster. *meta . . . utraque* 145: ablative of place from which, without preposition. The metaphor of a racetrack is common for the Sun, especially since he is imagined to drive a chariot and four swift horses. The two *metae* or turning posts are the east from which he rises and west where he sets. Ovid slows down the rhythm in 145 with four spondees just before introducing his main character.

146–
47
iuvenis . . . Hyantius: first of several epic circumlocutions designed to avoid naming the "hero." The adjective probably appears here for the first time in Latin; it means "Boeotian." Along with *placido . . . ore*, it frames the scene. Actaeon's serenity is designedly emphasized, in contrast to the common tradition about his violence and arrogance. He is almost an ideal Vergilian prince.

148–
49
Like the narrator in 143, Actaeon registers in 148 the bloody success of the hunt, and perhaps he distances himself from its cruel wastefulness. *fortunamque dies habuit satis* 149: one early fragment emended the accusative to partitive genitive with *satis*, but the change is unnecessary. In light of the narrator's introduction at 141, the statement here by Actaeon must seem ironic. He thinks of fortune as favorable and asks no more of it after his hunting successes; but fortune now has a crime to inflict on him. Its day has just begun.

149–
52
altera lucem / cum . . . Aurora reducet: the normally initial temporal *cum* yields to more significant words. Instead of saying "another day," Actaeon expands with a description of Dawn (which he will never see). *Phoebus utraque / distat idem terra* 151–52: variant on 145. *idem* replaces *ex aequo*, and *utraque . . . terra* replaces the racing image of the turning post with the limits of the earth.

153–
54
tollite lina: Actaeon's speech ends on the same word with which it began. That suggests not only Ovid's cleverness but also the prince's sense of order. The hunters have used nets to trap the deer: now they are to take them up. *intermittuntque laborem* 154: we have already had descriptions of tired hunters and the ways in which they relieve their toil. Ovid does not need to spell that out. However, earlier tired hunters rested only with drastic results. When Ovid stops here and turns to another hunter, he is either breaking or postponing a pattern.

155–
58
The poet begins an ecphrasis without indicating its pertinence to what has preceded. Actaeon has apparently been on a mountain (cf. 143); now the scene shifts, by this description, to a thickly wooded valley. There was a spring near Plataea, below the mountains, which the Greeks called Gargaphie. Ovid is the first to name the valley such. *succinctae . . . Dianae* 156: as the huntress goddess, Diana hitched up her long robes to facilitate the chase. In both 9.89 and 10.536, Ovid uses the phrase *ritu succincta Dianae* to liken other women to the goddess. *antrum nemorale* 157: this is the second cave in Book 3, and it acquires menace from the previous one. *arte laboratum nulla* 158: ostensibly, Ovid means only that it is a natural cave; but he also

refers to the contemporary Augustan delight in artificial caves, which were planned for aristocratic gardens, as later in eighteenth century England.

158–
60
Not content with praising the artlessness of Nature, the narrator argues that Nature is a superior artist, working with its own genius. It had constructed an arch from native stone. The dragon's cave also had an arch (cf. 30), the picturesque focus of its threat. *pumice . . . tofis* 159–60: ablative of material with the customary *ex* omitted. Both of these materials derive from volcanic regions; they were soft and easily worked.

161–
62
The spring matches the fresh water abundantly gushing near the dragon's cave in 31 (cf. 27); the similarity of the two settings implies similarity of trouble for Actaeon. *tenui . . . unda*: ablative of respect. The adjective, applied to water, means "clear." The transparency of water connotes freshness and purity, and it befits the virginal goddess. However, when Actaeon stumbles onto the scene, we can suspect a less dignified relevance in the word: he can see through the liquid the naked body of Diana, or so she suspects. In 162, Ovid completes his picture of false idyllic serenity. Right up to the very opening of the spring, grass grows and frames it. There is no mud, no rough stones: it is perfect, another masterpiece of Nature the artist. *hiatus* 162: accusative with perfect passive participle; cf. 1.265, 270.

163–
64
dea silvarum: Ovid invents a plausible epithet for Diana. *venatu fessa*: the tired huntress, like Callisto, has been the target for rape in earlier lines. However, Ovid created two tired hunters, and both settle down to relax. How is he going to bring them into relationship and make one victim, the other aggressor? The language of 164 is ostentatiously literary, putting special poetic emphasis on the site of Diana's bath.

165–
67
nympharum . . . uni: although this is the first indication of the presence of nymphs with the goddess, stories and paintings regularly assign her such companions; they attended her in the account of Callisto. *armigerae* 166: Plautus used this word in comedy, but Vergil treated it as an epic compound. Ovid's innovation is to use it for a female. This first nymph takes various items of hunting (each recalling the scene of Callisto's disarming before rest and rape, 2.419 ff.). Others take her clothes. *subiecit bracchia* 167: like a lady's maid, this nymph held out her arms so that the robe could be neatly laid out on them.

168–
70
It takes two maids to remove Diana's sandals. From the feet, Ovid jumps up to the head, where specially skilled Crocale arranges the hair for the bath. Normally, Diana wears her hair loose (*sparsos*), as her maids continue to do. But for obvious convenience during the bath, she has her tresses bound in a knot. Most readers recognize that Ovid indulges in anachronism here by describing Diana as an imperious Roman lady who is waited on by a large set of servants. *Ismenis* 169:

Theban, derived from the nearby river. Ovid invents the epithet. At
171, Diana, completely nude, with her hair properly arranged, is ready
for her bath. In the usual written and pictorial versions, she plunges
into a pool (exactly as she did earlier in 2.459). But Ovid has started
to describe her as a rich Roman matron, and so her bath must be in
Augustan style: servants must draw water in urns and pour it over her
as she stands. Thus, he adds five more attendants to the five he has
already allotted the goddess, and this time he ostentatiously names
them. The names are all Greek, several associated with water, and
they all have a mellifluous dactylic flow (except Ranis). The light
rhythm results in five dactyls in 171 and two initial dactyls in 172.

173–   *perluitur . . . lympha*: careful alliteration with liquid *l. solita*: cf.
76   *solebat* 163. *Titania*: Diana was granddaughter of the Titan Coeus by
her mother Latona. *ecce nepos Cadmi* 174: here, the poet suddenly
interrupts the sedate bath and switches our attention back to Actaeon,
now presented with another epithet that reminds us of the ominous
theme of precious family members (cf. 134, 138). *dilata . . . la-
borum*: this clause picks up 154, where we left the hunter. Now
perhaps we realize that Ovid did not give Actaeon there a setting for
rest, and he fills in the deficiency here by bringing him to Diana's
idyllic spot, as an unwitting intruder, not as a rapist. The details of
175, climaxing in the thematic *errans*, force the innocence of the boy
on us, the audience. In one of his poems from exile (*Tr.* 2.131 ff.),
Ovid used the innocence of Actaeon as in this version to parallel his
own guiltlessness in connection with Augustus. He thus seems to have
had a special feeling about this Theban prince. *sic illum fata ferebant*
176: more of the same emphasis, with *fata* serving loosely as the
equivalent of *fortuna* earlier in 141. Ovid has simplified a famous
line of Vergil, where the audience was offered by cautious Aeneas a
choice of explanations for the enthusiasm of some Trojans to bring
the horse inside the walls: *sive dolo seu iam Troiae sic fata ferebant
(Aen.* 2.34). The biased narrator allows us no choice here, nor is this
a situation with massive epic import.

177–   *qui simul intravit*: by using the relative as a connective with 176,
79   Ovid seems to continue his focus on Actaeon. But again he surprises
us by veering away from his "hero" at this key moment, when, if we
were in his shoes, we certainly would have reacted in *some* way.
Ovid denies us the satisfaction of attributing any reaction whatsoever
to the prince, thus by deliberate omission implying his lack of guilt.
rorantia fontibus antra: poetic plural, presumably to facilitate the
dactylic ending of the participle. The phrase summarizes details of
157–62. *sicut erant, viso nudae . . . viro* 178–79: the MSS early fell
into two camps over this passage. With the above text, Ovid does not
limit the picture of the nymphs "as they were," and so invites us to

recall the whole scene of the ten attendants collected around their mistress. He has not told us that they were also nude, nor do they seem so much concerned over their own nudity as that of Diana. A rival reading of good MSS gives *nudae viso*, which would presumably require punctuation after the first word and its grouping with *sicut erant*. The passage would then put the emphasis on the nude nymphs, who at sight of a man shrieked because of their nudity. That seems a misplaced emphasis, and the reading has been rejected. Ovid certainly wants *us* to picture the pretty nudes and their disarray, so as to wonder about Actaeon's response and be surprised and disappointed by its elision. We supply the erotic element that innocent Actaeon and irately virginal Diana have eliminated from the anticipated situation.

179– *ululatibus*: howling or shrieking of women that can fit a variety of
82 circumstances, though, as here, it often accompanies panic and distress. Vergil before Ovid in *Aen*. 7.395 described how women filled the air with shrieking. *circumfusaeque* 180: the passive functions in a "middle" or reflexive sense. The simple verb might ironically recall *fundunt* of 172 and point to the confusion caused by Actaeon. It also helps Ovid to compose a rare four-word hexameter here. *tamen altior . . . supereminet omnes* 181–82: Ovid exploits another famous passage of Vergil, who introduced Dido through a simile about Diana (borrowed in turn from Homer) and put special emphasis with the same final words on the imposing size of queen and goddess. In Vergil's simile, however, Diana, like Dido, grand and majestic, advances among her lesser companions. Cf. *Aen*. 1.498–502. In Ovid's passage, on the contrary, the tallness of Diana stirs our erotic responses (but apparently not Actaeon's). The taller the goddess, the less the nymphs shield and the more she exposes. Ovid fussily specifies, where Vergil does not need to, that we can see the goddess down to her neck.

183– Diana blushes with modesty and wrath, and Ovid develops that blush
85 pictorially by simile. He seems to refer to opposite times of day, sunset and sunrise. *ab ictu*: strictly speaking, the preposition is unnecessary. *purpureae Aurorae* 184: a rare double spondee so organized that hiatus occurs and metrical stress falls on the final syllable of the adjective, where the word is not accented; and thus the usual coincidence in the fifth foot disappears. Since red sunsets and colorful dawns strike us as beautiful, we may be lulled by this simile into eroticism and then be shocked, by Ovid's intention, at the drastic actions of Diana. *visae sine veste* 185: a deliberate understatement. As the narrator seems to attenuate the gravity of the situation, he actually broaches the basic theme of the story: the automatic disaster of those who see the forbidden.

186– *quamquam comitum turba stipata: quamquam* with participle renders

89   precisely our English "although closely pressed." Ovid is recalling
          the actions of Diana's maids at 180–81. Feeling still exposed, the
          goddess turns her body and her head sharply to keep prying eyes from
          seeing her sexual parts and her face. The famous statue of the crouching
          Venus seems to assume that that goddess has been intruded upon,
          too, while bathing and modestly tries to prevent erotic inspection. *ut
          vellet . . . sic hausit* 188–89: correlative clauses. "Much as she wanted
          . . . still she drew some water." The subjunctive is not normally
          employed in such clauses. Ovid may suggest, as Bömer believes, the
          form of Diana's wish (*ut vellem*), or he may seek a metrically useful
          alternative for *volebat* or *voluit*. *quas . . . aquas*: in his typical manner
          of creating suspense, Ovid puts the relative clause before its anteced-
          ent. Diana "had" water, of course, in the pool pouring over her nude
          body or immediately available in one of the urns of her attendants.

189–   Splashing Actaeon's face and hair, Diana immediately causes his
93   metamorphosis to start there (194–95), but she continues to change
          the rest of the body (196–97), to complete the deer-form. *ultricibus
          undis* 190: the water, personified, carries out the vengeful purposes
          of the goddess. *cladis* 191: objective genitive. *posito visam velamine*
          192: another delicate circumlocution for *nudam visam* (cf. 185). Here,
          Ovid uses ablative absolute. The most even Diana attributes to Actaeon
          is open boasting that he has seen her nude. This is a long way from
          the blasphemy or lust assigned him in earlier tradition. (That will
          differentiate him considerably from his cousin Pentheus later in Book
          3.) By starting the metamorphosis at the head, she rapidly robs him
          of the capacity of speech (cf. 210). *narres*: at first, this seems a jussive
          subjunctive, but then the delayed *licet* changes its syntax and reduces
          the certainty of narration.

193–   *sparso* 194: cf. *spargens* 190. *vivacis cornua cervi*: starting from the
95   horns that rise above the head, Ovid works his way down the external
          form of the deer, before focusing on key internal features (198 ff.).
          This phrase comes verbatim from Vergil *Ecl*. 7.30, where horns are,
          fittingly enough, dedicated to Diana. It was a fixed popular belief that
          deers lived a long life. Here, the adjective is ironic, because as a deer
          Actaeon will meet his death in minutes. Like Io in 1.640–41, he will
          be shocked to see his horns reflected in a pool (cf. 200–1). The next
          changes require in 195 broadening the human neck and tipping the
          human ears. In Hawthorne's *The Marble Faun*, and in the Roman
          statue that inspired the novel, the faun has tipped animal ears, the
          only external indication of his special nature. *cacuminat*: invented by
          Ovid for this line and used only here.

196–   Once she has started the changes in parts where the water splashed,
97   Diana continues on to parts where the water did not touch. *cum*

pedibusque manus: taking his viewpoint from the front of the beast, the narrator now registers what happens to the hands and arms, which become feet and legs, obviously forelegs. In converting a human biped to a quadriped, the imagination has no difficulty in changing legs to back legs: the dramatic change occurs when arms become forelegs, and the erect human being falls down on all fours. (Cf. the transformation of Callisto at 2.476 ff.) Loss of hands also means loss of the gesture of human prayer and appeal; which frustrates Io and Callisto and becomes emblematic of the fatal helplessness of Actaeon (cf. 240–41). *velat . . . corpus* 197: instead of indicating that the white human skin becomes a dappled hide, Ovid suggests that the human being is "veiled," as if enclosed, by the hide. Thus, he is able to continue with his special thematic situation: human consciousness struggling to cope with animal form and to communicate with its former human associates.

198– *additus et pavor est*: the verb echoes *addidit* at 191, as Ovid switches
99 from physical to psychological changes. Fear, characteristic of a deer, is antipathetic to the bold human hunter, and Actaeon is surprised and confused by what happens to him: he flees. *fugit Autonoeius heros*: the narrator seems to lighten the tone momentarily by catching the comic paradox. The epic epithet and the noun *heros* set up a context with which the verb clashes (cf. 2.676). The epithet creates another circumlocution to avoid naming Actaeon, here referring to his mother Autonoe, Cadmus' daughter. It is another flamboyant neologism of Ovid, used only here in Latin. The poet has packed much art into this line, including five dactyls to reinforce the speed of the unheroic flight. *cursu . . . in ipso* 199: in the act of running. Needless to say, a deer runs much more swiftly than a human being, and the man inside the deer is amazed to see how much ground he (ambiguity of *se*) covers.

200– *in unda*: since he has raced away, Actaeon does not see his new
1 reflection in Diana's spring. It must be in some forest pool, where he pauses. *vox nulla* 201: start of the fatal series of frustrations for the "human deer." He cannot voice his self-pity; later, he will not be able to call out his name (cf. 229–30).

202– *ingemuit*: Ovid echoes the scene where Callisto expresses her human
3 despair and frustration with bear-like groans (cf. 2.485–86). He assigns pathetic tears here to Actaeon, which he omits from the description of Callisto (because less surprising in a woman?). But he takes pains to comment in both cases on the original *mens* or human consciousness that survives the metamorphosis inside the animal form.

204– *quid faciat?* deliberative subjunctive. Ovid used the same phrase earlier
5 as his narrator intruded to invite the audience to share the uncertainty of Phaethon in 2.187. Often, as here, the words introduce a dilemma

(Latin, *dubitatio*) that can be explored. For the first person *quid faciam*, cf. Narcissus below at 3.465. The problem of this man-deer points to his double identity: as Actaeon, he wants to go back to the palace, but as deer he needs to hide in the woods. *hoc . . . illud* 205: usually, in Latin, these words mean respectively "the latter" and "the former" (i.e., the nearer and the farther) in reference to two previously stated alternatives. Thus, the prince's shame (and pride) interferes with his return to the palace, and the fear he has acquired as a deer deters him from facing wild animals in the woods.

206   *dum dubitat*: Ovid alludes to the rhetorical *dubitatio*, with which he is playing. *videre canes*: this settles all uncertainties. The deer will act, but will not be able to hide: he will have to race away again (cf. 228). Up to this point, Ovid has not mentioned the hunting dogs with Actaeon; he has been saving them for this key juncture and the grotesque "epic catalogue" with which he will list a gigantic pack of thirty-five hounds in 206–24, then add three more at 232. The names are all Greek, not because Ovid copied them from some handbook, but because he shows off his mastery of Greek and amuses his philhellenic audience in Rome. This catalogue is an Ovidian tour de force. Hyginus 181 greatly expands Ovid's list, attempting somewhat clumsily to arrange the dogs into males and females.

206–   Two hounds, *Spartan Melampus* and *Cretan Ichnobates*, start the
8   chase; both types are noted for speed. Their names mean "Black-foot" and "Tracker."

209–   Ovid supports the quick rush of the pack with three straight dactyls
10   in 209. The three names in 210 mean respectively "All-consuming," "Sharp-eyed," and "Mountain-ranging." *Arcades omnes* 210: this phrase looks like a clever variant on Vergil's *Arcades ambo (Ecl.* 7.4); Vergil was talking about two herdsmen, proper residents of pastoral Arcadia, whereas Ovid refers to three dogs.

211   The three names of this line mean "Deer-killer," "Hurricane," and "Hunter."

212   Feet are especially good for "Wing-foot," and the nose for "Chase."

213   *Hylaeus* ("Made-of-wood") had recently been struck, no doubt lightly, by the tusk of a boar.

214–   *Nape*'s mother has mated with a wolf; her name means "Wooded
15   glen." *Poemenis*, "Shepherdess," gets her name from her function described in 214. *Harpy* is an apt name for a hound.

216   *Ladon*, named for a river, has its flanks drawn up as it races along. Ovid devised the phrase and uses it metaphorically at 11.752 of a swift and maneuverable seagull.

217   This line consists exclusively of five names and connectives: "Runner," "Uproar," "Spotted," "Tiger," and "Courage."

218   Ovid varies the pattern with a neat chiasmus covering two hounds, *Leucon* ("Whitey") with white hair and *Asbolos* ("Soot") with black.

219   *Lacon*, like the Spartan that he is, has massive strength; *Aello*, as his
      whirlwind-name implies, runs swiftly.

220   *Thoos* means "Ready." *Lycisce* ("She-wolf") connotes ferocity in a
      hound. When Messalina, wife of the emperor Claudius, adopted that
      as her prostitute-name, it had other connotations. *Cyprio*: it is not
      clear whether this is a name or an adjective referring to the origins
      on Cyprus of this dog's breed.

221– Ovid spares us a name in 221 as he accumulates descriptive details
22   about *Harpalos* ("Greedy"), then continues in 222 with "Blackie" and
      "Soft-haired."

223– Another two-line unit, introducing the three offspring of a Cretan sire
24   and Laconian dam ("Furious," "Savage-toothed," and "Barker") as
      the genitive of description etymologizes the name.

225– *quosque referre mora est*: having devoted nineteen lines to this incred-
27   ible dog-catalogue, Ovid impudently smiles and says he will not waste
      time—though in fact he intends to list three more in 232–33. We
      might call this passage the first "Shaggy Dog Story." As if to prove
      his serious haste, the poet avails himself of five dactyls in 225 and
      lavishes detail on the savage course of the hounds over varieties of
      terrain, which grows increasingly wild and pathless with each new
      detail. Note especially 227.

228– Now Ovid returns to Actaeon-deer, whom he abandoned at 206.
31   Covering roughly the same terrain as the hounds, he nevertheless
      accumulates pathetic details that point up the paradoxical changes that
      have befallen him. The hunted beast was, less than an hour ago, hunter
      in these very places. Next paradox in 229, supported by alliteration: he
      flees his own "creatures," who recently cowered before him and obeyed
      his every command. Even more pathetic paradox: his human con-
      sciousness yearns to identify himself as Actaeon—here at last the
      name occurs, just as he has ceased to be Actaeon except to himself—
      but the quoted speech of 230 proves to be entirely imaginary. The
      reality is that he looks like a deer, and his physical features as a deer
      frustrate any emergence of his humanity. Hence, the poet captures
      the cruel irony in 231: not a word, apparently not even a sound,
      escapes the deer, and the air reverberates with the baying of the killer
      dogs. *animo* 231: dative of reference. The noun, synonymous with
      mens, reminds us of Ovid's special theme of dualism and frustration:
      the human consciousness persists, suffering and impotent, inside the
      animal form that conceals it.

232– As if to emphasize the sudden onslaught of the dogs, Ovid cleverly
33   introduces three new hounds, whose unexpected appearance he then
      explains in 234–35. Two of them leap on the deer's back, the third
      on his shoulder. Their names are epic-sounding compounds, the last

actually Homeric: respectively, "Black-haired," "Tamer-of-wild-animals," and "Mountain-bred."

234–
36

exierat: one early fragment and several good later MSS changed the singular here to plural, thinking that the poet should refer to all three dogs. But Ovid is providing a gloss on the last dog's name: it, and it alone, knows all the short-cuts in the mountains, because they are its native haunts. *dominum* 235: Ovid placed this word in the same metrical position as it had in 230, to stress the ironic result of Actaeon's effort to identify himself as master. *retinentibus illis*: ablative absolute. The sound effects in 236 would go with the savage tearing of flesh.

237–
39

iam loca vulneribus desunt: Ovid spares us the gory details of the reduction of the deer's body: he is exclusively interested in the human feelings inside all this savagery. In agony, Actaeon tries to groan humanly, but the sound emerges neither quite human nor entirely deer-like. *sonumque*: object of *habet* in 239. *quem . . . possit / cervus* 238–39: relative clause of characteristic qualifying the sound. *iuga nota*: another reminder of the irony noted in 228. *querellis*: the human lament that Ovid's audience knew especially from Roman elegy. However, Actaeon has lost the capacity to communicate as a human being.

240–
41

The desperately wounded Actaeon-deer wants to assume the pose and gestures of the suppliant. Ovid says he does succeed in kneeling—apparently on its forelegs (once arms)—but he lacks arms and hands to carry out the formulaic gesture. From the biased perspective of the narrator, the deer seems to be pleading with silent gaze as it looks around at dogs and hunters, but nobody else interprets the situation that way, alas for Actaeon. This scene has outdone that of Callisto's frustrated supplication in 2.477 and 487, but Ovid will still outdo this with Pentheus at 3.721 ff.

242–
44

Failing to establish authority over his dogs, Actaeon also fails to communicate with his hunting companions, who join in the kill. *rabidum*: this is the reading of two early fragments, against the prevailing *rapidum* of the later tradition. Considering that it is both more appropriate to hounds in hot pursuit and contact with the prey and also easily corruptible in a single letter, it should be accepted. *ignari* 243: Ovid presses the dramatic irony. *Actaeona* 243–44: the name twice in the same metrical position gives the suggestion of repeated calls to the "absent" friend.

245–
46

The poet explores the pathetic irony. The man inside the deer hears every word—that is the obvious point of the parenthesis at 245—that his friends loudly address to the forest, hears them criticize him as lazy for missing this prey that luck has presented them (*oblatae praedae* 246).

247–   *vellet*: subjunctive conveying the hopelessness of the wish (in a conces-
48   sive sense). Ovid neatly creates a pair of antitheses in the verbs *abesse*
      vs. *adest* and *videre* vs. *sentire*, which stress in the second terms the
      grim reality.

249–   The subject of the plural verbs is clear from the reference to the dogs
50   in 248. They swarm over the body and literally tear it to pieces in
      the typical ending of hunts whose only rationale is the chase and kill
      (not the meat). *dilacerant* 250: this picture of the human being torn
      apart by animals goes back to the pathetic image Ariadne conjures in
      her fear: *dilaceranda feris dabor* (Catullus 64.152). The narrator
      explicates the irony: the dogs rend their master literally *under* the
      deer's form. The human being is what counts; he was still there for
      killing.

251–   Heinsius took exception to these two lines and wanted to remove
52   them; but Ovid's narration turns from the innocent human victim to
      the needlessly vengeful goddess in order to invite our human protest
      and that of people within the narrative frame (cf. 253 ff.). *finita . . .
      vita*: ablative absolute. The final line of the story in 252 is nicely
      balanced around *fertur*, a verb that distances narrator and us from
      events. *pharetratae*: standard epithet of Diana the huntress; but ironi-
      cally the last time we saw her she was not wearing her quiver or
      anything else to lend her dignity.

SEMELE (253–315)

From Diana, whose harshness against Actaeon stirs mixed comment
in Thebes, Ovid turns to Juno, who nurses a grievance against Cadmus'
daughter Semele. Semele has become pregnant by Jupiter—Ovid
leaves the circumstances untouched—and Juno dedicates herself to
destroying this rival and the beauty of which she is so proud. Borrowing
a device that Vergil had employed, the poet invents a dramatic scene
where, disguised as Semele's loyal old nurse Beroe, Juno insidiously
persuades the naive girl to try to act out her rivalry: to ask that her
lover come to her in all the power and energy that he manifests to
his divine wife. Swearing by the Styx, Jupiter makes his typical foolish
promise before learning the details of Semele's wish, and so he must
carry out the desire of his beloved even though it will prove fatal.
When he does appear in full (or slightly attenuated) force, his divinity
is of course too strong, when revealed, for a mere mortal. Having
seen and experienced what is forbidden for a human being, Semele
is incinerated. At the last minute, however, Jupiter rescues the embryo
of the son, who will become irresistible Bacchus, and, after bringing
it to full term on his own body, entrusts the newborn to Semele's

sister Ino. The main details of this myth may be found in Hyginus 179 and Apollodoros 3.4.2.4.

253–   Picking up from *fertur* in 252, Ovid reports two kinds of reactions to
55   Diana's violence: extremes of approval and disapproval. As he has told the story, though, he requires our disapproval. *dignamque severa /virginitate* 254–55: we have seen that the issue was not a threat to virginity, either in Actaeon's actions and intentions or in Diana's own interpretation (cf. 192–93). These three lines function rhetorically as a proemial transition, by which Ovid achieves his focus, with *sola* 256, on Juno (cf. 1.579 ff.).

256–   The structure of 256–58 may be simplified as follows: *non tam . . . /*
59   *eloquitur quam . . . /gaudet. culpetne probetne* 256: Ovid has various poetic ways of dealing with alternate indirect questions, mainly to avoid an introductory conjunction such as *utrum* or *an*. In 1.578, he used no particle at all on the first member, followed by enclitic -*ne* on the second. Here, he uses enclitic -*ne* on both members. The two alternatives recapitulate 253–55. Juno focuses on the house of Agenor first because Cadmus' sister Europa had provoked her jealousy. *Tyria . . . paelice* 258: typical insulting way that Juno views the rape victims of Jupiter. *generis socios* 259: "other members of the family."

259–   *subit*: we might have expected *additur*. *gravidamque . . . Semelen*
61   260–61: pregnant Semele graphically encloses the seed of Jupiter. *iurgia*: we have heard of the raging complaints of Juno on the occasion of Jupiter's infidelity with Callisto (2.424), when he ignored them; later we heard her raging to Callisto (471 ff.). Now, Ovid decides to give us a fresh taste of her angry rhetoric, with obvious reminiscences of Vergil. The lead-in is decidedly unepic.

262–   Having led us to expect a long string of deserved abuse for Jupiter,
66   Ovid surprises us by having Juno abandon useless words and launch directly into plans for vengeance. The repetition of *iurgia* in identical position helps to emphasize the change of plan. *ipsa . . . ipsam* 263: Semele, stressed at key structural points of the line. Alliteration of the two verbs only serves to bring out more forcefully the increased harshness of Juno's actions. She piles up three conditional clauses as a way of claiming that her very being depends on the destruction of Semele; but the conditions contain language that destroys their validity and the justification of killing this rival. Both *rite* 264 and *decet* 265 introduce moral criteria that we in the audience use to question the goddess' behavior. There is no evidence that Juno was called *maxima* in Roman religious practice. The bejewelled sceptre connotes a queen. *regina Iovisque / et soror et coniunx* 265–66: Ovid copies directly from *Aen.* 1.46–7, where Vergil also has Juno speaking. But the

difference in contexts helps to mark the difference between the goddesses in the two works and undermine the regality of his speaker, as he intends. Thus, the addition to Vergil's passage, *certe soror*, turns Juno here into a simple shrew who herself questions the validity of her status as wife.

266–
67
Juno's rhetoric pretends with *at puto* to offer an excuse for Semele—which she then immediately will annihilate. The irony is that she blames the girl, as usual, for the *furtum* and *iniuria* that are obviously to be laid at Jupiter's account. By "brief injury," she means something like a one-night affair, quickly over, free from complications. But "omnipotent" Jupiter never lies with a girl whom he does not make pregnant.

268–
70
Juno, who ought to know better, blames Semele for getting pregnant, with a kind of self-serving reasoning that parodies many a chauvinistic outburst. She has been especially severe on Callisto at 2.471 ff. on the same grounds. In 269 the goddess reveals the basis of her jealousy: she has almost no children by Jupiter—and they are not very significant, the most important being lame Vulcan. *uno* 269: a certain correction for the MSS reading *uni*, which would be dative and refer to Juno (and be nonsense). *tanta est fiducia formae* 270: exact repetition of 2.731, both functioning as terminal sentiments. In the first case the poet so characterized Mercury on his way to visit Herse, somewhat slyly, but not a serious criticism. Juno, on the other hand, uses it to sneer at Semele and justify her wrath.

271–
72
fallat: supply as subject the final two words of 270. The subjunctive depends on *faxo*, a form that serves as the future (probably colloquial) of *facere*, which introduces a substantive clause of result (without *ut*). There is of course no indication, in Ovid's account, that Semele does in fact take excess pride in her beauty. That is Juno's hostile viewpoint. *nec sum Saturnia si non*: again, Juno reveals that her very identity depends on the most violent vengeance against this girl. She is far below the stature of Vergil's Juno, who was at least concerned with national issues. The run-on from two monosyllables and the late start of the condition go against practices of Vergilian epic. *mersa* 272: Semele's destruction is to be a kind of downward plunge into the world below; but she will definitely not be "drowned," as this verb might imply: she is doomed to be consumed by fire (cf. 309).

273–
75
ab his: an unepic way of marking the end of a speech; though we are lured into thinking that the prepositional phrase links with the verb, it functions almost independently, meaning roughly "after these words" (cf. 4.329). The verb goes with *solio*, ablative of place from which. Juno conceals her approach to Thebes, then dons disguise as old Beroe. The language of 275 recurs in closely similar fashion in 6.26–27, where Minerva becomes an old woman so as to approach Arachne in disguise.

276– Ovid recalls Vergil in this scene: he borrows with variation the lan-
78   guage for Juno's transformation from *Aen.* 7.416 ff. where Allecto
      turns into a old woman before approaching Turnus; and he gets the
      name Beroe from *Aen.* 5.620, where Juno's agent Iris becomes old
      in order to work on the Trojan women in Sicily. *sulcavitque cutem*:
      Vergil has *frontem . . . rugis arat. curva . . . membra*: Ovid catches
      the stooped posture of old women. *vocem . . . anilem*: although this
      phrase is unexampled, Ovid has fixed on a definitive feature of older
      people. Vergil had not carried his description so far. The nurse serves
      as a trusted intimate in drama and other literature from the time of
      Euripides' *Hippolytus*. She is a practical advisor and totally biased in
      favor of the person she has attended for years. Homer created a
      prototype in Euryclea of the *Odyssey*: loyal, but no advisor.

279– *ergo ubi*: these two words, with elision, form an initial dactyl, by
82   which Ovid moves the narrative on from the scene of disguise. *captato
      sermone*: ablative absolute. *diuque loquendo*: a loose ablative of means
      with the gerund, a metrically easy variation for *multisque locutis*.
      suspirat 280: a sigh often functions as a meaningful gesture among
      gossips and elderly friends. Here, Juno-Beroe acts out her concern
      and poses as mistrustful of Semele's lover, sighing on the basis of
      worldly wisdom. She implies that he has merely used the name of
      Jupiter to deceive gullible Semele. Both the run-ons in 280 and 281
      begin unusually late, in the sixth foot, giving special emphasis to the
      word and demonstrating the acting ability of Juno.

283– The next step in this malicious deception is to suggest that, even if
86   the man really is Jupiter, he should prove his love by revealing himself
      in his full majesty. *quantusque et qualis . . . tantus talisque* 284–85:
      coordinate clauses, but normal order reversed. Juno seduces the mortal
      girl into asking to be treated as herself. Ironically, as Juno has just
      complained, she herself does not get many amatory visits from her
      husband. Semele, thinking that she asks for something wonderful,
      really gets death as a mortal who cannot safely encounter the divine
      openly. *rogato*: future imperative, governs the indirect commands of
      286. *suaque . . . insignia* 286: Jupiter's most familiar attribute is his
      thunderbolt, not exactly a reliable weapon in Ovid's stories so far.
      When he appears to Semele melodramatically brandishing it, he causes
      her, against his will, to be incinerated.

287– *ignaram*: Ovid's regular note of dramatic irony. *formarat* 288: the
88   verb, part of the vocabulary of metamorphosis, suggests that Juno
      had worked a psychological change on Semele by her deceptive words:
      she formed her for destruction. Horace earlier, in *Sat.* 1.4.121, had
      used the clause *formabat puerum dictis* to honor the way his father
      shaped him morally. *sine nomine munus*: it is often a test of a lover,
      frequently used as a literary motif, to ask for a present without speci-

fying ahead of time the desired item. Omniscient Jupiter is much too stupid here to anticipate where he is being led.

289–
91
Like the Sun with Phaethon in 2.44 ff., Jupiter lets himself in for disaster by yielding foolishly to sentiment and binding himself in advance to grant anything. *nullam patiere repulsam*: identical with the Sun's appeal to Phaethon in 2.97 to choose anything else but the fatal wish that had already trapped his loving father. The attentive Roman audience might have caught this special irony. *quoque . . . quoque* 290: the meter, as well as the sense, shows that these two identical-looking forms are in fact two very different words. The first is the familiar substitute for *et quo*, ablative of degree of difference in relative purpose clause; the second is an adverb. *sunto*: future imperative in a solemn oath. Jupiter's silly seriousness here characterizes his submission to thoughtless lust. *Stygii . . . torrentis* 291: Ovid no doubt expects us to remember that Juno has planned for Semele to go down to Stygian waters (272); the two references to the Styx are interconnected.

292–
95
The use of two caesurae in 292 enables Ovid to develop three short phrases that capture Semele's predicament; we can't call it a "tragedy" because the narrator has not enlisted our feelings for her. And the five dactyls tend to make the situation rather light-hearted. *nimiumque potens*: all too proud. *qualem . . . talem* 293–5: echo and abbreviation of Juno's words in 284 ff. Notice how Semele in 293 livens up the language of her adviser when talking about the love-encounter. Bömer considers it an Ovidian "error" vs. 286 when Semele refers to Juno embracing Jupiter, but it is of course no such thing. Semele puts the emphasis where she feels it should go, thinking of herself as Juno, welcoming her lover.

295–
96
ora loquentis / opprimere 297: he wanted to put his hand over her mouth to prevent utterance of the fatal words. *exierat*: the tense indicates that the god's wish had come too late.

297–
301
ingemuit: the god too late regrets the trap he has created for himself and sorrowfully grasps the nature of Semele more clearly. *neque . . . potest*: the double negatives cause some difficulty, but, when the word order of the first clause is made parallel to that of the second—reverse *non haec*—it becomes easier to work out. Semele (*haec*) could not have chosen otherwise, nor could loving Jupiter, he believes, have sworn differently. *vultuque sequentia traxit / nubila* 299–300: without wasting further time on the feelings of Jupiter, without attributing to him and Semele a final understanding, Ovid moves rapidly on to the circumstances of her death. Jupiter, gloomy and sad, surrounds his head with clouds, which also happen to be the natural source of lightning. *quis*: dative plural. *inmixtaque fulgura ventis*: Ovid here offers a naturalistic, nonmythical explanation of harmless lightning,

which as Lucretius 6 and others argue, closely depends on the interaction of wind and clouds. *inevitabile fulmen* 301: the climactic term. As distinguished from *fulgur, fulmen* does damage, and it is Jupiter's characteristic weapon, but Ovid makes him wield it as if it were a blunderbuss. Ovid has invented the adjective for this context.

302–4   *qua . . . usque:* = *quatenus.* When we hear that Jupiter tries to lessen his powerful aspect, we might think he actually intends to save Semele. Ovid builds up a false expectation through 307, only to disabuse us. *quo . . . igne . . . eo*: Ovid has pulled the noun out of the clause where it logically belongs, with its demonstrative, and put it early in the relative clause, to help clarify the antecedent of *quo. Typhoea*: more commonly known as Typhon, he challenged and terrified the gods until Jupiter finally took him on. The language of 303 implies that the monster was downed and killed by the lightning bolt. However, in 5.346 ff. we hear that Typhoeus still lives, pinned under Mount Etna and breathing fire out its volcano. In order to fit the Greek accusative into the final position of the hexameter, Ovid avails himself of synizaesis, compressing the normally separate syllables *o* and *e*. For standard prosody of this accusative form, in four syllables, cf. 5.321, 325, 348. *feritatis* 304: partitive genitive.

305–7   *aliud levius fulmen*: Ovid, as we might suspect, is the only authority for this gentler bolt. It serves his purposes in creating false hopes for us in this oafish Jupiter. Seneca cites these three lines in *Q Nat.* 2.44.1, to contrast poetic invention with natural fact. *dextra Cyclopum*: the Cyclopes worked for Vulcan to forge, among other things, Jupiter's bolts. For a fuller picture of Vulcan's smithy, cf. *Aen.* 8.416 ff. Note the chiastic pattern of 306. *tela secunda* 307: Ovid affects to give these second-class bolts official status and nomenclature.

307–9   *domumque . . . Agenoream*: a flamboyant way of referring to the palace of Cadmus. Agenor never visited Thebes, and he banished his son when he failed to locate Europa (cf. 3.4–5). At the caesura after this adjective, the narrator jumps rapidly to his conclusion, ignoring all possible drama. *tumultus . . . aetherios*: a rather odd expression for the god's manifestation to Semele. This "heavenly uproar" could refer to a storm or a military disturbance; in any case, it lends no dignity to Jupiter or his supposed efforts to lighten the effects of his presence. *donisque iugalibus arsit*: Ovid shapes this grim ending into a folktale pattern to resemble the death that Medea meted out to her rival in Corinth, Creusa. Cf. the quick summary in 7.394: *Colchis arsit nova nupta venenis.*

310–12   *ab alvo / eripitur*: similarly, in 2.629–30, Phoebus snatched the embryo of Aesculapius from the womb of Coronis, whom he had shot dead. *patrioque . . . femori* 311–12: the long postponement of the noun adds to our incredulity. *si credere dignum est*: one of many passages in which Ovid calls attention to the incredible aspects of his stories while affecting to bypass our doubts. This exact formula comes from Vergil, who used it twice (in *G.* 3.391 and *Aen.* 6.173) to apologize for a mythical explanation of an event that could be naturally explained. Ovid uses other parenthetical appeals to (dis-)belief in conditional form, as here (cf. 2.330), or in questions (cf. 1.400). *maternaque* 312: neatly balances *patrioque*.

313–15   Ino, sister of Semele, briefly receives charge of the baby at birth; then, still a nurseling, it is entrusted (by Mercury, according to Hyginus 179) to the nymphs of Nysa in India. From there, Liber (Bacchus) as a young god will triumphantly return to assert his power in Greece. In the hymnal catalogue of divine epithets of 4.11 ff., we hear of the birth from fire and of *Nyseus* (13). Juno savagely avenges herself on Ino for her brief baby-care in 4.416 ff. Ovid uses a rare procession of four spondees in 313 to enhance the mood of secrecy. *cunis*: ablative of place. Cradle by metonymy stands for birth. For the present, the narrator sensibly abandons the large story of Bacchus in order to keep the focus on his narrative theme about the danger of seeing divine mysteries. Later, at 3.511 ff., the god reappears as the antagonist of his cousin Pentheus.

TIRESIAS INTRUDES ON THE MYSTERY OF SEX (316–38)

In the longer stories of Narcissus and Pentheus, which will soon follow, Tiresias the prophet will play an initial role as he gives a puzzling prediction of the fatal destiny of each young man. Ovid discovers in this short sequence a way of bringing him into the book, thematically apt though seemingly trivial. Too many readers have missed the thematic relevance and indeed condemned Ovid for superficiality. In his past, Tiresias was severely punished for disturbing a pair of snakes as they were mating. He was transformed into a woman (presumably to learn better the sanctity of sex). When after seven years he managed to restore himself to his original sex, he could be considered an expert on both males and females. That story overlaps with several of the topics so far developed in Book 3, especially with the central theme of trespassing on the sacred and being punished. But in addition, there are snakes embodying the sacred, as with Cadmus, and there are matters of sexuality, which link with Diana's savage protection of her modesty and can be related to the next story, that of Narcissus. Although these are the main thematic links with the rest of the book, Ovid affects to make them secondary, background to the principal tale involving Tiresias, namely his role as judge of a disagreement between Jupiter and Juno. In a foolish, teasing mood induced by drinking too much, Jupiter chauvinistically declared that women get more pleasure from sex than men do. (A similar claim is made by the speaker in *Ars Am.* 1.281 ff. that women have a more powerful *libido* than men.) Juno denied this crude allegation and no doubt showed that she did not think it funny. As a person known to have had sexual experience as both a male and female, Tiresias became the judge; and he sided with Jupiter. That was not very foresighted, and many people, male and female, would question the accuracy of his judgment. Juno, who had every right to disagree in view of the rarity of her *voluptas*, in marriage and extramaritally, and the all too frequent self-satisfaction of lustful Jupiter (most recently with Semele), became her typically angry self and blinded Tiresias—punishment for his "blindness" to women's rare sexual pleasure, at least as she knew it. Jupiter could not undo that condition, but he compensated him with prophetic knowledge, so that, in a metaphorical sense, Tiresias could "see" with his mind, much more clearly than others could visualize with their eyes. Throughout this brief section, then, which Ovid seems to play down by his casual and markedly unserious narrative manner, he keeps his attention firmly fixed on his major themes. Tiresias, in his four changes, each time repeats the experience of "seeing" the sacred mystery and suffering for or recovering from it. For routine versions of the myth, cf. Hyginus 75 and Apollodorus 3.6.7.

316–   A pair of *dum*-clauses, each carefully measured to a full line, start
17   this new story off on a falsely solemn note. *fatali lege*: there has been no indication that Fate constituted a significant factor in the story of Semele. *bis geniti . . . Bacchi* 317: first mention of the god's name, along with a compound epithet that comes from the religious realm. He is "twice-born" because, as we heard, he was taken from his mother's womb (first birth) and then brought to full term sewed in his father's thigh, from which he had his "second birth." In 4.12, the enthusiastic Thebans, referring to this miracle, hail Bacchus as *satumque iterum solumque bimatrem.*

318–   In contrast to the grave events on earth, the narrator describes the
21   gods at play in the heavens. *memorant*: he takes no authority for his tale. *diffusum nectare*: the liquid metaphor of the participle should be retained; Jupiter was pretty soused. *curas / seposuisse graves*: more false seriousness, as though in fact Jupiter had showed genuine concern about Semele and made useful moves to avoid killing her. The words suggest that the god practices the ideal Epicurean rules for controlling and conquering the cares of this world. Jupiter, however, who lives on carefree Olympus, has no genuine anxieties: that is one definition of divine existence, as Homer had long ago noted. Jupiter, pretending to dominate his "cares," is hypocritical, and, presuming to tease Juno about sexual pleasure, is a rat. *agitasse remissos . . . locos*: "engaged

in relaxed jesting." Although Jupiter may be in a playful mood, there
is no reason why Juno should be. Her only pleasure, not exactly
voluptas, in the poem so far, has been vengeance. *vestra*: note the
number; hence in 321 Jupiter refers to males. The insulting noun is
effectively postponed to the end of 321.

322– *sententia*: the opinion of a judge or, as here, a wise man with fair
23 understanding. Jupiter no doubt looks forward to lots of laughter when
Tiresias entertains the drinkers with a discourse on *voluptas* of the
two sexes.

324– Here the narrator inserts as explanatory background (324–31) the
27 account of Tiresias' bisexuality, before continuing with his main story.
quo magnorum viridi: the nouns for these three adjectives appear in
approximate chiastic order. *coeuntia*: proper verb for what sex manuals
once learnedly called *coitus*. It will be employed with clever ambiguity
in the frustrating dialogue between Narcissus and Echo below at 386–
87. *violaverat* 325: the basic meaning of the verb is "to do violence
to," but it is regularly used in contexts of impious violence or violation.
Ovid has carefully used the word and exploited the variant of the
myth that best fits his theme. In other versions, Tiresias was said to
have struck and killed or wounded the female. Thus, just as Cadmus
will pay the price for trespassing on inviolate ground (cf. 3.28) and
attacking the giant serpent, so Tiresias must be punished for violating
the mating snakes. Background pluperfect continues into 327. *factus,
mirabile, femina* 326: at the interjection, the miraculous change of
genders is effected in the alliterating words.

327– *octavo*: that is, *autumno* = *anno*, ablative of time. *eosdem / vidit*: he
31 violates their presumed mating a second time with his eyes and reasons
that he should violate it again with his stick. *vestrae potentia plagae*:
"the power of striking you"; subjective genitive *auctoris sortem* 329:
"the sex of the originator of the stroke." It would not seem that Tiresias
reasons correctly. He is punished the first time for doing violence,
from ignorance, to mating serpents. The sex change results from his
abuse of others' sexual pleasure (and usually because he particularly
attacked the female). But Tiresias reduces everything to mechanics:
striking serpents means sex change! It will happen every time! And
amazingly, his dim-witted reasoning works. *forma . . . imago* 331:
Ovid doubles his description of the reverse metamorphosis, framing
the line with the two words for shape. *genetivaque*: possibly the first
appearance of this word in Latin (although Cato may have used it in
a very different sense as an epithet of Phoebus). It refers to the shape
with which Tiresias was born. What we call the *genitive case* had not
acquired that technical name by Ovid's time. Ovid has probably
doubled his clauses so that he can spring on the admiring audience
his new word.

332–
35   *igitur*: Ovid resumes his story from 327, having provided necessary background. *lite iocosa*: the adjective links with *iocos* 320, but the narrator wrongly labels this a playful dispute: Juno takes it seriously. And well she or any woman might do. *pro materia* 334: in proportion to the situation. *fertur*: Ovid or his narrator does not make this assertion about Juno's anger on his own authority: others report this information and criticize Juno. *aeterna . . . nocte* 335: ablative of penalty. The juxtaposition of metaphorical *lumina* and *nocte*, which goes back to Vergil's description of death from combat in *Aen.* 10.746 and 12.310, alters the heroic context meaningfully to cover the loss of the light of the eyes in blindness.

336–
38   *at pater omnipotens*: Ovid has already used this resonant epic formula for Jupiter in 2.304 and 401, in both instances abusing the grand associations it had beforehand in Lucretius and Vergil. Here, the lusty deity who sacrifices all honor and dignity for personal sexual exploitation operates his so-called omnipotence under severe restrictions with Tiresias. The parenthesis asserts that no god, even Jupiter, can counteract the deed of another deity. All he can do is devise some kind of compensation. *lumine adempto* 337: Ovid revives a famous scene of *Aen.* 3.658, where blinded Polyphemus, a figure of pathetic horror, was first given that description. *scire* 338: infinitive used as direct object of *dedit*, itself governing direct object *futura*. Ironically, Tiresias has lost his eyesight as a sign that he woefully lacks basic knowledge about men, women, and sex, and Jupiter gives him a lesser knowledge, that of the future (which does neither him nor anyone else much good).

NARCISSUS (339–510)

Tiresias was not a member of Cadmus' family, and his sorrows at first have no connection with those of the Theban monarchy. Similarly, Narcissus, though a Boeotian, has no direct relationship with Thebes or Cadmus. Our narrator seems to have forgotten his announced subject and strayed off on idle material. However, in this substantial and carefully organized story, Ovid continues to explore his principal themes. Narcissus illustrates significant aspects of human sexuality and the danger of not understanding it; he frustrates desires, which his beauty rouses, and spurns love of others, male or female, which might have flourished, and he is left with futile self-love that inevitably proves suicidal. His discovery of himself, because of his prior snubbing of others, cannot lead to personal development, only to doom. Accordingly, in the narrative, the circumstances of self-knowledge become shaped like the events that brought Actaeon and Cadmus to misery. Narcissus experiences, apparently for the first time, the vision of himself—and it is fatal, predicted so from the start by Tiresias. More-over, he sees this fatal sight in a pool of an inviolate forest area. Like Actaeon, he must die, victim not of a violated deity, but of himself.

We possess no other extended narration about Narcissus, and, al-though some people argue that much of Ovid's achievement should be credited to a lost Hellenistic source, there is no evidence whatsoever for such material. Moreover, Ovid has woven into the myth of Narcissus, fool in love with his reflection, the tale of Echo, the nymph whose every verbal response depends on echoing (e.g., reflecting) the words of others. Ovid treats these two as opposites, Narcissus totally preoccupied with himself and Echo pathetically preoccupied with others, and he forces them into a doomed relationship. Echo falls in love with the boy and yet must vainly try to pursue her love in terms of his loveless words. She responds passionately to words that he speaks with no interest in her, and she misinterprets his passionless sentences, from which she is permitted to echo only final words or syllables, as invitations to love. When she follows up her misinterpreta-tion, and he spurns her, the rejection desolates her, and her body wastes away, leaving her nothing but a forlorn, helpless echo as we know the phenomenon. As Ovid presents the story of Echo, we tend to sympathize with her and view her as a victim of heartless, selfish Narcissus. However, she is also a victim of her own defective nature. Unable to be a complete person, forced to wait for others to speak first before she can utter a word—and then only according to the last words spoken by the other—Echo can never experience the mutuality of love, the ideal toward which Ovid's amatory theme in Book 3 points. But selflessness makes a stronger appeal then selfishness, and Ovid shows Echo, even after suffering rejection, capable of sympathiz-ing with and pitying the fate of selfish Narcissus.

Once he has narrated the scorning and metamorphosis of Echo and set up expectation of the merited punishment of Narcissus, Ovid moves into the second phase of his story. Narcissus, tired hunter, comes to an inviolate spot with a clear pool: he is like both Actaeon and Diana in situation, and so Ovid makes him play a double role as the mysteri-ous power whose being may not be safely seen (or known) and the sacrilegious intruder and spectator. Narcissus views his reflection in the pool and falls fatally in love with it and himself. Ovid develops the delusion of Narcissus, his false perception of the reflection as an other person, his crazy efforts to conduct a conversation with the image in the water. In contrast to Echo, he generates all the words and gestures in this imaginary relationship. Although at first he inter-prets the exact repetition of his movements of body and mouth as proof that this "other person" responds to him, eventually he realizes that the reflection is nothing but an echo of himself, devoid of body, feelings, and any existence that would provide him mutuality. Since for Narcissus, then, there can be nothing lovable apart from himself—and no gratification in this frustrating self-love—he can only waste away. He leaves a pretty but insignificant flower on earth as his physical memorial, and his vapid soul descends to the Underworld clothed in an airy version of his human beauty, which he persists in vainly admiring as it is reflected from the waters of the Styx. He is a victim of his own defective nature, at the opposite extreme from Echo. Love that proves to be nothing but self-love, that seeks self-gratification without true perception of another, is doomed. Self-centered beauty sooner or later dies, flawed in its humanity and deprived of lasting happiness.

Narcissus and Echo (339–401)

339–
40
ille: Tiresias, whose new-found fame as prophet provides the transition to this new story. *Aonios*: Boeotian; Ovid used the adjective once earlier at 1.313. *inreprehensa* 340: Ovid invents this word, along the lines of other Augustan neologisms, which negate a past participle. Its prominent position in the line and the sound-patterns that it initiates give a flashy epigrammatic quality to this transition.

341–
44
prima: nominative, framing the clause with its proper noun *Liriope*. *fide*: as indicated by *vocisque*, with which it is linked, this is genitive singular. It is an archaic form that Ovid uses to avoid normally trisyllabic *fidei*. *vocisque ratae*: "powerful prediction"; literally, the voice that proved true. *temptamina*: another poetic neologism, first used here, then again at 7.734 and 13.19. Evidently, the narrative tone has changed from the jesting manner of Jupiter with Juno. *caerula* 342: a parallel poetic form to *caerulea*. The two adjectives have the same meaning, and their usage depends on metrical considerations. Nominative singular feminine. *caerulea* has too many short syllables for the hexameter. Ovid is the first to name Liriope as mother of Narcissus; he may have based the name on flower-associations. It evokes a Greek word for lily. *flumine curvo / inplicuit*: in this and the following clause, Ovid suggests an erotic picture of a river that curves its waters, like arms, around the struggling nymph. The Cephisos flows into western Boeotia from the mountains of Phocis. Thus, the story of Narcissus takes place closer to Delphi than to Thebes. The first epithet Ovid uses for his hero is *Cephisius* at 351. *vim tulit* 344: this dactylic unit, followed by a complete stop, denotes perpetration of rape. It next occurs at 4.239. Ovid has another phrase, *vim parat* (cf. 2.576), which covers attempted rape that does not always succeed.

344–
Raped nymphs have become commonplace in the poem by now, and

46   we would expect Liriope to get pregnant, so Ovid can hurry forward
      to the birth of the child. *pulcherrima*: seems a gratuitous and ironic
      detail at the time of birth, but the nymph's beauty explains the lovabil-
      ity of her baby: he is beautiful, too. *nymphe 345*: some early scribes
      changed the Greek nominative to Latin *a*, but the meter, an emphatic
      sequence of four spondees, requires long *e*. As the story begins, the
      narrator acts as though love can inhere simply in physical beauty. It
      ends on a quite different note. The naming of Narcissus pretty much
      concludes Liriope's role.

346– *de quo consultus*: Ovid goes back to Tiresias and links him briefly to
48   Narcissus. We may assume that the mother Liriope consulted the seer,
      but the narrator does not actually say so. *esset . . . visurus*: separation
      of the two verbal units enables Ovid to shape 347 like a Golden Line
      and lend it solemnity. It is no accident that he uses a verb of seeing
      here. Narcissus will see a fatal vision long before he reaches a natural
      old age. *fatidicus vates 348*: Ovid reuses a solemn epic phrase from
      Aen. 8.340, where a prophetess unambiguously predicted the greatness
      of Aeneas' descendants. Tiresias' prophecy, on the other hand, baffles
      people, and it strikes us at first as a trivial inversion of the Delphic
      injunction to know oneself. In Greek moral thinking, as Plato's
      Socrates emphasizes, self-knowledge is the prerequisite of an ethical
      life, the most important goal for human beings. Self-knowledge en-
      ables us both to act in reasonable conformity with our true natures
      and to make intelligent changes in ourselves. Tiresias declares that
      self-knowledge will shorten Narcissus' life. How is that possible? The
      clue lies in the implicit meaning of "knowledge" in Tiresias' prophecy.
      Narcissus will not "know" anything more profound than that the figure
      he sees in the water is the reflection of himself. That discovery does
      kill him, granted, but it is not the self-knowledge that Delphi and
      moral philosophers meant. If he had arrived at Socratic self-knowledge
      or worked his way to it after this frustration, Narcissus could have
      led a useful, significant existence, even one that brought him love.

349– The narrator sounds as though he is merely interested in developing
50   a tale that proves the reliability of Tiresias. *exitus*: ambiguous here.
      The first meaning would simply be the outcome of events, but that
      leads to the second meaning: the outcome in connection with Narcissus
      is his strange madness and death (cf. 350). To explain those intriguing
      matters, the story then can explore Narcissus's life in considerable
      detail.

351– *ter ad quinos*: that is, *annos*. Since *quindecim* almost never fitted into
52   the hexameter, and Ovid did not want to try equally awkward *sedecim*,
      he creates an addition problem for us: $(3 \times 5) + 1 = 16$. Narcissus had
      reached his early teens, when some young men are equally attractive to
      males and females.

353–
55

For this wooing topos in Ovid, cf. note on 1.478. Catullus in his Epithalamium, 62.42 ff., seems to have created the anaphora formula that Ovid uses here. He had men argue from the analogy of a pretty flower, which is desirable only so long as it is in bloom, that young girls should yield to love. Ovid turns most cases of wooing into rejection. There is always a sensible answer to the impetuous selfishness of "Gather ye roses while ye may." Narcissus, however, is not sensible: he proves more selfish than those who desire his beauty. The careful balance between 353 and 355 is significantly interrupted by the parenthetical comment in 354, which explains the boy's nonresponsiveness as due to arrogance. The adjectives of 354 create an antithesis: hardness in Narcissus' personality negates the allure of his soft young beauty. The dichotomy, which Ovid will work out in the split between body and reflection, has been noted as of now. *superbia* 354: even worse but equally doomed with *fiducia formae* (cf. Semele at 270).

356–
58

The narrator has gone from pluperfect in 351–52 through perfect in 353–55, completing his sketch of the relevant background, and now he moves into the present. He introduces Echo, who falls in love with Narcissus under the typical amatory opportunity of a hunt. *agitantem . . . cervos*: we have just watched Actaeon driving deer, then himself being hunted down and killed as a deer. *vocalis* 357: before he names Echo, the poet introduces her dominant characteristic, her voice, and then explores its parameters. *nec . . . didicit*: since it is hardly a matter of "learning" to do these things but rather of having the capacity, we might have expected *potuit* or *poterat* (cf. 361, *posset*). The prefixes *re-*, occurring at the same metrical position in 357 and 358, both point to the basically responsive personality of Echo. *resonabilis*: Ovid has coined this word here as the definitive epithet to go with the name.

359–
61

non vox erat: after the earlier *vocalis*, this may seem puzzling. What is meant is that Echo was not *simply* a voice, not yet. The narrator points up the difference between the Echo of his initial story and Echo of our experience (and of later stages of the story, after 399 ff.). *usum . . . oris* 360: wide hyperbaton. *garrula*: Echo suffers a basic frustration. She has a passionate compulsion to communicate her feelings, but is hampered by being dependent on others' words. *verba novissima* 361: the longest response given in this story consists of four words (cf. 500), extending slightly more than a half-line.

362–
65

Echo has lost the capacity to initiate speech and conversation because Juno has punished her for what, to the goddess, was misuse of that ability. The nymph distracted the jealous deity with her chatter, deliberately babbling on so as to give her friends time to escape Juno's anger. *deprendere*: earlier, in 3.6, the narrator used this verb to ask who could catch Jupiter in the act. Juno always blames the girls for

Jupiter's amours, so here she aims to catch them. *sub Iove . . . suo* 363: until the reflexive adjective is added, after a pause, we might think that Juno merely means "out in the open under the sky" with the colloquial *sub Iove*. In fact, the phrase means that the nymphs literally lie "under Jupiter," in sexual intercourse. *prudens* 364: the deliberate plan of Echo sets up the *dum*-clause with subjunctive in 365.

365–69   Ovid doubles his clauses as Juno menaces *linguae . . . potestas* 366 and *vocis . . . usus* 367. The adjectives *parva* and *brevissimus* refer to the drastic limitations on Echo's power of speech. In the *tamen*-clause of 368–69, the slight possibilities are once again reviewed, in new terms. *in fine loquendi* 368: i.e., the final words spoken by others. *ingeminat . . . reportat* 369: these terms for repeating, echoing frame the line significantly.

370–72   *ergo*: resumptive, taking us back to the hunting scene at 356–57. *per devia rura*: remote, pathless stretches of the countryside provide standard locales for hunts (cf. 226–27). *vidit et incaluit* 371: the second verb adds a key new detail to the scene at 356: Echo grows hot with desire. Same words in 2.574 to describe the passion of Neptune (which, in his case, led to attempted rape). *sequitur vestigia*: the language suggests that Echo hunts the hunter. *quoque* 372: = *et quo*; ablative of degree of difference. *flamma propiore*: as the metaphorical "flame" that heats Echo's desires, Narcissus increases her passion (quite unconsciously) in proportion as she gets closer.

373–74   Ovid explicates his metaphor with a humble simile about firebrands. The elaborate opening by a double negative (*non aliter quam* instead of simple *ut*) leads to false expectation of epic dignity in the comparison. As with Echo, brands are brought ever nearer to the flame until (unlike her) they actually ignite. *summis circumlita taedis*: "smeared around the tops of torches." (They resemble huge matches.) *vivacia* 374: Bömer argues that this is a formulaic epithet that Ovid has clumsily borrowed from Vergil and the epic tradition. It seems better to take the adjective in connection with the image: the "lively" feature of sulphur is its sudden combustibility.

375–78   The poet briefly characterizes the frustration of this lover who cannot speak out her love spontaneously. *blandis . . . dictis*: ablative of manner (her words) or dative with the compound verb (his words that Echo vainly longed to respond to). Sweet words form Narcissus would liberate her love. *molles . . . preces* 376: more lover's talk, "soft requests" for affection. *natura repugnat*: a battle here rages between the will and the physical constraints of Echo's speech. *nec sinit, incipiat* 377: *sino* takes the subjunctive with or without *ut*. *quod sinit*: parenthetical clause, more commonly in prose rendered *id quod*. *sonos, ad quos sua verba remittat* 378: literally, "sounds to which she might echo back her own words." Subjunctive in relative clause of purpose.

It is partly true that Echo responds with "her own words," in that, though she only repeats what another has said (and only the final part of the speech), she impresses on them a special meaning.

379– Separated from his companions, Narcissus might be vulnerable to
82   attack, as Actaeon proved to be. Ovid starts off this episode with pluperfect in the first two lines, then moves into the present as he focuses on Narcissus' puzzlement over the echo. His question in 380 arises from a desire to locate his friends. In the chiastic ordering of the line, Ovid appropriately juxtaposes the hunter's query and the shortened form of Echo's repetition, which constitutes a reply. We can easily imagine how she converts the neutral question into her own feeling response. We are not to consider a multiple echo reverberating from many points in the landscape, but a single clear "response," from nearby, to judge from what Ovid said about the close pursuit by Echo. Narcissus, then, imagines that the echo is the free communication of an independent person (as he will later misinterpret the reflection in the pool to be the free response of a separate individual). *vocat illa vocantem* 382: instead of mechanically reproducing the exact words of each echo, the poet devises various clever methods of alluding to them. Here, he does not repeat *veni*, but conveys the special intention of Echo: whereas Narcissus looks for someone indefinite to tell him where his path lies, she specifically calls Narcissus for love.

383– *nullo veniente*: ablative absolute. *quid . . . me fugis?*: because nobody
84   appears after his previous command, Narcissus impatiently assumes that the speaker avoids him and asks why. With the very same words, again indirectly conveyed to us in 384, Echo speaks out her longing passion. When later confronted with his reflection, to which he mistakenly assigns personality, Narcissus will speak much the same words, but with a hopeless longing similar to Echo's here (cf. 455–56 and 477–78).

385– *alternae . . . imagine vocis*: a circumlocution for the echo-effect, but
89   Ovid so phrases it as to suggest by the visual term *imago* a connection between an echo and a reflection. That helps to link the two phrases of Narcissus' story. *coeamus* 386: Ovid exploits the difference between "getting together," merely to make a casual acquaintance, and uniting in sexual intercourse (cf. above 324). The first person plural liberates Echo to act optimistically on her response. *verbis favet ipsa suis* 388: in "favoring her own words," Echo happily acts upon them. *silva*: ablative of place from which. In the later story of Procris, when she lovingly moves through the underbrush in the woods to embrace Cephalus, he mistakes the sound for that of a wild animal and kills her. So Ovid recounts it in *Ars Am*. 3.731 ff. *iniceret sperato bracchia collo* 389: these words have an unmistakenly erotic meaning and indicate the intention of Echo. However, in the only previous use of

inicere bracchia + dative, Ovid was describing the hostile attack in 1.184 of the monstrous children of Earth on Olympus. Thus, what Echo means as a loving approach could be construed by a cold egoist like Narcissus as disgusting belligerence, an assault on his person! Echo, however, thinking that because of her own biased use of his words she has been invited to love, suffers terrible shock from his repulse.

390–   *ille fugit*: Ovid used the same words in identical metrical position at
92   228 to describe the vain flight of another hunter, Actaeon. The word order of 391 may be simplified as follows: *emoriar antequam sit*. Translate *emoriar* as future indicative; it is a strong assertion of intended action. *sit tibi copia nostri*: Fränkel called special attention to the importance of this clause in Ovid's story. Whereas Narcissus is so intent on denying himself to others that he proclaims his determination to die rather than giving Echo access to himself, she freely offers herself without reservation to him. By dropping the two opening words of Narcissus' outcry, which subordinate the clause (essentially negating it) to his death-wish, Echo converts the anticipatory subjunctive to a jussive, a genuine invitation to love to which he, in arrogant coldness, cannot accede.

393–   *spreta*: Ovid sketches out the main features of humiliation that result
95   from spurned love. Ashamed, Echo hides herself from all contact with people (393–94). However, her frustrated love torments her even more painfully.

396–   *corpus . . . curae*: of this alliterative pair, the agonized feelings take
99   priority and cause the body to undergo the metamorphosis that eventually eliminates it. The nymph Echo decomposes into nothing but a voice, the familiar bodiless echo (still endowed with love for vain Narcissus). *tenuant*: sleeplessness wears her down. *adducitque cutem macies* 397: she becomes gaunt and wrinkled. *sucus / corporis* 398: her vital juices evaporate. When nothing remains but voice and bones, these separate from each other, bones turning into stone (a reversal of the change of 1.398 ff.) and voice alone surviving to represent Echo's troubled personality. *vox manet* 399: at this point she becomes the echo the narrator and audience know (cf. 359–60).

400–   *inde latet silvis*: virtual repetition of the first hemistich of 393. Echo
401   hides and is no longer seen, because she no longer possesses a visible body. By contrast, she is universally heard: her entire identity inheres in her voice. *omnibus* 402: dative of agent with passive verb, common in Latin poetry.

Narcissus and His Reflection (402–510)

402–   In his transition, Ovid notes that Narcissus had frustrated not only
3   Echo but all potential lovers of either sex. *luserat* 403: not a sympathetic word for Narcissus' behavior. *coetus . . . viriles*: the tricolon

ends on the group that will continue the narration. A young man calls down divine punishment on the proud spurner. *coetus* has no independent existence from *coitus* nor a separate meaning; the orthography depends entirely on the metrical need for a long syllable that the dipthong provides. Thus, we should think back to 386–87 and translate "sexual relations with men," not "masses of men."

404–6

aliquis: Ovid has a rejected male curse Narcissus for two reasons: (1) he wants to keep Echo sympathetic and come back to her at the close, showing her still loving and able to generate a warm response from the youth's selfish words; (2) he perceives that when Narcissus falls in love with his own reflection, he loves a male; which would better justify a male's curse than a female's. Guillaume de Lorris, in his *Roman de la Rose*, greatly simplifies his Ovidian imitation and has Echo, a fine French lady, curse Narcissus with her dying breath, with the result that he falls in love with his reflection—de Lorris then omits Ovid's elaborate analysis of that love—and quickly dies. *manus . . . ad aethera tollens*: standard prayer gesture. *sic . . . sic* 405: careful echo of the anaphora in 402–3, to set up poetic justice. *amet . . . amato*: significant disposition to heighten antithesis. *precibus . . . iustis* 406: dative with compound verb. The narrator inserts his bias against Narcissus with the adjective *Rhamnusia*; Themis or Nemesis, the Greek goddess of divine punishment, had a famous shrine at Rhamnos near Athens.

407–10

Ovid abruptly moves into an ecphrastic description of an idyllic, unviolated, "virginal" forest pool (407–12). It has the typical start (*fons erat*) and the demonstrative close (*hic*) at 413. Except for the adjective *argenteus*, he characterizes the pool and its location entirely in negatives: no mud, leaf, animal, human being, or even sunray has "touched" it. *inlimis*: the pool's first adjective is coined for this passage. It never recurs in Latin. Although it adds a touch of poetic appeal to the remarkably clear water of this spring, it initiates the negatives that end by making the pool an appropriate symbol of Narcissus' personal negativity. The description of Diana's pool at 155 ff. differs noticeably. *aliudve pecus* 409: since she-goats have been listed in 408, this noun includes billy goats and sheep, as well as other barnyard animals.

411–12

The attractive grassy approach to the spring occurred in Diana's pool also (cf. 162). *sole . . . nullo* 412: the description ends on the negative note, instead of positively talking of cool shade. *passura*: future participle in present sense, used to fit the meter easily.

413–14

et studio venandi lassus et aestu: Ovid propels us once again into the formulaic setting of the tired hunter, probably at high noon. A strange kind of "violence" will occur here. *procubuit* 414: he fell forward to get a drink. *faciemque*: although a general word for appearance, this alliterative word prepares for the form that will appear as a reflection in the pool (cf. 416).

415–
17
sitis altera: the metaphorical use of thirst in love poetry was well established. Lucilius used thirsty Tantalus as a pardigm of sexual frustration, as Horace used him to define the foolish miser (*Sat.* 1.1.68). As Bömer notes, Ovid varies the metrical stress on the two different types of thirst here. *conreptus imagine formae* 416: while leaning forward to drink, Narcissus sees and becomes caught up with desire for his reflection. Ovid repeats these words in 4.676 to describe the violent onset of Perseus' love for Andromeda. If he failed to make clear in 416 what Narcissus saw, he ends any doubts in the verbosity of 417. *spem . . . amat* 417: reminiscent of the hopeless passion of Echo at 389. She tried to put hope into her echo; he imagines hope in his reflection. This time, frustration will arise not from the pride of the beloved but from physical absence.

418–
19
adstupet ipse sibi: Narcissus epitomizes the self-frustration that Ovid has repeatedly studied in the poem. The verb here renders the stunning effect of love at first sight, but, in order to capture the reflexive feature of this passion, the poet invents the compound form (with dative). Ovid also suggests by his choice of language that this love, which fulfills the curse, (cf. 405) constitutes, as elsewhere, a metamorphosis of the lover. Narcissus becomes trapped and motionless by the pool, a statue reflected. Romans used statues for this very purpose, as garden-planners do today. Some of the richer houses of Pompeii and the pool in front of the Serapeum at Hadrian's Villa provide good examples of Roman taste. The simile implies the lifeless beauty that Ovid sees in this whole story.

420–
21
humi positus: Ovid clarifies the stance of his figure for future artistic representations (such as the famous one of Caravaggio): Narcissus crouches where he has been drinking, thus leans over the water and creates the reflection. *geminum . . . sidus*: a good example of a metaphor interrupted by the apposition that explicates it. *dignos . . . crines* 421: Narcissus possesses fair long hair, as the youthful gods Bacchus and Apollo did in artistic representations. Now that Bacchus has been born, Ovid inserts a favorable reference to him at the first opportunity.

422–
24
inpubesque: at sixteen, Narcissus was hardly below the age of puberty; but the adjective had an extended meaning of "youthful," and here with the noun would mean "beardless." *eburnea*: Ovid uses this adjective of parts of the body that are "white as ivory." *decusque / oris*: "his handsome face." *mixtum candore ruborem*: the narrator talks of the general complexion of the boy and his reflection, an ideal blending of red and white, what we today sometimes call "a healthy pink." The same three words will recur in slightly different syntax at 491,

to register the loss of that complexion. *candore*: ablative of place where, omitting *in*. *cunctaque miratur* 424: after the chosen details of 420–23, the narrator can afford to generalize. *quibus*: ablative of specification. *mirabilis ipse*: the repetition, the apparent distinction between object and subject, makes the mirror effect and the paradoxical experience of Narcissus graphic. There will be much repetition of this type.

425–
26   In the four hemistichs of these lines, Ovid uses three different structures to present the reflection paradox: verb and reflexive pronoun, active and passive forms of same verb, active and intransitive forms of synonymous verbs. Even when he repeats his use of active and passive, he varies the grammar: using a relative clause first, then a subordinate *dum*-clause. The alliteration of 426 begins to imply that the narrator plays with the situation he has devised, with no sympathy with Narcissus.

427–
29   *fallaci . . . fonti*: he thought he was kissing a human face but, deceived by the reflection, he merely touched the water. For 428–29, the complex word order implies the awkward, frustrated effort. The order could be made more prosaic and perspicuous as follows: *quotiens in mediis aquis bracchia mersit captantia collum visum*. In addition to attempting a kiss, the lover is trying to embrace the neck. Although Narcissus would have ruined the reflection by plunging his arms into the water, the narrator does not utilize that detail here; later, at 475 ff., it will serve his purposes well.

430–
31   *quid videat, nescit*: so far, he has not fulfilled the fatal prophecy of self-knowledge (cf. 348). *quod videt*: relative clause placed, as often, before its antecedent, this time to force the balance with the first clause and entertain the audience by the varied syntax. *qui decipit incitat error* 431: the doubling and ambivalence demands Narcissus' investigation.

432–
33   Now the narrator, as though impatient and eager to clear up the confusion, apostrophizes Narcissus. Not that Narcissus is able to hear him across the fictional and temporal barrier. But the speech emphasizes the reality of the reflection, the vanity of the image, for our benefit, to distance us farther from this lover. *simulacra fugacia captas*: reusing the verb of 428, Ovid changes the earlier object (which was the physical neck) to insubstantial image. It will take the boy until 463 to understand this. *quod petis* 433: clarification of the paradox of 426. *quod amas, avertere, perdes*: Ovid compresses the grammatical syntax, in order to force three verbs into juxtaposition and suggest the speed with which, by a slight movement, the boy could destroy his beloved (rather emphatically dismissed as lifeless by the neuter *quod*). The first and third verbs make good sense together; the second

verb is a parenthetical imperative, where we would expect perhaps a
condition (*si averteris*) or gerund (*avertendo*), neither of which would
have fitted so neatly into the metrical line.

434–
36
repercussae . . . imaginis umbra: "the shadow or phantom of a re-
flected image." *nil habet ista sui* 435: a new perspective on the confu-
sion caused by the reflection. Whereas before Ovid played with the
reflexive opportunities of the reflection, e.g., that Narcissus kept
seeing and seeking himself, deluded that it was another; now the
alienated narrator argues that, as an entity generated from and identical
with the boy (*ista*), it has no substance of its own, no reflexive feature.
venitque manetque: note the distinction in tenses, which, in 436, will
be extended to a distinction of moods. If Narcissus left, his reflection
would quietly disappear—if only he could bring himself to leave.

437–
39
The apostrophe having accomplished nothing, the narrator continues
in the third person. He starts off with anaphora and alliteration, to
establish the fanatic quality of this devotion: it distracts the lover from
food and robs him of sleep. He will waste away, if he goes on like
this. *opaca fusus in herba* 438: whether this is a new stance (vs. 420)
is not clear, but it is more precise. *mendacem . . . formam* 439: Ovid
insists, with the philosophic tradition, that mere form lies. That is
especially true here, where form is nothing but reflection of form.

440–
41
perque oculos perit: the alliteration helps to call attention to the strange
way of dying, not simply *because of* the eyes, but actually *out through*
the eyes. *paulumque levatus*: since he had been sprawling face down-
ward on the ground, staring at the pool, Narcissus has to raise himself
in order to carry out the histrionic gesture toward the trees, to enlist
nonhuman nature on his side. Since he himself has been inhuman and
suffers the penalty for that, he gets little sympathy from us. And of
course the trees do not respond.

442–
43
io: an interjection that connotes a loud cry to someone. *crudelius . . .
amavit*: although "cruel love" is a familiar theme to Ovid and his
audience, it normally applied to love that was actively, not passively,
cruel. The unkind or heartless lover gets branded as "cruel." Cf.
1.617, 2.612, and (in the later words of Narcissus) 3.477. Probably,
then, we are to sense the irony of the usage here and, rejecting his
self-pity but remembering Echo, to classify Narcissus with other cruel
lovers. *latebra opportuna* 443: the woods provide a convenient place
for love. In the poem, however, the kind of love that has taken
place in that locale has been primarily rape. Thus, the trees to which
Narcissus appeals have indeed seen a great deal of "cruel love," much
crueler than this.

444–
45
tot agantur saecula: literally, "so many centuries have been passed
(of your existence)." Ovid turns into a passive structure an active
phrase, *agere saecula*, that Propertius coined in 2.2.16 on analogy

with the conventional *agere aetatem*. Narcissus simply means: "since you are so many centuries old." *tabuerit* 445: perfect subjunctive in relative clause of characteristic. Again, the selfish boy expects to generate pity by his rhetorical question and hear: "Nobody; you are uniquely pitiable." We have just watched his victim Echo waste away, so he cannot get from the inanimate woods or us the answer he wants.

46–
47
Chiastic ordering of the paired words on either side of the caesura in 446. *placet* 446: that is, *mihi*. Narcissus likes what he sees, but he cannot make contact. *quod*: as in 430, the neuter subtly alludes to what he does not recognize, that the reflection is nonhuman. Here, the personal pronoun *quem* would easily have fitted. *tantus . . . amantem* 447: a terminal sententia, like that in 1.60, occupying the second hemistich. The narrator has called attention to the *error* in much the same terms at 431, but without wasting any pathos.

48–
50
quoque: = *et quo*, introducing relative clause of purpose. Narcissus' self-pity now focuses on a common topic of love elegy, namely, lovers' separation. Normally, there is a geographical separation of great distance between frustrated lovers, when, for example, the girl goes off with a rival or the man to fight wars. At the minimum, a house door or a wall parts the lovers. None of those conventional obstacles exists here. *exigua prohibemur aqua* 450: "we are kept [from each other] by a tiny film of water." *cupit ipse teneri*: "he obviously wants me to embrace him." Narcissus continues to personify the reflection, to treat it as a separate being.

51–
53
The statement of 450 is now justified. *quotiens . . . totiens*: he draws false conclusions from the mirror effect. Although he means he tries to kiss that other boy, Ovid makes him say what in fact he does: he kisses the water! *resupino ore*: as Narcissus leans down to kiss the water, he sees the reflection strain to meet his lips, mouth up and head tilted back at the same angle that his is. *putes* 453: the speaker has forgotten his imaginary audience of trees (cf. 442 ff.) and now seems to address each one of us or anyone who will pity him. Subjunctive in incomplete unreal clause. *amantibus*: plural, because Narcissus infers from the reflection that "it" feels the same as he does. So they are mutual lovers, both frustrated.

54–
56
Now he turns to the water and addresses the reflection itself. *huc exi*: this imperative resembles *veni* at 382, which Echo tried to turn into a lover's appeal. Narcissus wants the beloved to "come out" of the water. *unice*: as Bömer notes, this adjective does not appear in the erotic vocabulary of Ovid or other love poets. It does not, then, have the conventional associations of modern "one and only." The vocative implies that Narcissus regards this form as the only *puer* he would familiarly address. And Ovid chooses it for its obvious irony: this deceived lover treats as unique what is only a double of himself.

petitus 455: the verb has already been used at 426 in an amatory sense. *abis*: unless Narcissus has made a move back from the water, he cannot have seen his reflection doing that either. *quam fugias* 456: subjunctive in relative clause of characteristic after negative antecedent. *et amarunt . . . nymphae*: using the nymphs to prove his lovability, Narcissus unconsciously reminds us of his transgressions against others' love. He deserves to experience rejection.

457– *spem . . . nescio quam*: Echo had vain hopes, too (cf. 389). *promittis*:
58   Narcissus sees "promises" where of course there are none from another, only his own vain desires and interested looks. The corresponding verbs of 458 describe what we know is the mirror effect, reflection, which the lover interprets as spontaneous response. *ultro*: a fatal illusion, not an observed fact. As long as Narcissus can attribute an independent personality and series of free actions to this shape, it remains a possible love object.

459– Repeated verbs in corresponding clauses allow Ovid to lay out the
62   lover's delusion. *adrides*: "response" to laughter. *me lacrimante* 460: ablative absolute does not define the logical connection with the surrounding context. However, Narcissus infers from the simultaneity of identical tears that his tears cause the "other" to cry. *motu . . . oris* 461: the lover becomes a lip-reader of his reflection, which of course moves its lips as he does. This line slows down with four spondees. *formosi*: the standard word in Roman elegy for lovable beauty. Here, its basic sense reminds us that the reflection and its mouth are nothing but empty forms. *verba refers* 462: a reminder of Echo? She responded to his words, but not as he meant them; now he imagines a sympathetic response where there is none.

463– Significantly, the moment he reminds us of Echo and verbal response,
64   the curse becomes fulfilled. *iste ego sum*: "I an what I have been calling 'you'." Here the divided being(s) resolve themselves into the single Narcissus, as he realizes the truth of the reflection and the cruel fact about himself, which also fulfills Tiresias' original prediction. *nec me . . . fallit imago*: a sharp distinction from what he said at 454. Using the fire metaphor in 464, he verbalizes his understanding of the situation the narrator objectively described in 426. *mei* 464: nice use of the objective genitive, distinguished from the meaning of *meo*.

465– *quid faciam?* Ovid has the desperate lover lay out his problem in the
66   familiar rhetorical form of a dilemma. Cf. Actaeon at 204 ff. *roger anne rogem?* Translate with the active verb first: "woo or be wooed?" It is likely that Ovid changed the order for metrical reasons. Deliberative subjunctive. *quid deinde rogabo?* No sooner has he shaped his difficulty as a dilemma than Narcissus must discard it as invalid. There are not two separate people or two independent actions from which he can choose. *quod cupio, mecum est* 466: the third word should be

rendered very literally; "what I yearn for, I have right here *with me*." These words, spoken under other circumstances, would be a happy declaration that one's fondest desires have been achieved. Picking up on that ambiguity, Ovid has Narcissus articulate his condition in language that recalls his earlier rejection of Echo: *ante emoriar quam sit tibi copia nostri* (392). Having sworn he would die rather than give himself to her, Narcissus finds himself in total possession of himself—and so miserable that he will die. *inopem me copia fecit*: Ovid correctly exploits the related etymologies of adjective and noun. The noun derives from an abandoned archaic adjective, *co-ops*, meaning "abundant." Wealth has paradoxically made him poor, because in acquiring the reflection, he has lost a viable lover. This is a poor version of the self-knowledge that Delphi and Socrates advocated, but it is all that limited Narcissus can muster.

67–
68
As the first human lover that Ovid has presented, Narcissus finds himself in a paradigmatic state of hopelessness, doomed to defeat by the conditions of his being. It is typical of such lovers to express the vain wish—"if only . . . "—with the hopes that these conditions be altered. In 467, then, he wishes to separate himself from his body, that is, to create two individuals out of the present one and so make mutual love possible for himself. That wish will be granted in quite a different fashion: he will die and be permanently disconnected from his physical being, which in turn will be lost as a human body. *votum . . . novum* 468: ever the self-conscious lover, Narcissus calls attention to his unique desire. By definition, it might be said, lovers always desire to be together, to die together in times of danger. (Cf. his complaints in 455–56.) Here he wants the opposite.

69–
70
Abandoning these verbal conceits before they become too much for us, Narcissus faces approaching death. The *dolor* that was mentioned at 448, and the wasting away, first noted at 437 ff., have taken their toll. *primoque extinguor in aevo* 470: a rare use of first person passive of this verb; Ovid has appropriated this whole clause from his *Her.* 8.121. In referring to the boy's premature death, it uses a metaphor that links the snuffing of the light of life and of the flame of love.

71–
73
In the final lines of this soliloquy, which began at 442, Narcissus still cannot abandon his fixation on there being two separate individuals. Note the careful structure of 471, divided at the caesura into two corresponding halves. *posituro*: dative depending on *mihi*. Death is no severe burden since he will get rid of his severer pains. On the one hand, he imagines himself as released. But on the other hand, there is *hic qui diligitur*; and for that person he would like to have a long life! As it is, the two of them will end up united in death *anima in una* (473). In putting things that way, Ovid lets the boy trivialize the love language of mutual lovers and also that of close friends who,

as Horace shows us, could call each other "half of their soul." Cf. Horace of Vergil, *animae dimidium meae (C.* 1.3.8), and Maecenas, *te meae partem animae* (C. 2.17.5).

474–
76
male sanus: the narrator has resumed control of the story, and he immediately produces a more objective evaluation of this young fool. *male* is a common poetic alternative for *non* or the negative prefix *in-*, and is often chosen for metrical reasons. Here, Ovid especially aimed for five dactyls and narrative speed after the slow self-pity of Narcissus' speech. *turbavit aquas* 475: this is the first time that Ovid has taken advantage of his opportunity to describe the effect on Narcissus of seeing the reflection disappear or be disturbed. He could have done it earlier, for instance, when the boy kissed the water (cf. 451) or when he was weeping over the pool (cf. 459–60).

476–
79
It is evident that Narcissus' self-realization lasted only a short time, before he sank back into his delusion about the separate existence of the reflection. Here he passionately apostrophizes the vanishing form, in much the way he addressed it in 454–55. It is a cruel beloved who heartlessly forsakes his lover! *tangere non est* 478: *est* + infin. = *licet* or, as here, "it is possible." Cf. 453, where Ovid writes *posse tangi*, using the passive. Narcissus at least knows now that it is impossible to touch the reflected form; he asks only to be allowed to look at it. *misero . . . furori* 479: aware of the madness that confirms the narrator's foreshadowing at the start (cf. 350), he invites our pity with the adjective. Like an addict, he seeks to "feed" his mad addiction, aware but out of control.

480–
81
dumique: = *et dum*. A casual transition from direct speech by the boy back to narrative. *dolet*: the pain of hopeless love (cf. 471, 452) rather than of physical sickness. *summa . . . ab ora*: from the top edge. Ripping one's robe from top to bottom is a standard gesture of despair among Greeks and Romans. Proserpina will rip her dress as she is kidnapped by Pluto in 5.398. The immediate result of Narcissus' gesture is that his comely chest is bared, and the poet can launch into his Golden Line at 481 (enhanced by alliteration) over the next gesture, beating the breast. *marmoreis* 481: earlier, the boy had been compared to a statue of Parian marble (cf. 419).

482–
85
pectora . . . percussa: careful repetition from 481, in chiastic order. *roseum . . . ruborem*: together with the marble-white hands, this composes a scene mixing red and white, a favorite Ovidian combination (cf. 422–23). The simile of 483–85 introduces two types of fruit, apples and grapes, which, before reaching ripeness, appear of mixed colors or purplish. That is the color of his bruised skin, and the reference to immaturity points to the premature death of this young man. *parte / parte* 483–84: both ablative of specification, chiastically

disposed. *variis . . . racemis*: the grape clusters show a variety of colors.

86–
87
quae: the chest (pectora 481) being beaten. *liquefacta rursus*: the participle is ablative with *unda*. Ovid derives a unique meaning from the verb, which regularly means "turn into liquid." What he intends to convey is that, after having been disturbed and nonreflecting (cf. 475–76), the pool, once again clear, becomes able to reflect the boy's image. He extends the sense of *lique-* by analogy with adjective *liquidus* and verb *liquesco*, both of which carry connotations of being clear and transparent. *non tulit ulterius* 487: this language regularly applies to violent indignation, but here denotes the intolerable agony of Narcissus' special *furor*.

87–
90
A second simile helps to convey the rapid disintegration of the lover. Wax melts near fire or a flame; morning frost melts away in the sunshine. Similarly, under the burning effect of the internal fire of hopeless passion, Narcissus wastes away. *intabescere*: cf. *tabuerit* (445). *attenuatus* 489: Ovid reminds us of the way Echo earlier was weakened (cf. 396). The fates of these two become linked again as both prove victims of futile passion.

91–
93
In 491, the narrator picks up the colorful phrase of 423, only to deny now that it is valid. Dying Narcissus has simply turned pale. One negative after another dismisses elements of his former physical beauty. *visa placebant* 492: cf. 446. *nec corpus remanet* 493: Ovid means that the special body, so desirable in Echo's eyes, had wasted, but some body still survives, until finally at 509 the narrator reports its complete disappearance. Now, he carefully brings Echo back, taking his cue from the relative clause, in order to contrast her other-directed love with the self-fixated passion of Narcissus.

94–
96
quae: nominative; the relative immediately picks up from the name of Echo. *quamvis*: limits the two adjectives that follow in the line; *indoluit* (495) is an independent verb. She has greater reason to suffer and to resent her suffering, because it was caused by the person she loved, yet she grieves *for him*. *miserabilis* 495: perhaps the narrator now concedes that Narcissus is pitiable, but I prefer to think he is emphasizing Echo's impressionable feelings. *eheu*: whereas Narcissus emotes in self-pity, Echo takes and transforms his speech, injecting it with her own feelings of loving sympathy. *resonis . . . vocibus* 496: reverting to the echo effect, Ovid reminds us of the epithet he coined for her at 358, this time coining the adjective *resonus*.

97–
98
Ovid describes another gesture of grief and despair, which Narcissus used: he beat his upper arms with his hands; cf. 4.138. In echoing that sound, which is wordless, Echo should have had some trouble, inasmuch as she had no arms to beat.

499–   *solitam . . . spectantis in undam*: Narcissus is still staring into the
501   pool as he utters his last words. Soon, however, it will be a different
       body of water that he sees; cf. 505 below. *heu frustra dilecte puer*
       500: again, we judge the words differently according to who is speak-
       ing them. *dictoque vale* 501: ablative absolute, the second word, of
       course, being indeclinable. *vale inquit et Echo*: since scansion of the
       first *vale* is short, long, Ovid has to do something special with the
       second *vale* here; he scans it short, short. This is a rare but permissible
       shortening in hiatus (rather than using elision). Ovid ingeniously imi-
       tates Vergil's *Ecl.* 3.79, but adds the echo situation. Thus, where
       Vergil had the effect of a repeated "Farewell" seemingly die out, Ovid
       has the echo, dying out, imply the death of Narcissus.

502–   *caput . . . submisit in herba*: since he was sprawled on the grass,
3   staring into the water, Narcissus merely slumps to the earth in death.
       domini mirantia formam 503: self-admiration and self-delusion con-
       tinue right up to the moment of death (cf. 424).

504–   *se . . . spectabat*: Ovid does not explain how the incorporeal being
7   could look at himself. We can hypothesize that Narcissus went down
       to the Underworld with an *umbra*, which would have a visible form
       though no physical substance. In theory, that could produce its own
       reflection in the Styx. In any case, this mirroring of insubstantiality
       compounds the folly of the boy. He is even less sympathetic in death
       than in life. *planxere*: a basic mourning gesture is beating the breast.
       Ovid will repeat this verb twice in 507, at the beginning (with the
       more familiar form of perfect 3rd person plural) and the caesura.
       sorores / naides 506–7: since Narcissus' father was Cephisos, the
       water-nymphs whom he sired would be the boy's sisters. Cutting hair
       for women was another act of mourning. At 507, Echo again seems
       to violate her verbal limitations and echo a physical blow that would
       logically require her to have a body to beat (cf. above 497–98).

508–   In the trisected 508, Ovid lists three items for a funeral. The most
10   important item, however, is lacking: there is no body. *croceum florem*
       509: the narcissus replaces the dead boy. As Ovid describes it, it has
       white petals around a deep yellow center and much resembles the
       daffodil (to which its species is closely related). Not a significantly
       lovely flower, merely pretty. Narcissus' metamorphosis is an
       anticlimax.

PENTHEUS (511–733)

The longest story of Book 3 is the last. It takes us from the dubious
elegiac pathos of Narcissus to the level of traditional tragedy, for
Pentheus was the subject of Euripides' last play, the *Bacchae*, and of

lost dramas by the Romans Pacuvius and Accius (to name but three poets). Euripides' plot is summarized in Hyginus 184, and Apollodorus 3.5.2 gives the main details of the story without noting Euripidean influence. While Ovid surely knew the *Bacchae*, he chose not to follow its deeply tragic construction and its concentration on the cruel victory by Dionysos/Bacchus over arrogant young Pentheus, who trusted in merely human power. In this story, the god plays no role— he appears only in an inserted tale—and the antagonists of Pentheus all possess less power and menace by themselves than he does. The spokesman for the god, a character never imagined by Euripides, proves to be a simple, pious sailor; and Pentheus meets his death at the hands of weak women, whom he despises, torn apart according to tradition by his mother and aunts, but without the obvious instigation of sadistic Bacchus. Whereas Euripides ends his tragedy not with the death of Pentheus, but with the contrast between Dionysos, gloating, unfazed, and totally triumphant, and Agave, carrying the bloody head of her son and slowly realizing the human horror of her "inspired actions," Ovid leaves the dismembered corpse of Pentheus in the mountains and returns us quietly to Thebes, where reverence for Bacchus reasserts itself.

Although, then, he consciously mutes the disturbing tragic note, Ovid does utilize the dramatic mode. He pits one character against another, most notably Pentheus vs. Acoetes, and he uses dramatic speech rather than narrative description. In every episode but the last, speech dominates; the longest speeches, those of Pentheus (531–63) and Acoetes (582–691), perform key functions of characterization and thematic elaboration. From the disproportion between the two speeches, we can reasonably infer the narrator's bias. Thus, although Pentheus dies in a horrible manner like his cousin Actaeon, as we are reminded at 720, Ovid, ever attentive to nuanced distinctions, makes clear that Bacchus does not resemble petty, spiteful Diana, that his worship has validity, and his persecutor was psychologically and morally warped.

Pentheus vs. Bacchus (511–76)

In this first part, Pentheus opposes reception of Bacchic rites in Thebes, despite the warnings of Tiresias and the instinctive piety of his people. Indignant and horrified by what he considers unpatriotic sacrilege, Pentheus harangues the populace. Ovid changes tragic issues to the more familiar ones of Augustan propaganda and Vergilian epic, as Pentheus speaks for native Roman values of manliness and martial preparedness against the alien vices of effeminacy and religious fakery that he attributes to Bacchus and his corrupt followers.

511–
12
cognita res: the news of Narcissus' death. *vati*: Tiresias. Ovid repeats the opening device of the previous story, except that Tiresias volunteers his prophecy in the form of a warning, which Pentheus spurns. At the end of this narrative, the prediction has been completely fulfilled. Past tenses indicate that these two lines serve as transition and background.

513–
16
Echionides: Pentheus was son of Cadmus' daughter Agave and of one of the humanized dragon's teeth, Echion, of the snaky name. The patronymic gives him epic status at first. *ex omnibus unus*: his unique contempt for Tiresias ushers in his unique opposition to the god, as if he felt challenged by any distinction. *contemptor superum* 514: this phrase defines the young king as a parallel to Vergil's Mezentius, called *contemptor divum* in *Aen*. 7.648 (same metrical position). Vergil represents without modification the impiety and savagery of his king, but he does not refuse him tragic grandeur at the end. *superum*: genitive plural. *praesagaque*: Vergil introduced this word into Latin, and used it memorably in connection with the doom of Mezentius. Ovid's audience might catch the echo (cf. *Aen*. 10.843 and *Met*. 2.124 n.). *tenebrasque . . . obicit* 515–16: Pentheus shows himself despicable from the start by mocking Tiresias' disability as well as his proven reliability. *lucis ademptae* 515: cf. above 337.

516–
18
canis: in plural, a substantive. Ovid strengthens the contrast between contemptor and prophet by also noting the difference between wise old age and foolish youth. *felix* 517: since this is a contrary-to-fact condition, Tiresias predicts that Pentheus will be *infelix*. The details will be spelled out in future indicative at 522–23. *ne Bacchica sacra videres* 518: negative purpose clause. Ovid reminds us of his overriding theme for Book 3: the fatal result of seeing a sight that is taboo.

519–
20
namque dies aderit: a formula dear to epic since Homer. *auguror*: Ovid always treats this verb as deponent, in contrast to Vergil and others. *novus . . . Liber* 520: Tiresias refers to the newly divine status of Pentheus' cousin, not his rather recent birth.

521–
23
fueris dignatus: future perfect indicative, in a simple future condition. Tiresias is totally confident of his words. *lacer spargere* 522: the verb is future passive. Ovid picks up the adjective in the fulfilling scene at 722, using the verb *lacerata est*. The details of the prediction, both gory and horrible because of the involvement of Pentheus' relatives, enrage Pentheus here, but prove all too true.

524–
26
Changing the negative condition of 521 to a statement of fact in 524, Tiresias also adds the key word *numen*, to insist on the divinity of Bacchus. *sub his tenebris . . . vidisse* 525: Pentheus' impermissible taunt of 515–16 is ironically turned against him. Tiresias has better "vision" than this fool. *proturbat* 526: Pentheus knocks the blind man over while he is still speaking. This is the first occasion when Pentheus scorns warnings.

527–   *dicta*: picks up *dicentem* in 526. *aguntur*: "they are acted or worked
28   out." *Liber adest* 528: this fulfills 520. *festis fremunt ululatibus*: the
       verb implies a wild, even animal sound, but the adjective makes it
       clear that the noise is happy. In other contexts *ululatibus* would have
       negative associations. Here, though the howling is wild, it is neither
       ungodly nor miserable. The same howling ushers in the death scene
       of Pentheus at the end (706).

529–   Ovid specifically informs us that men are there with the women—
30   these are not just female bacchantes—and aristocrats along with
       humble folk. A large cross section of the Theban populace welcomes
       the god; and Pentheus would have done well to do so, too. *ignota ad
       sacra* 530: here, Ovid plants the seeds of Pentheus' disaster. If he
       fails to honor the god (521), then in his impiety he will spy on the
       sacred rites (518).

531–   *quis furor*: a speech suddenly erupts in opposition to the general
32   Theban piety, and only after a line and half do we learn that Pentheus
       speaks. Branding the piety of his populace as "madness," he himself
       acts like a madman. The same opening by an impious rogue occurs
       at 641 and at 6.170 (where Niobe starts haranguing her reverent fellow
       Thebans). *anguigenae*: this epithet, invented by Ovid for this context
       (and imitated only by Statius), is meant as a patriotic appeal to national
       origins by Pentheus, but affects us differently. The snake whom he
       depicts as the noble forefather of Thebes has hardly been represented
       as such at 32 ff. *Mavortia*: this adjective for Mars is mainly reserved
       for poetry, to provide a grandiose, metrically useful equivalent for
       Martia. *Mavors* was the archaic name for Mars. In declaring the
       Thebans "offspring of Mars," Pentheus is made by Ovid to echo
       Roman patriotic rhetoric. Mars was also the originator of Rome, by
       his rape of Ilia, and the adjective *Mavortia* occurs early in the *Aeneid*
       (1.276) in connection with the walls that Aeneas and his descendants
       will raise in Latium.

532–   *aerane*: Pentheus starts a long rhetorical question, fixing on what he
37   considers the disgraceful paraphernalia of worship, but ignoring the
       religious essence. Bronze cymbals, employed by exotic cults, those
       of Bacchus and of Cybele, offended conservative Roman feelings.
       Catullus and Lucretius had developed this poetic theme before Ovid.
       adunco tibia cornu 533: the flute of animal horn was associated in
       the Roman mind, too, with the imported rites of Cybele. Same phrase
       when Bacchus manifests his power at 4.392. Cymbals and flute pro-
       duced unholy sounds, to the ear of this Roman Pentheus. *magicae
       fraudes* 534: nothing in the narrator's objective description of the rites
       justifies this biased assertion. The foe of religion regularly sneers
       about superstition and magic. *quos*: the result clause, which Pentheus
       announced by *tantum* (532), begins here, but the orator inverts its

order for effect and first inserts a resonant relative clause, piling up his negative anaphora, before elaborating a series of prejudicial subjects of the verb *vincant* (537). The construction of this periodic question is significant for Pentheus: he surrounds the Martial symbols of which he approves, but which he feels are threatened, by biased details about Bacchic worship, the challenger of his revered traditions. *bellicus*: the adjective will recur at 704, when Pentheus is ironically compared to a spirited horse inspired by the war-trumpet (on the verge of death). *femineae voces* 536: the narrator scrupulously told us that men and women together participate in the reception of Bacchus. Pentheus exhibits typical male prejudice, identifying the enemy exclusively with women. *obscenique greges* 537: it was a common claim that alien cults indulged in sexual orgies. The Greek thought this about bacchantes; the Romans borrowed and magnified the prejudice as they stamped out the Bacchanalian rites in 186 B.C.; and the generation of Varro, Lucretius, and Catullus could imagine all kinds of obscenity among the eunuch priests of Cybele and her Roman worshippers. *tympana*: drums went with alien Asiatic practices, notably those of Cybele, in the Roman mind. *vincant*: deliberately sardonic use of the military metaphor.

538–
40
vosne . . . mirer: alternative deliberative question, coordinate with *vosne* (540). Pentheus divides his appeals between the older and younger generations. The verb professes shocked disapproval. *longa per aequora vecti*: unmistakable allusion to several passages in the *Aeneid* (1.375, 3.325, and 6.355) where the same last three words, in the same metrical position, refer to the troubled voyage of the Trojans toward Italy. Impious Pentheus poses as a super-patriot and abuses the true values of Vergil's poem. He is a Mezentius, not an Aeneas. *profugos . . . Penates* 539: again, allusion to the story of Aeneas, but the popping alliteration and rhetorical phrasing mark the difference between Pentheus and Aeneas. The Theban ruler never mentions his grandfather Cadmus, but we know that he did not carry Penates and that his refugee status arose not from fate or war or plan, but incidentally because, not locating Europa, he fell under his father's curse (cf. 3–5). *sine Marte capi* 540: Pentheus chooses to compare the arrival of Bacchus to a military conquest. Thus, for him the older men are "cowardly."

540–
42
vosne: since this is an alternative question, we are to assume the same verb *mirer* as in 538. *acrior aetas*: the special "keenness" that Pentheus seeks in his contemporaries will be militancy. The relative clause of 541–42 sets up invidious antitheses between items of war and alien cult-paraphernalia. The thyrsus, a stick wreathed with a garland and tipped with a pinecone, recurs at 712 when Autonoe attacks her son.

543–
By turning the snake into the Founding Father of Thebes and urging

46   the populace to be mindful of its heritage, Pentheus patently abuses
       current Augustan rhetoric. It is as if a Roman orator should hail as a
       foundation-symbol the wolf that raised Romulus and Remus (an animal
       that Livy and others suggested might in fact have been a human
       prostitute!). *illiusque . . . serpentis* 544–45: the hyperbaton delays
       the anticlimactic word to the end—a snake whose acts have been
       perverted into the equivalent of a hero's deeds. *animos* 544: appropriate
       language for a human being who has been metamorphosed, but mere
       anthropomorphism in this case. *multos perdidit unus*: this sounds like
       Hollywood heroism, one man against many; but it does not bear much
       resemblance to the narrator's account. *pro fontibus* 545: more slanting
       of facts. Noble self-sacrifice in defense of national values fits neither
       the dragon nor the actions that Pentheus tries to force on the Theban
       men. *vincite* 546: an echo of 537. The king promises victory, not
       heroic death.

547–   *fortes . . . molles*: prejudicial rhetorical antithesis, quite familiar in
50   our contemporary patriotic harangues. *patrium . . . decus* 548: the
       serpent is the "forefather" in this warped paradigm. *vetabant*: indica-
       tive has satisfactory sense, but most editors suggest that Ovid uses
       the indicative in place of imperfect subjunctive in a contrary-to-fact
       condition. Since the rejected form would have been metrically similar
       vetarent, I believe that the poet employed the heightened vividness
       of the indicative. *stare diu* 549: Pentheus rigs the situation into a
       crisis over the very survival of Thebes. Thebes will survive, but he
       will not. Thus, he returns to his antithesis between war and this
       religious "invasion." He would prefer to have violent warfare rather
       than this insidious cult. War is simpler and cleaner, according to too
       many rulers, even today. His details suggest the assault on a besieged
       city (such as Aeneas' Troy).

551–   *essemus miseri*: Pentheus proceeds with a present contrary-to-fact
52   statement. Using the first person plural, he rhetorically includes the
       Thebans in his biased reactions. They would suffer misery in defeat,
       but at least it would be glorious defeat. He then goes on to vary the
       idea in two additional clauses: *querenda* vs. *celanda*, tears vs. shame.

553–   *at nunc*: Pentheus shifts to future indicative, to make a seemingly
56   confident—though inaccurate—assertion. *puero . . . inermi*: division
       of the phrase makes the delayed adjective, in the final position, more
       effective. Pentheus' unmilitant cousin especially irritates him. The
       list of martial attributes in 554 becomes swamped by two lines of
       corrupt items the king dreams up and emphasizes by alliteration. They
       add up to a picture of Asiatic decadence that Roman moralists often
       decry. Iarbas sneers at Aeneas' "dripping hair" (*Aen.* 4.216) as does
       Turnus (12.99–100). Crowns or garlands go with Bacchus and other
       gods' celebrations; softness suggests effeminacy here, but not always.

Purple in its most precious form comes form shellfish of Asia Minor. It and gold thread were exotic luxury goods. Anchises made a rich gift to Latinus of a chlamys woven with gold thread (*Aen.* 8.167).

557–
58   *quem*: the hated "boy" Bacchus. Pentheus moves into threats of instant action. *modo vos absistite*: parenthetical remark addressed to the crowd of Thebans, whose opposition or disapproval the king recognizes here. Cf. the stated reactions at 564–65 below. *cogam*: "force" will be applied at 562 (arrest) and 694 ff. (imprisonment, attempted torture and execution). *adsumptumque . . . commentaque* 558: the key participles are linked by double *-que*, as Pentheus charges as a religious fraud the divine birth that the narrator has already asserted. Euripides' Pentheus made a similar charge, and sometimes Semele's sisters voiced jealous insinuations about her "immorality."

559–
61   *Acrisio*: dative of possession. *animi*: partitive genitive. Acrisius, king of Argos, is most famous for intervention to punish his daughter and grandchild Perseus, sired by Jupiter and the "Golden Rain." He was duly destroyed for that. Ovid refers to another violence by Acrisius, otherwise unknown to our various sources, which makes the Argive king a model for Pentheus' impiety. Pentheus, of course, attributes courage to Acrisius, but we are to reject that view. *vanum / numen*: careful separation by enjambement. *claudere portas*: the doors are being shut against an "enemy" (the king's view), not against a relative, friend, or lover. In 561, we have the antithesis rhetorically rigged. Pentheus will refuse to be "frightened" by this "stranger." As for "all Thebes," contrary to the king's bias, it shows no fear of Bacchus, but simple reverence.

562–
63   *ite citi*: the rhetoric changes into abrupt tyrannical commands, only later explicated by the parenthetical stage direction. *ducemque*: the king means the "leader" who, in his opinion, poses as the god Bacchus. Instant obedience is regularly demanded by rulers. *abesto* 563: future imperative, giving the command special insistence.

564–
65   Public reaction to the speech and orders is negative. Ovid singles out the grandfather Cadmus and Athamas, husband of Ino (who had nursed the baby Bacchus for a while—cf. 313–14—and could attest to his divine origins). Pentheus might listen to his male relatives; besides, the females are in the mountains with other worshippers of Bacchus. *turba surorum*: a group not specifically defined, but either other members of the family and court or the general populace. These people represent a second warning to Pentheus, which he wildly dismisses.

566–
67   Two clauses each in two lines repeat the paradoxical picture of regal impatience and irritation. Note the alliterative patterns and the implicit metaphors in the words. Ovid could have launched into a simile about a wild horse, refusing to be reined in, but he preferred an image of greater violence and dehumanized power.

68–   *sic ego . . . vidi*: starts a simile, not with the usual conjunction *ut* or
71   *velut*. Instead, it introduces the personal viewpoint of the narrator and
      the anachronism of his own Roman time. The subject of the simile,
      a mountain torrent, is studied from two antithetical aspects, each
      occupying two lines. When it meets no obstacles, the water moves
      fairly smoothly; but, when obstructed, it becomes more violent, a
      perfect symbol of Pentheus here. Thus, the final word before the verb
      at 571 is *saevior*, a reminder of the comparative *acrior* at 566. *trabes*
      570: not boards, but whole trees that have been uprooted and swept
      down by the flood. They get tangled in each other and make a dam
      for other debris. *tenebant*: Ovid abandons indirect discourse, and uses
      imperfect indicative to stress the chief points of the simile. Understand
      illum (the torrent). *obice* 571: last of three words with the prepositional
      prefix *ob-* in this simile, all emphasizing opposition.

72–   *ecce*: the dramatic device, like a floodlight, focuses attention on the
73   next scene, which follows without preparation on the simile that closes
      the episode of Pentheus' wild oration. *cruentati*: these bloodstained
      men are the *famuli* whom the king ordered at 562 to find and capture
      the ringleader. We would expect them to explain the blood, namely,
      resulting from some battle that they had before they could lay hands
      on their captive; but Ovid assumes that we know enough of the
      traditional story to deal competently with this brief allusion. He says
      nothing more. *Bacchus ubi esset*: subjunctive in indirect question with
      quaerenti 573. The king keeps asking where Bacchus is, trying to see
      him, but his own stubborn disbelief prevents him and his slaves from
      recognizing the god's presence.

74–   *comitem famulumque sacrorum*: this character, who will name himself
76   as Acoetes at 582, is introduced as an independent servant of the
      god's rites, in appearance entirely different from the ringleader and
      boyish "god" they were hunting. Some scholars believe that this
      nevertheless is Bacchus in disguise, playing the role of the Stranger
      in Euripides' tragedy. However, Ovid's Acoetes is no sinister figure,
      but another warner. Euripides' Stranger gives no warning story, but
      he teases and lures Pentheus to destruction, revealing himself as the
      god in disguise, malevolently bringing down punishment on the unbe-
      liever. *manibus post tergo ligatis* 575: ablative absolute. The scene
      is reminiscent of that in *Aen.* 2.57 ff., when shepherds bring Sinon
      before the Trojans. Sinon tells a destructive lie, whereas Acoetes
      recounts a story that could, if heeded, save Pentheus. Line 576 gives
      us details about the captive that show the narrator's viewpoint: it
      serves to guarantee that this is not Bacchus, but a loyal follower.
      Pentheus will ask him why he frequents Bacchic rites (581), and he
      will give a lengthy explanation of why he—and implicitly the king—
      should do so. *Tyrrhena gente* 576: ablative of origin without preposi-

tion. The Tyrrhenians are understood by Ovid here to inhabit the coast of Lydia. Herodotus 1.94 reports that these people abandoned their homes and sailed away, eventually arriving in northern Italy and settling down to become the Etruscans, regularly called Tyrrhenian by Latin writers.

Pentheus vs. Acoetes (577–700)

In this second part, Pentheus faces a second major warner and opponent and, by angrily spurning him, too, seals his doom. The character Acoetes occupies the role played by Dionysos, who poses as a Stranger in Euripides' play and lets himself be temporarily captured. Ovid has a different design for Acoetes. He rejects the Euripidean model and turns instead to the Homeric *Hymn to Dionysos*, which represents a nameless pilot protesting against the impiety of his pirate shipmates. Expanding that Homeric prototype carefully, Ovid gives it dramatic substance by speeches and vivid action, and then utilizes every opportunity to elaborate a description of metamorphosis.

577–78   Fixing on the angry eyes of Pentheus, Ovid depicts the savage tyrant, who decides on punishment before hearing a case. The long explanatory speech of Acoetes, which tells us in the audience much about him and his gentle god, merely serves to irritate the king as it postpones his anger's satisfaction.

579–81   *aliis documenta dature*: the Romans, who were strong believers in the force of example, would have heard the argument for capital punishment as a deterrent (for the living). A tyrant would favor such a theory. *tuaque . . morte* 580: again, careful and effective hyperbaton across the line-break. However, this opening is hardly calculated to secure compliance from the prejudged victim. Pentheus asks four pieces of information of this stranger. He gets the first three in two lines, but he hears more about the rites of Bacchus than he calculated, with no benefit and increasing impatience. Acoetes echoes the final two words of 581 at the end of his explanation, at 691.

582–83   *metu vacuus*: a brief characterization of the speaker as fearless sets him up in sharp antithesis to angry, menacing Pentheus. Ovid will expand that antithesis. Acoetes begins with his name, as ordered; but then he omits his parents and tells the name of his homeland. From what he next tells us of the humble status of his parents (583), it is evident that he omits their names as beneath the proud king's notice. Maeonia is a coastal region of Lydia, identical, for the purposes of this poem, with the Tyrrhenian territory.

584–85   *non mihi . . . reliquit*: within this framing hyperbaton, Ovid inserts subject, three objects, and a relative clause of purpose. The three nouns at the end of 584 all have different functions. The father, surrounded by the fields and oxen that he did not have, seems to disappear from significance, only to reemerge in the next lines as a simple fisherman. *arva* and *iuvenci* come after the words and clause to which they belong, as an anticlimax.

586–
87
pauper et ipse fuit: this might mean that the father was poor as the son evidently is (in appearance). It seems more likely that Acoetes uses the conjunction late, in reference to what he just said above: the father did not leave him any land or farm animals, and in fact he owned none since he was poor. *linoque . . . hamis . . . calamo* 587: line, hook, and rod define a fisherman. Ovid divides their functions. Hook and line deceive the fish; the rod pulls them in as they jump and try to get away.

588–
91
ars . . . census erat: a witty way of saying that all his "wealth" consisted of his fishing skill. Normally, *census* refers to substantial riches, those of a Roman senator, for example (cf. 7.739 and 8.846). Ovid uses this same disclaimer of wealth in introducing the poor father of Cretan Iphis in 9.671. In the next three lines, he elaborates his conceit: *artem* at the end of 588 leads us to the "wealth" mentioned in 590–91. *quas habeo* 589: relative clause before antecedent (*opes*), as often in Ovid. *nihil . . . reliquit* 590: echoes 585. Since water would be for the Romans and Greeks one of the most common public commodities, Acoetes inherited no material item at all. In contrast to the warped serpent-heritage that Pentheus has adduced, this man admits his simple background without shame.

592–
94
mox: imprecise temporal indication, it suggests that Acoetes did not long pursue his father's occupation. *scopulis . . . isdem*: fishermen are regularly depicted in literature and art as fishing from rocks, when on land. The fishing rod had not developed then to allow casting and reeling. Acoetes finds that a dull existence, as do many nonfishers today. *addidici* 593: not a poetic word; Ovid seems to have been the first, and one of few, poets to use it, here and earlier in *Am.* 2.5.56. The prefix *ad-* occurs with special meaning: Acoetes is learning something additional to his modest nautical lore as fisherman. *regimen . . . flectere* 594: the noun literally means "rule, command." It is only by metonymy that, in connection with ships, it refers to that part of the vessel that steers the craft, the rudder. Acoetes learns how to be a shipmaster and pilot the boat.

94–
96
Oleniae . . . Capellae: Olenos of Aetolia had a daughter Aege who, in accordance with her name's Greek meaning, turned into a goat. Later, she became a star, set in the constellation Auriga; its appearance coincides with the coming of rain, an important detail for any competent navigator to know. *Taygetenque* 595: one of the seven Pleiades, a group on which sailors of the Mediterranean much relied. *Hyadasque*:

group of five stars, whose rising and setting synchronized with rain (hence, the Greek name). *Arctonque*: the Big Bear, to translate the name. This is what Callisto became after her final transformation. Greeks and Romans had other names for this prominent constellation, such as *Septentriones*. It helped sailors determine north. Other key data for navigators (596) include marking the winds and familiarity with good ports.

597–
99
forte: another casual connective. We may assume that, having learned his new craft, Acoetes has found employment as pilot and is on a voyage of some sort. *Delon*: since the destination is Delos, island of Apollo, and a stopping point is the island of Chios, not far from Lydia, the voyage has started in Acoetes' native Lydia, and they sail westward. *adplicor* 598: this passive form renders our intransitive sense of "put in." *dextris . . . remis*: scholars argue whether the adjective means "to the right" (and thus gives us significant information about the route that the ship has taken) or "dextrously, successfully." If we take Ovid literally, then rowing with right oars at the last moment would have little relevance to the original course the vessel *sailed*; it seems more likely that the poet signals a successful arrival in port. Continuation of the passive forms through the end of the sentence begins to suggest that Acoetes presents himself as being acted upon, not as an independent agent.

600–
602
nox: again, the story leaps over a gap. We can fill it in by realizing that Greek voyagers did not spend a night at sea unless they had to, so the landing in Chios came at nightfall. They ate a meal and bedded down on the shore near their boat, which they had drawn up on the beach. *exsurgo* 601: as a good captain, Acoetes is first to rise and get the sailors into action to take advantage of the daylight. *laticesque . . . recentes*: fresh water is absolutely critical for saltwater sailors. *viam . . . undas* 602: Acoetes apparently knows this port and its resources, so he points out the route to the spring.

603–
4
quid aura . . promittat: subjunctive in indirect question. Acoetes climbs a low hill to check the wind. The three units that divide 604 suggest the dedicated efficiency of the captain.

605–
7
adsumus en: in response to Acoetes' call, the sailors appear and one of them cheerily announces: "Here we are." Thus, Ovid introduces his modernized version of the Homeric Hymn to Dionysos. In the Greek, the god was wandering along the seashore when Tyrrhenian pirates suddenly landed and kidnapped him. The hymn names none of the sailors. Ovid, on the other hand, letting one of the crew narrate the event, can justify naming many of them. And they are ordinary sailors manning a ship that sails to Delos on presumably normal trading purposes. When they kidnap Bacchus, then, the sailors are gratuitously evil; and when they reject and mutiny against their prudent, reverent

captain, they serve as clear warning prototypes for Pentheus. *utque putat* 606: the *-que* links the next clause (*praedam . . . forma*) with the previous. Ovid uses *ut putat* as a parenthetical note of ironic foreshadowing. *praedam*: predicate noun. The sailors wrongly believe that they have found an easy captive for ransom. *virginea puerum . . forma* 607: Ovid emphasizes the youth of Bacchus with ablative of description, making the god considerably younger, less virile and impressive, to begin with. His scene owes much to kidnapping situations of Greek and Roman comedy that involve children.

608–
10   *mero somnoque gravis . . . videtur*: Acoetes, as narrator, registers the imprecise impressions that he had when first seeing the boy. From these random details, he drew the inference that he was involved with an immortal being. We can perhaps detect some hints of Bacchus, but we have no reason as yet to agree with his rather simpleminded credulity. Ovid has organized this quite differently from the Hymn, where the captive, who cannot be fettered, awakens by that clear miracle the Greek pilot's belief. *cultum faciemque* 609: precisely what Acoetes saw, he does not say. *quod credi posset* 610: relative clause of characteristic after the negative.

611–
13   *dixi sociis*: there are two speeches in the Hymn: those of the prudent pilot and of the captain; the latter's answer cows the former into silence. Ovid represents Acoetes warning the sailors (as his narrative tries to warn Pentheus). *quod numen . . . sit* 612: subjunctive in indirect question. *isto*: the demonstrative points to the boy that all the sailors ("You") are so interested in. Careful repetition of the clause, now in the indicative, insists on the propriety of *numen*. *quisquis es* 613: in a conventionally reverent manner, Acoetes then addresses the child as a god, unable to name him precisely. *adsis*: standard request of a deity. In the end, Bacchus does favor the efforts of the captain alone, since he is pious, but reveals his presence to the others as a punisher.

614–
16   *des veniam*: when he tries to intercede on behalf of the crew, they abruptly dismiss his prayer. *mitte*: simple verb for the usual *omitte* (+ infinitive). The story introduces non-Homeric Dictys and his rare ability to climb to the top yards and slide down on the ropes. Elaborating the impiety of the crew, Ovid expands the fifty-eight lines of Homer to ninety-five in Latin. *quo . . . ocior* 615–16: ablative of comparison.

617–
20   Acoetes names four other crew members, giving a few key details about two of them. *flavus . . . Melanthus*: an oddly playful description, which receives emphasis from the inserted apposition. (He looks out for rocks and reefs.) The name in itself means "Blackie" in Greek, yet Acoetes calls him blond! *et qui . . . Epopeus* 618–19: as is customary in well-organized lists, the final item receives special expansion.

Moving up the relative clause and delaying the name all contribute to the climax. Epopeus, whose Greek name identifies him as overseer, sets the time for the rowers and encourages them on. Ovid specifies that he uses his own voice. In modern representations of Roman galleys and their slave-rowers, incorrectly the overseer has a drummer to pound out the rowing rhythm. *hoc omnes alii* 620: all the crew thus adopts the irreverence of Dictys in 615. *praedae tam caeca cupido est*: terminal sententia, filling the second hemistich. Ovid has taken a Lucretian phrase about blind ambition, *honorum caeca cupido* (3.59), and substituted the thematic word *praedae* (cf. 606).

621–
23

sacro violari pondere: although it seems odd that a profane object such as a ship could be "violated" by something sacred, Acoetes refers to the regular incommensurability of the religious and ordinary spheres. Since the god does not belong on the ship, his unwilling presence will cause the pollution and eventual peril of the boat. The next time we see this verb will be when Pentheus' mother leads the "violation" of her son (cf. 712). *pars . . . maxima iuris* 622: in defense of pious propriety, the captain tries to assert his supreme authority. The crew, respecting neither right nor authority, react with fury. Like Pentheus, they know no restraint. In the Homeric Hymn, the pilot alone objects to piracy, but, being only another sailor, he quickly returns to duty, terrified by the captain, who voices the pirates' greed and villainy.

623–
25

furit audacissimus: verb and adjective characterize the doomed blasphemer. *Tusca pulsus ab urbe* 624: Ovid invents an especially violent character to begin the mutiny and briefly sketches a story of Lycabas' exile from his Etruscan city for a nameless but heinous crime. The details resemble the facts that Vergil reports about Mezentius, tyrant of Etruscan Caere, and how his people rose up against and exiled him (*Aen.* 8.483 ff.) Thus, Lycabas takes on the same allusive identity as Pentheus, and he acts similarly.

626–
28

dum resto: at 623, Acoetes reported that he tried to block entrance on the boat to those who were dragging the "sacred" captive. *guttura . . . rupit*: without saying a word, the violent seamen "smashed" Acoetes in the throat. Had he actually "broken" the throat, the captain would have died. *excussum misisset* 627: typical Latin use of subordinated participle with verb where English would use two coordinate verbs. "He would have knocked me out of the way and pushed me into the water." *si non*: in conventional epic, it is unusual to begin enjambement with two monosyllables starting a new grammatical unit in the sixth foot. Ovid's unorthodox device gains the result of negating the effects of Lycabas' fury at the last moment. *quamvis amens* 628: Acoetes was "out of his mind" not because he was furious also, but because nearly unconscious from the blow. *in fune retentus*: he was holding on to a rope apparently, as he blocked the passage, and, even though stunned, he still maintained his grip. The four spondees here produce a complete pattern of rhythmical disagreement, to enhance the sense of struggle.

629– *inpia turba*: once again, Acoetes makes clear that the entire crew
31   agrees in the kidnapping of the god, the rejection of pious warning, and in the violence against the captain. *Bacchus*: Acoetes tells his story with total naivete. So far, he has in no way proved that the boy is divine. When he names the god, he does so from his bias, a slant that would understandably irritate Pentheus. The parenthetical insistence on Bacchus' identity in 630 would increase the king's annoyance. *veluti* [= *velut si*] . . . *solutus / sit* 630–31: the unreal condition reminds us that, when Acoetes first saw the boy, he registered details of a dubious "appearance" (cf. 608–9). Now, the curious befuddlement disappears.

632– *quis clamor*: Bacchus is apparently acting. He asks about all the uproar
33   (cf. 630), but Acoetes wants us to believe that the god has been fully conscious the whole time. So he is testing the crew by his questions. When he asks where they are taking him, he gives them a chance to be honest, but they lie.

634– *Proreus . . . dixit*: another sailor named; the Greek etymology points
35   to his position at the prow. He pretends to be concerned for the boy. *quos . . . velis* 634–35: subjunctive in indirect question, depending on *ede*. *terra*: ablative of place where. *sistere*: second person singular future passive. Proreus makes an absolute promise that he knows they will not fulfill.

636– *Naxon*: accusative in Greek declension, place to which. Although
37   the Homeric Hymn does not mention Naxos, Dionysos had a long association with this island by Ovid's time. Here he found and overwhelmed Ariadne after Theseus abandoned her. It is located in the mid-Aegean, well south and slightly west of Chios. In the carefully balanced halves of 637, the boy ingenuously offers the sailors hospitality at his home.

638– *fallaces*: again, Acoetes prejudices the narrative. Foreswearing by the
39   gods to a god constitutes serious perjury. *meque iubent* 639: as part of their deceptive act, the sailors order their captain-pilot ostensibly to carry out the boy's request and steer for Naxos. Of course, they have no business giving orders to their own shipmaster. But he simplemindedly believes them serious.

640– *dextera*: this nominative is the reading of a few MSS and regarded
43   as "more difficult" by contrast with ablative *dextra*, which would then be repeated at the caesura. Ovid starts with the adjective, then changes his form and syntax at the caesura to achieve pleasant variety. For a ship heading due south or somewhat west, Naxos would lie on the

right, definitely not in sight. *lintea danti*: Acoetes was not himself handling the sails; he was steering the boat and giving general orders about the sails. *demens* 641: each epithet applied by the crew to Acoetes tends to be more appropriate to the sailors themselves. *quis te furor*: we can supply a verb like *agit*. The question reminds us of the opening question of Pentheus at 531 and stresses the similarity between impious king and seamen. The real madness is that of the impious. They are afraid that, if they do go to Naxos, they will be punished, if not by the boy's relatives, then by their own captain appealing to the authorities. *laevam* 642: they want him to steer north away from Naxos. *quid velit* 643: subjunctive in indirect question. *aure*: the poet omits the preposition *in*.

644–
45
obstipui: Acoetes' surprise is more than the usual; it involves shock and horror, it seems, at the irreverence of these sailors. *aliquis*: we would say, "someone else." *moderamina*: the tiller by metonymy. Different from the word's usage in 567. *scelerisque artisque* 645: a good example of zeugma. Both words depend on *ministerio* as objective genitives, but they result in quite different, conflicting senses, not, as the double *-que* suggests, in similar meanings. Practice of his art, as steersman, will involve him in the practice of evil, which Acoetes wants to avoid.

646–
49
cunctis: further emphasis on the united impiety. *inmurmurat*: Vergil used this verb, apparently inventing it, in *G.* 4.261. Ovid uses it here and three other times in the *Met.* only. Whereas Vergil made it a metaphorical sound of the wind, Ovid restricts the usage to the muttering of human beings. *Aethalion* 647: the Greek name for this new character suggests a smoky flame; and he is a "hothead." *te . . . in uno*: Aethalion is sardonic about what he believes is Acoetes' pride in his uniqueness. *Naxoque . . . relicta* 649: within the ablative absolute, Ovid has inserted the main point, that the ship is turned in the opposite direction.

650–
51
deus inludens: more intrusion by the pious narrator, who interprets the boy's words and actions as those of the god Bacchus. Acoetes is now convinced that the god was playing with his kidnappers. *tamquam*: understand *si* and an unreal condition to fit the god's charade. *e puppi pontum prospectat* 651: from the stern, the boy looks south in the direction that he wants to take and, with nautical knowledge far beyond his childish years, realizes that the sailors have deceived him. The prominent alliteration with *p* has a disturbingly unserious effect; perhaps it adds to the sense of the god's play-acting.

652–
55
flenti similis: here, the narrator confidently assures us that the god was acting. However, at 656 he reports that his own reaction at the time was to weep himself. That suggests that he was not then entirely sure of the god's playful pretence or of his omnipotence in relation

to these blackguards. The tearful speech that the narrator now records appears to be the pathetic protest of a helpless single child against a mass of brawny young men. *non haec mihi*: anaphora planted in the same metrical positions in 652 and 653. *poenam . . . gloria* 654: ironically contrasting terms that will soon be reversed, as the young Bacchus will exult and punish these sailors.

656–
57
flebam: Acoetes admits that he was taken in by the act and honestly wept himself. *lacrimas . . . nostras*: the tears of the two only provoke mocking laughter from the crew, again labeled *inpia* by the narrator (cf. 629). In a hurry to get away, they undertake strenuous rowing. (Or they may in fact be rowing against the wind.)

658–
61
Acoetes intervenes with further pious claims, as he prepares us for the epiphany of the god and the miracles he performs. *per . . . ipsum*: by the god himself, as the parenthetical addition indicates. *praesentior*: remember that Acoetes is addressing Pentheus, so that the present tense can refer to Bacchus' definitive presence in Thebes, as well as to Bacchus in the story's frame. This could have been a special warning to Pentheus, who, however, remained obdurate. *tam . . . vera . . . quam veri maiora fide* 659–60: "as true as [they seem] incredible." *fide*: ablative of comparison, governing objective genitive *veri*. Literally, "greater than the belief in their truth." The first incredible event follows: the ship, though being strenuously rowed, stops dead in the water. *si . . . teneret* 661: subjunctive in contrary-to-fact. We are invited to imagine a naval drydock, so as to picture this fantastic event.

662–
63
admirantes: the sailors are made by the narrator to testify to the miracle. *perstant*: they persist in their impious behavior, and their struggle is reflected in the series of spondees of 662. *velaque deducunt* 663: now it appears they were not using their sails (in spite of 640). *geminaque ope*: wit prepares us for the untragic sequel of metamorphosis.

664–
65
With all the dramatic dialogue, description, and narratorial intrusions, Ovid has distanced himself from the Homeric Hymn. Now he moves back to it as he develops the way Bacchus reveals himself. But he has much greater interest in the various possibilities of metamorphosis, aboard the boat and affecting the sailors. *hederae . . . corymbis*: the first manifestations are harmless and not at all frightening. In Homer, a lion appears, representing the god's power, and chases the sailors to the back of the boat, from which in their terror they leap into the sea, where without more ado or individualization they turn into dolphins. Ovid's language, by its poetic prettiness, removes all menace from Bacchus. The ivy and grape clusters do, however, interfere with the two means of locomotion.

666–
ipse: the god. Acoetes does not tell us what the god himself looked

67   like, whether the same or different from the "boy" (who he realizes
     was acting). He merely adds to his attributes a crown of grape clusters
     and a harmless "spear" enveloped in vine leaves (cf. 542). At 712,
     it will be called by its more technical name, *thyrsus*. *racemiferis*:
     Ovid has invented this epic-looking epithet. He tries it once more in
     the *Met*. and in the contemporary *Fasti*.

668– Tigers, lynxes, and panthers became associated with Bacchus in Helle-
69   nistic times, when India and Indian beasts were linked with his myths.
     simulacraque inania: these empty, hence imaginary forms, though
     specifically connected with the lynxes, may well apply to the other
     animals. Acoetes, at least in retrospect, regards the threat of these
     creatures as entirely fictive, more of the god's play. Note that the
     verb *iacent* emphasizes their quiet, unmenacing position; unlike the
     lion in the Hymn, which is the god himself and pounces on and kills
     the pirate-captain, these beasts do nothing but pose. *pictarumque
     . . . pantherarum* 669: panthers, like leopards, were spotted. The
     alliteration that enhances the framing effect resolves into a double-
     spondee in the final word.

670– *exsiluere*: whereas the Homeric sailors flee from the lion to the stern
72   of the ship, then leap overboard, here the sailors only jump up.
     Acoetes' explanation, madness or fear, leaves unclear the god's effect.
     Did he drive the men crazy? *primusque Medon* 671: Medon begins
     the series of metamorphoses; his name means lord or ruler in Greek.
     nigrescere: a poetic word that was ably used by Vergil; Ovid makes
     it serve for human changes (cf. 2.581). The poet teases us by providing
     only a few inconclusive details here: the body turning black and the
     spine being forced into a curve. These hardly add up to a dolphin.
     But he intends only to expand these details, never to name the resulting
     dolphin. The poet's playfulness with his audience goes well with the
     relative playfulness of the god. *expresso . . . curvamine* 672: the nor-
     mally erect human torso is bent over by a forced arching of the spine.
     Dolphins mentioned in 2.265–66 receive the epithet *curvi*.

673– Lycabas, the violent Etruscan of 623 ff., reappears to receive his
75   punishment. He may be mocking Medon or merely expressing his
     surprise. I prefer the first: it makes the concentration on the immediate
     transformation of his mouth more apt. *lati rictus* 674: the wide, seem-
     ingly smiling mouth of dolphins appeals to modern anthropomorphic
     cartoons. At 685, the school of dolphins that was the crew is considered
     to be playing in the water. *panda . . . naris*: effective separation. A
     snub nose is another standard feature of the dolphin: cf. below *repan-
     dus* 680. *cutis durata*: the same skin that, in the case of Medon, grew
     black. Now, we know it is black, hardened, and scaly: that begins to
     suggest a fish.

676– Libys was named at 617. When he keeps wildly pulling on the oars,

78   in spite of their resistance—they were wound about with ivy—his
        metamorphosis focuses attention on his hands. They shrink in size
        and become fins, with ease, as the five dactyls of 677 imply. Poor
        Libys watches this happen to himself; but we are not invited to imagine
        his feelings.

679–   *alter*: Acoetes has named ten of the crew of a total that at 687 he will
82   reveal was twenty. In this final individualized vignette, before he
        proceeds to generalize, he leaves the man anonymous. *ad intortos
        . . . funes*: the sailor intended to grab the twisted or braided ropes
        and try to escape. *bracchia non habuit* 680: Ovid likes to describe
        the frustrating loss of arms in metamorphosis, but usually in the
        context of attempted prayer (cf. Io in 1.636). Prayer is beyond these
        sailors. *truncoque . . . corpore*: with a seemingly limbless body. We
        have already heard of the loss of hands and arms, and we can imagine
        the similar loss of legs. *in undas . . . desiluit* 680–81: at last, the
        individual features can add up to a dolphin, and this victim leaps into
        his new habitat. Thus, Ovid links up with the Homeric Hymn, which
        had wasted no effort on the description of metamorphosis. *falcata*: as
        this fish dives into the water, the last one sees of it is the tail, curved
        like a sickle or, more poetically put (682), like the half-moon.

683–   *undique dant saltus*: the rest of the crew, also dolphins, follow this
84   first one and, from various parts of the ship, dive into the water. The
        description then fits the known antics of dolphins, which regularly
        dive and jump out of the water as they move along.

685–   *inque chori ludunt speciem*: the language here indicates that this meta-
86   morphosis is not cruel, tragic, or ugly. The fish register no pathos;
        Ovid insists that they play around like a comic chorus. That nuance
        receives stress from *lascivaque*. And the final detail of their blowing
        seawater from their broad nostrils corresponds to the way children
        play in the bathtub.

687–   *de modo viginti*: supply *nautis*; the numeral is indeclinable. Left alone,
89   Acoetes reports his shaken condition in four overlapping units, of
        which *trementi / corpore* (688–89) qualifies *gelidum*. *vixque meum*
        689: "hardly myself or in my right mind."

689–   *firmat deus*: alone, Acoetes faces the contriver of all these miracles,
91   who surely he can now call a god. Moreover, the god speaks with
        authority and enables the single man to get the ship to Naxos. His
        speech consists of two imperative clauses. *Diamque tene* 690: Dia is
        an archaic name for Naxos. Since *Naxonque* would be metrically
        equivalent to the archaic form, it would appear that Ovid is testing
        the audience's command of mythology. The final line of Acoetes'
        speech firmly answers the menacing query of Pentheus in 581. Note
        the different tenses of the two verbs: on Naxos, Acoetes says he joined
        the cult of Bacchus, and ever since he *has been* a regular adherent.

Involvement in the cult was not, it should be remembered, part of the god's command, but a definite act of free will and firm belief.

692–93   *longis . . . ambagibus*: this phrase for a lengthy, involved story goes back to Lucretius 6.919 and 1081 (the latter with the same placing of the words in the hexameter) and *Aen.* 1.341–42. Ovid will use it again at 4.476, where he will copy Lucretius more closely. Pentheus chooses to regard the entire warning story about the sailors and Bacchus as a mere digression. *vires absumere* 693: the king claims that Acoetes dragged out his tale long enough to make his anger lose its force. This reading of the infinitive is regularly accepted as the more difficult and likely one for this passage (vs. the easily assimilated form *assumere*, which would point to the build-up of his wrath).

694–95   Again, Pentheus fires a series of violent commands to his attendants. *praecipitem . . . rapite*: emphasis on instant action, as before at 561, enhanced by the procession of five dactyls. *cruciataque . . . corpora*: plural for singular, to get some convenient dactyls. Only one body is to be tortured. *demittite nocti*: the verb is Heinsius' certain correction for MSS *dimittite* (which carries the wrong connotation of "liberate"). Dative in poetic syntax instead of the prosaic preposition + accusative.

696–98   *protinus abstractus*: the first command is obeyed to the letter. *solidis . . . clauditur in tectis*: presumably, this strongplace was to serve as the scene of torture. Hence, the additional details about the cruel devices in 697–98. The narrator establishes a bias against the tyrant.

699–700   *sponte sua*: emphatically repeated in the initial position of the line, though the two clauses are of quite different length. The narrator reports a miracle, but, unlike Acoetes, not having been present at the event, he distances himself and credits the story to tradition. At this point, Acoetes disappears from the narrative. He has been miraculously saved for his piety, as earlier aboard the ship, and we assume that the same Bacchus helped him. In Euripides' tragedy, the Stranger who defied Pentheus was also imprisoned and escaped, but violently, in something like an earthquake. He then returned and lured Pentheus to death in the mountains. Ovid makes sure that Acoetes plays no such role and that the god himself never manifests himself visibly in the destruction of Pentheus, who decided freely to violate the mysteries of Bacchus in the mountains.

The Death of Pentheus (701–33)

The inevitable end of Pentheus' impiety, prescribed by myth, is his grotesque death. After the playfulness with which Bacchus punished the Tyrrhenian sailors, the cruel dismemberment of the young king may seem an excessive penalty. To some extent, the manner in which the narrative operates provides palliation of the god's actions,

if we require it. Bacchus, who has nowhere so far definitively inter-
vened in Theban affairs, does not manifest himself at the king's death.
He does not lead Pentheus to the rites, nor does he make a final
comment claiming a superiority that is above human judgment. We
can, if so inclined, regard the grotesque killing as an exclusively
human act, one that naturally results when a disbeliever intrudes on
passionate believers.

701–   *perstat Echionides*: echo of the first scene, at 513, though Pentheus
3   now gets a verb that stresses his stubborn impiety (cf. 662). *sacra*
        702: the ominous word in Tiresias' prophecy. Cithaeron is south and
        some distance from Thebes, nearer Plataea. We may assume the sound
        of the bacchantes drew the king to the fateful spot. However, the
        narrator's language for the singing carries no pejorative associations,
        not yet.

704–   *fremit*: the spirited sound of a horse would be a neigh. Ovid anachronis-
7   tically refers to a Roman battle, where a trumpeter sounds the charge
        to the cavalry. Pentheus, in this simile, retains his militant associations,
        though reduced to an animal. *longis ululatibus* 706: a typical sound
        of bacchantes (cf. 528). *recanduit ira* 707: the anger, which supposedly
        died down during Acoetes' narrative, has heated up again.

708–   For the final scene, Ovid uses a short ecphrasis, to focus attention,
9   centering events in a field, which is surrounded by trees and opens up
        "in the middle of the mountain." Here the bacchantes have collected, to
        sing and conduct the rites of Bacchus. Ovid jumps to the detection
        of Pentheus spying.

710–   *oculis . . . cernentem sacra profanis*: this epitomizes the continuous
13   theme of the book and fulfills Tiresias' words at 518. After giving us
        the object of action in 710, the narrator uses *prima* prominently at
        the start of 711 and 712, but postpones its noun *mater* until the final
        word of the clause, to achieve maximum suspense and then shock.
        No sooner does she spot the spy—whom she considers a wild animal—
        than she rushes wildly at him and hurls her thyrsus. *violavit* 712:
        although the thyrsus does little harm, the point is that the mother is
        the first to attack her own son and start the process that will lead to
        his bloody death.

713–   *geminae . . . sorores*: Autonoe and Ino. Agave is crazed and sees
15   Pentheus as a huge boar that must be slaughtered as part of the Bacchic
        rites.

15–   *ruit omnis in unum / turba furens*: this crazy hunting down of Pentheus
18   is reminiscent of the pursuit of Actaeon-turned-deer by his dogs; but
        this is an even worse kind of "hunt." *trepidumque . . . iam trepidum*
        717: repetition of the adjective seems clumsy and un-Ovidian to some,
        and they would like to change the first instance—one could think of

praedamque, rapidaeque, or *rapideque*—but no emendation has won wide support. And we can make sense of the repetition: Ovid first used the word almost expectably, but, by repeating it, he calls attention to the psychological change in militant Pentheus, who had appealed so shrilly to the manliness of his citizens. The four units introduced by *iam* fulfill what Tiresias predicted in 525. With four spondees in 718, Ovid slows down the rhythm and edges us toward tragic solemnity.

719– *saucius*: attacked by all the women, Pentheus has sustained unspecified
20   wounds, but still can cry out to his relatives. *fer opem*: standard appeal for help (cf. 1.380 and 546), which no human being and few gods would ignore. Autonoe, to whom he speaks, does not recognize the nephew nor even recall her dead son Actaeon, whose death was so similar. As bacchantes, the women have lost all maternal sense.

721– *quis Actaeon*: supply *esset* or *sit*. *dextramque precantis / abstulit*: a
22   shocking enjambement, the most grotesque answer yet to prayer (but cf. 2.477–78 and 3.240–41). *Inoo . . . raptu*: because the name of Ino declined somewhat awkwardly for the hexameter, especially in the ablative poets tended to substitute an adjectival phrase with *Inous -a -um*. Aunt Ino has outdone Autonoe: she has wrenched off the left arm and then torn it to pieces (*lacerata*). This is the mutilation predicted by Tiresias (522), that pieces of Pentheus would be scattered "in a thousand places."

723– *non habet infelix . . . bracchia*: cf. Tiresias' ironic use of *felix* (517).
25   For the lack of arms in metamorphosis at the agency of Bacchus, cf. 680. The dismemberment of Pentheus constitutes a cruel type of "metamorphosis." *quae . . . tendat*: relative clause of purpose, which has included its antecedent. *trunca . . . vulnera* 724: a striking phrase to catch the picture of this bloody, limbless torso. It is totally different from the limbless body in 680–81 of the sailor who was changed into a sportive dolphin. *adspice, mater* 725: the final words Ovid attributes to Pentheus are a desperate and vain appeal to his mother to pity his wounds.

725– *visis*: supply *vulneribus*. The sight stirs no pity in the dehumanized
28   mother; instead, she exults as a totally possessed bacchante. *ululavit*: this sound has acquired more and more disturbing associations: cf. 706 and 528. The wild movement of neck and hair in 726 prepares us for the insane violence of 727. *avulsumque . . . conplexa* 727: use coordinate verbs in translation. The mother tore off his head and held it "lovingly," not as a mother would embrace her dear son, obviously, but as a hunter would clutch a prized trophy. *opus hoc* 728: it is not certain whether Agave says this feat—displaying the head—is her victory, or that this feat of destroying the imagined boar (Pentheus) is the victory of them all. I prefer the first alternative as more melodra-

matic. The final "victory" takes the military imagery from Pentheus'
grasp and lodges it with the women. Unlike Euripides, Ovid never
records the return of Agave to human and tragic awareness.

29–
31
Ovid introduces at the end a disturbing simile to summarize what
happens to Pentheus. For two quiet lines, he takes us into a familiar
scene of seasonal nature, when wind blows the turned foliage from
a tall tree in autumn. This is a scene of considerable beauty, to most
eyes. Colorful leaves litter the ground, and the tree, more than a trunk,
stretches its leafless branches (arms) to the sky, a temporary skeleton.
It is, then, with some dismay that we hear the poet using this ordinary
and pretty picture to clarify the dismemberment of the king. The wind
which snatches leaves from the tall tree turns into the unspeakable
hands of the women which wrench apart the limbs of Pentheus. That
does not make the death of the young man pretty: it spoils the natural
beauty. Something unnatural and inhuman has occurred here.

32–
33
exemplis monitae: Pentheus, who was going to turn Acoetes into a
sadistic lesson (cf. 579), missed all the warnings that his elders and
Acoetes were giving. As a result, he has himself become an example
in death. *sacra frequentant*: echo of 691 and 581. The populace agree
with Acoetes. *Ismenides* 733: no longer a nymph sired by the Ismenos
river (cf. above 169), but the Thebans in general. The reference to
incense and altars implies organized worship within the city, operating
in entire freedom, now that repressive Pentheus is dead.

NOTES TO BOOK 4

Having eliminated two of Cadmus' grandsons in Book 3 and intro-
duced Bacchus, a third of irresistible power, Ovid follows the spread
of Bacchic influence to nearby Orchomenos. There, the three daughters
of Minyas oppose the god, as Pentheus had in Thebes, and, trans-
formed into bats, duly meet their fate (1–415). At this point, Juno
reappears, to take more vengeance on Cadmus' family: she enlists
Tisiphone and the malignant might of the Underworld to destroy
Cadmus' last daughter Ino and her family (two more precious grand-
sons). That leaves Cadmus desolate and alienated from the Thebes
he had founded for his family. He departs into self-chosen exile, and
reaching Illyria, willingly welcomes the predicted metamorphosis as
a snake (416–603). In the remainder of the book, Ovid effects a
transition to Perseus, also a son of Jupiter's amours, whose grandfather
Acrisius, in sharp contrast to Cadmus, questioned the paternity of not
only Perseus but also Bacchus. Beginning the story of Perseus, then,
the poet covers the rescue of Andromeda and the killing of Medusa
(604–803), but leaves to Book 5 the great battle with Phineus for
possession of Andromeda as wife.

THE DAUGHTERS OF MINYAS CHALLENGE BACCHUS (1–415)

Ovid ended Book 3 by concentrating on the way the Theban women
(*Ismenides* 733) responded to the death of Pentheus by devout worship
of Bacchus. He begins Book 4 by focusing on the contrasting behavior
of the daughters of Minyas. They do not live in Thebes, but in
Orchomenos, perhaps forty miles northeast, but still in Boeotia. With-
out naming the new locale, Ovid simply juxtaposes the impious three
girls to the reverent female population of Thebes. At 31–32, he will
emphasize the contrast by using patronymics in successive lines. The
unbelieving trio refuse to participate in the holiday declared to honor

410

Bacchus: while the rest of Boeotia engages in prayers and hymns to
the god, with which the narrator himself affects to identify (17 ff.),
they profane the holy day by stubbornly carrying out their usual tasks
of weaving. To keep their work from seeming tedious, they agree
each to tell a story. The three tales that Ovid assigns them constitute
evidence of their irreverence, but their contents raise subtle problems
about the relative merits or dignity of divine and human beings in
Ovid's poetic world. The Minyeides may be foolish and arrogant to
challenge Bacchus (who seems more appealing then other Olympians
we have so far encountered); but their narratives suggest what the
Ovidian narrator has also been suggesting: that human beings have a
richer, more responsible sense of emotion (especially love) and of
ethics than the gods have. Thus, their stories perform a more telling
challenge of divinity in general than the women themselves can mount;
and, when they turn into bats, we can recognize their guilt without
ignoring the powerful implications of the stories which almost uncon-
sciously they have presented. We shall examine each of the stories
(Pyramus and Thisbe, the love affairs of the Sun, the warped passion
of Salmacis) as we come to it.

Introduction to the Minyeides (1–54)

Ovid marks the stark antithesis between the impious three women
and the otherwise total unanimity of female Boeotians in devoted
worship to Bacchus. He develops a hymn, in which his narrator soon
joins, then shows the Minyeides doggedly working on the holiday.
As they smugly boast of serving a better deity, Minerva, and of
performing useful tasks, they also decide on storytelling. The first
narrator is nameless. She considers a number of topics (43 ff.) and
finally fixes on one for a reason that seems entirely unimportant, in
view of the dramatic context: it is not a familiar story (53). That seems
to have been true, for Ovid's audience, but that claim obscures the
reason why he told it; it is his first account of human love. The story
of Pyramus and Thisbe has become one of the best-known tales of
Ovid and world literature ever since because of the insights it gives
on that subject.

at non: unusual opening for a poetic book. It suggests an unbroken
narrative continuity with the previous book. *Alcithoe Minyeias*: though
she appears as the ringleader here, Alcithoe will be kept waiting to
tell the third story (274 ff.). The usual patronymic for the sisters is
Minyeides, which yields a singular form *Minyeis*. Since the initial
vowel of the next word did not allow lengthening of final *-is*, Ovid
created his own variant, to produce two long syllables at the end.

Minyas, the girls' father, founded and ruled Orchomenos. *orgia*: Vergil had used this word twice of the wild nocturnal rites of Bacchus (*G.* 4.521 and *Aen.* 4.303), but neither he nor the narrator here thinks of the rites prejudicially as "orgies." *adhuc temeraria*: "rasher still." *progeniem . . . Iovis*: since the narrator guaranteed the divine birth of Bacchus and also has just shown punishment of Pentheus' blasphemy, Alcithoe is rash indeed. *inpietatis* 4: objective genitive with *socias*.

4–6   *festum*: noun; Ovid uses the plural at 33. *celebrare sacerdos*: finite verb *iusserat* is delayed until 8. *inmunesque operum* 5: the holy day required all regular work to be suspended. Violation of this commandment subjects the Minyeides to punishment. *pelle* 6: bacchantes wore fawnskins, as can be seen in vase paintings. *crinales solvere vittas*: in religious rites, women would be required to have their hair loose, so the fillets bound about the head would be untied.

7–9   Garlands for the head would not be particular to Bacchic cult, but familiar in various celebrations. The thyrsus, on the other hand, belongs specifically to bacchantes; cf. 3.712. Chiastic arrangement juxtaposes *coma* and *manibus*. Pluperfect verbs of 8–9 indicate that the priest's words function as background to the next scene, which has present tenses. *laesi . . . numinis* 8: the "injury" would be disrespect.

9–12   *parent*: by placing this verb first in the sentence, without any connective, Ovid stresses the instantaneous response of obedience by the other women. *telasque* 10: Ovid appends -*que* to five words in a row here; but the first two (in 9) go with an earlier verb. Here, the lengthening of the normally short syllable, by analogy with Homeric procedure (as in 1.193), caused the scribes of the MSS some confusion. Only a few refrained from "correction." Since women characteristically worked at the loom, the three nouns here all refer to separate aspects of weaving. Whereas the obedient women stop their weaving, we soon find that the Minyeides persist in working at the loom (cf. 32 ff.). In 11–12, the Thebans begin their worship of Bacchus, with incense, then prayer. The narrator cites some of the epithets with which they call upon and honor the god. *Bromiumque* 11: the Greek word alludes to the noisy celebrations of Bacchic rites. *Lyaeumque*: another Greek epithet, which refers to the relaxing effect of wine (much like Latin *Liber*). The fact that -*que* is hypermetric might suggest that Bacchus even now causes relaxation of normal rules. In 12, by three compound expressions, the prayers refer to the miraculous circumstances of Bacchus' birth (by fire, inseminated a second time, and given a second mother), which the narrator has already rendered for us at 3.308 ff. *bimatrem* 12: Ovid's invention here.

13–15   *additur his*: singular verb, ostensibly with the first member of a list of more epithets. *Nyseus*: we heard in 3.314 how the nymphs of Nysa in India raised the young Bacchus. *indetonsusque*: the long hair of young Bacchus regularly marks him out, with Apollo, in statues and pictures. Ovid's epithet is his own creation, unique to this passage. *Thyoneus*: Ovid seems to borrow this from Horace *C*. 1.17.23, where we first find it in connection with Bacchus. *Lenaeo* 14: this adjective derives from the Lenaean festival in honor of Dionysos (one of the two occasions for comic performance in Athens). *genialis consitor uvae*: Ovid seems to vary Tibullus 2.3.63, *iucundae consitor uvae*. That guarantees that the adjective goes with *uvae* here. Only in these two passages does *consitor* occur. Bacchus' connection with grape-growing needs no emphasis. *Nycteliusque* 15: supposedly a compound of two Greek words (*nykto-* and *teleios*) that refer to the nocturnal rites of the god. The word appears in Latin, however, before we find it in surviving Greek. Ovid had already used it in *Ars Am*. 1.567. The poet uses five mellifluous dactyls to render his four epithets in 15. *Eleleus*: this word appears only here, but Ovid had used a somewhat similar form, *Eleleides*, in *Her*. 4.47 to refer to worshippers of Bacchus. It connotes the wild cry with which they called on the deity. *Iacchus*: a name especially associated with Dionysos at Eleusis, cited by Herodotos in connection with the Battle of Salamis. Roman writers used it from the time of Cicero, Lucretius, and Catullus. *Euhan*: probably inspired by Lucretius 5.743, where a line about Bacchus ends *Euhius Euan*. The epithet, like *Eleleus*, derives from one of the standard outcries in Bacchic rites, *euhoe* or *euae*.

16–17 The narrator now ends his list conventionally, alluding to the *plurima nomina* that he might have included. At the end, he apostrophizes the god by his standard Latin epithet *Liber* 17. The apostrophe could be a conventional poeticism, but Ovid makes it lead into an extensive addition, in which the narrator, seemingly inspired by the Theban reverence, proceeds with his own prayer.

17–21 *tibi enim*: in Greek and Roman prayers (and in many Christian prayers that follow their form), after the section which reviews and selects the appropriate name or epithet for the deity, comes a section introduced by an explanatory conjunction and what is called *hymnal* repetition of personal or relative pronouns to present some of the god's attributes and feats. The narrator intrudes, then, with his personal beliefs at this transitional point. *inconsumpta iuventa est*: eternal youth, an appealing aspect of Bacchus' deity, receives stress here and in the next phrase. The adjective is Ovid's invention for this context; he uses it twice more, without imitators. Many MSS omit *est*, and then *NP* change the noun to *iuventus*. But the text should stand as is, with the poetic noun *iuventa* and the verb. *puer aeternus* 18: the phrase, which Jungian psychology has developed for its own purposes, appears only here in Latin. *alto . . . caelo*: ablative of place where. *conspiceris*: not a reference to a star in the sky, but rather to the fact that Bacchus lives with the other gods in Olympus. *cornibus*: to stress the potential for violence in this god, poets and artists often assigned horns to his head. Cf. Tibullus 2.1.3, Propertius 3.17.19, and *Fast*. 3.499–500. Without the horns, Bacchus would seem more "virginal." *Oriens tibi victus* 20: these conquests of the East were closely connected in Macedonian and Alexandrian propaganda with the campaigns of Alexander the Great. *tibi*: dative of agent. *adusque*: a poetic variant for the prosaic *usque ad*. It goes with the ecstatic diction of this context. *decolor* 21: the brown skin of Indians earned this epithet from the ethnocentric white-skinned Romans. *cingitur*: the Ganges, which flows along the northeastern border of modern India down to Calcutta, hardly "rings" India, unless we imagine it linked with the Indus (which perhaps Ovid suggests). Heinsius found an emendation *tingitur* that he proposed to adopt, but it is more clever than necessary.

22–25 Three acts of punishment for impiety are mentioned in 22–23, two of which we have heard about already, the death of Pentheus and the metamorphosis of the Tyrrhenian pirates into dolphins. As the story of Pentheus was narrated, however, Bacchus played an invisible role. To declare here simply that Bacchus slaughtered Pentheus is either to imply that he acted through Pentheus' mother and aunts, the actual killers, or to incline to a different account, such as that of Euripides' *Bacchae*. *bipenniferumque Lycurgum*: Lycurgus was king of Thrace, another who resisted the rites of Bacchus. His story appears in *Iliad* 6.130–40, Apollodoros 3.5.1.3, and Hyginus 132. The axe in this Ovidian epithet, first used here, was brandished by Lycurgus in his attack on the god and his followers, then on the vines that had been planted in his kingdom, and then, when he was driven mad, on his own wife and son. Eventually, Lycurgus himself was killed, more by the indirect will of the god than by any direct action of his. *biiugum . . . lyncum* 24–25: the hyperbaton of these two words encloses the separated word-pairs of the rest of the clause. The speaker describes the pair of lynxes that drew Bacchus along in a car; his ability to dominate them indicated his power not only over sacrilegious human beings but also over savage animals.

25–27 Behind the triumphal car of the god, in many representations, as here, follow his familiar attendants, the female bacchantes and the male satyrs. Then, two lines are devoted to Silenus, old and drunk, staggering along on foot, uncertainly propped up by a staff, or clinging precariously to an ass. Ovid later uses Silenus, whose age and drunkenness cause him to lose contact with the train of Bacchus, to initiate the tale of King Midas in 11.85 ff. *pando . . . asello* 27: the ass was not easy to sit on, being crookbacked.

28–30 The narrator, ignoring the very instances of opposition that he has just mentioned (perhaps because they failed), ends by recording the universal welcome that the god receives. He conveys it by the sounds of worshippers: the shouts of the young, cries of women, and the tones of various musical instruments. We have heard Pentheus speak scornfully of these very instruments (3.532 ff.). *longoque foramine buxus* 30: this pipe of boxwood corresponds to the *tibia* mentioned by Pentheus; it has a long series of holes that allow for variety of notes.

1–35 The narrator, having identified with the feelings of the Thebans and inclined our sympathies in that direction, now withdraws and refocuses on the Theban worshippers. From their obedient piety, at the caesura of 32, he turns to the sacrilege of the Minyeides. *solae* 32: regular transitional word, often in Ovidian priamels, by which the narrator gets to his main characters (cf. 3.256, 4.607, 6.421). *intempestiva . . . Minerva* 33: the phrase spans this rare four-word hexameter, which also has the maximum number of slow spondees. We are not to think that the girls reverently worship the goddess Minerva, on a day not set aside for her; they are, in a sense, using her name in vain, for it stands in antonomasia for weaving, one of her favored spheres. In 34–35, the narrator lists typical actions of weavers: drawing out the wool into usable thread, twisting it into a ball, moving up to the loom, and hurrying servants in their tasks.

6–39 *una*: never named. *deducens pollice filum*: Ovid repeats some technical terms of 34. The verb reminds us that Greeks and Romans posited a relationship between weaving and poetry and often transferred to the latter terms from the former. Thus, the poet "weaves" and "spins" his imaginative fabric of words. Here, the girls are parallel to the poet himself. *commentaque sacra* 37: same sneer in Pentheus' tirade against Bacchus at 3.558. *frequentant*, with *sacra*: a thematic phrase for the followers of Bacchus, Acoetes, and the Thebans; cf. especially 3.732. The girl convicts herself of folly by these unconscious echoes. *Pallas . . . detinet* 38: the ambiguous clause suggests that Minerva claims and receives her piety, which contrasts favorably with the worship of charlatan Bacchus. However, as noted above, the goddess' name functions merely as a trope for the profane act of weaving. The girls in fact violate the holy day. *utile opus* 39: the utility of the work is irrelevant, since this day demands cessation of all such tasks. *vario sermone*: the noun suggests discussion, whereas in fact what ensues is a set of three uninterrupted stories. However, the adjective points to a literary criterion that does operate, namely, *varietas*, Alexandrian pursuit of novelty and variety.

0–41 *perque vices*: "by turns." *quod . . . non sinat*: relative clause of purpose. Storytelling will be an antidote to boredom. *in medium*: in public, aloud for all to hear. *vacuas*: the ears are "open," "idle," and "free" for listening to stories.

42–46 The proposal gets a favorable reception. Invited to begin, the proposer
casts around for suitable material. *quid . . . referat* 43: subjunctive
in indirect question. Homeric bards regularly chose songs from a wide
repertoire, but any storyteller tends to do so. *dubia est* 44: the narrator
announces a *dubitatio* i.e., a listing of options, which gradually leads
up to the topic selected. Instead of adding the usual conjunction *an*
to introduce the alternatives, Ovid moves directly to the subjunctive
verb. For this form of compound indirect question, cf. 1.578. *de te,
Babylonia*: here is a case of apostrophe that, unlike the prolonged
address to Bacchus in 17 ff., hardly implies any feeling for Dercetis.
Ovid is getting around a metrical problem: the vocative provides him
with a desirable short final syllable. Dercetis was one of the names
of the Syrian goddess Atargatis. The details of this exotic myth are
summarized: the goddess became clothed in scales and metamorphosed
(*versa . . . figura* 45–46,, key clause that frames the entire account)
into a fish. As a fish, then, the Palestinians believe she swam through
the waters. *motasse* 46: this is Merkel's almost certain correction of
the MSS reading, *mutasse* (which makes no sense here, though it is
understandable why an early scribe changed the unfamiliar verb to
one usually appropriate in this poem).

47–48 *illius filia*: the daughter of Dercetis was the notoriously amorous
Semiramis. The narrator mentions only her metamorphosis into a
dove, which lived its final years in a lofty dovecote. Fuller stories of
both mother and daughter would have included the love affairs that
preceded their transformations. *sumptis . . . pennis*: an allusive refer-
ence to the change into a winged bird.

49–51 The third rejected story involves a bewitching sea-nymph who used
spells and potions to change young men into fish. This parallels the
tactics of Circe, who transformed men into beasts. In the end, the
nymph suffered what Circe as a goddess could avoid: she herself was
turned into a fish. Since the other two tales have an Eastern locale,
and that of Pyramus and Thisbe will happen in the city that Semiramis
built, Babylon, it is generally assumed that this nymph and her fish-
victims also belong to the Near East. The artful storyteller displays
her literary mastery by considering only novel Eastern myths, all
featuring women. *tacitos* 50: fish are notably mute, even when fish-
ermen inflict horrible torment on them.

51–54 *an . . . ut . . . ferat*: the previous two stories have been cited with
the conjunction pair *an ut*; so Ovid continues that overall construction,
but inserts a relative clause between *ut* and its verb, to focus our
attention on the berries that, once white, became black. Notice the
delay of the subject to the final word. *contactu sanguinis*: tragic
foreshadowing. To judge from what we know of the three rejected
tales, our nameless storyteller chose the narrative with the greatest

pathos and amatory appeal. *hoc . . . haec* 53: a nice example of anaphora. The second demonstrative has been attracted into the gender of *fabula*. *vulgaris*: this girl pays lip service to Callimachus and indeed chooses an exotic tale, but she lacks Alexandrian or Neoteric subtlety. Vergil expresses similar desire for novelty in *G*. 3.4: *omnia iam vulgata*. *orsa* 54: supply *est*. This verb, which conventionally announces any epic speech, as in Vergil, has a root sense of "starting to weave." Ovid may revive that sense here, to suggest the parallelism of weaving a tale and a tapestry.

Pyramus and Thisbe (55–166)

This sweet and sentimentally "tragic" story of ill-fated love has won many admirers, for the story in itself and for the mastery of the Ovidian storyteller. Pyramus and Thisbe emerge as naive lovers, idealized as extraordinarily beautiful young people, but otherwise undefined, who face a number of symbolic obstacles to their happiness, and finally, in confusion and passion, can achieve union only through suicide. We pity them, but we do not feel compelled by the narrative to identify with them or their rather unrealistic love. Apart from the distorted love of Narcissus for his reflection, this is the first story in the *Met.* that focuses exclusively on human love. Although it does not directly challenge the myths of Bacchus, who is no lecher like his father Jupiter, it does indirectly deny the god and insist on the importance of human beings and their activities. Pyramus and Thisbe, unlike Bacchus and other gods, are not self-centered and amoral: they kill themselves for love, to join the beloved in death, if not in life. Their being is nothing without the other; what they seek is not selfish pleasure or humble worship from another, but permanent union of soul and body. Such a goal was silly and irrational in the case of Narcissus: it means a lot in the case of these two lovers, for their passionate, if mistaken, suicides carry more conviction than the plaintive disintegration of the pretty young Boeotian. However, Ovid draws a portrait of love here that needs extensive improvement. It is the program of the *Met.* to explore human love through a large variety of narratives, a program so obvious that the poem has been called an "epic of love." Thus, naive presentation of love here can function as the beginning of a progressive exploration; but naiveté can also serve to reflect on the person of the female narrator Ovid created and the situation in which the stubborn, impious Minyeides have placed themselves. Naive human love is sweet and a pleasant subject for women spinning, but is it an admirable or viable alternative and reaction to a powerful, largely benevolent god like Bacchus? Isn't there something rather "spinsterish" in this sentimental tale? Shakespeare, at any rate,

consciously improved on it when he incorporated it into his dramas
of love: he mocked its easy pathos in *A Midsummer Night's Dream*,
using it as foil for a better-informed kind of love; and in *Romeo and
Juliet* he placed youthful passion in a fuller context that gave the final
suicide genuine power.

We do not know where Ovid found this story. It is not a myth, for
it ignores the gods and serves the girls as a substitute for divine cult;
a humanly devised tale, it attempts to give significance to human
beings. Its locus in Babylon and the Eastern locale of the other stories
of the Minyeides indicate a handbook source of near-Eastern narra-
tives. Whatever the source, Ovid has fully subordinated the story to
his complicated purposes.

55–58   *alter / altera* 56: having given her main characters exotic non-Roman
names (Pyramus taken from a river in Cilicia), the narrator repeats a
basic pattern of allotting them their one identifiable feature: "story-
book" beauty. *quas*: typical appearance of relative before its anteced-
ent. *contiguas* 57: this unfamiliar word, preserved only in *LM*, has
been corrupted in other MSS to the common *continuas*. The houses are
not "continuous," for they do not share a structural wall; neighboring
properties, they share a garden or perimeter wall. *ubi dicitur*: the last
of five dactyls in this line, as the narrator locates the action expansively
in Babylon. *coctilibus muris* 58: the mud-brick walls of stoneless
Eastern cities, especially one so large and important as Babylon, struck
the imagination of Greek (and Roman) travellers, who were used to
fortifications of stone, plentiful in the West. Propertius in 3.11.21–
24 had already described Semiramis' walls in greater detail, as so
wide that two chariots could meet and pass in their corridor without
difficulty. This extraordinary female was mentioned in 47 above. She
married Ninos, founder of Nineveh, and Ovid places his tomb (88)
outside the walls of Babylon, to serve as a meeting place for the
lovers.

59–62   *notitiam . . . vicinia*: the narrator uses abstract nouns to account for
that typical romantic situation of girl meeting boy. As a result, their
portrayal involves little realism, and their love seems stereotyped at
the start. *primosque gradus*: that is, of love (the noun retrospectively
implied by 60). *taedae . . . iure* 60: by right of the torch (metonymy
for marriage). *coissent*: as in the interchange between Echo and
Narcissus in 3.386–87, this verb refers to the union of love and
sex, which is the goal of lovers. But the contrary-to-fact subjunctive
establishes the special theme of this story: these lovers fail to unite
in life, dogged by a series of frustrations, and only death brings
them together to share the same ash urn. *vetuere patres* 61: another
stereotypical situation, which the narrator passes over: parental opposi-

tion to young love. We hurry on with the speaker, but we miss the dramatic detail such as audiences get in *Romeo and Juliet*, and so cannot feel much for these two lovers. In the balancing half of 61, the narrator introduces the stereotypical antithesis between external ritual, such as weddings, over which fathers can exert total control, and the internal state of mind and the feelings of love, which operate spontaneously and free of parental restrictions. *ex aequo* 62: Ovid is not describing the standard comic or elegiac situation, where a male of the upper classes has fallen in love with a girl of no social pretensions, whether a pauper or a courtesan. Thisbe is as good as Pyramus, and the bar to their happiness comes from their fathers, not from any defect or neglect on their parts. They are equal in merit and in love. This entire line, with its slow spondaic rhythm, emphasizes the perfect match of their feelings. *captis . . . mentibus*: since for Ovid, the *mens* constitutes the key to personality, this phrase succinctly indicates the way love has transformed the pair and, by capturing their minds, has negated family loyalties. In later stories, he will explore the tension between love and family (especially fathers) with powerful detail; here, it is a brief, standard motif.

3–64 These two lines create a false sense of conventional rebellion against parental restrictions. *conscius*: instead of this vague generalization, we can imagine an appointed *custos* or maid for the girl, perhaps a *paedagogus* for the boy. When such are absent, the two converse. Nothing leads us yet to expect the physical barrier to their intimacy that is posed by the wall. The rhetorical organization of 64, with the balancing words juxtaposed at the caesura, implies that the growing "heat" of this concealed love may successfully defy the stereotypical stern fathers.

5–66 Now the narrator introduces a new piece of scenery: a wall of uncertain height, which allows conversation, but in a way too public and subject to parental observation and even hearing—it is not one of Robert Frost's good neighborly walls. Ostensibly, then, it parallels and symbolizes the unbending opposition of the fathers, owners of the property and deliberately separated from each other by this barrier. *tenui rima*: the crack symbolizes the breakdown of family hostility, which, positively or negatively, is pursued by this naive love of Pyramus and Thisbe. *cum fieret* 66: "when it was being made."

7–70 *vitium*: this "fault" in structure proves to be an opportunity for the lovers. The objective fathers would call it a flaw; the lovers find it sympathetic and so personify it and the wall. *nulli*: dative of agent with perfect passive participle. *(quid non sentit amor?)* 68: the parenthesis both implies the special sensitivity of love and, by the rhetorical question, starts to suggest the narrator's engagement with it. *vidistis amantes*: now she apostrophizes the lovers and thus moves herself

and us into the scene. This is the first action that she has attributed
to them, and she emphasizes it. *vocis . . . iter* 69: since they have
already been talking openly across the wall, it is necessary to explain,
in 70, what special function this "route for the voice" serves. *tutaeque
. . . murmure blanditiae minimo* 70: the pair want to exchange love-
talk privately without being overheard, and the crack provides them
a "safe" route. The word for love-talk, *blanditiae*, along with the
synonymous phrase *blanda verba*, has earlier described the false words
of seduction employed by Apollo in 1.531 and Neptune in 2.575,
spoken and discarded in favor of outright violence against the desirable
human victim. Here, the words are honest, the love mutual, and no
one-sided lust or violence ensues.

71–73   The narrator sets the scene for the first words we hear from the lovers:
a chiastic arrangement of the two at the wall in 71, mutual efforts to
catch each other's breath through the chink in 72, both actions in
pluperfect to prepare for the imperfect of regular past speech in 73.
invide . . . obstas 73: they personify and apostrophize the wall, which,
though they have made it a special means of communication, they
now represent as an obstacle.

74–75   *quantum erat*: "how little it would have been." *quantum*, when used
colloquially this way, has the ironic sense of *quantulum*. The imperfect
indicative has the force of subjunctive contrary to fact. *toto . . .
corpore iungi*: the desired goal of the lovers, never to be achieved in
life. *ad oscula danda pateres* 75: it is too much to ask that the wall
let them achieve bodily union—that would mean the very destruction
of the wall—but with a slight enlargement of the crack they might
be able to kiss each other.

76–77   The complaint changes to prudent professions of gratitude for what
they actually have, *verbis . . . transitus* 77, if not *corporum coitus*.
But dissatisfaction persists and soon drives the lovers to bold action.

78–80   *diversa . . . sede*: ablative of place where: they are on opposite sides
of the wall. *sub noctem* 79: "toward night." They would have been
willing to settle for kisses, but now their natural goodnight kisses are
frustrated. The wall does not let them be felt. Unfinished business for
the next day.

81–82   Ovid uses one of his formulaic pairs of lines to announce the next
morning (cf. 3.600–601, 7.100 and 835).

83–85   *solitum . . . locum*: the wall. *murmure parvo*: as an echo of 70, this
phrase indicates that the lovers are whispering through the crack.
questi 84: having been prevented from kissing, they start from where
they left off the previous evening, with complaints. *nocte silenti*:
following Vergil (e.g., *Aen.* 4.527 and 7.87), Ovid puts this phrase
at the end of the line and gives an *i*-ending to the participle. This is
the only instance of the phrase in the *Met.*, but in other works, when

the phrase occupies the fourth and fifth feet, he uses *silente*. The choice seems due to Vergil and euphony. *fallere custodes* 85: in Roman elegy, a girl frequently deceives her guards in order to join her lover. Here, the action is mutual. The narrator devotes three more clauses to clarifying the details of departure from house and city, rather needlessly, it would seem, except that all this apparent exactitude ends in unexpected failure.

86–90 They make precise plans, again very fussily, over the meeting place, once they have emerged from the city. The narrator has little realistic sense of love when she concentrates on these details and ignores the feelings of the lovers. *lato . . . arvo* 87: ablative of place. *spatiantibus*: dative of agent. *busta Nini* 88: the funeral monument of Semiramis' husband. In other stories, Ninus' tomb stands more reasonably outside Nineveh, the city he founded and named. In any case, it is an ominous spot for a lovers' tryst. *lateantque sub umbra / arboris* 89: this proves to be the key element of the elaborate plan, the tree where they hope to meet in love, but where they will miss each other and thus meet in death. The spinster-narrator leaves implicit that they will be hiding from observers (especially grim fathers) while making love, so long prevented; that the shade of the tree has nothing to do with the sun (since it is night), but will keep them from being exposed to the moonlight (cf. 99). *niveis . . . pomis*: as soon as she has mentioned the tree, the Minyeid pauses to describe it. This is the very tree whose aetiology has determined her choice of the story in 51–52, where she cited the *poma alba* that would turn black. Here, it is named a mulberry, in full bloom with its white berries. By locating it next to a cool fountain, the narrator produces for our imagination a *locus amoenus* that seems appropriate for nighttime landscape. *contermina* 90: Ovid's invention earlier for 1.774.

91–92 *pacta placent*: in this laconic alliterative phrase, the narrator includes all that she specified in 84 ff. Again, she ignores the feelings and words of the lovers. Then, she announces nightfall with a formulaic passage matching that for daybreak. The sun seems to set in western waters and the moon or night to emerge from water also, but in the east. *tarde discedere visa*: though in fact the day is rushing past, it seems slow to Pyramus and Thisbe.

93–96 *callida*: like elegiac lovers, Thisbe is clever in pursuit of love. *versato cardine*: the narrator retraces her path selectively over the agreed-upon arrangements. With *fallitque suos* 94, she covers 85. *adopertaque vultum*: Thisbe tries to avoid being recognized. The details of 95 correspond to the plans of 88–89. *dictaque sub arbore* 95: the tree that has been both agreed upon and extensively described for the audience as the focus of interest. It is important for the sentiment of the story that Thisbe arrive first: to indicate her eager passion. The

narrator, however, does not account for her earliness or Pyramus' late-
ness: she focuses on basic difficulties in the way of this innocent love.
audacem faciebat amor 96: the power of love is rendered here as a kind
of metamorphosis, which makes a naturally timid girl bold. It is an
amatory commonplace that love (or Venus) favors the bold. As he under-
takes a perilous challenge, Hippomenes declares: *audentes deus ipse
iuvat* (10.586); and indeed Venus sees that he prevails. Ironically,
Thisbe's audacity immediately collapses before a new threat.

96–98   With *ecce*, a lioness makes her surprise dramatic entrance and starts the
grim theme of death. The last three words of 96 might have fitted the
expected arrival of Pyramus, but 97 totally alters the situation. Like
the wall, this lioness is a highly melodramatic barrier. *caede* 97: ablative
of means with *oblita*, the noun of slaughter standing in metonymy for
the blood that flowed from the cows and smeared the lion's jaws. *rictus*:
familiar internal accusative; cf. 1.265. *depositura sitim* 98: having ac-
quired a massive thirst from its bloody meal, the lion heads for the spring
(which now ceases to be a sign of the idyllic spot).

99–
101   *ad lunae radios*: the narrator introduces the moon at the moment when
it serves her purposes. *Babylonia*: it is not clear why this epithet is
here. It would seem to "heroize" Thisbe and compare her to an epic
character. Since at this very moment she loses her boldness and flees,
I suspect a touch of Ovidian irony. *obscurum . . . in antrum* 100:
caves, along with springs and isolated trees, form regular backdrops
for Ovidian country scenes, as for contemporary wall paintings. Thisbe
withdraws to a new spot of hiding after the first has proved too
dangerous. *tergo* 101: ablative of place from which with *lapsa*. *vela-
mina*: clothes of any kind; here, the outer cloak that the girl took
against the evening chill (cf. *amictus* 104).

102–
4   *lea saeva*: by using the brief poetic alternative for the Greek loan
word *leaena*, Ovid can add the standard fairy-tale adjective to the
beast. *ut . . . sitim . . . conpescuit*: equivalent to English pluperfect.
The action of this clause precedes all other verbs in the sentence. *sine
ipsa* 103: it is hard to take this expression as seriously intended. It is
simply too clever, exhibiting no special sympathy for Thisbe. *ore
cruentato* 104: all that water drunk could have washed the gore from
the lion's jaws, but no. So it tears the cloak and wipes blood on to
it, leaving for Pyramus apparently clear evidence that his Thisbe has
been torn limb from limb by some wild beast.

105–
8   *egressus*: same verb as for Thisbe in 94. *vestigia vidit*: by the moonlight
presumably, the lover spots animal tracks around the spring. *expalluit*
106: obvious sign of fearful anxiety for Thisbe. *vestem*: the narrator
repeats the information of 104, but now we see how it fits into the
love story.

108–   To give desired sentimentality to the end of her tale, the narrator

12   attributes to Pyramus one speech, then later gives a pathetic death
         speech to Thisbe (142 ff.). These are the only individualized state-
         ments of either lover. *una duos . . . nox perdet amantes*: the speech
         opens with a reference to an amatory commonplace, the union of two
         separate lovers in death. We have already heard a travesty of the idea
         in Narcissus' claim (3.473): *nunc duo concordes anima moriemur in
         una*. But Pyramus' assertion is validated in the final line, when the
         two, after funerals, are joined in a single ash-urn (166). Alcyone in
         11.388 defines her love for Ceyx in the same terms. In the third story
         by the Minyeides, Salmacis pursues a kind of union that perverts the
         amatory ideal, as the echo of this theme reminds us (cf. 4.371 ff.).
         longa dignissima vita 109: unlike divine rapists, who enjoy themselves
         and leave their victims to misery and even death, the human lovers
         defined here by Pyramus (and travestied by Narcissus earlier) wish
         for their beloved life even at the cost of their own (cf. 3.471–72).
         nocens anima 110: Pyramus takes guilt on himself and needlessly
         blames himself for the (supposed) death of Thisbe. *plena metus* 111:
         partitive genitive. *iussi nocte venires*: subjunctive in substantive clause
         of command. Normal usage with *iubeo* expects the infinitive, and a
         few scribes have automatically emended to *venire*; but the personal
         form here carries more pathos (and is *lectio difficilior*). It is of course
         an exaggeration for Pyramus, in his self-blame, to say that he "ordered"
         Thisbe to come to this spot. As we heard earlier, they eagerly worked
         out the arrangements together (cf. 84 ff.).

112–   *divellite corpus*: in passionate despair, Pyramus apostrophizes the
15   lions of the region, seeking to join Thisbe in the same cruel death
         that he has inferred from her torn and blood-stained cloak. *scelerata*
         113: more undeserved self-recrimination. *sub hac . . . rupe* 114: a
         little more detail about the scene; it has a tall rock as a backdrop (a
         common feature of wall paintings). *timidi* 115: genitive of possession
         modifying the subject infinitive *optare*. Pyramus means that it is
         cowardly only to wish for death and not to act on the wish by suicide,
         as he now proceeds to do.

115–   The narrator interrupts at this suspenseful moment with melodramatic
17   stage directions, to add to the sentimentality. The cloak, which has
         caused the entire misconception, now becomes the object of Pyramus'
         passion, a substitute for Thisbe. *pactae . . . arboris umbram* 116:
         earlier words are echoed (cf. 88–91) as the action moves back to
         center stage, under the fateful mulberry. *dedit . . . dedit* 117: pathetic
         repetition. Thisbe will herself spend tears and kisses on dying Pyramus,
         without return.

118–   *accipe nunc*: he addresses the cherished cloak. Thinking it bathed in
21   Thisbe's blood, he offers it his blood, too. In a somewhat similar
         way, Peleus offers a blood sacrifice to his friend Crantor, saying

inferias . . . accipe (12.367–68), as he kills the warrior who has slain Crantor. *quoque erat accinctus* 119: an item of Pyramus' costume, which the action requires, is now named. *quoque = et quo*. The relative clause, as often in Ovid, provokes interest by preceding its antecedent. *in ilia ferrum*: the phrase is stereotypical for any fatal wound into the center of the body below the rib cage; Ovid has already used it for Cadmus' killing of the Boeotian dragon at 3.67 and will use it later for Perseus' killing of the sea-monster at 4.734. When Romans fell on their swords or when today Japanese commit hari-kari, this vital area is the target. There is a problem in punctuation at the end of this line. Editors regularly use a comma, presumably because the understood object of *traxit* in 120 is also *ferrum*, and they treat *nec* as the connective between the two verbs. However, Ovid uses *nec mora* only as an independent unit, to start a line or sentence and introduce an independent clause, not to connect clauses (cf. 1.717 and 3.46). It means nothing more than "without delay" or "immedi-ately." Thus, the correct punctuation at the end of 119 is a period. The narrator is trying to deal with the unusual gesture of dying Pyramus when he yanks the sword out of the wound. No ordinary suicide would do such a thing, and he has no explicit reason for doing so himself, but the story needs the weapon to be out of the wound, so that the blood may gush high up to the branches of the mulberry. Pyramus here acts more like a warrior wounded in battle, who pulls the offending weapon out of the wound and heroically tries to fight on. Cf. *Aen.* 10.486–87, where Pallas, fatally wounded by Turnus in the chest, wrenches the spear out, but then collapses and dies, unable to continue. *iacuit resupinus* 121: same phrase in 12.324 for a standard position of dying or reclining. *cruor emicat alte*: this high spurt of blood, though fantastically dramatized, is realistic. Doctors have experience of the force of blood that can spout from a major artery. I have been assured that it would be possible for such a jet to reach a height of six or seven feet briefly, high enough, then, to strike the mulberries. The narrator elaborates on this important gushing blood, to emphasize the height and power it attains, by reaching for a simile. However, she picks a simile that is notably anachronistic and, because of its technical nature, flagrantly "unpoetic." When a water pipe bursts, water pressure can make the water gush out in a considerable fountain. In modern times, the phenomenon often occurs in cities when construc-tion crews accidentally break a main pipe or a hydrant is knocked over by a truck. The result is a literal geyser. The question is, then, what effect is Ovid seeking. Earlier critics, who have simply been shocked and disapproving, and therefore attributed to the poet an artistic mistake or bad taste, must be regarded as themselves mistaken. Since the archaic Boeotian could not have known about the Roman

122–
24

water system (to which Ovid probably refers), I believe that he is intruding the anachronism and the technical unpoetic details as a way of sabotaging the Minyeid's naive narrative. This spurt of blood turns into a ridiculous geyser that demands a corps of plumbers. We don't really care how precisely the blood struck the berries—the less detail, the better, on the whole—but the narrator seems more interested in this trivial aetiology than in the love story that is its main justification for Ovid's audience. *vitiato . . . plumbo*: lead pipes (replacing iron of an earlier time) are mentioned by Augustan writers like Vitruvius and found in Italian excavations. A flawed pipe would burst, as they do today. Seneca, in *Q Nat.* 1.3.2, mentions the problems, but no poet other than Ovid ever does. To compare a human artery with a lead pipe is plainly reductive. *tenui stridente foramine* 123: the hissing of water as it poured through a break was often noted by the Romans, but again the sound is grotesque when applied to the blood from Pyramus' wound. *eiaculatur* 124: since this (or possibly *Fast.* 1.270) constitutes the first appearance of this verb in Latin, and the noun *eiaculatio* did not exist in ancient Latin, any sexual inferences drawn from the word must be regarded as anachronistic and heavily biased by modern emphases. Ovid has simply created a new word that stresses the lance-like appearance of a jet of liquid, water, or blood. He uses the verb once more in 6.259 to produce an even more inventively grotesque effect than here: an arrow that pierces the artery in the throat is forced out of the wound, and the blood then spouts high into the sky! A few later prose writers pick up this word; no poets do. *ictibus aëra rumpit*: the narrator's persistent attention to this jet permits her to conclude the simile with this exaggeration.

125–27 *arborei fetus*: this poetic circumlocution for the mulberries seems to be derived from Vergil *G.* 1.55 (where it simply meant the fruit of trees in general). *adspergine*: another Vergilian poetic word (used of water in *Aen.* 3.534), which this speaker applies flamboyantly to the bloody spray (cf. 3.85–86). *caedis*: the metonymy for *sanguinis* allows the meter to proceed somewhat more easily. *in atram / vertuntur faciem*: the aetiology uses the normal language of Ovidian metamorphosis. Although it often proves true that *ater* carries more emotional overtones than *niger*, it is incorrect to assert that for this passage: the narrator chose the other word in her introduction at 52. So the choice may be due to metrical considerations, not special significance. The narrator, in her fussiness, proceeds in the second half of 126 to correct the impression of a definitive metamorphosis. Although the details she has given would have satisfied most audiences as entirely consistent with the miraculous ways of aetiology, she now implies that the blood only temporarily stained the mulberries, and she resorts to pseudo-botanical lore to suggest that the tree roots were also soaked in gore, that thus the living sap rose from these roots, up into the branches, and finally into the berries, to stain them purple. Here, the tale might have ended, for it has achieved its announced goal. Fortunately for us, however, the speaker has much closer interest in Thisbe than in Pyramus—whose blood mainly preoccupied her—and so she adds a sequence that balances the *Liebestod* of the man, to create, almost in spite of herself, a true romance.

128–
30

metu nondum posito: Thisbe is reintroduced indirectly, but appealingly, after her departure in 100–01. Main verb and subject pronoun appear in 129; here in 128, we focus on her struggle to meet her beloved in spite of her substantial fears. She does not think of herself or even let timidity rule her actions: human love is mutual commitment, concern for the other along with oneself. It puts divine love to shame in Ovid's poem. *oculis animoque* 129: the double-noun phrase suggests the nature of human love as more than merely physical. *vitarit* 130: perfect subjunctive in indirect question. The narrator hits upon pathetic irony skillfully here. Little does Thisbe know that her lover has drawn fatal conclusions about her dangers and that she will never tell him of her lucky escape.

131–
32

utque . . . sic: regular coordinating Latin construction, which here could be rendered by English "although . . . still." She recognizes the spot she had left and the shape of the tree, but is puzzled by the color of its berries. *an haec sit* 132: indirect question. Three monosyllables ending the hexameter are unusual for epic; the tone of this passage is, in fact, evidently unepic.

133–
36

dum dubitat: Ovid likes this line-opening (cf. Actaeon at 3.206) and the sudden way he can then resolve hesitation. *tremebunda*: she sees the spasmodic movements of dying Pyramus, whom she does not recognize from a distance. *cruentum*: another powerful adjective focuses attention on blood before the narrator provides the nouns. Thus, we can follow the slow, grim process by which Thisbe discovers her tragedy. Here, her first instinct is to start back, in fright, turn pale, and shiver with alarm. The double comparison, the second an extended simile, reveals the sympathetic emphasis that the female narrator gives to her heroine. The whiteness of boxwood appeals to Ovid (here and at 11.417) as a useful symbol of human pallor. He liked and perhaps inverted this analogy between human shivering and the way a light breeze ruffles water. He repeats it in *Am.* 1.7.55–56 and *Her.* 11.75 ff. *tremit* 136: Thisbe's tremor corresponds significantly to that of her dying beloved. The reading is preserved, perhaps as an emendation, by a few MSS; most give *fremit*, which has nothing to do with the simile and surely is a wild sound for Thisbe at this stage of uncertainty.

137–
38

remorata: this time, Thisbe stays to find out precisely what has frightened her. *cognovit*: her state of recognition, incomplete at 131, is now all too precise. *percutit . . . lacertos* 138: Ovid has described this gesture of profound grief earlier in the case of Narcissus at 3.497–98. Thisbe's selfless grief corrects the egoism of the former.

139–
41   *laniata comas*: another standard gesture of female grief, earlier assigned to one of Phaethon's sisters (2.350). *corpus amatum*: the various forms of words for love in this narrative are undoubtedly deliberate. We cannot imagine a god embracing the dying body of a mortal he or she had hoped to possess, with genuine concern for the mortal. *vulnera supplevit lacrimis* 140: here, I believe, Ovid marks his separation from this female narrator, who now proceeds to overdo the picture of Thisbe's pathos. The closest that Ovid as narrator comes to this scene is in his representation of the grief of Hecuba over Polyxena in 13.490: *lacrimas in vulnere fundit*. But that is far from the fantastic image the Minyeid has concocted: it is as though Thisbe replaced all that blood that has spattered the berries and soaked the ground with her copious tears, literally filling up the wounds! Not content with her conceit, the narrator goes on to insist on the mixing of tears and gore. *oscula figens* 141: this is the moment when Thisbe finally gets her kisses, equally unsatisfactory—or even more so—as the final kisses that Pyramus lavished on her lifeless cloak.

142–
44   The narrator had assigned Pyramus a speech of about eight lines and then, after a dramatic description, one last line. To Thisbe here, she allots an appeal of three lines, which elicits a slight response before death from her lover, then a long lament and suicidal decision of fourteen lines. Thus, Thisbe seems to be twice as important to the narrator as Pyramus. *clamavit*: Bömer suggests that Ovid refers with this verb and the repeated vocative to the ritual of *conclamatio*, in which relatives and friends, for several days before a funeral, would call out to the corpse of the dead. That might be a subsidiary nuance, but the main emphasis rests on the terrible shock Thisbe feels at recognizing the body and her attempt to make it live and respond to her. She does not accept Pyramus' death, and indeed he is not quite dead. *mihi*: dative of separation. *carissime* 143: this vocative is preserved by *F*, but the other MSS give *carissima*. Thisbe wins more readers by treating her lover as "dearest" than by calling herself egotistically his "dearest." The corruption from vocative to nominative is also easier to explain than vice versa. In her anguish, she begs him to answer and also to lift his head. He can do neither, but he does show that he has heard her.

145–
46   *ad nomen Thisbes*: the narrator ingeniously reveals that the dying man pays no attention to his own name, but he does stir at Thisbe's. *oculos iam morte gravatos*: the main MSS tradition corrupted the adverb into a preposition, most commonly *in*, but *NU* have *a*. There is no good reason for any preposition, but every reason for the temporal adverb.

Vergil, Livy, and Ovid himself (cf. 5.658) all use *somno* with the
participle and no preposition. Ovid has merely gone one step farther
with this noun. He may also be thinking of dying Dido in *Aen.* 4.68–
89, who tries to lift her heavy eyes and fails, as Anna lovingly cares
for her. *visaque . . . illa* 146: the ablative absolute stresses the fact
that the last sight Pyramus has before death is of Thisbe. Their love
momentarily postponed death by keeping him alive. But Thisbe will
not let death permanently separate them: she will join her lover in
death. *recondidit*: the narrator tersely indicates, when Pyramus closes
his eyes again, that he has died.

147–   *quae*: continuing from the final pronoun of 146, the story immediately
50   shifts the focus back to the narrator's heroine, delaying, as often, the
        less important conjunction. *ense / vidit ebur vacuum* 148: it seems
        odd that Thisbe checks the scabbard and sees that it is swordless, but
        misses the sword, which we have heard that Pyramus drew from the
        wound (so presumably would still grasp in his hand or have let fall
        visibly nearby). Cf. above 119–20. However, she quickly reacts to
        the discovery that her lover has stabbed himself; and the rhythm
        appropriately speeds up in 148 with five dactyls. *manus . . . amorque /
        perdidit*: an instance of zeugma where the poet does not use his wit
        ironically, but seriously to represent the real power of human love.
        fortis: Thisbe calls attention to her unusual courage, which matches
        that of Pyramus, and makes her hand and love capable of the same
        act. *in unum / hoc*: a highly effective, but unepic division at enjambe-
        ment. Most of the MSS missed the point and adopted *haec*, to go
        leadenly with *manus*. The narrator does not want to emphasize the
        hand so much as the love, which gets the demonstrative in the next
        clause.

151–   *persequar*: a loyal companion of Ino will declare her intention to
53   follow her presumably dead mistress in 4.551–52. *miserrima*: Thisbe
        can now devote some attention to her own pathos. *causa comesque*
        152: another zeugma, enhanced by alliteration, and still serious. The
        rhetorical level rises in this speech, a legitimate ascent to tragic diction.
        A major point is made in the paired clauses that follow, where both
        lines 152 and 153 end with the same words, whose meaning has been
        radically changed by the colliding juxtaposition of the two forms of
        posse at the caesura. All those barriers and separations, which seemed
        transitory, have apparently been rendered final by death, whose power
        Thisbe for a moment ruefully concedes as unique, before she retakes
        the power, denying death a victory. *nec* 153: position and emphasis
        can be captured by "not even."

154–   *hoc*: prepares for the noun-clause of 156–57. *amborum verbis*: Thisbe,
57   ready to join Pyramus, insists that she speaks for them both. *estote*

rogati: apostrophizing the parents (and more particularly the forbidding fathers) of them both, she uses the future imperative, which lends her death-request special solemnity. *miseri* 155: the narrator lets Thisbe spread pathos to the whole family. *certus amor* 156: a phrase of tragic irony. The love has been definite, but it has been rendered uncertain and powerless until this moment, when Thisbe's action, matching the premature act of Pyramus, at last secures the union the two sought. *iunxit*: echo of the lover's vain request of the wall at 74. *conponi* 157: the compound could be pressed in translation, i.e., "buried together."

158–61 *at tu*: in a last apostrophe, Thisbe addresses and personifies the mulberry tree and puts a final touch on the aetiology. Her tragic gravity is enhanced by the three spondees. *miserabile corpus*: her insistence on the wretchedness of the scene becomes linked in 159 with the theme of union, two in one; cf. 108. *signa . . . caedis* 160: although Thisbe has not explicitly shown that she knows what has happened to the tree, we do, and so she may be expected to have worked out her confusion after 131–32 without our being told. *pullosque*: a dark and therefore appropriately funereal color. *gemini monimenta cruoris* 161: aetiologies regularly combine a causal explanation with a commemorative purpose. As she prepares to die, then, Thisbe brings in the desire to be remembered. While sparing us another scene of blood spurting into the tree, she links the new color of the berries with the bloodshed of them both, emphasized by *gemini*.

162–63 *aptato . . . mucrone*: this is the point of Pyramus' sword, which she has located. *pectus sub imum*: underneath the rib cage, where the sharp point would enter easily (cf. above 119). *incubuit ferro* 163: Dido's suicide at 14.81 uses the same words and metrical position. The narrator has reduced her engagement with Thisbe, so she does not linger over the heroine's death.

164–66 *vota tamen tetigere deos*: Thisbe has not prayed to the gods at all, which is not surprising, considering the personality of the narrator. What is somewhat surprising is that she is said to have touched the gods.Thus, what could have been assigned to the benevolence of the tree or the special working of nature has here been specifically credited to unnamed gods. When Alcithoe tells the third story, her heroine does pray to the gods, at which the narrator remarks with words that echo 164: *vota suos habuere deos* (373). The stories implicitly contradict the blasphemy against Bacchus. *pomo* 165: the technical word for mulberry, *moro*, would have fitted into the same metrical position, but Ovid preferred the more general word. *permaturuit*: invented for this line; imitated by Hyginus 136 in a passage about the mulberry. Ovid makes the story end not with the aetiological detail, but with the amatory success, such as it is, achieved by the lovers in death, their ashes inurned together. Although the parents were not present to hear Thisbe's last wishes, they have instinctively acted to grant them.

The Loves of the Sun: Clytie and Leucothoe (167–270)

After a short interval, a second Minyeid named Leuconoe begins her diverting tale. She announces her subject without the affected hesitation that characterizes the sister who preceded her and, as we shall see, Alcithoe after her: *Solis amores* (170). That might lead us to expect that she would concentrate on the Sun and his amatory exploits. However, as her sister had turned the love between Pyramus and Thisbe into a heroic portrait of the girl Thisbe, so Leuconoe places her emphasis on two mortal women who suffer for love, whether forced on them or eagerly embraced. The Sun merely dithers.

She begins with the familiar Homeric story about the adulterous affair of Venus and Mars, which served to characterize the basically frivolous morality and sexual behavior of the gods, in sharp contrast to the full commitment of Pyramus and Thisbe, but also to set the Sun up as a prude and informer who deserves to suffer a similar fate. Although he has involved himself in numerous loves and currently has Clytie passionately devoted to him, the Sun initiates another liaison, with the Persian princess Leucothoe, whom he approaches in disguise and essentially rapes. In her jealousy, then, Clytie informs on Leucothoe to her father, who reacts with typical male violence and intolerance, buries the daughter alive, and thus causes her death. This story does not have the easy, amusing outcome of Mars and Venus' adultery. Whereas the gods were somewhat embarrassed for a while, but eventually were released and departed none the worse, Leucothoe perishes. The divine rapist feels some regret as he watches, yet does nothing but make her a shoot of future frankincense. Clytie has no opportunity to profit from informing or to enjoy unrivaled love. The Sun ignores her. Abandoned and frustrated, she changes into a heliotrope, a kind of sunflower, which keeps turning lovingly and vainly toward the indifferent Sun. The final emphasis of Leuconoe, then, rests on miserable Clytie, whose love, persisting in the flower she has become, poses a sharp contrast to the selfish and transitory amours of the divinity.

The affair of Venus and Mars was universally known and admired in the Greco-Roman world. Ovid himself had recounted it earlier in *Ars* 2.561–92, and here he uses that familiar tale ingeniously to introduce the unfamiliar main narrative, the triangle of Clytie, the Sun, and Leucothoe. There is no evidence that any Greco-Roman writer had ever told (or even known) this latter story, and the novelty of the account, along with its Persian locale, has persuaded scholars that it came from the same "handbook" of exotic tales that the other two sisters seem to quarry.

167–   *desierat*: the narrator fills in the space between stories rapidly. Pluper-
68   fect verb occupies the first dactyl and a half, putting the first tale in the background. Ovid continues with a series of uninterrupted dactyls to the central caesura of 168, changing to the perfect for the new speaker, Leuconoe.

169–   *hunc . . . Solem*: careful delay of the noun, to collect its full associa-
70   tions and to set up the chiasmus that follows. Leuconoe implies a climax, rising from human to divine love. In fact, morally gauged, this divine love sinks far below that of Pyramus and Thisbe. And the mortal women show up the triviality of the god's love. *siderea* 169: though often used of the night stars, this adjective can properly apply to any of the bright astronomical bodies, by day or night. *qui temperat*: the verb implies the controlled, intelligently controlling power of a god such as the earlier Augustans, Vergil and Horace, represented. Love quickly makes the Sun intemperate.

171–   *adulterium Veneris*: the preliminary details in Homer were so well
72   known that Leuconoe did not need to elaborate. The use of this prosaic word from the law courts, to brand the behavior of Venus, only reveals the double standard with which male deities operate in sexual matters. *videt hic deus omnia primus* 172: another final hemistich that carefully repeats words. It gives the false impression that Leuconoe venerates the god and his powers. However, he sees here only to inform against Venus, acting on motives that gain little human respect; and he falls into the pattern of Phoebus' bird (cf. 2.545), who saw and reported adultery to Apollo and suffered grievously for it. Next, the Sun will see Leucothoe and become blindly infatuated by her beauty (194 ff.).

173–   *facto*: ablative of cause. *Iunonigenaeque*: dative, antonomasia in pa-
74   rodic epic form, to refer to Vulcan, Juno's son. The long word enables Ovid to limit this line to four words, an unusual form. (There are only three such lines in Book 4.) *furta . . . furti* 174: although Venus deceived Vulcan several times with Mars, Ovid may have been as much influenced here by metrical considerations as by the desire to insist on multiple adultery. The "place of deception" was, as Homer tells us, the marriage bed of Vulcan. Hence, it was easy for the god to lay his artful trap there, once he learned the truth.

174–   *at illi . . . excidit*: dative of reference. The verb, serving both *mens*
76   and *opus*, produces a typically witty Ovidian zeugma, to capture the absurd posture of the jealous god. He cannot control his mind or his work at the forge. The same verb registered in zeugma the shock to Phoebus when informed of Coronis' adultery in 2.602.

176–   Vulcan's helplessness does not last long, as he immediately proceeds
79   to vengeance. *graciles . . . catenas*: the adjective is a key word, for
       the god must devise a trap so fine and so inoffensive-seeming that it
       will catch the divine pair. *quae . . . possent* 177: relative clause of
       purpose; the pronoun in the neuter covers the gender of all three
       antecedents. *elimat* 178: he works it out artistically. Ovid uses this
       verb only here; no other poet tries it. The long parenthesis, which
       enhances the suspense, also attests to the admiration of Leuconoe for
       handicraft (more than for love). She thinks of weaving as a possible
       parallel. *vincant*: subjunctive in future less vivid apodosis. *quae pendet
       aranea* 179: relative typically placed by Ovid before antecedent. The
       spider is the insect paradigm of a weaver, and as such will be later
       explained in 6.5 ff. in Arachne's metamorphosis.

180–   *utque . . . sequantur*: substantive clause of result; the subject is neuter
81   plural referring to the trap (cf. 179); the nouns here are accusative
       plural. *momentaque*: the slightest movement (of the lovers) will spring
       the nets and catch them. *circumdata* 181: neuter accusative plural, of
       the trap. Ovid and other Latin writers subordinate with the participle
       instead of using a coordinate verb (e.g., *circumdat et*). *arte*: Leuconoe
       stresses the craftsman's skill: cf. below 183.

182–   *coniunx et adulter*: the prudish narrator stresses the immorality of the
84   gods. *nova ratione* 183: ablative of manner. The unique delicacy of
       Vulcan's art, earlier noted by Leuconoe, now achieves its purpose.
       in mediis . . . amplexibus: the scene receives graphic emphasis, be-
       cause the guilty pair are in fact, in the hexameter, caught in each
       other's arms.

185–   *Lemnius*: Vulcan was especially revered on Lemnos. *valvas . . . ebur-*
87   *nas*: since ivory was precious, these inlaid doors indicate a rich aristo-
       cratic home, as befits a god. *ligati / turpiter* 186–87: the moral adverb,
       delayed by enjambement, adds emphasis and again characterizes the
       prudish Leuconoe. In the earlier account of *Ars Am.* 2.561 ff., the
       male narrator appeals to our sensuality, brings out the amusement of
       the gods at the enviable plight of Mars, and finally draws the "moral"
       that love, once exposed, rages more freely.

187–   *aliquis*: Homer in *Od.* 8.333 ff. originates this situation by a conversa-
89   tion he reports between lusty young Apollo and Hermes; the latter
       would eagerly exchange places with Ares (Mars). *non tristibus*: with
       Victorian-like sanctimoniousness that misreads the *Odyssey*, Leuconoe
       rebukes the triviality of these gods. Homer's narrator, on the side of
       sexual pleasure, mocked the pains and art of Vulcan. *risere* 188: the
       laughter of the gods over such "disgraceful behavior" offends this
       warped narrator, but her criteria merely add to her folly. The final
       line is a clever rewriting of the line with which Ovid introduced the

same story at *Ars Am.* 2.561: *fabula narratur toto notissima caelo.*
Leuconoe has carefully not announced her story as supremely familiar;
that would conflict with her and her sisters' Callimachean pursuit of
novelty. And she has given the Homeric-Ovidian tale a new emphasis
and chosen it to introduce a novel story, that of Leucothoe, the Sun,
and Clytie.

190–
93

indicii memorem: objective genitive. Venus devises a punishment to
fit the Sun's offense as an informer (*index*). *Cytherea*: the island of
Cythera, south of the Peloponnesos, was a special location of Venus'
worship. Ovid seems to have invented this adjective, and this is the
one passage where the word functions as a substantive. *tectos qui
laesit amores* 191: Leuconoe, who has declared her topic to be the
loves of the Sun, has presented him as a violator of secret love,
and he will now become a victim of similar frustration, like Venus.
Hyperione nate 192: a standard epic circumlocution for the simple
monosyllable *Sol*. Same phrase at 241. Earlier, at 1.10 and 2.118,
Ovid has called the god *Titan*, by the race of his father Hyperion. At
this point, Leuconoe begins an apostrophe to the Sun that extends to
the end of 211. Such a device often characterizes the manner of the
elegiac poet. And she is jumping to the next phase of her story, to
record how first Venus makes the prudish god a passionate lover.
However, where the elegist would normally use the apostrophe to
suggest sympathy with the lover, Leuconoe betrays no such kindred
feeling. Her cold clinical description of the transformation of the god
by love seems rather to imply contempt for this foolish male. *radia-
taque lumina* 193: sunlight is regularly represented as shining in rays.
The ancient artists gave the god, when shown anthropomorphically,
a radiate crown, as Ovid does earlier in 2.40–41. Here, he may also
imagine the rays to be shooting from the eyes. Cf. the damage to the
eyes cited at 195–97.

194–
97

nempe: Leuconoe answers her own rhetorical question caustically, at
the expense of the inept god. In juxtaposed clauses, with careful
repetition, she makes clear that love, such as the god feels, has
metamorphosed him and weakened his divine powers. *ureris igne
novo* 195: this fiery god has been victimized by a superior fire. *omnia
cernere debes*: sardonic reminder of the resonant relative clause with
which she first hailed the god at 172. In the next two lines, she works
out the antithesis: that the god focuses exclusively on a single girl.
The name of this girl, Leucothoe, otherwise unknown, makes her
sound very much like the narrator Leuconoe, and that may not be
accidental.

197–
99

modo . . . modo: these balancing clauses record the erratic behavior
of the Sun (normally the most predictable of heavenly bodies). He

rises too early and sets too late, all so as to see the beloved longer. But the speaker avoids exact balance, spinning out in 199 a radical effect: normally short days of winter become lengthened!

200–
201
deficis: the height of erratic action is an eclipse, for which ordinary people, except for astronomers and the well-educated, lacked an explanation, and regularly interpreted the phenomenon with superstitious dread. Here, Leuconoe trivializes the eclipse and the love-smitten Sun with it. *vitium . . . mentis*: in many human metamorphoses, the *mens* resists and survives the physical transformation, as was the case specifically with Callisto and Actaeon. At other times, the mental defect explains allegorically the form into which the person is changed, as, for example, Lycaon into a bloodthirsty wolf. So here the "eclipse" of the rational part of the Sun causes his light literally to be eclipsed. *transit* 201: a standard verb in metamorphoses. It is comically inappropriate that the effect of his love on the Sun should cause worldwide panic.

202–
3
lunae terris propioris: Leuconoe learnedly refers to the natural explanation for a solar eclipse, which occurs when the moon comes between the earth and the light of the sun. *terris* dative with adjective *propioris . . . palles*: here, she turns to the anthropomorphic representation for the eclipse, using a word that typically describes the wan face of the lover. *facit . . . amor*: metamorphic vocabulary for the transforming power of love.

204–
5
To fix the special attraction of Leucothoe, the narrator lists three favorites of the Sun: Clymene, whom we met as Phaethon's mother in 1.756 ff.; Rhodos, whose close connection with the Sun was commemorated on the island of the same name; and Perse, mother of Circe. All three are connected to Eastern locations and thus can lead up to Leucothoe. *Aeaeae* 205: adjective referring to the island, usually placed in the Tyrrhenian Sea south of Rome off Terracina. Circe haunts that area later in *Met.* 14.320 ff., when she pursues and transforms the reluctant Picus.

206–
8
Clytie . . . despecta: Clytie is another new character in extant myth, a necessary part of the triangle we are to watch. She is the last of the foil women, who prove the unique power of Leucothoe's beauty. The participle nicely picks up the ocular side of the Sun's love: he does not look at Clytie (or looks down on her) because he has eyes only for another. The passionate desire of Clytie, not exemplified in human women so far in this poem, may be an Ovidian clue to the narrator's personality. It contributes to the wretched triangle. *Leucothoe . . . fecit* 208: the priamel reaches its end to focus on Leucothoe, who incarnates the metamorphic effects of love.

209–
Having named the lovely heroine at 196 and 208, the narrator now

11   proceeds to give her a brief description as she takes center stage. *gentis odoriferae*: Ovid picks up the adjective from Vergil or Propertius, to give the heroine an "epic" introduction. The East in general was considered the source of incense; that geography will be narrowed down at 212. *formosissima*: typically, a beautiful maiden has a beautiful mother, but then she surpasses her mother in loveliness. Cf. the opening of Horace, *C.* 1.16: *o matre pulchra filia pulchrior. quam . . . tam* 211: the usual order is inverted, to get the final stress on the girl, and is solemnized by four spondees.

212–   *Achaemenias*: anachronism for mythical times; the Achaemenids ruled
13   Persia after Cyrus in the sixth century. But this adjective establishes the locale. *Orchamus*: presumed Oriental name, otherwise unknown. *Belo* 213: the name is Eastern and seems to be a Greek version of the deity known as Baal. In myth, the father of Danaus and also the father of Dido (cf. *Aen.* 1.621) were so called.

214–   Leuconoe now establishes the particular occasion for the encounter
16   between Sun and maiden. *Hesperio*: the Sun sets in the west, so we imagine a special pasture there for his tired horses. The detail is leisurely; the narrator does not have a very real sense of passionate love and dwells on what interests her. *ambrosiam pro gramine* 215: animals in divine service need divine fodder. *ea*: the ambrosia, nominative singular. *ministeriis* 216: ablative of cause with *fessa. labori*: dative of purpose. Ovid produces a striking echo of this passage in his description of benevolent Sleep in 11.624–25, *qui corpora duris / fessa ministeriis mulces reparasque labori.*

217–   The language here is ostentatiously grand and "epic," especially to
18   describe the horses munching on their food, a somewhat parodic preface to the behavior of the romantic "hero." We must not miss the fact, of course, that the Sun, having set in the west, now rapidly and counter to nature makes his way to the east at night, to "shine" in a most inappropriate and premature way. *thalamos . . . amatos* 218: Leuconoe could have said *amatae*, but the transferred epithet, while being conventional, could also indicate the vague quality of this love or her sense of it.

219–   In assuming the shape of Leucothoe's mother, the Sun goes one step
21   lower than Jupiter, who raped Callisto after posing as Diana to get close to her (cf. 2.425 ff.). The mother would be trusted even more than the goddess. *et inter*: the unusual enjambement separating preposition and complement also enhances the impression of haste on the Sun's part. *ad lumina* 220: artificial light of lamps. The scene is lovingly set by Leuconoe, because it parallels her own setting (though it is not yet evening in Boeotia). Her Golden Line in 221 catches the formulaic scene of weaving; it closely echoes a line in *Her.* 18.37.

Moreover, in Roman literature, weaving with one's servants represents
a quintessentially chaste activity (for the male audience). Cf. Ovid's
picture of chaste Lucretia in *Fast*. 2.741 ff.

222– *ceu mater*: the lover stays in his role at first, restraining unmotherly
24 signs of his love even in his kisses. The gesture automatically implies
the fidelity he intends to abuse. *arcana* 223: this word can apply to
religious mysteries as well as to human secrets of all kinds (from
military to amatory). What is plain to Leuconoe and her audience is
that the god abuses his position to force Leucothoe, against her will,
into a shameful secret. He wrecks this chaste setting. *neve*: unorthodox
start to enjambement; a clue to the Sun's lust. *matri* 224: dative of
separation. The lover exploits his disguise.

225– *paruerant*: quick Ovidian development, as the single pluperfect verb
28 clears the room and lets the main action proceed. *sine teste*: there is
a wicked pun available in this phrase—look up the meaning of *testis*—
especially since the god masquerades up to now as a woman. Indeed,
he does not emerge as a male—we are to imagine how—until after
his pompous speech, at 231. *ille ego sum* 226: a formula of boastful
self-identification. It is used seriously in the apocryphal lines added
to the start of the *Aeneid*. More typically, we find it employed to
make fun of self-introductions of lovers, especially gods, whose erotic
purposes rob them of dignity. Propertius set the pattern for Ovid in
the speech of Hercules in 4.9.37. Apollo, approaching Daphne at
Met. 1.513 ff., uses different words to accomplish the same purpose
of self-advertisement. The three relative clauses sound like the god's
praise in hymns and prayers, except that in this comic case the god
praises himself, in order to perpetrate an act that diminishes his moral
stature as deity. *omnia qui video* 227: Leuconoe naughtily repeats this
divine trait from 195 and 172. It marks how far the god has declined.
mundi oculus 228: at 197 we have heard how this feature has deterio-
rated. *mihi, crede, places*: the abruptness with which the speaker
moves from his credentials to his egotistic purpose makes him indeed
an incredible lover. He rushes on without considering or encouraging
any verbal response from the girl, in voluble dactyls. Leuconoe does
not enlist the least sympathy with his selfish feelings.

228– *metuque*: ablative of cause. Leucothoe does not speak, but she is
29 terrified, and her weaving becomes totally disrupted, a foreshadowing
of the rape that ensues.

230– *ipse timor decuit*: the lascivious god pays no attention to the fear, but
31 his desire is whetted by the way it enhances her beauty. Ovid has
earlier broached this erotic motif describing the Rape of the Sabines
in *Ars Am*. 1.126, and it also appears in the rape of Europa in the
contemporary *Fast*. 5.608 (*et timor ipse novi causa decoris erat*). It
is a grotesque fact, not lost on Ovid, that the victim's fear spurs on

the rapist. The Sun's response, then, is to change back to male form and prepare to rape. *solitumque nitorem* 231: the noun, which denotes the typical brightness of the solar orb, also can refer to the physical attractiveness and elegance of human beings, therefore of this anthropomorphic figure. Horace talks of succumbing to the *nitor* of Glycera in *C.* 1.19.5.

232–33   Still wordless and frightened, Leucothoe lets herself be raped. *victa . . . vim passa* 233: this is definitely rape, not love, and certainly not mutual love. The narrator leaves us with that stark impression, not bothering to describe the departure of the "victorious" Sun and his carefree return to the heavens (which go without saying, to judge from other rapist gods.) Nor does she spend any time on the rape victim.

234–37   *invidit Clytie*: now we discover why Leuconoe especially emphasized Clytie at 206 ff. The "wound" that pained her then turns into militant envy. *neque . . . fuerat*: this explanatory parenthesis, typically occupying two hemistichs, reveals how much she loved the Sun. *paelicis ira*: objective genitive. Clytie, though herself no legitimate wife or mate, deludes herself into thinking that her love is so privileged that any other woman loved by the Sun must be a base concubine, a rival against whom any attack is just. *vulgat adulterium* 236: this is the point where Venus secures her condign vengeance on the Sun, who informed on her adultery. But in the description of Leucothoe and in her subsequent lament (238–39), emphasis falls exclusively on rape. Where there is mutual consent and pleasure, as in the affair of Venus and Mars, one can use the term *adultery*, but not where the girl is coerced. Clytie's envy distorts the situation, and the sufferer turns out to be the girl, already a victim, not the rapist. That may indeed be Clytie's purpose, but it makes us dissatisfied with the punishment of the Sun, with the quality of his love, and with the moral system operating in Ovid's world. *diffamatumque*: the prosaic word occurs in Ovid only here; length and long syllables enable the poet to limit the hexameter to four words. *parenti / indicat*: thus, both Clytie and Sun (cf. 190) are informers, and Clytie will in her turn suffer for her slander.

237–40   Fathers are typically intolerant toward their daughters, when they become involved, even against their will, in an affair or even when they resist the parent's choice of a marriage partner. The father of Perimele, raped by Neptune, is equally savage; cf. 8.592–94. *inmansuetusque*: this striking adjective, invented by Ovid for *Her.* 17.37 and used here and twice more in the *Met.*, emphasizes the preceding *ferox*. This father behaves barbarously. This is stressed by the contrasting pathos of the daughter, vainly appealing with gestures that Ovid regularly assigns to pathetic victims: *precantem / tendentemque manus*: At first, it might seem, she appeals to her father with out-stretched hands, but in fact she is trying to catch the attention and intervention of her "lover." Ironically, he who claims to see all and has been so focused on her before raping her is otherwise occupied. The accumulated participial clauses, which continue with a third into 239, enhance the picture of Leucothoe as victim and leave us in suspense as to the father's action against her, until *defodit*. Burying alive was not a legitimate Roman punishment for adultery, except for Vestal Virgins, so this father, ignoring the fact that Leucothoe was raped, behaves indeed like a savage barbarian, and the narrator properly brands him such. Not only does he bury her deep in the earth, but he heaps a huge mound over her body, as if to commemorate it.

241–42   *dissipat hunc*: too late, after the damage has been done, the Sun intervenes, ineffectively. We might expect much from the way the narrator sets up this divine action. Smashing the mound, the *iter* with its promising purpose clause, and the apostrophe by Leuconoe to the buried girl could have led to romantic rescue.

243–44   Changing tenses to imperfect, the narrator reveals that all the effort was too late. *enectum*: though this word properly means "killed," "utterly dead," and was popular with the Comic poets in such an extreme sense, it came to be attenuated as "worn out," "tormented." That weaker meaning operates here. The apostrophe ends by being addressed to a corpse.

245–46   *illo*: ablative of comparison with *dolentius*. Calling the Sun by his epic title as charioteer, the narrator gives him some grandeur, but only after the fatal fact of his rape and indifference, which proves that he had no deep feeling for Leucothoe. *Phaethonteos . . . ignes* 246: we are reminded of the elaborate story of Book 2. Ovid as narrator there rendered the Sun far more convincingly as a father than Leuconoe has portrayed him as lover here. *vidisse*: the all-seeing god has become pretty miserable with what he sees.

247–48   The Sun tries to revive the corpse with the heat of his rays. *si queat* 248: "if he could possibly do so"; almost parenthetical.

249–51   *fatum conatibus obstat*: once a human being has died, it stands contrary to nature and destiny for her or him to return to life. Aesculapius runs afoul of this law in 2.643 ff., and Orpheus uses his music to set it aside and recover Eurydice for a moment. *nectare odorato sparsit* 250: same clause in 10.732, where Venus tries to save something living from the beloved body of Adonis. The Sun sprinkles not only the body but also the earth, to make sure that the plant breaks through to the open air. *multaque praequestus* 251: indicating a long, conventional speech of elegiac content, the narrator gets succinctly to the three words that form the point, as far as she is concerned. *tanges tamen*: the adversative adverb suggests an entire clause, such as: "though you have perished."

252–
55
inbutum . . . delicuit: the body, so much desired and so selfishly abused, now dissolves into liquid. It is little compensation to Leucothoe and an insignificant victory for the Sun that the narrator records. *odore*: picks up the participle of 250 and prepares for the generation of incense. *virgaque . . . turea* 254–55: the hyperbaton postpones the key identifying adjective until all words but the main verb have been amassed. *surrexit*: this would seem to fulfill the Sun's prediction of 251, but, to achieve proper emphasis, the narrator goes on to mention the mound (which she had reported demolished at 241) and has the growing plant shatter it again!

256–
58
The death of Leucothoe and the ineptitude of the Sun turn the narrator's attention to the remaining member of this triangle, Clytie. *quamvis . . . / . . . poterat*: although indicative forms of *posse* often in Latin substitute for subjunctive, Ovid himself frequently uses *quamvis* with indicative (cf above 1.686 n.). The clause suggests Leuconoe's sympathy for Clytie and a love that excuses all. *auctor / lucis*: another circumlocution for the Sun, now very distant from her, not as "epical" as the phrase promises. *Venerisque modum*: in sharp contrast to her passion, cited at 234–35, the Sun ended his sexual visits. Thus, Clytie who, unlike Leucothoe, was more than willing has her passion snubbed and becomes one more victim of the Sun's inept and selfish so-called love.

259–
61
tabuit: Ovid has recorded the metamorphic effect of rejected, frustrated passion in the stories of Echo (cf. 3.393 ff.) and Narcissus (3.487 ff.). *ex illo*: the pronoun is neuter, referring to the end of the Sun's love. *dementer amoribus usa*: the adverb is rare and unpoetic, occurring only here in Ovid. It should mean she has handled her love crazily and be a simple (self-?)condemnation. However, it could also mean that her total experience of love, as lover, victim, and jealous informer, has driven her out of her mind. It is that loss of rational control, at any rate, that makes her ripe for transformation. *nympharum inpatiens* 260: in situations like this, fellow-nymphs regularly surround the disconsolate one and try to comfort her, always in vain. Because of the elision, early scribes dropped the negative prefix, and medieval tradition transmits *patiens* here. Later scribes corrected that error in some MSS. Ovid has not used this formulaic context earlier in the poem, but he elaborates it in narrating Byblis' love and metamorphosis (cf. 9.652 ff.). The sympathy shown by the nymphs toward Byblis tends to suggest that of the narrator, too. *sub Iove*: the details that follow fit the standard Ovidian picture of emotional desolation; sketched out earlier for Echo and Narcissus, they are fully deployed

with Byblis. *sedit humo nuda* 261: meter guarantees that the adjective agrees with *humo* (a variation on locative, as in 4.121). *nudis incompta capillis*: the narrator repeats her adjective and rounds out her pathetic picture with detail about the bareheaded, disheveled heroine.

262–65 *expers undaeque cibique*: cf. Narcissus at 3.437–38 and Orpheus at 10.73–75. The conventional claim is that the mourner abstains from food and water and feeds her-/himself with tears. *nec se movit* 264: this motionless state foreshadows transformation into a rooted plant. *euntis / ora dei*: the face of the Sun as it moves across the sky. *vultusque . . . flectebat*: this final evidence of volition and of the survival of her love becomes the defining quality of the flower into which Clytie turns (cf. 269–70).

266–67 *ferunt*: as often, the narrator backs off and attributes the account of metamorphosis to an anonymous source. *haesisse*: direct result of the immobility of 264. To account for the colors of the new flower, we learn that the typical white and red that Ovid frequently emphasizes in his human characters suffer mutation. The white, exaggerated by the pallor of frustration and lack of food, becomes the light green of flower-leaves (*exsangues . . . herbas* 267).

268–70 *est in parte rubor*: the red remains as the picturesque center of a plant that closely resembles a violet and replaces the face of the girl. Ovid does not describe the sunflower that Van Gogh painted and so many of us admire: it is too large and has the wrong colors. The heliotrope, on the other hand, is a delicate small plant, violet-like in some species; as the Greek name implies, it turns on its stem by day toward the sun. *suum . . . Solem* 269–70: the story ends with an ironic touch of sympathy for the Sun's lover (but not for the Sun or his kind of love); Clytie, though metamorphosed, still retains her passionate delusions and still identifies the fickle star as "her love." With the wide hyperbaton, the narrator stresses the pathetic irony. *mutataque servat amorem*: this clause captures the twin themes of change and continuity. Normally, *servo* refers to physical continuity. Here it applies to the essential emotion of Clytie's being, her love, which puts to shame what was supposed to be Leuconoe's main interest: the "loves" of the Sun.

Alcithoe Chooses the Unique Story of Salmacis (271–388)

After the audience of sisters and maids has registered its interest in Leuconoe's complex tale, Alcithoe takes over. Very ostentatiously, she lists a series of stories that she rejects as too familiar (*vulgatos* 276). Although some of them have not come down to us, they all have Greek locales. Rejecting them, Alcithoe moves east to Caria in Asia Minor for a tale that she claims will entertain by its pleasant novelty (*dulci . . . novitate* 284). It is definitely novel, unknown to

Greco-Roman writers before Ovid; but why she considers it "pleasant" is not at all clear. I doubt that Ovid agrees.

Alcithoe proposes to give an aetiology, pronounced Callimachean that she is, to account for the strange powers of the spring of Salmacis to enervate males who touch its waters. This amazing blight, which was familiar to the curious long before Ovid, constitutes the frame of the tale of metamorphosis which functions as the main part of the account and, as Alcithoe asserts, is indeed novel. Salmacis is both spring and nymph, but primarily the latter, the inhabitant of a transparent fountain (which reminds us of where Narcissus met his erotic disaster, 3.407 ff.) who goes around in provocatively transparent clothing. Unlike the nymphs Ovid has previously described (Daphne, Callisto), she has no interest in hunting or Diana; which implies what is the case, that militant virginity does not appeal to her. When a handsome boy, son of Hermes and Aphrodite, wanders into her neighborhood, she aggressively woos him, with words such as those Odysseus used to charm Nausicaa. But the innocent, virginal boy has no interest in love. To prevent him from running away, Salmacis pretends to leave, but merely hides and spies on him. He strips and plunges into the spring, and she, fired by desire, plunges after him, uttering the typical cry of "victory" (356) that we have only heard from a male deity as he proceeds to rape. They wrestle for their separate goals, she for sexual intercourse, he for his virginity, and Alcithoe, after prolonging the contest with three similes, depicts the result as inconclusive, until Salmacis prays to the gods for help, asking that they never let the boy escape from her. That is a perverse and selfish prayer, which twists the idea of love as a physical and spiritual union; and Ovid has made it, in spite of Alcithoe's delight with it, as unappealing in its way as Narcissus' crazy infatuation with his reflection in his fountain. Worse still, Alcithoe lets the gods grant this perverse prayer. Salmacis gets her permanent union with the reluctant boy, through a monstrous metamorphosis, not sexual intercourse and definitely not a child. The boy becomes a mix of male and female characteristics, turning into what was known then—and still is—as a hermaphrodite (the name derived from his parentage). Salmacis has won an ugly victory. The boy has been unmanned, turned into a half-male (*semimas* 381, *semivir* 386) and half-female. Hellenistic art played with this hermaphroditic figure and left us a well-known type: a recumbent young nude, lying prone, with body slightly turned so that the curious and the prurient, unsure of the nude's sex, could discover, with well-calculated surprise and interest—if not the "delight" that Alcithoe predicted—female breasts and male genitalia!

When the metamorphosis is complete and Salmacis' prayer and victory total, she disappears from the narrative—returning to be the merely watery spring of the subsequent aetiology—and Hermaphroditus, her forlorn victim, speaks from his perspective of deprivation, as one who has suffered in the waters of the spring. As if he has been radically envenomed by his own agony and rendered permanently envious of all other young men who have a natural future ahead, he, too, prays to the gods, to his own parents, to grant that any male who hereafter bathes in the fountain of Salmacis will be turned to a *semivir*, that is, lose his masculinity and become permanently sterile. And so it happens: this second perverse prayer acts as the aetiology that Alcithoe promised. She has given us a tale that makes us consent to her coming punishment: she has described a gross rape by a female, has made unnamed gods ratify the "victory," and then has depicted the male victim devoid of pathos, actuated by Schadenfreude that again gets the gods' approval. We are meant to reject this view of love, of women, and of the gods and prefer the vision of Bacchus that Ovid has created for us.

271–
73   Ovid starts his transition by briefly recording the audience reaction to Leuconoe's story. *dixerat*: for this unepic Ovidian formula to close a speech, cf. 1.367. *factum mirabile*: standard language for the marvel of metamorphosis. *pars* 272: Ovid reports a divided response in the audience, as he did at the death of Actaeon at 3.258 ff. The other two sisters and the various maids (cf. 35) are all blasphemous, but some restrict their impiety to Bacchus, denying him the status of a true god.

274–
75   *poscitur*: when someone is called upon to speak or sing, this is the conventional verb; cf. 5.333. The silence of the other sisters as Alcithoe prepares to start matches the earlier scene of Leuconoe's beginning (cf. 168). *radio . . . percurrens* 275: formulaic details about the weaving process. Ovid describes the way the weaver runs the shuttle through the threads stretched on the loom.

276–
78   *vulgatos taceo*: Alcithoe starts out with a *praeteritio* (cf. the verb at 284), in which she briefly sorts through and discards some story topics, which act as foil to the one she finally selects. The criterion for selection is novelty vs. familiarity. In this, she agrees with the Callima-chean tastes of her sisters (cf. 53). The first tale is one that is indeed well known, that of the loves of the shepherd Daphnis. Vergil, in *Ecl.* 5, takes the death of Daphnis and the general lamentation of Nature as his subject. Alcithoe refers to a version where a jealous nymph turns him into a stone for infidelity. She mentions this first: because it parallels the recent story of Clytie (cf. *paelicis ira* 235 and 277, *dolor* 257 and 277).

279–
80   *ut . . . fuerit*: subjunctive in indirect question. *naturae iure novato*: metamorphosis is here represented as an innovation in nature. *ambi-*

guus . . . vir 280: Sithon, otherwise unknown, sounds too much like Hermaphroditus for Alcithoe.

281–82 *te*: object of *praetereo* in 284. Traces of the story of Celmis survive, but they do not preserve much more than what Alcithoe deigns to mention here. Celmis, once a faithful attendant of baby Jupiter on Crete, where his mother hid him from his murderous father Cronos, was later transformed into steel by the same Jupiter, when he questioned the god's deity. The Curetes of 282 also lived on Crete and devotedly attended Jupiter; Alcithoe knows of a story of how they were born of the rain.

283–84 Finally, we hear of two flower-metamorphoses which this narrator rejects: that of Crocos, who was presumably a handsome boy like Narcissus, to judge from the pairing in *Fast.* 5.225–27, and that of Smilax, a nymph who became a plant that we today call bindweed or smilax. With a story perhaps like Leucothoe, too repetitious, she had to be bypassed. *dulcique animos novitate tenebo* 284: although Alcithoe undoubtedly holds attention with an exceedingly novel story, it proves less and less *dulcis* as she proceeds.

285–87 Two indirect questions, followed by *discite* in 287, outline the aetiological frame of this story, within which Alcithoe elaborates an expansive metamorphosis. *infamis*: a general reference to notoriety of any kind; it has no automatic connotation of sexual impropriety. Hence, Alcithoe explains the terms in the second clause. *male fortibus*: the adverb serves as a colloquial negative (cf. *male sanus* 3.474), and normally this phrase would simply mean "cowardly". However, Ovid has stretched it farther, to mean "what saps the strength of men." *enervet . . . remolliat* 286: the unusual subject finds Ovid using here first a rare word, then an invented word (which prepares us for the synonymous verbs at 381 and 386, where the narrator actually gets to the aetiology). *causa latet* 287: justification for this aetiological account. *notissima*: cf. the use of the same adjective in 189, to contrast with the novelty of the narrator's story. At the start, we think of Salmacis as nothing but a spring with ruinous powers.

288–89 *Mercurio*: dative, technically indirect object of *enutrivere* 289: the meter makes it difficult for Ovid apparently to join the two parents in a coordinate ablative construction, so he escapes to this. The god's name might also remind us of the story of Venus trapped in the bed (above, 186 ff.). It was Mercury who wished he could be *turpis* in place of Mars, and now it appears that he did eventually have that good luck. *Cythereide*: wishing to use the epic antonomasia, but not having a form that would quite fit the meter here, Ovid creates his own neologism. Cf. 190. *Idaeis . . . antris* 289: we start in Crete, in much the same locale where the infant Jupiter was raised (cf. 282), but we rapidly move eastward to Lycia and Caria. *enutrivere*: another

444   OVID'S *Metamorphoses*

word invented by Ovid. He is letting Alcithoe show her verbal, if not
her moral, finesse.

290–   *facies in qua materque paterque / cognosci possent*: it might seem
91   that the narrator merely indicates that the boy resembles both his
divine mother and father. However, she is also probably referring to
that special age of adolescents when, to poet and lover, it was hard
to decide whether they were male or female. Ovid has already de-
scribed the "virginal appearance" of young Bacchus at 3.607 and the
sexual ambiguity of Narcissus (a closer prototype for Hermaphroditus)
at 3.351 ff. Later, he will make much of the *facies* of Atalanta (8.322–
23) and Iphis (9.712–13) that indicates sexual uncertainty. Ambiguity
here could foreshadow the ultimate cruel metamorphosis. *nomen* 291:
the long name, based on that of the parents, does not easily fit the
hexameter; Ovid saves it for 383, when it has become, more than a
name, a generic type.

292–   *tria . . . quinquennia*: for fifteen to sixteen as the particularly romantic
95   age for *pueri*, cf. Narcissus (3.351–52). *montes . . . patrios*: looking
back at 288–89, we can figure out that Mount Ida is meant. If we
cannot, the following ablative absolute clears up the puzzle. *ignotis
. . . ignota* 294: Bömer calls attention to the way Ovid locates the
anaphoric adjective, so that they receive different metrical stress. The
open pleasure of the young wanderer is a common story motif. *studio
minuente laborem* 295: that enjoyment reduces the sense of work is
a truism which Ovid liked to stress. He uses almost these same words
in 6.60 of Arachne's weaving.

296–   *Lycias urbes*: Lycia lies in southwestern Asia Minor due east of Crete
99   and Rhodes. *propinquos / Caras*: the Carians live in the area north
of Lycia. On the coast is the city of Halicarnassus, home of Herodotus
and Mausolus, also site of the fountain of Salmacis. *stagnum*: else-
where (310, 388), the narrator calls it *fons*. It is the typical idyllic
spring, such as Ovid elaborately describes for Narcissus at 3.407 ff.,
where virginity is mirrored but also threatened. Its transparency makes
it a lovely spot for a swim, but makes a nude swimmer strikingly
lovely, too. It is not marred by reeds or other marshy growth.

300–   *perspicuus*: Ovid uses this adjective elsewhere only at 5.588, to de-
301   scribe the water where Arethusa bathes and encounters a rapist. *vivo /
caespite*: for the grassy margin framing the idyllic spring, cf. 3.411.

302–   *nympha colit*: this nymph, who will be named at 306, is Ovid's or
4   his exotic handbook's innovation, which allows this story to develop
the typical dualism for rivers and springs: as inanimate bodies of water
and as living beings, male or female. We will continue to focus on
Salmacis the nymph now through 379, until the metamorphosis, being
completed, yields place to the aetiology. *nec venatibus apta*: Alcithoe
defines the nymph in negatives, to indicate how she differs from the

usual nymph (such as those Ovid has represented in Books 1–3, e.g., Daphne or Callisto). She is no huntress, does not use the bow, and is unique in being unknown to Diana. That signifies that she does not avoid the haunts of men, does not fanatically dedicate herself to virginity, or, to put it in positive terms, she is entirely open to love, sex, and marriage. *contendere cursu* 303: we have seen no nymphs yet compete in racing, but Ovid presumably intends this, too, as an indication of virginity. The exemplary runner, who preserved her maidenhood by competing with suitors, is Atalanta; Ovid will tell her story in 10.560–680. *naiadum* 304: this classifies Salmacis specifically as a water-nymph.

05–7   *sorores*: the sister-nymphs of Salmacis serve to remind us of their typical pursuits and the symbolism of chastity. In 306, they mention the names of two standard weapons of hunting, then in 307 refer clearly to the hunt. *duris* 307: this added adjective (vs. 302) points up the contrast with Salmacis' *otia*. She exhibits the leisure-time behavior of a young Roman lady in Ovid's day.

08–9   A good example of Ovid's skill in repeating the main parts of neighboring lines, to forward the narrative. Once again, Salmacis negates the views of her sister-nymphs.

10–12   By contrast, she devotes her attention to prettying herself, implicitly for a man. The characteristic mode of the chaste nymph is neglect of her looks, to let her hair blow in the breeze, only loosely filleted, to bathe *after* hunting, never to consult a mirror. *fonte suo*: the reflexive plays with the dualism of nymph and spring. *formosos*: the adjective, common in the descriptions of elegiac beauties, alerts us for erotic events. Like the courtesans of Roman elegy, Salmacis prepares herself for a lover. *Cytoriaco* 311: Ovid invented this adjective here, and he uses it again at 6.132, when Minerva strikes Arachne angrily with the boxwood shuttle. Mount Cytorus, in northeast Asia Minor, was noted as a source of boxwood, from which various wooden implements were carved. The scribes, being unfamiliar with this new word, "emended" it into *Cytheriaco*. Here, though Salmacis may be dedicated to Venus, there is less reason to connect her comb with that goddess of Cythera than with the mountain where boxwood grew. *spectatas consulit undas* 312: typical Ovidian subordination, where we would coordinate. "She looks at the water to see what suits her." In open landscape, nymphs cannot of course be carrying mirrors around, so Ovid regularly has them (or characters like Actaeon and Narcissus) discover what they look like by checking their reflection in a nearby pool or quiet spring. Salmacis, however, is the first who does this as part of her regular elegant toilette.

13–14   *perlucenti . . . amictu*: the narrator takes advantage of the fact that the spring has highly transparent water, to imagine the nymph of the

spring, on the grassy bank, wrapped in a diaphanous robe, like many
an elegiac courtesan, ready for a lover (cf. *lucentis* 297). *mollibus*
314: this word, emphatically repeated, defines the soft, sensuous
interests of Salmacis that contrast sharply with the hard, chaste atheti-
cism of the hunt. *incubat*: indolence further characterizes the leisure-
loving ways of this prototype courtesan.

315–   *legit flores*: picking flowers is a typical part of girls' play, but it
16   regularly serves as the occasion when a maiden, separated from the
protection of parents and home, is especially pretty and vulnerable to
an impetuous male. Europa is picking flowers on the shore when
Jupiter seduces her (2.861), and Proserpina is doing the same thing
when Pluto kidnaps and rapes her (5.391 ff.). Thus, Salmacis' descrip-
tion here ends on an ambiguous note, as if she might be vulnerable.
When the narrator, then, introduces a male at 316, she starts false
expectations that she cleverly thwarts, with what she believes is "sweet
novelty" (cf. 284). The male is only an inexperienced and innocent
puer. What develops, then, is a rape of the boy by the impetuous,
lustful nymph. *cum puerum vidit* 316: the *cum*-inversum structure
enables the narrator to stress this moment as she brings the two key
actors, so far separately presented, together. *visumque*: for anadiplosis
or doubling of a word like this at the central caesura, cf. 1.33 n. The
sight of the boy ignites Salmacis' desires, a variation of "love at first
sight," which so far has activated only rapist males (and Echo). Cf.
Circe's warm response later to the sight of Picus (14.349–51).

317–   *nec tamen ante adiit*: for the concessive adverb, as an eager lover
19   pauses to check on his or her appearance, cf. Mercury before ap-
proaching the home of Herse in 2.732 ff. The verb here has been
used at 258 in a context of erotic visitation, too. The details of feminine
preparation parallel those of Mercury's masculine *cura* and evoke the
courtly world of Augustan Rome. *formosa* 319: as noted at 310, this
adjective belongs especially to elegiac heroines, so it indicates the
amatory purposes of Salmacis.

320–   Since this story shows the nymph wooing and ravishing the young
24   man, she speaks first and uses amatory ploys that seem appropriate.
Note that unlike the gods she does not boast of her importance. On
the contrary, she flatters her prey as possibly a god himself. This and
the trend of Salmacis' speech derive from Odysseus' first words to
Nausicaa on Phaeacia in *Od.* 6.149 ff. The Greek hero was not trying
to seduce the girl, but to flatter her and thus secure help in a strange
land. Which indeed he did. But Homer shows that the flattering words
of Odysseus did evoke an amatory interest in the girl, something like
a first crush. *potes esse Cupido* 321: the erotic purposes of the speaker
reveal themselves in her image of the boy as the god of love himself.
When Odysseus compared Nausicaa to a goddess, he chose Artemis,

beautiful but chaste. (Vergil, alluding to the same scene of *Od.* 6, depicts Aeneas first seeing Dido as Artemis/Diana in *Aen.*1.498 ff.) *sive es mortalis* 322: the alternative, that she is dealing with a human being, is in fact the working hypothesis of Salmacis (as of Odysseus before). This second option, then, receives more elaborate development, in the form of a priamel (322–26). The family of the addressee is individually counted lucky to have such a paragon of beauty, but only as a preface to the marriage partner (if such there be). *qui te genuere*: relative clause precedes the antecedent. Salmacis affects great seriousness in 322–23, slowing down the rhythm with spondees. *frater felix* 323: Odysseus also mentioned brothers at 6.155. Salmacis' mention of a brother, in this heavily alliterated line, plus sister and nurse, does not evoke dynastic pride but her own sensuous feelings. The boy's siblings were lucky because they could get close to him and touch him. *quae dedit ubera nutrix* 324: presumably a conventional way for a woman to express her envy of another, usually a mother. There is a parallel in the admiring words of an unnamed woman about Jesus in *Luke* 11:27: *beatus venter qui te portavit et ubera quae suxisti.* Ovid has twisted the topos in an erotic direction by choosing this sensuous nymph as speaker. Note how the spondaic rhythm of 323 dissolves into dactyls in 324 as the imagination of Salmacis becomes excited.

25–
26   *longeque beatior*: here, Salmacis' obvious emphasis points to the capping term of the priamel. For a different way of working the same theme about the lucky mate of another, cf. Catullus 51 and the Sapphic poem he translated.

27–
28   The final two lines of her speech set off Salmacis decisively from the Odyssean prototype. Odysseus added two lines after mentioning the possible husband of Nausicaa, by which he decorously expressed general admiration again for her slim beauty, without erotic suggestions. *furtiva voluptas*: Salmacis proposes adultery, utterly unfazed if the boy happens to be married. And if he is not, she proposes marriage, as a means of getting him into bed with her. *ego sim* 328: supply *sponsa* from 326. That plainly is not a conventional proposal; the nymph resorts to patently feminine ploys to achieve the same results as the male gods earlier.

29–
30   The narrator maintains her jaunty style, as she returns to narrative and the contrast between nymph and boy. *rubor*: the blush of innocence, as the parenthesis of 330 makes definite. (*nescit enim, quid amor*) 330: a variation, as Bömer notes, on a topos, for which Vergil *Ecl.* 8.43, *nunc scio quid sit amor*, provides the Latin prototype. The virginal soul does not know what love is; the new lover suddenly realizes what it is; and the disappointed lover learns, alas, too well what love is. Thus, Ovid delineates Medea's initial innocence in 7.12 ff. by having

her wonder whether what she is feeling about Jason is love. *erubuisse decebat*: ironically, the boy's implicit compunctions only make him more desirable. For a similar narrative touch, cf. above 230: the fear of Leucothoe made her only more certain to be a victim of the Sun's rape.

331– Alcithoe elaborates on the boy's blush with a triple simile. The first
33 comparison, to apples, has been used earlier to describe the flush (also *rubor* 3.482 ff.) that came over Narcissus' white skin when he beat himself in despair. *aprica . . . arbore*: ablative of place from which. The adjective evokes a sun-bathed tree. Since it takes apples months of sunshine to grow ripe, the reference is to autumn. *ebori tincto* 332: the first poetic allusion to dyed ivory occurs in *Il.* 4.141 ff., but Ovid takes his inspiration from Vergil's adaptation of the Homeric simile to the blush of Lavinia in *Aen.* 12. 67 ff. *rubenti . . . lunae* 333: the narrator refers to the moon in eclipse, when superstitious people would anxiously beat bronze cymbals to "help" recover its white form. As with many tricola, this third item in the simile-pattern proves the longest.

334– *poscenti*: the datives of the two participles in 334–35 serve as indirect
36 objects of *ait* in 336. *sororia saltem / oscula*: the phrase, emphasized by alliteration and the inserted adverb, makes its first literary appearance. However, it must have been a common topos in Rome, as it is in the modern world, for chaste affection. Ovid reuses it in 9.539 for the kisses of Byblis, true sister of Caunus, which are incestuous, not sisterly in intent. Salmacis tries to win erotic kisses by deception, and Alcithoe tops the "maternal" kisses counterfeited by the eager Sun at 222. *eburnea* 335: the adjective, anticipated by 332, first appeared in the description of Narcissus' fair neck at 3.422. Narcissus and Hermaphroditus have much in common. Salmacis' first efforts to overwhelm the boy by affection, impulsiveness enhanced by the five dactyls, stop when he protests. Not for long, however. *an fugio* 336: this is the reading of β*M*; in *NU* we find what looks like a scribal corruption, *aufugio*, and in the majority of the MSS *aut fugio*, which I take to be an emendation of the corruption. The boy has started 336 with a question in present indicative (not the deliberative subjunctive); and it is correct grammar for him to continue his alternative questions, introduced by *an*, with the same syntax. *tecumque . . . ista relinquo*: "Do I leave you and your place?" Another reference to the dualism of nymph and pool. If we insist on a noun for *ista*, we can find it in the next line in *loca*.

337– *locaque*: a good example of the way Ovid avoids the formulae for
40 opening and closing speeches, which were well defined by his predecessors in epic. Here, he begins the speech abruptly, then adds -*que* to the first word, so as to provide a connective to the tiny word of

speaking *ait* in 338 (cf. 1.757 for an early example). *hospes* 338: withdrawing verbally as well as physically, Salmacis addresses the boy as a stranger, not as Cupid or a cute little "brother." *gradu . . . verso*: "walking in the other direction." *tum quoque* 339: "even so," she kept looking back with longing. *recondita*: she hides in or behind bushes. Elsewhere, Ovid tells us, in 7.840, of how Procris, spying from the bushes, was fatally speared by her husband Cephalus. Salmacis here crouches down on hands and knees. *flexuque genu submisit* 340: this is the closest that Ovid or any Roman up to his time comes to the Latin expression behind our word "genuflect." Even so, it caused the scribes trouble. The noun *flexu*, ablative of means, does not normally cover the bending of a bodily part, so the scribes tried to turn the noun into a participle, mostly going for ablative *flexoque*, which would drag *genu* wrongly into the same case. Ovid says that she brought her knee down (to the ground) by bending.

0–
3
at ille: suddenly in the fifth foot the focus shifts to the boy, who thinks himself alone. *inobservatus* 341: invented by Ovid earlier for 2.544. *herbis*: the grass that rings the spring (cf. 301). *in adludentibus undis* 342: the notion that waves and water "play" was common in Latin from the time of Cicero. However, Ovid adds a nuance of seductiveness to the play. The waters of Salmacis' spring are luring the boy into love-play. Ovid repeats this scene of the virginal innocent testing water with the foot before stripping in his later account of the rape of Arethusa at 5.592–95.

4–
5
blandarum . . . aquarum: the adjective continues the implicit personification of the spring, which is "gentle" and "inviting" exactly as Salmacis the nymph would like to seem. The picturesque quality of 345, designed to fix a key instant of the narrative, receives emphasis from the verbal organization. Note the sensuous choice of adjective.

6–
7
placuit: this verb can be used often by Ovid as an understated way of denoting the erotic pleasure that a lovely form gives to the imagination. Thus, the Sun declared to Leucothoe at 2.228: *mihi places*: and then he proceeded to rape (as Salmacis here). *exarsit: flagrant* 347: two synonymous verbs, on either side of the central caesura, double the reactions of the eager nymph. It is easy to interpret the reference to her blazing eyes, especially because of the simile, as a description of sunlight dazzlingly reflected from the surface of water. But the fire-image primarily signifies sexual desire. Unfortunately for the nymph, her desire is not shared, and the mirror-comparison does not signify that the boy's heat is reflected as is the sun's. Rather, the interposed mirror suggests the frustration of contact between nymph and the object of her eager gaze. Alcithoe indulges in a large number of similes hereafter; they form an aspect of her self-conscious artistry.

0–
vix iam sua gaudia differt: for the difficulty of a lover in restraining

51   passion, cf. Jupiter inside the bull-form as he gains control of Europa (2.863) and Tereus as he contemplates his unwitting prisoner Philomela (6.514): *vix animo sua gaudia differt*. *amplecti* 351: this "embrace" serves as the central focus of the next lines, until it becomes permanent at 377. *amens*: because of her lust, her *mens* no longer operates morally.

352–   *applauso corpore*: the boy strikes his body with his palms as swimmers
55   often still do, to prepare themselves for cool water. *alternaque brac-chia ducens* 353: a conventional description of the hand-over-hand stroke of most swimmers, long before the era of the Australian crawl or the other named strokes of modern aquatic skills. *translucet* 354: Lucretius seems to have been the first to use this verb, in 4.332, in a series of mirror problems that employ various verbs compounded with *trans-*. He was describing how light is passed from one mirror to another around the corners of rooms in a house. Alcithoe's meaning differs strikingly: consistent with her thematic interest in transparency (297, 313), she calls attention to the way the boy's white body gleams in the clear water. And she adds a double simile to enhance the picture. Glass, which was much more precious and prized in Ovid's day than now, was often used to enclose another lovely work of art or nature. Looking through glass at a statuette of ivory or at white lilies implies some of the desirable loveliness of the boy's body to Salmacis as it shimmered in the spring. *eburnea*: cf. 335 and 332.

356–   *vicimus*: Ovidian metaphor for the rapist. Tereus will exult with this
57   word as he ensnares Philomela in 6.513. Jupiter after raping Callisto departs as *victor* (cf. 2.437). Here, however, the image proves ironic; it serves only to introduce the theme of violent erotic conflict, where any victory seems dubious. *meus*: the understood noun is *puer*. *omni / veste procul iacta*: the wildness of Salmacis' stripping should be contrasted with the calm, orderly undressing of the boy (345). *inmitti-tur*: this verb, too, is stronger than *desilit* (353). "She throws herself into the middle of the spring," not testing the temperature or diving neatly. Latin passive here renders Greek middle voice (or reflexive).

358–   Note the emphasis on struggle in 358, especially the personification
60   of kisses by the adjective "resisting." *subiectatque manus* 359: having held him so as to snatch kisses, Salmacis now uses her hands to fondle him, reaching up from below. *invitaque pectora tangit*: the adjective suggests more resistance. Although we might expect Ovid to use the act of breast-fondling regularly where males rape females, in fact such a description occurs only in 8.606, in a passage that many scholars suspect is an interpolation. After all, our expectations may be due to our different cultural conventions. *circumfunditur* 360: this verb reminds us that Salmacis, both water and nymph, can "pour around" him all by herself.

nitentem: from *nitor*, another verb with military overtones. The two participles, which focus our attention on the desperate efforts of the boy to fight Salmacis off, are quickly negated in 362 by the initial verb and the triple simile. *inplicat* 362: repeated at 364, as the erotic human embrace (351) turns into the coils of a constrictor snake. *quam*: Ovid generally treats *serpens* as masculine especially in Books 3 and 4, where the Theban snake is so important. Here, he used feminine, presumably because Alcithoe is comparing Salmacis to the reptile. *sustinet ales*: the simile starts off deceptively, as though the snake is the object of the eagle's violence and doomed. However, if we look more closely, and especially if we peek at the parenthesis, we see that the emphasis falls on two contrasting movements: that of the eagle straining to climb into the air (and the boy to get to the surface) versus that of the snake to wrap the bird up and stop its flight (and of Salmacis to pin the boy's resisting limbs). *illa* 363: the snake. In typical descriptions and representations of birds and snakes, the eagle grasps the snake with its talons. Alcithoe imagines a snake so immense and powerful that, though apparently so held, it still has the strength and expanse to wrap itself around the head, legs, and wings. The first simile suggests a rather even contest, but the next two convey the likelihood of Salmacis' victory.

intexere: Alcithoe chooses a verb appropriate to her weaving as a metaphor of the nymph's clinging and the way ivy twines around a tree. Twining ivy is a conventional symbol of devoted female love; it has no negative connotations in Latin like our "clinging vine." It is the only one of the three similes that does not connote aggressive conquest. *sub aequoribus* 366: this final simile implies the perverse feelings and behavior of the nymph, using the same watery locale. Instead of flying skyward like an eagle, the boy has been trapped beneath the water and is likely to drown. He is not lifting his enemy, but has become the enemy and prey and is trapped in the tentacles of the octopus (more numerous and more victorious than the snake's coils). *polypos*: the basic Greek word from which this Latin derivative comes had a short first syllable. However, there were epic forms with a dipthong and Doric forms with omega, and Latin treats the first syllable invariably as long in extant literature. *hostem*: the metaphor exposes the true meaning of any rape-relation. The rapist is a conqueror, but not heroic; the victim is an enemy; and there is no "love" but only exploitation, brutalization, murderous warfare. *continet* 367: cf. the first verb describing Salmacis "holding" the struggling boy (*tenet* 358); she is now in control. *flagellis*: the arms or tentacles of the octopus looked like flailing whips to the Romans.

perstat Atlantiades: the "epic" language ironically suggests that the boy continues a heroic resistance, which, however, Alcithoe's heroine

Salmacis will master. As great-grandson of Atlas through his father Mercury, Hermaphroditus has a remote right to this circumlocution. *sperataque gaudia*: cf. 350. *denegat* 369: other poets did not like this word, but Ovid chose it for its initial dactyl and its sense of emphatic refusal. *commissaque*: this verb describes the joining of two separate or normally irreconcilable elements, as the two legs of Cadmus turn into the tail of a snake (4.579) or man and horse unite to form a centaur (12.478). Salmacis' close hold on the boy anticipates the metamorphosis. *corpore toto*: the phrase occurred earlier in 4.74, where the lovers Pyramus and Thisbe longed to be so joined. Thus, this total bodily union by Salmacis with the boy should denote sexual intercourse, the pleasure that she sought, but it describes instead the final frustration: physical juxtaposition without union or love.

370–
72

pugnes: concessive subjunctive with *licet*. Salmacis is determined to crush the "fight" out of the boy. *inprobe*: an interesting and significant use of this moral term. As Bömer remarks, it is being transferred by the guilty rapist to her innocent victim; we would normally expect, as Ovid makes happen in *Ars Am.* 1.665, the victim to cry out against her attacker and call him a "wretch." Moreover, Alcithoe lets Salmacis brand the boy as the guilty scoundrel, since rapists frequently claim that *they* are the victims (and male judges often excuse rape as "provoked" by the female). *non . . . effugies* 371: same words in same metrical position at 14.355, spoken by lustful Circe as she exerts her will over Picus. *ita di iubeatis*: jussive (precative) subjunctive. Salmacis asks the gods to confirm her confident assertion. This resembles the prayer formula in third person plural, *di faciant* + subjunctive with or without *ut*, and several scribes automatically "corrected" *et* to *ut*. What Salmacis prays for sounds remarkably like the prayer at the end of the modern marriage service: "Those whom God has joined together, let no man [person] put asunder" (cf. *Genesis* 2:24). We have no examples of such a statement accompanying Greek or Roman weddings, but lovers could make an oath of fidelity along these lines, as Bömer notes, citing Propertius 2.6.41–42. The ironic point here is that this is a perverse prayer for ratification of a perverse union, a total travesty of love and marriage. And yet the gods grant the request and create a monstrosity! Alcithoe's sweet novelty has reached its nadir. *istum . . . isto*: this demonstrative almost surely has an overtone of anger and frustration; it does not refer to any personal connection between the gods and Hermaphroditus. (He will pray to his parents next.)

373–
75

vota suos habuere deos: although this could be a gnomic generalization, which the following *nam*-clause applies to Salmacis, readers regularly interpret it as a particular comment about the nymph. "Her prayers had their special gods (to answer them)." Ovid used the same clause (but preceded by *ultima* in the previous line) of Myrrha's last wishes. However, there is all the difference in the world between the remorse of Myrrha and the violent determination of Salmacis, and Ovid expects us to be shocked at the gods here, but not when they pity Myrrha. We might think of Alcithoe as trying to outdo her first sister in her finale. The last prayer of Thisbe, that she and Pyramus be finally united in the ash urn, was a tearjerker that gained our and the gods' sympathy: *vota tamen tetigere deos* (4.164). Alcithoe twists the true heroine-lover's prayer into something ugly, then caps the earlier statement (in the same metrical position) with the horrifying blasphemy about Salmacis' success at dominating the boy. *mixta duorum / corpora* 374: because of Salmacis' efforts to possess the other's body, their limbs are visibly mingled, ready for the metamorphosis that now unites them in one organism. Again, sexual and marital symbolism gets distorted. *facies inducitur illis / una*: emphatic enjambement. The single visible form makes the mutuality of love and marriage impossible. Love has become warped and pursued a destructive result, much as Narcissus' love for himself ended in suicide. Possibly Ovid alludes here to Aristophanes' playful allegory in the *Symposium* about the origin of love. Alcithoe allows no playfulness in her sterile bisexual hermaphrodite that emerges from this union of male and female. The union is unnatural, nonmutual, and Salmacis' "victory" (such as it is) receives no triumphant expression, whereas the misery and degradation of the boy cry out.

375–
79 *conducat . . . ramos . . . cernit* 376: the modern practice of punctuation disrupts a not unusual Latin organization, where the accusative functions with both verbs. Alcithoe refers to the normal agricultural practice of grafting, but she uses a nontechnical word, in order to emphasize the connection between *inducitur* 374 and the action of the grafter. The bark that joins the main stock and the new branches resembles the *facies* that becomes one over the two human beings. *pariterque adolescere*: the branches grow together into the stock, but, unlike Salmacis and her *puer*, the result is a fruitful, productive tree, not a sterile hybrid. The farmer has a valid and realizable intention; Salmacis and her gods have illicitly produced a freak. This is the last of Alcithoe's similes. *conplexu coierunt* 377: the prefixes are deliberately chosen. This phrase should denote coitus, passionate sexual intercourse. Since, however, there was no real love nor a successful rape, the language that now describes the union depicts a monstrous hybrid. *forma duplex* 378: Salmacis has achieved the very opposite of satisfactory love and sex. Instead of winning the heart and *mens* of the boy to mutual love, so that their separate bodies could then give and receive pleasure in intercourse, she has forced an unnatural physical melding that destroys sexual differentiation and ignores the incompatibility of feelings. Ovid strongly emphasizes in this poem that love results from the symbolic union of the mind and emotions, not mere physical linkage. *nec femina . . . nec puer*: the words touch upon the modern ideal of feminism, the sharing of male and female sensitivities and roles, but Alcithoe's program should affront feminists today as much as it does males. The androgynic ideal differs radically from a hermaphrodite. *nec utrumque et utrumque videtur* 379: Ovid has let Alcithoe be witty as she sums up the metamorphosis, but I doubt that he shares her wit or pleasure in this *novitas*. Salmacis and her gods have eradicated the valid and precious individuality of two people.

380– *se*: object of *fecisse* 381: subject is *liquidas . . . undas*. With the
82   mythical metamorphosis narrated and complete, we return to the aetiology and a more objectively natural viewpoint. Without referring to the nymph Salmacis again or allowing the boy to show any awareness of the episode that, as we have seen, caused his change, Alcithoe presents him as one who reckons himself the victim of inanimate water and directs his anger and frustration against other innocents, not against the guilty nymph nor the poisonous water of the spring nor even against the weirdly amoral gods. *semimarem* 381: the unusual nature of this story finds Ovid and Alcithoe lacking a vocabulary of synonyms to denote the double nature of the hermaphrodite. Traditionally, the "half-male" indicated by this term was a eunuch, not an actual blend of male and female. In a still different sense, Ovid plays with the sexual ambiguity of Caeneus in 12.506, letting an enemy also sneer at him as an effeminate. *mollitaque*: supply *fuisse*. Softening of the boy's limbs might not necessarily result from the union of male and female, at least in Alcithoe's mythical account, but in practice the hermaphrodite was represented with a soft, girlish body, and male prejudice interpreted loss of full masculinity as a kind of effeminization or "softening" of male toughness. We do not need to conclude, however, that Alcithoe and Ovid have lost control and fallen into inconsistencies; they are not talking about the fairly common effeminate, who looks unisexual but behaves with sexual ambivalence, but are using some of the terms of effeminacy, as well as of eunuchs, to describe the special quality of the hermaphrodite. *manus tendens* 382: familiar prayer gesture (cf. 238). Up to now, Ovid has regularly employed *tollere* with *manus* (e.g., 2.487) and *bracchia* with this verb (e.g., 1.635–36). *non voce virili*: in the aftermaths of metamorphoses, Ovid likes to register some changes as the transformed being resorts to prayer. Often, as with Io or Callisto, since the girl has become a beast, she starts off with a frustrated gesture, lacking hands and arms to extend. Then, she has no human voice any longer, so she cannot say her prayer aloud. Io finds herself mooing; Callisto feels her prayer.

Here, the boy speaks with a changed voice. The physical union of the two beings does not allow for vocal differentiation (as it does for sexual dimorphism), unless we imagine a voice like that of teenagers, which sounds now treble, now baritone. The more likely voice is that of the effeminate, unusually high for the average male.

383–
86
Ovid names Hermaphroditus only at the end of the story, as he does with key names in other stories, where he teases and flatters the mythological expertise of his audience. Here, also, the delay of the long and awkward name enables him to use it once at the precise moment when the boy has become what the mythical name signifies. *nato date*: we now discover that the prayer goes to the divine parents of Hermaphroditus. *vir . . . semivir* 385–86: Ovid had prevented Alcithoe from using this witty pairing above at 380–81, but now he lets her do so. Again, this word for "half-man" does not conventionally refer to the rare hermaphrodite. It can apply variously to semihuman monsters like the centaurs, to unmanned people like eunuchs, and to unmanly males like cowards and effeminates. Thus, at *Aen.* 4.215, Vergil lets Iarbas sneer at the sissified companions of Aeneas (with their Trojan unRoman way of dressing). Again, the context indicates that Ovid has pressed the word to apply to the special physical nature of the hermaphrodite. *mollescat*: Alcithoe, having prepared us with *mollita* above at 381, now completes the announced aetiology: cf. 286. The prayer is formally correct and addressed to known deities, but it strikes us as morally depraved. The boy has learned nothing from his suffering except the desire to have others share his misery.

387–
88
motus uterque parens: Alcithoe makes the divine parents blindly acquiescent, like the anonymous gods of Salmacis, ready to inflict pain without reason on human beings. *nati . . . biformis*: one final stretching of regular usage to cover the special duplicity (cf. *forma duplex* above at 378) of this creature. Normally, the adjective referred, as it does at 2.664, to the human-animal doubling of species like the centaurs. *incerto* 378: the frequently reliable family of βMN has *incesto*. Paleographically, the corruption could have occurred either way, so the question is: which seems to be an attempted, but misguided, "correction" of the other? I believe that *incerto* is the text of Ovid, because that adjective applies to the sexual ambiguity of the hermaphrodite, the subject of this story. Livy talks of a baby whose sex was hard to discern, using this word; and Juvenal at 15.137 describes a boy with such long hair that he looked like a girl, whose sex could not be inferred from his face (*ora incerta*). On the other hand, *incesto* normally has the meaning of sexually criminal and perverse in behavior, which is not the definition of a hermaphrodite nor the kind of person this Hermaphroditus is. Alcithoe has declared the spring *infamis* (285), but notoriety does not automatically connote incest or other sexual

depravity. It is quite bad enough to lose masculinity, as this boy has done and others will after him. The correction has come, then, I suspect, from a scribe who insisted on labeling the hermaphrodite, a sport of nature, as morally perverse.

The Metamorphosis of the Impious (389–415)

Still persisting in violating the holy day by their weaving, the three sisters suddenly watch their work area being taken over by the presence of Bacchus. Mysterious sounds and scents are followed by the weaving of ivy and grape clusters over loom and tapestry. There is nothing threatening about this divine assertion: like the advent of Bacchus to the Tyrrhenian pirates in Acoetes' account, it is firm but nonviolent. Without registering the sisters' reactions, Ovid proceeds to their transformation. Daylight has turned to dusk, when eerie lights flash in the house and unreal beast-shapes roar. Terrified, the Minyeids try to hide, and in the darkness of evening they appropriately turn to bats. They have violated daylight; now they become creatures of the night, not true birds, but squeaking flying mammals. Their new name, *vespertilio*, which does not easily fit the hexameter, derives from the word for evening, *vesper*.

389– *finis erat*: a typical transitional formula, Ovidian and not epic; it allows
90   the narrator to move quickly forward. *dictis et*: the MSS disagree on the division of the words here, several early ones offering *dicti sed*. Both the singular noun and the conjunction are inelegant. *Minyeia*: another special adjective created by Ovid for this story. *urget* 390: same verb at 4.35. Ovid trisects this line and thus lists three impious acts of the women. *spernit*: same verb at 3.513 to characterize Pentheus' rejection of Bacchus. *festum*: so the holiday is described at 4.4 and 33.

391– *tympana cum*: Ovid develops a long *cum-inversum* period down to
93   398, to stress the start of metamorphosis. These drums, already mentioned at 4.29, are typical of unRoman ecstatic rituals. *non apparentia*: although drums beat, neither they nor drummers can be seen. *et adunco tibia cornu* 392: same phrase at 3.536 in Pentheus' scornful catalog of Bacchic paraphernalia. *tinnulaque aera* 393: Ovid refers to the familiar exotic cymbals (cf. 4.30), adding a rare poetic adjective that he uses only once elsewhere. The incense, which concludes this description, had for the Romans connotations of exotic luxury. Myrrh was imported.

394– *resque fide maior*: another variable formula to introduce an incredible
95   metamorphosis (cf. Acoetes' words at 3.659–60). *virescere*: dead wood becomes alive and green. *inque . . . faciem* 395: this + genitive

provides a typical formula of change. Ivy regularly announces Bacchus (cf. 3.664). *frondescere vestis*: an unusual collocation, to stress the way the living power of the god takes over the inanimate, futile work of the women.

396–
98

Ovid analyzes the metamorphosis of the weaving into its constituent parts and appropriate changes. Each verb, except for *adcommodat*, is one of the variants for the process. *pars abit in vites*: the tapestry, which Ovid has not described, turns partly into a grape vine. *fila . . . palmite*: threads become vine-shoots. *pampinus*: vine-leaves sprout from the warp on the loom itself. *purpura . . . uvis* 398: the purple dyed into the thread becomes the appropriate color for grapes that appear on Bacchus' vines. *pictis*: "colored," but not artificially: they are "painted" as if by Nature.

399–
401

Ovid defines the time of twilight, without yet explaining that it is the time of bats. Notice the way he draws in his audience by the apostrophe of 400. *nec . . . sed* 400–401: concerned for precision, the narrator insists that it is neither daylight nor darkness, but a blending of both. *dubiae*: night is "doubtful," as darkness has not yet eliminated the light.

402–
4

quati . . . ardere videntur: an illusionary earthquake and bright flash-ing lights occur. Ovid does not state that Bacchus has caused this phenomenon, so that the effect noted in the death of Pentheus—that the god does not play the strong intrusive role given him by Euripides—continues here. Bacchus' will is evidently being worked out, but he is not an assertive egotist like other gods. The illusion continues in 403, as the growing darkness of the home is illuminated, it seems, not only by torches but also by menacing red fire. The house seems to be burning. *falsaque . . . simulacra* 404: in 3.668 Acoetes described the empty forms of wild beasts that appeared on his ship and frightened the sailors. Here, the beasts produce a threatening howl, to increase the effect.

405–
6

At last, Ovid turns to the sisters and their reactions to this realistic horror show: they try to hide, to avoid the menace from torches and fire. That will become characteristic behavior of the bats into which they will change. *fumida*: the smoky atmosphere comes from the seemingly burning objects. *diversae* 406: in various directions, not as a group.

407–
8

As they hide in panic, metamorphosis begins. *parvos . . . per artus*: as Bömer notes, Ovid implies that the human limbs have been made tiny (to fit bat-dimensions) and then a membrane has been stretched between "hands" and "feet." *tenuique includunt bracchia penna* 408: with this reading, the subject is the women. The passive with *bracchia* as subject would have been better, if the meter had allowed it. Their arms, confined by the membrane, form wings. Many MSS, which often tried to "correct" the transmitted text, have changed the reading to *tenuesque . . . pennae*, so as to make the wings the subject. They would have done better to change the verb to singular *includit*, thus allowing *membrana* to continue as subject.

409–
11
nec . . . scire sinunt tenebrae: Ovid avails himself of the darkness to ignore further details of metamorphosis. The reduced bodies and the special membrane-wings provide enough data. *pluma*: these are not birds, so their "wings" are not equipped with feathers. *perlucentibus alis* 411: Ovid refers to the transparency of the membrane. The modern scientific name for the bat family is chiroptera, from Greek, meaning "hand-winged." Bats are the only mammals capable of flight.

412–
15
conataeque loqui: Ovid regularly thematizes the loss of the human voice when men or women are changed into animals. This motif goes back to the first metamorphosis, that of Lycaon in 1.233. Cf. Io at 1.637, Callisto at 2.483, Actaeon at 3.201, etc. *minimam et pro corpore*: cf. *parvos* above, 407. Bats squeak like mice. *peragunt . . . stridore querellas* 413: Ovid imagines that the shrill noise of the bats is a complaint of the sisters over their metamorphosis. *tectaque . . . celebrant* 414: this connects with 405. Though bats, the sisters within still haunt their old home. Bats, we know, often make their nests in the dark parts of ceilings or attics, but also in caves. *lucemque perosae*: hatred of light continues the theme of 406. *a vespere nomen* 415: that is, *vespertilio*. As often, Ovid concludes his metamorphosis with an aetiology of the Latin (or Greek) name. Cf. 2.675, where Ocyrhoe, changed into a mare, assumes the name of Hippe.

THE RUIN OF CADMUS' LAST DAUGHTER, INO (416–542)

The punishment of the Minyeids gives a false sense of conclusion, as though not only Bacchus has won due recognition, but also the remnants of his line have gained tranquility. The families of two daughters of Cadmus, Autonoe and her son Actaeon, Agave and her son Pentheus, have been desolated; and a third daughter, Semele, mother of Bacchus, has perished. That leaves only Ino, her husband Athamas and two sons to carry on Cadmus' heritage. Although she helped nurse Bacchus after his birth and participated in the dismemberment of Pentheus, Ino is presented as guiltless, happily immune so far from Juno's hostility. (In other versions, she is culpable for having doubted the divinity of Bacchus.) But Juno has been biding her time. Now, offended by what she construes as Ino's pride in Bacchus, she dedicates her efforts to destroying her. This involves going down to the Underworld and enlisting the help of the Fury Tisiphone, sister of Allecto (whom Vergil used in *Aen.* 7 to carry out Juno's destructive purposes against the Trojans). Ovid develops the second of his long allegorical descriptions: cf. Minerva's visit to Envy in 2.760 ff. Hellish Tisiphone comes up to Thebes and implants Madness in Athamas, who then believes that his wife and children are lions to be hunted down and killed. He kills one son, Learchus, and Ino, also maddened, picks up the second, Melicerte, and dashes for the sea, calling on Bacchus. When she reaches a cliff overlooking the water, she jumps with Melicerte to what she supposes will be her death. However, Venus intervenes to save her grandchild: she persuades Neptune to turn the two into minor sea gods, Ino into Leucothea, Melicerte into Palaemon. They are considered benevolent, so the conclusion of their mortal misery appears a consolation.

Ovid tells a story that he has selectively organized from traditional details and personal improvements, to carry his unique stamp and look forward to Senecan tragedy. Ignoring entirely a version in which Ino was evil stepmother to Athamas' two children by his first wife (and thus deserved to suffer the loss of her own two), he uses an account that also appears in Apollodoros 1.9.2 and 3.4.3.5 and, somewhat garbled, in Hyginus 1–4. It tells of how Juno drove Athamas mad, and he attacked his son. Ovid does expand the account by a large central section (4.432–511) that permits him to vie with Vergil and pursue his allegorical interests in Tisiphone and Madness. Thus, he ends up with a brief traditional tale in two phases of about sixteen lines each, which frames his own episode of grotesque Tisiphone, a brilliant tour de force of eighty lines. Probably later, in *Fast.* 6.483–502, Ovid narrated the simple story, without a large central section.

Juno Determines to Destroy Ino (416–31)

16–19   *totis . . . Thebis*: whereas earlier, after the punishment of Pentheus, there were three notable exceptions, the Minyeids, to the public honor for Bacchus, now it is unanimous. *matertera* 417: Ino. Her insistent praise of Bacchus naturally irritates Juno. We do not hear what happened to Autonoe and Agave after their sons' deaths; but, as Ovid says, Ino alone had been exempt from grief like theirs.

20–21   *adspicit hanc*: a common opening formula for Ovid; same words in 2.443, same verb with masculine pronoun at 2.748, 3.356 and 577. Notice how the picture of proud Ino is developed before the identity of the angry watcher becomes clear. *et alumno numine* 421: Bacchus, Ino's nephew and nurseling, comes as a significant afterthought. The ablative is a loose poetic one of specification.

22–23   *nec tulit*: Juno's typical intolerance shows up at 549 again, at the end of this story. *et secum*: as Bömer suggests, Ovid is probably alluding to the famous first soliloquy of Juno in *Aen.* 1.37 ff., which begins *haec secum*. This Juno appears much pettier than Vergil's goddess.

de paelice natus: she immediately focuses on her typical irritant, the bastard child of Jupiter. Same words and situation in the case of Callisto's Arcas at 2.469. In 423, she reviews some of the successes of Bacchus, which Ovid has already narrated, starting with the transformation of Acoetes' impious crew into dolphins; cf. 3.670 ff.

424– *laceranda . . . viscera matri*: the death of Pentheus (3.701 ff.), whose
25   head was torn off by his mother Agave. Dative of agent. *novis . . .*
      alis 425: the adjective refers in typical language to the metamorphosis of the sisters into bats; cf. above 411.

426– *nil poterit . . . haec una potentia*: it is characteristic of Juno to rail
27   against her impotence, then to do something drastic. *flere*: since it is a convention, and Ovid himself has already declared it at 2.621–22, that gods never weep, Juno is guilty of exaggeration in her rhetorical questions.

428– *ipse docet*: Bacchus' contrivance in the death of Pentheus "teaches"
31   her, Juno says, how to proceed. Her parenthesis, reusing the verb, makes a slogan of her methods. *furor valeat* 429: the power of madness, certainly not a healthy force, showed itself in the delusion of Agave that her son was a boar to be killed. A similar delusion will be inflicted here on Athamas. *Penthea* 429: adjective, probably invented by Ovid, with a long second syllable. *stimuletur . . . furoribus* 430–31: the metaphor of the goad is regularly used of the effect of emotions on rational behavior; cf. the ruinous effects of Clytie's jealousy at 4.235. The noun goes with both verbs of 430. *per cognata suis exempla*: "after the pattern of her relatives," i.e., her sister Agave. Ovid has moved up the reflexive adjective so as to achieve the maximum antithesis with *cognata*: Ino will be driven by her own madness. The name of the victim is saved by Juno (and Ovid) until the very last, both to make the speech more sinister and to tease the audience's familiarity with myth.

Juno Pays a Visit to Tisiphone and Requests Help (432–80)

432– *est via declivis*: Ovid begins a brief ecphrasis, in the formulaic manner,
33   with *est* + noun; it will end with the demonstrative adverb *illac* at 435. This downward route is the reverse of the heavenly route of the first ecphrasis (*est via sublimis*) at 1.168. Same three words later at 7.410. *funesta . . . taxo*: the yew, because of its deadly berries, had a poetic association with the Underworld. *nubila*: simply dark (because of the dense foliage). *infernas . . . sedes* 433: Vergil used this at 8.244 to characterize the hellish aspect of Cacus' cave; Ovid relegated Narcissus there in 3.504. *muta silentia*: the phrase, duly shortened, seems to have been suggested by Lucretius 4.583, *taciturna silentia* (applied to the nighttime).

434–   *Styx . . . iners*: since Ovid mentions only one river of the Underworld,
35   the Styx receives an epithet usually reserved for the calm, "dead"
   waters of the Cocytus. Its wet mist is a commonplace. *simulacraque
   functa sepulchris* 435: an expansion of the previous *umbraeque re-
   centes*. These dead have received funerals. The same phrase appears
   at 10.14 when Orpheus visits the dead.

436–   Ovid has in mind Vergil's description of Aeneas' visit to the Under-
38   world in *Aen*. 6.268 ff. Instead of showing this strange world through
   the visitor's eyes and feelings (as Vergil did with Aeneas), Ovid
   reduces the interest of the setting to its effect on the newly dead,
   who grope their way to their final destination. Vergil emphasized the
   colorlessness of the scene, and "winter" is a traditional symbol for
   death. *loca senta*: to Dido, Aeneas had spoken of the cheerless route
   he had taken to visit her (*per loca senta situ, Aen*. 6.462). *qua ducat*
   437: the MSS divide here on the form of the relative. Those that often
   have suffered scribal "improvements" offer *quod*, which would refer
   to *iter*. The more difficult reading of others, *qua*, would continue
   with anaphora and use the same subject *iter*. *Stygiam . . . urbem*:
   Vergil had described one part of the Underworld, Tartarus, as a mighty
   fortification (*Aen*. 6. 548 ff.). He had assigned this area to the greatest
   sinners, and here he had placed Tisiphone (6.555); but he had barred
   Aeneas from entering, declaring that it was forbidden to anyone pure
   (563). Ovid intends to urbanize the entire scene of the dead, but to
   concentrate on Tisiphone's locale (where ironically his not so pure
   Juno does enter). *regia Ditis* 438: this reference to royal power might
   suggest a political order that would assign the dead to appropriate
   places, but Ovid skips over that traditional element.

439–   *mille . . . aditus*: since Death is the end of us all, its city can symboli-
42   cally be said to have a thousand approaches, all open gates (cf. Tibullus
   1.3.50). Ovid takes a familiar Greco-Roman idea and adapts it to his
   metaphor. *utque fretum . . . flumina* 440: Ovid has already described
   the creation of rivers and their course to the sea in 1.39 ff. He uses
   this same simile in almost identical words at 8.835, but in trivializing
   fashion to render the grotesque appetite of Erysichthon. *nec ulli /
   exiguus populo est* 441–42: "it is not too cramped for any mass of
   people." Ovid sounds, no doubt deliberately, like a traffic engineer,
   interested only in the crowd-capacity of this place, whereas Vergil's
   emphasizes with the same *turba* (*Aen*. 6.305) the pathos of death
   (which we feel).

443–   After a summary line about the aimless wandering of the shades, Ovid
46   divides them perfunctorily into four groups, using *pars* in anaphora
   three times and, for variety, *partem* the fourth. *exsangues . . . umbrae*:
   the phrase comes from *Aen*. 6.401, where Vergil had Cerberus, bark-
   ing, terrify the shades. *forum celebrant* 444: Ovid Romanizes the city

even more, as if the dead continued the activities that characterize the forum. *imi tecta tyranni*: Ovid has used alliterative *tecta tyranni* of the palace of Lycaon (1.218) and of the domain of Neptune (1.276). The adjective he here adds, *imi*, is clever, but hardly a subversive allusion to Augustus, as has been suggested. Augustus did not live in a palatial home, and the palaces of the Palatine Hill did not come into existence until the times of his successors. Ovid merely refers to the way courtiers in every period haunt the seat of royal power. *artes . . . exercent* 445–46: the MSS tradition indicates convincingly that 446 was not in the Ovidian text that survived into the medieval period; the earliest evidence for it appears in corrections added to earlier MSS in the twelfth century. Then, it was adopted into later copies. Although it is probably a Humanist creation, it seems to be the work of someone who knew Ovid and recognized what the context required. Rather than leave a useless lacuna, I prefer to cite the ably conceived line as worthy of Ovid. To leave 445 as the intended end of the description of the dead would require taking *celebrant* with *artes*, which seems awkward after the way it has been used with the two objects in 444. I find no examples in Latin of that noun with the verb. Ovid does use the noun with *exercere*, however, in 2.618. These arts are presumably some of the noble activities that Vergil depicted in Elysium. Although some scholars object to the punishments taking place inside this City of the Dead and suspect the "incompetent Humanist interpolator," they argue from Vergil's, not Ovid's, account. Vergil had reserved Tartarus for the damned, as I noted above at 437, and he made pious Aeneas bypass it. Ovid, on the other hand, reorganizes all the details and subordinates the separate locales of Vergil so as to lead up, not to Elysium, but to his version of Tartarus, Juno's destination and a place where she easily and naturally (and fitly) enters. Thus, the fourth group of the dead provides an apt transition to the intended object of Juno's trip. The "interpolator," if he is such, is right on target.

447–48   *sustinet ire*: the main verb implies the extent of Juno's power; for a negative use, cf. the description of Apollo's inability to continue his wooing words in 1.530. *illuc*: perhaps the City of the Dead in general, but more specifically the place of the Damned. The build-up continues with the ablative absolute clause (reminiscent of the clause applied to Jupiter who gave up all for lust of Europa, *sceptri gravitate relicta* 2.847). Then the parenthesis sabotages the goddess. She "gave up so much" to her anger and hatred. Ending the sentence with her Vergilian tag, *Saturnia Iuno*, only clarifies her pettiness beside her epic prototype.

449–52   *sacro . . . corpore*: the adjective connotes, on the one hand, the supposed venerable majesty of the queen of the gods, but, on the other, the real weight of the deity; and Ovid thereby achieves a comic inconsistency that he exploits with the initial verb of 450. In 9.270, he playfully comments on Hercules' *augusta gravitate* as the hero achieves apotheosis. Similarly, he treats Cerberus with unserious precision. Vergil had placed him at the entrance to the domain of Dis, where those who crossed the Styx landed, and he had given him the poetic attribute, *latratu trifauci* (6.417). Building on that and choosing to imagine that all three heads bark simultaneously, Ovid spells it out in 451 with *tres . . . simul*. What a nuisance of a watchdog! *sorores / Nocte . . . genitas*: Juno addresses Allecto at *Aen.* 7.331 as *virgo sata Nocte*; and at 12.845 the poet himself reviews the three children of Night.

453–   *carceris*: Ovid turns the traditional Tartarus into a Roman prison.
54   *adamante*: Vergil has the columns of Tartarus made of solid iron (6.552). For Ovid, it is an incidental topos. Line 454 is virtually Golden, apart from the preposition; the picture, however, is ostentatiously grotesque—combing snakes from the hair. Ovid's sharp sense of strange detail has made original use of the fact that the Furies have snaky locks.

455–   *quam*: Juno. Ovid implies that, in the gloom, it is difficult to make
56   out the identity of visitors. *Sedes Scelerata vocatur* 456: the poet borrows the name and scene from Tibullus 1.3.67, but he makes a change. This *Sedes* is not simply the place of punishment for evil, as in Tibullus, but also the actual seat from which the Furies rise to greet the goddess (cf. 453).

457–   Tibullus listed some of the standard Damned at this point, and Ovid
59   follows his lead, almost certainly adapting the description of Tityos from Tib. 1.3.75–76. Vergil had a fuller version in *Aen.* 6. 595–600. Tityos, a Giant, tried to rape Latona and was dispatched by her son Apollo. His punishment is to be chained to the earth, spread out, so that his lusty liver may be daily attacked and consumed by vultures, as he suffers agony. Each night, it grows back, so that he may suffer the same agony again. *novemque / iugeribus*: the enjambement, which is Ovid's improvement of Tibullus, helps to bring out the huge area over which Tityos' body sprawls. Ablative where we would have expected accusative of extent of space. Tantalus comes next in Tibullus' list, too. As son of Jupiter, he was privileged to banquet with the gods. But when he betrayed their secrets to mortals, he was plunged into Hades. There he suffers a kind of torment that has generated our word *tantalize*: immersed in water up to his neck, Tantalus can never quite get any to drink: as soon as he tries to bend down to get some liquid, it seeps away from him. Overhead, a tree covered with luscious fruit stands, and a branch seems within reach, until he stretches out his hand to pluck the fruit: then, a breeze blows it just out of reach. Tibullus mentioned only the water, so Ovid has "corrected" his omis-

sion. In amiable fashion, he apostrophizes the Damned (and also facilitates his meter). *quaeque* 459: relative + *que*; with *arbor*.

460– Sisyphus, robber king of Corinth, whom Theseus killed, was com-
61 pelled as his punishment to roll a huge boulder up to the top of a steep hill. Before he could ever quite get there, however, it became too heavy for him, and, when he lost control, it rolled back, obliging him to start his eternal task again. Tibullus leaves him out of his abbreviated list; Vergil may refer to him anonymously at 6.616; but Lucretius, in his allegorization of the punishments of Hell, has a long explanation of Sisyphus (3.995 ff.) as the paradigm of the ambitious politician. *petis . . . urges*: Ovid refers to the two phases of the punishment in an order that reverses the usual: Sisyphus goes back to get the rock or he shoves it. The apostrophe and alliteration inspire Ovid later to an even finer effort: *inque tuo sedisti, Sisyphe, saxo* (10.44). Ixion had tried to rape Juno and was bound to a wheel by Jupiter; its perpetual turning was his proverbial punishment. Ovid has already fixed on the two phases of Sisyphus' misery, and so he contrives a similar two-phased sorrow for Ixion on the wheel, more witty than grave: he keeps fleeing and pursuing himself! That might perhaps suggest that Ixion himself plays the two roles in rape: the rapist (his crime) and the fugitive victim.

462– *suis letum patruelibus*: the word order emphasizes the shocking crime,
63 murder of cousins. That phrase and the feminine subject unmistakably alert the Roman audience to the Danaides, the notorious fifty daughters of Danaus and granddaughters of Belus king of Egypt, who resisted the marriage forced on them by their uncle and, on their wedding night, killed their new husbands. However, the poet postpones naming them as long as he can, and then he invents a special patronymic, *Belides*. The problem was to solve the intractable metrical difficulty of *Danaides*, which in Latin has three successive short syllables. In his lengthy narrative about these girls and their one heroic sister Hypermnestra (who alone spared her husband, *C.* 3.11), Horace uses the periphrasis *Danai puellas* (23), a device adopted by his contemporaries. *repetunt quas perdant* 463: in the antithesis of the two verbs, Ovid again captures the eternal frustration of the damned. The final word of the entire construction, *undas*, makes graphic the hopeless loss of what is needed, being also the "antecedent" which the poet typically delays. The Danaides were condemned perpetually to draw water in jars pierced at the bottom; the water leaked out as quickly as it was drawn.

464– *acie . . . torva*: the "grim look" of angry, threatening characters,
66 especially gods, is a commonplace of dramatic scenes, and Ovid uses it often. He has already worked this topos with the adjective + *vultus* (2.270) and *lumen* (2.752), and he will have *oculis* in 5.92. This

seems to be the only time that *acies* serves his purposes. *ante omnes* 465: Juno especially studies the hated Ixion (above, 461), and Ovid cleverly uses his mythological lore to give her a special argument for her proverbial anger. She turns to Sisyphus, who is a son of Aeolus— Ovid calls him *Aeolides* in 13.26. That reminds her of Athamas, also a son of Aeolus and therefore brother of Sisyphus. (There was still another brother, Salmoneus, whom Vergil plants among the Damned in *Aen.* 6.585 ff., but that is a special entry in the usual catalogue, and Ovid chooses to ignore it.)

466–
69
Juno's speech might be public, but it resembles the angry soliloquy in *Aen.* 1 rather than the open outrage of *Aen.* 7. Tisiphone would be moved only to delight by the goddess' indignation. Mainly, then, Juno talks to herself. Her fury is conveyed by the sputtering alliteration of 467. *superbum* 467: not warranted in what Ovid has told us. As often, Juno distorts the situation to serve her rhetoric and wrath. *cum coniuge* 468: Ino was proud of her nephew Bacchus (cf. 420–21), but not in a way to show scorn for Juno.

469–
71
Juno makes her request to Tisiphone, and Ovid, having sufficiently characterized her demonic passion in direct speech, quickly summarizes her exchange with the Furies. *causas odiique viaeque*: zeugma. Ovid joins the conventional traveller's theme, why he or she has come (cf. 2.33, 511 and 549 for the phrase *causa viae*), to the question provoked by Juno's ranting speech: why she hates Athamas so much. The genitive nouns, being of different relevance to *causa*, produce the witty result. *quidque velit* 470: as the third member of the tricolon, the indirect question goes aptly with the implicit questions suggested by the zeugma. *quod vellet*: we would have expected imperfect indicative, but Ovid has let the mood be attracted into subjunctive. The verb then takes a noun clause with *ne*: "what she wanted was, that not . . ." Juno has two goals, both of which she will achieve by this one alliance with Tisiphone: the long-range one of ending the kingdom of Cadmus and the immediate purpose of driving Athamas murderously mad. *furores* 471: cf. 431.

472–
73
confundit: the poet gives the impression of the jumbled argument that the irrational goddess produces, a mix of commands, promises, and prayers. The speeches that Vergil assigns to Juno amply define her rhetoric. *Iunone locuta* 473: ablative absolute, with skillful choice of the deponent verb, which then can take an object.

474–
75
canos . . . turbata capillos: "with her white hair mussed." Ovid makes this accusative serve in common both as one of respect (or Greek) with the participle and as direct object of *movit*. *reiecit ab ore colubras* 475: at 454, the Furies were combing snakes out of their hair, that is, combing their snaky tresses. Here, the hair and snakes seem to be falling down over the mouth of Tisiphone, so she tosses it (them)

back. The gesture of tossing the hair can be quite theatrical, and we may suspect that Ovid has wittily adapted a flamboyant move of contemporary Roman speakers.

476–
78
longis . . . ambagibus: same phrase in same metrical positions at 3.692. All business-like, Tisiphone refuses to beat around the bush with her response. *facta puta* 477: "consider done." *inamabile regnum*: Vergil had used this adjective of the Styx both in *G*.4.479 (at the time of Orpheus' descent) and then again in *Aen*. 6.438 for Aeneas' visit. Ovid makes the Underworld in general hateful and destructive of love. Ironically, though, Juno has brought her hate down to Hell and invoked the Furies to vent it on the "better sky," to which she departs just ahead of Tisiphone.

479–
80
laeta redit: Juno so rarely achieves a moment of happiness in Roman epic that Ovid must be referring irreverently to the end of Vergil's epic (*Aen*. 12.841–42), where she gained satisfaction from an arrangement with Jupiter (not the Furies) for the future of Italy. *lustravit* 480: Iris purifies Juno, who, it appears, has been tainted by contact with the Underworld. However, Ovid has left the impression that Hell was precisely where this vengeful goddess belonged.

Tisiphone Goes into Action (481–511)

True sister of Allecto, Tisiphone follows the pattern that the former had set for her in *Aen*. 7.341 ff. when she helped Juno start the war against the Trojans in Italy. Although Ovid builds up the scenic horrors here, Tisiphone simply ruins an innocent family of typically unheroic Ovidian victims, not significant epic personalities like Vergil's Amata and Turnus.

481–
85
The symbols of murder and madness are heavy in the attributes of the Fury: a torch and robe both dripping with red blood and a snake used as belt. *induitur . . . incingitur* 483: note that the first verb takes the Greek accusative, whereas the second has an instrumental ablative. The four abstract forces that accompany Tisiphone all have a symbolic function: Grief will desolate both Ino and her parents and eventually end Cadmus' reign; Panic and Terror (cf. 488–89) will be the immediate result of this demonic band; and Madness will carry out the purpose articulated by Juno at 471. *trepido . . . vultu* 485: the hectic, agitated look of the crazy.

486–
89
constiterat: i.e., Tisiphone's mere presence on the threshold caused the doorposts to shake. *Aeolii* 487: Athamas is a son of Aeolus; cf. 465 n. *infecit*: the malevolent Fury causes a "sickening pallor" to spread over the maplewood, as a foreshadowing of what will happen to the human residents. *Solque locum fugit* 488: since there is an

absolute opposition between the Sun and this creature of the Underworld, daughter of Night, wherever she appears she drives the sun to flight. Turning to the reactions of Ino and Athamas in the remainder of 488–89, the narrator registers their terror in paired clauses.

490–
92

obstitit . . . obsedit: both verbs, with compounding prepositions, emphasize the way Tisiphone malevolently blocked the exit of her victims. *infelix*: she will cause misery. *distendens* 491: spreading her arms helps the Fury to prevent escape through the doorway, especially since live snakes are coiled around. Ovid has enhanced his ugly picture here by the Golden Line organization and framing alliteration. *caesariem . . . colubrae* 492: in case we have forgotten 454 and the snake-haired Furies, the narrator explains his first clause with the second and adds framing alliteration.

493–
94

parsque . . . pars: we focus on the snakes, shaken out, like long hair, to "grace" her shoulders and breast. *lapsae*: they seem to slither free and actually coil hissing around her breasts. Three short clauses in 494 trisect the line at the alternate caesurae. *coruscant* 494: the third verb, which captures the swift flicking of the snake tongue, represents a unique touch of the poet. He takes a verb that is usually transitive and much-used by Vergil to describe the brandishing of weapons, but intransitively refers to the flickering light of things, and applies it to the menacing movement of the reptile tongue. That he sought a special meaning here is demonstrated by the fact that he nowhere else uses this verb.

495–
96

abrumpit: recalls the actions of Allecto in *Aen.* 7.346 ff., but he presses in a grotesque fashion the image of the snakes, as though they grow on the head of Tisiphone and so have to be yanked out by the "roots." Whereas Allecto hurled a single snake into the heart of Amata, Tisiphone has two victims and must use twice as much ammunition. *pestiferaque* 496: this epic adjective, which Ovid uses first to describe the monstrous Python of Delphi at 1.459, a typical poisonous snake, now receives a clever application as the hand, which holds and throws the poisonous reptile, becomes "pestiferous." Throughout this scene, the poet's eye fixes on details that improve on the traditional poetic repertoire, but do not engage us with the potential horror. *raptos*: careful use of the simple verb after the compound form in 495.

496–
99

illi: the line-end and enjambement emphasize the new subject, the snakes. *Athamanteosque* 497: to achieve this rare four-word hexameter, Ovid uses the adjectival form of Ino, as in 3.722, to get around the genitive, and creates this parallel form for Athamas. *inspirantque graves animas* 498: although many good MSS offer *animos*, the phrase of the Vergilian model, *vipeream inspirans animam* (*Aen.* 7.351), proves that the snakes breathe their noxious breath into the mortals. Only with the next sequence and *mens est*, do we hear how these fantastic snakes operate: they poison the mind. In this way, Ovid accounts for a symbolic metamorphosis. *sentiat ictus* 499: relative clause of characteristic. Ovid has adapted the word for the "striking" of ordinary snakes.

500–
5
attulerat secum: not content with the destructive results of her own snakes, which were quite sufficient for Vergil's Allecto, Tisiphone has brought along a monstrous blend of hellish poisons. In this detail, Ovid adds to the allegorical symbolism and attenuates the dramatic realism. In 501, he attributes poison to Cerberus, who usually appears as a terrifying three-headed dog, and associates him with a poisonous Viper, whom later at 7.408 he makes Cerberus' mother. In 502–3, he lists various aspects of madness, which are mixed in with this special poison. Those of 503 point to the insane crimes that will soon occur. *trita* 504: Ovid visualizes the ingredients as ground down to a powder and blended like chemicals. *sanguine*: fresh blood, found in Hell, provides a useful and symbolic base for the mixture, which was cooked like the proverbial witches' brew, stirred with a green stick of hemlock (a final poisonous flourish of the ingenious poet). When in 7.262 ff. Medea cooks up her brew to rejuvenate Aeson, she stirs it with an aged branch, which quickly becomes green to indicate the properties of the liquid (280).

506–
7
vertit . . . venenum: the MSS all give this verb, which has troubled some scholars, who have emended it to *vergit*. Although Lucretius 5.1010 did have the phrase *sibi venenum vergebant*, he did not mean that people poured poison for themselves (as would be useful here), but that they misused poison, accidentally applying or turning it against themselves. Ovid seems to be developing his topic of symbolic metamorphosis (madness) with a favorite thematic phrase, *vertere in* + accusative. But instead of saying the Fury turned their hearts into poison, he says that she turned poison into their hearts. *furiale*: this adjective prepares for the *furor* sought by Juno (471, 431; cf. 512).

508–
9
face iactata: for the torch, cf. 482. Tisiphone whirls it round and round her head. The use of this added symbol of madness comes from *Aen.* 7.456 ff., where Allecto attacked Turnus with a brand. Ovid's insistence on literary allusion and on allegory give his scene a distinctly non-Vergilian quality. Hence, the rhetorical juxtaposition in 509, *ignibus ignes* (as in 2.313).

510–
11
victrix: Vergil had given the same epithet to Allecto as she triumphantly addressed Juno (7.544) after completing her ruinous mission of starting the Italian war. *iussique potens*: "having achieved what she was ordered to do." Ovid remembers Vergil's reference to Allecto as *promissi potens* (7.541). *inania magni*: the first adjective suggests a poetic mocking of the second. *recingitur* 511: careful reminder of 483. Tisiphone marks her return by removing her snake girdle.

THE MAD PARENTS GIVE JUNO HER VENGEANCE (512–42)

Ovid's version here of the destruction of Ino and her family differs considerably from the story he composes on the same subject in *Fast.* 6.485 ff. In that narrative, Athamas goes crazy first; when he kills Learchus—no details given—Ino sadly gives the boy burial, then grabs up Melicertes from his cradle and rushes out, now insane both from fear and grief, and throws herself off the cliff.

512–
14
Aeolides: Athamas (cf. 465 n.). *media . . . in aula*: Ovid has left the setting vague until now. Madness here gains emphasis from the royal hall in which this crazy "hunt" will take place. Hunting, we recall, has been the death of two other children of Cadmus, Actaeon and Pentheus, both turned into beasts of prey by angry deities or mad pursuers. *io comites* 513: like mad Agave (3.713), Athamas calls for his hunting friends. Juno's malevolent imitation is working. *visa est mihi* 514: a nice example of ironically ambivalent Latin. As a true passive with dative of agent, which no doubt is what Athamas means, he has sighted the animals; but it can also mean to us that these "animals" only seem to be such to him. The lioness, of course, is Ino; the two cubs, his and her two children.

515–
19
utque ferae: genitive agrees with case of *coniugis*, the wife he now pursues as an animal. *amens*: cf. 299, where Tisiphone attacked Athamas' *mens* with her snake. *ridentem et . . . bracchia tendentem* 516–17: as often, Ovid describes the pathetic actions of the object of the main verb in a series of participial clauses, without revealing the violent verb that nullifies the child's gestures. He laughs at his father and holds out his arms in affection, not, as is more common with this phrase, in desperate appeal (cf. the similar pathos of young Itys in 6.640 ff.). *Learchum . . . rapit* 516–17: in other versions, Athamas actually hunts his son and kills him; Apollodorus 3.4.2.5 reports that he shot him down with arrows, believing that he had a deer as prey. The verb starts to take us away from the fantasy of hunting, which Athamas has voiced at 513–14, and Ovid switches to the image of a slinger, who whirls his sling and its projectile around his head a few times, then launches the stone (cf. David confronting Goliath). This is a unique description of a hand sling; elsewhere, Ovid describes the way the lead shot, when propelled through the air from a machine, especially the Balearic sling, grows hot (e.g., 2.727–28). In 9.216 ff., in an obvious variation on this double tradition, Hercules swings young Lichas around his head like Learchus here, then hurls him towards Euboea, at which Lichas, utterly terrified, congeals into ice! *discutit* 519: Athamas does not launch his son, as the sling-simile

might lead us to expect, but he smashes his brains out on a rock. The long-delayed verb, in initial position, is highly effective.

519–24 *concita mater*: with the grotesque death of Learchus, Ovid quickly changes his focus to Ino, who is in a violent emotional state, for which the poet uncertainly offers us a choice of explanations: either it is anguish over what has happened to her baby or mad frenzy like that of Athamas. The subsequent narrative never allows us to decide. *exululat* 521: the wild, uncouth howl that Ino utters need only imply her violent emotional state, but it can also prepare us for her Bacchic fantasy. Bacchantes howl in this fashion (cf. 3.528 and 725). *passisque . . . capillis*: hair left free to blow and toss in the wind is regularly an indication of disturbed passions; cf. 2.238 and 6.531. *teque . . . parvum . . . Melicerta* 522: the narrator apostrophizes the one remaining son and adds an adjective to generate pathos. The cry to Bacchus in 523, as the narrator specifically notes at 521, comes from an insane woman, not from the once-proud aunt. About to cause the boy's death, the mother is innocent as Agave, mother of Pentheus, was shown to be, when under the power of Bacchus (cf. 3.710 ff.). *Iuno / risit* 523–24: the goddess' laughter, emphasized by enjambement, is sadistic and disgusting. She has achieved her goal: cf. 428. *hos usus praestet tibi*: "these benefits or advantages (which you are enjoying) let Bacchus go ahead and provide you." *alumnus*: the final word, suspended by the verb of saying, rings sardonically by contrast with its earlier appearance at 421.

525–27 Ovid jumps forward to set the scene for the tragic suicide. The details are conventional: a cliff that hangs over the sea, its lower part hollowed out by the surf, but its summit projecting out over the water. He adds in 526 that, where the cliff is hollowed, it protects the water beneath it from rain! The clever paradox conveniently distracts us from the plight of Ino and son.

528–30 *occupat hunc*: since we have been through a miniature ecphrasis, the pronoun refers to the opening noun, *scopulus* (525). Ovid likes to use this verb to position someone in a particular place. At 1.667 he represented Argus taking a seat on a tall hill. In the parenthesis, the poet explains how Ino suddenly made it all the way to the top of the cliff, and blandly credits her madness. Craziness has its uses! *seque . . . mittit onusque suum* 529–30: Ovid employs marked hyperbaton to set up the suicide of Ino, then adds a second victim, *onus*, referring in metonymy to the baby she carries (cf. 522). *percussa recanduit unda*: a shocking change of focus and short-circuiting of our feelings. The narrator coolly looks at the way the water grows white with foam when the bodies strike it, but he refuses to waste feeling on the tragic souls.

531– *inmeritae neptis*: Venus was mother of Cadmus' wife Harmonia,

33 therefore grandmother of Ino. The innocence of Juno's victim, at least to a rival goddess, receives strong emphasis. *patruo* 532: Neptune, as Ovid quickly ensures that we know in 533. Neptune intervened against Juno, of his own accord, in the storm of *Aen.* 1 and, in response to Venus' appeal, in *Aen.* 5.779 ff. *blandita*: Venus is flattering and cajoling her uncle, but the format of her speech is that of a prayer, beginning with honorary epithet, followed by a relative clause listing some of his powers. *proxima . . . potestas* 533: the three brothers, Jupiter, Neptune, and Dis, divided up the universe: Jupiter got the major power with heaven and earth; Neptune was next with the waters; and Dis third with the Underworld. Since Ino now has plunged into his waters, Neptune can exert himself legitimately for her. *cui caelo*: two different datives. The relative goes with *cessit*, and the noun with *proxima*.

534– *miserere meorum*: Ovid tends to use the two Latin verbs *misereor*
35 and *miseror* as metrical variants with the same meaning. The first, as here, serves him primarily in prayers; the second, as above in 531, provides participles. Note also the alliteration. *iactari* 535: we last left Ino splashing into the water from the high cliff, enough to have killed most people. This verb implies that she and her son are still alive, tossed on the waves. *Ionio inmenso*: Ovid allows himself hiatus and then a double spondee (cf. 3.184) with a Neoteric flair that undermines Venus' supposed pathos. This "Ionian Sea" makes trouble for those who wonder about its relation to landlocked Thebes. Such a sea would be conventionally that part of the Mediterranean which stretched between Greece and southern Italy. It is clearly placed in *Aen.* 3.210–11, and Ovid himself in *Met.* 15.699–700 seems to refer to the crossing from Greece to Italy. It may be better to allow Ovid to be poetic and vague than to argue that Ino made it down to the Corinthian Gulf and that Ovid conceives of that body of water as part of the Ionian Sea.

536– *dis adde tuis*: she asks that the two victims be transformed into sea
38 gods. This is the physical metamorphosis that follows the dramatic changes of insanity that have dominated the narrative. *gratia*: this word has political overtones in Rome, and Ovid exploits them here in this scene of artful negotiation. Venus claims, then, that she has some "influence" in the sea. *si . . . spuma fui* 537–38: a good instance of Ovid's naughty use of a conditional clause. Formally, the condition should refer to a fact and therefore enhance the statement of 536. But logically we are entitled to inspect the if-clause and its mythological marvel (especially as stated here), and the doubts it inspires undercut the claim of 536. To hear Venus boasting of her origin as a bit of foam stirs humorous doubts. These doubts increase when we follow out the myth of her "birth." If born in the sea, then she was not the

daughter of Jupiter but of Uranus, and the vital force came from the genitals that Cronos had cut off his father and thrown into the sea. The story is less pretty than we would assume from the lovely painting by Botticelli; it also raises a question about her relation to Neptune. Thus, the if-clause produces a series of problems. *Graium . . . nomen* 538: the MSS tradition early became corrupt, making the easy mistake of reading *i* as *t* (encouraged by *gratia* 536) and ending up with *gratum*. Late medieval scribes recognized the error and corrected it: Venus refers to the etymology of her Greek name, Aphrodite, the first part of which comes from the Greek word for foam.

539– *adnuit oranti*: this language recognizes the context of prayer and
42 fulfillment. *illis*: ablative of separation. *quod mortale fuit* 540: Ovid here first uses a topic which he likes to employ somewhat irreverently when dealing with apotheoses. Human beings supposedly possess a mortal and immortal part, namely, body and soul. But Ovid plays with other distinctions between gods and human beings, which do not always point to superiority of the divinities. Mortals have moral compunctions, for example, whereas gods do not; mortals do not practice such vicious vengeance as we have seen vented by Juno. *maiestatemque verendam*: the only other context of the poem where Ovid uses this noun is 2.847, where Jupiter blithely abandons his "majesty" to pursue a sordid love affair, raping Europa by means of an animal form. Thus, Jupiter implicitly preferred a bestial body for himself and a mortal body for his beloved to the so-called venerable majesty of divinity. With that passage in mind, then, we may doubt that Ovid really wants us to admire the exchange of mortality for this kind of greatness. Later, he tends to undermine "majesty" even more, by using as a synonym *gravitas* and thus emphasizing the "weightiness" of the new god. When Hercules puts off his mortal limbs in 9.268 ff., Atlas (who carries the heavens on his shoulders) feels the unusual weight! For the apotheosis of Romulus in 14.824 ff., Ovid devises a different way of removing the mortal body. *nomenque simul faciemque novavit* 541: the verb, thematic in metamorphosis, covers in the two objects the physical change and the aetiology of the new names, which Ovid specifies in 542. We can imagine for ourselves how sea-gods differ in appearance from mortals. *deum* 542: the interlocked word order helps to emphasize the close association of mother and son as gods.

JUNO ALSO PUNISHES INO'S COMPANIONS (543–62)

Ovid introduces a story about Ino's friends who criticize the harshness of Juno. In anger, she transforms most of them into stone statues, frozen in their attitudes of grief, wilfully aiming to preserve them as "monuments of her savagery." A few, however, change into water birds that skim over the waves. Though the story is not original, we can see familiar motivations that inspire Ovid: he likes to register a terminal comment on events from contemporary onlookers, and he often likes to note how sympathy for a victim leads to metamorphosis for friends. The grief of Phaethon's sisters in 2.340 ff. illustrates the latter; the judgment of Diana's destruction of Actaeon in 3.253 ff. or the hesitation about how to judge Daphne's transformation in 1.577 ff. exemplifies the first. Here, he combines motifs by making the friends' judgment the cause of their metamorphosis, a further sign of Juno's anger.

543–
44
Sidoniae: it has been some time since we have been reminded that Cadmus and a few male companions (3.129) came from Sidon to found and settle Thebes. These women can hardly be first-generation Sidonians; after all, Ino was born in Thebes. At the end of this episode, Ovid more properly calls them residents of the Ismenus (562). *secutae / signa pedum*: Ino had fled wildly from Thebes to the mysterious Ionian Sea. Her loyal friends try to track her down. *primo videre novissima saxo*: Bömer carefully notes that Ovid fell into inconsistency here, because one does not leave tracks in solid stone. But he assumes that *primo . . . saxo* refers to the farthest rock over the water. We could rescue Ovid, I think, by arguing that he means the first rock of the cliff. There, though the trail disappeared, it was not hard to guess the rest.

545–
48
nec dubium: the irony is, of course, that no death, but metamorphosis has occurred. *Cadmeida*: earlier (3.287) a substantive with a Greek declension; here an adjective. *deplanxere* 546: as if affecting a high "epic" style, Ovid invents this compound, using it again only at 14.580. The prefix emphasizes the usual gesture of grief (cf. 2.584), and also contributes to alliteration. *scissae cum veste capillos*: more "poetic" style, accusative with past participle, as we have often seen with *indutus* (cf. 1270). Although he could have used present *scindens* and avoided the showy syntax, Ovid insists on this sequence: first fierce gestures of grief, tearing the hair and ripping down the dress, then pounding of the bare breast. *iustae . . . saevae* 547: dative with *deae* 548. Vergil made "savage Juno" a byword in his epic; and Ovid has already introduced the adjective at 2.470, when Juno victimized Callisto. *invidiam fecere*: "they caused her ill-will."

548–
50
convicia: mortals rarely get away with abuse of gods. *non tulit* 549: a favorite opening dactyl for impatience and indignation (cf. 1.753). *maxima . . . saevitiae monimenta*: the women regard Ino as an instance of Juno's unfair savagery, so she malevolently promises, apostrophizing them, to make them her supreme example (as if to outdo Vergil's

Juno). *res dicta secuta est*: events confirm her words. For this motif, cf. the narrator's comments after Tiresias' grim prophecy about Pentheus at 3.527.

551–
53
praecipue . . . pia: Juno starts her attack malevolently on the companion who best exemplifies *pietas*. The gods' refusal to honor prayers and to reward good people, the many ways in which *pietas* is thwarted and warped and *inpietas* triumphant, are insistent themes of Ovid. *persequar*: interruption of the short speech by the verb of saying separates the verb, perhaps significantly, from its fulfillment. *datura* 552: caught as she prepares to jump from the cliff, too, the woman turns into a sensational statue. *cohaesit* 553: as stone, she became united with the stone of the cliff.

554–
57
altera: a second, not of two, but of several. *solito . . . plangore*: the participle reminds us of the formulaic nature of the action. *temptatos . . . lacertos* 555: Ovid regularly picks up the main verb of a first clause and turns it into a past participle at the beginning of the second, but here he does something bolder. He has been talking about beating the breast, so we would expect *temptata* with or without *pectora*. That does not facilitate his meter, so he glides to another formulaic gesture: beating the upper arms (cf. 4.138). The woman went from one violent gesture to another or—irony encouraged by the conjunction *dum*—missed her breasts and hit her arms! *sensit riguisse*: the narrator stresses the sensations of this victim, changed at this critical moment of grief, expecting to strike a yielding part of her body and instead getting bruised on herself, a stone! *illa* 556: a third friend. *manus . . . tetenderat*: this histrionic gesture, implying grief and despair, as the pluperfect indicates, becomes background, ironically, when the hands turn to stone. Line 557 echoes 556, with the key change of *saxea*.

558–
60
huius: a fourth. *laniabat . . . crinem*: the formulaic gesture, mentioned above at 546, of tearing the hair. The continuous action of the imperfect will also be nullified in 559 by petrifaction. *duratos subito digitos* 559: the suddenness of the change is to be experienced by the reader (hence, *videres*). The fingers that claw at the hair remain, thwarted, to define this statue. *quaeque* 560: having given us a substantial list of victims, the narrator introduces a summary pronoun. The rather unusual pattern of four spondees helps to emphasize the way the lively gestures have been slowed down to stony immobility. As a statue group, these women epitomize the grotesque savagery of Juno.

561–
62
pars volucres factae: although the narration seemed to end at 560, we now hear of a different kind of metamorphosis inflicted on others. Birds serve as a common symbol of grief, with their piercing cries and seemingly restless flight, and for that reason Ovid may have added them. *nunc quoque*: regular topos (cf. 1.285) for suggesting continuity

between the original person and the changed form. *destringunt* 562: as Bömer notes, Ovid probably invented this verb, for both the *Met.* and contemporary *Fast*. It captures here the way the wing tips of a water bird brush the waves.

CADMUS BECOMES THE PREDICTED SNAKE (563–603)

When Cadmus carried out the Delphic commands to found a city and killed the snake that interfered with his efforts, he heard a mysterious voice that foretold his metamorphosis into a snake (3.97–98). Now, having apparently lost all his children and grandchildren, overwhelmed by misery, he and his wife leave this evidently cursed location at Thebes and travel northwest over the mountains into Illyria. There, still meditating on his misfortunes, he suddenly suspects that the snake of Mars at Thebes might have been sacred (*sacer* 4.571). At the thought, he invokes the gods' vengeance on himself and starts to turn into a snake. The process is unusually long, for the poem, and Ovid invites our humorous reactions, especially to the overdone anguish of Harmonia. She, too, finally asks to share his fate, and, after a grotesque scene in which Ovid lets her clasp the Cadmus-snake to her bosom, she gains her wish. Remembering their lost humanity, they remain harmless to people.

There are no full versions of this episode that have survived before Ovid's. Euripides let Cadmus' change be predicted at the end of his *Bacchae*, but it was not a scene that could be dramatized—or should be, as Horace *Ars P*. 186 insists. In addition, then, to Ovid's account, Apollodoros 3.5.4 and Hyginus 6 offer brief summaries. Cadmus eventually escaped his reptile form and ended up on the Islands of the Blest or in Elysium.

63–
68
nescit Agenorides: Cadmus is reintroduced with the same patronymic used for his first appearance at 3.8. Like the friends of Ino, he does not know of her apotheosis and infers the worst. *luctu serieque malorum* 564: as foreshadowing of this moment, Ovid warned in 3.131 ff. that Cadmus only seemed happy, and then he introduced Actaeon as "the first reason for *luctus*" (139). Now, Cadmus has many more occasions of grief. *ostentis* 565: also with *victus*. Ovid's narrative does not make clear what these many portents are. One such portent could be the snake, which Cadmus himself will mention at 571 ff. Perhaps Ovid expects us to assume that Cadmus also experienced the divine interventions at Thebes registered in Books 3 and 4. Euripides, for example, gave Cadmus a role in his *Bacchae*. *exit / conditor urbe sua* 566: the enjambement brings out the pathos of the departing city founder. *tamquam . . . premeret*: conditional clause of comparison.

fortuna . . . sua: Cadmus thinks Thebes itself accursed, failing to recognize that he himself carries the curse of Juno's hatred. Again, Ovid has broached this theme at the start (cf. 3.135 ff. and 141). *longisque erroribus actus*: once again, as he sets out on his wanderings, Cadmus becomes like Aeneas. Ovid uses the same words for Aeneas at 15.771, but in each case he draws on Vergilian language such as that at *Aen.* 6.532. *profuga* 568: another Vergilian echo, as at 3.7.

569– *malis annisque graves*: "weighed down by troubles and by age." The
70 mixture of literal and metaphorical usage for the adjective makes this a case of zeugma. *releguntque . . . labores* 570: Ovid evidently uses this verb as a synonym of *retractunt*. They are talking, not reading. The choice was influenced by the alliteration.

571– *sacer . . . serpens*: as noted in Book 3, Ovid developed an implicit
75 theme about mortals who saw what was sacred and hence taboo. That began with the serpent killed at the spring and emerged in the mysterious words of 3.98: *serpentem spectas. et tu spectabere serpens.* But nowhere did the narrator call that snake "sacred." *vipereos . . . dentes* 573: for the interruption of an adjective-noun unit by its apposition, cf. 2.515. Ovid had used the same words together at 3.103, then added the apposition in conventional manner. *cura deum* 574: the gods can punish or reward; hence, this phrase recurs at 8.724 to refer to the blessings conferred on the pious couple Philemon and Baucis. Cadmus did not know that the snake was under the care of Mars. After all his miseries, however, he asks to be made a snake under the protection of the gods: that is preferable to being a fate-blighted human being.

576– *serpens . . . alvum*: Ovid skillfully copies the words of Cadmus'
80 prayer in 575 to stress its fulfillment here. As above at 556–57, he utilizes the synonymous verbs *porrigo* and *tendo*, but here for obvious metrical reasons. Cadmus feels some of the metamorphosis in 577–78, namely, scales growing on his hardened skin and spots dappling it. He of course does not feel the colors, but Ovid wants us to see them. We subsequently learn that this is a harmless reptile, but the colors fit a deadly one, too. The one Cadmus killed was *caeruleus* (3.38). *cadit pronus* 579: this expands slightly on the first details of 576. Cadmus is flattened on his belly and chest. *commissaque . . . crura*: up to this point, arms and legs remain, and Ovid now proceeds to deal with them in a way that detracts from the sympathy of this transformation. Here, the legs become joined and then turned into the tapering tail of the snake. Artful hyperbaton enables the poet to describe the change and actually create the tail before he identifies the legs from which it was formed.

581– Having disposed of the legs, Ovid deals with the arms. We are invited
85 to picture this strange creature, stretched out prone on the ground, its

legs just now grown together, oddly waving its arms and talking! *bracchia tendit*: having developed a chiastic pattern to call attention to the arms, Ovid uses them for the histrionic gesture of loving appeal by husband to wife. *lacrimis . . . fluentibus* 582: the narrator affects to be a sentimental "tearjerker." *adhuc humana*: the transformation seems to be moving from the tail up, so the human face and voice still survive, for a while. *accede . . . accede, miserrima* 583: the repetition and the "pathetic" adjective, along with Cadmus' copious tears, all add up to mock-tragedy. After all, he is getting what he requested. Emphasis on touching the human part that remains, which he spells out in the details of 584–85, also invites us to smile because of the grotesque realism. *manumque / accipe* 584–85: holding the hand is a common final act of love to the dying. The distinction between dying and this awkward metamorphosis becomes the basis of humor. It is notable that, after calling so much attention to the arms and hands, Ovid says nothing about what happens to them (except at 592). That may be because the snake has no corresponding part into which they could turn.

586–89 *vult plura loqui*: loss of human voice now becomes the poet's focus, presented here as frustration of the desire to achieve human communication. The tongue, split or forked, as we say, can no longer produce recognizable words. *questus* 588: when the last human part of Cadmus tries to achieve pathetic complaints, all he can muster is hissing. *natura* 589: the essential constitution of this snake that once was articulate Cadmus.

590–94 Ovid turns attention to Harmonia, who speaks in a hysterical fashion to the snake. *nuda . . . feriens . . . pectora*: she has ripped open her dress and started beating her breasts in the conventional manner of those wildly grieving. *mane* 591: Ovid chooses a comic verb. The wife wants the husband to "stay," i.e., not to disappear by metamorphosis. *his exue monstris*: as though Cadmus has "put on" his new snake form, she asks him to "take it off." In 592–93, she goes into a series of breathless and ridiculous questions, which Ovid emphasizes by assigning five dactyls to both lines. *dum loquor, omnia* 593: from her words, we can infer that the transformation is complete at this point. *eandem . . . anguem* 594: she means the same kind of snake, not the same snake.

595–97 *lambebat*: it is not normal snake behavior to lick anything or anybody. Ovid contrasts this harmless, even loving action with the restless, menacing movement of most snake tongues. *veluti cognosceret* 596: conditional clause of comparison; cf. above 566–67. We are to assume that Cadmus' love survives inside the snake form. *dabat amplexus* 597: a snake "embraces" with its wreath of coils; those of the constrictor usually connote hostility, not love.

598–   *adest aderant*: juxtaposition of two forms of the same verb makes the
601   two-word parenthesis all the more objective in its precision. *terretur*:
       Ovid depicts the expected reaction to the snake and its apparent "attack"
       on Harmonia. Then with abrupt enjambement, he shows Harmonia
       strangely unfazed, caressing the reptile like a lover. *permulcet* 599: the
       verb can describe fondling a person or petting an animal. Ovid makes
       it plain that we are to see only a conventional crested snake, despite
       what Harmonia believes. *iuncto volumine* 600: although the old couple
       are now united in metamorphosis, Ovid chooses details that lack full
       sympathy. He represents them as coiled together, a union that many
       would find grotesque. *serpunt*: typical verb for snake movements. *nem-
       oris . . . latebras* 601: these hiding places in the woods regularly protect
       creatures from men.

602–   *nec fugiunt hominem*: unlike other snakes, this pair does not find
3   human beings hostile. *quidque prius fuerint* 603: indirect question.
       The snakes retain their human memory and disposition; they remember
       that they were human beings once. *placidi . . . dracones*: the adjective
       is emphatic; every snake so far in Cadmus' experience has been
       menacing and destructive, and these gentle ones bring his story to a
       quiet close. For another special snake that was peaceful and innocuous,
       cf. the description of the harmless snake that visited the altar for
       Anchises in Sicily, *Aen*. 5.84 ff.

THE ADVENTURES OF PERSEUS (604–803)

Ovid makes a transition to Perseus and his exploits by several
superficial connections. Cadmus and his wife are proud of their grand-
son Bacchus and his divine status, Perseus' grandfather denies the
divinity of Bacchus and also that Jupiter sired Perseus; and finally,
Cadmus and Acrisius (Perseus' grandfather) trace their roots back to
the same distant ancestor: Cadmus through Agenor to Poseidon, and
Acrisius through three intermediaries to Belus (Agenor's brother) and
so to Poseidon. Ovid will refer to that remote relationship at 772 by
illicitly using the patronymic *Agenorides* for Perseus. Grandfather
Acrisius merely provides a frame for Perseus' adventures, which Ovid
typically develops for their own interest.

Although Perseus is best known as killer of Medusa, Ovid begins
his story just after that event, as Perseus was flying home. Cruising
above North Africa, the hero dropped blood from the Gorgon on to
the sands of Libya, which caused them to swarm with snakes. Then,
he proceeded to the kingdom of Atlas, who greeted him so suspiciously
and violently that Perseus felt obliged to use the Gorgon's head to
sedate him permanently as a stone mountain (621–62). Once more
soaring aloft, the hero soon spotted the distress of Andromeda, Ethio-

pian princess; deeply infatuated with her beauty, he rescued her from the sea monster and claimed her as his bride (663–739). Preparations were made for the wedding, including a premarital banquet, at which his hosts persuaded Perseus to tell how he killed Medusa and why she alone of the Gorgons had snakes for hair (765–803). Here, Perseus' narrative stops and Book 4 ends, leaving for Book 5 the entirely different narration of the disturbed wedding.

Ovid has deliberately shaped his account so as to minimize our concern with the conquest of the Gorgon, sliding it in briefly—he assigns it less that fifteen lines—after expatiating on the encounter with Atlas (which is more usually connected with Hercules) and the romantic rescue of Andromeda. He has also created a connection with Cadmus' misfortunes that ignores the usual account of Perseus' origins and the character of Acrisius. Both Hyginus 63–64 and Apollodoros 2.4.1 ff., in their review of the full myth of Perseus, start from the prophecy to a relatively harmless old Acrisius that his daughter Danae would give birth to a son who was destined to kill Acrisius. When he tried to prevent that fate by barring Danae from marriage and shutting her up in a secure tower, Jupiter came to her in a golden shower, raped her, and thus sired Perseus. Still trying to avoid the inevitable without committing murder, Acrisius had Danae and her baby sealed in a wooden case and thrown into the sea, where, he hoped, they would die. Saved and raised at the court of King Polydectes on the island of Seriphos, Perseus grew to manhood and went on the dangerous quest for the head of Medusa. In the usual story, then, when Perseus did return victorious, he accidently killed his beloved grandfather, who was admiringly watching him compete in a discus contest, by hitting him with the discus. Ovid's details about impious Acrisius (which he had already introduced at 3.559–60) would seem to call for punishment of the blasphemer, as Pentheus, for example, was punished. But for Ovid, when the opportunity arrives, Acrisius will have ceased to be thematically relevant.

Transition to Perseus (604–20)

04–
6

ambobus: the two snakes, formerly Cadmus and Harmonia. Ovid has attributed to them some vestiges of humanity inside their snakeskins, and so here he imagines them feeling consolation. *versae . . . formae*: objective genitive. *nepos* 605: Bacchus. *debellata . . . India*: for Bacchus' conquest of India, cf. the hymn in his honor, 4.20–21. The verb occurs only here in Ovid; other Augustan writers use it to describe real, not mythical warfare. *positis . . . templis*: we have only heard about altars for Bacchic worship. Temples for Dionysos in Greece or for Bacchus or Liber in Rome were not common. The narrator, with

his flowing five dactyls, seems more interested in forcing a transition
than in achieving accuracy.

607–
9
Abantiades . . . Acrisius: Acrisius was son of Abas and grandson of
the single good daughter of Danaus, Hypermnestra. The patronymic
also refers to Perseus at 767a. *ab origine . . . eadem* 607: the identical
origins of Acrisius and Cadmus are explained above in the introduc-
tion. The three extra generations on Acrisius' side prove that Ovid
has artificially forged this link. *qui . . . arceat* 608: relative clause
of characteristic. For this peculiarly Ovidian version, cf. 3.559–60.

609–
11
genusque . . . non putat 610: Ovid begins a new thought and launches
into unorthodox enjambement, then a transition to Perseus, Acrisius'
grandson. The indicative, a more difficult reading, is supported by
good MSS, whereas a few less trustworthy ones have tried to continue
the subjunctive. *deum*: though this appears in the same metrical posi-
tion and looks the same as *deum* of 609, it should be read as genitive
plural (= *deorum*). *neque enim*: the explanatory particle suggests now
the priority, for the narrator at least, of the story of Perseus. Because
he doubted Jupiter's role in siring his own grandson, Acrisius was
predisposed to doubt the paternity of Jupiter in connection with
Bacchus. Ovid hurries along in 610 with five dactyls (as above in
601, 603, 606, and 607). He does not want the meter to slow him or
us down. *pluvio . . . conceperat auro* 611: the narrator so words his
relative clause that we cannot be sure whether he merely summarizes
the familiar myth about Jupiter or whether he invites us to consider
it a preposterous story that Danae told Acrisius and he understandably
doubted.

612–
16
Acrisium: connected by hyperbaton with *paenitet* 614. The temporal
adverb *mox* is vague. In fact, Ovid will never describe Acrisius'
moment of deserved regret. *praesentia veri*: the narrator seems to
foreshadow a conclusion like that of Pentheus' impiety, which Tiresias
predicted. *violasse deum* 613: his irreverence toward Bacchus (cf.
608–9). *non agnosse nepotem*: this alliterative negative formulation
conceals the whole story about sealing Perseus and Danae in a chest
and throwing them into the sea, to die. It also reiterates the theme of
grandsons sired by Jupiter. *inpositus . . . caelo* 614: Ovid has already
used these words to describe the apotheosis of Callisto and Arcas
(another son of Jupiter). So here he refers to Bacchus, now definitely
become a god in heaven. But that serves primarily to set up a parallel
for Perseus, chiastically elaborated: the hero is in the air, a mortal
flying! *viperei . . . monstri* 615: the entire line gives a showy poetic
circumlocution for the familiar end to the Gorgon episode. The hero
flies home with the snaky head. *aëra carpebat* 616: Ovid seems to
vary a regular phrase, *carpere viam/s* or *iter* (cf. 2.549 and 3.12), in
order to catch the oddity of this flying traveller. *stridentibus alis*: same

phrase in *Aen.* 1.397 describes the flying of swans. Perseus' wings whistle, presumably, because of the speed of his flight. Ovid assumes we know that these wings were not naturally grown from the back, but tied to the feet at the ankles. He will describe them at greater detail in 665–67 and give them their technical name of *talaria*.

**17–
20** *victor penderet*: from the perspective of one looking up, birds often seem to hang in the sky. The noun points up the paradox of this "bird," who is also a hero. *harenas*: the sands refer literally to the stretches of Libyan desert that abounded in snakes. Lucan makes dramatic use of this snake-infested locale in 9.696 ff. *quas . . . exceptas . . . animavit* 619: participial subordination. Translate as though Ovid wrote *excepit animavitque*. The Gorgon's blood has life-giving properties, though monstrous, which contrast with the life-destroying, petrifying power of her dead stare. *unde* 620: Ovid goes on from the mythical metamorphosis to an aetiology.

Perseus and Surly Atlas (621–62)

**21–
24** *per inmensum*: Ovid has invented this phrase, but he has picked up the substantive for heavenly spaces from Lucretius, e.g., 1.74. *ventis discordibus*: the "brawling winds" were a poetic commonplace; Vergil has the same expression in *Aen.* 10.356. Perseus' aimless, wind-swept flight has been invented by Ovid; one result is that the hero arrives at Atlas' land like an exhausted, needy voyager. *exemplo nubis* 622: "like a cloud." Clouds do scud around the sky, but hardly the way Perseus is said to travel; and it is odd to imagine the slender mortal as a large dark rain cloud. Driven off course, deep inland, Perseus looks down on totally land-locked regions, then supposedly on the entire world. Ovid is taking great pains to keep us and Perseus from his next adventure.

**25–
26** The poet ends this sequence by explaining what he means by the "whole world." Perseus is carried to the four quarters: north and south in 625 (in terms of the Bear constellations, associated with cold, and Cancer, which prevails in the hottest part of the year), west and east in 626 (in the familiar terms of setting and rising sun).

**27–
30** *veritus*: like a sailor, Perseus distrusts aerial navigation by night. *Hesperio . . . in orbe* 628: the hero stops in the west, but in North Africa, not in the Italy that Aeneas first knows as Hesperia. *regnis Atlantis*: the apposition interrupts the phrase it qualifies (cf. 4.573). *petit requiem* 629: this modest request for hospitality should have been granted. It will be repeated in direct speech at 642. *dum . . . evocet*: subjunctive in temporal clause. The names of Lucifer and Aurora connote the next morning.

31– *cunctis*: dative of reference with *praestans*. *corpore*: ablative of speci-

34   fication. Atlas (whom Ovid briefly mentioned at 2.296) is a giant,
      son of Iapetus like Prometheus (cf. 1.82). *aequora subdit* 634: the
      western sea provides water for the thirsty horses. *fessos . . . axes*:
      the noun by synecdoche refers to the chariot of the Sun; the adjective
      is transferred from the horses or their driver. Have we forgotten that
      in 2.296 Atlas already supported the axle of the sky?

635–   *vicinia nulla premebant* 636: Ovid uses singular *vicinia* as a collective
38   noun, meaning "neighbors" (as in 2.688), and thus allows himself
      a plural verb. From Atlas' perspective (which is that of a solitary
      misanthrope), neighbors would put unwelcome pressure on his exis-
      tence. The poet represents him as a miser or hoarder of his wealth,
      which especially consists of the famous golden apples. There is no
      mention here of a special garden or the Hesperides nymphs who guard
      the apples. The gold receives strong emphasis in 637–38, notably
      in 638, where the repetition and the four spondees concentrate our
      attention.

639–   Perseus' speech is brash and conceited. Without any polite words to
42   Atlas, he gives him a choice of two reasons for admiring him: his
      birth as son of Jupiter or his deeds (*rerum* 641). On the basis of these
      two claims, which do not impress Atlas, he makes his brusque request
      for hospitality. In 640, note the chiastic pattern that brings the repeated
      forms of *generis* together. In 641, Perseus pompously uses four spon-
      dees to make his marvelous claim; then, he hurriedly launches into a
      series of dactyls in 641.

642–   *vetustae / sortis*: objective genitive with *memor*. Ovid seems to have
45   invented this prophecy; its effect is to give Atlas some justification
      for spurning Perseus (whose rudeness Ovid has taken pains to estab-
      lish). *Atla* 644: according to Bömer, the only instance of this vocative.
      The MSS disagree as to the spelling; this seems to qualify as the more
      difficult reading. *auro*: the key word, ablative of separation, is placed
      at the line-end for emphasis. *hunc praedae titulum* 645: the demonstra-
      tive has been transferred from *praedae*. *titulus* regularly, as here,
      acquires the meaning of "glory" or "reputation" by metonymy, from
      the inscription or title that commemorated great deeds. We have some
      doubts as to the greatness of the feat. *Iove natus*: the oracle means
      Hercules; Perseus' egotistic identification seems to make him the
      villain prophesied.

646–   *id*: the prophecy. *clauserat*: Ovid continues pluperfect background
48   tenses that began at 643. The ring of mountains around the orchard
      appears to be another of his inventions. *draconi* 647: the guardian
      snake, well established for this myth before Ovid, is a familiar motif
      in such stories (cf. the snake guarding the Golden Fleece). Dative
      both as indirect object and agent. *arcebatque* 648: the tense changes

to imperfect to indicate continuity in this exclusiveness. Atlas seeks security from strangers as well as neighbors (cf. 636).

49–
52
huic: Perseus. *gloria rerum*: Atlas picks up Perseus' boastful remarks (641) and contemptuously dismisses them as lies. Initiating a pair of clauses in anaphora, Ovid postpones the common verb until the end of 650. Atlas does not deny the birth of Perseus (unlike impious Acrisius, 610–11), but he menaces the young hero with the failure of his "glory" and father. Then, without waiting for the youth to respond, he proceeds to act like a bully, confidently relying on the difference in their sizes. Ovid sets up the scene by devoting 651 entirely to the violent behavior of the giant, then using 652 to portray the mild actions of Perseus as the innocent object of violence. *placidis miscentem fortia dictis* 652: Perseus for the moment displays the nobility of a true Roman: he talks peacefully, firmly, and courageously.

53–
56
viribus: ablative of respect. Ovid carefully repeats the word in the same position within the parenthesis that follows. As usual, mere brawn fails to win in this poem. However, Perseus' reliance on his "secret weapon" seems far too sadistic to win our favor. *parvi* 654: genitive of value. *gratia . . . munus*: the second term, being unexpected, involves grim irony. Had Atlas welcomed Perseus and recognized his connections (*gratia*), then a gift from the visitor or an exchange of gifts would have been customary. The "gift" that Perseus now offers is anything but real. *laevaque a parte*: this direction may have overtones of the sinister and magical, but the proffered hand would be the left (for Perseus would have his sword in his right). *Medusae*: in hyperbaton with *squalentia . . . ora* 656. *ipse retro versus* 656: Perseus turns away so as not to be subject to petrification from the Gorgon's eyes. Much will be made of this motif in the battle against Phineus' supporters in 5.179 ff. Perseus will warn his allies, as he pulls out the head: *vultus avertite vestros.*

57–
60
The metamorphosis briefly described. *quantus*: Ovid omits the coordinate and self-evident *tantus*. The chain of mountains named Atlas stretched from the Atlantic across North Africa to near Carthage. Vergil had introduced an anthropomorphic Atlas range into *Aen.* 4.246 ff., for Ovid to appropriate here. His Atlas also had "shoulders" and "beard." Ovid more specifically allocates the transformation of the human parts: the hair into trees or foliage on the mountain slopes; the hands that have molested the guest (cf. 651) into long ridges, together (more logically) with the towering broad shoulders; the head into *cacumen*; and finally bones into the stony substance of the mountain (a reversal of the miracle that Pyrrha and Deucalion achieved after the Flood).

60–
altus: participle. *sic di statuistis* 661: the poet apostrophizes the gods

62   who, he reveals, have for some reason intervened at this point and
       turned this giant-mountain into something they can put to use. *omne*:
       repeats the adjective of 660 in the same position, but now in effective
       enjambement and hyperbaton. Here, Ovid catches up with the anachro-
       nism of 2.296, where Atlas was already supporting the sky on his
       shoulders.

Perseus and Andromeda (663–764)

       Ovid's principal story about Perseus concerns his heroic rescue of
       Andromeda. It is a typical Ovidian account of love, with the usual
       touches of good-humored irony, combined with the fantastic defeat
       of a monster. Andromeda's mother Cassiope (cf. 738) invidiously
       compared the beauty of the Nereids with hers, and they complained
       to Neptune, who sent a sea-monster to plague the coast of Ethiopia.
       Consulted as to how to rid themselves of this monster, king Cepheus
       and his wife learn that only by sacrificing their daughter Andromeda
       to the *belua* can they free their land. Andromeda, chained to a cliff
       by the sea, awaits her doom as Perseus chances to fly overhead. It is
       love at first sight. His inquiries about her lead to his heroic resolve
       to win her hand by destroying the monster. Which he proceeds to do,
       without resorting to Medusa's head. Ovid's genial, humanized account
       probably goes back to Euripides' romantic tragedy of 412, which
       Aristophanes also comically exploited in *Thesmophoriazusae* of 411.
       Apollorodos covers the details in 2.4.3.2 ff.

663–   The final verb of 662, *requievit*, which referred to the skies resting
65   on Atlas, also implied that Perseus, having overcome all opposition,
       gained the night's rest he sought (629, 642). In his transition, Ovid
       assumes that the night has ended and our hero starts the day. *clauserat
       . . . ventos*: the winds (cf. 621 ff.) that had so hampered Perseus' flight
       the previous day have died down, shut up by Aeolus (*Hippotades*); cf.
       Aen. 1.52 ff. The patronymic is a unique construction of Ovid, to
       tease the mythical lore of his audience. *admonitorque operum* 664:
       this appositional phrase teases some more, being placed considerably
       before its proper noun. Lucifer, the morning star, reminds human
       beings to be about their daily tasks.

665–   *pennis . . . resumptis*: talaria or ankle-wings, alluded to in 616, but
67   named at 667 below. Perseus untied them at night. *teloque . . . unco*
       666: special hooked sword used by the hero, known as *harpe* in Greek.
       aëra findit 667: he is flying once again (cf. 616).

668–   *circumque infraque*: this "epic" doublet of adverbs flamboyantly refers
71   to the many peoples everywhere below, from which Ovid will select

in 669 the Ethiopians. *Cepheaque*: Cepheus, ruler of Ethiopia, here introduced as an adjective. *maternae . . . linguae . . . poenas* 670–71: Andromeda is the innocent victim of her mother's blasphemy. *iniustus*: Ovid, as a follower of Euripides, denies the justice of the oracle's penalty. A few MSS miss that point and prosaically make the adjective modify *poenas*.

672–
75

quam: Andromeda. *simul*: conjunction (in prose, *simul ac*). *bracchia*: Greek accusative. This scene of the maiden chained to the cliff was often reproduced in Roman wall paintings. *Abantiades*: Perseus, a distant descendant of Abas (cf. 607). What follows, 673–75, is an unusually long parenthesis, which amusingly interrupts the normally close association of (first) seeing and loving. The narrator intrudes the fussy facts that compare the girl to a marble statue and thus invite the audience to refer to its own familiarity with artistic versions of this story, in sculpture and painting. Only slight movement of her hair and some fearful tears betray the distinction from perfect art. *marmoreum . . . opus* 675: Andromeda had a beautiful body, white like marble, nude like most statues. The adjective was used in 3.481 (cf. 419) to convey the beauty of Narcissus. *trahit . . . ignes*: Perseus "catches fire" with love. For a few moments, though, he remains unaware of his condition.

676–
77

et stupet: Ovid more commonly registers the stunning effect of sudden passion by *obstipuit*, a verb which he uses in the similar situation of Mercury in flight, who spots Herse at 2.726. *et visae*: most of the MSS have meaningless *exiguae*, which some then have inadequately emended to *eximiae*. That implies that there was hopeless corruption in the MSS tradition and that this reading, which catches Ovid's meaning, is a medieval emendation. The connective *et* is needed, and the participle *visae* and *formae* seems perfect. Same phrase in 3.416 to render the violent start of Narcissus' love for his reflection. *quatere* 677: another sign of corruption in the tradition appears here, where most early MSS were deceived by the elision and transmitted *quater*. The wings that Perseus almost fails to flap, remember, are those on his heels. *oblitus*: Ovidian characters forget necessary actions or things under traumatic emotional stress. Perseus' prototype is Callisto, who almost forgets her arrows after the rape (2.439). In 13.763, Polyphemus, overcome by love, forgets his herds, *oblitus pecorum*.

678–
81

stetit: the flier has descended to the earth and taken up a position near Andromeda. *o . . . digna*: the exclamation sets up a speech more courtly than passionate, as Perseus wittily advocates the metaphorical "chains of Love" for the captive. *cupidi . . . amantes* 679: implicitly, though he reveals his own desires, the speaker idealizes mutual love and satisfaction. *nomen terraeque tuumque* 680: although this is hardly the moment for Andromeda to give the formulaic account of her home and family, Perseus acts like a courtier at a tea dance! The critical information lies in the next indirect question of 681.

681–
84
Like Perseus, who seems overly formal for the situation, Andromeda cannot break out of the virginal mode that society prescribes for her, even at the risk of her life. Since she has not officially been introduced to this man, it is "improper" for her to speak to him. *virum virgo* 682: emphatic juxtaposition. *modestos . . . vultus*: the exact nature of the girl's embarrassment is left to our erotic imagination. In ancient wall paintings and more recent pictures, artists regularly represent Andromeda as chained nude to the cliff. Whether that is the motive or she simply wants to avoid meeting the passionate look of Perseus, the girl hoped to hide her face. *si non religata fuisset*: Ovid develops a motif made famous by Vergil *Aen.* 2.405 ff., who described Cassandra, prevented by bonds from making the gesture of supplication, as appealing to heaven with burning eyes. Later, in some Christian accounts of female martyrs, Vergil's and Ovid's scenes will be reused. *quod potuit* 684: supply *id* as antecedent; this is our parenthetical phrase "what she *was* able to do." Ovid smiles rather than evokes real pathos here: Andromeda may fill her eyes and so block out the sight of the man, but she hardly conceals any part of herself except her eyes from him.

685–
88
instanti: grammatically connected with *indicat* 688. The two words, then, frame the entire sentence. *delicta*: what finally conquers the girl's reserve is her anxiety not to be misinterpreted, as though she were concealing some guilty acts on her part. Again, Ovid projects us into the wrong world, urbane Roman society rather than this exotic adventure. The echo of 680 in 686 gets rid of those formulae, and in 687, alluding to 670, the girl answers the query of 681: her mother's pride in her own beauty and her foolish boasts have doomed the daughter to pay the price.

688–
90
Without giving Perseus a chance to reply, Ovid rushes on in the narrative with a simple *et* as connective. In fact, in the ablative absolute he suggests that Andromeda had more to say when the monster loudly called attention to itself. *inmenso . . . inminet* 689–90: alliteration reinforces the picture of the huge beast that sprawls over the water. In case we need it, Ovid repeats the alliteration and the idea in a second clause in 690.

691–
94
Andromeda's reaction to the monster, a piercing shriek, is rendered in five long syllables. The narrator then turns attention to her father Cepheus and her mother Cassiope, who stand uselessly by. *iustius illa* 692: because of her guilt (cf. above 671–72 and 687). *nec secum auxilium, sed . . . fletus / plangoremque ferunt* 693–94: similar to the effect of zeugma. Practical aid is what Andromeda needs at this

juncture, not a futile show of tears and breast-beating. *Auxilium* uses the common verb in an entirely different manner from the other two objects.

695–
96
cum sic hospes ait: cum-inversum clause abandons the vain parental despair to focus on the intrepid stranger, who speaks with heroic confidence. Perseus acts as brashly here as earlier with Atlas. *longa . . . tempora . . . brevis hora*: standard antithesis of the hero, who dismisses tears and anxieties, declaring: "There is no time to lose" or "This is not the occasion to waste on tears," etc. Perhaps with deliberate antiheroic irony, Ovid assigns Perseus the longest possible line of five dactyls in 696. *ad opem . . . ferendam*: gerundive; the hero stresses the necessity for action.

697–
701
hanc: he points to chained Andromeda. *peterem*: regular word for wooing and asking parents for the hand of a girl (cf. the wooing of Daphne at 1.478). Perseus expresses total confidence that his parentage and his conquest of Medusa would establish his superiority over all rivals. Little does he know that Andromeda has already been betrothed to another, Phineus, brother of Cepheus, who will make his dramatic and violent appearance at the opening of Book 5. *illa*: ablative of origin (like *Iove*). Danae's connection with Jupiter is described by Perseus in the ponderous four spondees of 698 that supposedly turn rape into something grand; but Perseus' viewpoint is not shared by poet or audience. *auro* 698: cf. 611. *Gorgonis anguicomae Perseus superator* 699: there was no need for Perseus to repeat his name so ostentatiously after 697, except that he is driven to assert his importance. The words with which he makes his claim here reinforce his pomposity: Ovid has invented the second and fourth words, to give Perseus a false self-chosen epic patina as he acts out the role of the elegiac lover. *et alis*: the unusually late start of the run-on makes this claim sound almost breathless: I can fly, too! *praeferrer . . . gener* 701: a series of spondees, seven heavy syllables, are dissolved by the noun and its short syllables, as if Ovid were letting Perseus, in spite of his arrogance, suggest the anticlimax that he is.

701–
3
tantis / dotibus: the noun comes as a surprise in this context of marriage, because a suitor does not offer a dowry to the bride, but gets one. However, the word has the secondary sense of "endowments" or "special gifts, especially of nature," and so proud Perseus proposes to offer the listed assets (his birth and heroic feats) to his bride and her family. *meritum*: a meritorious action that is especially appropriate to the situation. He will spell that out in 703. *faveant modo*: subjunctive in proviso clause. *paciscor* 703: although it may seem that Perseus gives an unconditional promise to rescue Andromeda, the succeeding lines prove that an agreement or *pactum* exists, recognized by both parties. He promises to save the girl if the parents promise to make

him their *gener*. Thus, we might translate: "I guarantee that your daughter (if you engage her to me) will be saved by my heroism."

704–   *legem*: the implicit condition, that they will marry Andromeda to
5   Perseus if he rescues her. *et orant*: this clause adds new detail; it does not function with the previous object. The desperate parents resort to tearful prayers in the presence of this confident teenager. *super* 705: "in addition." Having already promised their daughter, the parents now add a royal dowry, if only Perseus can pull off the seemingly impossible. Which of course he can.

706–   *ecce velut navis*: while we have focused on the parents and Perseus,
10   the monster, seen approaching in menacing fashion in 689–90, has moved ever nearer. With *ecce*, Ovid directs our eyes back to it and compares it to a steadily approaching enemy warship. In its movement through the water, its fearsome size, and probably its dangerous jaws (which resemble the battering "beak" of the ship), the monster is like the ship. *sulcat* 707: it creates a furrow or, as we say, "plows" the sea. *acta lacertis*: a reminder that the only steady motive power for ancient ships came from rowers, not from the wind. *dimotis . . . undis* 708: this ablative absolute picks up the sense of *sulcat*. Ovid unbalances his simile to focus on the distance between monster and victim. *Balearica . . . funda* 709–10: Ovid has already in 2.727 referred to this slingshot, which Balearic islanders made a striking weapon of the Roman army. In both cases, he indulges in anachronism, which somewhat undermines the epic pretensions of this scene. What the range of the sling was, we are not told; evidently, though, the monster was close. *medii . . . caeli*: partitive genitive with *quantum*. "As much air as a Balearic sling could pass through with its propelled lead shot."

711–   As in 695, Ovid uses *cum*-inversum to focus his narrative. *tellure*
13   *repulsa*: Perseus pushes off from the ground and launches himself into the air. Ovid says "into the clouds," but that would hardly allow his shadow to be projected on the surface of the sea, as it is in 712. The chiastic word patterning in the two clauses of 713, along with the assonance, calls our attention to the literary art of the narrator rather than to his narrative.

714–   *Iovis praepes*: with more epic grandiloquence, the poet introduces a
17   new simile, about an eagle attacking a snake. The eagle is Jupiter's bird (cf. 6.517), but Ovid has chosen the periphrasis here aptly, since Perseus is also Jupiter's winged son. The hostility between eagles and snakes provided a regular source of comparisons: Ovid used one to render the struggle of Hermaphroditus in 4.362 ff. to free himself of Salmacis. *praebentem Phoebo . . . terga* 715: the snake is innocently sunning itself. That does not exactly agree with the actions of the monster, and so it confuses our attitude toward the beast. *occupat*

aversum 716: the eagle catches its prey unawares. *neu = et ne*, introducing a negative purpose clause. In 717, Ovid concludes his elaborate figure with a Golden Line, which begins with a fine epic compound. The talons that the eagle drives fast into the snake's neck as it launches its sneak attack are immediately likened to the sword that Perseus buries in the sea monster.

718–20   *celeri . . . volatu*: the flight of the eagle and of Perseus is alike swift. *praeceps*: echo of *praepes* 714. *terga ferae* 719: cf. *terga* 715. The wound to the right shoulder is serious and agonizing, but not fatal. *Inachides* 720: another epic circumlocution for Perseus. It refers to the Inachus River in Argos, where he was sired. *curvo tenus . . . hamo*: Ovid has already described this special sword at 666 and will again at 727. Partway up the blade was a hook or sickle-like projection. So the hero has flown down from nowhere and suddenly plunged the blade up to the hook in the right side.

721–23   *laesa*: i.e., the monster (*fera*). Ovid describes two antithetical movements, high into the air or plunging down into the sea, before he resorts to still another poetic comparison. *versat* 723: like the boar, which turns to face and then hurl itself against its attackers, the monster swings head and body around to locate Perseus. *circumsona*: more "epic" display, as Ovid coins a compound.

724–27   *ille*: focusing again on the hero, Ovid shows him reacting to this effort of the beast to turn and crunch him with its jaws. Using his advantage of flight-mobility, Perseus darts here and there, quite out of reach, and attacks one exposed spot after another. It is hardly a fair or heroic fight. *nunc . . . nunc . . . nunc* 725–26: this triad of easy attacks corresponds to the triad of vain efforts (stressed by repeated *modo* in 721–22) to fend Perseus off. *terga . . . obsita conchis* 725: like a ship or a whale, this sea-creature has its back covered with barnacles. *desinit in piscem* 727: it ends in flukes of a fish, as does the whale's body. Although the tail is far away from the dangerous jaws, Ovid does not seem to realize how dangerous it could be in itself and how little damage a wound to it would cause.

728–29   *mixtos cum sanguine fluctus*: like badly wounded animals during hunts, this monster starts to cough up blood, as well as floods of water, for a suitably epic effect. This causes the only danger Perseus incurs, for his winged ankles become soaked by the bloody spray and start to lose their levitation! Later, Icarus is warned by his anxious father Daedalus to avoid flying too close to the water for the same reason (cf. 8.204–5).

730–32   *bibulis . . . talaribus*: dative with *credere*. The wings have indeed drunk too much and are soaked. *conspexit scopulum* 731: although we would expect this cliff to be the one to which Andromeda is chained (since the monster heads for her), Ovid seems to have in mind a series of cliffs along a rocky coast, and this particular one supposedly gives Perseus a special perch to complete the kill before the beast reaches Andromeda. The description follows a stereotype: when the water is calm (*stantibus*), the cliff towers above the sea, and, when it is rough (*moto*), the waves bury it.

733–
34
nixus eo: the hero lands on the cliff. There, hanging on with his left hand to the outcrop closest to the water, he hacks at the helpless, dumb beast, which is brainlessly swimming much too close. *ter quater* 734: these twelve final wounds suggest mere slaughter. We might compare the unheroic killing of an African elephant or indeed modern techniques for hunting whales. *repetita per ilia*: he drives his weapon again and again into the vitals.

735–
39
cum plausu clamor: ablative of accompaniment instead of the less convenient *plaususque*; the verb treats them as double subject. As Ovid jumps to the public joy, we are of course to assume that the monster has died. *superasque deorum . . . domos*: the sound not only echoes around the shore but also reverberates high into the sky to Olympus itself. *generumque salutant*: although Ovid postpones the subjects to 738, we can easily infer that Andromeda's parents are here carrying out their part of the bargain of 703–5. The four words that comprise 737, a rare organization, give the lapidary effect of a proud inscription, an effect emphasized by the prosaic, political overtones of *servatorem*. Ovid suggests, I think, that Perseus has not achieved the monumental success usually associated with the "savior of the state" in the late Republic. Everything this "hero" does and the claims made by or about him are exaggerations. *resoluta catenis / incedit virgo* 738–39: released from her chains, Andromeda finally walks free. Here, we might have expected to return to the love situation that earlier motivated Perseus. Ovid refuses to gratify such expectations.

740–
43
ipse: Perseus pays no attention to his lovely prize. He produces a sharp anticlimax by washing his hands! That concern for cleanliness, in itself comic at this point, allows Ovid to stray off naughtily on a rather pointless metamorphosis. *anguiferumque caput* 741: to inflate the importance of the Gorgon's head, Ovid uses this compound adjective only here; he seems to have borrowed it from his admired mentor Propertius 2.2.8. Since Perseus has to put down the head to wash his hands, Ovid can devise a clever mythological explanation for the scientific puzzle of ancient times: why the coral plant becomes petrified. To keep the hard ground or sand from damaging the head, Perseus places it on a protective layer of branches and leaves. *natasque sub aequore virgas* 742: named at 750 as coral. Modern science describes coral as a variety of sea animals whose skeletons form a hard stone-like material. The red coral of the Mediterranean, well known to Ovid and his contemporaries, is now commercially produced in banks off

Algiers, Tunis, Sicily, and Sardinia. *Phorcynidos* 743: Medusa and the other Gorgons were the daughters of Phorcos, a son of Neptune. Ovid seems to have introduced to Latin this form of the patronymic; the more familiar one, shorter by a syllable, will occur at 775, when he calls the Graiae, also Phorcos' daughters, *Phorcidas*.

744–46   *virga*: shift to the singular, vs. 742. *bibulaque . . . medulla*: ablative of specification with *viva*. The living coral has a soft, watery pith. However, as soon as the Gorgon's head touches it, it becomes hard, like the coral that Romans bought for decorative purposes. *novum . . . rigorem* 746: the adjective implies a completed metamorphosis. Ironically, the result reverses Perseus' intentions: he tried to use live coral to protect from hard surfaces the head that now itself has caused the soft mat to become stone-like.

747–49   *pelagi nymphae*: sea-nymphs or nereids; it is not clear why they are here with Perseus. Being semi-divine, they are immune to the Gorgon's danger and so can play around with impunity. They set out to repeat the marvel, like modern scientists who reproduce experiments. *idem contingere* 748: "to achieve the same result," i.e., make the soft branches hard. *seminaque . . . iterant* 749: Ovid imagines that this single marvel originates a plant species for many regions. The nymphs take the seeds from the hardened coral and scatter them on the water, enacting the growth cycle and hardening of the branches picked by Perseus. Thus, more coral and seeds appear.

750–52   *nunc quoque*: familiar tag to emphasize continuity after metamorphosis (cf. 1.235). In this instance, Ovid is explaining how today the hardening of coral takes place without the Gorgon: the seeds have acquired from that first contact with Medusa a permanent propensity to petrification outside the water they grow in. *capiant ut* 751: subjunctive in result clause. Ovid delays the conjunction *ut*, which in prose would have been initial. *tacto . . . aëre*: it is no longer necessary to touch Medusa's head. *quodque*: in prose, this would be *et id quod*; the connective links the two subjunctive verbs, *capiant* and *fiat*. The final line of this sequence, 752, becomes through Ovid's artistry a superb— we might say lapidary—epigram in chiasmus: *vimen . . . erat, fiat . . . saxum*.

753–56   *dis tribus*: Perseus assumes center stage again and makes final preparations for his marriage with Andromeda. He chooses to honor Jupiter, Mercury, and Minerva, because each helped him achieve his previous successes. Jupiter sired him; Mercury and Minerva treated him like a brother. Mercury fitted him with his sword and wings; Minerva gave him advice, and eventually she will receive the Gorgon's head as one of her fearsome attributes. *focos*: three sod altars where he could make burnt offerings (cf. *ara* in 755). *bellica virgo* 754: Minerva is often at war. In 755–56, Ovid will reverse his device, naming the goddess, but using a poetic epithet for Mercury. The goddess typically receives a female animal; Mercury has a male one, inferior in size to the bull given almighty Jupiter. Chiastic organization in 756.

757– *Andromedan et*: accusative in Greek declension to avoid elision. The
62 conjunction is explanatory, not additive. The main point is that Perseus is motivated only by love, not by ambition, and so he considers the girl alone as the proper reward of his heroism. He does not hold Cepheus to his promise to award him the throne (cf. 705) as dowry. *rapit* 758: although the verb regularly works with rapes, here it merely indicates the passionate speed with which the marriage occurs. *taedas*: wedding torches. They are held by favorable deities, who bless the marriage. For ill-omened deities with such torches, cf. the wedding of Procne and Tereus (6.430). *praecutiunt* 759: Ovid has invented this compound for this passage; neither he nor any other classical writer uses it again. The gods lead the wedding procession, shaking the torches. *satiantur*: this personification suggests that the altar fires hunger for incense. *sertaque dependent tectis* 769: garlands of flowers festoon the ceiling. After these decorative details, Ovid focuses on the music produced by a variety of instruments, made more impressive by polysyndeton.

762– *reseratis . . . valvis*: now, as if revealing for the first time that the
64 festive preparations have occurred behind closed doors, Ovid opens these doors and displays the splendor for the guests, the lords of Cepheus' court. *atria tota patent* 763: Latin writers describe the interior rooms of Greek and mythological homes and palaces in Roman terms. Cf. Vergil's comment on Priam's palace, exposed to view by the assault of Neoptolemus: *atria longa patescunt* (*Aen*. 2.483). *Cepheni* 764: although this word has no etymological connection with Cepheus, its resemblance to the king's name allows Ovid to use it, whatever its original meaning and derivation, to suggest the subjects of Cepheus.

Perseus Finally Tells about Medusa (765–803)

Ovid has managed to ignore the most popular story connected with Perseus, while elaborating material he himself has invented, which falls well below the usual heroic level. Now, he goes through the death of Medusa, but in a tired, indirect manner that robs the tale of its customary heroic delight. Perseus, in fact, does not get a chance to speak directly until he answers a question about the origins of the Gorgon, details which do nothing for his heroic pretensions, but remind us rather of Ovid's favorite erotic themes.

765– *epulis functi*: Ovid quickly passes over the standard description of an
67 epic banquet, to focus on the after-dinner stories. The subject of *functi* and the main verbs is the wedding party as a whole. The participle

takes the ablative. Food and plentiful wine dispose the guests to conversation. *Lyncides* 767: Perseus, who has been identified by several other patronymics (cf. 673 and 720), is here connected with his ancestor Lynceus, the only son of Aegyptus to be spared by his Danaid wife, Hypermnestra, by whom he sired Abas and the line that has come down to our hero. He asks for information about the people and land to which he has come.

767a–
68

These lines do not appear in any major early MSS, but have been added in the margin of some by later hands. We assume that some scribe, who did not realize that Perseus was *Lyncides*, tried to fix the text by creating a short conversation, question and answer, between *Abantiades* and *Lyncides*, with the absurd result that Perseus is talking to himself! The interpolator was also attempting, with *unus narrat*, to provide a clear antecedent for the relative *qui* in 769 (suggested by 790–91?).

769–
71

qui simul edocuit: someone has answered Perseus' geographical queries. It may be one of the Ethiopians, as the interpolator suggests, or Cepheus himself, whose admiration for his new son-in-law could well express itself in the question that follows. As is usual in Ovid and other poets, *simul* is a conjunction. *fortissime . . . fare*: as Ovid leads us to expect a grand epic narrative, he soars into epic language. Perseus is invited to regale his audience with a tale like the one told by Odysseus, about his courage and intrepid skill. *crinita draconibus ora* 771: an epic circumlocution for Medusa's head with its snaky locks.

772–
75

narrat: this verb introduces a tale in indirect discourse, a format that reduces the personal drama of the hero. It continues through 786, and then Ovid adds three more lines. The story starts out briskly, with five dactyls in both 772 and 774. *Agenorides*: still another patronymic for Perseus, last used in 563 for Cadmus. *gelido sub Atlante*: the Gorgons were regularly located in myth in the far west, here at the foot of Atlas, which Ovid anachronistically treats as a mountain, despite his earlier story at 627 ff. *esse locum* 773: in direct speech, this would have been *est locus*, start of an ecphrasis. *munimine molis*: poetic word, with its -*men* ending, and alliteration add up to more epic show. Ovid describes the natural fortress of a cliff-enclosed valley. *geminas . . . Phorcidas* 774–75: these two daughters of Phorcos are sisters of the Gorgons, called Graiae or the Gray Ones. They are old, toothless, and share a single eye between then, and they function as grotesque guardians of the Gorgons.

776–
81

id: the single eye. Four spondees place heavy emphasis on this feat. *astu*: Perseus' trick, taught him by his brother Mercury, the master thief, was to seize the opportunity when the eye was being passed and neither Graia could see. He interposed his own hand and grabbed the eye. The purpose was to hold it ransom until the Graiae told him where to find Medusa. Ovid skips intermediate details and, with a mere -*que* as connective, quickly takes us to the barren realm of the Gorgons, in the middle of 777. *abdita . . . saxa* 777–78: the narrator collects three descriptive participles before he supplies the noun. *simulacra* 780: Medusa has created something like a statue gallery of men and animals by her petrifying gaze. Later, in 5.211, Ovid will describe the result of Perseus' use of her head against his enemies as a kind of "art museum." *ferarumque*: hypermetric -*que* elides with the first word of 781.

782–
86

se tamen: in contrast to the many men who had failed and become stone, Perseus follows Mercury's advice and never looks directly at Medusa and her fatal eyes, but uses his shield as a mirror to guide his movements. *horrendae . . . Medusae*: this phrase in hyperbaton frames the clause. *quod*: although we would expect *quem* (and several MSS have so changed the prevailing reading), Ovid makes the relative refer to the bronze, the key aspect of the shield. *aere repercusso*: usually, the participle applies to the image that is reflected from a mirror surface, not, as here, to the reflecting surface. Ovid has extended its usage. *formam adspexisse*: literally true. Perseus gazes at the form in the mirror, not the real body. *gravis somnus* 784: from earliest versions, it was recognized that, with all his weapons, mirror, and wings, Perseus still could have done nothing unless Medusa was asleep, she and the snakes in her hair. *eripuisse caput collo* 785: this is the moment toward which the detailed account has been working; it is spoiled by its brevity and vagueness. "Snatching" the head from the neck makes it seem too easy. When other narrators imagined the moment, they recognized that Perseus would be anxious and feel awkward using the sword in a mirror. Some of them had Minerva appear and actually guide the indirect stroke of the sword, which hacked off the head amid much blood and snake-hissing; and one could even add screams from Medusa. Ovid has sabotaged the hero's own account of his so-called *virtus* (cf. 770). *pennisque fugacem*: at the central caesura, the narrator races on, without pausing to admire his feat, appending minor details of the monstrous births, Pegasus and Chrysaor, from Medusa's blood. Apollodorus 2.4.2.9 explains that Poseidon (Neptune) had impregnated Medusa and so was the father of this pair. Ovid reports at 798 the rape of the maiden Medusa (before she became a snake-headed Gorgon), but makes no express connection with Pegasus' birth. Pegasus is most famous as the winged steed of Bellerophon, a story which Ovid does not narrate. He only mentions, at 5.262, Pegasus' connection with the spring of Hippocrene on Mount Helicon, started by his hoof.

787–

longi . . . cursus: Ovid spares us the details, some of which he has

89   already supplied at 614 ff. by his odd chronological organization. *non falsa*: the narrator seems a bit too eager to remind us of his fictional achievement in the poem. *sub se . . . ab alto* 788: an obvious allusion to his flying, which he clarifies in 789 for those who need it. The two lines form a doublet: what Perseus saw below and above him as he flew through the air.

790–   *exspectatum*: a certain correction made by late medieval scholars to
92   the transmitted *spectatum* (an error resulting from the elision). Ovid plays with a formula of narrative situations, according to which the audience is so charmed by the story that it wants it to go on and on. Ovid might also perhaps inject a note of sophisticated irony at the inadequate way Perseus has told his tale. *sola sororum* 791: in other versions and in earliest Greek art, the Gorgons all alike have snake hair. Medusa's distinction is that she was born a mortal and therefore could be killed. However, Ovid is getting at a problem in the myth, namely, how a girl who was raped by Neptune for her beauty became such a horrible monster. His little story here, which brings back snakes and a vengeful female deity, rounds off the shape of Book 4, though doing little for Perseus. *alternos . . . angues* 792: the picture is deliberately, I think, "precise." Every other hair on Medusa's head is a snake! Bömer protests that such detail does not fit the traditional frightfulness of the Gorgon; but that is Ovid's point. The poet has slipped out of the epic mode, and he is now combining the elegiac and aetiological.

793–   *hospes ait*: Perseus ends the book speaking as a learned expert, a poet
97   like Ovid with an Ovidian theme. *scitaris digna relatu*: archaic verb and ablative of the supine establish the didactic tone. *causam* 794: announces an aetiology. *forma*: ablative of specification. We immediately focus on the once-outstanding beauty of Medusa, which forms such a sharp antithesis with her fearsome ugliness as Gorgon. *spes invidiosa procorum* 795: formulaic reference to the many suitors who, in fairy stories, vie for the hand of the beauteous princess. Cf. the situation of Daphne in the first such story, 1.478–80. Ovid takes over this entire line at 9.10 to characterize Deianira's attraction. *illa* 796: the narrator has described Medusa before clearly identifying her. *in tota*: supply either *virgine* or *forma*. *capillis*: ablative of comparison. Perseus is explaining the snake hair, so he artfully focuses on it as especially worth attention from the start. *inveni qui* 797: since Perseus has known Medusa only as a Gorgon, he poses as a scientific researcher, who has located a witness of the maiden's lovely tresses. The indefinite antecedent of *qui* justifies the subjunctive in *referret*.

798–   *pelagi rector*: periphrasis for Neptune. *templo vitiasse Minervae*: the
801   verb, carefully set in the middle of the phrase about Minerva's temple, emphasizes the shocking affront to the goddess and her essential

chastity. What Medusa was doing in the shrine, Perseus does not say, but we should probably assume that she was acting reverently and modestly. Of Neptune, though, we have to think the worst: his lust has defiled the temple and a worshipper, and he has made her vulnerable to the angry goddess. *aversa est* 799: in turning away, Minerva anticipates the necessary response to monstrous Medusa and her severed head. *castos aegide vultus . . . texit*: Ovid anticipates another part of the story by mentioning the aegis, a shield behind which she conceals her irate embarrassment, before that part of her armor became decorated with Medusa's head (cf. 802–3). *neve*: = *et ne* (+ negative purpose clause). *inpune*: as usual, the deity punishes the innocent victim of rape, and the rapist goes unscathed. In 801, Perseus, concentrating on the question, limits himself exclusively to the metamorphosis of human hair to snakes. How Medusa got from temple to barren North Africa or how she acquired the power to petrify, he ignores.

802–
3

nunc quoque: this formula for continuity after metamorphosis has recently been used at 750. Here, however, it causes a temporal problem. If Perseus, as most readers believe, continues to be narrator to the end of Book 4, then he is guilty of anachronism, for the snakes on the aegis imply the presence of the entire head of Medusa (as in artistic representations). But Perseus himself has the head—it provokes this query—and he will need it as his super-weapon until 5.249. Ovid has no serious objections to anachronism, and we may let these two lines stand as Perseus' words. Alternatively, since Perseus completed his required task at 801, we could close the quotes there and assign these final lines to the poet-speaker, who brings us up to the present to end the book. *pectore in adverso* 803: the aegis "now" becomes a frightening decoration. The head of Medusa, prominently placed on it, looks at the foe and petrifies him. *angues*: final word of the book, repeating the key term of the question of 792, provides a ring to frame this narrative.

NOTES TO BOOK 5

Ovid continues the story of Perseus without a break dividing the book boundaries, starting with *dumque* as if to insist on the temporal consistency. He immediately plunges us into an "epic" battle at the wedding banquet, which harks back to the battle between Odysseus and the Suitors during the feast in the palace at Ithaca, but takes its motivation and vocabulary more patently from the rivalry between Turnus and Aeneas for the hand of Lavinia. When the battle has ended, the banquet hall is littered with corpses and statues, for Perseus has had to resort to his trusty Medusa-head to save his life from the superior numbers of his foes (1–235). Ovid briefly follows the hero back to his mother on the island of Seriphos (–249), then transfers our attention to Minerva (who supposedly has been attending Perseus, her brother, up to this point). Minerva flies to Mount Helicon near Thebes and there begins a long conversation with the nine Muses. She first explains her visit: she wishes to see the site where Pegasus, whose "birth" she has observed while accompanying Perseus, has created the Fountain of Hippocrene (–263). After visiting it, then, she congratulates the Muses on their happy location and activity. But they have just escaped a frightful danger and report the failed attempt of Pyreneus to rape them, which resulted in the rapist's deserved death (–293). However, all that serves merely as preface to a much longer account, of how the Muses engaged in a poetic "battle" with upstart human rivals, the Pierides, and conquered them. The victorious Muses give us the full text of their winning song—as daughters of Memory, of course, they can recall it in exact detail. Thus this book consists of two different battles: a violent battle along grotesquely epic lines among male warriors and a passionate poetic contest among proud and temperamental female singers. The four hundred lines Ovid devotes to the latter imply which he finds more interesting.

PERSEUS' BATTLE WITH HIS RIVAL PHINEUS (1–235)

The banquet and conversation have been going along amiably so far, with geographical queries from the polite guest Perseus and scientific inquiries from the Ethiopians. The bride has been ignored, and so has the jilted groom Phineus, who suddenly announces his presence and grievance by invading the feast with a gang of supporters and hurling his spear at hated Perseus; this in spite of a passionate speech by Cepheus protesting his threats of violence. He is a poor parody of Turnus, whose motives for fighting Aeneas included his fiery claim upon Lavinia. When Phineus' spear misses its target, the battle is on. Cepheus helplessly departs (a poor parody of Latinus), and Perseus stands virtually alone against more than a thousand! In these unequal conditions, nevertheless, he happily and with total impunity dispatches one enemy after another, by a series of differentiated and grotesque wounds. After killing more than twenty single-handed, he begins to realize that the sheer number of enemies will overwhelm his *virtus* (177), and so at last he decides to use his super-weapon: he pulls out Medusa's head and starts waving it in the direction of the foe. Rather quickly, then, the enemy host becomes a petrified army; a final group of two hundred has their fighting stopped cold (209), and only Phineus, their ringleader, remains. Unlike the sympathetic Turnus at the end of the *Aeneid,* Phineus, unwounded but craven, desperately begs for his life; and Perseus, unlike the fierce and complicated Aeneas, taunts his enemy before turning him into a statue, captured in a final pose of abject cowardice (234–35).

Although Euripides composed an *Andromeda,* a fair number of whose fragments have survived and might have inspired Ovid in this sequence, I take the position that Ovid should be credited with developing the rivalry between Perseus and Phineus into an epic battle along the lines of Vergil's recent model. Even later, for example, Apollodorus dismisses the situation, which Ovid finds so opportune, in a single sentence, and reduces the battle to a mere plot (which Perseus quickly petrifies, 2.4.3.5). The chief critical question is: what has Ovid aimed at and achieved in this "epic" battle? Has he raised the tone of his poem and ennobled Perseus; has he, on the contrary, made a mockery of epic warfare in general (and Vergil's in particular) by his emphasis on the crazy odds of a thousand to one and on the grotesque variation in wounds that have no sense or ethical relevance, thereby reducing Perseus to a sardonic bully? I shall argue for a more nuanced interpretation, but I leave the details to the line-by-line commentary below.

1–4   *dumque ea . . . commemorat:* a direct link with the story that Perseus has been telling at the end of Book 4. *Cephenum* 1: genitive plural; for the word, cf. 4.764. *Daneius heros:* Ovid uses the epic periphrasis, a matronymic adjective + *heros*, to catch Perseus like others in a doubtfully heroic situation. Other such heroes weep (2.676) and flee (3.198). *fremida . . . turba* 2: an alternate later reading, *fremitu . . . turbae*, added to many MSS in a second hand, weakens Ovid's emphasis on the invasion by the roaring mob. The scribes took exception to Ovid's word *fremida*, which he invented here; it is unknown anywhere else in Latin. *qui canat est clamor* 4: Ovid has altered normal word order (*est clamor qui canat*) in order to achieve an approximate chiastic arrangement of the two clauses in 3–4, both dependent on *est clamor* as relative clauses of characteristic. He here implies what he clearly states in 5: that the marriage feast has been disrupted and perverted into a scene of battle; happy songs have become sounds of war.

5–7   *versa:* metamorphosis of scene. *adsimilare freto possis* 6: the poet invites his audience, in apostrophe, to develop a simile along the lines of a stormy sea. This rare extension of the verb acts to put us in a self-conscious "literary" attitude from the start. The analogy between raging seas and war is as old as Homer and conventional in all subsequent ancient epics. Vergil uses it repeatedly. *saeva quietum:* careful juxtaposition of antithetical terms. *rabies* 7: properly, the madness of dogs and thence of any wild animal or human being. Propertius had written *saeva canum rabies* (3.16.17). Vergil makes the winds, penned in by Aeolus, a pack of animals (*Aen.* 1.52 ff.). *exasperat undis:* Ovid remembers Vergil's phrase for a winter storm, in the same line-position: *asperat undas* (*Aen.* 3.285).

8–9   *his:* the band of intruders. *Phineus:* identified at 13 as Cepheus' brother. *temerarius:* the narrator quickly establishes Phineus as the villain. *fraxineam . . . hastam* 9: this weapon focuses attention until it is finally thrown in 32. Ash provides a regular wood for spears.

10–12 Phineus asserts his arrival, with egotistic *en, en adsum*, like the first of the piratical band that kidnapped Bacchus in 3.605. *praereptae coniugis ultor:* the language of Turnus who, in *Aen.* 9.138 complained of the injury done him (*coniuge praerepta*). He proceeds to abusive sneers and threats, focusing on Perseus' wings (which he diminishes to feathers) and the story of Jupiter becoming a golden rain to sire the hero (which Acrisius also doubted). In fact, Phineus plays a very small part in the battle that ensues, and he reveals himself a contemptible coward at the end.

12–15 *conanti mittere:* before Phineus can throw his spear, his brother addresses him, and he stands poised to cast throughout the speech (13–29), then resumes his action. *quid facis? . . . quae . . . furentem / mens agit* 13–14: for a similar pair of protesting questions, cf. 3.641. In this case, Cepheus correctly defines Phineus' actions as *furor* and emphatically alliterates with *facinus*. After the near-anaphora of *quid . . . quae*, he changes to *haec . . . hac* in 14–15. *dote:* Cepheus produces a rhetorical question that, with this word, focuses on the chief irritant of his brother. Phineus owes no dowry to Perseus and has promised none. It is Cepheus, in fact, who in 4.705, when Perseus swore to save Andromeda, held out to him the rule of Ethiopia if he succeeded; and ironically that was the bride and the dowry that belonged previously to Phineus. (This parallel to Turnus justifies his outrage as a man robbed of his bride). Cepheus plays here the role of a casuistic Latinus, arguing a poor case to persuade the victim to accept political "necessity."

16–19   Cepheus becomes tendentious and dishonest, using rhetoric in place of fair, brotherly persuasion. *quam:* Andromeda. *verum si quaeris:* it is obvious from this argument, that Cepheus has no interest in the "truth." There may be valid reasons for letting Perseus have Andromeda and thus depriving Phineus, but it cannot be denied that he has taken her from Phineus. The triple anaphora in 17–18 with *sed* enables the rhetorician to list three causes that exculpate Perseus. He refers to events (alluded to in 4.670 ff.) that led to the anger of the Nereids, to the oracle of Ammon that doomed Andromeda, and to the sea-monster who almost devoured her. *corniger Ammon* 17: Ammon, god of the oracle of Cyrene, was represented as having ram's horns, an attribute that was appropriated later by Alexander and his successors. *exsaturanda* 19: only instance of this expressive verb in all Ovid's poetry. Some critics claim that the poet uses the future passive participle not to denote necessity, but simply the future. That is incorrect. Cepheus is arguing indeed that necessity forced on him the disaster of letting Andromeda be eaten by the monster, from which Perseus saved her. He had to give his daughter to the *belua,* and then he had no choice but to offer her to Perseus as the price of her rescue.

19–21   *rapta est:* picks up Phineus' term *praereptae* (10) and trivializes the sense of loss that the jilted suitor feels. Phineus is expected to agree that, once his bride was doomed to feed the monster, she was lost to him. That would be true, of course, if she had in fact been eaten. But she was not. Cepheus swiftly deals with that objection and puts his brother in the wrong in the *nisi*-clause of 20–21. As if Phineus is *crudelis* and insists that Andromeda die by pressing his claim to her hand! That is more rhetorical prestidigitation from Cepheus.

22–23   *scilicet:* a standard beginning to a sardonic argument. Cepheus continues from the fabrication he has developed in 20–21, and Ovid continues with his imaginative construction of a mythological *controversia.* With no sense of shame at his own ineffectiveness or at the guilt of Cassiope, Cepheus pictures his brother tamely watching while Andromeda was chained to the cliff, offering no heroic help though he was both uncle and fiancé of the girl. That makes Phineus complicit in the awarding of the girl to Perseus, implies the father.

24–26 *insuper:* as if everything he has said adds up to a terrible indictment of Phineus, Cepheus protests that his brother has the further effrontery to be angry at the marriage of Andromeda to Perseus. Again, that is unscrupulous twisting of facts. *praemiaque eripies* 25: suddenly the verb that had been the basis of Phineus' argument is snatched away from him and used to condemn his actions. He has been rhetorically turned into the *raptor! si . . . videntur . . . petisses:* in this mixed condition, scholars disagree as to whether the conclusion is subjunctive in contrary to fact or jussive. The different translations indicate the nuances: "If the prize really seems so grand to you (now), (a) you would (then) have pursued it, or (b) you should have pursued it then." Whichever feels more invidious is what Ovid wanted Cepheus to be saying. *ex illis scopulis:* Cepheus himself has become so trapped in his devious rhetoric that he obliterates the sense of his supposedly cherished daughter as an animate being, chained to a cliff, and lapses into neuter plural and the metonymy of *praemia*.

27–29 *nunc:* i.e., inasmuch as Phineus failed to seek his reward at the right time. *qui petiit:* Perseus, the successful suitor who did seek and gain the bride. *haec non orba senectus:* in this flagrant appeal for the audience's sympathy against his brother, Phineus focuses on his pathetic old age rather than on Andromeda's safety—he has betrayed the fact throughout that he is nothing but a sinister old egotist. *quod* 28: neuter singular now, since *quae* would be elided; Cepheus is still referring to *praemia*/-*um. et meritis et voce est pactus:* the logical order has been inverted here by the sly speaker, and he uses the verb freely with the first noun. Translate: "He contracted for verbally and earned by his deeds." The verbal contract (cf. 4.703) was fulfilled by Perseus, so he earned its terms, namely, Andromeda. Cepheus could have made his case more palatable by apologizing to his brother and showing how desperate concern for the girl had made him agree to any bargain, but he cloaks his own part in the "contract" and hides behind a mask of pseudolegalism. *non tibi sed certae . . . morti* 29: behind the rhetoric of this virtual zeugma is the final bit of dishonesty of Cepheus. The different status of the personal pronoun and the impersonal noun of "death" reveals how the king claims to have dismissed his brother's importance and prior claim: death simply replaced Phineus, he suggests, and in those circumstances a contest between death and Perseus obviously demands the choice of Perseus, the savior and life-giver. Although the death he refers to is that of Andromeda, his choice ends up a not very sympathetic challenge to his brother and a provocation of the death that Phineus now attempts.

30–33 *ille nihil contra:* Phineus does not resort to slick words, but to action. Ovid has rigged sympathy for him against Cepheus (if not against Perseus), but he rapidly fritters it away. Thoroughly irate at the self-serving words of Cepheus, Phineus hesitates as to whether he should use the spear on brother or rival Perseus. *petat hunc* 31: the poet changes natural word order so as to place the pronoun in the same metrical position as it occupied in 30. Prose order would be: *ignorat (an) hunc petat an illum*. In 32–33, Ovid develops suspense and anticlimax, with two clauses focusing on the mighty effort taken to hurl the spear—we don't know which target has been chosen—then the adverb *nequiquam* that sabotages all that male might, and finally the name of Perseus to identify the nonvictim.

34–37   Ovid makes no attempt to awaken sympathy for Perseus. He does not do what Vergil regularly does, namely, describe the flight and sound of the spear, to make us feel what it would have been like to be its target. Instead, having already warned us it was vainly thrown, he jumps to where Perseus suddenly sees the weapon sticking in the couch next to him. The hero, about whose heroism Ovid has already planted doubts, shows his readiness to plunge wildly into combat, but with none of the humanity and sanity that we would want in an Augustan hero. He could have protested against this violence and tried astutely to stop it, but he is *ferox. teloque . . . remisso* 35: he uses the weapon that Phineus has supplied against the enemy. Like the abortive efforts of Phineus, those of Perseus are built up impressively in 35, then negated in 36 by the contrary-to-fact clauses. Essentially, Phineus ducked to avoid the spear, an action that stirs the narrator's indignation. His outrage focuses on what he chooses to regard as a paradox, that the altar shielded Phineus, that the sacred place benefited the unholy criminal! At this point, the narrator exhibits as much bias as Cepheus.

38–40   *non inrita cuspis:* since the spear hit somebody in the enemy ranks, the narrator asserts that it was not vainly thrown. The victim, Rhoetus, has the name of a centaur in 12.271 ff., a scene where Ovid describes the banquet battle between Lapiths and Centaurs. Such similarities invite us to compare the two descriptions. Here, the narrator pursues the gory death. Someone, perhaps Perseus, yanks the spear out of Rhoetus' forehead, where it has stuck, and in his death-struggles the man kicks over dining tables and spatters them with blood. No sound to make the scene real, only movements to create a vivid but dispassionate picture. The narrator is full of quick ethical judgment, but pitiless.

41–43   *ardescit vulgus in iras:* the mob of Phineus' supporters rage over the death of one of theirs. They aim their spears at Perseus, of course, but many of them also blame the king (as did Phineus after that speech). The situation clarifies the differences between Cepheus and honorable, ineffective Latinus in *Aen.* 7. Latinus spoke fairly; sympathetic to Turnus, whom he really liked, he tried to stop a minor fight from developing into war; and popular feeling, not animosity against himself, overwhelmed his weak old age. This Ethiopian mob wants to kill its king, who is unattractive even if not deserving death.

43–45 *limine tecti / exierat:* Cepheus slips across the threshold out of the banquet hall, more a coward than a noble but ineffective resister of violence. He has abandoned his beloved son-in-law, but, even worse, scurried away without concern for wife and daughter, the supposed justification of all his questionable actions against Phineus. *testatus iusque fidemque:* Ovid echoes the scene in *Aen.* 7.593 ff. where Latinus legitimately invokes the gods as witnesses. The behavior of Cepheus seems a pious sham. He has acted from no convincing ethical position, nor has he effectively attempted to dissuade his brother or to prevent this violence. *ea* 45: subject of *moveri.* The five dactyls of 45 reinforce the glibness of his excuses.

46–47 *bellica Pallas:* Minerva; cf. 4.754. *protegit aegide:* here, too, as in 4.799, Ovid treats the aegis as a shield. It wards off the many spears aimed at Perseus. Not until later will it be decorated with the head of Medusa and become almost an offensive weapon, to turn enemies into stone. Minerva here plays the role of Athena during the battle in Ithaca at the banquet, when she helps Odysseus against the suitors.

47–50 *Indus Athis:* this second member of Phineus' band adds to its exotic impression. He comes from India, and his name echoes that of Cybele's devotee from Asia Minor in Catullus 63. *flumine Gange / edita:* we learn that Athis' mother is daughter of the Ganges and gave birth to him under water, but Ovid gives us none of the usual data (i.e., rapist deity) about his father. *Limnaee:* the final *e* in a Greek name is long. The name itself is unique; it represents a conjectural emendation by Magnus of the many variants in the MSS. A Greek adjective meaning "marshy" inspired the conjecture. *egregius forma* 49: male beauty has no relevance to warrior qualities, but Homer, in his brief presentation of Nireus in *Il.* 2.671–75, pointed up the antithesis sharply: the most handsome Greek warrior after Achilles, Nireus had little strength and so found few men to follow him. Vergil developed the motif differently, and Ovid followed him here. In *Aen.* 9.176 ff., the poet features the pair of friends: Euryalus, the younger, most handsome of the Trojans, and Nisus, somewhat older and more experienced in battle. The two end up dying together, when young Euryalus gets trapped and slain by the Italians and Nisus decides to avenge his death and die with him. Vergil makes their death highly significant and engages our feelings for them; Ovid introduces Athis and his friend Lycabas as a pretty episode, of next to no significance in this utterly meaningless battle. *divite cultu:* handsome Athis wears rich clothes, like a dandy in Rome, not a mythical warrior. *bis . . . octonis* 50: since *sedecim* hardly fits the hexameter, Ovid amuses the audience with a little multiplication. *adhuc . . . integer:* a phrase of Horace *C.* 3.7.21, which indicates the amatory connotations of the adjective. Someone who is "untouched" in this sense, is a completely loyal lover, undistracted by interest in other possibilities. Thus, we can detect the hand of Ovid slyly watering down the epic power of Vergil's Euryalus, turning his Athis into a richly dressed, elegiac figure of contemporary Rome (trivial in comparison with his Trojan archetype).

51–55   *indutus chlamydem Tyriam:* as often, *indutus* functions as a Greek verb in the middle voice, capable of taking the accusative. Athis "has on" a chlamys (cf. 1.270). The chlamys was a cloak especially associated with Greek soldiers, even generals; but it has earlier in the poem adorned Mercury at 2.733 on his courtly visit to Herse. He had a gold fringe, too, like Athis. Ovid seems to be recalling Dido, also, who wore a Sidonian, artfully fringed chlamys and much gold jewelry to the hunt with Aeneas in *Aen.* 4.137 ff. What should be a military cloak becomes, by its lavish adornment and poetic associations, the cloak of a modern, rather unmilitary dandy. *aurata monilia* 52: emphasis on gold, together with necklaces, turns Athis into an extravagant, exotic effeminate. Roman men did not wear necklaces. Thus, Juvenal 2.85 indignantly denounces the Roman transvestites, almost a century after Ovid, who *posuere monilia collo. madidos murra . . . capillos* 53: more prejudicial detail appropriate to despised Eastern ways of oiling and scenting hair. Iarbas sneered at Aeneas for his "dripping hair" (*Aen.* 4.216), and Pentheus derided Bacchus in almost exactly these words, *madidus murra crinis* (3.555). The point of such charges is that anyone who fixes his hair that way is soft and averse to masculine activities like war. Yet here Athis sidles out to fight with scented locks! He is ridiculous. We are not to think that the Romans did not oil and perfume their hair: they did, but for occasions of urbane, peaceful amusement. Horace refers to a boy with scented hair in *C.* 1.5 who is deeply involved in a love affair with Lydia, and he makes no hostile comments about the hair, because it is appropriate for love. Similarly, in *C.* 2.7.6–8, he calmly reports that he and a friend Pompeius enjoyed drinking together, wore garlands on their heads, and had hair oiled and scented with Syrian perfume. But he makes clear that they did that when not on military duty. *curvum crinale:* some kind of hair band or ornament. This is a unique use of the substantive *crinale,* and presumably Ovid refers to a kind of jewelry appropriate to women. For all this Eastern corruption of dress, Athis possesses military skills, both with spear and bow. That is the surprise conclusion of this sketch in 54–55. His greater ability as archer explains his choice of weapon in the next lines.

56–58   *flectentem cornua:* Athis, now become the object, is bending the bow. The same phrase occurs at 1.455 for Cupid as archer. Evidently, Athis aims at Perseus, but Perseus, now the subject, decisively stops his warfare. *stipite . . . in ara* 57: the narrator has been indignant at the way Phineus used the altar, but he makes no protest when Perseus actually plunders and thus profanes the same altar. Ovid, I think, expects us to distance ourselves from this narrator and his "hero" Perseus. The model for this situation may be found in *Aen.* 12.298–300, where, as the broken truce lets loose a fierce battle around the still-smoking altars, one man uses a burning brand on another's face and beard. For Vergil, this symbolizes the work of *furor impius,* but he is too skillful to make the point in detail. Ovid has created a narrator here who does not respect Vergil's thematic symbolism and so presents in Perseus a travesty of Vergilian heroism. Using this situation as a type scene, Ovid repeats it in the battle of Lapiths and Centaurs at 12.271 ff., again to sabotage the claims of the narrator (specifically identified as Nestor) to understand ancient heroism. *confudit . . . ora* 58: our hero smashes Athis' skull and totally destroys his handsome face amid the fragments of bone. The narrator made sure that we didn't like this Eastern dandy, but he has not made us like Perseus' savage killing either.

9–61 *laudatos . . . vultus:* we now get a second perspective on Athis' death, that of his close friend Lycabas. The participle fits Lycabas, who has admired the handsome face of Athis and therefore is appalled at the disfigurement of that beauty. *iactantem:* not yet dead, the boy, in his agony, writhes about with his shattered, bloody face. *Lycabas iunctissimus* 60: Ovid has already used the name Lycabas at 3.624 for one of the most villainous Tyrrhenian pirates, and so probably intends to create mixed responses to this lover by the name. The superlative adjective appears here for the first time in Latin and may be a sign of exaggeration. *veri non dissimulator amoris* 51: in elaborating on the close friendship and love of Lycabas, the narrator uses a double negative formulation. The verbal noun *dissimulator* occurs rarely in Latin; Sallust and Horace used it before Ovid, in political contexts, where dissimulation constitutes a devious strategy. Lycabas receives praise for Roman forthrightness, a quality that he will now demonstrate by his vain efforts to avenge his beloved Athis.

2–64 *exhalantem . . . vitam:* earlier of Priam in *Aen.* 2.562. Vergil added the ablative phrase *crudeli vulnere,* which Ovid has slightly altered. *quos . . . arcus* 63: cf. 55–56. Taking up Athis' bow, Lycabas defines himself as his friend's avenger.

5–68 *nec longum . . . laetabere:* again, Ovid borrows from Vergil; cf. *Aen.* 10.740, where the same words, in different metrical position, are addressed by a dying foe to Mezentius, correctly; for the Etruscan soon fell before Aeneas. Here, however, Lycabas' words lead to his own undoing, and nothing happens to Perseus—another instance of Ovid's ironic use of Vergil to define the injustice and impiety of his

poem's world. *invidiae . . . laudis* 66: partitive genitives. Since Per-
seus has said nothing and shown no signs of exultation or boasting,
it is not evident that Lycabas' angry words are just. *dixerat, emicuit*
67: usually, Ovid introduces *et* between two such verbs, where, as
here, the first in pluperfect establishes subordinate background to the
second, a main verb. *nervo:* the bowstring. *penetrabile telum:* Ovid
borrows from a famous sequence of Vergil, where Turnus menaced
Pallas with his spear in these words, then threw the weapon and indeed
pierced his chest fatally (*Aen.* 10.481). Ovid reduces the weapon to
an arrow, then makes it miss its target, merely piercing the cloth of
Perseus' robe. For all his Vergilian words, then, Lycabas proves an
anticlimax, another easy victim of Perseus. *vitatumque . . . perpendit*
68: the two verbs define the vain results of Lycabas' show of heroism.
He fails to equal Nisus; having not avenged Athis, he becomes a
grotesque corpse.

69–73 *harpen:* last seen when buried up to the sickle in the sea-monster
(4.720). This is the first time Perseus has resorted to a weapon of his
own. *Acrisioniades* 70: a unique patronymic, invented here to fill up
an entire half-line pompously and to imply the disparity between the
epic "name" and the unepic behavior of the pseudo-hero Perseus.
There is a similar disparity between the significant self-devotion of
Nisus and the sentimental incompetence of Lycabas. *oculis . . . na-*
tantibus 71: the image is Vergilian (cf. *Aen.* 5.856), but Ovid has
shifted its application from sleepiness to the moment before dying.
His cleverness is pointed up by the alliterative use of the metaphor
nocte, which symbolizes the darkness of death. *circumspexit* 72: "he
looked around for." When he sees Athis, he collapses on him. *seque*
adclinavit: the first known use of this verb in Latin, it brings the two
friends together in a touching group, Lycabas resting familiarly against
the body of Athis (as he must often have done when alive). *iunctae*
solacia mortis 73: subjective genitive, rare with *solacia.* Since Lycabas
falls so far short of Nisus in *Aen.* 9.441–45, Ovid exaggerates senti-
mentality and explains the meaning of his death. That he wants us to
compare the truly epic scene with his unepic version is guaranteed
when later, in the battle of Centaurs and Lapiths, he does the same
thing, featuring the confused tangle of legs and bodies of two "devoted"
centaurs (cf. 12.393 ff.).

74–78 *Suenites . . . Phorbas:* from upper Egypt comes Phorbas, otherwise
unknown son of unknown Metion. Same name for a centaur in 12.322.
Amphimedon 75: comes from even farther away in Libya to support
Phineus. Ovid presumably picked his name from the set of evil Suitors
in *Od.* 22 and 24. *avidi committere pugnam:* the poet sets up another
anticlimax to ruin the epic language. Rushing forward to engage

Perseus, they slip ridiculously in the blood that has soaked the ground. The pratfall quickly results in their death at the efficient hands of the murderous Greek. Again, Ovid ostentatiously borrows from a well-known scene of Vergil, which also involved Nisus, in *Aen.* 5.328–33. During a race in Sicily, he slipped in blood shed by a bull during sacrifice, and Vergil made that scene involving another's blood foreshadow the fatal bloodshed of 9.441 ff. Ovid's vocabulary closely parallels that of Vergil, but the effect of his scene sharply diverges. *surgentibus* 77: whereas this motley pair rise to be killed, Nisus rose to trip up another runner and so enable Euryalus to come in first. *ensis:* the *harpe* again. To give inappropriate elegance to these deaths, Ovid organizes them with a neat chiasmus in 78.

79–84 *Actoriden:* Ovid applies the patronymic of Homeric Patroclos to the insignificant Ethiopian Erytus, to set up another anticlimax. We might be expecting, from the negative start, that Erytus played a more heroic and successful role than the pair of clowns that preceded; but Ovid reduces the difference to a matter of fatal weapons. Later, at 13.273, he uses this patronymic properly of the Greek hero. *bipennis / telum:* Ovid continues to use *telum* loosely for "weapon." We are not to imagine that he considered the axe a throwing weapon, like an Indian tomahawk in some Westerns. *altis / exstantem signis:* in contrast to Erytus' menacing weapon and to the efficient one with which Perseus has just dispatched three enemies, Ovid elaborately describes for more than two lines the giant mixing bowl with which the Greek will smash Erytus' skull. If he were trying to be more realistic and less grotesque, it would seem that Erytus would at least have had time to swing his axe while Perseus was maneuvering his unwieldy weapon into position; unless, that is, our hero hit him unawares, from the side or rear! The first detail about the bowl stresses its decoration in high relief; *signis* refers to any artistic representation. *multaeque in pondere massae:* genitive of description and ablative with preposition instead of simple ablative of respect. Ovid stresses the heaviness of the bowl in 81 by four spondees (the first such collocation in Book 5). *tollit . . . inflig-itque* 82–83: notice the different positions of the verbs in their respective clauses and metrical lines; Ovid slowly prepares us for the sudden smashing of Erytus' head. Fighting the Centaurs, Theseus in 12.235 ff. smashes a similar crater down on a foe of similar name, Eurytus. *rutilum vomit:* in the context of a banquet, it would not be unusual for an inebriated quest to vomit up red wine after imbibing from the crater. Ovid uses the association of scene and weapon to allude to that possibility. He probably recalls *Aen.* 9.345 ff. where Rhoetus, hiding near a crater from which he has liberally drunk, is stabbed in the chest by Euryalus and proceeds to vomit up a mixture of wine and blood. *resupinus humum . . . pulsat* 84: like Pyramus in 4.121 and 133–34, Erytus falls backward and beats the ground in his death pangs. Ovid, however, focuses our attention on the smashed head.

85–88 Having lavished detail on Perseus' killing of six men in the past fifty lines, Ovid quickly lists six more easy victims. He gives the first the honor of an entire line, allots half-lines to the next two, and obliges the final three to share 87. As Otis noted, the poet apes the form of epic, but the epic style of naming these people is meaningless in this anti-epic context. *Semiramio:* Ovid invents this pretentious adjective and character who comes all the way from Babylon. Even more exotic are the men of 86: Abaris from the Caucasus Mountains and Lycetus from the neighborhood of Thessaly's Spercheus River. (The epithet is Ovid's invention for this grand setting.) Perseus fights ragtag elements of the entire savage world. *intonsumque comas* 87: participle and Greek accusative give the illusion of another epic epithet, but the long-haired type fits more closely the world of Roman elegy. Helices' name does not appear in earlier literature or myth. Phlegyas' name is well-known; his prototype sired the Centaurs. Clytus seems merely a convenient filler. The metrical organization of this list in 85–87 puts emphasis on speed: five dactyls in 85, four in 86 and 87. *exstructos morientum calcat acervos* 88: the unheroic arrogance of Perseus emerges patently in this action. He has downed six men in a heap before him, and now he scornfully kicks that heap. The *Ilias Latina,* which much admired this battle, appropriated the entire clause as well as the final half-line of 84.

89–91 *concurrere comminus:* since his men have failed so dismally at hand-to-hand combat, cowardly Phineus dares not risk himself. He tries his spear again, aiming ineptly. *expertem frustra belli* 91: Ovid extracts ironic emphasis for peace-loving Idas with four spondees.

92–96 Ovid builds a picture in 92 that the remainder of the scene destroys. We seem to have two savage warriors facing each other, but Phineus has already been well defined as a coward, and Idas has refrained from battle for unknown but suspicious reasons that belie his stern look and words now. *in partes . . . abstrahor* 93: "I am forced to take sides." *hoc vulnere* 94: Idas' furious threat, which Ovid stresses by four spondees and the juxtaposition of the two forms of *vulnus,* results in nothing; the demonstrative points to nothing. *remissurus* 95: Idas planned to hurl the spear back at Phineus, as Perseus did in 35. *de vulnere telum:* same phrase and same situation in *Aen.* 9.486, but Vergil's infinitely more impressive and heroic Pallas puts unwarlike Idas in the shade. *sanguine defectos . . . artus* 96: the limbs are drained of blood because, as we may assume and the analogy of Pallas proves, when the spear was yanked out, blood poured from the wound.

97–99 *tum quoque:* Ovid introduces a second fatality on Cepheus' side. *post regem primus:* i.e., second only to king Cepheus. Hodites is also the name of a centaur at 12.457. *Prothoenora* 98: rare name, but useful to Ovid for its contribution toward the dactyls of this line. The easy, speedy killing fits modern movies better than ancient epic. We do not even know on which side this victim and his killer were. But in 99, with *Lyncides,* we are back with the main killer, Perseus (cf. 4.767).

99–
02 *grandaevus . . . Emathion:* aged Emathion, opposed to this fighting, can only be one of Cepheus' banquet guests. The epic compound should command respect. *aequi cultor timidusque deorum:* two phrases with objective genitives, chiastically disposed, to stress the justice and piety that Ovid intends to show being defiled. *loquendo / pugnat* 101–2: paradoxical phrase, promoted by the enjambement, which Ovid then explains. Emathion is what we might call a militant pacifist, and he denounces this resort to weapons.

03–
6 Having set up the situation, Ovid destroys it with elaborately grotesque detail. Chromis predictably appears also as a barbarous centaur in 12.333. *amplexo . . . altaria:* it was a common gesture of pious supplicants and desperate fugitives to embrace altars, and it became a commonplace of theatre and dramatic poetry. Butchery of an old man at the altar had its finest prototype for Ovid in the death of Priam (*Aen.* 2.550 ff.). But Ovid destroys the nobility of Vergil's scene by concentrating on the severed head and the incredibly voluble tongue. *decutit* 104: emphatic placing of special verb. This seems to be the first use to refer to a human beheading; Ovid has worked from the tale of Tarquin, whom both Livy in 1.54 and he himself in *Fast.* 2.707, portray with this verb knocking off the heads of flowers, in order to convey to his son that he should execute similarly the leaders of Gabii. *incidit arae:* the head on the altar epitomizes for Ovid the frustration of piety. No other Latin writer quite equaled the daring of 105. *exspiravit* 106: in the same metrical position as *exsecrantia* above, it provides the grotesquely appropriate comment on the old man's unbelievable final words. The head, no longer connected to the chest and lungs, still breathes its last into the fire and thus, I suppose, fans the flames!

07–
10 *hinc:* on the side of Perseus, from among the fellow-banqueters. *gemini fratres:* Vergil has used the same words in *Aen.* 7.670, to introduce twins from Tibur in a solemn epic catalogue. Ovid will use the phrase again in another mock-epic setting at 8.372, to describe the abortive heroism of Castor and Pollux. Here, too, he is comparing these twins to the Dioscuri, as reference to boxing "gloves" makes evident. *invicti vinci* 108: with the enjambement, Ovid completes his deceptive build-up, then immediately starts to dismantle it. Juxtaposition of two forms of *vincere,* contrary-to-fact condition, and four spondees all combine to dismiss boxing (*caestibus,* ironically in the

same position in successive lines) and insist on the supreme power of swords. *Phinea* 109: adjective with three long vowels. *manu:* up to now, Phineus has been afraid to venture into hand-to-hand battle (cf. 89), but the Latin (especially, *enses* 108) implies that he used his sword on the unlucky twins. *Cererisque sacerdos:* Ovid selects another vignette of affronted *pietas*. The model and a significant amount of his language come from a notorious scene of impiety in *Aen*. 10.537 ff. where Aeneas, outraged by the death of Pallas, attacks a priest, who is in full sacramental dress, and "sacrifices" him there on the battlefield. This scene has none of Vergil's power.

111–
13   The poet apostrophizes the next victim, perhaps because he was a kindred spirit? *non hos . . . ad usus:* bards do not belong amid fighting, as Homer showed in the case of Phemius in the *Odyssey. sed qui . . . moveres* 112: relative clause of characterization with nuance of purpose. *pacis opus:* apposition that precedes, in common Ovidian fashion, the idea it explicates (cf. 2.340–41). *cum voce:* since this is an instance when the accusative *vocemque* would have fitted the meter, it seems that Ovid deliberately avoided the obvious wit of zeugma. *celebrare . . . canendo* 113: alliteration dignifies the bard's calling and completes Ovid's set-up.

114–
18   *quem . . . adstantem . . . tenentem:* Ovid now changes Lampetides into object, describes his harmless behavior as entertainer, and then makes him the victim of the violence. *inbelle:* he holds no weapon, but an innocent pluck for his lyre. *inridens* 115: the sardonic attitude of this murderer makes this killing especially disgusting. *Stygiis . . . manibus:* the interruption of the short speech with the verb of saying seems to mirror what the speaker says and carries out: he cuts short the bard's song at the banquet and dispatches him to the Shades (where, for all we know, he may have continued singing). *mucronem . . . fixit:* although the noun regularly signifies, in Ovid and other writers, the sword point, it would seem that here Paetalus has thrown a spear, whose point has pierced the left temple. The location of the bard at a distance (114) and the verb *fixit* combine to require a spear cast. *digitis morientibus* 117: a novel expression, as Ovid personifies the musician's fingers and lets them bathetically epitomize his death. *retemptat:* a devoted bard to the end, Lampetides struggles to go on with his lyre-playing to the death. *casuque* 118: the first time in the poem when Ovid uses this word to comment on a scene of melodramatic irony. He will repeat the device at 6.359 and 7.84. Supposedly, the bard has been engaged in a tearful, pathetic song when he was fatally wounded, so it becomes most appropriate for him to take up that tune again.

119–
22   *nec . . . inpune . . . cecidisse:* Lycormas avenges the bard. This infinitive echoes the verb of 117. *raptaque . . . repagula* 120: ablative

absolute. He grabs a heavy wooden bar that serves to bolt the great right door of the banquet hall. He apparently strikes Paetalus from the rear, for he hits the vertebrae of his neck and fells him like a sacrificial bullock. Animals were downed by a blow from a hammer that smashed in their skulls.

23– *laevi quoque robora postis:* the next warrior tries to imitate Lycormas,
25 by grabbing the bar from the left door. He shares his name Pelates with a centaur in 12.255; he originates in North Africa, far from Ethiopia. *temptanti* 124: balances the active verb of 123 and starts the report of the fatal halting of Pelates' efforts. *dextera:* he has reached for the bar with his right hand, so that becomes the ironic target of another spear. The point pierces the hand and pins it to the wood. *Marmaridae* 125: this Corythus comes from North Africa, too, from Marmarica near Carthage.

26– Abas' name will be given a centaur in 12.306. He has an easy, helpless
27 victim and slashes his side. Unable to fall like others fatally wounded, Pelates hangs dying from the door.

28– Melaneus, a centaur in 12.306, has a name that suggests dark skin,
31 but comes from Persia. Dorylas, named as a centaur in 12.380, comes from Libya in North Africa (which in Ovid's day was a rich source of wheat for Italy). *ditissimus agri* 129: phrase borrowed from the description of Sychaeus in *Aen.* 1.343 or of Camers, a battle-victim of Aeneas in 10.563. Ovid elaborates the irony of futile wealth in war. *turis acervos* 131: scribes early were surprised by the alliterative word for incense and emended to *farris,* an expected term for grain. But Ovid's point is that with his vast wealth Dorylas has bought up huge quantities of exotic incense from the East, accumulating it in heaps! He is evidently one of the guests, not a warrior ready for battle; and Perseus will avenge him (cf. 138).

32– *in obliquo . . . inguine:* another ugly wound. The spear drives into
36 his groin from the side, i.e., from an unexpected quarter. In other scenes, as when the chauvinistic braggart Ancaeus is felled during the Calydonian hunt in 8.399 ff., a wound to the groin has special aptness. *letifer ille locus* 133: epic compound and alliteration add to the effect of this half-line. *vulneris auctor:* name postponed to 135, so that we can see in our imaginations the throes of his victim that he watched in 134 and sharply distance ourselves from his crude exultation. *singultantem* 134: Ovid was thinking of the first known use of this verb, in this precise form and similar battle context, in *Aen.* 9.333, where a victim of Nisus sobs out his last bloody breaths. *versantem lumina:* rolling the eyes is a common sign of agony. Ovid uses the phrase again in 6.247 of the death-throes of two Niobids. *Bactrius* 135: Halcyoneus comes from Bactria on the borders of India. *hoc . . . terrae:* partitive genitive; "this portion of earth." *de tot agris:*

with its clear recollection of 130, Ovid emphasizes the ironic fate of all rich people, indeed all human beings, who end up, whether as ashes or corpses in coffins, possessors of a tiny plot of land. *corpusque exsangue:* same phrase for a corpse in 2.647.

137–
39
hastam . . . raptam: the situation differs from that of Idas (cf. 95–96), who pulled out the spear that had wounded him and intended to throw it back at the enemy—in vain. Dorylas has fallen, so his avenger, Perseus, yanks the weapon from the corpse and throws it at Halcyoneus. *Abantiades* 138: cf. 4.673 and 5.236. Ovid sketches out the grotesque wound and forces us to linger over it with the four spondees of 139. *in partesque* 139: the *-que* would belong on *eminet* in most other writers, even poets.

140–
43
manum Fortuna iuvat: a perversion of the Roman saying that Fortune favors the brave or bold. Turnus used the motto as a rallying cry in *Aen.* 10.284, where the second and third words here have the same metrical position. Ovid contrasts the heroic ethic of true epic and this urge of Perseus to inflict ugly wounds on negligible enemies. The victims this time are brothers with alliterative names—Clanis will be a centaur in 12.379. *una diverso* 141: key terms juxtaposed at the caesura. For the grim joke when brothers, especially twins, are distinguished by different fatal wounds, there will be a long future, notably in Lucan. *Clytii per utrumque . . . femur* 142–43: somehow, Perseus has secured two more spears; he hurls one with such incredible force that it pierces both thighs of Clytius. As for the other, Ovid euphemistically says that Clanis "bit" it, enough to indicate that the spear went in the open mouth or from the side through the cheeks. The narrator's insouciance is suggested by the rapid five unelided dactyls.

144–
48
After lingering over these three kills of Perseus, we hear in a single sentence of four more. Ovid spares us the details of the wounds and concentrates on the piquant in the victims' background. Celadon (a centaur in 12.250) comes from Mendes on the Nile Delta. Astreus has a checkered origin: an identifiable Palestinian mother, but an unknown father. The chiastic order of detail in 145, ending with the disgraceful, may well imply that the mother was a prostitute. Aethion enacts the ironic fate of other epic seers (e.g., Rhamnes in *Aen.* 9.327–28): he failed to foresee his own death or, as Ovid puts it, he misread an omen. We might wonder why any seer would have joined the murderous band of Phineus. *caeso genitore infamis* 148: Agyrtes has killed his father and earned eternal notoriety, but there must have been some accident or extenuating circumstance, or else he would have been a public pariah.

149–
51
plus tamen exhausto superest: "there is more remaining than what has been accomplished." The narrator reduces all those bloody deaths to an impersonal neuter singular: *exhausto,* ablative of comparison.

omnibus unum: Ovid likes this antithetical pair. Perhaps the most outrageous example occurs in 10.317–18, where Orpheus too wittily plays with Myrrha's unique desire for her father. Here, we focus on the incredible odds confronting Perseus: a thousand vs. one. The narrator works hard to slant our attitude in his hero's favor. The intruders fight, he asserts, for a cause that fights against the right. *meritum* 151: Persius' earned reward to marry Andromeda. *fidemque:* the promise of Cepheus to his daughter's savior.

52–
53 *hac pro parte:* Perseus' side, which the narrator adopts as his own with the demonstrative. *socer frustra pius:* like Vergil's Latinus. Cepheus left the hall at the start of the battle (43–45), so his "favor" amounts to very little. Andromeda and Cassiope, however, seem to have remained, and they contribute a series of piercing screams. In effect, Perseus fights alone (149, 157).

54–
56 *sed sonus . . . superat:* just as we begin to imagine the halls echoing the women's shrieks, the narrator declares that they are drowned out by the clash of arms and groans of the wounded and dying. *pollutosque . . . penates / sanguine perfundit* 155–56: note the alliteration. The household gods have been polluted because an important family occasion, the celebration of a wedding, has been disrupted by Phineus' murderous intrusion. *renovataque:* Bellona keeps renewing the battle, spurring on Perseus' foes.

57–
59 The narrator describes the incredible plight of the hero, one against a thousand: weapons whiz around him everywhere, but not one touches him or his armor! *hiberna grandine plura* 158: ablative of comparison. It is evident that the narrator inhabits southern regions, to be able to use *winter* hail as an example of thickly falling missiles. Farther north, it would be more accurate to refer to heavy winter snow or springtime pelting hail.

60–
63 With his back to a solid column, like the conventional hero in the cinema who protects his back, Perseus continues to fight fearlessly, unscathed, killing many. *adversaque in agmina versus* 161: he faces the mass of attackers. This heroic stance is the reverse of the coward's position, who turns his back (and tail) to the enemy, exposing himself to ignominious wounds if he does not run away. *instantes; instabat* 162: stylish Ovidian juxtaposition at the caesura of different forms of the same verb in related clauses. Molpeus comes from Chaonia, which is not the famous region in Epirus where the shrine of Dodona stood, but rather a place in Syria mentioned otherwise only once in ancient sources. All other followers of Phineus come from either Africa or Asia. Echemmon is Arabian.

64–
66 In an epic simile, Ovid uses two lines to describe the situation of a tiger, then in 166 assigns it the anthropomorphic "doubt" that will facilitate the connection with Perseus. What is notable, though, is the

fact that the supposedly outnumbered, hard-pressed hero is trans-
formed into a beast of prey that has no constraints on its savage desires.
We might rather have expected the beast surrounded by hunters, a
favorite Homeric analogue for the warrior in difficulty. But this narra-
tor never makes Perseus convincing. *auditis . . . duorum . . . mugiti-
bus armentorum:* Ovid uses hyperbaton to frame the two lines with
the two adjectives and their nouns. He also gives special attention to
the second line, which consists of four words only, the first invented
by Ovid for this passage (also in 6.459 and *Fast.* 6.588) and the last
a double spondee. *diversa valle* 164: although the normal interpretation
would assume that the two herds bellow in a valley different from
the one where the tiger stands, the battle context suggests that we
should treat the singular here as standing for the plural. Thus, just as
Perseus looks to left and right and wonders which foe he will attack
first, so the tiger hears sounds in two valleys on either side of it and
cannot decide which herd to attack. *utro . . . ruat, et ruere . . .
utroque* 166: chiastic arrangement of pronouns and verbs. In contrast
to 165, this line has eight words and five dactyls. As the animal,
which has stopped to listen and work out its problem, moves into
action, the rhythm speeds up.

167–   *dextra laevane feratur:* for this simplified treatment of the alternative
69   indirect question, cf. 1.578. Perseus quickly disposes of Molpeus on
        the left, wounding him, it seems, with still another spear that pierces
        his shin. He flees, in a most awkward manner, one imagines, and the
        hero turns to meet the attack of Echemmon from the right.

170–   *furit:* the rage of this warrior translates into total ineptitude and absurd
73   failure. The narrator seems to construct a serious danger for Perseus
        in 170, but that quickly shatters. The four spondees of 171 slow down
        the action as this oaf awkwardly raises his sword to stab Perseus'
        throat and strikes instead the column (cf. 160), shattering his weapon.
        The narrator then contrives a grotesque result: the sword blade, sepa-
        rated from the handle by the shock, rebounds from the column and
        pierces Echemmon's throat. That is apparently "poetic justice."

174–   Since the wound is not fatal, Perseus has his heroic opportunity.
76   But now Echemmon appears an abject, easy victim. *inertia frustra /
        bracchia tendentem* 175–76: Ovid frequently shows the failure of
        suppliants, with special grimness. He has used the two words of 176
        in the same metrical position in 4.517 as mad Athamas seized his son
        (who was holding out his arms affectionately) and killed him. Soon
        Phineus will make the suppliant gesture (215) to Perseus and be
        malevolently spurned. For the rejection of the defeated warrior's ap-
        peal, Ovid has a Vergilian model in *Aen.* 10.595–96. *confodit:* answer
        to the prayer; Perseus stabs him, perhaps repeatedly, in his help-
        lessness. The hero turns out to be an unworthy tiger (cf. 164).

77–
80

virtutem turbae succumbere: the clause defines a common situation, where one brave man cannot finally prevail against superior numbers, but the abstract terms here invite our inspection. It is not at all evident that Perseus has truly personified *virtus.* His victories have been too easy, one-sided, and grotesque. When he resorts to the Gorgon's head, all heroism vanishes. *auxilium . . . ab hoste petam* 178–79: confident Perseus can afford to jest menacingly about the "reinforcements" he uses. Medusa was once his self-chosen enemy. Now she generously supplies him with her petrifying head, according to our hero. *siquis amicus adest* 180: friends present would be Andromeda, Cassiope, and other invited guests. However, it is odd that the enemies could not have used this warning, too.

81–
83

quem moveant: subjunctive in relative purpose clause. *oracula:* an alternate reading, *miracula,* early came into existence. Apparently, the scribes did not understand that Thescelus was reacting to the implicit prediction in 179–80, and they imagined a reference to the marvelous transformations that will now take place through petrification. But Thescelus did not know this yet; he found out too late. *utque . . . parabat* 182: carefully chosen conjunction; from this point, Perseus' enemies will be halted in the moment of action, transformed into striking statue poses. Thescelus is the "javelin-thrower." *signum de marmore:* especially suggestive of a statue. Elsewhere, the stone is flint (e.g., 199) or not specified (e.g., 202). It is significant that Phineus is meant by Perseus to be a special "memorial" (227) and so turns into marble (234).

84–
86

animi plenissima magni: like Thesculus, full of foolish words and pride, Ampyx is filled with high spirit, which becomes quickly negated by Perseus' super-weapon. *inque petendo* 185: the moment when the pose is frozen. Now we have a "swordsman." The poet focuses on the right hand with its weapon; it stops moving. *nec citra . . . nec ultra* 186: an unusual doublet for "not at all." Literally, "neither inside nor beyond," the phrase might better be applied to the weapon than to the hand that holds it; that is, the sword stopped threatening to pierce the hero and to come out the other side of his chest.

87–
90

Nileus starts off as though of noble birth, with an epic compound to add dignity in 187; but then the narrator destroys his pretensions with *ementitus* 188. Ovid is the only Latin poet to have used this word, which otherwise belongs to prose. The narrator brings Nileus down to reality: either he is a bastard (cf. 145) or he lies about an ignoble father. Compounding his deception, the fool uses his shield to urge his false claim. *flumina septem:* like *septemplice* in 187, refers to the seven streams of the Nile Delta. *partim, partim* 189: chiastic arrangement of metals and adverbs at caesura. Four spondees add to the impression of false solemnity. *nostrae primordia gentis* 190: the moment of peak irony as Nileus invites Perseus to look at his shield, the counterfeit blazon of his origin; but he will look at the Gorgon, fatal reality in the hand of Perseus.

191–
94
solacia mortis: Ovid likes this versatile motif, and he has already used it during this battle at 73, to refer to the real consolation that Lycabas felt in dying with Athis. In epic, it is supposed to be a comfort to have been killed by a great(er) hero. Aeneas offers that as solace to the corpse of Lausus in *Aen.* 10. 829–30; it does not necessarily convince Vergil's audience, any more than it impressed the unhearing dead. (Ovid lets Achilles offer similar *solamen mortis* in 12.80–81 after an undistinguished, almost ridiculous victory over Cygnus.) Here, however, Nileus has the effrontery to predict his victory and its solace, which rests on his fake origins. *tanto . . . viro* 192: it can only be appropriate that he become *nullus vir sed saxum.* The narrator focuses on the braggart mouth of this blatant liar, which fails to enunciate the end of its sentence, frozen forever trying to impress others with Nileus' unreal manliness and nobility. *credas* 194: we are invited to picture the statue.

195–
97
A fourth fool, Eryx, shows no sympathy for his petrified companions, but berates them for cowardice. *vitio . . . animi, non viribus:* antithesis heightened by alliteration, both words dependent in different ways on *torpetis* 196. He thinks their transformation is psychological and temporary; it needs only shame to change them back into real men. *incurrite* 196: Ovid will remind us of this with *incursurus* 198. *magica arma moventem* 197: Eryx, while sneering, admits here that the Gorgon does possess significant power.

198–
99
Having called for a charge against the Greek, Eryx is rendered immobile, fixed in a stance of one about to move. Each of these "statues" reminds one of Hellenistic art and its emphasis on unbalanced, twisted bodies. *silex* 199: this somewhat unfamiliar word has been changed in many MSS to the easier verb *silet. armataque . . . imago:* he has become an artistic representation of a warrior.

200–
2
ex merito poenas subiere: the narrator confidently assesses blame. *miles erat Persei* 201: an apparent inconsistency with earlier information (e.g., 149) that our hero fought single-handed. He obviously did not pay attention to the warning of 179–80. *saxo concrevit oborto* 202: the description poetically suggests that the stone spreads and congeals over the body.

203–
6
Astyages: the most famous holder of this name was the Mede grandfather of Cyrus; this is another Asian. *ense ferit: sonuit . . . ensis* 204: the surprising result of the sword-blow gains effect from the chiastic pattern that juxtaposes the verbs. *tinnitibus . . . acutis:* the sounding sword is framed by this phrase, which registers high-pitched metallic noise instead of the groan of wounded Aconteus. *stupet* 205: standard

response to metamorphosis. *naturam . . . eandem:* he turns into stone of a specific kind. *marmoreoque . . . in ore* 206: Ovid aims for "lapidary lines" to fix the stance of each new statue. Cf. 199, where also he uses *manere* and alliteration on *m*. *manere* fits nicely any transformation into a lifeless entity. *mirantis:* Astyages becomes fixed ironically in an expression of amazement, but at another's metamorphosis, unaware of his own.

:07– 9 *nomina longa mora est:* it is a common device for a poet, embarked on an epic catalogue, to break it off, as though intent on getting on with the story and not boring the audience. Ovid does this with his mock-epic dog-catalogue in 3.225. Here, the narrator, with aristocratic bias, refuses to dwell on the fates of ordinary (*media de plebe*) warriors. In 208–9, by wittily altering *restabant* into *riguerunt,* he summarily reduces two hundred living bodies to stone. We might wonder what happened to the rest of the thousand he so wildly cited at 157.

:10– 14 *iniusti . . . belli:* the narrator represents Phineus as condemning himself in Roman terms of waging an unjust war and therefore deserving harsh punishment. However, this has been no "war"; it has been total slaughter and defeat for Phineus. *quid agat?* 211: Phineus' dilemma is posed indirectly. *simulacra:* his allies have become statues in various poses. *quemque vocatum / poscit opem* 212–13: double accusative with *poscere. sibi proxima tangit / corpora* 214: although *sibi* could be taken with *credens,* the caesura before it and the regular association of *proxima* with the dative make it more likely that *sibi* goes with the following word. Phineus touches the lifelike statues near him to convince himself of the hopeless truth.

:14– 27 *avertitur:* Phineus is reduced to grotesque grovelling, forced to twist his head away as he talks, yet to assume the suppliant position. He is the first to follow Perseus' warning (cf. 179); but because he is no friend, Perseus will still petrify him. *confessasque manus* 215: the hands admit defeat and so plead for mercy. This is a special phrase devised by Ovid to emphasize the pathos of Phineus. *obliquaque bracchia:* because he has turned away, yet wants to hold out arms toward Perseus, he cannot stretch them directly. The double object of *tendens,* two parts of the suppliant's arms, overstates the case. Readers often compare this scene with the end of the *Aeneid* where the fallen Turnus addresses his victor in humility, and it may be that Ovid was thinking of that, so as to expose the cold cruelty and unheroic behavior of Perseus. Vergil contrived an especially powerful scene with an unusual pair of objects (930–31): *supplexque oculos dextramque precantem / protendens; oculos* does not normally go with this verb. *vincis* 216: Turnus said *vicisti* to Aeneas (936). He made a brave appeal to his enemy, whereas Phineus behaves and talks like the coward he is. Turnus was facing death; this man trembles before

a worse fate, petrifaction. Thus, instead of concentrating on the hero's
poised sword, we watch what he does with his unheroic super-weapon,
the Gorgon head. *tuaeque . . . Medusae:* these paired words frame
the desperate appeal, whose anxiety is implied in the unusual enjambe-
ment. *saxificos:* Ovid has invented this word, an epic formation in a
context of antiheroic, unepic emotions and behavior. *quaecumque ea:*
supply *est,* which a few MSS tried to substitute unnecessarily for *ea.*
As often, the antecedent of the relative, here *Medusae,* follows.

218–   In 218–19, Phineus denies that hatred or ambition motivated him; and
22   in fact the narrator has not attributed them to him. *pro coniuge* 219:
as indeed he stated when he rushed in (cf. 10). *causa . . . meritis
melior tua, tempore nostra* 220: Phineus reduces the issue to a single
witty line that jingles along with five dactyls and plays with the ethical
term "better" and two very different ablatives of specification. Cepheus
earlier in his self-justifying speech to Phineus had begun and ended
by insisting on the merits of Perseus (14, 28). Phineus concedes that
point, merely stating that he had priority (which does not count for
much, he also implies). *non cessisse piget* 221: "I am not ashamed
to have been defeated." The negative goes with *piget. praeter / hanc
animam:* ending the line with the preposition and separating by en-
jambement preposition and its complement take away dignity from
Phineus. *tua cetera sunto:* future imperative balances present impera-
tive *concede,* but perhaps tries to make Perseus' spoils, "everything
else," specially impressive.

223–   *talia dicenti neque . . . respicere audenti:* the dative participles change
26   Phineus into victim awaiting his end. Ovid again reminds us that his
supplication is made in a twisted position (cf. 214–15). Normally,
the suppliant counted on the appeal of his eyes as well as his hands
and words. *quod . . . munus:* effective hyperbaton and heavily ironic
choice of noun after the delay. *timidissime* 224: this contemptuous,
ungracious superlative balances the flattering one used by Phineus at
221. The victor continues to sneer with *inerti* 225. *pone metum* 226:
this parenthetical comment, although elsewhere potentially reassuring,
does not work that way, I think, here. It is another sneer; otherwise,
the rapid way in which the "hero" announces his real intentions in
the following line would not be dramatically consistent. *nullo . . .
ferro:* not Phineus' chief fear.

227–   *dabo monimenta:* by omitting the pronoun of the second person singu-
29   lar and obscuring the relation between Phineus and these lasting monu-
ments, Perseus teases and gloats over his helpless victim. His sardonic
mood differs totally from the righteous anger that moves Aeneas in
his final action against Turnus. Perseus gives nothing *to* Phineus except
humiliation and death. He makes *of him* a lasting memorial for the
supposed pleasure of Cepheus and especially of Andromeda. *soceri*

. . . *nostri* 228: Phineus will permanently be trapped in a family now dominated by his rival, whose father-in-law, remember, is Phineus' very brother. *se sponsi soletur imagine* 229: Perseus cruelly suggests that Andromeda will mourn the loss of her ex-fiancé Phineus and, as other heroines in literature cling to a locket or a photo of a lost lover, so Andromeda will roam through this gallery of twisted statues to find consolation in the most twisted and cowardly of the lot.

230– *Phorcynida:* cf. 4.743. *transtulit:* he quickly moved the head so as
31   to have it stare at the averted face of Phineus. *trepido . . . ore* 231: the narrator continues to be as cold and pitiless as Perseus.

232– *conanti sua vertere lumina:* Phineus tries to make another evasive
35   turn, but too late. *cervix / deriguit:* the details of this metamorphosis start at the neck and quickly work upward to the parts of the all too expressively terrified face. Panic becomes frozen on the statue. *oculorum . . . umor:* Phineus cries with fear. The less heroic he is represented, the less heroic Perseus strikes us. The final two lines, with the attributes they assign to each of the physical parts, emphasize the suppliant who has been so basely spurned. That is indeed the eternal memorial of Perseus' achievement.

TRANSITION: MINERVA VISITS THE MUSES (236–93)

Ovid follows Perseus back to Greece for two final minor episodes, ignoring Andromeda entirely and never letting the pseudo-hero settle down "happily ever after." Nor does he round off the motifs that he had defined at the start (cf. 4.607 ff.), where Perseus' grandfather Acrisius was contrasted unfavorably with Cadmus and seemed headed for the same doom as Pentheus. It was well known that Perseus did indeed kill Acrisius, by accident, unwittingly serving as agent of divine displeasure. Instead of reporting that episode, Ovid tells us that Acrisius was overthrown and exiled by his evil brother Proetus (238–39), and so Perseus can be cast as noble avenger of his grandfather. That happens in Argos. Perseus continues on to Seriphos (where his mother Danae is, though Ovid ignores that fact) and punishes king Polydectes for the same kind of disrespect that has characterized all his enemies, from Atlas to Phineus: belittlement of his heroism. As we might expect, he uses his antiheroic weapon, Medusa's head. These stories, both cited as early as Pindar, may be found, with variations, in Apollodoros 2.4.3.6 ff. and Hyginus 63–64.

Having been reunited with his mother on Seriphos, Perseus traditionally had no further need for magical aids: he gave back his wings to his "brother" Mercury and donated the head of Medusa to his "sister" Minerva for her aegis. Ignoring that fact, Ovid merely says that Minerva flew off for a brief tour to Helicon, to see where Pegasus

had made the Fountain of Hippocrene with his hoof. This visit brings
the goddess into contact with the Muses, and a courteous exchange
of compliments ensues. Though happy with their spot on Mount
Helicon, the Muses have been having trouble with hostile intruders.
First, the tyrant of nearby Daulis, Pyreneus, tried to rape them and,
chasing them when they fled, fell to his own death. Second, and more
serious, the Pierides challenged the Muses' essential role as singers.
The second episode will be the concern of the remainder of this book
(294 ff.); the former, apparently first told and perhaps invented by
Ovid, serves merely as an introduction. Ovid uses familiar motifs in
a cursory fashion, and he forces a metamorphosis into the story by
reporting that the Muses escaped by "taking wing" (288). Since the
Muses are not known to have been winged or to have been depicted
so, Ovid seems to have taken pains to make them briefly bird-like
both to provide an explanation of Pyreneus' death and to assimilate
them momentarily to their rivals, the Pierides, who have been turned
into birds as punishment.

236–   *victor Abantiades:* the last time Perseus received this epic patronymic,
38   he was styled *ultor* (138) and savagely wounded an enemy. In 237,
        he will become a more political "avenger." *patrios . . . muros:* Argos,
        where he was sired. Since Jupiter raped Danae and vanished, the
        adjective refers not to his father, but his fatherland. *inmeriti . . .
        parentis* 237: his grandfather Acrisius (cf. 239). These selected details
        completely change our earlier impression of the man.

238–   *Acrisioneas* 239: Vergil had invented this resonant patronymic adjec-
41   tive in *Aen.* 7.410 and used it to create a four-word hexameter; Ovid
        follows his pattern to describe an infamous, unepic usurpation. Note
        the alliteration. *quam . . . arce* 240: relative before antecedent. All
        Proetus' military advantages cannot cope with a super-weapon. In
        241, ending this episode, Ovid flashes a Golden Line and an "epic"
        neologism: the compound *colubriferi.*

242–   The poet turns to a new episode and main character, Polydectes,
45   whom he apostrophizes in 242. The form seems to suggest respect,
        but that rapidly vanishes in 243 ff. Seriphos, an island in the Aegaean
        more than a hundred miles east of Argos, would normally be, and
        was in fact in other versions of Perseus' chronicle, the first stop for
        the traveller returning from Ethiopia. *virtus per tot spectata labores*
        243: the participle was regularly used by Romans with abstract nouns
        like this in inscriptions and political slogans. Thus, Ovid's phrase
        casts Perseus in biased political terms. We have already questioned
        the claim of *virtus* at 177. *mala mollierant* 244: it is not clear what
        "evils" Ovid refers to in this alliterative clause, but he probably means
        Perseus' heroic troubles. The metaphor of "softening" prepares for

the petrification of an all too "rigid" personality (cf. *durus*). *iniqua
. . . ira* 245: Ovid piles up stereotypical details of a tyrant deserving
punishment.

246– *detrectas:* Ovid is the first poet to bring this sense of the verb, associ-
49   ated with political propaganda and electioneering, into verse. The
detractor is not a likable person, especially when, as here, he belittles
assured deeds. *Medusae . . . necem:* Proetus had actually sent Perseus
on what he expected to be the fatal quest, to get Medusa's head, so
now he sneers at the hero's proud report. *pignora veri:* he will prove
he tells the truth; objective genitive. *parcite luminibus* 248: Ovid
naughtily borrows this clause from a totally different context in
Tibullus 1.2.35, to warn Perseus' friends to look away (cf. 179).
Tibullus was asking passers-by not to spy on his amatory activities.
The only friends Perseus has on Seriphos are his mother Danae and
Polydectes' brother Dictys. Indeed, Apollodoros has the petrification
of the king take place at a banquet, where all his courtiers share his
fate. Ovid avoids repetition of what happened in Ethiopia. *oraque
regis / ore . . . silicem . . . fecit* 249: final use of Medusa, which
combines the witty repetition of forms of *os* with the just reduction
of this bloody, hard man to a bloodless flint.

250– *aurigenae:* Ovid's invention here was imitated only at the end of
52   antiquity by Sidonius. It of course refers to the shower of gold by
which Jupiter impregnated Danae. Epic in form, it goes with the
epithet for Minerva, *Tritonia,* in the same line. Leaving Seriphos in
a cloud, Minerva heads for Thebes, which takes her northwest past
Cythnos and Gyaros on her right.

253– *via . . . brevissima:* i.e., the most direct route; as we say, "the way
55   the crow flies." *virgineumque Helicona* 254: the adjective prepares
us for the Muses and their endangered virginity. Same adjective at
274. *monte potita:* "having reached that mountain." *constitit* 255:
i.e., she stopped her flying and lit on earth. *doctas . . . sorores:* as
exemplary singers, the Muses have the ideal asset of contemporary
Roman poets: they are erudite in the Alexandrian tradition.

256– *novi fontis:* Minerva has heard the story of the new marvel, a metamor-
59   phosis recently produced by Pegasus after his birth from Medusa's
blood (cf. 4.785–86). *nostras pervenit ad aures:* Ovid models this
courtly conversation on a famous clause of *Aen.* 2.81, which differs
only in using the adjective *tuas,* where Sinon lies to the Trojans. The
two contexts differ so radically that Ovid must expect us to enjoy the
discrepancy. He repeats the words in *Fast.* 3.661. *Medusaei . . .
praepetis* 257: a very pompous circumlocution for Pegasus, who is
in some sense the "bird sprung from Medusa." *is mihi causa viae*
258: most often, the traveller does not volunteer information, but
provides it in answer to a query (cf. 2.38 and 5.11). *mirabile factum:*

a metamorphosis evokes a standard reaction of amazement. *vidi ipsum* 259: as Minerva was with her brother Perseus throughout his perils, she personally viewed the genesis of Pegasus.

260–63   The Muse recognizes that Minerva has not come to pay a visit, but shows thorough politeness: the goddess is most welcome on any account. *has . . . domos* 261: this place where the Muses live; we are not to think of any buildings. *vera . . . fama* 262: Urania confirms the report mentioned in 256. *est: est:* careful repetition on either side of the caesura, with the emphasis on the second occurrence. The Greek name *Hippocrene*, which means "horse-fountain," refers to its origin. *latices . . . sacros* 263: it is customary to regard the spring of the Muses as "sacred," because it causes poetic inspiration. *deduxit:* although a Muse is subject, and the verb frequently functions in passages about poetry, notably the proem to this poem in 1.4, Urania has no immediate poetic purpose. She guides this tourist down the mountain to the valley where the spring happens to be. However, Ovid assigns her a "generic" verb. Soon she is poetic.

264–68   *quae:* Minerva. *mirata . . . factas:* the goddess satisfies her expressed desire to see *mirabile factum* (cf. 258). *silvarum . . . antiquarum* 265: this impressive line uses the same devices as 165. It confines itself to four resonant words, and it ends with a double spondee. In fact, except for the fourth foot, there are nothing but spondees, to suggest the slow, admiring survey of the scenery by Minerva. The details of 266 amount to an idyllic Eden. *studioque locoque* 267: this doublet, which the Muse takes up at 271, refers to the poetic activity of the Muses and to their place of residence. For the moment, we focus on the second, less important and traditional detail, namely, place. *Mnemonidas* 268: the Muses are daughters of Memory, whose Greek equivalent is Mnemosyne; Ovid seems to have invented this matronymic from a rare Mnemone.

269–72   *virtus opera ad maiora:* in her flattering response to the goddess, the unnamed Muse commits a number of humorous errors, which no doubt Ovid planned. She attributes *virtus,* the noble basis of masculine, human greatness, to a female deity, then declares that that odd quality took the goddess away to "greater tasks," with a phrase that might well remind an attentive audience of how *maius opus* (e.g., in *Aen.* 7.45) signifies a greater poetic work. Minerva, of course, has a specially masculine nature from birth, but it does not emerge very nobly from this description. She has turned back on poetic art to pursue activities that, up to now, the poet has depreciated. *gratam sortem* 272: after recapitulating in 271 much of 267, the Muse continues with a synonym for *felices,* declaring her lot precarious. *tutae modo simus:* proviso clause.

273–   *vetitum . . . nihil:* the parenthesis expresses the generalization of a

75   prude, that nothing is safe from evil, especially her precious chastity.
      omnia terrent / virgineas mentes: although this could be a general
      statement of fact, we should understand *nostras.* All virgins do not
      fear everything, but these rather odd Muses do. *ante ora . . . vertitur:*
      she keeps imagining that she sees Pyreneus, never having totally
      recovered from her scare.

276– *Daulida:* Daulis lies on the principal road to Delphi from Boeotia.
78   Delphi itself lay within the territory of Phocis. *Threicio . . . milite:*
      Pyreneus had invaded from the north and occupied this key region.
      In 277, his power emerges as cruel and unjust, like that of a tyrant.
      templa . . . Parnasia 278: the Muse jumps without connective from
      political conditions of the time to the particular event that involved
      her and her sisters, when they travelled to Delphi. There are no temples
      on Mount Parnassus; that place connoted Delphi, the most famous
      site nearby, with a major shrine of Apollo. The Muses and Apollo
      have a common interest in poetry, so their visit occasions no surprise.
      vidit euntes: as the nine virgins pass through his domain, the tyrant
      notices them eagerly.

279– *veneratus numina:* Pyreneus recognizes the travellers as deities and
82   so goes through the formulaic reverence required when men encounter
      gods. The poet shaped this ironically as a Golden Line. In retrospect,
      the Muse comments on Pyreneus' deceptive look; at the time, the
      Muses were indeed deceived. *cognorat enim* 280: syncopated pluper-
      fect in the parenthesis sets the recognition as background. The narrator
      is explaining how the ruler was able to address them with the same
      grand term as earlier the poet used (268). *consistite:* seemingly polite
      invitation for the traveller to stop and rest (cf. 255). *tecto . . . meo*
      281–82: hyperbaton frames the whole infinitive clause, including the
      intrusive parenthesis. The invitation proves especially attractive in
      view of the bad weather.

282– *minores . . . superi:* using these relative terms, Pyreneus affects to
86   be especially pious and eager to welcome the gods, as other human
      beings before him had shown hospitality to visiting deities. Ovid has
      recorded one such visit that was ill-fated and indeed an apt prototype
      to this one: the host tried to do violence to his divine guest. That was
      Lycaon in 1.216 ff. A more reverent host appears later in the person
      of Philemon and his wife in 8.626 ff. Ovid may be twisting the words
      of Evander, who invited Aeneas into his humble home and encouraged
      him by saying that a god, Hercules, had entered there earlier. Here,
      Pyreneus appeals to precedent to invite a god, not a man. *tempore:*
      the weather helps to persuade the Muses to accept the invitation.
      primasque intravimus aedes 284: the first part of a Roman house
      included the atrium, the social center of a home, where virgins could
      properly risk themselves. There, polite conversation might take place

with no expectation of compromise, as in a modern living room.
desierant imbres 285: without giving any details of events during the
storm, the Muse leaps to the end of the rain, which she describes
with a poetic flourish that shows no sense of the story's shape. The
North Wind clears the skies, as it did earlier after the torrential rains
that produced the Great Flood (1.328–29). The poetic display includes
in 286 a Golden Line, more play with the metaphor of battle, and
alliteration.

287–   *inpetus . . . fuit:* supply *nobis.* They were ready to continue their
90   journey. *claudit:* it might have been more clever for Pyreneus to have
acted during the storm, but that is not the way this story goes. *vimque
parat* 288: same clause in 2.576 to refer to attempted rape. When the
verb changes to *tulit* (3.344 and 4.239), the rape is perpetrated. In
such expressions, Ovid stresses the violence of rape and ensures our
alienation from the rapist. *quam:* the intended force of *vim. sumptis
. . . alis:* Ovid twice uses a similar ablative absolute, *sumptis . . .
pennis* (4.47, 6.96) for bird-metamorphoses. As noted above, the
Muses elsewhere are never represented, in art or story, as winged or
birds. Thus, Ovid has presumably added this motif to his novel tale.
secuturo similis 289: since similarity really does not operate here—
Pyreneus definitely lacks wings—these two words mean little more
than simple *secuturus. stetit arduus arce:* since the Muses have soared
away into the air, the pursuer climbs to the highest point of his city,
the citadel, with the crazy intention of launching himself after them.
The adjective has mock-heroic associations, as it regularly served
Vergil to represent the tall stature of his heroes in battle. Ovid earlier
used the final two words at 2.306 in a scene involving Jupiter. *eadem*
290: Ovid neatly compresses Pyreneus' foolish words into a single
epigrammatic line—which has the same idea as Ruth's statement of
piety to her mother-in-law, but means something entirely different—
and yet, by separating this word from the rest of the statement, he
suggests the failure of this "sameness."

291–   *vecors:* this word, which lacks all poetic overtones in Latin, conveys
93   the puritanical Muse's contempt for Pyreneus. *summae . . . turris:*
for his first and last "flight" the man has chosen the highest point
on his battlements. The Muse continues with a grotesque, exulting
description of his death that makes her a fitting companion for the
narrator of Perseus' feats. *discussisque ossibus oris* 292: cf. one of
the first wounds inflicted by Perseus at 5.58 and a similar one in the
battle with the centaurs, 12.252. *tundit humum moriens* 293: the Muse
echoes another agonizing wound to the head by Perseus at 5.84.
scelerato sanguine: recalls the powerful poetry of Vergil at the end
of the *Aeneid,* when Aeneas expresses demonic anger against fallen

Turnus (12.949). The vengeful Muse here relishes the fact that the ground is soaked with the villain's blood.

THE MUSES AND THE PIERIDES (294–678)

The remainder of Book 5 presents a sprawling account of the Muses' difficulties with a rival set of maidens who challenge their poetic talents. Feeling much more menaced in this respect than by poor Pyreneus, they accept a contest, which leads predictably to the defeat of the mortal singers—how could human rivals surpass deities? In due course, these enemies become birds, too. However, although the outcome of such a contest is predetermined, the narration of the process of defeat allows Ovid to intrude a dissident opinion and leave his audience in doubt about the superiority of the Muses as poets and persons. Not that their challengers appeal to us: they are loud, arrogant, and—to judge from the brief summary of their singing entry—simply insulting. But the Muses prove equally obnoxious and incompetent, I think, by their poem; and we suffer it *ad nauseam* for more than three hundred meandering lines.

In direct antithesis to the blasphemous Pierid song about gods who resort to theriomorphism in order to escape the danger of monstrous Typhoeus (319–31), one of the Muses sets out to hymn the glory of the goddess Ceres (341–661). Here is the strange structure of the hymn:

1. Formal invocation of Ceres (341–45).
2. Punishment of Typhoeus in Sicily provides a locale (–358).
3. Jupiter's brother Dis carries Proserpina off from Enna (–408).
4. He returns to Hades with his prize despite nymph Cyane, who feels so offended that she weeps herself into a fountain (–437).
5. Ceres, an anxious and hysterical mother, hunts day and night, everywhere (–508):
   a) pausing for a drink (near Athens), she gets angry at a saucy child (Ascalabos) and turns him into a gecko (446–61);
   b) later, she finds Persephone's girdle in the waters of Cyane and angrily curses the entire earth to a grain-famine (465–86);
   c) she encounters the nymph Arethusa at her fountain in Syracuse, learning, with a minimum of digression, that Proserpina is living as wife and queen in Hades (–508);
6. Ceres storms off to Olympus to complain to Jupiter, who is Proserpina's father. He mildly offers a compromise, which she intends to reject (–533).

7. But Proserpina had violated a taboo and eaten in Hades (–538).
8. A wretch named Ascalaphus informed on her, and she punished the spy by turning him into an ill-omened horned owl (–550).
9. A contrasting bird-metamorphosis: the friends of Proserpina, afflicted with grief, turn into the sweet-voiced Sirens (–563).
10. Now Jupiter imposes an arrangement: Proserpina will divide the year between her "husband" and her mother Ceres (–571).
11. Feeling mollified, Ceres asks for more of the personal story of Arethusa, who earlier had suppressed it out of consideration. The nymph tells a long tale of attempted rape (–641).
12. Ceres at last considers the earth that she has cursed. She assigns to Triptolemus the task of recultivation and of teaching to primitive peoples the art of agriculture (–647).
13. Triptolemus encounters the Scythian king Lyncus, who violates the laws of hospitality, so Ceres turns him into a lynx (–660).
14. She then orders Triptolemus to fly back to Athens (–661).

This structural scheme indicates that the Muse does not know how to produce an effective narrative; she cannot refrain from getting herself involved in secondary tales of metamorphosis, which distract us from the supposedly main narrative and present unattractive qualities of both Ceres and Proserpina; far from maternal and loving, the Ceres of this hymn seems a self-indulgent egotist, who is quick to punish others, even a foolish child. The Muse has projected upon the goddess a personality that fits her own twisted and unloving attitudes, a paradigm of the powerful, vengeful goddess that, activated in the Muses, will turn the Pierides into nasty, unmusical daws. So we end by questioning the verdict of the acquiescent nymphs of Helicon: was it an earned victory of poetry? Is it not perhaps the poet of the *Met.*, Ovid rather than the Muse, who raises the questions about true poetry and proper divinity?

As Hinds shows, Ovid and his audience were familiar with the Homeric Hymn to Demeter, which serves as the framework for the Muse's effort. In *Fast.* 4.417 ff., Ovid used the occasion of the Cerealia in April to praise Ceres and tell of the Rape of Proserpina. Though not in hymn form, it retains its focus much more evidently than what we have here in *Met.* 5. And Ceres emerges less as a vengeful deity than an understandably concerned mother. Here, the poet has devised his own manner of presentation, choosing to introduce a situation of rivalry and bitter competition, which distorts the nature of the traditional hymn. It also makes an ineffective poetic structure and an unappealing major character, Ceres, whom the Muse tries to honor to answer the Pierides' dishonor. The metamorphoses, which form the most overt intrusion in the hymn and derive from post-Homeric,

Hellenistic poets like Nicander, expose the inadequacy of the Muse, *but also* enable a better poet to continue his regular topic and to characterize Ceres and the Muses as vengeful deities, who use metamorphosis cruelly and thoughtlessly for self-satisfaction. This *is* an artful composition; but the artist conceals himself behind the stumbling Muse.

The Pierides: Challenge and Song (294–331)

294–
97

loquebatur: the sequence of tenses indicates that, as the Muse was talking, the birds came up and started chattering, to interrupt her. *voxque salutantum* 295: Minerva has not seen any birds, and, when she hears voices that say something like *salve,* even though the sound comes from the tree branches, she looks for human beings. Whatever species of birds these are—and Ovid leaves scholars uncertain—they have the capacity to imitate human speech. Persius, Prol. 9, refers to the teacher who *picamque docuit nostra verba conari. suspicit* 296: the poet does not identify the subject as Minerva before the end of 297. *linguae quaerit . . . unde sonent:* word order radically upset from normal prose arrangement. Ovid has no metrical reason for changing the position of the first two words; he probably wanted to reflect the puzzlement of the goddess over these strange tongues, the way their sound triggered her query.

298–
99

ales erat: initial dactyl, first of five, with emphasis on the surprising answer to Minerva's expectations. We might have wondered why Ovid shifted from plural *linguae* of 296 to singular *hominem* in 297. It was not a metrical requirement of 297, but it prepared for this compact singular *ales* here in 298. There is no need to claim that Ovid is using the word as a collective singular. He pointedly goes from *ales* to the exact number and species. "It was a bird; in fact, nine magpies!" *imitantes omnia picae* 299: Ovid will return to this description at the end of the book (678–80). There, he refers only to the imitation of all human sounds. The only other source for this story of the Pierides is fixed by Antoninus Liberalis 9 as Nicander in Book 4 of his *Heteroioumena:* Liberalis' summary describes a very different contest, in which we learn nothing of the songs themselves, but only of the way the natural world of Helicon reacted, gloomily to the Pierides, sunnily and spring-like to the Muses—that was the obvious verdict. The losers then become nine different birds, with no particular connection to what they boasted of being before. Ovid has gone well beyond Nicander and incorporated the challengers carefully into his total scheme.

300–
4

miranti: the poet lets the goddess express the standard response to the marvel of metamorphosis (even before she knows of that event).

deae dea: Ovid wittily epitomizes this female conversation. *victae certamine* 301: announces the dramatic context, and Ovid broaches a topic that extends into Book 6. By inserting this unit inside *volucrum . . . turbam,* Ovid suggests that the defeat of the Pierides resulted in their increasing the bird-species. *Pellaeis dives in arvis* 302: Ovid, like Nicander, locates Pieros in Macedonia, adding to the brief data preserved by Liberalis that he was a rich inhabitant of Pella (also birthplace of Alexander the Great). The wealth accounts for the pride if not also for the number of his daughters. Adding to the epic introduction of the foe, the Muse develops a formal description of the mother Euippe (not mentioned by Liberalis). The subtle implication behind placing these rivals in Macedonia is that since they are barely Greeks, they could hardly presume to superiority over the Muses. Their presumption, then, proves their low state of culture. *noviens, noviens* 304: careful juxtaposition at the caesura of two different clauses, as *est, est* above, line 262. Nine human sisters somehow seem more surprising than the nine divine sisters, the Muses.

305–7 *intumuit numero:* having just mentioned childbirth, Ovid uses a verb that often applies to the swollen state of pregnancy; now, however, it refers to foolish pride over the nine children that resulted from those numerous pregnancies. Vain pride over many children will characterize the contest in Book 6 between Niobe and Latona. As mother of Apollo and Diana, Latona has only two children, but they avenge her. In this story, Euippe remains innocent; it is the children themselves, who, though they deserve no credit for the result, preen themselves over their nine. *perque tot . . . et per tot* 306: the poet skillfully places the same words in different relative metrical positions to vary his rhythm. We can perhaps imagine the proud parade of these Pierides down from Macedonia to Helicon. *committit proelia* 307: a standard expression in prose histories for the beginning of battle. Ovid has used a slight variant at 5.75. The Muse, remember, applies these pretentious military metaphors to this singing contest.

308–11 *indoctum . . . volgus:* Ovid assigns to the Pierides an arrogant Hellenistic put-down (borrowed from Propertius 2.23.1) of the Greek audience. This reverses the usual Greek scorn of Macedonians. *vana dulcedine:* in other contexts, the sweetness of song "captivates" its audience. Here, the Pierides sneer at sweetness, as some modern music-lovers depreciate the melodic works of the nineteenth century. *siqua est fiducia vobis* 309: questioning another's confidence makes an impression of over-confidence, which foreshadows disaster. *Thespiades* 310: the Muses live near the village of Thespiae by Mount Helicon. *nec . . . vincemur* 311: the Muse has already forecast their defeat at 301. *totidemque sumus:* anticlimactic assertion, which the Pierides mistakenly think is significant.

311–
14
cedite: the verb takes ablative of place from which without the preposition. *fonte Medusaeo* 312: fountain of Hippocrene, created by the hoof of Pegasus, as we have seen at 256 ff. The pretentious, Alexandrizing Pieridies produce a flamboyant hexameter, with hiatus here at the central caesura, a series of unusual words, and more hiatus at the end. Aganippe is a fountain, like Hippocrene, on Helicon. Its adjective, referring to Boeotia, had a short *i* in 3.147; here, the *e*, true to its Greek origin, remains long. The terms proposed by the Pieridies were that either the Muses would yield them control of Helicon or they would yield up their Macedonian home to the Muses. Had they then accepted defeat gracefully, there would have been no metamorphosis. (In Nicander, they become birds directly as a result of their defeat, for having challenged the deities.) *ad Paeonas usque nivosas* 313: they will leave the cities of the plain, like Pella, and move into the snowy mountain regions of the west. *dirimant . . . nymphae* 314: since the Pieridies propose the judges, they should not have protested their decision.

315–
17
turpe . . . turpius: the prudish Muse has an extreme sense of turpitude: it includes yielding to a rival. Ovid stresses the point by chiastic ordering of adjective and infinitives, which allows him to dispose both adjectives effectively at the beginning of successive lines. *electae . . . nymphae:* jumping over many imaginable intervening incidents, the Muse proceeds to the swearing in of the judges (cf. 314). *per flumina:* this oath implies that the nymphs are naiads. *vivo . . . sedilia saxo* 317: these three words appear without a break in *Aen.* 1.167 to describe the nymphs' haunt on the African coast where Aeneas has landed. Vergil's epic setting contrasts ironically with this Ovidian one.

318–
20
sine sorte: in a well-ordered contest, the competitors would draw lots to determine the order of their singing. Here, true to her aggressiveness, the Pierid contestant just insists on being first and proceeds to deliver her harsh invective. *quae se certare professa est:* "the one who claimed to be the contestant." *bella . . . superum* 319: Ovid briefly narrated these wars against the Giants in 1.151 ff., with open bias for the gods and against the "impious challengers." He ignored entirely there the special menace of Typhoeus (usually called Typhon). Customarily, the Gigantomachy of myth symbolized the struggle of Civilization against Barbarism, of Order against Disorder; and this struggle could be more specifically defined as Athens vs. the hordes of Persia or, in Ovid's time, as Augustan Rome vs. its selfish and self-destructive past. When, then, the Pierid ennobles the Giants and sneers at the gods, she inverts a theme of high contemporary significance for Ovid's audience. Not that the gods have appeared so far in Ovid's poem as worthy of respect. In fact, the Pierid follows up some of the very themes that the poet of the *Met.* himself has broached.

falsoque in honore: remember, it is the indignant Muse who makes this assertion. *extenuat . . . facta deorum* 320: slighting the actions of the gods balances the so-called false honor of the Giants and epitomizes the inversion of usual roles. The adjective attached by the Muse to the gods, *magnorum,* brings out the paradox: she expects magnitude, not lightness, in connection with gods.

321–
24

emissumque . . . Typhoea . . . caelitibus fecisse metum 322: supply a verb like *canit* (319), as the Muse now summarizes the rival song in indirect discourse, until 327, when she ends with direct quotation. The story of Typhoeus (commonly Typhon) had been included in Book 4 of Nicander's *Heter.,* which Antoninus Liberalis 28 summarizes; another extensive version is preserved by Apollodoros 1.6.3 ff. To avenge the dead Giants, Earth mated with Tartarus and produced the most fearsome monster ever to confront the gods. They fled in terror, as the Pierid sings, to Egypt and, when Typhon pursued them, they tried to conceal their identity by assuming animal forms. Here and in 325, the monster's name appears in the Greek form of the accusative, which fits melodiously into the fifth foot. *cunctosque:* new subject of the infinitive; supply *deos. donec . . . ceperit* 323–24: subjunctive with subordinate clause in indirect discourse. The purpose of this episode is to explain the theriomorphic or animal shape of Egyptian deities and to associate them directly with Greco-Roman gods. Apollodoros does not describe individual shapes, but Nicander did before Ovid. Both, however, agree that Zeus (Jupiter) was not among the cowardly metamorphizers; he persisted in the war against Typhon and eventually overcame him, pinning him helplessly under Mount Etna in Sicily. The Pierid fabricates a fearful role for Jupiter, so as to ignore the war's true ending. Later, the Muse will carefully correct her omission (cf. 346 ff.).

325–
28

terrigenam: this epic compound, which alliterates with the name, is properly assigned, as the Earth was Typhon's mother. Ovid earlier used the word of the Dragon Seed's growth that Cadmus produced at Thebes (3.118). *se mentitis superos celasse figuris* 326: the Pierid produces a biased version of the myth, which both Nicander and Apollodorus report in neutral tones; they were not interested in exposing the cowardice and subhuman qualities of the gods, but rather in connecting them with the animal-shaped deities of Egypt. Thus, in Nicander appeared a list of correspondences, like that given by the Pierid, without prejudice. Elsewhere in Ovid's poem gods resort to animal form to pursue erotic desires, like Jupiter with Europa in 2.846 ff. They are not abject cowards. *dux . . . gregis* 327: in order to demonstrate more clearly the shocking blasphemy of her Pierid rival, the Muse gives what purports to be the final five lines of that song as a direct quotation. The lines lack shape and effective conclusion, a fact that is probably due more to the Muse's angry, abbreviated report than to the actual form of the Pierid entry. The first divine metamorphosis asserted by the blasphemer directly contradicts other versions, where Jupiter remained untainted, unchanged, to prosecute the ultimately successful war against Typhon. The god is supposed to have become a ram; for this phrase, cf. later 7.311. *nunc quoque formatus* 328: the Pierid uses one of the formulae of continuity after metamorphosis (cf. 1.235) to account for the representation of Jupiter Ammon of Libya. Herodotus comments on this ram-faced Egyptian Jupiter in 2.42. *nunc* is somewhat anachronistic, but it fits the perspective of Ovid's audience. Besides, Ovid has let Cepheus refer to *corniger Ammon* at 5.17.

329–   The theriomorphic list of the Pierid agrees in general with that of
31   Nicander, but is shorter. *Delius in corvo est:* the biased "art" of the Pierid involves slighting the metamorphosis by special verbs and reduction of the gods to epithets. First, then, Apollo is literally inside a raven and Bacchus inside a goat. Ovid has earlier connected the raven with Apollo in his story of how it was turned back for clumsy informing (2.535 ff.). Bacchus' connection with the goat in sacrifices and tragedy was well known to Ovid's audience. The construction of 330–31 centers on a single common verb *latuit*, which takes ablative of the animal form used, so that the demeaning picture of gods hiding inside, and by means of, a bestial shape becomes effectively fixed. Each line sets up a pair of deities in chiastic order: the animals get emphasis by framing the line and gods that they graphically and literally enclose or hide. Only Venus is named outright; otherwise, the Pierid contemptuously refers to Diana, Juno, and Mercury by circumlocutions. Diana, taking cat-form, resembles Egyptian Bubastis, protectress of cats. The Egyptians mummified cats, as Herodotus 2.67 notes. The connection between Juno and cows in Egypt is most dubious, and Nicander, who knew better, did not mention her metamorphosis. Ovid lets the Pierid make the claim, because Juno regularly received a cow in Roman and Greek sacrifices and because her familiar Homeric epithet was understood to mean "cow-eyed." Juno's Egyptian parallel, Isis, does not have a cow-form. That Venus took fish-form seems again Ovid's invention. Nicander ignores the goddess in his list, and her connection with fish comes not from Egypt, but from the Near East. Ovid has already briefly referred to a myth in which an Eastern Venus, Dercetis, turns into a fish (2.44–46). Mercury changing into an ibis was reported also by Nicander. This god was compared to the Egyptian Thoth, who supposedly invented letters, music, and other key features of human culture and was regularly represented with the head of an ibis. Herodotus reports in 2.67 that corpses of ibises were buried at his sacred city

of Hermopolis. Once again, we should remember that the Pierid did not stress the religious continuity between Greek and Egyptian deities, but the craven abandonment of anthropomorphism by the gods in favor of a bestial shape that fitted their subhuman natures. Hence, the anger of the proper Muses.

Transition (332–40)

332–
34
ad citharam: to the accompaniment of the cither or lute, a favorite instrument of Apollo himself. *moverat ora:* pluperfect to show that the song has ended. *poscimur* 333: "it was our turn." *Aonides:* living on Mount Helicon, the Muses are to be considered Boeotians. Ovid has taken the more common adjective *Aonius* (cf. 1.313 and 3.339) and made it a pompous new epithet for the Muse to flourish. It recurs at the end of the episode at 6.2. *sed forsitan:* the Muse takes the story to a suspenseful moment, at the start of the new song, and then pretends to be concerned for the time of her audience. Once she traps Minerva into urging her to continue, she stretches her report of her sister's effort over 320 lines. The bias is significant: the Pierid song in truncated and indirect report takes fourteen lines. *nec . . . vacet* 334: synonymous for *otia non sint* in 333.

335–
36
refer ordine: Minerva requests that the Muse report the song in the order it was sung, and so the Muse gives it word for word. *consedit in umbra* 336: she sits down comfortably in the pastoral setting and prepares to enjoy a good song.

337–
40
refert: picks up Minerva's verb in 335. *summam certaminis uni:* as one Pierid represented those nine sisters (cf. 318), so the Muses entrust their defence to one of their band. Named as Calliope at 339, she is traditionally the principal Muse, goddess especially of epic poetry, but also of other genres for Roman poets. *inmissos hedera collecta capillos* 338: "having gathered her freed hair together with ivy." As often, Ovid uses the past participle with an internal accusative (*capillos*), like the Greek middle voice. He has not elsewhere so used this verb. *querulas . . . chordas* 339: the plaintive sound may point ahead to a pathetic topic, more fit for elegy than for epic. *praetemptat pollice:* a similar clause describes Orpheus preparing to perform at 10.145. *percussis . . . nervis* 340: having lightly tested the strings, Calliope launches into her song, vigorously striking the same strings. The four spondees promise something great.

Opening Themes: Praise of Ceres, Dispraise of Typhoeus (341–55)

341–
45
prima Ceres: it is no accident that Calliope chose to feature Ceres in responding to the Pierides. Their song depicted Earth as enemy of the gods, spawning a monster to challenge their power. Their Earth was

a geological force, responsible for cataclysms, earthquakes, sudden appearances of mountains, and other violent and unpredictable disturbances. The answer to that view of Earth is the benevolent personality of Ceres, who in Latin inherits the associations, if not the name, of Greek Demeter (= Mother Earth). She rules over productive land; she fosters agriculture and meets the basic food needs of human beings. She works with the gods, in kindly maternal manner, to make the world better, the earth more bountiful. Thus, a hymn in honor of Ceres implicitly denies the truth of the Pierid vision, that Earth fostered Disorder. In a style often used in hymns and prayers, Calliope starts out with a series of lines in anaphora, repeating the word *prima,* and listing different benefits of the goddess. (She echoes and expands a single line about Ceres as the first to train farmers in Vergil, *G.* 1.147.) Instead of repeating the goddess' name, however, the singer in 342 replaces *Ceres* with *dedit,* in the same metrical position, to produce a more impressive anaphoric unit. In fact, the anaphora caused the scribes to confuse similar-looking line-beginnings, so that part of the tradition omitted 342. The goddess taught men to plow, and, once farming had focused mankind on the path to civilization, she gave gentle food and laws. These are the laws that enhance communal living. *Cereris sunt omnia munus* 343: Calliope summarizes her vision of this supremely munificent deity, a perfect antithesis to the extreme terror of Typhoeus. *illa canenda* 344: the "inspired poet" often describes herself or himself as under powerful obligation to sing a specific topic. *carmina digna dea* 345: the third word is ablative. Continuing the language of the hymnal invocation, the Muse ends by praying to compose a song fit for this goddess, then reverses the idea by altering the syntax of the same three words.

346– *vasta . . . insula:* now the Muse starts out to develop her themes in
48   an odd way, beginning with a near-Golden Line—the verb in the middle consists of two words. She slyly "finishes" the story of Typhoeus and demolishes the Pierid blasphemy, but gives no indication of the connection with Ceres. *ingesta:* because Typhoeus was so large and formidable, it took an entire island, anchored by the colossal mass of Etna, to pin him down. *subiectum . . . Typhoea* 347–48: in the Pierid song, Typhoeus has been the subject of vigorous verbs, and the timid gods have been the objects; Calliope reverses the grammatical pattern: Typhoeus is reduced to impotent foe, brought low for aspiring too high.

349– *nititur . . . pugnatque:* like *Furor impius* in *Aen.* 1.294 ff., who
53   struggles to free himself of his bonds and cause more trouble, Typhoeus in this version fights against his restraints. Calliope pictures his form sprawled and weighed down by the limits of Sicily. We are to imagine him, then, lying on his back, with his body extending almost directly

from east to west. His head and shoulders rest roughly in the middle of the east coast, under Mount Etna (352). His right arm stretches to the north, and Cape Peloros, the northernmost point, pins its hand (350). Calliope calls it Ausonian because it lies just across the Straits of Messina from the Italian mainland. His left arm stretches south; at the southernmost cape of Pachynos, which Calliope amiably apostrophizes, its hand is pinned (351). At the western end of Sicily, the legs, which stretch some 150 miles, are pinned down by Lilybaeum. The monster beneath Etna provides a mythical explanation of the live volcano and constant earthquakes in this and other parts of the island. *eiectat . . . vomit* 353: typical metaphors for anthropomorphized volcanoes.

354–
55 *remoliri:* inventing a verb to react against *molibus* (347), the Muse and Ovid poetically show the vain struggles of the subdued monster under the island. *devolvere corpore* 355: he tries to roll off his body (ablative of place from which, not means) the weight of the cities and mountains, and, as the Muse says in 356, that means earthquakes.

Dis and the Rape of Proserpina (356–437)

The clever Muse has had the intention all along of working her way from this most improbable beginning back to Ceres. The earthquakes cause concern to Dis, lord of the Underworld, and, when he emerges to check his foundations, he becomes a victim of Cupid and falls passionately in love with Proserpina as she wanders over the meadows of Enna picking flowers. She of course is Ceres' beloved daughter, so when he carries her off to Hades, he inevitably plunges Ceres into inconsolable grief. Thus, at the end of this episode, Ceres will return as central character (438), having languished offstage for over ninety lines. But the role the Muse somewhat incompetently assigns her does not exemplify the benevolent qualifies exalted in the invocation.

Nobody else that we know ever told the Rape of Proserpina, a familiar story, as Calliope does. Scholars who believe that Hellenistic poets like Callimachus invented everything we cannot otherwise explain assign to the Alexandrians credit for the novelties in this version. On the other hand, those who insist on Ovid's brilliant originality give him full credit here. Calliope introduces Dis as a careful monarch anxious, like Jupiter after the disaster of Phaethon, to check the structural security of his kingdom (cf. 2.401 ff.). As he reviews the damage, like Jupiter before him, Dis becomes the victim of love, quite literally the target of Venus and her son Cupid. (This is a motif that Ovid worked with Apollo and Daphne but is new to this story.) Since he has been victimized, Dis does not act like other over-sexed gods: without describing the depth of his passion or the way he plans his rape, Calliope races over the gamut, from love at first sight to rape, in one line (395). And she devotes her attention almost exclusively to Proserpina and to the nymph Cyane, who vainly tries to halt the escape of Dis.

We have other versions of this myth that permit us to ascertain the innovations of Ovid's narrative. In addition to the Homeric hymn and prose of summaries by Apollodorus 1.4.5 and Hyginus 146, Ovid himself, almost at the same time as he was working on this passage, was developing an account, in connection with the Cerealia of *Fast.* 4, of the same rape (417–620). In that other account, he does not motivate the rape in any way whatsoever, but he does place Ceres at her favorite shrine of Enna in Sicily and Proserpina in her company. Both Apollodoros and Hyginus state that Dis or Pluto wanted to marry Proserpina and that Jupiter collaborated with him in his desire, so that, when it appeared certain that mother Ceres would not allow her daughter to live in the grim Underworld, Jupiter encouraged his brother to carry the girl off. In reading Calliope's account, then, we shall see that the innovations that she introduces help to characterize her as narrator and relate her idea of Ceres to her own situation of conflict.

356–   These lines facilitate the transition from Typhoeus to Dis and the rape-
58   story. *rex . . . silentum*: Ovid takes poetic license and forms the genitive plural of the participle without the ending in *-ium*. The description of the dead as "quiet" is traditional, but it enhances this context, because the noise of the shuddering earth worries the king of this silent Underworld. *pateat . . . retegatur* 357: the verbs are synonymous, but the second is more expressive. As we know from news coverage of modern earthquakes, the earth does radically gape. Ovid's description of Dis' dread of yawning openings through which light would come down to its comfortable dark was anticipated by Vergil in *Aen.* 8.242 ff., and Ovid seems intent on varying some of his predecessor's successes. *inmissusque dies trepidantes terreat umbras* 358: cf. *Aen.* 8.246, *trepident inmisso lumine Manes.* Both poets like the conceit of the dead frightened by light, a reversal of the usual theme that, as ghosts, the dead terrify the living in the dark.

359–   *metuens cladem*: Calliope is at pains to stress the fearful personality
61   of this Underworld king, who thinks a little light is a major "disaster." *tenebrosa sede*: ablative of place from which, without preposition. The adjective points up the darkness that Dis is trying to protect. *tyrannus*: used without apparent distinction along with *rex* (356). *atrorum . . . equorum* 360: Dis appropriately has a team of black horses. *ambibat . . . cautus fundamina* 361: this description seems

to characterize Dis less as king than careful house-owner or engineer. Although the noun is a typical alternative in the hexameter for an intractable word ending in *-mentum*, the description cannot be labeled "poetic" or "epic." Love is definitely not on the ruler's mind at this point.

362–
64

exploratum satis est: supply dat. *regi*; Ovid uses an impersonal construction to shift from Dis to his oppressors, Venus and Cupid. *depositoque metu . . . vagantem* 363: the ablative absolute refers to the calming of the fear that Calliope has so stressed; once that fear has been abandoned, Dis wanders idly, like a tourist. Similar description of Jupiter after he checked on the damage from Phaethon's blaze (cf. 2.403–5). *Erycina*: Venus, introduced unexpectedly by Calliope into the story, with an epithet referring to her worship on Mount Eryx in Sicily. The narrator will follow up the epithet skillfully in 364 and place the goddess on "her mountain." Eryx lies in the far west of Sicily, so Dis has indeed wandered miles from the center of geological instability near Mount Etna on the east coast. It does have a commanding view of the landscape, and Calliope makes Venus seem like a powerful queen on her throne. *natumque . . . volucrem* 364: winged Cupid. Ovid recalls the speech of Venus to Cupid in *Aen.* 1.663 ff. It provided an "epic" model for this unepic version of divine causation.

365–
68

arma, manusque, meae, mea, nate, potentia: cf. this over-elaborate passage, its three appositions and five dactyls, with the first line of Venus' speech in *Aen.* 1.664: *nate, meae vires, mea magna potentia*. Calliope economically follows up all the military language in 366, *cape tela*. The vague sense of *tela* quickly becomes defined in 367. *inque dei pectus* 367: mention of a god as target comes momentarily as a surprise. *molire sagittas*: present imperative. Vergil had already extended the verb's meaning, so that its general sense of "setting in motion" could become "hurling" or "shooting." *cui . . . regni* 368: the whole relative clause identifies for Cupid (alluding to the tripartite division of the universe by Jupiter, Neptune, and Dis) the god mentioned in 367. *fortuna novissima*: Dis got last choice, so won the least desirable of the three lots.

369–
72

Cleverly exploiting the tripartite universe, Venus appeals to Cupid in hymnal/prayer form—note the anaphora with *tu*—and argues that the love god dominates the masters of two-thirds of the universe, namely, Jupiter and Neptune. With a slight assertion of his irresistible power, he could master Dis and thus control the entire cosmos. *victa domas* 370: participle (in neuter because of the third object in 369) and subordination where English likes to coordinate, for *vicisti domasque*. *regit qui*: reversal of prose order not simply because of the meter. The change moves a strong verb prominently forward, and it places the subject *qui* in the same position as *tu* of 369, repeating *numina ponti. imperium profers* 372: Venus has introduced imperialistic metaphors above, and she climaxes them with this clause. We are seeing a clever extention of the goddess' role as *Venus victrix. agitur*: "it's a question of."

373–77   *et tamen in caelo*: here, the goddess backtracks to point out that her domination of the Olympian gods is not absolute. That argument enhances her request of Cupid, but it also cleverly works into Calliope's plan for a transition to Proserpina and Ceres. She sets Dis and Proserpina before Cupid's mind as a dual target by which her "empire" will be aggrandized. *quae iam patientia nostra est*: the MSS tradition early became corrupted in this line because of this unexpected parenthetical clause, and it transmitted *quoque*, not *quae*, to limit *caelo*. But that word is otious; it goes over the boundary of the central caesura awkwardly; and it leaves the relevance of *iam patientia . . . est* imprecise. Scholars of the seventeenth century conjectured *quae*, which subsequently has been found in a few late MSS (perhaps also a conjecture of the time). Suggested translation: "something that we have long been enduring," or "and we have just had to endure it." If the passage had not been parenthetical but terminal, Ovid would have used a more familiar organization with the abstract, e.g., *haec iam patientia nostra est* (cf. 4.427) or *tanta est patientia nostra* (cf. 1.60). *spernimur* 374: emphatic placing of the verb in the initial dactyl, to register the lack of respect, as Venus sees it, for her divine prerogatives of love. *vires minuuntur*: the verb, which Romans regularly used in political contexts, refers to loss of prestige. Venus' attitude here toward virgin deities is an inversion of the usual honor assigned to Minerva and Diana for their chastity, also to the Roman Vestals who duplicated this virtue. *iaculatricemque Dianam* 375: same hemistich in *Fasti* 2.155, where it forms part of a four-word hexameter and, I think, was written first. As a huntress, Diana would have been expected to use a spear, although she most characteristically appears as archer, with bow, quiver, and arrows. *abscessisse* 376: we might have expected a verb with the political overtones of "revolt" or "secession," but this one simply means depart. *virgo . . . erit* 376–77: the noun, focus of Venus' animosity, is predicate nominative. *si patiemur*: the future tense makes clear the logical relationship with *patientia* in 373. Venus intends to put a stop to what she considers an intolerable situation, which has lasted too long; therefore, the future endurance will not take place, nor will young Proserpina be a virgin much longer. *spes adfectat*: the verb can have neutral or prejudicial meaning, and we may suspect that querulous Venus intends it her to be invidious: Proserpina and her older models pursue an evil goal! Calliope is hardly glorifying any gods in this sequence.

378–   *socio . . . regno*: Venus keeps insisting on the political aspects of the

81   power of love that they share. That turns *gratia* also into a political term, "influence." Their mutual advantage, the goddess suggests, requires Cupid to act as she says. *iunge deam patruo* 379: Calliope makes Venus put the situation in such bald terms as to raise the thought of virtual incest. When later Claudius married his niece Agrippina, it was a scandal in the Roman court. The verb chosen by Venus also looks forward to marriage rather than rape. Again, the Muse chooses a version that varies from most others, in which Jupiter abetted, if he did not actually plan, his brother's possession of Ceres' and his shared child. Neither version magnifies the gods. *pharetram / solvit*: Cupid immediately acts on his mother's words; he opens the quiver on his shoulder and picks an arrow. How this will join divine maiden to uncle (cf. 379) still remains to be seen. The last time we saw Cupid in operation, he used arrows to produce in Apollo a passion for Daphne that could not be gratified (1.463 ff.). *de mille sagittis / unam*: a hyperbolic description of the capacity of Cupid's quiver.

381–   *sed qua*: ablative of comparison, which governs the next two clauses.
84   *quae magis audiat* 382: understand *ulla est* as antecedent; this is relative clause of characteristic. *oppositoque genu* 383: he braced his knee against the bow and bent it. That sounds reasonable, but, as Bömer demonstrates, an archer does not so bend the bow as he prepares to shoot; for he would never be able to fire the arrow. It seems that Ovid has fused a picture, perhaps suggested by a famous work of art, in which Cupid bent his bow with the help of the knee as he strung it, with this moment of bending the bow as the arrow is about to be launched (where only arm and hand strength operate). *cornum*: cornel wood often was chosen for good bows. *hamata* 384: the arrow that struck Apollo in 1.470 was equally sharp, but this one, being barbed, is intended to stick fast and permanently wound.

385–   *Hennaeis . . . moenibus*: we have heard that Dis roams around Sicily
87   (363) and that Venus and Cupid have spotted him from Mount Eryx at the western end of the island. Now, the scene shifts to Enna, almost in the center of Sicily, perhaps ninety miles to the east of Eryx. It was a famous shrine of Ceres, but Calliope says nothing of that fact— it was well known to Romans. *lacus est . . . altae . . . aquae*: this genitive of description, because of the hyperbaton, caused the scribes much dismay, which was compounded by the unfamiliar proper noun, *Pergus*. Since lakes are rare in Sicily, it helped to make the spot idyllic. But it does not appear in other earlier descriptions of the Rape. Ovid, who almost surely had visited the site during his youthful Sicilian tour with his friend Macer (cf. *Pont.* 2.10), is then providing personal information. *Caystros / carmina cygnorum*: the Muse fills the water with swans, using the well-known example of the Cayster River of Asia Minor, a favorite theme of poetry. The triple alliteration

does not enhance the sense of haunting song. *edit*: the river produces
swan songs which, more correctly, come from the birds. There is no
need to accept the variant reading *audit*, a conjecture to make the text
easier.

388–
91

silva coronat aquas: "woods ring the lake." Calliope describes the
setting as a *locus amoenus*. The woods shade the lake and make it a
perfect refuge in the heat. *ut velo* 389: an anachronism, linking mythi-
cal times with first century Rome, where awnings were spread over
the theatre on sunny days to improve the comfort of the audience.
(The practice continued under the Empire, for example, with the
Flavian amphitheatre.) *frigora . . . flores* 390: the Muse aims for a
chiastic pattern and alliteration of the two objects. Otherwise, there
is no essential reason to connect branches and ground. *Tyrios*: since
Tyre on the Levant was a source of purple dye, the adjective here
frequently meant simply "purple." Readers began to misunderstand
this sense in the eleventh century, and introduced the emendation
varios, clever but unnecessary. *perpetuum ver est* 391: this clause
epitomizes the loveliness of the spot. It is well-watered, shaded, cool,
and bright with spring flowers.

91–
95

quo . . . luco: Calliope has started an ecphrasis in 385 with *lacus est*,
and the formal structure of such descriptions calls for the poet to
maintain focus on that first noun. However, instead of reverting to
Lake Pergus and telling us about an event on or in the water, the
Muse shifts her attention to the flowery woods. She turns from *lacus*
to *lucus*. At this point, framed by the grove, Proserpina is first named
for her dramatic entrance. But Calliope does not say why she is at
Enna or where her mother Ceres (last mentioned in the invocation at
343) can be found. In two pairs of clauses linked by repeated *dum*,
the innocent virginal pleasures of the girl who gathers flowers emerge;
the main clause will spoil all these effects. *puellari* 393: the Muse
makes no effort to describe the beauty of Proserpina; her focus is on
her girlish behavior. *aequales* 394: friends and attendants share her
enthusiasm for flowers. They will be noticed again (551 ff.), when
Calliope will recount their metamorphosis. *simul visa est dilectaque
raptaque* 395: emphasis on Proserpina as passive victim rather than
on Dis as active agent. The Muse crowds three verbs into a line and
thus compresses the whole event. Love at first sight is covered by
two verbs, and in the third the narrator races to the abduction, omitting
all the steps in between. This is not the familiar rape of earlier books,
where Jupiter, for example, gratified his lust and fled; Dis has matri-
mony in mind, as the traditional version indicates.

96–
99

properatus amor: the clever Muse comments on her compression of
incident in 395, and the five dactyls support the sense of speed. *dea
territa*: Proserpina in her fear. *maesto . . . ore* 397: the hyperbaton

allows the Muse to put in the girl's mouth, so to speak, the words that she utters. In the Homeric hymn, she first calls out to her father Zeus, and then out of desperation to her mother. Here and in the *Fast.*, Ovid has her appeal only to Ceres. *ut summa vestem laniarat ab ora* 398: ripping one's robe from the top margin is a conventional gesture of grief. Ovid had almost the same words, only a different verb, for Narcissus in 3.480. This verb exploits the syncopated pluperfect. *tunicis . . . remissis* 399: earlier, at 393, we heard that Proserpina used the fold of her robe to hold the flowers she had picked; now, when she tears open the robe, it no longer can keep its burden, and they fall out. The detail is a calculated symbol for her loss of girlish pleasures and innocence. No such dramatic effect in *Fast.* 4.448: the girl simply rips her dress at the bosom.

400–
401
tantaque simplicitas: the only occurrence of this abstract noun in the *Met.*, but it does appear often in the elegiac works of Ovid. Most Ovidian lovers prefer more sophisticated women, but remember, this is Calliope speaking. In several previous contexts, the poet uses a *sententia* like this as a terminal comment. But the *-que* shows that it is introductory here. We might expect a result clause, but the Muse prefers asyndeton.

402–
4
raptor: first use of this word in the *Met.*, since this is the first case of abduction as opposed to rape. It will be used in 6.710 of Boreas, abductor of Oreithyia, and in 6.518 of an eagle that has flown off with a rabbit. *currus*: plural to avoid elision; for singular, cf. 360. *nomine quemquem vocando*: a charioteer, whether in flight or in races, regularly calls each horse by name to get the maximum speed. *tinctas ferrugine* 404: same phrase for the poison hand of Envy in 2.798. All things connected with the Underworld are dark or black.

405–
8
olentia . . . stagna Palicorum: driving southeast toward Syracuse, Dis passes through a region of small volcanic lakes near Palike. It was a natural marvel of Sicily that Ovid had visited on his student tour, as he states in *Pont.* 2.10. The smell of sulphur was prominent, as is typical of such spots. In 407–8, the erudite Muse alludes to Syracuse obliquely. Colonists came there in the eighth century from Corinth (ruled by the family of the Bacchiadae) and founded the city (which originally was an island called Ortygia) that enjoyed two harbors. The so-called Great Harbor was the scene of the final naval battle that destroyed the Athenian Expedition in 413 B.C.

409–
12
est medium . . . quod coit . . . aequor: the Muse learnedly locates the next scene, postponing the key noun until the end of 410. She refers to the Great Harbor, which is all but closed (hence, *coit . . . inclusum*) by points of land, one of them (Ortygia) having the Fountain of Arethusa at its end, the other having the Fountain of Cyane. *Cyanes* 409: Greek genitive. *Pisaeae Arethusae*: the Muse shows off her

metrical skill by resorting to hiatus + the four-syllable proper name at the line-ending. Later, she will use Arethusa's name five times, but always at an earlier point in the hexameter that does not necessitate such bravado. We do not yet know it, but the Muse is preparing us for Arethusa's subsequent importance. *a cuius stagnum . . . nomine* 411: the Muse has graphically inserted the word for pool or fountain into the phrase about the derivation of its name. *celeberrima*: 412: the fame of Cyane was never widespread; Ovid is the first known Latin writer to mention her. Thus, he may be making the Muse claim too much here as she introduces a story that does not, at first sight, seem very pertinent to her program.

413–   *gurgite . . . medio*: ablative of place from which. *summa tenus exstitit*
16   *alvo*: the prudish Muse robs this moment of all its beauty by making us focus on the top of the stomach. Almost surely, Ovid is letting her "correct" the more interesting picture that Catullus created in 64.18, when he described sea-nymphs rising from the waves and for the first time revealing their bare bodies to mortal eyes, bare down to the breasts (*nutricum*). Cyane is asexual herself, bent on halting an outrage to Proserpina. As soon as she spots the girl (*deam* 414), she grasps the situation and acts. *nec longius ibitis* 414: we might say: "Halt right there!" Notice the plural; in 415 she addresses only Dis. *invitae Cereris* 415: it was a feature of the earlier tradition that Ceres opposed the marriage of her daughter and Dis. But the Muse has created an entirely different background, so that Ceres' opposition is only hypothetical at this point. Hence, Cyane can go on as though Dis has failed to use proper procedures: *roganda, / non rapienda fuit*: all he needed to do was ask for Proserpina's hand! The contrasted verbs, emphasized by alliteration, are so different in connotation that Cyane's linking of them raises a smile at her silliness. In a reversal of this situation, Boreas, reflecting on his failure to win Orithyia by wooing, declares in 6.700–1: *socerque / non orandus erat mihi, sed faciendus Erechtheus*, and proceeds to abduct the girl.

416–   *quodsi conponere magnis / parva mihi fas est*: Cyane resorts to a
18   traditional comment on improper comparisons. Vergil used it to apologize for comparing bees to gigantic Cyclopes in *G.* 4.176. Using much of Vergil's language, then, Ovid invites us to feel the ineptitude of Cyane and of her narrator the Muse, when Cyane boldly compares herself with a god, her trivial love affair with the passion of Dis. She then names her lover, Anapis, the god of the nearby Sicilian river of that name. He supposedly loved like Dis and had only to ask to achieve success. *exorata . . . nec . . . exterrita* 418: again, Cyane presents a pair of alliterative verbs to define her contrast.

419–   *bracchia tendens*: instead of the usual gesture of appeal, Cyane at-
20   tempts a gesture of halting. As the chariot thunders towards her, it

can easily be imagined how effective the nymph would be in stopping the fierce and passionate god. *haud ultra tenuit Saturnius iram* 420: as Saturn's son, Dis gets this adjective along with Jupiter (cf. 1.163). Like his sister Juno, regularly called *Saturnia*, he is quick to anger; his restraint has lasted only for Cyane's short speech and her feeble effort to prevent his passage.

421–
24

in gurgitis ima: Cyane has been described as rising from the middle of the pool (413), so now the savage Dis whips his horses directly at her, into her fountain. *contortum . . . sceptrum . . . condidit* 422–23: he hurled his sceptre and buried it deep in the ground, thereby creating an entrance to Tartarus. *pronos . . . currus* 424: plural for singular without metrical necessity. The car is drawn headlong by the horses. *medio cratere*: a volcanic opening, metaphorical use of the noun first attempted by Lucretius 6.701 and next by Ovid here; literally equivalent to the modern crater.

425–
29

The Muse has introduced Cyane in order to feature her "virtuous" behavior and now her outraged feeling of offense. She offers, then, one model of female probity approved by Calliope. Beside the abduction of Proserpina, she especially resents the insult to her own status as fountain-nymph. Angry Dis has "ridden rough shod" over her rights, smashing his way through her to Tartarus, and she feels nullified. Silent grief in Ovidian women regularly expresses itself, as here, in tears; and extreme grief often dissolves the mourner into a body of water. That is the ultimate fate of Byblis in 9.655 ff. In this book, Arethusa's fear also turns her into a fountain (632 ff.). *quarum . . . in illas . . . aquas* 428–29: relative clause before antecedent. *magnum . . . numen*: a proud exaggeration: Cyane was a minor deity of a minor fountain, certainly nowhere near on a par with Dis, whom she presumed to halt. *extenuatur* 429: the other Muse has used this verb in 320 to protest the way the Pierides slighted the *great* gods. Now, Cyane is reduced from supposed "greatness" by her own hurt pride. Although Calliope respects her for this, we need not follow her. *molliri membra videres*: Minerva and we are invited to imagine the sight and sympathize. The process of metamorphosis required that all hard parts of the nymph turn into water. Calliope rather labors the point by mentioning limbs, bones, and finally finger- and toenails!

431–
35

Not content with the preceding four lines, the Muse feels impelled to elaborate this insignificant transformation for seven more. *primaque*: we hear of three stages, namely, this, *post haec* (434), and *denique* (436). *de tota*: supply *forma. tenuissima*: whatever is of least substantial nature would be first changed. The adjective connects with *extenuatur* (429). The list of 432 includes some pretty substantial parts, as Cyane is changing at her extremities, slowly melting into nothing but water. The Muse miscalculates her effects: this is more grotesque by far than pathetic (as she seems to consider it). *brevis . . . transitus* 433–34: she has to assert the logic behind her narrative of metamorphosis: a fussy, unnecessary "accuracy" for a better poet-singer. In 434–35, more parts are listed, larger ones, closer to the center of the body. *tenues . . . rivos* 435: the adjective continues to be thematic. *abeunt evanida:* the verb regularly denotes change from one substance to another; the adjective goes with all four subjects, but especially with *pectora.* For Calliope and most of her audience, female and male, the disappearance of that part would be supremely sad.

436–37   *vitiatas . . . venas:* like other bodily parts, the veins have been ruined, drained of their blood supply, which has perhaps leaked out of them as through cracked pipes. The Muse resorts to alliteration here rather tastelessly as she completes her otiose description. Water replaces blood, and nothing material remains of Cyane. *quod prendere posses* 437: again, Calliope attempts to draw in her audience (Minerva). The goddess is assured that Cyane has become totally liquid, thus ungraspable. Cyane might have been a woman who, like Eurydice in 10.58, slipped out of the grasp of her lover; and yet Calliope has not made her a woman anyone would want to hold.

Ceres Reacts (438–508)

We have heard Proserpina calling out to her mother (397), but Calliope has never told us where Ceres is nor whether she heard her daughter's cries. Now, we are to infer that indeed she did learn of the girl's abduction, because she has been searching for her everywhere as she finally enters the narrative. Calliope leaves the route of her search vague, contrary to the usual tradition, and narrates a new story about an impertinent boy whom the "maternal" goddess angrily turns into a gecko; that, instead of the more kindly stories connected with her visit to the cult site at Eleusis. Wandering back to Sicily, she finds the girdle of Proserpina floating in Cyane's fountain and, despite the uncertain significance of that clue, she reacts with fury and instantly curses the innocent crops and labors of the farmers. Arethusa then surfaces from her nearby fountain and mildly rebukes Ceres for her violence (490 ff.). She tells the wild goddess that Proserpina is being detained in the Underworld as consort of Dis.

438–39   *pavidae . . . matri:* dative of agent with passive verb. Ceres is introduced without name, in terms of her relationship, and she receives an adjective that could be sympathetic. *omnibus est . . . omni quaesita* 439: an artful use of anaphora and hyperbaton of the two verbal elements.

440–   *illam non . . . non:* another anaphora to stress the ceaseless movement

43   of Ceres, with a doublet of Dawn and Evening Star to suggest the
entire day. Dawn is given an ablative of description: her wet hair
refers to early morning dew. *illa*: now Ceres dominates as the vigorous
subject. *pinus . . . succendit ab Aetna* 442: exploiting Typhoeus
pinned under Etna and breathing out fire (cf. 353), without expressly
referring to him, Ceres ignites a pair of torches at the volcano to light
her search through the dark night. *inrequieta* 443: cf. 441.

444–   Two more lines to tell us that the goddess searched all day, too. *dies*
45   *hebetarat sidera*: an unusual conceit, that the light of day "blunted"
the star(light). *ab occasu solis . . . ad ortus* 445: if Calliope had
reversed the words for setting and rising, she would have created
confusion between an indication of time and geographical location.
But we normally do not denote time by the span between sunset and
sunrise. Ceres is travelling eastward. In *Fast.* 5, Ovid follows the
goddess' route in detail, until she finally arrives in Athens (467–503).

446–   *fessa labore*: Calliope will reuse this phrase to describe Arethusa in
50   618. And Ovid has it in a context similar to this at 6.340, where he
presents tired, thirsty Latona. *conluerant* 447: the Muse has picked
out an odd word—only here in Ovid—and used it in an unusual
manner. She seems to mean that no water had touched Ceres' mouth,
but the Latin says that no fountains had washed her face. Calliope
too often slights the goddess by her inept poetic efforts. *tectam stra-*
mine . . . casam: the *cum*-inversum clause focuses our attention on
this simple thatched hut. *fores pulsavit*: the verb implies the violence
of Ceres: she pounded on the doors; it was no polite knock. Cf. the
imperious banging of Minerva with her spear on the doors of Envy
(2.767). *anus* 449: this poor old woman has the role of Misme in
Nicander 4, who did not make her old, since she has a young son
Askalabos, who becomes the victim of the goddess. *divamque videt*:
Calliope does not say the woman recognized her thirsty visitor as a
deity, and presumably she did not. She merely shows the meager
hospitality within her means to an unknown, needy traveller. *dulce*
dedit 450: the adjective functions as substantive, distantly anticipating,
as Bömer suggests, modern Italian *dolce*. Misme offers Ceres a sweet
drink, on which she has sprinkled toasted barley. This passage is the
only one where Ovid refers to barley, and indeed, except for an
undeniably satirical passage in Persius 3.55, it seems to be the only
poetic mention of the grain. Calliope has made the goddess resort to
a peasant drink.

451–   *duri puer oris et audax*: Nicander calls him Askalabos; Ovid may
52   have omitted his name, to avoid confusion later with another culprit,
Ascalaphus (cf. 539). The descriptive genitive refers to the rude speech
of countryfolk. *avidamque vocavit* 452: the unmannerly child laughed
at the way Ceres thirstily drank and proceeded to insult her, as children

often do in their naiveté. Nicander even had him suggest to his mother that she ought to give Ceres a larger container.

53– *offensa est*: the goddess takes offense and behaves more childishly
54 than this impudent boy. *neque . . . epota parte*: ablative absolute. The mockery of the child spoils her pleasure in the drink, and she stops. *loquentem . . . perfudit*: hyperbaton allows the Muse to place the verb in the middle of the splashed parts of the drink and thus graphically stress the picture of Ceres' inappropriate rage. She threw the drink in the boy's face. *cum liquido*: ablative of accompaniment with *polenta*. Clumsy Calliope preferred to dwell on this special scene rather than on the traditional picture of kindly Ceres at Eleusis gently nursing a baby boy. She evidently admires a goddess who can be powerful in her wrath, regardless of provocation.

55– *conbibit os maculas*: the Latin suggests that the child, in his turn, is
58 greedily drinking, as it describes the way the barley spots his face. *quae modo bracchia*: the relative is not feminine singular, but neuter plural and would, in prose, have followed *bracchia*. The altered word order enables Calliope to show off her wit in the change from *bracchia gessit* to *crura gerit* 456. The new tense goes appropriately with the transformed body part. Sparing us a detailed metamorphosis, Calliope mentions the tail (456), the diminution of size (457–58), and finally compares the result with that of a small lizard. *ne sit vis magna nocendi* 457: the boy, once changed into a reptile, cannot verbally injure any longer, but he might use his mouth to bite if he remained of human size. One set of good MSS actually changes the gerund to *loquendi*. He ends up harmless, a few inches long, living off flies. Pointed contrast of *magna* and *brevem*, reinforced by *parva* and *minor* in 458.

59– *mirantem flentemque et . . . parantem*: typical Ovidian construction.
61 The three participles introduce the character most powerfully affected by this metamorphosis, not the nasty child, but his fond, anguished old mother. Her instantaneous grief puts all the histrionics and particularly this tantrum of Ceres to shame. Again, the Muse has miscalculated: we do not approve of this kind of retribution, in a deity who resorts to it or in one who sings admiringly of it. A mother is deprived of her child pitilessly by a goddess who seeks hers. *latebramque petit* 460: he acts like a true lizard. *aptumque colori*: one set of useful MSS offers *pudori*. Although we can understand the drive to put an ethical interpretation on the metamorphosis, the name does not refer to disgrace, but to the patterns on the lizard's hide (= *color* or complexion). *nomen habet . . . stellatus* 461: the Latin name of the lizard is *stellio*. Although the word could have fitted the hexameter, e.g., at the beginning of the line, the Muse displays her art in the Alexandrian manner dear to Ovid, by offering instead the aetiology of the name. On the

back of this lizard, Romans saw star-patterns, and hence from *stella* they derived *stellio*. In the Roman world, the lizard's name was metaphorically applied to cheats and unscrupulous tricksters; that image has nothing to do with this bratty boy.

462–
63 *quas erraverit undas*: supply preposition *per* from the previous phrase; subjunctive in indirect question. The difference between the detailed travelogue of *Fast.* 4.467 ff. and 563 ff. and the total indifference to such data by Calliope is striking. Traditionally, Ceres did wander by foot over many lands, but she did not swim or sail across the water: she flew above it in her winged chariot. *dicere longa mora est* 483: we might praise the Muse's poetic restraint, except that, when we inspect what she does with the space saved, we do not find a tighter, better organized narrative. *quaerenti defuit orbis*: the singer justifies abbreviation with the conceit that Ceres ran out of places to look for Proserpina! Its wit tends to create distance from the goddess.

464–
67 *Sicaniam repetit*: at length, she returns to her starting-point and the scene of the "crime." *ad Cyanen; ea* 465: Ovid could have used relative *quae* instead of the demonstrative, but that would have risked the ambiguity of referring either to Ceres (incorrectly) or Cyane. *mutata*: although the Muse has tiresomely described how the nymph softened into water (427 ff.), she has in store the detail about how change frustrates human speech. *os et lingua volenti / dicere* 466–67: the Muse feels the pathos of Cyane's plight, who acted on behalf of Proserpina; but there was no pity for the sudden inarticulateness of jeering Askalabos. *nec qua loqueretur habebat* 446: relative clause of result, the relative being the adverb. Cyane had no way of talking.

468–
70 *signa tamen . . . dedit*: the wordless fountain did manage to effect some communication. *notamque . . . zonam* 469, 470: hyperbaton so wide, that the Muse covers the place and the way Ceres picked out the girdle. *gurgite sacro* 469: Calliope adds a dubious epithet to slant her narrative. Many fountains are sacred, but there is no warrant for calling Cyane such (cf. 573).

471–
73 *tamquam tunc denique raptam / scisset*: the participle might seem to agree with *quam*, but that would be an error. It is not the girdle that has been abducted, but Proserpina, for whom the floating girdle is a "tragic" symbol. The context clarifies the reference, as it does in 474 with *ubi sit*. *inornatos laniavit . . . capillos*: since up to this point, there has been no indication that Ceres had disturbed her coiffure, I take the adjective as predicative; "she tore her hair into total disorder." This is the moment for histrionics. In 473, with excessive repetition of *p*-sounds, the Muse catches the excess of another gesture of grief, except that she has not added the conventional information that the

breasts are bare. Cf. the nymphs around Diana in the forest pool, 3.178–79, or Narcissus, 3.481.

4– *ubi sit*: subject is Proserpina. *terras . . . omnes*: inevitably, the Muse
7   suggests how unreasonably, not how grieving, Ceres is. She has to vent anger; she does not know how to behave with decorum in her sorrow. The earth, her element, is totally guiltless; on the contrary, the gods of the sky (Jupiter) and of the world beneath the earth (Dis) have conspired to marry the girl to Dis. *frugum munere* 475: Ceres had given agricultural techniques and grain crops to mankind (cf. 341 ff.). *vestigia damni* 476: the girdle. Instead of being thankful for information, the goddess typically blames its source.

7– *saeva . . . manu . . . irata*: the adjectives are crucial for interpretation.
0   Ceres acts savagely and destructively, breaking plows, killing farmers and oxen. That is far crueller than the traditional behavior assigned to Demeter in the Homeric Hymn. There, having failed to move Zeus/ Jupiter to behave like a father to Proserpina, the goddess retires from Olympus and refuses to help the farmers, so that they incur a terrible famine (cf. 302 ff.). But her effect is passive, not ruinously active, as here. *parilique . . . leto*: the hyperbaton encloses the victims. *fallere depositum* 480: the Muse resorts to a commercial metaphor, as if blighted fields deny the treasure of crops that have been deposited (planted) with them. We might question the propriety of such a poetic conceit here.

1– *fertilitas terrae . . . vulgata*: the Muse refers to the far-famed produc-
3   tivity of Sicily, one of the main sources of grain for the Roman metropolis. *falsa* 482: connects with *fallere* 480. *primis . . . in herbis*: as the crops push up first shoots, they die. Ovid has the same phrase in *Fast.* 4.645 in connection with Ceres' disappointment of farmers. *modo . . . nimius, nimius modo* 483: chiastic pattern at the caesura (plus five dactyls) enhances the doublet of destructive forces, which serve as an extension here of Ceres' fury.

4– *sideraque ventique*: imitating the Homeric manner, the Muse contrives
6   a double-*que* unit and lengthens the first one simply because of Homeric practice. All the natural forces of crop failure work for Ceres here, and each verb connotes her hostility. *avidaeque volucres*: same phrase, same metrical position, in 7.549, where birds, eating corpses, add to the horror of a plague. *lolium tribuliqu* 485: rare technical words for rustic curses, thorns, and darnel. Vergil introduced them into Latin poetry together in *G.* 1.153–54, and Ovid is recalling them and their context. The Muse seems to flaunt her "poetic" sources, and at the same time she lets the meter run along (as at 480 and 483) with five dactyls that slight the seriousness of the situation. *triticeas messes* 486: Vergil also first used this phrase, in the singular, in *G.* 1.219.

inexpugnabile gramen: resonant adjective continues the theme of war against human beings.

487–
91
Eleis Alpheias: as Calliope introduces a new character, she makes a flourish of Hellenistic erudition that ill accords with her stated purpose. Both words have unique features. We know that we are not in Greece or Greek waters, and *Eleis* should refer to Elis, the site of the Olympic Games. It does not; later, the Muse will tell us how these waters got to Syracuse. The substantive *Alpheias* is Ovid's invention. It is neither a patronymic nor a geographical term, as its form suggests. Arethusa, the nymph being introduced, postpones her explanation of the connection with Alpheios—most Romans knew the story of her unwilling involvement with the lusty river—until later (572 ff.). We are to assume, it appears, that angry Ceres remains by the fountain of Cyane near Syracuse, where she was shocked by the sight of the girdle. Accordingly, nearby Arethusa (cf. 409) can exert her influence, a wise, articulate replacement for Cyane. Like Cyane in 413, she rises in her waters and tries to deter the wild deity's progress. *rorantesque comas* 488: as a long-haired swimmer today, she brushes her wet hair back from her eyes and face to her ears. Realistic detail of a humble type reduces this scene to an everyday chat between women. *toto . . . orbe* 489: ablative of place where. *virginis . . . et frugum genetrix*: the zeugma with the two objective genitives focuses attention on the maternal qualities of Ceres, which we have come to question. Arethusa queries Ceres' treatment of her earth and crops, if not of her daughter. *siste labores*: the imperative implies Arethusa's feeling of superior wisdom in the situation. Ceres' "toil" includes her futile wanderings (cf. 446) and wild efforts to punish the innocent. *tibi fidae . . . terrae* 491: Arethusa rebuts the goddess' charge that the whole earth is "ungrateful" (475). *neve . . . violenta irascere*: a second imperative rebukes Ceres for unjust anger.

492–
94
nihil meruit: i.e., it was totally innocent; indeed, it was an unwilling victim (*invita*) of the abduction. *pro patria supplex* 493: the reasonable speaker Arethusa quickly moves to check the thought in Ceres that she speaks on behalf of her Sicilian fatherland, personally involved in its miseries. No, she is an unbiased voice of reason. *Pisa mihi patria est* 494: carefully aligning *patria* with its form in 493, the nymph clears up any misunderstanding. Pisa is a town of Elis near Olympia.

495–
97
peregrina: as a stranger, Arethusa implies her freedom from uncritical bias. *gratior omni . . . terra solo*: ablative of comparison; the whole clause rebukes Ceres' careless use of *ingratas* 475. *hos . . . penates / hanc habeo sedem*: Arethusa, who finally identifies herself by name, treats her fountain site as a proper Roman home, with its own Penates. The anachronism is Ovidian. *mitissima serva*: again, the imperative

urges reason on the unreasonable, pressing her to recover her basic nature (cf. 342). At present, Ceres is *inmitis*, so the epithet is either a reminder of what is lost or part of the imperative desire for the future.

498–
01
mota loco: ablative of place from which. *per aequoris undas / advehar*: reminiscent of Vergilian *diversa per aequora vectos* (*Aen.* 1.376, 3.325). *Ortygiam*: the peninsula of Syracuse, at the end of which Arethusa's fountain is located. She will answer her own indirect question at 640, using the same two opening words, but in the indicative. *narratibus*: Ovid created this word here as the Muse self-consciously teases her audience with a delayed story. In fact, she has no reason to drag the narrative into Ceres' hymn. But as we shall see, Ceres cannot restrain her curiosity (572 ff.), even if it means she has not yet done her benevolent duty and restored the crops. *curaque* 500: ablative of separation. *vultus melioris* 501: genitive of description. As the nymph realizes, the primary goal is to transform Ceres from a raging to a kindly goddess again.

501–
5
pervia tellus: the efficient nymph gets to the point. She has to explain how she could see Proserpina in the Underworld. Since she presents herself as flowing from Elis to Syracuse, she can declare that she has a subterranean course. *ablata . . . hic* 502–3: refer to the starting and ending points of her journey. *desuetaque sidera*: because of the long underground trip, she has not seen stars overhead. *Stygio . . . gurgite* 504: it is not necessary to press this phrase and assume that Arethusa flowed into the waters of the Styx; she does flow in subterranean regions close enough to the Styx so that she could see what was going on with Proserpina there. The calm revelation of 505 contrasts sharply with Ceres' wildness. Ovid has let Calliope introduce a new means for telling the mother what happened to her daughter. In the Homeric Hymn 74 ff. and in the somewhat close version that Ovid uses in *Fast.* 4.583–84, Ceres consults the all-seeing Sun, who duly reports that Dis has abducted her child and holds her in Hades. Homer has him add good masculine advice—which she of course rejects—that it really is a suitable match. Using Arethusa instead, Calliope can ignore the rape itself; the nymph expresses no opinion about that deed, but she soberly criticizes the wrong-headed actions of Ceres in blighting the earth. And she can report seeing what the Sun above could not see, the present condition of the girl. She believes that Proserpina has done rather well for herself—and a woman's opinion carries more weight here than that of the Sun, a male deity.

506–
8
illa quidem . . . sed: the structure of these three lines neatly makes the point that Proserpina has indeed suffered and that the nymph feels for her (506), but on the contrary—*sed* three times—she has achieved a status that should make her and Ceres quite satisfied. *neque adhuc*

interrita: cf. *territa* 396, the girl at the first moment of the abduction. *maxima mundi* 507: alliterative reinforcement of the admiring claim that Proserpina is the "greatest woman" of the Underworld, that is, in her role of queen. All this is collected and reiterated in 508, enhanced by the procession of solemn spondees.

Still Angry, Ceres Demands Satisfaction of Jupiter (509–71)

In the Homeric Hymn, once she learned, quite early, of how Hades, with the connivance of Zeus, had taken Proserpina away, Demeter refused to have anything to do with Zeus or the other Olympians and remained inconsolable on earth, primarily in the neighborhood of Eleusis. Zeus sent messenger after messenger to her (313 ff.) to get her to calm down and accept the situation, but she refused to do so until she had her daughter back. When that was granted and she realized that Hades had a hold on her (because Proserpina had eaten some pomegranate seeds down there), she listened to the last messenger, her mother Rhea, and went up to Olympus to negotiate a final settlement. Calliope changes the action. As soon as Ceres gets the facts from Arethusa, she pays no attention to the plea for Sicilian crops, but storms up to Olympus to upbraid Jupiter. Ovid also has her complain to Jupiter in *Fast.* 4.585 ff., but he describes her in far gentler tones, as less imperious and more sympathetic.

509–
12
mater: Calliope emphasizes the mother in action, to the exclusion of *frugum genetrix* (cf. 490). *stupuit ceu saxea*: for the stunning effect, which seems to turn one momentarily into stone, cf. Orpheus' reaction to the loss of Eurydice in 10.64 ff.: he resembled men who became petrified. *attonitae* 510: another synonym for consternation. Note the adjectives 511, *gravi gravis*. They enact a contest in which the first finally conquers the second: *dolor* drives away *amentia*, "insensibility, unconsciousness." *auras . . . aetherias*: in *Fast.* 4.497–98, Ceres uses her chariot to fly over the sea from Sicily to Greece, but Calliope ignores this vehicle until the goddess needs it to fly to Olympus, with angry urgency.

512–
17
toto nubila vultu: this novel expression captures the gloomy look on Ceres' face, putting it in metaphorical terms that stress her alienation from the usual sunshine of the Olympians. She is a "stormy" presence among the cheerful, carefree deities. *passis . . . capillis* 513: the unkempt hair disturbs the elegant decorum of the gods also. *invidiosa*: full of ill-will herself, Ceres will aim to spread ill-will; our words "envy, enviable, envious" are quite inappropriate here. All in all, Ceres is unsympathetic in this scene; Callisto once again has miscalculated her characterization. *pro . . . meo . . . sanguine* 514–15: since

mea . . . nata would create no metrical problem, the Muse has presumably resorted to this metonymy, to produce this impersonal tone. The hyperbaton ends in an unexpected term. *supplex*: Ceres announces her role, but she does not maintain the pose. *proque tuo* 515: a neat echo of the previous line, using the *-que* in a different way. This is the start of her hateful strategy, questioning Jupiter's paternal feelings. *si nulla est gratia matris*: it is not hard to imagine the tone in which this condition is spoken. Ceres, though sister of Jupiter, is not his wife, as his other sister Juno is; so she cannot claim special favor and risk the notorious jealousy of Juno. In the next contest, Arachne will weave a pattern of illicit divine amours, as her challenge to the goddess Minerva, and Jupiter's rape of Ceres in the form of a horse, will be noted (6.118–19). *nata patrem moveat* 516: Ovid does not mention Jupiter's approval of Dis' abduction in his account, so Ceres cannot openly complain, only voice these catty arguments. *precamur*: the appropriate verb, but the "prayer" itself is a nasty insinuation. Jupiter does not hold Proserpina cheap; he thinks about her marriage in a different manner than Ceres, arranging what he believes is a good family match with his royal brother.

8–
2

quaesita . . . reperta: Ceres will start doing some rhetorical twists with the verb *reperire* in 519–20, so she fixes its meaning here as the opposite of "seeking." Then she tries the infinitive as predicate accusative: a good example of the infinitive doing the work of the gerund in this case. Using her nasty conditional sentence structure again (cf. 515), she sardonically turns finding into a more extreme opposite: namely, losing her daughter more decisively (because of the apparent truculence and inaccessibility of Dis); or, to put it differently, merely knowing where the girl is and how totally lost. This whole speech, as we can see, stresses the wild feelings of Ceres; she shows no real understanding of the emotional situation of Proserpina, even though Arethusa had given her some indications (cf. 506). *quod rapta* 520: supply *est*. Ceres ignores the acts of abduction and subsequent rape, because she really does not think of her daughter except as a pawn in her marriage plans. Ovid assigns her much the same argument in *Fast.* 4.589 ff. *praedone marito* 521: = Fast. 4.591. The phrase is Ovidian, but the idea goes back to the theme of Paris who stole Menelaus' wife Helen; Vergil adapts it to the propaganda of the Italian war in his epic. In a scene that anticipates this one, Amata protests to her husband Evander his plan to marry off their daughter to Aeneas instead of to Turnus; and she falsely accuses Aeneas as *praedo* (7.362). *filia . . . tua est, si iam mea filia non est* 522: maintaining her whining tone to the end, Ceres closes with still another false protasis. The rhetorical calculation emerges in the almost perfect chiastic pattern of the key elements. She ends virtually as she began in 515–16. As she manipulated the word *find*, she here jumps to the opposite extreme with *daughter*, and again she implies how little real maternal feeling she has.

523–
28
commune est pignus: without giving us any indication of the tone or manner in which Jupiter responded, Calliope has him focus immediately on the spurious division of father and mother by Ceres and dismiss it as such. *nomina rebus . . . vera* 524–25: Jupiter, having disliked the way Ceres abused meanings, claims that he will correct her definitions. However, he does the same thing she has done, in the opposite direction: putting good names on misdeeds. These gods practice rhetoric on each other; they do not communicate honestly. So Calliope again slights the deities in her song. *non hoc iniuria . . . verum amor*: not a satisfactory assertion. Dis' so-called "love" has committed an outrage in the process of violent abduction. *nobis . . . pudori*: double dative. In answering Ceres' assertion that Proserpina does not deserve a brigand as her mate, Jupiter merely denies the match is a disgrace, but implicitly he means that it is in fact an honor. *tu modo . . . velis* 527: all that is necessary, he suggests, is for Ceres to will the opposite meaning. Again, male rhetoric answers female rhetoric. *ut desint*: the clause has an adversative sense; e.g., "leaving aside the other advantages." *Iovis fratrem* 528: Jupiter's egotism suggests to him a dominant argument, which neither Ceres nor we, who have seen the trivial ways in which his majesty has operated, would be inclined to accept.

528–
32
non cetera desunt: more rhetoric, as the god brings back into play the factors he had just dismissed, in chiastic order. *sorte* 529: ablative of respect; except for the luck of the lot, which gave Jupiter mastery of the heavens and Dis power in Hades, they are equal. *discidii* 530: objective genitive. The word refers to any separation, commonly to divorce. Jupiter affects to yield to Ceres, putting her in the wrong as an interfering mother. We are never told that the god knows he is safe in making this condition, but it is a likely suspicion in the case of such sly omniscience. *repetet . . . caelum / lege tamen certa* 531: the confident future is immediately countered by the "but" of *tamen*. *si nullos contigit*: a good example of a mixed condition. The perfect indicative, which represents an actual deed in the past, has the power to negate a promise. *Parcarum foedere* 532: the Fates represent a universal law (of nature) above ordinary human law, binding even on the gods. *cautum est*: technical legal terminology, "it is decreed or stipulated." Jupiter uses law whenever it serves his purposes.

533–
36
Cereri certum est educere natam: heedless of the arguments of the father (which did not deal with her own feelings nor the interests of the girl), Ceres fastens only on the permission to get the girl back. *non ita fata sinunt* 534: synonymous with 532, fate and the Parcae

being alike. *ieiunia . . . solverat*: pluperfect introduces a flashback, which takes us into two digressive metamorphoses, from which Calliope returns to the main narrative, thirty lines later, at 564. This expression (also in *Fast.* 4.607) for appeasing hunger is pretentious. *dum simplex errat in hortis*: Calliope has imagined an unusual occasion when Proserpina breaks her fast; other writers do not picture Dis as owner of a palace or villa beautified by cultivated gardens. As the adjective, which echoes 400, emphasizes, along with the key verb of 536, Calliope has placed the girl in an analogous context, and she picks fruit in Hades just as simple-mindedly as she had plucked flowers at Enna. It follows, then, that the result will prove similar. She artfully makes 536 a Golden Line to impress us. *puniceum . . . pomum*: an alliterative, artificial phrase, framing the line, for the fateful pomegranate that frustrates Ceres. The Romans called this fruit the Punic apple, referring primarily to the bright red color of both skin and seeds inside. That was the Phoenician color because of the connections the Punic ancestors in Phoenicia had with the production of purple dye. Calliope has flamboyantly altered the usual expression, *Punicum malum*. Cf. *Fast.* 4.608. *curva*: the branches have bent under the weight of the fruit.

37–
41
sumptaque . . . septem . . . grana: accusative object. These seven seeds mystify readers as much as the three seeds that the poet specifies the girl ate in *Fast.* 4.607. The Greek sources, the Homeric Hymn and Apollodorus 1.5.3, say that wily Pluto tricked the girl into taking a single seed—it is enough that one was eaten. We could suspect Calliope of creating this mystery by her poetic interest in alliteration. *presserat* 538: euphemism for chewing. *Ascalaphus* 539: the Homeric Hymn, having no interest in irrelevant metamorphoses, does not mention this person. Proserpina herself tells her mother the story, without any spy-informer. Ovid is our earliest source for this tale (which also appears in Apollodorus 1.5.3), but he may well not have originated it. The fact that Apollodorus assigns the boy a mother named Gorgyra and has other differences suggests that Ovid used a known story, which had some minor variants. And Calliope may have added to those. Strictly speaking, an informer is superfluous for the operation of the Fates: the violation of their law would produce the automatic penalty. This informer assumes a situation more like that of human law, where the authority has to condemn the violation formally on the basis of evidence. Then, we can watch the familiar theme of informer punished by transformation; cf. Aglauros and Battos in Book 2. *Orphne*: Calliope gives the mother a Greek name that connotes darkness, as is appropriate for her habitat. Rapable nymphs in Hades constitute a Hellenistic innovation, which Calliope, after her recent experience, deems worthy to develop. *haud ignotissima* 540: on the

contrary, the Roman audience had probably never heard of this nymph. *atris* 541: natural adjective for anything in the gloomy Underworld. In some MSS, scribes corrupted this to *antris*, as if nymphs, babies, and caves go well together (cf. 3.314, 4.289).

542–45 *vidit et indicio . . . ademit*: repeating the verb of 539, Calliope closes her genealogy of the boy and resumes the narrative. She is so vague about how this "information" functions that she fails to say to whom the boy reported—a key detail in most such accounts. *regina Erebi* 543: Proserpina. In Apollodoros' version, Demeter (= Ceres) continued her angry vengeance and herself punished the act by burying Ascalaphos under a rock. *profanam / fecit avem*: the adjective applies to the bird, not the witness. She turns him into an owl (*bubo*), such as haunted Dido in *Aen.* 4.461 ff. *sparsumque caput . . . lympha*: the rage of the daughter closely parallels that of her mother in 453–55, not by accident presumably. Calliope likes women who express their rage against brats and refuse to suffer insults. The initial detail of the metamorphosis is complete in one line, 545, with apt final emphasis on the large eyes of the owl. Like unnamed Ascalabos, this male is reduced to tiny size, but is left with his ill-omened voice.

546–50 *ille sibi ablatus*: by the transformation, Ascalaphus is taken away from himself; and Calliope hereafter concentrates on the bird aspects, with little interest in the Ovidian theme of continuity or human resistance to becoming an animal. *amicitur in*: normally, Ovid and others Latin writers use a simple instrumental ablative with this verb. The Muse exploits a metaphor common in metamorphosis: the human being puts on a "cloak" of tawny wings. But her choice of verb is unique in Ovid. Similarly, her verbs are striking in 547: he grows into his head as it becomes a larger part of his total body (though in fact it is smaller than the human head; the rest of the body is much smaller); and he hooks his long toenails into talons. The exact syntax of accusative *ungues* 547 with the passive verb remains under dispute. *vixque movet . . . pennas* 548: during daytime, when this owl could be seen in antiquity, it seemed to be perched motionless and sleepy. We now know that night birds like owls do rest by day. Sunlight virtually blinds them. *per inertia bracchia*: the feathers, which appear on humans in metamorphosis, subsequently become part of the wings. The adjective added to the arms characterizes them after the feathers have been added: arms have lost their former functions and are rendered inactive in human terms. In 549–50, the Muse belabors the ugly meaning of this bird-change, with words that imply her total approval of the action. Each line consists of half-units, usually with prejudicial adjective at start. Line 549 exploits alliteration; 550 strikes a sober final note with four spondees. Calliope declared Ascalaphos "cruel" (542), on the dubious grounds that he robbed Proserpina of her return—

regardless of her eating the seeds—but the satisfaction she takes in this metamorphosis makes her crueler.

551–
53

Calliope now modulates to an even more gratuitous metamorphosis, which proves, in spite of her intention, to reflect poorly on Ceres. She links two bird-metamorphoses with Ceres and Proserpina. Having described the punishment of Ascalaphus, she can declare that his change has a reasonable explanation. It is the unreasonable change of loyal friends and expert singers, the Sirens, that now concerns her. *vobis* 552: the Muse shows her bias by apostrophizing the women, whom she elliptically identifies as the daughter of Achelous. This river and his daughters, located in western Greece in Acarnania, welcomes Theseus and his companions in 8.549 ff. He would seem very remote from the scene of Proserpina's rape, at first. In fact, after the Sirens were metamorphosed, they were assigned to dangerous rocks in the sea off Italy. In *Odyssey* 11.165 ff., the Greeks pass the Sirens after leaving Circe and before they reach Scylla and Charybdis, the straits between Italy and Sicily. That was interpreted as a voyage south along the west coast of Italy. Sailing in the reverse direction, north from Sicily, Aeneas passes the rocks of the Sirens, with their piles of bleached sailors' bones, just before he lands at Cumae in *Aen.* 5.864 ff. And in fact, the isle or isles of the Sirens were identified with islands outside the Bay of Naples. Calliope still provides weak motivation for the personal connection between the Sirens and Proserpina (554–55), but at least we can glimpse a geographical connection. *unde / pluma pedesque avium* 552–53: supply *sunt* for these noms. The Muse appears to be analyzing the total bird-change of human women, but then she stops: feet and features, including wings, are the extent of the new bird form (unlike the complete owl, Ascalaphos). *cum virginis ora geratis*: concessive subjunctive. The Sirens, like the Harpies, are bird-monsters: they retain the face of a girl, and speak and sing with the alluring voice of females. Calliope then asks why they are part-bird, robbed of their feminine beauty.

554–
55

Calliope proposes an answer to her first question with a second. Perhaps the Sirens were among the nameless companions of Proserpina mentioned at 394? (They play no part at all in *Fast.* 4.) *doctae Sirenes* 555: here, the Muse betrays her special interest. These Sirens are expert singers like the Muses (cf. 255). In fact, their mother is usually named as one of the Muses, whether Terpsichore, Melpomene, or Calliope herself. Remember that Ovid introduced the unique story of how the Muses temporarily assumed bird form to escape a rapist. With that bias, we can understand why Calliope will construe this bird-change as a reward and emphasize the survival of the most precious aspect of the Sirens, the superlative human voice.

556–

quam: Proserpina. *toto . . . orbe*: like Ceres, they hunted her all over

60   the world (cf. 462–63). The Muse slows down the start of her solemn
story with four spondees. *ut vestram sentirent aequora curam* 557:
they were going to hunt for her on the sea, too. Calliope words this
in a special way, to suggest that the sea would actually "feel" their
concern for their friend. *alarum insistere remis* 558: again, her verb
fits oddly with the metaphor for flying that she utilizes. It is traditional
to think of oars as resembling wings, and Lucretius, then Vergil, had
talked of wings as oars. Later, in 8.228, describing the fall of Icarus,
Ovid will say that his arms lacked "oars" and so could not catch air
and stay aloft. But "standing upon the oars of wings" is an odd picture.
She means that the Sirens wished to sail over (= above) the waves
on or by means of wings (as oars). *facilesque deos* 559: friendly,
compliant gods, who grant wishes; same phrase in 9.756. Hyginus
141 did not understand this metamorphosis as a reward—there are
good reasons why—and he turns it into punishment, inflicted by angry
Ceres on these companions for not preventing the abduction. *artus
. . . flavescere pennis*: a variant on Calliope's phrasing in 546, also
a reminder of 553, the opening of this story.

561–   *ille canor mulcendas natus ad aures*: the musical ability of the Sirens
63   has only been alluded to in *doctae* 555. Now, the Muse treats it as
something particularly to be preserved. But these Sirens whom she
apostrophizes so favorably as sister artists are notorious as monsters
who use their art to lure men—and I use the gender properly—
to destruction. These are men-haters who, like powerful Ceres and
Proserpina, successfully vent their hatred on their victims. Only
Odysseus was able to sail past unharmed and still enjoy their song.
tantaque dos oris 562: Calliope cannot refrain from repeating her
praise of their "talent." Apparently, then, the benevolent gods decided
that such a gift should not be lost to the world in spite of the bird-
change. *virginei vultus* 563: this alliterative phrase closes the ring
with 553. *vox humana remansit*: this is the essential continuity given
to the once totally feminine Sirens. Now, we can review the antithesis
that the Muse has contrived between Ascalaphos and Sirens. They have
been rewarded for fidelity to Persephone, whereas he was punished for
informing against her; both have become bird-like, but he is now an
ill-omened owl, whereas the Sirens have preserved their seductive
voices and musical charm. However, Calliope has passed over in
silence the ruinous use to which that charm was put by the bird-
monsters. The Sirens symbolize for Ovid's readers aspects of women's
power that Calliope especially prizes. Their destructivity could be
considered far worse than that of Ascalaphos.

564–   *medius fratrisque: medius* + two genitives renders English "between
67   a and b." Calliope has to simplify the complicated relationship with

Ceres, who is the mother of the bride and victim of Jupiter's lust, but she secures a neat opposition between brother and sister, a perfect dilemma for Jupiter. *ex aequo . . . dividit* 565: an absolutely even division solves the dispute ideally. It also makes sense of the agricultural year of growth and rest, with which Ceres is identified. *dea* 566: Proserpina. *regnorum numen commune duorum*: she belongs as deity alike to the kingdoms of Dis below and of Jupiter above. The chiastic pattern of 567, with its juxtaposition at the caesura of *totidem* twice, epitomizes the phrase of 566.

8–
1   *vertitur . . . facies et mentis et oris*: Calliope registers a metamorphosis in the psychological state (*mentis*) and in the facial expression (*oris*), using zeugma. Ceres has been a prey to violent emotions, once specified as *amentia* (511), and the unhappy face has been noted by Arethusa (501) and Calliope. Thus, Ceres (who is the subject, not Proserpina) gives up irrational anxiety and fury, returns to a reasonable state of mind, and begins to smile again. *Diti quoque maesta* 569: Calliope has already assigned this epithet to Ceres at 564. She seems to mean here that Dis, knowing she hated him and the marriage, would not normally have been able to pity such a venomous mother-in-law; however, in this situation, Ceres has been truly piteous, enough to move even Dis (We may not agree with her assertion.) *laeta deae frons* 570: the adjective not only sets up the common image of sunshine after rain, but it also reminds us of its basic agricultural application to the fertility of fields, which, as we shall see, Ceres will finally think to restore (642 ff.). *tectus aquosis / nubibus*: a reminder of the way Ceres arrived in Olympus, hateful and *nubila vultu* 512).

Ceres Indulges Herself with Arethusa's Story (572–641)

Much relieved after the recovery of her daughter, Ceres wants only to divert herself: she completely ignores her responsibilities to the farmers, fields, and crops. So she calls on Arethusa to give her promised story (cf. 498 ff.) and explain why she changed her abode from Elis to Syracuse. Arethusa proves to be another virgin who escaped rape, like the Muses, but had to be transformed into water in order to do so. Unintentionally, then, she could have personal significance for Ceres, because she speaks of feelings she had when threatened with rape—what Ceres has ignored in the experience of her daughter while being totally preoccupied with her own feelings. Calliope expatiates for some sixty-five lines on this tale because Arethusa is a kindred spirit. Few nymphs manage to escape the lust of determined gods and survive as animate beings. Arethusa is a rare heroine, defeater of a rape attempt. Ovid frequently echoes the earlier story of Daphne and Apollo te offer a meaningful parallel.

572–   *alma Ceres*: same phrase in *Fast*. 4.547. Here, it suggests that Ceres
76   has resumed her traditional character as kindly mother of Proserpina
       and of the crops (cf. 489–90). However, she still ignores the farmers'
       needs until she has satisfied her curiosity about Arethusa. *secura*:
       another indication of change (cf. 500). *quae tibi causa fugae* 573:
       supply *sit*. Note that Calliope apostrophizes this exemplary female as
       she had the Sirens, to show her bias. She also anticipates information
       that, hitherto, Arethusa has not supplied. She did not mention "flight,"
       only a distant move. We will now hear of a desperate race to escape
       rape, not of political flight. *sacer fons*: the first time in the *Met*. that
       a final monosyllable has been preceded by a word of more than one
       syllable (except where *est* or *es* has followed a word, with which it
       becomes linked by elision, e.g., *petita est* 580). The result here is a
       jerky final rhythm. Why Calliope should seek such a rhythm as she
       calls attention to this "sacred fountain" is not clear. When Ovid ends
       14.515 with *semicaper Pan*, we can assume that he is having fun
       with the goatish god Pan. Ovid's use of double monosyllables in the
       final foot is rather bold and casual (e.g., 1.452, 499, 696), but its
       effect falls on the enjambement, not on the conventional rhythm.
       Calliope had called the water of Cyane's fountain "sacred." *conticuere
       undae* 574: as the fountain-nymph prepares to launch into her minor
       tale, Calliope reaches for epic emphasis and varies Vergil's famous
       opening of *Aen*. 2: *conticuere omnes*. The difference between the
       audience and genuinely serious account of Aeneas and this erotic story
       of Arethusa with its idle audience makes Calliope's pomposity silly.
       We are to imagine that the splashing fountain waters fell silent while
       the fountain spoke. *sustulit . . . caput*: the Muse had given Arethusa
       a similar opening action earlier (487). *siccata capillos*: a slightly
       different gesture with the hair from that assigned in 488. Another
       internal accusative. *fluminis Elei* 576: the river Alpheos of Elis. The
       three-syllable adjective was well established in Augustan poetry; how-
       ever, it struck scribes as odd, who tried to "improve" the text by
       substituting *Alphei, narravit amores*: Calliope tells us the theme she
       perceives in the story, anticipating the words of the nymph. Another
       story of a god's lust would seem to be counter-productive to the
       Muse's supposed defense of divine majesty. However, as we have
       seen, she tends to confine her defense to the feminine gender.

577–   *in Achaide*: in Greece, as opposed to Sicily or Italy, for instance. *me
79   studiosius* 578: ablative of comparison with adverb that only Ovid
       uses in poetry, here and in 579. It may well be that its choice reflects
       the special literary vocabulary of the Muse. Haunting the woods and
       laying nets connote hunting, and the huntress is the exemplary virgin.
       Arethusa defines herself implicitly as Calliope would want.

80– *quamvis*: with indicative (cf. 1.686). *formae . . . fama*: the beginning
81   of significant alliteration, which in 581 plays on the difference between
     fortis and *formosa*, so frustrating to the nymph. The theme goes back
     to Daphne in 1.489, whose beauty fought against her desire to remain
     a chaste huntress. *nomen* 581: synonymous with *fama* above.

82– *facies*: another synonym for beauty; it gives Arethusa no pleasure,
84   for she obviously is no city-bred coquette. *quaque . . . dote* 583:
     relative clause before "antecedent," in typical Ovidian style. *rustica*:
     Arethusa describes herself with an epithet that is usually pejorative,
     especially in the urbane society of Augustan Rome. But neither she
     nor Calliope apologizes for her rustic virtue. *dote / corporis*: this
     physical "endowment" again refers to her beauty. *crimenque placere
     putavi*: "I thought it a crime to please (males)"; the infinitive is object,
     and the noun is predicate nominative.

85– *lassa . . . aestus*: two basic motifs for the type-scene of sexual violence
86   in idyllic setting. The narrator starts with a tired hunter or huntress
     in the heat of the day. Cf. Callisto in 2.417 ff. Calliope will fit
     Arethusa to that context. *Stymphalide silva* 585: ablative of place from
     which. Stymphalos, its lake, and its forest lie in eastern Arcadia, no
     more than thirty miles from Corinth, but fifty or more miles across
     rugged mountainous terrain from the Alpheos River. No wonder the
     huntress is tired after ranging so far from home. *aestus erat* 586: same
     words for the setting of another noontime tragedy in the woods at
     10.126; Ovid first used them to begin *Am.* 1.5., introducing Corinna
     and his virtual rape of her.

87– *invenio*: here, the literal meaning of "come upon" is better than "find,"
89   because the huntress does not consciously look for this water, but it
     meets her needs when she chances upon it. *sine vertice*: the water
     flows without any sign of eddies or current; it is quiet water. *perspicuas
     ad humum* 588: transparent to the bottom. Cf. Salmacis' pool (4.300),
     which was inviting to Hermaphroditus for a cooling swim. Similarly,
     the spring where Diana bathed after her hunt was *perlucidus* in 3.161.
     Calliope lets Arethusa wax "poetic" here and add a pretty clause to
     emphasize the transparency and clarity of the water: *numerabilis* occurs
     only here in Ovid's poetry and otherwise among contemporary poets
     only once in Horace. *vix ire putares* 589: Arethusa gains credence
     with Ceres, and Calliope with her audience and judges, by this apostro-
     phe. The infinitive cleverly qualifies *euntes* of 587; because of its
     calmness, the water does not seem to move.

590– *dabant . . . umbras*: in the heat of the day, the idyllic spot must
91   provide shade as well as water. Willows and poplars commonly grow
     near water. *sponte sua natas* 591: it is a convention of place-
     descriptions that nature is superior to art, so natural features win more
     approval than artificial beautifications. *ripis declivibus*: dative. The

banks that sloped down to the water, well-shaded, made the river a very alluring spot.

592– *accessi*: Arethusa acts immediately at sight of all the river's attractions.
95 Without even sitting or lying a bit to enjoy the cool shade, without stopping for a drink (like Narcissus), she thinks of a swim. *poplite deinde tenus* 593: she tests the water in two stages, first with her foot, then wading in up to her knees. *recingor*: Calliope and Arethusa use this verb in a daring way. Ovid likes to mention loosened robes, whether for ritual ceremonies or for love, with the phrase *tunica recincta*. Nowhere else does he use a personal passive of this verb; nowhere else does he extend the loosening or ungirding so succinctly and mean the removal of all clothes; but the further detail of 594–95 leaves no room for doubt that Arethusa is appropriately bare as she re-enters the river to swim. *salici . . . curvae* 594: a willow sapling or perhaps only a branch, from the thicket mentioned at 590. The nymph has returned to the bank to leave her clothes.

595– *dum ferioque trahoque*: a description of wild thrashing, not the elegant
98 swimming that is taught and practiced today. But swimming was not a graceful art in ancient times. What one noticed—and still observes today in untrained swimmers—is violent movement of the arms, as the flounderer tries to keep head above water and make progress. *excussaque bracchia iacto* 596: more frantic flailing of the arms. There is no attempt to make fun of Arethusa's swimming; everybody swam in this awkward fashion, and nobody "swam" very long or very far. *medio sub gurgite murmur* 597: here, we can see the relevance of saying, in 587, that the water flowed "without a murmur." A murmur now, in the middle of the river, beneath the surface, would frighten the happy swimmer. *insisto propiori margine* 598: the verb, which places the narrator suddenly on the nearer bank of the river (where her clothes are not), leaves to our imaginations how she dashed, frightened and nude, to the shore. Ablative of place where; cf. similar syntax in 558.

599– *quo properas*: a metrically useful unit that Ovid tries in a variety of
600 situations of unwise or unwished haste (e.g., *Am.* 1.13, *Fast.* 6. 563). This is the only instance in which a lover so addresses his elusive victim, but the victim does regularly try to escape hurriedly (cf. 1.510). *suis Alpheus ab undis*: typical separation of the river-god and his river waters. Since the audience knows the story of Alpheos and Arethusa in some form, if not exactly this one, the sudden identification of the river (cf. 576) occasions no surprise. *rauco . . . ore* 600: the adjective suits harsh sounds of animals, birds, or waves; it is anything but musical or normally human. Thus, for Calliope, it connotes a male's brutal, roaring violence; and for Arethusa it should mean the lustful bellowing of the male animal.

601–   *sine vestibus*: Arethusa quickly explains why she was still naked and
3   why that provoked more ardent pursuit from Alpheos. *fugio*: picks
         up the previously unexplained *fugae* 573. *paratior* 603: she is not
         ready and willing, but her nudity makes her, against her will, more
         vulnerable.

604–   Calliope goes into an unusual double-simile, offering alternative per-
6   spectives depending on whether Arethusa or Alpheos is subject or
         object. *ferus*: wild like a nonhuman animal or bird. For the comparison
         between love-pursuit and the chasing of a weak animal or bird by a
         predator, cf. Apollo chasing Daphne in 1.533 ff. For dove, hawk, or
         eagle, cf. 1.506 and 6.529 ff. Regardless of the subject, however,
         the affective focus of both similes falls on the panic of the dove:
         penna trepidante 605, trepidas 606. That is to be expected when the
         inner narrator is the victim Arethusa and the outer narrator, Calliope,
         has shared her experience.

607–   Calliope has Arethusa sketch a fantastic chase-route all over Arcadia,
9   which scholars have calculated to cover more than 150 miles and a
         variation between lowest and highest points of a mile and a half.
         usque sub: this seems to vouch for the incredible. Orchomenos lies
         in central Arcadia; Psophis is in the northwest, on the slopes of
         Erymanthos; Cyllene rose in the far northeast, 50 miles away; the
         folds of Maenalia take us 50 miles due south to the vicinity of Tegea;
         cool Erymanthos rises in the northeast again, 60 miles away; and
         Elis would be another 20 miles east of that. *Cyllenenque*: Calliope
         embellishes her geographical list with a double-spondee. In 608, she
         works in five dactyls to fit the speed of the chase. *currere* 609: infinitive
         used as direct object (accusative of the gerund).

610–   *tolerare diu cursus*: immediate comment on the preceding line, as an
11   accusative noun does the work of the previous infinitive. *viribus inpar*:
         ablative of specification. Mortal Arethusa could not hope to compete
         with a god in strength and endurance, a nymph against a lusty male
         deity.

612–   *tamen . . . cucurri*: instead of proceeding to her point, however,
13   Arethusa records more desperate running up and down and all over.
         qua via nulla: more fantastic motifs. Ovid uses the same words in
         3.227, when dogs pursue Actaeon.

614–   *sol erat a tergo*: this notation should indicate a rough time of day and
17   the direction of the chase. Shortly after noon (586), Arethusa aroused
         the lust of Alpheos, who began to pursue her. Now, the sun is no
         longer overhead, but lower on the western horizon, producing long
         shadows. Hence it must be early evening before sunset. If the sun is
         in the west, then the chase must be roughly heading eastward. *timor
         illa videbat* 615: the demonstrative, a loose neuter accusative plural
         (where, if meter had permitted, feminine accusative singular [i.e.,

umbram] would have been natural), caused the scribes trouble. Some of them assimilated the case to that of *timor*, hence *ille*. Arethusa resumes stressing her terror (cf. 598), which may have had the para-doxical power of seeing, i.e., of making her imagine the menacing shadow and closeness of her pursuer. *sonitusque . . . terrebat* 616: she did not imagine the pounding footsteps, which definitely registered on her sense of hearing. The *-que* links with the following *et*, to offer a pair of real menaces. *vittas adflabat* 617: she could feel his hot breath on her hair. Daphne has Apollo similarly breathing on her locks in 1.542.

618–
20
fessa labore fugae: cf. Daphne 1.544, *victa labore fugae. fer opem*: regular appeal for help of any kind in the *Met.* and used by Daphne in 1.546. In other stories, the poet has carefully prepared us for such a cry, mentioning the relative god involved. Here, Calliope has to backtrack and explain why the nymph called upon Diana. She lets Arethusa style herself *armigerae* in 619, then add a relative clause to tell us (pretending to remind Diana) of her services. The motif, in itself, performs a familiar function, because, from Daphne on (cf. 1.476), the chaste huntress was by definition a devotee of Diana and regularly enrolled in her hunting parties (cf. Callisto). Diana had an *armigera* in 3.166. The scansion of *Diana* with a long *i* is an archaic doublet that Augustan poets occasionally appropriated to make meter.

621–
25
mota dea est: same words in 1.381 to render the pity of the goddess Themis and answer to prayer. Sometimes Ovid specifies divine re-sponse and action in metamorphosis; often, not. Here, Calliope lets Arethusa express her confidence that Diana did act on her behalf. *spissis . . . e nubibus*: Diana was apparently on Olympus, so descends from the heavens to help, grabbing a cloud on the way. We might protest that Calliope has talked only of heat and sunshine, and "thick clouds" seem like a desperate stage device; on the other hand, between mortals and gods on Olympus, there is regularly a thick veil of atmo-sphere. Arethusa now enjoys the same concealment provided for Aeneas when he first entered Carthage and Odysseus before him at the court of Alcinous. *lustrat* 622: subject delayed until 623; "he looks at." *caligine tectam*: Ovid likes this phrase (1.265, 2.233, 6.706). In the latter, ironically, he has the rapist use the cloud's concealment to get at his prey. *ignarus* 623, *inscius* 624: frustrated Alpheos becomes a comic figure in this feminist account. Some critics find 623–24 repetitious and propose deleting 623, but they miss the deliberate purpose of the Muse to make the male silly. *bisque . . . et bis*: more ostentatious repetition and emphasis on frustration. Calliope also avails herself of triple hiatus, to isolate each *io* and to make sure the second naming exactly matches the first in rhythm. It is notable in this story that the Muse does not let the god say anything personal to Arethusa

(unlike Apollo with Daphne): he is no courtly lover, only a vague
pursuer who vainly calls to the fugitive (cf. 599).

626–   *quid mihi tunc anima . . . fuit*: Arethusa invites her audience to sympa-
29   thize, and Calliope slants her song. Ovid likes this rhetorical strategy;
          he first used it in *Her.* 11.87 and has it twice more in this poem
          (7.582 and 14.77). Another double simile focuses exclusively on the
          supposed feelings of weak animals of prey, lambs facing wolves and
          rabbits hunted by hounds. *agnae*: dative of reference, parallel to *mihi*.
          stabula alta 627: a common phrase in Vergil, then in Ovid to refer
          to farm buildings and stalls. Here, their height keeps the wolves out.
          In *Aen.* 9, Turnus, as he tries to break into the Trojan encampment,
          is twice compared to a wolf eager to steal lambs from their pen (59
          ff., 566 ff.). Daphne, fleeing from Apollo, is compared to a rabbit
          trying to escape a dog (1.533 ff.). *vepre latens* 628: effective detail.
          The Muse has made us imagine the rabbit cowering in the thorns, not
          daring to move. A unique picture in Ovid.

630–   *abscedit*: the narrator, in her emotionality, fails to specify the change
31   of subject and thus forces us into engagement with the story as we
          sort these details out. *vestigia*: since the footprints stop at the cloud,
          the god, not altogether stupid, keeps his eye on that, like a watch-
          dog or a human hunter. The Muse resorts to zeugma in the double
          object of 631.

632–   *obsessos*: metaphorically, the nymph in the cloud is under siege.
36   *sudor*: a unique origin of a fountain and perhaps not an entirely
          successful touch of the Muse. Pools of anxious sweat do not have as
          much sympathetic appeal (at least, today) as torrents of tears; cf.
          Cyane at 427 ff. and Byblis in 9.655 ff. Based on other instances
          where the altered human being has lost the capacity to speak and/or
          the mouth, we can assume that it is a special effect for her to describe
          her own transformation. Although Diana concealed her from Alpheos,
          nothing in what follows proves that the goddess effected the metamor-
          phosis, and we may rather assume that fear accounts for this rather
          grotesque change. The initial alliteration of 632 becomes a technique
          of 633, too, which is largely repetitive, except for the strange color
          of the sweat. It is becoming more like water for a fountain. (cf. Cyane
          at 432). *movi, manat* 634: effective use of alliterative verbs at the
          caesura. Afraid to move inside the cloud and to leave footprints for
          her tracker, she finally does move, and shows a trail of water. *eque
          capillis / ros cadit*: the preposition often emphasizes how *from* one
          material or part arises another; but the verb seems to denote simply
          water falling from the hair before complete metamorphosis. Calliope
          has practiced this description, with Cyane, so she lets Arethusa merci-
          fully abbreviate it. *in latices mutor*: the only such usage of this key
          thematic verb in the poem. Similarly, this is the only fountain, formed

by metamorphosis, that retains a head, hair, and voice (cf. the inarticulate condition of Cyane). However, the story of Salmacis in 4.285 ff. provides ample precedent for the dual viewpoint toward water and fountain-nymph (as for river and river-god).

636–38 *amatas / amnis aquas*: assonance to point up this odd conceit. The river did not recognize the water, never having seen it before, but the object of his desire in the water. *positoque viri quod sumpserat ore*: Arethusa has never described the appearance of her pursuer; the most she has said is that she saw or imagined his shadow (614–15) and felt his breath. That presumably warrants these lines about changing from human back to watery form. *se mihi misceat* 638: witty ambivalence in wording. It could refer to the simple confluence of bodies of water or the sexual congress of two very human, lusty bodies.

639–41 *Delia rupit humum*: Diana now intervenes again after the metamorphosis to arrange the final escape. The earth opens and swallows watery Arethusa (but not Alpheos), and she flows under the sea to emerge far away at Syracuse. Arethusa had already told about the *pervia tellus* (501) and the subterranean caverns (502), but in a different context, promising that she would later explain how she came to Ortygia (499). *cognomine divae / grata meae*: Ortygia was the early name of Delos, where Diana and Apollo were born, and its adjectival form became an epithet for the goddess, as in 1.694. The island portion of Syracuse, which may have been named merely because it resembled or sheltered quails, pleasantly reminds the nymph of her goddess. Arethusa, closely associated with this great city, with her beautiful head decorated some of its finest coins.

Mighty Ceres Brings the Song to an End (642–61)

642–44 *dea fertilis*: Calliope assigns Ceres an epithet appropriate for her agricultural function, as the Muse returns to her proper subject and the goddess to her responsibilities. *admovit . . . coercuit* 643: Ceres herself yokes the snakes and fits the reins. *medium* 644: with double genitive, cf. 564. Since Calliope has made the geography of earlier wanderings vague and ignored the traditional stop at Eleusis (which in *Fast.* 4 required a chariot to cross the sea from Sicily), she now takes Ceres there.

645–47 *Tritonida . . . urbem*: the city of Athena, called *Tritonia* in 5.250 and 270. *misit . . . Triptolemo*: although the syntax might seem the familiar one of direct and indirect object, we really need Ceres driving the chariot. Translate: "She steered the chariot to Athens to Triptolemus." Poetic dative instead of *ad* + accusative. *partimque . . . partim*: the adverbs help to stress both dative adjectives that frame this sequence. Hence, hyperbaton in 647 to *recultae*. The young man is going to introduce grain cultivation to some places and revive it in others where Ceres' blight (474 ff.) has taken effect. Triptolemus is barely mentioned in the Homeric Hymn 474, as one of several Eleusinians to whom Demeter taught her mysteries. In *Fast.* 4. 549 ff., Ovid puts Triptolemus as the baby of Metaneira, in place of the traditional Demophon. Ceres then predicts (559–50) that the boy will grow up to be the first to plow, sow, and reap the products of the earth. The role that he plays in Calliope's song was traditional in cult myth and art long before Ovid. Cf. Apollodoros 1.5.2 and (for garbled details) Hyginus 147. However, using that role, Calliope reduces the benevolence of Ceres, to concentrate on her vengefulness.

648–
50   *Scythicas . . . oras* 649: ignoring the second part of the mission, to restore grain production to such places as Sicily, the boy heads directly for a nonagricultural region, namely, Scythia. Hyginus 259, who tells this part of the story briefly, in fact carelessly changed Scythia to Sicilia. Scythia, southern Russian today, eventually did become a major grain-growing region. Lyncus, who tries to murder his guest, resembles the first villain and object of metamorphosis in the poem, Lycaon (cf. 1.216 ff.) *penates* 650: metonymy for *domum*.

551–
54   *qua veniat*, etc. The king asks the typical questions permitted a Homeric host, of which the second, *causamque viae* (cf. 2.33, 511), is the most important. Triptolemus answers the other three in reverse order (another Homeric touch), saving until last the reason for his trip. *veni nec puppe*, etc. 653–54: elaborate and riddling response to the initial query. First he denies using normal means of travel; then he offers an alliterative circumlocution for his miraculous flight.

555–
56   *dona fero Cereris*: Triptolemus finally explains his purpose, outlining the benevolent side of Ceres in line with Calliope's preface (cf. 341–43). He refers, of course, to the grain seeds (646) which he carries for farmers to sow. *frugiferas messes* 656: the compound served in Ennius' *Annales* to refer to the earth, and Cicero used it to embellish his prose. Line 656 echoes 343 earlier, with both *fruges* and *alimentaque mitia*. It seems to be Calliope's point that men (gender intentionally chosen) keep affronting Ceres and other women, obliging the kindly goddess to change into a severe but just avenger. Thus, the program of the hymn becomes altered.

557–
59   *barbarus*: used accurately and prejudicially of a non-Greek by the proud Muse. In the tale of Tereus of 6.422 ff., the word will recur to define the Thracian origins of Tereus and his savagery. *invidit*: Lyncus wants to play the grand role that Triptolemus has. *muneris*: in 343, Calliope declared all things Ceres' *munus. hospitio recipit* 658: the king shams hospitality to get his guest in his power. *somnoque gravatum*: Lycaon planned to attack Jupiter (*gravem somno* 1.224).

559–   *conantem figere pectus*: at the caesura, Calliope changes the syntax

61   and makes Lyncus the object, vainly attempting murder as Ceres intervenes. She quickly transforms him into a lynx (*lynca* 660, Greek form of accusative). *rursusque per aëra*: back to Athens. The singer says no more of Ceres' beneficence; the evil Scythian has apparently ended it. *Mopsopium iuvenem* 661: Triptolemus is given a florid epithet as Athenian (also in 6.423), to make Calliope's final line somehow impressive. *sacros agitare iugales*: another ostentatious "poetic" clause for the finale. He is driving the team of snakes (cf. 642), but the Muse assigns him a verb that elsewhere Ovid never uses for driving a team—its connotations are too disorderly and violent—and a substantive *iugales* that Ovid elsewhere only employs in connection with marriage. In short, the poet implies that this is Calliope's effort, not an Ovidian line. Rarely does Ovid end a story so lamely, with nothing but stylistic flourishes.

The Contest's Results: Victory and Metamorphosis (662–78)

662–   *finierat*: Ovid introduced this pluperfect form, metrically useful at the
64   beginning of the line, as a short unepic formula for closing a speech (cf. 1.566, 2.103). *doctos . . . cantus*: the narrating Muse prejudices the case, to prepare for the verdict of the nymph-judges. *maxima*: more bias. She did not introduce Calliope that way at 337. *deas Helicona colentes* 663: we could hardly expect mortals to defeat goddesses in any contest, and the nymphs prudently gave a unanimous verdict. Luckily, they did not have to explain the artistic basis of their judgment.

664–   *convicia victae / cum iacerent*: at this point, we return to the unfinished
68   story begun at 300, namely, how and why human beings became birds after losing a singing contest. Abusive language is the common reaction of losers, and deities in Ovid, very thin-skinned, respond violently to any abuse (cf. Juno at 4.548). Two stories of Book 6 continue this motif in different ways: Niobe and then the Lycian farmers insulting Latona. *dixit*: some early MSS read *dixi*, thus assigning our nameless narrator the major role. That seems less likely than for Calliope, proud of victory, to react angrily at these protests. *supplicium meruisse* 666: she refers not to the agreed penalty, that the Pierides retire to the mountains (313), but rather to punishment they deserve for challenging divinity. *maledictaque culpae / additis*: close to our expression. "You are adding insult to injury." The Muse claims in 667 that they are not allowed by these nasty mortals to be tolerant, a self-serving claim. (Venus also, in 373, complained about her abused *patientia*.) The Muses act out the quick-tempered conception of divinity that Calliope has admiringly assigned to Ceres in her song. *qua vocat ira* 668: though "righteous anger" can be documented, it is usually absent where the perpetrator claims it.

669–
72
rident Emathides: the Pierides have already been connected with Ema-
thia (313). The scribes were hopelessly confused by this substantive,
which Ovid introduced to Latin here. Heinsius brilliantly solved the
corruption and restored the text. It is a nice dramatic touch to have
the arrogant Pierides mock the threats of Calliope, then actually move
forward to scratch the Muse's eyes. *conantesque* 670: as in 659 above,
this participle announces in Ovid an abortive effort. *magno clamore*:
ablative of manner. *protervas / intentare manus*: having carefully
given a prejudicial attribute to the Pierid hands, the narrator then
cleverly starts the metamorphosis with them. *pennas exire per ungues*:
sharp, dangerous fingernails lose their power as they sprout feathers.
adspexere 672: Ovid likes to record the fact—and imply the shock—
of characters who see themselves or others in metamorphosis losing
use of body parts (cf. 4.590 ff). From the nails, the eye travels to the
arms, which turn into the defining features of birds, wings.

673–
76
The narrator and her sisters have caused this metamorphosis. She now
calmly reports details that a human being hears with sympathy for
the afflicted. The Pierides do not just see and react to their individual
disfiguration: they grieve for each other. *rigido concrescere rostro /
ora*: Calliope has insisted on the beak that more or less took over
Ascalaphus' face (544–45), but she omitted that detail from the meta-
morphosis of the admired Sirens in 559 ff. Here, the beak destroys the
once-feminine face. *volucresque novas*: cf. 301. They were destined to
depart to the mountains, but now they merely join other birds in the
forest. *volunt plangi* 675: the infinitive serves to connote a series of
grief-stricken actions that Ovid usually conveys with the active verb.
The closest such prototype is when Coronis in 2.584, describing her
reaction to gradual transformation as a bird, says that she tried to beat
her bare breasts with her hands, but suddenly discovered that she had
neither hands nor breasts. *per bracchia mota levatae*: the movement
of the arms to vent grief is frustrated and becomes instead the flapping
of wings that launches the Pierids into the air. So, too, Coronis at
2.587. *nemorum convicia* 676: the raucous voices of these magpies
make them metonymically and aptly the "insults of the woods." As
far as the egotistic Muse is concerned, this is poetic justice. *picae*:
the final word of the metamorphosis-account gives the new genus.

577–
78
These last two lines deal with the continuity between Pierides and
birds, as the formula *nunc quoque* indicates. Note *prisca* and *remansit*.
raucaque garrulitas 678: the Muse sneers at the principal qualities of
her ex-rivals. They were harshly voluble as women, so now they are
ceaselessly harsh-chattering birds. They eagerly talked nonsense (in
belittling the gods and challenging the universe's top singers); now
they are imitative birds (299), saying things that, to them, are meaning-
less. What the Muse ignores and what the poet noted from the begin-

ning is that they lament their fate (298). Thus, the final assertions of this speaker represent self-serving propaganda. Ovid and his audience, more generous to fallible mortals, less admiring of quick-tempered, vengeful deities, are not likely to be deceived by the strident anti-male, anti-human themes of the Muse.

INDEX

569